TELEVISION AFTER TV

CONSOLE-ING PASSIONS

Television and Cultural Power

EDITED BY LYNN SPIGEL

TELEVISION AFTER TV

Essays on a Medium in Transition

Edited by Lynn Spigel and Jan Olsson

DUKE UNIVERSITY PRESS   DURHAM & LONDON 2004

© 2004 Duke University Press.

All rights reserved. Printed in the United

States of America on acid-free paper. ∞

Designed by Rebecca M. Giménez.

Typeset in Adobe Minion by Keystone

Typesetting, Inc. Library of Congress

Cataloging-in-Publication Data appear

on the last printed page of this book.

2nd printing, 2006

This volume is part of a research
project funded by the Institute for
Futures Studies, Stockholm. Additional funding has been generously
provided by the Bank of Sweden
Tercentenary Foundation.

The editors would also like to
express their gratitude to Sten
Frykholm and Lasse Nilsson, both
formerly at the Television Archives,
Stockholm.

CONTENTS

LYNN SPIGEL **INTRODUCTION**

What is television's future? Today, at a moment of rapid technological change, this question pervades industry boardrooms,
university classrooms, and popular culture alike. To be sure,
television—as an institution, industry, and cultural form—has changed
significantly from its earlier incarnations. In the postnetwork, post–
public service media systems, television as we knew it is something else
again. Yet, as the title of this book suggests, even while mutated in form
television remains a central mode of information and entertainment in
our present-day global culture, and it appears that it will continue to do
so for many years to come. Understanding what is new about the medium thus demands an understanding of both its past and present.

Television After TV contains a mix of historical, critical, and speculative essays that explore television's rise and its transformations over the
past fifty years. Mostly concerned with U.S. and European contexts, the
authors in this collection address both commercial and public service
traditions, and they evaluate their dual (and some say merging) fates in
our global, digital culture of "convergence." This book explores television's pasts, presents, and futures from a broad historical perspective by
showing how the current transformations in media delivery systems simultaneously transform and sustain familiar patterns of U.S. and European television cultures. The essays contribute to a number of salient

debates in television and cultural studies by examining changes in media industry practices, program production, and traditional modes of broadcasting; changes in television's textual forms, modes of reception, and relations to everyday life; relationships of television and new media to nationalism, citizenship, and globalization; and questions regarding the role that critics, activists, and teachers play in the old and new media environments.

In the last ten years, television has reinvented itself in numerous ways. The demise of the three-network system in the United States, the increasing commercialization of public service/state-run systems, the rise of multichannel cable and global satellite delivery, multinational conglomerates, Internet convergence, changes in regulation policies and ownership rules, the advent of HDTV, technological changes in screen design, the innovation of digital television systems like TiVo, and new forms of media competition all contribute to transformations in the practice we call watching TV. Indeed, if TV refers to the technologies, industrial formations, government policies, and practices of looking that were associated with the medium in its classical public service and three-network age, it appears that we are now entering a new phase of television—the phase that comes after "TV."

As the cable and broadcast networks struggle to compete for audiences (which are now divided among hundreds of channels and distribution platforms), new program forms emerge and multiply. In the late 1980s and 1990s, in response to changes in industry, policy, technology (especially the introduction of VCRs), and audience viewing habits, terrestrial British television extended its schedules and targeted groups (including housewives, the elderly, and youth) with new program types.[1] In her chapter in this volume Charlotte Brunsdon considers how these changes in scheduling and demographics relate to changes in Britain's traditional notions of "quality." As Brunsdon demonstrates, in the late 1990s British television redefined its traditions of "public service" with "lifestyle" programming—from decorating to gardening to cooking shows—that were scheduled in the 8–9 time slot and aimed at diverse taste cultures of middle-class consumers (especially women and gay men).

Meanwhile, in numerous national contexts, cable networks from Animal Planet to the Food Network to the Travel Channel exemplify the transition from a "mass audience" of traditional broadcasting to the present-day tactics of narrowcasting. As Graeme Turner has argued, these cable networks create viewer loyalty by associating themselves with particular genre types, and they often recombine older broadcast genres for the niche demographics of contemporary TV (for example, Animal

Planet's *Emergency Vet* is a hybrid of the nature show and *ER*-type medical drama).[2] Lisa Parks's essay in this volume considers a further permutation of this trend by exploring the rise of interactive cable networks like Oxygen and the short-lived DEN, which organize their schedules around (their perception) of the taste cultures of particular demographics (women and youth, respectively).

The rapid rise of reality TV is also a function of the new television marketplace.[3] First associated in the late 1980s and early 1990s with crime/accident magazine-format programs like NBC's *Unsolved Mysteries*, CBS's *Rescue 911*, or Fox's *Cops*, and then mutating into "docusoaps" like MTV's *Real World* and the BBC's *The Living Soap*, reality TV is now a broad generic label used to describe unscripted (although edited-for-drama) programs that recombine the old genres of broadcast television (from game shows to soaps to beauty pageants to documentaries) into a relatively low-cost, high-rating, and internationally marketable alternative to more traditional prime-time series.[4] The global reach and international cross-pollination of the format is evidenced not only by U.S.-British licensing deals (as with *Who Wants to Be a Millionaire?*, *Survivor*, *Big Brother*, or *Weakest Link*), but also by examples like Sweden's *Expedition Robinson* (the Swedish prototype for *Survivor*) and shows like India's *There's Someone* (a marriage-broker show in which couples and their families get to know each other, and which is somewhat of a prototype for the U.S. show *Married in America*). As this last example suggests, at the present moment the genre has morphed into highly contrived, serialized spectacles where real people acting as themselves play out increasingly "perverse" scenarios.[5] In the past several years, audiences have seen castaways eat pig brains on *Survivor;* rock stars curse (with family values) on *The Osbournes;* Britney wannabes sing out of tune on *Pop Star* and *American Idol;* women trade places on *Wife Swap;* and singles play the "dating game" Olympics on the *Bachelor*, the *Bachelorette*, *Joe Millionaire*, and *Mr. Personality*, the latter of which was hosted by the (ironically cast?) Monica Lewinsky.

Although some advertisers are still reluctant to associate their products with the tabloid environment offered by reality TV shows,[6] the programs often outperform traditional fiction series and news magazines, at least among the much-desired 18–49 and 18–34 demographics.[7] According to the BBC *News*, in January 2003 *Wife Swap* picked up almost two million viewers while the BBC's once high-profile army series *Red Cap* lost almost a million viewers.[8] In the United States, *Variety* reported that during the final full week of the February 2003 "sweeps" rating period, "barely 35% of the programming aired by the Big Four consisted of original scripted series." Instead, the networks ran news magazines, movies, seven hours' worth of Michael Jackson, and a "whopping 22.5 hours of reality vs. 19 hours of dramas and just 5 ½ hours of sitcoms." As *Variety* further reported, writers and actors were worrying about whether they would even have jobs in a few months.[9]

In addition to occupying network time slots, reality TV has become a favorite topic among news outlets that increasingly package cultural criticism as a mode of "infotainment." In early February 2003 I counted at least twenty-seven news stories (in the press, on the Net, and on television) remarking on the cultural significance of reality TV. In an amusing exchange, ABC's *Nightline* featured host Ted Koppel asking author Kurt Vonnegut whether or not reality TV signaled the end of civilization. Vonnegut replied, "Well, what makes you think we have a civilization? My Lord, to act as though we have this precious thing which could be damaged? What can happen to it that hasn't already happened to it?"[10] While the reality craze might indeed be less "revolutionary" than it now appears, the widespread industrial and cultural anxieties it has generated indicate that at the present moment of transition, uncertainty is one of the only certainties in the television industry.

The changes afoot are felt not only in the "factual" sector. Even traditional scripted series have changed considerably in the multichannel program environment. As John Caldwell's essay in this volume demonstrates, television producers have developed a battery of techniques with which to lure the smaller audiences that are divided across the channels. Scripted series often include highly hyped one-off episodes, like the live version of *ER* (a practice referred to in the industry as "stunting"). Jeffrey Sconce's essay shows how these new production practices—along with a more TV-literate generation of fans—have fostered changes in the way fiction series construct story worlds. As he argues, 1990s hits like *The X-Files* and *Seinfeld* often strayed from their series bible to present "stand-alone" fantasy episodes that were promoted as "appointment" TV (the backward-moving *Seinfeld* is a case in point). And while television has always mixed genres and recombined narrative materials (a point that Todd Gitlin made in 1983),[11] contemporary television genres are increasingly hybrid (for example, the WB network, which targets a "youth-identified" public, recombined horror, science fiction, comedy, and teen TV in its hit series *Buffy the Vampire Slayer*—later on UPN).[12]

Traditional modes of sponsorship are likewise up for grabs. Channel surfing, VCRs, and new digital systems like Philip's TiVo make advertisers especially nervous that viewers will skip past their commercials.[13] In view of this, William Boddy's essay demonstrates how contemporary television is (ironically) looking more and more like the days of early broadcasting when advertising agencies (which had produced the shows) integrated commercial content into program narratives. Only now, Boddy claims, in addition to the intensive use of conventional product placement and single-sponsor "infomercial" programs, the industry is moving toward "virtual product placement" in which sponsors digitally insert products into programs that they think will be good sales environments (thus, hypothetically, an advertiser could digitally insert a box of Pampers into the episode of *Friends*—now in rerun—where Rachel gives birth).

Moreover, television's convergence with the Internet means that audiences often see TV promotional materials and ads on their computer screens. In December 2000 the AC Nielsen Company reported that 36 percent of all Web users were consuming "streaming media" (which include commercials, movie trailers, and promotional materials for TV shows) at home.[14] As T. S. Kelly, director of Internet Media Strategies at NetRatings, puts it, "Streaming consumption is closely linked to huge media events . . . such as the Super Bowl, Olympics, and Election 2000."[15] Net convergence also enhances opportunities for what John Caldwell in his essay describes as "branding"—the increasing attempt of networks, program producers, and advertisers to stamp their corporate image across a related group of media products, thereby creating a "franchise" akin (if not as yet legally the same as) trademark and trade dress in the fast food industry. Dating back to early broadcasting (Disney's television/theme park ventures in the mid 1950s is a prime example),[16] branding has become so widespread that even corporations traditionally associated with educational media and public service are now increasingly profiling their "brand" across related media venues (the National Geographic Channel, the *Sesame Street* franchise, or the BCC's 1995 campaign for "Our BBC1" and "Our BBC2" are just some examples).

Changes in programming and sponsorship are met with similar changes in the entire culture of "watching TV." As networks make way for the Net, audiences dip in and out of an immersive sea of interface postings, surfing past the interplay of news headlines, TV promos, chat rooms, media criticism, weather reports, advertising pop-ups, and self-help columns as these flash across the increasingly segmented computer screen. According to the *U.S. Statistical Abstract,* in 2001 audiences divided their time across a number of media outlets: 93.6 percent of U.S. households used television; 73.1 percent used cable; 84.4 percent used radio; 79.3 percent used newspapers; and 52.1 percent used the Internet (these figures vary greatly, of course, according to income, race, and age).[17]

Moreover, as Henry Jenkins observes of convergence culture, "all evidence suggests that computers don't cancel out other media; instead computer owners consume on average significantly more television, movies, CDs, and related media than the general population."[18] In what Jenkins and others refer to as "transmedia storytelling," content is designed to appear across different media platforms so that we can now access our favorite media "franchises" and characters in multiple storytelling universes (Barbie now appears as a doll, a CD-ROM fashion model, a home video, a comic book, a magazine, a McDonald's giveaway, and an art object to be looked at in world-class museums). Clearly linked to the industry strategy of "branding" (although with a more positive spin on it), transmedia storytelling is not just child's play; it is also aimed at adult demographics (Martha Stewart's various cooking shows, magazine, and home decor products, and Delia Smith's BBC cooking show, best-seller books, and product endorsements make them both transmedia storytelling figures with enormous appeal).

Meanwhile, the television image has itself become increasingly multidimensional and fractured by different kinds of textual materials that all coexist (albeit in incongruous ways) on the same screen. Some TV sets allow viewers to watch several programs at once (at least on pop-up postage-size images) while news programs (since 9/11) provide continual "crawl" at the bottom of the screen. More generally, the stylized graphic displays, digitized image processing, painterly quality, and/or overproduced images that John Caldwell first attributed to numerous 1980s fiction, news, and reality programs have now become standard modes of production.[19]

In this multimedia/multi-image context, audiences are learning new "viewing protocols" that allow them to interpret TV images in relation to the textual materials found on the Net and/or on fragmented parts of a single screen. As images multiply on a variety of delivery systems and platforms, who knows what audiences are seeing—much less thinking—anymore? I will leave this issue to the social scientists; from my point of view the more interesting problem is precisely the uncertainty. Television—once the most familiar of everyday objects—is now transforming at such rapid speeds that we no longer really know what "TV" is at all.

In the face of these changes much of the existing literature in television studies now seems as dated as network shows like *Dallas* (and, sadly, unlike *Dallas* TV scholarship can't even be repackaged as camp). When teaching many of the "greatest hits" of television studies, I often notice that my students readily object to the aesthetic/cultural theories that were developed for terrestrial broadcast systems and the old hand-dialed, pre-VCR television sets. Accordingly, many of the authors in this volume revisit some of the central theoretical premises and debates in television studies, exploring ways to understand television at this moment of transition.

Some authors in this volume reconsider television aesthetics and cultural form with regard to changes in transmission, technology, and everyday reception by audiences. William Uricchio explores how remote controls, video gaming, and "smart" television services like TiVo demand that we rethink television's aesthetics of "liveness" and "flow" (a term Raymond Williams first used to describe the unfolding of programs and commercials across the schedule and the viewer's perception of the stream of materials).[20] For example, TiVo makes it possible to capture and pause programs during their live transmission, while also allowing audiences to pattern their own scheduled flow of programs. While Uricchio considers the changing conditions of television technology, flow, and reception in domestic contexts, other authors emphasize the need to rethink the theories of everyday life and spectatorship that were developed in relationship to the family audience watching TV at home. Anna McCarthy's essay considers the way television has become part of the visual culture of "waiting" (in the public spaces of doctor's offices, airline terminals, and train stations). In these instances, television becomes a crucial dynamic of the experience of time and boredom in late capitalism, although McCarthy also describes how some artists and activists use television to seize the moment in public waiting places.

Other authors in this volume contribute to and develop recent discussions about television, global space, and diaspora.[21] In his essay David Morley uses theoretical insights in critical geography to account for the way our increasingly mobile forms of audio/visual culture have contributed to changing perceptions of space and place in everyday life. In addition, numerous authors in this volume (Morley, Brunsdon, Curtin, Hartley) reconsider theories of television's relationship to citizenship and nationalism that were developed in the context of the U.S. network system and the BBC but don't necessarily explain the present-day multichannel "niche" audiences and global satellite delivery systems.

Despite our collective attempts to revisit the theoretical, historical, and critical paradigms of television studies, I do not mean to imply here that we should relegate the scholarship of the past to a "dinosaur club" of television theory. Indeed, many of the authors in this volume return to and rely on the pioneering work in television studies—especially Raymond Williams's groundbreaking *Television: Technology and Cultural Form* (1974).[22] Yet, while the essays in this book are obviously in dialogue with previous media theories and historians, they also represent a collective effort to reconsider the goals of media scholarship and, in particular, to propose new ways of accounting for television's past, present, and possible futures. As John Ellis (himself a pioneer television scholar and producer) argues, although television will continue to play an important role in society it is now in an "age of uncertainty" that presents new challenges for artists and critics alike.[23] Like Ellis, the authors in this volume rethink television in this moment of uncertainty. While we are indebted to the scholarship of the past, we all attempt—in a variety of ways—to reconsider the project and purpose of television studies both inside and outside the academy.

Television studies in the humanities has always been a hybrid, interdisciplinary venture, drawing on fields of inquiry that often are at odds with one another. As it developed in the 1970s and 1980s in the anglophone university and publishing industry, it drew on at least five critical paradigms: the "mass society" critique associated with the Frankfurt school and postwar intellectuals such as Dwight MacDonald and Herbert Marcuse; the textual tradition (to borrow John Hartley's term)[24] associated with literary and film theory; the journalistic tradition associated especially with theater criticism (in the United States this tradition formed a canon of quality and golden-age programming); the quantitative and qualitative mass communications research on audiences and content; and the cultural studies approaches to media and its audiences. Although these traditions developed differently in different national contexts, they all formed a discursive field—a set of interrelated ways of speaking about TV—that continue to affect the way we frame television as an academic object of study.[25] In addition, insofar as the rise of television studies in the humanities coincided with the rise of feminist theory and critical race theory, much of the scholarship has been informed by theories of difference, identity, and subjectivity.[26]

In the 1970s and 1980s (the truly formative years of television studies) British cultural studies was particularly important in redirecting the kinds of questions that scholars posed about television. Above all, cultural studies (in conjunction with the changing paradigms of mass communications research) played a major role in redefining the established assumptions about media's relation to its publics. Instead of thinking of television as an ultimate source of power that affected audience behavior and consciousness "en masse," the major innovators of cultural studies (Raymond Williams, Richard Hoggart, and Stuart Hall) insisted on looking at what audiences did with the media—how media formed the means through which people (especially in the British context, the working classes) expressed their culture.[27] (It should be noted here that developments in mass communications research—especially the interest in "uses and gratifications"—also refined early "hypodermic" models of media effects.)

Following this view, many television scholars in the humanities steadfastly eschewed notions of a "mass audience" on the grounds that, as Williams suggested,[28] the term "mass" served as the twentieth century equivalent of the word "mob." With reference to the British working classes, Williams (*Culture and Society 1958; The Long Revolution, 1961; Communications, 1962*) and Hoggart (*The Uses of Literacy*, 1958) demonstrated that industrially produced media are not simply enforced on the "masses" but rather are used by people as a material source for communication and the creation of communities.[29]

Later, in the 1970s, work at the Centre for Contemporary Cultural Studies and, in particular, Stuart Hall's influential essay "Encoding/Decoding," provided a theory of circuits and reciprocal relationships between media and their audiences. Following the work of Antonio Gramsci, Hall argues that media are "hegemonic" institutions that work to secure social consensus by incorporating dissent and conflict. Yet he also argues that this does not mean that audiences necessarily always respond to and interpret media texts in the same way. Rather than simply being affected or persuaded by media messages, audiences "decode" media according to their own social backgrounds and identities. Because of this, audiences do not all necessarily accept the dominant ideologies offered in mainstream media.[30]

This early work in British cultural studies set an agenda for television scholars in the years to come. Rather than thinking about audiences as faceless mobs with scientifically predictable responses and behavior, television studies has used a more anthropological idea of audiences as cultures.[31] And rather than thinking about mass media as "captains of consciousness" or sources of propaganda and persuasion, television scholars interested in ideology are more likely to use the more nuanced concept of "hegemony" to explore how television texts voice but usually conservatively resolve social contradictions and dissent.[32] Beginning in the late 1970s, feminist critics from film/literary studies and from British cultural studies focused particularly on the "everyday" aspects of television (especially soap operas), and many feminist critics were and continue to be interested in the internal contradictions that its hegemonic operations impose. In particular, feminist critics have explored the way television reinforces patriarchy while also providing women (or the female consumers TV addresses) with pleasurable ways to fantasize against the grain of patriarchy. In this pursuit, feminist critics have often used methods of narrative analysis and/or psychoanalysis imported from film theory (associated, for example, with the pioneering work on soaps by Tania Modleski), and they have also used qualitative audience research (associated, for example, with the innovative work on *Dallas* by Ien Ang, who combined an analysis of audiences with narrative and ideological analysis of the show).[33]

It would, of course, be entirely misleading to say that all of television studies has revolved around this cultural studies dialogue on hegemony, audience resistance, and pleasure. Certainly, television studies has always been much more varied and fluid than this brief sketch suggests. Numerous people have written about the industry, aesthetics, and globalization, and many have been more influenced by the continental theories of Baudrillard and Virilio or by Jürgen Habermas's theory of the public sphere than by British cultural studies. Foundational books such as Horace Newcomb's *Television: The Most Popular Art,* John Fiske and John Hartley's *Reading Television,* John Ellis's *Visible Fictions,* Todd Gitlin's *Inside Prime Time,* and David Morley's *Family Television,* as well as groundbreaking anthologies such as Newcomb's *Television: The Critical View,* E. Ann Kaplan's *Regarding Television,* Patricia Mellencamp's *Logics of Television,* and Robert C. Allen's *Channels of Discourse* all represent the breath and scope of inquiry into the medium throughout the 1970s and 1980s.[34]

So too, over the course of the 1980s, as British cultural studies traveled to the United States, many of its complexities (including its sustained critique of ideology and power) were often dropped in favor of searching for audience pleasures and subversive readings. In its most deeply caricatured form, cultural studies (and television studies by proxy) often came to signify a certain brand of work that simply embraced mass culture by locating "resistance" everywhere, refusing to analyze fully the constraints imposed by the culture industries. What ensued was a rather polarized debate over the degree to which popular media reproduce dominant ideology and consumer alienation versus the degree to which the media provide people with the "tools" through which to make their own culture and even "resist" the status quo.[35]

By 1990 this cultural optimism/cultural pessimism debate was so associated with television studies that when the *Voice Literary Supplement* featured a long cover story on the history of academic television studies (an amazing turn of events in the first place), reporter Linda Benn represented the evolution of the field as a long march toward the optimistic claims of cultural studies. Benn argued that a new generation of academics had turned away from a highbrow disdain for television and toward an optimistic embrace of popular culture, epitomized for Benn by the work of Andrew Ross, Lawrence Grossberg, and especially John Fiske.[36]

Reading Benn's *Voice* article a decade later, I can't help but think how quickly this history has itself become history. In other words, while critics in the late 1980s and much of the 1990s were preoccupied with the relative value of media, more recent television scholarship has for the most part dropped the debate altogether. Indeed, rather than asking if media does bad things to people, or conversely whether people do good things with media, the "hot" topics of debate have shifted elsewhere—largely toward a focus on "new media."

It is not that the previous debate about culture, ideology, and audience resistance was in any way resolved. Nor did the debate naturally evolve into this new one. To be sure, media professors still ask their students to read seminal literature in cultural studies, and television studies per se continues to be a varied and vibrant field of inquiry.[37] But today the passions that once made tempers flare have shifted toward a passionate engagement with new technologies, which often are assumed to be tantamount to the "future" itself.

This shift in emphasis is not merely a product of the exhaustion with a certain set of questions and modes of analysis that characterized television and cultural studies in their formative years. More troubling, at its worst it is a shift away from an analysis of the present—from the material and actually existing conditions of media culture—toward a kind of "retro-avant-gardism" that resonates with modernity's great faith in technology. Anything that works differently from the old stuff—and especially if it works in ways mysterious to most people—is instantly considered for its radical utopian potential. I am not speaking just about the likes of Bill Gates and Steve Jobs. I am also referring to the people in the academy who seem to think that as long as their presentation is on PowerPoint then it is by nature better than any other kind of presentation, especially one that is just plain talk. Today, if Moses went to the mountain the Ten Commandments would have to be etched on Power-Point for anyone to take them seriously.

There are more important implications than just academic narcissism, however. In his review of the literature on new media theory, Kevin Robins in *Into the Image* highlights the way present-day virtual reality (VR) enthusiasts imagine cyberspace as a kind of digital Disneyland, a place of (bland) utopian sameness that denies all conflict and difference in social reality. By critiquing such cybervisionaries as Jaron Lanier, Timothy Leary, Brenda Laurel, and Michael Benedikt, Robins challenges their "age-old" dreams of transcendence, commonality, and transparent identification with make-believe others on the Net. Rather than building a vr version of the bland, orderly "neutralized city" of Disneyland, Robins argues that we need to conceptualize vr's possible worlds by starting from the real-world social conflicts around us: "We must recognise that difference, asymmetry and conflict are constitutive features of that world. Not community."[38] In other words, it might be more useful to consider how new media can be used within the actually existing imperfect present—a world where conflict is rife and should be featured as a constituent element of a culture (cyber or otherwise) rather than denied in appeals to a (not actually existing) democratic ideal. This doesn't mean that we can't strive for a more democratic use of media; instead it cautions us against platitudes and utopian appeals to "disembodiment" (the transcendence of race, sex, gender, and other physical realities) on the Web.

From a historical perspective, this "transcendent" utopian discourse on new media seems frighteningly consistent with what James Carey and John Quirk have called the "mythos of the electronic revolution,"[39] a myth they trace back to the advent of nineteenth-century inventions (the telegraph, the telephone, etc.) but that equally applies to the current stories we tell about new electronic communications. These stories tend to fetishize technologies—to abstract them from their social, industrial, and political contexts—in favor of imagining wondrous futures that bear little relation to the worlds in which technologies actually take shape. In his essay in this volume, Jostein Gripsrud considers this utopian discourse on new media in the context of contemporary European television, and he argues that this faith in new technologies is part of a more general embrace of commercialism and neglect for the democratic traditions of public service broadcasting.

That said, the flip side of technological utopianism is the dystopian "doomsday" view that technology will ruin our world. The various "moral panics" about the new digital media (especially with regard to children) often distort what are extremely complicated questions about media effects—questions that are often hotly contested among humanists and social scientists alike. Politicians often act as if these contested questions were answers and present them to the public as if they were fact: video games will make kids violent; the Internet will give kids access to adult secrets; computers lead to a lack of physical exercise and "healthy" outdoor fun—all claims that were, by the way, variously made about previous media forms, including the novel, movies, radio, and television.

This is the new media paradigm at its worst. At its best, however, the study of new media eschews both retro-avant-gardism and dystopian moral panics in favor of a critical engagement with what is actually going on here in the media-saturated present. From this perspective, scholars have explored how Internet culture shapes concepts about the public sphere; how it rearticulates (and at times replicates) gender, sexual, class, and racial struggles; how it provides alternative modes of "gathering" as communities; and/or how it reconstructs the politics of national borders and our sense of place.[40] David Morley's essay in this volume deals with this last issue with regard to the way television and new media technologies relate to mobility among world populations and an increasingly "dislocated" sense of home.

In addition, numerous critics have demonstrated how people are making use of interactive digital technologies for communication with and among one another. Building on cultural studies' long-term interest in the "active" audience, scholars have explored fan uses of the Net, showing how audiences use chat rooms and message boards to discuss their ideas about programs, create their own stories, and even protest network cancellations of favorite shows.[41] Although it is important to recognize that chat rooms are not outside the logic of consumption (indeed, the "official" sites are sponsored by the industry), it is clear that the Net has made it more possible for audiences to form reception communities and at times voice opinions not heard on the major media outlets. As Priscilla Peña Ovalle's essay in this volume demonstrates, Mexican Americans have launched the Web site Pocho.com, which critiques racial stereotypes on commercial television. So, too, various grassroots organizations are using digital media against the grain of the traditional media. Anna Everett's essay is a case study of black women's political use of the Internet to organize protests during the Million Woman March in 2000. At the time of this writing, the global antiwar movement is likewise using the Net to organize both virtual and physical marches against Washington, while groups like MoveOn.org and the National Network to End the War distribute information via Web sites and/or e-mail on a regular basis.

Yet, it is equally important to note (as many of the aforementioned critics do) that the ability to use the Net is circumscribed by our consumer model of technological access and the politics of the digital divide. In July 1999 the Digital Divide Summit held by the U.S. Secretary of Commerce demonstrated that numerous Americans were "falling through the Net." Despite signs that upper-income blacks are purchasing home computers, "the 'digital divide' between Whites and most minorities continues to grow."[42] Moreover, Logan Hill argues that even if low-income groups and minorities gain access to the Web (particularly with the advent of Community Technology Centers in schools, libraries, and low-income housing communities), the digital divide should not be measured just in terms of online access. "Universal Access," he argues, "isn't just about being able to surf the Web, it's about the ability to participate and compete in a technology-driven industry and society. Information-poor communities not only miss out on interesting content, they do business at a severe disadvantage, in what Manuel Castells describes as 'information black holes': information goes in, but it doesn't come out."[43]

To be sure, at this moment in history politicians and executives are doing everything possible to "consolidate" the media under a handful of corporate giants. The overturning of the 1970s syndication and copyright rules in the early 1990s meant that broadcasters no longer had restrictions on the production and ownership of programming. Following this, the Communications Act of 1996 lifted many of the then-existing limits to corporate ownership of broadcast channels. Although, as Robert McChesney notes, the act used the rhetoric of democracy and choice to justify corporate conglomeration, by 1997 "the preponderance of U.S. mass communication [was] controlled by less than two dozen enormous profit-maximizing corporations."[44] And, of course, in the 1980s the three major U.S. broadcast networks were taken over by parent corporations, and in the 1990s they become part of media conglomerates that also variously own cable networks, film studios, syndication companies, radio stations, print media, book publishers, video outlets, dot-coms, theme parks, and the like.[45] The broadcast networks have in recent years also sought partnerships and/or shares in large commercial search engines such as Yahoo, AOL, and Infoseek.[46]

In 2003 these deregulation policies reached a crescendo when the Federal Communications Commission (FCC), led by the laissez-faire sensibilities of Chair Michael Powell, lifted longstanding restrictions on media ownership by, for example, loosening restrictions that prevent a network from owning stations that broadcast to more than 35 percent of U.S. households (the new rules expanded that to 45 percent); by loosening rules that limit the number of television stations that one company can own in any given market; and by eliminating the newspaper/broadcaster cross-ownership restrictions in markets with nine or more TV stations. Powell's agenda was hotly debated within the FCC by opposing commissioners, by a well-organized activist campaign, and by the U.S. Congress, which in fact (at the time of this writing) is overturning these new FCC rules. Perhaps in this regard, at least for the moment, the FCC's laissez-faire policies will be tempered by a more complete consideration of the effects of deregulation not only on business practices and fair competition but also on the culture of television itself.

Certainly, market-driven policies and corporate mergers raise important questions regarding diversity, access, freedom of speech, and the general corporate control of everyday life.[47] While FCC chair Michael Powell and many industry executives seek to legitimate further deregulation and increasing conglomeration on the basis that the old ownership restrictions have outlived their usefulness in the new TV market, others (including FCC Commissioner Michael Copps as well as various industry leaders and spokespeople) disagree, arguing that the presumed cornucopia of channels does not necessarily deliver diversity of quality and viewpoints. (And note that cable is still a luxury item that not everyone owns—it it used by roughly 70 percent of U.S. households.)

Moreover, given the global nature of media markets, the situation in the United States has ramifications across the Atlantic. On hearing of the new FCC rulings in June, senior BBC executive John Willis delivered an impassioned speech to the Royal Television Society in which he warned that the relaxation of U.S. ownership rules could turn British TV into "a wasteland" (echoing, of course, the oft-cited phrase coined by FCC Chair Newton Minow in 1961). While Willis admitted that America's "well-resourced system . . . has produced some of the world's greatest television programs," he nevertheless added that much of U.S. TV's commercially driven fare was "bland and tasteless," that the "apparent [freedom of] choice is just a tawdry illusion," and that "the lesson from America is that if news and public affairs are left purely to the market, it will most likely give the government want it wants." (He especially attacked the news coverage of Iraq, calling Fox news a "military cheerleader.") Given this, Willis warned that allowing groups like Viacom or Disney to control ITV or Channel Five would be a "careless risk."[48]

While Willis and others direct their attention to issues of program quality and the right-wing bias of news coverage, in the United States it is also clear that a diversity of channels hasn't (as some media conglomerates claim) produced more cultural diversity. In this volume, John Caldwell discusses how the conglomerate structure of the industry has led to strategies of "tiering" (in which a conglomerate can devote a channel to, say, women or youth), but in effect this has served to fragment audiences into demographic "ghettos." He also discusses the way people of color continue to find themselves in genre "ghettos," such as the notorious placement of black talent in the sitcom form or in reality shows like *Cops*—where representation is anything but desirable. Caldwell argues that these corporate strategies are not the same as diversity of point of view, nor do they equal diversity in terms of authority over production and self-representation.

The historical treatment of African American publics in the multi-channel system is telling in this regard. Faced by cable competition and shrinking audiences, U.S. broadcast networks began to feature more black-cast programming. In particular, this was a strategy used in the late 1980s and early 1990s by Rupert Murdoch (CEO of News Corp.) in an attempt to build audiences for the start-up Fox Network. In 1993, Fox was airing more black shows than had been offered by any network in U.S. television history, but by 2000 no black-cast comedy appeared on the network. Explaining this turnabout, Krystal Brent Zook in *Color by Fox* argues that Fox's embrace of black culture was first and foremost a business plan devised to install the company as the "fourth network." Zook writes that Fox "ultimately found ways to profit from the cultural production and consumption practices of African-Americans . . . [and] also manipulated, to the collective detriment of black people, government infrastructures designed to balance the racially distorted playing field of media ownership. When such infrastructures threatened to limit Murdoch's monopolistic domination . . . he simply had them removed."[49] In turn, this meant the removal of the black-cast shows that no longer helped the network to jockey into position.

As the Fox case demonstrates, even while more competition in the multichannel universe can at times create more space for underrepresented groups, this is subject to business strategies that often are not necessarily "progressive." Considering the entire U.S. television landscape, Beretta Smith-Shomade astutely comments in *Shaded Lives* that even though we tend to think that the current multichannel system offers a multitude of black-cast programs, this "perceived abundance" is not borne out by the numbers, which demonstrate percentagewise an "actual lack" of people of color both in front of and behind the camera.[50] Meanwhile, according to a study recently conducted by the UCLA Chicano Studies Research Center, the statistics are particularly skewed when it comes to Latino populations, who make up only 4 percent of regular prime-time characters on network television, even though they are the largest minority group in the United States (and a majority of the population in Los Angeles where most prime-time TV is produced).[51]

Moreover, as so many critics have suggested, it is not just the number but also the kind of representations and narrative logics that matter.[52] While this is a complex problem, it is clear that the current multichannel landscape is not a world of infinite diversity but rather a sophisticated marketplace that aims to attract demographic groups with spending power. Even minority networks like BET (owned since 2000 by Viacom) or Telemundo (owned since 1998 by Sony Pictures Entertainment in conjunction with other corporate shareholders) are first and foremost concerned with reaching a consumer constituency so as to attract advertisers. As Herman Gray and Smith-Shomade argue, television tends to level all differences and internal struggles in communities of color and to address racialized groups as homogeneous consumer types—for example, the African American audience is imagined as one block rather than a group composed of different social, political, and class interests.[53] In the multichannel universe, this kind of homogenization of various publics has become a way to turn the smaller "niche" audiences of cable into a marketable "brand" (e.g., Lifetime or Oxygen are the "women's" channels; BET is the "black network").

In addition to concerns about source and program diversity, the new conglomerate business structures—coupled with ever-sophisticated technologies of marketing—have spawned debates about privacy and the increasing corporate control over everyday life. A case in point is the recent scandal over TiVo. As reported by the BBC, "TiVo users found the machines, which record programmes onto a hard drive, had stored trailers and commercials from Discovery Channel two nights a week. They had also set themselves to Discovery Channel by default the following mornings."[54] Needless to say, the Discovery Channel is part owner of TiVo.

Although cases like this are striking for their blatant corporate will to brand every artifact of culture with publicity for another, it is not as yet exactly clear what these new conglomerate structures and industrial practices will achieve. While George Orwell's *1984* is still the major "script" for thinking about everyday life in television culture, it is not at all clear that the media are as "organized" as they seem. As David Harvey argues with respect to post-Fordist industrialization generally, we are faced with a kind of internal contradiction between consolidation and fragmentation (in Harvey's analysis big industry now is based on labor forces that are increasingly decentralized and "flexible" as opposed to the old industrial factory model of lifelong wage earners working for monopolies).[55] This kind of contradictory logic between corporate consolidation on the one hand and increasing fragmentation on the other is true of the postindustrial media industries and their labor forces. John Caldwell's contribution to this volume details the new realities of fragmented and flexible labor forces in television/new media production culture by demonstrating that media producers are actually extremely uncertain about their future, so uncertain that they tend to adopt what he calls "ritualistic" business practices and protocols.

Industrywide uncertainty not only influences business practices but also affects cultural values about the relative worth of television as a public service and form of sociality. In his volume *On Television* (a series of lectures that he had delivered on French TV), the late Pierre Bourdieu spoke out against the commercial imperative in news and information programming. He argues: "In the 1950s, television in France was openly cultural; it used its monopoly to influence virtually every product that laid claim to high cultural status . . . and to raise the taste of the general public. In the 1990s, because it must reach the largest audience possible, television is intent on exploiting and pandering to these same tastes." Considering Bourdieu's own intellectual oeuvre on the sociology of art and taste (which in turn has been very influential in television studies), this might seem like a rather odd position. He ends his thought, however, in a more characteristic fashion: "I don't share the nostalgia professed by some people for the paternalistic-pedagogical television of the past, which I see as no less opposed to a truly democratic use of the means of mass circulation than populist spontaneism and demagogic capitulation to popular tastes."[56]

In Britain, where John Reith's notions of "public service" and "educational uplift" formed a key historical trajectory for the BBC, new regulatory policies and the related 25 percent minimum quota on independent production initiated a "quasi-market" consumer-demand philosophy that now governs terrestrial broadcasting.[57] The change from a "cultural uplift" mission to one of consumer choice and regulated market competition has in turn refueled debates about television's artistic and cultural purpose. Even Channel 4 (which was created in the early 1980s through an act of Parliament and became known for providing cutting-edge programs that catered to minority tastes and interests) has been criticized for becoming more predictable and conservative in view of increased market competition.[58] In other words, although British broadcast policymakers have used the rhetoric of market competition, independence, and "choice," none of this rhetoric is self-evident. As in the U.S. system, market competition (even regulated markets) does not necessarily mean greater diversity or better TV.

In the United States, where public television has historically been "ghettoized," the term "quality" has nevertheless played a central role in policy discourses and in the industry at large. As I suggested earlier in my discussion of reality TV, news organizations debate the demise of culture on a daily basis (or at least turn this cultural debate into marketable infotainment). This rather cynical conflation of culture and commerce has a long history in U.S. broadcasting: since the early 1950s the major national networks used cultural programming and appeals to "quality" as a way to legitimize their oligopoly business practices.[59] But in the current TV marketplace the term "quality," which is often tied to branding, has new instrumental uses and commercial ramifications.

Meanwhile, for television critics, who have long debated the cultural hierarchies and prejudices associated with the term "quality," the issues are in no way self-evident. Although it is, of course, important to understand the limits imposed on representation by markets and their regulation, it is also clear that stories, images, and audience interpretation are never strictly ruled by the logic of the market. In this regard, despite my rather lengthy incantation of the current media-conglomerate marketplace, it is just as important to remember that issues of culture and meaning-making are "messy," unpredictable, and in no way understood through market analysis alone. As so many studies have shown, audiences make sense of popular culture in unexpected ways—and often in ways that have little to do with the cultural hierarchies of producers and critics. Moreover, as suggested by the quote from Pierre Bourdieu, rather than looking back at the old broadcast systems and wishing for the return of traditional notions of "quality" (which were mostly formed on the basis of the tastes and interests of the broadcast elites), it seems that this moment of change gives critics an opportunity to consider the quality debates anew—an opportunity that both Charlotte Brunsdon and Jostein Gripsrud take up (although from different perspectives) in their essays.

In all of these ways, the new television universe—and the critic's role in it—looks considerably different from the old one. In order to understand the changes afoot, we should not simply analyze the present but rather attempt to understand television within the "long view" of its historical meaning and place in cultures. Along these lines, television historians have attempted to map "alternative" histories of the medium—diverging, for example, from the evolutionary models, chronicling efforts, and industrial/technological/policy focus associated with groundbreaking broadcast historians like Erik Barnouw or Lord Asa Briggs.[60] In the late 1980s and early 1990s, a new generation of historians built on the efforts of the previous generation by rethinking political and economic history and by redirecting analysis to issues of the cultural/social history of everyday life.[61]

More recently, historians have explored television through a number of perspectives. In *Radio, Television, and Modern Life*, Paddy Scannell reformulates the "object" of historical analysis by moving from the industry and technology per se in order to analyze how the broadcast vernacular (modes of talk and presentation) changed ideas about everyday life and nationhood in Britain. John Caughie's *Television Drama* takes television out of the familiar historical story of technology, industry, and policy, and places it into the broader sphere of postwar British modern theater and literary movements. Laurie Ouellette's *Viewers Like You?* places the history of PBS within a Foucauldian framework of "governmentality." Steven Classen's *Watching Jim Crow* rethinks the history of the famous case of WLBT in the civil rights era through oral histories with African American activists who were engaged in the struggle against the racist policies of the Jackson, Mississippi, station. Jeffrey Sconce's *Haunted Media* traces the history of the idea of "tele-presence" and "liveness" from the telegraph to the Net. And Chon Noriega's *Shot in America* maps the history of independent Chicano film production through an alternative history of PBS.[62] In this sense, historians are not just "adding more" to television history but rather are rethinking the goals of television history itself by attempting to break with familiar historical narratives and to place the medium within new contexts of past experience.

Building on these efforts, a number of essays in this volume consider television culture within a larger historical perspective. John Hartley's essay places television into a broad history of the "republic of letters" and the construction of citizenship from print through the electronic age. Through this history Hartley argues that the antitelevision stance adopted by many elite institutions (the academy foremost among these) often proceeds on the rhetoric of cultural preservation and democratic access but in the end fits into a longer history of attempts, on the part of elites, to police the interpretative and cultural practices of modern publics. Michael Curtin rethinks the entire project of writing television history from a "nationalistic" perspective—that is, the major ways the histories of the medium have been written. Instead, he argues that the rise of national television systems should be studied cross-culturally, and to this end he presents a broad cultural geography of the television age by comparing the fates of three "media capitals"—Chicago, Hollywood, and Hong Kong—over the last fifty years. William Uricchio explores the history of television aesthetics and spectatorship by mapping broad changes in television technology—from the old living-room console to remote control to the new "smart" television systems. William Boddy considers the new digital interactive television systems in the context of previous failed attempts to introduce interactive systems, thereby demonstrating that technological "revolutions" are never simply technology driven, but rather occur within broader industrial, regulatory, and cultural/social conditions.

Jan Olsson and I both return to the early days of television, and by taking a more microhistorical case study approach we both attempt to revise longstanding notions about the relationships among commercial culture, public service, and the "high" arts that have underwritten television histories. Jan Olsson challenges the "great divide" thesis that sees commercial broadcast systems as the antithesis of public service/state-run systems. Instead, through a detailed case of study of the innovation of Swedish television in the 1950s, Olsson shows how Sweden's public service model was from the start based on and designed to emulate U.S. commercial media. In the process, Olsson makes us question the nostalgic idealism that runs through recent critiques of the commercialization of European broadcasting. In my essay I argue that we need to understand television history within the broader context of the history of postwar visual culture, especially the merger between "high" and "low" art. I explore how the Museum of Modern Art in New York envisioned television as a potential way to lure suburbanites (especially housewives) into the urbane world of modern art, and I show how the museum tried to create a popular/vernacular form of modernism by creating its own commercial TV production company and several television pilots.

Taken together the essays in this volume provide a diverse exploration of television and its convergence with new media. To be sure, not all authors agree on the political and social consequences of television and our contemporary culture of convergence; instead the book displays a range of questions, positions, and research agendas.

The authors in this volume write at a moment of considerable uncertainty, anxiety, and confusion, not only about television per se but about what television scholars themselves can do and what role they can play in media culture, in teaching, and in producing ways of thinking about media. In *On Television,* Bourdieu addresses the ironies of a world where going commercial no longer signifies for intellectuals any sort of compromise but instead demonstrates the ultimate "legitimation." Bourdieu particularly discusses how television journalists create an "on-call" roster of intellectual authorities who speak at speeds that defy thought. Television, he argues, "rewards a certain number of fast-thinkers who offer cultural 'fast-food'" and banal clichés delivered at sound-bite speed. Obviously, the fact that Bourdieu went on television to deliver this critique suggests that he did not simply mean that intellectuals should avoid the mass media, nor did he think everyone in the audience fell for these jingoistic tactics. Instead, his book warns against the seductions of being a celebrity professor and against accepting at face value television's presentation of authoritative knowledge.[63]

In the case of U.S. intellectuals it seems just as important to note that universities are themselves often ruled by the logic of the market. The history of academic television studies and television archives is very much intertwined with the formation of industrywide groups (for example, the Emmy-granting Academy of Television Arts and Sciences) and industry initiatives to create canons of "quality" television (and also "quality" criticism).[64] As Julie D'Acci suggests in her essay on the role of television studies within the university, television critics work not in an ivory tower of idealism but rather in the material conditions of the contemporary (superconsumer-oriented) university with its battles over enrollment dollars and hiring lines, and, I would add, with its webs of corporate and government funding that make certain objects and topics more possible to study than others.

Building on D'Acci's insights I want to conclude here by considering the peculiar situation that television scholars occupy at this moment of transition. Despite the field's considerable achievements over the last three decades, television studies in the humanities has been only reluctantly incorporated into university life. When I was in graduate school in the early 1980s I worked as a teaching assistant for a professor who began every class by admitting that having a Ph.D. in Television Studies was just a step up from being a doctor of refrigerators. On the one hand her self-deprecating humor was a strategy for dealing with the struggle, still ongoing, of choosing to study a seemingly trivial and obvious, and always-objectional object. On the other hand her joke was much less funny when we consider that at this same time in history Mark Fowler (President Reagan's FCC chair and a great proponent of deregulation) claimed that television was pretty much no different from a toaster (and who needed to regulate toast?).

Since the early 1980s television studies has been increasingly institutionalized, and people like myself found jobs in film schools and communication schools where we became the first generation (now followed by another) to benefit from the previous generation's struggles. Yet even while television studies has been somewhat institutionalized, there is no doubt that the cultural prejudices against television still significantly impact the debates on the medium. The continued denigration of television as a hopelessly "low" medium has the unfortunate effect of making us blind to its successes and potential. Making matters worse, in the year 2003 even to speak of the medium's "artistic and educational potential" sounds so steeped in the rhetoric once used to promote public TV (now a radically compromised and severely underfunded venture) that no one seems able to envision much of a future for television at all.

Perhaps for this reason, at the current moment many people in the humanities tend to value anything called new media as a somehow more high-end field of culture and thus worthy of study. Moreover, the political/moral debates about the Internet, the military applications of new media, and our culture's general love affair with new technologies make government grants more available and the whole pursuit more lucrative and prestigious for universities. Despite the fact that the new media are technologies of mass distribution, it has somehow become more legitimate to study anything that comes over the Internet (including TV shows) than it is to study television itself.

A similar bias, if somewhat differently articulated, is registered in the *U.S. Statistical Abstract*, compiled by the U.S. Census Bureau. In a section titled "Arts, Entertainment, Recreation" the bureau measured "adult participation . . . in selected leisure activities" for 1999. The activities selected by the bureau include the following in order of their popularity: "dining out; entertain friends or relatives at home; reading books; barbecuing; play cards; go to beach; attend music performances; baking; cooking for fun; go to bars/night clubs; surf the net; crossword puzzles; picnic; go to museums; go to live theater; zoo attendance; board games; video games; dance/go dancing; photography; billboards/pool; electronic games (not TV)."[65] Notice that this list does not include TV (in fact, it rules out TV) nor does it include movies as part of the adult activities that constitute leisure activities. While the *Statistical Abstract* offers no justification for its omission of TV and film, the absence of these media is especially interesting considering the presence of "surfing the net," "video games," and "electronic games (not TV)." Indeed, the data reported in this study are complied according to an underlying assumption that TV and movies are fundamentally not like the Net, video games, or electronic games. The underlying assumption that guides this study is more obvious when we consider the rest of the list. As the report explains, the selected pastimes are "activities" that people do. In this context, both TV and movies do not qualify as activities. If this seems reasonable, it is less so when we consider that other spectator amusements—live theater, musical performances, and museum going—are counted as activities. But why is watching a play considered to be an activity, while going to the movies or watching TV is not?

The answer is that there is no answer. The *Statistical Abstract* is not simply reporting data, it is also making value judgments about what counts as a form of active culture and what doesn't. No matter what is on the Net (and of course TV shows and movies are major content for the Net), the fact that we "surf" it somehow makes it "active" and thus comparable both to "high" cultural activities like going to the theater and museums and to homespun cultural hobbies like card playing, crossword puzzles, or cooking for fun. For those of us who think of the Net as a branch of media culture, listing it alongside cooking and baking is a bit like the old *Sesame Street* song "One of These Things Is Not Like the Other." But, if we regard the *Statistical Abstract* as (to use Foucault's terminology) an "ordering of things," then it is obvious that the Census Bureau is putting the Internet and video/electronic games into an altogether different discursive "series"—a completely other chain of meaning—than would media scholars. These state-sanctified ways of counting, dividing, and mapping media culture are worthy of study in their own right. For now, however, I simply use this example to suggest that television, film, and new media scholars need to come to terms with the way governments conceptualize media and media publics at this moment of transition.

Indeed, as this Census Bureau document suggests, what is at stake is the very definition of culture itself. And in that regard anyone interested in television should think seriously about how the medium has consistently been represented as "not culture" (whether that be interpreted as high art or as hobby culture). In fact, if you flip further through the *Statistical Abstract,* you will find that television is "counted" (as it has been since the 1940s) not only in sections regarding the entertainment industries, technology, and communications, but also in a section on "manufactures." In other words, television is counted as an appliance in the home. Hopefully, the essays in this book will be of interest to everyone who thinks that television is different from a toaster or a fridge.

NOTES

1. Karen Lury, *British Youth Television: Cynicism and Enchantment* (London: Oxford University Press, 2001), pp. 19–20.
2. Graeme Turner, "The Uses and Limitations of Genre," and "Genre, Hybridity, and Mutations," in *The Television Genre Book,* ed. Glen Creeber (London: British Film Institute, 2001), pp. 4–6.
3. Richard Kilborn traces the term "reality TV" to the appearance of *Unsolved Mysteries* in 1987. See his "How Real Can You Get? Recent Developments in 'Reality' Television," *European Journal of Communication* 9.4 (1994): 421–39. The term is now applied to a diverse group of programs including reality game shows, "shockumentaries" like

When Good Pets Go Bad, serialized reality shows with social experiment themes like *The Real World* and *Survivor,* or reality celebrity shows like *The Osbournes.*

4. The recent cycle of reality TV was spurred by the international success of the reality game shows *Who Wants to Be a Millionaire?, Survivor,* and *Big Brother.*

5. In an informal conversation (on January 7, 2003) with Susan Lyne, then head of ABC Prime Time Entertainment, I learned that the network offers people about nine times their yearly salary to appear on serialized reality programs.

6. In February 2003 *Variety* reporter Josef Adalian wrote: "Just last month [Jeff] Zucker (NBC Entertainment President) told a group of TV critics that reality 'has its place on NBC . . . in the summer.' Within a few weeks, Zucker—like webheads all over town— was tearing up his primetime sked to make room for new unscripted series" ("TV Nets Struggle to Get Grip on Reality," Variety.com, February 23, 2003. In this same article Adalian also notes: "ABC may be doubling its ratings on Thursday with [the reality series] *Are You Hot?,* but the net doesn't seem to be luring many A-list advertisers to the show." More generally, advertisers have a "taste-level" problem with reality programming. John Mandel, co-CEO and chief negotiating officer of Mediacom, says, "There's a ton of advertisers that won't go near certain of the reality shows because they find them not an appropriate environment" (cited in Louis Chunovic, "Advertisers Face Reality," *TelevisionWeek,* January 27, 2003, p. 10).

7. For example, *Joe Millionaire* delivered Fox's highest ratings in its time slot in eight years among adults 18–49 and total viewers. (In the 18–49 group its score increased 248 percent from the time slot's average.) (Leslie Ryan, "Are Short-Run Reality Series a Long-Term Fix?" *Electronic Media,* January 13, 2003, pp. 1A and 55).

8. See "Wife Swap Show in Ratings Surge," *BBC News,* news.bbc.co.uk, January 22, 2003. For more, see "ITV Scores Big with Reality TV," *BBC News,* news.bbc.co.uk, January 22, 2003; "Wife Swap," *Guardian Unlimited,* mediaguardian.co.uk, 8 January 8, 2003.

9. Adalian, "TV Nets Struggle."

10. For a description of the *Nightline* episode and the citation of Vonnegut, see "Rats for Ratings," abcnews.com, June 18, 2001. Note that even while Vonnegut refused the "end of civilization" thesis, he called the producers of TV "scumbags." In early February 2003, CNN ran a news package probing the question of whether or not American culture was in decline. One of the segments was specifically devoted to reality TV.

11. Todd Gitlin, *Inside Prime Time* (New York: Pantheon, 1983).

12. For more on television genres and their recent transformations, see Creeber, *The Television Genre Book.*

13. In a humorous article on this topic, Henry Jenkins points out that Turner Broadcasting System CEO Jamie Kellner characterized television viewers who used video recorders to skip commercials as being guilty of "stealing" broadcast content (Jenkins, "Treating Viewers as Criminals," technologyreview.com, July 3, 2002).

14. "Nielsen: Streaming Media Usage Spikes 6.5 Percent," internetnews.com, December 12, 2000.

15. T. S. Kelly, cited in ibid.

16. Christopher Anderson, *Hollywood Television: The Studio System in the Fifties* (Austin: University of Texas Press, 1994).

17. "Multimedia Audiences—Summary: 2001," *U.S. Statistical Abstract,* no. 1104, section 24 (2002): 699 (this report was compiled by Mediamark Research Inc., New York, spring 2001). The smallest group of television users was in the 18–24 group (90.5 percent) and increased in increments by age (the 65-and-over group used television most: 96.9 percent). Television use was relatively stable by income groups (92.4 percent in households earning less than 10,000; 93.6 in households earning more than $50,000); but cable viewing was much higher (for obvious reasons of cost) in the higher-income group (in households earning less than $10,000, 53.8 percent reportedly used cable while that figure rose to 81.6 percent in the households earning over $50,000). The biggest difference occurred in Internet use. Only 18.1 percent of the households earning less than $10,000 used the Internet compared to 73.9 percent of households earning $50,000 or more. When measured by race, television use was relatively stable (it varied only about 1 percent) whereas Internet use showed the highest variations (about 20 percent). Asians accessed the Net the most (67.2 percent); followed by whites at 53.8 percent; Spanish-speaking populations at 41.5 percent; and blacks at 37.4 percent. (The figures also included a category titled "other," presumably a "catch-all" category of various unspecified races and nationalities.) Net use also varied greatly with educational levels: 76.5 percent of college-educated people accessed the Net versus only 16.3 percent of people without a high school diploma. These figures indicate that the digital divide is still a reality, and that television—especially terrestrial broadcasting—is still the most widely used medium across all demographics. For more on the "digital divide," see Benjamin M. Compaigne, ed., *The Digital Divide: Facing a Crisis or Creating a Myth?* (Cambridge: MIT Press, 2001). This book contains the report "Falling through the Net: The Digital Divide" by the National Telecommunications and Information Administration, which concludes that Asians and whites of higher income and education "are far more connected" and that the "information gap between the information haves and have nots is growing over time" (p. 25).

18. Henry Jenkins, "Transmedia Storytelling," technologyreview.com, January 15, 2003. Jenkins notes that for the younger generation especially, participation in media culture has become a matter of "hunting and gathering" across media platforms.

19. John T. Caldwell, *Televisuality: Style, Crisis, and Authority in American Television* (New Brunswick: Rutgers University Press, 1995). Note, however, that what Caldwell referred to as "zero degree" television (or TV that presents itself as "unstylized") is still operative, especially in some sitcoms, game shows, and factual programs and talk shows.

20. For Raymond Williams's discussion of flow, see his *Television: Technology and Cultural Form* (1974; Hanover, N.H.: Weslyan University Press, 1992). While widely used, Williams's theory of "flow" had been criticized, even during the classic network and public service era in which it was devised. As early as 1982, John Ellis claimed that Williams's imprecise and problematic definition of the term "flow" allowed for misuse and misreadings of the concept (Ellis, *Visible Fictions: Cinema, Television, Video* [London: Routledge and Kegan Paul, 1982], pp. 117–19). In *Television Culture* (London: Methuen, 1987) John Fiske embraces much of Williams's analysis but suggests that within his theory of television flow Williams had an implicit preference for literature, and he argues that Williams didn't seriously account for the way U.S. broadcasters create scheduling flows and draw audiences for advertisers (pp. 99–105). In "Raymond Williams and the Cultural Analysis of Television," *Media, Culture, Society* 13 (1991): 153–69, Stuart Laing summarizes these and other criticisms of flow, claiming that "the problem with 'flow' is that it is a concept which was asked to do too much—to cover too many diverse aspects of the medium" (p. 167).

21. For examples of this literature on globalization and diaspora see Marie Gillespie, *Television, Ethnicity, and Cultural Change* (London: Routledge, 1995); Purnima Mankekar, *Screening Culture, Viewing Politics: An Ethnography of Television, Womanhood, and Nation in Postcolonial India* (Durham: Duke University Press, 1999); and David Morley and Kevin Robins, *Spaces of Identity: Global Media, Electronic Landscapes, and Global Boundaries* (London: Routledge: 1995).

22. Williams, *Television*.

23. John Ellis, *Seeing Things: Television in the Age of Uncertainty* (London: IB Tauis, 2000).

24. See John Hartley, *Uses of Television* (London: Routledge, 1999), chapter 6.

25. Marshall McLuhan is a perfect figure through which to understand how this network of critical paradigms began to coalesce in the 1960s. McLuhan's *Understanding Media: The Extensions of Man* (New York: McGraw-Hill, 1964) drew on mass society, textual, and to some extent, previous journalistic critical paradigms while also referring back to a sociological tradition of thought (associated with his teacher, Harold Innis) that was particularly interested in the ways communication technologies had changed relations of social space over the course of ancient to modern civilizations. McLuhan's work, and slogans like "cool media" or "global village," made him into the quintessential media scholar of his generation. As it turned out, however, despite his charisma his particular mode of inquiry did not do much to shape the field of television studies in the years to come. Instead, McLuhanism was eclipsed by the textual traditions of literary and film studies, and especially by what came to be known as cultural studies. (And note that in *Television* Williams attacked what he perceived to be McLuhan's technological determinism.)

26. For discussions and bibliographical references to feminist film theory in these formative years, see the introduction to Charlotte Brunsdon, Julie D'Acci, and Lynn Spigel, eds., *Feminist Television Criticism: A Reader* (Oxford: Oxford University Press, 1997). Although previously there had been studies about race on television, some of the first studies to use critical race theory and cultural studies insights to analyze race and ethnicity in television programs include Sut Jhally and Justin Lewis, *Enlightened Racism: The Cosby Show, Audiences, and the Myth of the American Dream* (Boulder: Westview Press, 1992); George Lipsitz, "The Meaning of Memory: Family, Class, and Ethnicity in Early Network Television Programs," in *Private Screenings: Television and the Female Consumer,* ed. Lynn Spigel and Denise Mann (Minneapolis: University of Minnesota Press, 1992), pp. 71–109; and Herman Gray, *Watching Race: Television and the Struggle for "Blackness"* (Minneapolis: University of Minnesota Press, 1995).

27. It should be noted here that postwar developments in mass communications research also refined the dominant "hypodermic" effects model toward an interest in what people do with television (by way of selection, uses, group dynamics involved in viewing, etc.). In other words, in reciting this short history I in no way want to suggest that mass communications was the direct opposite of cultural studies, even if the paradigms have since been "othered" and polarized in ways that obscure historical connections and the general history of ideas about communications and culture. David Morley's early book, *Nationwide Audience: Structure and Decoding* (London: BFI, 1980) (one of the first books on the television audience associated with the Centre for Contemporary Cultural Studies), relates a history of the field, showing how changing paradigms within U.S. and British mass communications moved from the hypodermic model of media effects to an emphasis on audience interpretation and use and the social dynamics of viewing.

28. Williams considered the term "mass" to reflect an elitist, antidemocratic way of thinking about culture, and he wanted to find alternative ways of speaking about communication media that would allow for their democratic potential. Williams first expressed his antagonism to the word "mass" and the mass communications paradigm in *Culture and Society, 1780–1950* (1958; New York: Columbia University Press, 1983), and he elaborates on it in *The Long Revolution* (London: Chatto and Windus, 1961) and in *Communications* (Harmondsworth: Penguin, 1962). Throughout his career he continued to resist the term, a position he rehashes in the first chapter of *Television*. James W. Carey elaborates on Williams's rejection of the term "mass" and the mass communications paradigm in *Communication as Culture: Essays on Media and Society* (Boston: Unwin Hyman, 1989), pp. 40–41. See also my introduction to the reprinted Volume of Williams's *Television*, pp. ix–xxxvii.

29. Williams, *Television*. Richard Hoggart, *The Uses of Literacy: Aspects of Working Class Life with Special Reference to Publications and Entertainments* (Harmondsworth: Penguin, 1958).

30. Stuart Hall, "Encoding/Decoding," in *Culture, Media, Language,* ed. Stuart Hall et al. (London: Hutchinson, 1980), pp. 128–38. An earlier version of the essay circulated as "Encoding and Decoding the TV message," Centre for Contemporary Cultural Studies mimeo, University of Brimingham, 1973. See also Stuart Hall and Paddy Scannell, *The Popular Arts* (London: Hutchinson Educational, 1964).

31. Morley's *Nationwide Audience* developed insights in British cultural studies by studying the variety of audience responses to the British program *Nationwide*. Several years later he wrote his influential *Family Television: Cultural Power and Domestic Leisure* (London: Routledge, 1986), which demonstrated the value of studying television audiences within their natural habitat (i.e., the home) in order to understand the way family dynamics (especially gender) can influence the experience of watching TV. In addition, feminist cultural studies of the 1980s—notably, for example, Angela McRobbie's "Settling Accounts with Subcultures: A Feminist Critique," *Screen Education* 34 (1980): 37–49; Janice Radway's *Reading the Romance: Women, Patriarchy, and Popular Literature* (Chapel Hill: University of North Carolina Press, 1984); and Ien Ang's *Watching Dallas: Soap Opera and the Melodramatic Imagination* (London: Methuen, 1985) influenced the direction of qualitative and/or ethnographic audience-based research on television.

By the early 1990s, a major (if not *the* major) preoccupation of television scholarship was with the analysis of audience cultures, not only within the context of hegemony but also within the context of poststructural theories of "everyday life." Michel de Certeau's *The Practice of Everyday Life* (Berkeley: University of California Press, 1984) provided fertile ground for media scholars interested in how people actually use the goods of late capitalism to make their own cultural expressions out of the products of mass culture. See, for example, Fiske, *Television Culture;* and Henry Jenkins, *Textual Poachers: Television Fans and Participatory Culture* (New York: Routledge: 1992). Fiske was also influential in applying Mikhail Bakhtin's work on preindustrial popular culture and the "carnivalesque" to discussions of television, audiences, and pleasure (see *Television Culture*). For overviews and analyses of cultural studies on audiences in this period, see David Morley, *Television Audiences and Cultural Studies* (London: Routledge, 1992), and Roger Silverstone, *Television and Everyday Life* (London: Routledge, 1994).

32. See, for example, Todd Gitlin, "Prime Time Ideology: The Hegemonic Process in Television Entertainment," *Social Problems* 26.3 (February 1979): 251–66; Horace Newcomb and Paul M. Hirsch, "Television as a Cultural Forum," in *Television: The Critical View,* 6th ed., ed. Horace Newcomb (New York: Oxford, 2000), pp. 561–73; Tania Modleski, "The Search for Tomorrow in Today's Soap Operas: Notes on a Feminine Narrative Form," *Film Quarterly* 33.1 (1979): 12–21; Lipsitz, "Meaning of Memory"; Gray, *Watching Race.*

33. Modleski, "Search for Tomorrow"; Ang, *Watching Dallas.* For other influential scholars in feminist cultural studies and criticism of the 1970s and early 1980s, see, for example, Carol Lopate, "Daytime Television: You'll Never Want to Leave Home," *Radical America* 11.1 (1977): 32–51; Dorothy Hobson, *Crossroads: The Drama of Soap Opera* (London: Methuen, 1982), and "Housewives and the Mass Media," in Hall et al., eds., *Culture, Media, Language,* pp. 105–14; Charlotte Brunsdon, "Crossroads: Notes on Soap Opera," *Screen* 22.4 (1981): 32–37; and Michelle Mattelart, "Women and the Culture Industries," *Media, Culture, and Society* 4.2 (1982): 133–51. Note as well that Radway's *Reading the Romance,* while about romance novels, was influential for feminist television scholarship. For a detailed bibliography, see Brunsdon, D'Acci, and Spigel, *Feminist Television Criticism.*

34. Horace Newcomb, *Television: The Most Popular Art* (Garden City, N.Y.: Doubleday, 1974); John Fiske and John Hartley, *Reading Television* (London: Methuen, 1978); Ellis, *Visible Fictions;* Gitlin, *Inside Prime Time;* David Morley, *Family Television* (London: Routledge, 1985); Newcomb, *Television;* E. Ann Kaplan, ed., *Regarding Television: Critical Approaches—An Anthology* (Frederick, Md.: University Publications of America, 1983); Patricia Mellencamp, ed., *Logics of Television; Essays in Cultural Criticism* (Bloomington: Indiana University Press, 1990); and Robert C. Allen, ed., *Channels of Discourse: Television and Contemporary Criticism* (Chapel Hill: University of North Carolina Press, 1987). This is by no means an exhaustive list of the work for this period but rather is an attempt to show the variety of critical methods. In fact, television studies has also been very much a field in which journal essays have had as much influence as books; see, for example, essays such as Nick Browne, "The Political

Economy of the Television (Super) Text," *Quarterly Review of Film and Television* 9.3 (summer 1984): 174–82; and Jane Feuer, "Melodrama, Serial Form, and Television Today," *Screen* 25.1 (1984): 4–16. In addition, the British Film Institute has published a number of influential monographs about television.

35. Although I think it wrong to reduce all of his work to this "trope," the cultural populism side became especially associated with John Fiske, who was often positioned (and indeed sometimes positioned himself) as the polar opposite of the equally caricatured pessimism of the Frankfurt school, especially Max Horkheimer and Theodor Adorno's seminal "The Culture Industry: Enlightenment as Mass Deception," in Max Horkheimer and Theodor W. Adorno, *Dialectic of Enlightenment: Philosophical Fragments,* ed. Gunzelin Schmid Noerr, trans. Edmund Jephcott (1944; Stanford: Stanford University Press, 2002). For essays that discuss and debate the value of cultural studies, see, for example, Michael Budd, Robert Entman, and Clay Steinman, "The Affirmative Character of American Cultural Studies," *Critical Studies in Mass Communication* 7.2 (1990): 169–84; Meaghan Morris, "Banality in Cultural Studies," in Mellencamp, ed., *Logics of Television,* pp. 14–43; and Ron Lembo, "Is There Culture after Cultural Studies?" in *Viewing, Reading, Listening: Audiences and Cultural Reception,* ed. John Cruz and Justin Lewis (Boulder: Westview Press, 1994), pp. 33–54.

36. Linda Benn, "White Noise," *Voice Literary Supplement,* December 1990, pp. 14–16. The cover of this issue of *Voice* sported the headline "Reading Television."

37. For books published on a variety of topics on television in the last five years, see, for example, Ellis, *Seeing Things;* Hartley, *Uses of Television;* Ellen Seiter, *Television and New Media Audiences* (London: Oxford University Press, 1999); David Morley, *Home Territories: Media, Mobility, and Identity* (London: Routledge, 2000); Mankekar, *Screening Culture;* Robin R. Means Coleman, *African American Viewers and the Black Situation Comedy: Situating Racial Humor* (New York: Garland, 1998); Arvind Rajagopal, *Politics after Television: Religious Nationalism and the Retailing of "Hinduness"* (Cambridge: Cambridge University Press, 2001); Ron Lembo, *Thinking through Television* (Cambridge: Cambridge University Press, 2000); Jason Jacobs, *Intimate Screen: Early British Television Drama* (London: Oxford, 2000); Beretta E. Smith-Shomade, *Shaded Lives: African American Women and Television* (New Brunswick: Rutgers University Press, 2002); Lury, *British Youth Television;* Daya Kishan Thussu, ed., *Electronic Empires: Global Media and Local Resistance* (London: Arnold, 1998); Christine Geraghty and David Lusted, eds., *The Television Studies Book* (London: Arnold, 1998); Anna McCarthy, *Ambient Television: Visual Culture and Public Space* (Durham: Duke University Press, 2001); Laurence A. Jarvik, *Masterpiece Theater and the Politics of Quality* (Lanham, Md.: Scarecrow Press, 1999); Jostein Gripsrud, ed., *Television and Common Knowledge* (London: Routledge, 1999); Charlotte Brunsdon, *The Feminist, the Housewife, and the Soap Opera* (Oxford: Oxford University Press, 2000); Lynn Spigel, *Welcome to the Dreamhouse: Popular Media and Postwar Suburbs* (Durham: Duke University Press, 2001); Margaret Morse, *Virtualities: Television, Media Art, and Cyberculture* (Bloomington: Indiana University Press, 1998); Kristal Brent Zook, *Color by Fox: The Fox Network and the Revolution in Black Television* (New York: Oxford University Press, 1999); John Corner, *Critical Ideas in Television Studies* (Oxford: Oxford University Press, 1999); Jeffrey S. Miller, *Something Completely Different: British Television and American Culture* (Minneapolis: University of Minnesota Press, 2000); Tamar Liebes and James Curran, eds., *Media, Ritual, and Identity* (London: Routledge, 1998); Jacques Derrida and Bernard Steigler, *Echographies of Television,* trans. Jennifer Bajorek (Cambridge, Eng.: Polity Press, 2002); Lisa Parks and Shanti Kumar, eds., *Planet Television: A Global Television Reader* (New York: New York University Press, 2001); James Friedman, ed., *Reality Squared: Televisual Discourse on the Real* (New Brunswick: Rutgers University Press, 2002); Donald Bogel, *Prime Time Blues: African Americans on Network Television* (New York: Farrar, Straus and Giroux, 2001); Marybeth Haralovich and Lauren Rabinovitz, eds., *Television, History, and American Culture: Feminist Critical Essays* (Durham: Duke University Press, 1999); Aniko Bodroghkozy, *Groove Tube: Sixties Television and the Youth Rebellion* (Durham: Duke University Press, 2001); Toby Miller, *Television Studies* (London: BFI, 2002); Sasha Torres, ed., *Living Color: Race and Television in the United States* (Durham: Duke University Press, 1998); Graham Roberts and Philip M. Taylor, eds., *The Historian, Television, and Television History* (Luton, Eng.: University of Luton Press, 2001); Joshua Gamson, *Tabloid Talk Shows and Sexual Nonconformity* (Chicago: University of Chicago Press, 1998); Kevin Glynn, *Tabloid Culture: Trash Taste, Popular Power, and the Transformation of American Television* (Durham: Duke University Press, 2000); Janet Staiger, *Blockbuster TV: Must-See Sitcoms in the Network Era* (New York: New York University Press, 2001); Siegfried Zielinski, *Audiovisions: Cinema and Television as Entre'actes in History,* trans. Gloria Custance (Amsterdam: Amsterdam University Press, 1999); Lyn Thomas, *Fans, Feminisms, and "Quality" Media* (London: Routledge, 2002); Robert C. Allen and Annette Hill, eds., *The Television Studies Reader* (New York: Routledge, 2003); John Caughie, *Television Drama: Realism, Modernism, and British Culture* (Oxford: Oxford University Press, 2000); Laurie Ouellette, *Viewers Like You? How Public TV Failed the People* (New York: Columbia University Press, 2002); Steven D. Classen, *Watching Jim Crow: The Struggles over Mississippi TV, 1955–1969* (Durham: NC; Duke University Press, 2004); Jeffrey Sconce, *Haunted Media: Electronic Presence from Telegraphy to Television* (Durham: Duke University Press, 2000); and Chon A. Noriega, *Shot in America: Television, the State, and the Rise of Chicano Cinema* (Minneapolis: University of Minnesota Press, 2000). For books related to media industries and policy, see note 47.

38. Kevin Robins, *Into the Image: Culture and Politics in the Field of Vision* (London: Routledge, 1996), p. 101.

39. James W. Carey and John J. Quirk, "The Mythos of the Electronic Revolution," in Carey, ed., *Communication as Culture,* pp. 113–41.

40. See, for example, Ananda Mitra, "Virtual Commonality: Looking for India on the Internet," in *Virtual Culture: Identity and Communication in Cybersociety,* ed. Steven G. Jones (London: Sage, 1997), pp. 55–79; Logan Hill, "Beyond Access: Race, Technology, and Community," in *Technicolor: Race, Technology, and Everyday Life,* ed. Alondra Nelson and Thuy Linh N. Tu (New York: New York University Press, 2001), pp. 13–33; Nina Wakeford, "Networking Women and Grrrls with Information/Communication Technology: Surfing Tales of the World Wide Web," in *Processed Lives: Gender and*

Technology in Everyday Life, ed. Jennifer Terry and Melodie Calvert (London: Routledge, 1997), pp. 51–66; Guillermo Gomez-Pena, "The Virtual Barrio @ the Other Frontier: (or The Chicano Interneta)," in Nelson and Tu, eds., *Technicolor,* pp. 191–98; Ella Shohat, "By the Bitstream of Babylon: Cyberfrontiers and Diasporic Vistas," in *Home, Exile, Homeland: Film, Media, and the Politics of Place,* ed. Hamid Naficy (New York: Routledge, 1999), pp. 213–32; Chris Berry, Fran Martin, and Audrey Yue, eds., *Mobile Cultures: New Media in Queer Asia* (Durham: Duke University Press, 2003); Beth E. Kolko, Lisa Nakamura, and Gilbert B. Rodman, eds., *Race and Cyberspace* (New York: Routledge, 2000); Ravi Sundaram, "Beyond the Nationalist Panopticon: The Experience of Cyberpublics in India," in *Electronic Media and Technoculture,* ed. John T. Caldwell (New Brunswick: Rutgers University Press, 2000), pp. 270–94.

41. Henry Jenkins, "Do You Enjoy Making the Rest of Us Look Stupid?: Alt.tv.twin peaks, the Trickster Author, and Viewer Mastery," in *Full of Secrets: Critical Approaches to Twin Peaks,* ed. David Lavery (Detroit: Wayne State University Press, 1995), pp. 51–69; Susan Murray, "Saving Our So-Called Lives: Girl Fandom, Adolescent Subjectivity, and *My So-Called Life,*" in *Kids' Media Culture,* ed. Marsha Kinder (Durham: Duke University Press, 1999), pp. 221–38; Susan J. Clerc, "DDEB, GATB, MPPB, and Ratboy: *The X Files'* Media Fandom, Online and Off," in *"Deny All Knowledge": Reading the X-Files,* ed. David Lavery, Angela Hague, and Marla Cartwright (Syracuse: Syracuse University Press, 1996), pp. 36–51; and Matt Hills, *Fan Cultures* (London: Routledge, 2002), especially "New Media, New Fandoms, New Theoretical Approaches," pp. 172–84.

42. U.S. Department of Commerce, National Telecommunications and Information Administration, *Americans in the Information Age: Falling through the Net,* report presented at the Digital Divide Summit, December 9, 1999, and posted at Web site digitaldivide.gov. See also Compaigne, *The Digital Divide.*

43. Hill, "Beyond Access," in Nelson and Tu, eds., *Technicolor,* p. 29.

44. Robert McChesney, *Corporate Media and the Threat to Democracy* (New York: Seven Stories Press, 1997), p. 6.

45. Disney now owns ABC (along with, for example, the Disney theme parks, radio stations, cable networks like ESPN and Lifetime, retail outlets, feature film companies, newspapers, and magazines). In 2003 industry rumors suggested that the Multiple System Operator, Comcast, would bid for the Walt Disney Company, but these rumors were laid to rest in 2004. CBS is owned by Viacom (which also owns, for example, Paramount Studios, cable networks like MTV and Nickelodeon, theme parks, and radio stations); NBC is owned by GE (which entered into a joint venture with Microsoft and owns MSNBC and in May 2004 merged with Vivendi-Universal); and Fox is owned by Rupert Murdoch's News Corp. (which owns, for example, Fox Broadcasting, Fox News Channel, Fox Sports Network, motion picture companies, magazines like *TV Guide, Elle,* and *Seventeen,* book publishers, and numerous newspapers, thereby delivering entertainment and information to at least 75 percent of the globe). Meanwhile, media conglomerate Time Warner owns a large number of cable channels, production companies, home video companies, magazines, music companies, and book publishers (for example, HBO, Cinemax, TNT, Comedy Central, E! Entertainment, Black

Entertainment Network, Time-Life Video, Warner Brothers Television, and the Book of the Month Club, to say nothing of its notorious deal with AOL). With telephone and cable operators acquiring and partnering with media corporations and moving into content, the synergy among these sectors is even more pronounced. These ownership structures make these media organizations more like the vertically integrated movie studios of the classical period because they have controlling stakes in all sectors of their industry—production, distribution, and exhibition—and thus reap the obvious benefits of owning multiple and related companies, which reduces risk and increases opportunities for synergy between different companies in the umbrella corporation.

46. Obviously, the great instability of the technologies market (including, of course, the fate of AOL and the AOL–Time Warner merger) begs us to ask new questions regarding the future of media conglomeration and convergence (an issue that John Caldwell addresses in this volume).

47. See Patricia Aufterheide, *Communications Policy and the Public Interest: The Telecommunications Act of 1996* (New York: Guilford Press, 1999); Patricia Aufterheide, ed., *Conglomerates and the Media* (New York: New Press, 19978); McChesney, *Corporate Media;* Ben H. Bagdikian, *The Media Monopoly,* 6th ed. (Boston: Beacon, 2000); and Dean Alger, *Megamedia: How Giant Corporations Dominate Mass Media, Distort Competition, and Endanger Democracy* (New York: Rowman and Littlefield, 1998).

48. Steve Clark, "Willis's Wasteland Warning," variety.com, June 17, 2003.

49. Zook, *Color by Fox,* p. 101.

50. See Smith-Shohade, *Shaded Lives,* p. 38. The NAACP's 1999 protest against the networks' color-blind fall lineup is a famous case in point of this continued "actual lack."

51. "Latinos Hardly Visible on Prime Time Television, UCLA Study Finds," press release, UCLA Chicano Studies Research Center, April 3, 2003. For the actual study see www.sscnet.ucla.edu/csrc.

52. See, for example, Gray, *Watching Race;* Torres, *Living Color;* Bogle, *Prime Time Blues;* Smith-Shomade, *Shaded Lives;* and Zook, *Color by Fox.*

53. Gray, *Watching Race;* Smith-Shomade, *Shaded Lives.*

54. "TiVo Criticized for 'Invading Privacy,'" BBC News, bbc.co.uk, February 13, 2003.

55. David Harvey, *The Condition of Postmodernity: An Enquiry into the Origins of Cultural Change* (Oxford: Basil Blackwell, 1989).

56. Pierre Bourdieu, *On Television,* trans. Priscilla Parkhurst Ferguson (New York: New Press, 1998), p. 48.

57. Central here were the Peacock Report (London: Peacook Committee, 1986); the 1988 White Paper *Broadcasting in the 90s: Competition, Choice, and Quality,* Cm. S17, London, HMSO, 1988; the 1990 Broadcasting Act; and the internal restructuring of the BBC. For a discussion of the market, see Simon Deakin and Stephan Pratten, "Quasi Markets, Transaction Costs, and Trust: The Uncertain Effects of Market Reforms in British Television Production," *Television and New Media* 1.3 (August 2000): 321–54.

58. See Karen Everhart Bedford, "Britain's Hybrid TV Network, Channel Four, Supports Its Mission with Advertising," *Current,* November 25, 1996 (reprinted on current.org). Meanwhile, producers interpret the 25 percent quota on independent production in ways that conflate "quality" with profit. In February 2003, *Variety* reported that "U.K. commercial networks ITV and Five outlined their commitment to public service broadcasting . . . by publishing programming goals for 2003." Among the "public service" commitments were the promise by Channel Five to broadcast better movies (including *Gladiator* and *Charlie's Angels*) and more one-hour U.S. drama series. Further, ITV1 expected to exceed its 25 percent independent production quota with factual and documentary series at a minimum of 91 hours (note that reality TV shows are counted as factual programming). See Debra Johnson, "ITV, Five list '03 Goals," variety.com, January 29, 2003.

59. See Vance Kepely Jr., "The Weaver Years at NBC," *Wide Angle* 12.2 (April 1990): 46–63; and "From 'Frontal Lobes' to the 'Bob and Bob Show': NBC Management and Programming Strategies, 1949–65," in *Hollywood in the Age of Television*, ed. Tino Balio (Boston: Unwin-Hyman, 1990), pp. 41–62. It should be noted that "quality" TV, or what counts as quality, changes over time (see Caldwell, *Televisuality*, chapter 1).

60. Erik Barnouw, *Tube of Plenty: The Evolution of American Television* (New York: Oxford University Press, 1975); Asa Briggs, *Sound and Vision: History of Broadcasting in the United Kingdom*, vols. 1–4 (Oxford: Oxford University Press, 1979).

61. William Boddy, *Fifties Television: The Industry and Its Critics* (Urbana: University of Illinois Press, 1990); Susan J. Douglas, *Inventing American Broadcasting, 1899–1922* (Baltimore: Johns Hopkins University Press, 1987); Michelle Hilmes, *Radio Voices: American Broadcasting, 1922–1952* (Minneapolis: University of Minnesota Press, 1997); Anderson, *Hollywood Television;* Carolyn Marvin, *When Old Technologies Were New* (Oxford: Oxford University Press, 1998); Cecelia Tichi, *Electronic Hearth: Creating an American Television Culture* (New York: Oxford University Press, 1991); Marybeth Haralovich, "Sit-Coms and Suburbs: Positioning the 1950s Homemaker," in *Private Screenings: Television and the Female Consumer,* ed. Lynn Spigel and Denise Mann (Minneapolis: University of Minnesota Press, 1992), pp. 111–41; Lipsitz, "Meaning of Memory"; and Lynn Spigel, *Make Room for TV: Television and the Family Ideal in Postwar America* (Chicago: University of Chicago Press, 1992).

62. Paddy Scannell, *Radio, Television, and Modern Life* (Oxford: Blackwell, 1996); for the other books see note 37.

63. Bourdieu, *On Television*, p. 29.

64. Lynn Spigel, "The Making of a Television Literate Elite, in Geraghty and Lusted, eds., *The Television Studies Book*, pp. 63–85.

65. U.S. Census Bureau, Statistical Abstract of the United States, 2001, sec. 26, "Arts, Entertainment, and Recreation," Fig. 26:1, "Adult Participation During Last 12 Months in Selected Leisure Activities: 1999," p. 752.

PART ONE

INDUSTRY, PROGRAMS, AND

PRODUCTION CONTEXTS

This first group of essays considers the historical changes in television's economics, production, and program forms, particularly regarding convergence, digital media, and the reorganization of the television industries. Collectively, the essays consider how technological and economic transitions are effecting changes in television's visual and narrative formats. They also analyze the industry and its programs in light of the larger social and cultural contexts in which programs are produced—especially with regard to globalization and the changing nature of the demographic groups targeted by contemporary advertisers.

In "Convergence Television: Aggregating Form and Repurposing Content in the Culture of Conglomeration" John Caldwell takes an in-depth look at contemporary production practices and, from an anthropological point of view, he argues that in order to understand the changes afoot we need to analyze the culture of production. Caldwell observes that despite its conglomerate structure, the contemporary television industry is in practice actually made up of many smaller companies locked into a "willed affinity." This willed affinity is a convenient unifying front for the industry as long as it guarantees stable markets and economies of scale. But in an ever-changing production climate of new technologies, delivery systems, and modes of consumption, unity does break down. When faced with uncertainties wrought by instability and change, the production community resorts to a set of industrial rituals and icons that are shared among practitioners and that eventually find their way into the expressive forms on television itself. From this point of view, Caldwell examines the place of the syndication industry in the new culture of TV-Internet convergence, and he considers how program forms are generated by new economics of convergence and conglomeration. In particular, he outlines an emergent set of industrial strategies and ritual exchanges among industry practitioners (including, for example, what the industry now calls the "repurposing" of program content, as well as new forms of "branding," "merchandise augmentation," and labor practices like "writing by committee"). All of these practices, Caldwell argues, affect the aesthetics and stylistics of contemporary TV forms.

Charlotte Brunsdon's "Lifestyling Britain: The 8–9 Slot on British Television" focuses on the genre of "lifestyle" programming that increasingly came to occupy the weekday 8–9 P.M. time slot on broadcast terrestrial television in Britain in the late 1990s. Composed of pedagogical programs on cooking, gardening, and home improvement, the time slot provides a key way to understand the changing patterns of production; the changing ideas about "newsworthiness" and "quality" programming; the "feminization" of network terrestrial TV; and the interplay of consumerist and civic identities in Britain's new media environment. Brunsdon proposes that this often overlooked and trivialized genre of lifestyle TV turns out to be an exemplary object of analysis for understanding the relationship between television and the nation today. By placing the genre into a broader historical context she considers both the paternalistic ways in which lifestyle programs had been imagined in the older BBC public service system, as well as the way the more contemporary commercial programs expand the definition of "lifestyle" to include broader, and she thinks potentially more progressive, definitions of citizenship that encompass the traditionally "feminized" spheres of home and homemaking. In this regard, Brunsdon's essay also resonates with the issues of commercialization and the public sphere, a topic that various essays address throughout the volume.

Also concerned with changes in television genres and forms, Jeffrey Sconce's "What If?: Charting Television's New Textual Boundaries" looks at recent trends in Hollywood TV series architecture. He focuses on programs that include fantasy episodes that are more or less freestanding from the series as a whole. By taking examples from science fiction, comedy, and drama Sconce shows how contemporary programs play with their story worlds, providing highly improbable episodes such as the "backwards" *Seinfeld;* an original *Star Trek* crossover story in *Star Trek: The Next Generation;* and the many stand-alone fantasy episodes of *The X-Files.* Rather than being embedded in dream sequences (as in *Moonlighting*'s famous "Taming of the Shrew" episode) or amnesia plots (as with the longstanding practice in soap operas), these "what if?" episodes often offer no plausible narrative motivation. Instead, they play on new forms of viewer literacy, in particular the kinds of fan activities that go on now in chat rooms on a regular basis. In the end, Sconce sees these "what if?" episodes as driven by numerous factors, not only viewer literacy and fandom on the Web but also industrial scheduling practices, narrowcasting, new forms of TV production and "authorship," new patterns of first-run syndication/distribution, and the increasing market for TV adaptations in feature film production. Sconce asks us to question why realism is increasingly punctured and how this relates more widely to modernist and postmodernist aesthetics, as well as why audiences no longer seem to expect a series to maintain its realist artifice.

William Boddy's "Interactive Television and Advertising Form in Contemporary U.S. Television" explores the history of interactive television—its various false starts, its transformations into WebTV, and its most recent manifestations in "smart" TV systems that allow viewers to digitally store, record, and pause live TV programs on demand. Looking especially at Microsoft's endeavors in the field, Boddy considers how that company promoted WebTV (which did not succeed as rapidly as Bill Gates hoped) and its more recent interactive system, Ultimate TV. Like Philip's TiVo and Sony's Replay, Ultimate TV offers viewers interactive capabilities, including the ability to bypass advertisements. Boddy then explores the television industry's panic over the possibility that viewers will indeed zap out commercials, and he shows how producers and advertisers are rethinking the relationship between commercial messages and program narrative. In particular, he considers the way companies are digitally inserting products into television narratives—a technique of "virtual" product placement that recalls the "integrated ad" pitches of early radio and 1950s television.

Lisa Parks's "Flexible Microcasting: Gender, Generation, and Television-Internet Convergence" considers the mergers between new and old media in relation to narrowcasting and identity politics, especially the politics of gender, generation, and class. By detailing current business initiatives for convergence technologies, Parks shows how the networks (both broadcast and cable) are tailoring programs to suit the mergers between computers and television. Parks pays particular attention to cable networks and Internet sites that target niche demographics, using Oxygen (a women-led cable network that features interactive technologies) and the short-lived DEN online entertainment network (aimed at youth) as examples. She demonstrates how gender and generation are key sites for the construction of convergence culture, but she also discusses some of the problematic politics at stake. Parks asks us to consider how current business practices and discourses around convergence ultimately return to well-encrusted notions of television's status as a "lowly," "feminine," "passive," and "immature" form of culture while promoting the computer as "high," "masculine," "active," and "mature." She warns that such ideological binaries work to disengage us from television and from active concerns about its future even while it continues to be a primary source of entertainment and information for many populations around the world.

JOHN CALDWELL **CONVERGENCE TELEVISION:**

AGGREGATING FORM AND REPURPOSING CONTENT

IN THE CULTURE OF CONGLOMERATION

I was on a panel called "Profiting from Content," which was pretty funny considering no one thinks we can.—Larry Kramer, CEO, CBS Marketwatch.com, quoted in *American Way*, December 15, 2000

"The New Killer App [television]"—title of article from *Inside*, December 12, 2000

With the meteoric rise and fall of the dot-coms between 1995 and 2000, high-tech media companies witnessed a marked shift in the kind of explanatory discourses that seemed to propel the media toward an all-knowing and omnipresent future-state known as "convergence." Early adopters of digital technology postured and distinguished their start-ups in overdetermined attempts to promote a series of stark binaries: old media versus new media, passive versus interactive, push versus pull. These forms of promotional "theorization" served well the proprietary need for the dot-coms to individuate and to sell their "vaporware" (a process by which products are prematurely hyped as mere concepts or prototypes before actual products are available, all in an effort to preemptively stall the sales and market share of existing products by competitors). Both practices—theorizing radical discontinuity with previous media and hyping vaporware—proved to be effective in amassing inordinate amounts of capital and in sending to the sidelines older competitors that actually had a product to sell. The tenor of this techno-rhetorical war changed, however, after the high-tech crash. Many observers now recognized that a phalanx of old-media players had, in fact, steadily weathered the volatile shifts during this period, and they did so with greater market share and authority than ever before. Far from being eclipsed by digital start-ups, television engaged and even welcomed the threat, proving that its historic prowess in entertainment, programming, and the economic realities of electronic media distribution gave it a set of comprehensive corporate skills well suited to tame the wild speculations of the dot-com world. Bankruptcy-prone media event/entities like DEN and pop.com might have garnered industry buzz as hip synergy-targets at Sundance, but television-Net initiatives had the National Association of Broadcasters, a wealth of prestige programming, adaptable technical infrastructure, and thousands of profit-focused electronic media facilitators and affiliates that were already "networked." In frustrated attempts to force the technical hand of "broadband" convergence, many newly tempered visionaries now conceded what had earlier only been a nagging hunch: a workable broadband network may already be in place—something called television.

Make no mistake, television did not assume its formidable position as a major player in digital media by having mastered and controlled the instabilities of the new technologies and practices. Far from it. The shift to digital created tremendous anxieties and a series of abortive responses from broadcasters because it threatened many of the most central tenets that had made the industry profitable over several decades. Consider, in this regard, how digital technologies have threatened the very centrality of TV's historic cash cow: syndication. Most academic histories of television focus almost exclusively on network television and ignore the fundamental role that the sale of independently produced series to individual and affiliated stations have played in the history of the medium. While the popular press typically conflates syndication with "reruns" of network shows, this gloss overlooks the vast number of series sold directly (usually for off-prime-time) across both domestic and international markets. Such syndication rights have for many years stood as central deal makers or breakers in television negotiations and development. The advent first of multichannel cable competition and then of digital technologies continues to threaten the place and value of syndication rights in the industry.

While the trades have spent considerable ink in hand-wringing speculation on the impact of Web "surfing" and "browsing" on advertising and sponsorship (which, in turn, has had considerable impact on the form that convergence has taken in television), less attention has been paid to the impact that those same user behaviors have had on syndication. New products/services like octopus.com, for example, give users the ability to download software that allows the user to click-and-compile sites and fragments of sites that the user wishes to view on a regular basis. This, in essence, automatically rips image/sound/data "content" from numerous commercially sponsored, proprietary, and advertised sites and compiles the gleaned material daily (without ad banners, buttons, or secondary matter) as a personalized site/document that can be distributed and forwarded at will by the octopus compiler. The impact of this kind of counter- or "meta-browsing" is not lost on commercial developers and dot-com investors worldwide: even the best-laid Web-design e-strategies, subscriptions, and e-commerce schemes are worthless if one's proprietary content ends up "republished" on the screen of any user who wishes to reconfigure and "syndicate" it. Owners lose control of revenue streams, user tracking, headlines, and ad impressions as users (now) automatically edit, personalize, and distribute content. Nervous Web developers and content owners ponder whether to counterattack themselves against meta-browsing, as they did with Napster and Scour for their "infringements." Portals that contractually promise their clients exclusivity and control of the context in which their content is seen, for example, can now no longer guarantee that the same content will not appear alongside their competitors' content.[1] Unlike the first generation of "unruly" analog users who threatened ad rates with VCR time-shifting and remote-control surfing, digital meta-browsing means not only that editorial control is in the hands of users but that it is also immediately and widely distributable by others. The syndication industry will again have to reinvent itself to insure profitability, even as advertisers have had to reinvent strategies in the face of personalized "bots" that aggregate and individuate content automatically for viewer-users. Given this kind of dynamic, it is clear that new modes of media delivery and television-Net convergence also have an impact on television's textual forms and the ways we relate to television itself.

AN "AESTHETIC" OF CONVERGENCE TV?

Even though ours has been characterized as a "postnetwork" or "post-television" era, television as an institution has proven resilient in adapting to a series of fundamental economic, technological, and cultural changes. In this essay I examine how the proliferation of forms in American television since 1990 developed through a pattern of industrial negotiations by practitioners. My intent here is both to describe a series of changes in television's textual forms and to reconsider methods of aesthetic analysis in television studies itself. By describing how various "cultures of production" mediate economic and cultural instabilities, I hope to shift the focus of analysis from aesthetics to notions of performance (how form is sociologically and industrially produced) and then to notions of "distributed cognition" (or how TV form emerges from broad but unstable networks of codified and contested industrial rationality). By doing this I intend to demonstrate the importance of a broad range of activities I group under the term "critical industrial practice." In addition, I want to show how these practices animate the industrial shift toward tactics of "aggregating," "migrating," and "repurposing" content.

Efforts to delineate a television aesthetic certainly stood as reasonable in what is still seen as the network era, a period of very real industrial oligopoly and apparent narrative homogeneity; a period perhaps constituted by the very "mass" culture premise in academia that somehow construed TV as one thing. In the 1970s and 1980s, attempts to nail down a television "aesthetic" (although this apparently archaic word was seldom used) were wide ranging. Critical scholars explained TV form by reference to a set of privileged generic modes and structural tropes;[2] to essential forms of distracted and fragmented subjectivity;[3] to semiotic taxonomies and descriptive schemes;[4] or to overarching narratological paradigms.[5] Within this broad movement to finally take seriously and to systematically understand television form, many scholars also insisted that such forms only made sense if understood within the logics of industry, ideology, and political economy.[6] This subsequent move to ground television critical studies historically demonstrated how televisual screen form was also fully complicit in programming tactics and political economy.[7]

These two critical phases fit well with the respective objects of analysis with which theory chose to tangle. The initial deconstruction by academic television studies of a common television form in the 1970s and early 1980s matched the overdetermined way that the networks themselves made television out to be one thing as well in the age of "broadcasting." Subsequently, the integration of political, economic, and cultural history with textual analysis in the late 1980s and 1990s came at a time when diversity was being industrially produced in an overdetermined way in a multichannel era known as "narrowcasting." These scholars fought the utopian gloss of endless diversity promised in the new age of cable and postnetwork television by taking television to task as a more fully historical phenomenon. Yet, I would argue, the current imbrication of digital technologies and the Internet with television further shatters the authority that either of these two models—broadcasting or narrowcasting—can have on critical analysis. To understand dot-com/TV permutations, TV-Web synergies, multichannel branding, and marketed poses of "convergence," scholars need to pay as much attention to the communities and cultures of production as they do to either political economy or ideologically driven screen form. The instabilities at play now—in labor relations, technological obsolescence, runaway production, and production economies—make the earlier advent and threat (to television) of HBO, CNN, and MTV seem moderate by comparison. It is within this present instability that the interplay between screen form, critical-industrial competence, and socio-professional interactions are most evident. Studying television's "production of culture" is simply no longer entirely convincing if one does not also talk about television's "culture of production."

UNEASY NEIGHBORS: THE TENTATIVE AFFINITIES
OF LOCAL PRODUCTION CULTURES

It is useful to consider the forms of convergence television not as mere textual or stylistic preoccupations but as Geertzian examples of "local knowledge."[8] Far from monolithic, the television industry is actually comprised of many very different local industries locked into a world of "willed affinity." This affinity stands as a convenient common front for "the industry" only as long as business relations can guarantee stable markets and economies of scale. Recent changes in technology (immersive stylistics, nonlinear editing, computer generated imagery [CGI], and digital interactivity) have heightened the facility and prowess of professionals even as they have threatened substantive changes in the ways that TV is made, delivered, and consumed. Faced with threats of industrial instability, local production communities mount a wide range of discursive, iconic, and ritual forms to (therapeutically) work through institutional anxieties and to (cognitively) rationalize and respond to threats to practice.[9] These industrial rituals and icons—circulated among practitioners to make sense of change—also directly impact and animate the program texts that audiences see at home.

While many media theorists spent their time speculating on polar oppositions between "push" media (TV) and "pull" media (digital media and the Net),[10] fewer recognized one increasingly obvious trend: television had long been making itself a "pull" medium (through interactivity), even as it merged and conglomerated in an unequivocal bid to make the Internet a viable "push" medium through the deployment of programming and advertising strategies.[11] Unlike television's smug but naive disregard of cable in the early 1980s—an upstart that ultimately hijacked over half of the TV audience—television was now, in effect, "covering its bets." That is, TV continued with its tried and proven success at programming, production, and marketing, even as it simultaneously invested in an array of start-ups and new technologies that could—if successful—ultimately cripple television. The unashamed investment by NBC, for example, in two new corporate enemies that promise to abolish TV advertising—the personal video recorder (PVR) companies TiVo and ReplayTV (whose PVR units allow viewers to skip ads in programs stored on their hard drives)—bear out this logic of planned corporate bet covering and equivocation. President Bob Wright of NBC laid out the preemptive logic of this kind of legal, boardroom surveillance: "[Our] company invested in both TiVo and Replay in part to keep track of the mayhem they could cause. We thought it was smart technology, but we weren't sure how it would be deployed."[12]

With this strategy, Wright and NBC brought to programming in the digital age the wisdom "that one should keep one's enemy close," but all of this pushing and pulling and merging and jockeying for position in the face of digital had a far different effect on the ground and in the industries. That is, the studios, network control rooms, story sessions, and guildhalls in Los Angeles and New York all began to evidence great anxieties and volatilities during this period. Members of the television production communities arguably faced a far more uncertain future than those above them in the boardrooms. For while Hollywood and television have jumped into digital with great public confidence, the lived communities that comprise those public fronts have had to navigate and negotiate change in ways that have substantively transformed what television looks like and sounds like in the age of digital.

Televisual form in the age of digital simply cannot be accounted for without talking about the institutional forces that spur and manage those forms. Before returning at the end of this essay to consider the broader questions that tie televisual change to issues of conglomeration, labor, and changes in advertising, I will lay out here what I consider to be five fundamental changes in the look of television that have been driven by the institutional instabilities that I described above. These five elements include ancillary textuality (repurposing, migrating content); conglomerating textuality (convergence texts, TV/dot-com sites); marketing textuality (branding); ritual textuality (pitching, writing by committee); and programming textuality (stunting, sweeps). Even though the industry emphasis on some of these forms and strategies prefigured and continues alongside the widespread digitalization of television, all the forms aspire to the very conditions and endgame that digital formats discursively anticipate in what might be called the age of "convergence television." In this way, the institutional practices described in the next section (repurposing, branding, pitching, stunting, and syndication) might be thought of as "protodigital" institutional strategies insofar as they both prefigure and bridge television's current and final transition to digital technology and digital content.

FORMS OF CONVERGENCE TELEVISION

"UPN's fate is still in the air, but for the time being, the network's affiliate body isn't interested in becoming a dumping ground for rehashed Viacom and CBS programming."[13] So went the spin as the UPN affiliate station group owners fought back attempts by its new takeover owners, Viacom and CBS, to use the sixth and weakest network as a dumping ground for syndicated and repurposed content, like MTV's recycled series *Celebrity Deathmatch*. In stressing the need to maintain its brand even after takeover, UPN President Dean Valentine stated that "re-purposing clearly doesn't work toward that end."[14] While the trades treated this stand as a corporate merger threat, UPN's resistant pose functioned more to show how conglomeration threatened another fundamental component of American television: syndication, or what has come to be known as repurposing and migrating content. The prospects of an endlessly expanding multichannel market in the 1980s and 1990s changed the way studios and production companies thought about their television product. During the network era of the 1960s and 1970s, TV shows aired, reran, and came and went in a descending temporal sequence defined by their initial air-date hyped by a major network. Reruns and second-run syndication deals simply allowed program owners to collect the remaining surplus value of series in the less prestigious worlds of distribution outside of both prime time and the networks. But then cable television in the 1980s and the Internet in the 1990s demonstrated—far more dramatically than the networks would have liked—that the real programming game in town was not going to be about initial air-dates, but about syndication rights.

With the flurry of dot-com activity attached to studios and networks in the late 1990s, the syndication lesson was further underscored: an endless "ancillary afterlife" was now a possibility for all shows; if not in off-prime-time, then in digital form; if not on or with the parent corporation, then with a subsidiary corporation.¹⁵ At least four changes are apparent in the new business and discursive practices that media corporations began deploying in trades and industry gatherings. All of these changes in symbolic capital encourage and stimulate the volatility of televisual form and the extensions and permutations of program texts. First, the "shelf life" of a show or series became increasingly important to program owners and networks in deciding which shows to develop. Syndication possibilities and foreign distribution in particular are now always very much on the mind of producers and executives, so much so that such perspectives encourage a "collage" approach to series development and a penchant for aggregating an ensemble of actors and story lines that will travel across national boundaries. In this way, first-run syndicated shows like *Acapulco Heat* mixed elements of *Baywatch* and *James Bond*, as well as Latin American and an international ensemble of European and American stars, to give the series "legs" in international distribution. Meanwhile, Pamela Anderson's *V.I.P.* mixed elements of *Baywatch, James Bond, Charlie's Angels*, and soft-core porn to cut across restrictive, demographic segments in the domestic market.

Second, studios and companies began to publicly refer to their archives as "legacy" holdings. No longer simply backlot warehousers of old program masters, prints, tapes, and dupe negs, studios like Universal and Warner Bros. hired professional archivists even as they remastered everything in the vaults for the new ancillary uses. Third, after the FCC relaxed the financial-syndication rules that had placed strict limits on the number of syndicated shows a network could own since the 1970s (rules that had once protected syndication rights for independent producers), the networks now used their position as the gatekeepers of broadcast to leverage increasingly more control over the syndication rights of programs. By the late 1990s independent program producers without "sweetheart deals" frequently complained that the networks were favoring their own in-house productions (over independently produced programs) when it came time to make the tough decisions about how, when, and what series to green-light, schedule, promote, or cancel. Fourth, two other paradigms began to eclipse the central importance traditionally assigned to the network broadcast as the primary benchmark of value: the lucrative possibilities of migrating content and program repurposing.

Consider the repurposing possibilities that emerged when the heretofore traditional NBC took on the market-share challenge of cable and digital. At least initially, the network news division drove the proliferation of NBC texts by repurposing news stories and talk shows for CNBC, MSNBC, and the MSNETWORK. Corporate heavyweights Microsoft and

NBC cooked up these kinds of synergies in a cross-media/cross-delivery onslaught, and by 2000 NBC threw down the gauntlet to even bigger globalizing Net success stories AOL and Yahoo when it rebranded its own online Internet activities (then named snap.com) as a comprehensive, one-stop entertainment and shopping Web service called NBCi. All of the erstwhile hype about how "new media" would replace "old-media" dinosaurs like network television now carried little credibility at GE/NBC. A place at the new media table would be assumed by NBC even as CNN and ABC/ESPN/Disney had done. Bits and pieces of hybridized news-anchor Brian Williams now show up in the form of migratory texts customized and endlessly individuated as e-content for NBC, MSNBC, CNBC, MSNETWORK, and NBCi.

Consider the daunting programming challenge that was ably met by this repurposing and hybridizing process. Not much more than ten years ago, NBC had but one half hour of network prime-time news to fill. Now the corporation has to program hundreds of hours per day with "new" programs across various electronic and digital networks. With a much lower cost to produce per minute than that of dramatic or entertainment programming, news production on videotape proved to be the perfect vehicle for this new corporate focus on repurposing. Tape, after all, can be endlessly recut and graphically stylized in digital postproduction. By 2000, the widespread use of digital servers (allowing random and multiple access to image and sound) makes the task of finding and incorporating archived file footage far less daunting. It also allows various divisional iterations of NBC nearly simultaneous access to the same footage and graphics. Also, unlike the textual "resistance" that an hour-long narrative arc in a prime-time show or a movie of the week places in the face of would-be abridgers, cutters, and repurposers, news is sound-bite and image driven, making it far more suited to the cable and Web programmers, who must tackle their urgent obligation to cut-and-paste, reformat, and extend "content."

The rhetorical shift from talking about productions as "programs" to talking about them as "content" underscores the centrality of repurposing in industrial practice. The term "content" frees programs from a year-long series and network-hosted logic and suggests that programs are quantities to be drawn and quartered, deliverable on cable, shippable internationally, and streamable on the Net. At industry summits, conventions, trade shows, and trade journals a newer generation of market-conscious "developers" at NBC, ABC, CBS, Time Warner, and Paramount spread the gospel of "repurposing content" and "migrating content" to this or that "platform." The old media corporations—defined historically by the entertainment experience of the screen, the narrative, the star, and the genre—now work to calculate, amass, repackage, and transport the entertainment product across the borders of both new technologies and media forms.

A second trend that has fueled the volatility of televisual form in the digital area might best be termed convergent or "conglomerating textuality," a practice that is apparent in numerous TV/dot-com sites. Through this practice entertainment companies intend to recapture, in the words of Michael Hiltzik, both "their brands (and) their business."[16] The term convergence is much bandied about now in almost every media and industry forum. The megaconvention of the National Association of Broadcasters (the NAB, an "old media" association guarding the interests of television stations nationwide) in Las Vegas in 2000 was anointed and hyped as the "convergence marketplace" by its sponsors. Everyone seems to believe in the imminent arrival of convergence but many still disagree about what the principle will mean in practical terms. "Broadband" (a big enough digital "pipeline") is currently the key word for the trigger delivery system that will allow for the transmission, multiplexing, and interaction of multiple streams of digital content. But the computer industry has always envisioned broadband as an extension of its focus on data management, interactivity, communications, and gaming while the motion picture industry has added broadband to its equation and plans for the domestic delivery of "electronic cinema."

Meanwhile, the television industry (and far more so than either the computer or film industries), brings to the groundswell of anticipation for broadband and the Internet its obsession with advertising, sponsorship, and programming. Of the three industries, television is more effectively mastering e-entertainment than either the film or high-tech worlds. Rather than focusing on the goal of HDTV (high definition) which it publicly (and ironically) whines about (because of the high cost of shifting from analog to high definition), television executives immediately saw in broadband an alternative—the possibility of "multiplexing." Ever focused on bottom-line profitability, broadcasters intended to exploit multiplexing's ability to offer simultaneous and ancillary digital streams (data, image, sound, interactivity). These ancillary channels promise to further engage and activate the audience, thereby bringing more of the viewer-user's dollars back to the programming source. Multiplexed content now inludes everything from background information, stock quotes, commentary, ancillary image and sound streaming, and the numerous forms of merchandizing that are inevitably glommed onto the ostensible focus of television's broadband transmission: the program or content.

Rather than place its bets on high resolution and cinematic illusion and effects, TV has argued for low resolution—a gambit that allows it to program, quantify, and stream far more than one channel of content. Television has also always been defined by and demeaned because of its "clutter." Television's presence on the Net carries on this fine and dubious distinction, but few critics of the ad banners and graphic morass that make the Net cluttered acknowledge that television has also always known how to take electronic clutter to the bank. Once again on the Net, and faced with the lure of high resolution alternatives favored by digital cinema (which would enable video-on-demand delivered digitally in the form of pay-per-view or subscription), many current TV-Net initiatives have opted for the far more complex, and lucrative, form of multiplexed broadband streaming.

Web sites for TV operative on the Net demonstrate the complicated strategies by which television in the digital age continues to extend its historical niche as a form of entertainment commerce. The most effective Web sites for TV succeed by keeping viewer-users engaged long after a series episode has aired, and this requires greatly expanding the notion of what a TV text is. Shows accomplish this through at least six on-line strategies: "characterized" proliferations of the text; "narrativized" elaborations of the text; "backstory" textuality; "metacritical" textuality; technological augmentations; and merchandizing augmentations. Dawsonscreek.com, for example, offers to its Web fans numerous possibilities to interact by utilizing each of these six modes. It makes special efforts, for example, to benefit from characterized proliferations by providing users with Web access to the "personal lives" of its many characters and actors. The wind-swept icon of one character, Joey, seductively entices users to "click here" to delve more into her personal life. At the same time the site also enables visitors to explore all of the show's four main characters through their "computers" (which appear as convincing simulations of Microsoft Windows icons and layout). To convince viewers that they are actually in the position to access the television characters' computers, the site's design graphically mimics "real" computer environments. Each week one of four different desktops is featured so that visitors can voyeuristically peak into a range of digital artifacts from the characters: "private" e-mails, AOL-style "instant messaging" chats, journals, and even (faux) trash cans. Through this interchange, visitors to "Dawson's desktop" are set up and positioned as unseen "hackers," secretly surveying not just the characters' personal computers but the characters' "real-time" Web chat as well, scripted and naturalized to mimic the kinds of dialogue viewers have experienced on the televised show proper.

The Web site also sets up access opportunities for "intimacy." Users can find out, for example, who's on Joey's Christmas list or what she has written in her "college essay." This kind of backstory elaboration fleshes out character biographies in far more detail than could be done in a broadcast episode, and it makes the users better narrative decoders of the series as well. Users are thus sutured into the world of the characters throughout the week through variously coded Internet activities. Having in one episode departed from the fictional town of Capeside, Andie has ostensibly been sending her friends postcards "from Europe" (Tuscany, Milan, Florence). The show then allows real users to sign up to receive an e-mailed postcard each time Andie reaches a new city or location in Europe. This kind of narrativized elaboration of the text works by allowing the narrative arc of the show (and the narrative reception of the show) to "continue" outside of the show itself. In further linking the electronic and virtual fiction with the user's real electronic activity, the Web site then allows those same recipients to "forward" Andie's post-cards to their own friends by using real e-mail addresses. This device is an effective mechanism that allows the producers to further aggregate fans for the show— with virtual e-mail triggering a proliferation of "real" e-mails through the fan base.

The show's Web site also utilizes technological augmentations of the text to secure an ongoing relationship with viewers in "off-air" time. By downloading or utilizing QuickTime or Real Video motion-image pro-tocols, the site invites viewers to take a 360-degree "virtual tour" of the show's Potter's Bed and Breakfast (a real set in the production, but a fic-tional building on the show). This augmentation thereby enables viewers to live vicariously in a constructed diegetic world and space outside of the show. They do so, furthermore, in a "place" that allows them to "book reservations" and to "read the guest book" in order to discern the identi-ties of other guests that have stayed at the B&B. Technological augmenta-tions also include another "fictional" Web site accessed through a link (Capesidehigh.com) that lets the visitor read a "real" newspaper printed at the show's fictional high school. After listening to the show's theme song on Real Audio (another downloadable extension) users can then purchase the music online (crossing yet another technical format).

The merchandizing augmentations on Dawsonscreek.com most fully betray the centrality of e-commerce in Web site design and operational practice. In the early years of the Web, television and film producers were publicly content to justify their expensive Web site initiatives as loss leaders or as a form of "value-added" to their existing entertainment properties or content. With the growing ubiquity of online shopping, however, TV Web sites now almost always exploit one of the few proven methods of returning capital on the Net. The Dawsonscreek.com online "store," for example, features sale items for the high-school-bound user: student planners, key chains, buttons, and locker magnets are sold in a way that extends the show's text into the fans' very real spaces—spaces far from either Hollywood's Capeside or the user's home and Internet connection. Users on the site are encouraged to "shop the creek" for novels, collector's books, and posters to pin up on bedroom walls. With improved streaming technologies and software links now embedded during video postproduction, many shows now go a step further by allowing viewers to immediately click on a sweater, garment, or prop worn or used by an actor. Doing so allows the user to purchase, ship, and import a show artifact to the very nondiegetic world of the audience. In this way, convergent mechandizing augmentations work to narrativize the world of the user rather than vice versa.

If merchandized augmentations smack of complete viewer co-optation by the producing entity, another mode counterposes commerce with a format that is in many ways more critical. Metacritical augmentations such as TVGuide.com and E! (Eonline.com) are among the most popular television Web sites, offering as they do scheduling information, critical reviews, news items, and bits of backstory. Many successful Web sites have learned valuable lessons from composite print-broadcast-online entities like these. Such sites suggest that criticism and analysis—even when negative and internalized—help fuel the entertainment machine. In this way, Dawsonscreek.com is like the official X-Files and MTV sites. All allow the viewer-user to weigh in with critical analysis and dialogue on the given series. These critical reflections are solicited both through fan chat rooms and with contests and polls that allow viewers to vote on, in dawsonscreek.com for example, such nonofficial PR spins as "the worst part of season four."

As I have argued elsewhere, any interactivity (good, bad, or indifferent) is economically valuable to producers and has been a defining goal of broadcast television since its inception in the 1940s.[17] These six recurrent forms of online textual elaboration, proliferation, and augmentation—all simultaneously operative in suceseful TV Web sites like Dawsonscreek.com and Thexfiles.com—also provide producers, studios, and advertisers with an expansive text that dwarfs the traditional thirty- and sixty-minute time slots of traditional shows. Convergent TV Web sites, therefore, represent a kind of model for the mutating, migrating, and aggregating textual ideals of contemporary industrial practice.

The next industrial trend that has altered the very way that television looks and sounds is "branding" (marketing forms). The venerable "eye" of CBS (which was known in the 1950s and 1960s as the "Tiffany" network due to its high quality news division) and the once proud "peacock" of NBC easily ruled the roost of public consciousness as corporate symbols that stood above all sorts of lesser fare in the network era of the 1960s and 1970s. Yet, by the mid 1990s, a large array of multichannel competitors had taken away the very viewership base that made the eye and the peacock almost universally recognized symbols in households across America. A few years earlier this decline in viewership and brand identity forced a boardroom shakeup at CBS, a takeover by GE of NBC, and a takeover by Capital Cities of ABC. A few years later a second wave of takeovers and mergers followed when the same networks were the takeover targets of Viacom (CBS) and Disney (ABC), and, in 2004, Vivendi-Universal merged with NBC. With upstarts like HBO, MTV, CNN, ESPN, Fox, WB, and UPN "cluttering" up corporate identities along with program choices in viewer living rooms, the major TV networks all embarked on public campaigns to "rebrand" themselves. The simple, stable, historic marquees of "quality" of CBS and NBC no longer seemed (to use Brandon Tartikoff's terms) to bring acceptable numbers of viewers into the network tent.

Of course, branding has been an obligatory marketing staple of corporate business strategies outside of broadcasting for many years, as any MBA student can attest. And while NBC once had the brand identity and loyalty of, say, Coca-Cola, it no longer did by the early 1990s. The lion's share of critical and public attention for branding was garnered by ABC in its "yellow campaign" starting in 1997. No longer even an issue of typography and logo, ABC simply plastered the color yellow on every promo in print, broadcast, or billboard, along with ironic and knowing tag lines that mocked everything from the moronic tastes of parents ("This is not your father's TV") to the exaggerated claims of mental decline (that TV is mind numbing and lowers literacy) and physical decline (programs for couch potatoes) attributed to television by concerned consumer advocates and liberal watchdogs. True postmodern irony might be the well-earned reputation of actual programs on and by MTV, VH1, and SCTV, but even if it did not have comparably hip programs ABC could still front itself as postmodern by making irony and pastiche a part of every institutional and promotional self-reference. In the end, ABC showcased itself by making the network packagers (rather than the production community) the authoring source of irony, and it signaled this new and very visible ever-presence with a branded Pavlovian yellow promotional hue.

While ABC's yellow campaign scored notoriety and endless news-hits for rebranding—in everything from the *Wall Street Journal* and *New York*

Times to *Entertainment Tonight* and the tabloids—the most extensive onscreen overhaul of a network began in 1994 by NBC in its "NBC-2000" campaign (a campaign that set the standard for the subsequent rebranding at both CBS and ABC). The campaign by NBC involved far more than a specific color and ironic tag lines. The smug confidence of the networks about their initial prowess in the multichannel flow had eroded to the point of crisis by the mid-1990s. With their drastic loss in market share, the three major networks now needed a way to make not just audiences but also industry members aware of the power and benefits that came with the network "family." The networks were in a state of crisis, with prognostications of demise or merger forming a steady rhetorical flow in the trades. In 1995 and 1996, NBC counterattacked by borrowing President Bush's much-maligned "thousand points of light" mythos. Research showed that the traditional four-letter station call-letters were simply too complicated for most viewers to remember. The response? Local stations owned by the national network were to drop the "K" and "W" nationally (as in "KNBC, Burbank"), and adopt the NBC plus channel number ("NBC-4, Burbank") as a simpler designation and common logo. These nationally aired station/network identifications that focused on local affiliate stations, however, show the full extent to which anxiety about the network's future ruled the corporate enterprise.[18] As the camera scans a graphic map of the country in one set of spots, hundreds of points of light mark the network's "214 affiliates nationwide, including KJRH-2 Tulsa, Oklahoma."

This campaign, not illogically, followed soon after the much publicized "abandonment" of CBS by a number of longtime affiliate stations— network-affiliate "traitors" as it were—who opted for the rising fortunes and hipper programming of the newer fourth network, Fox. The celebration and symbolic construction of a network "family" by NBC can thus be seen as a kind of preemptive corporate strike. It was, in essence, industry damage-control aimed at vigorously reasserting the aura of network authority and quality. Not since the 1950s had the networks had to work this hard to teach viewers and stations about the benefits of national network affiliation. These kinds of mediating video texts, then, also function as shorthand corporate reports for anxious affiliate stations who may have considered jumping ship. The top-down model of prestige programming—which includes Hollywood television and network news—always promises to guarantee the welfare of the affiliate family members broadcasting out in the provinces.

The kind of aggressive and heavy-handed damage control evident in these spots came as part of a broader range of marketing "innovations."

Indeed, NBC had also induced consent on the part of program producers to include the NBC logo "inside" scenes from aired programs themselves. This gambit amounted to a very clever sort of blackmail because program producers for years had complained that license fees from networks were never fair (that is, never paid for the actual cost of program production). These costs were ultimately only covered through later syndication revenues that went directly to the producers' companies. Here NBC was subtly forcing its partners to erect televised billboards inside episodes that NBC had not fully paid for. Apparently, the long-term financial prospects of NBC were both significant and enough in jeopardy that program providers realized that their fates were ultimately affected by the "health" of the network that first launched them. By eliminating commercial breaks between shows, and by asking for network IDs within diegetic scenes, the network could promise greater viewer carryover from show to show. Program providers could certainly appreciate this tactic—if the networks "hammocked" them between strong, proven shows. But the real lesson of these programming moves lies in the public consciousness of the notion that the fates of program producers, the network, and the affiliate stations were all very much intertwined. Both the network "family-of-stations" ID campaign and the tactic of intradiegetic branding with logos stand as very public ways that television mediates and negotiates changes, even as it mollifies insecurities in the industry.

In a quintessential moment of feigned nonpartisanship, *Today* host Katie Couric announced on the NBC-2000 demo tape that viewers were about to see the network's most dramatic makeover ever.[19] Visual evidence that something *had* changed in the aesthetic ways that the major networks did business came in the segment that followed, which summarized NBC's 1994 campaign to overhaul its corporate logo and identity. The makeover also initiated a proliferation of intermediary video forms, all designed to drive home and publicly "manage" the overhaul in the audience's mind. The marketing machine of NBC simultaneously flooded the programming world with intermediary texts that both legitimized and analyzed their "new" look and "attitude."

The once staid and venerable NBC "commissioned" cutting-edge artists—what they termed in the NBC-2000 demo tape as the biggest names in design and animation—to draft, engineer, sculpt, and animate the look that expressed its newfound attitude. Mark Malmberg, the computer-artist guru behind the cyberfilm *Lawnmower Man*, fused the network with Grateful Dead electronics. David Daniels—"bad-boy" artist (in the mind of perky host Katie Couric) and A-list director of music videos and claymation spots for Honda—touted his network offering, or what he called "psychedelic meatloaf in motion." Resurrected 1960s pop-art cast-off Peter Max repeatedly grooved about the "free reign" that enlightened NBC had given him to express himself. Painter Joan Gratz, in turn, stepped forward to render the network's logo monograph on electronic "impressionism."

The darker side of postmodernism came in full force, as well, in the form of J. J. Sedelmaier and John Kricfalusi. Seidlemaier spun his logo from the brain-numbed animated "slacker" aesthetic of *Beavis & Butt-Head*. Kricfalusi, originator of the *Ren & Stimpy* flatulent aesthetic in cartoons, toyed with the interviewer even as he explained to the network audience his vision of the network peacock: "Colorful things come out of his butt." To bring full circle the bad-boy, cutting-edge master code of the corporate makeover, NBC awarded broadcast exhibit to two nonprofessional artists who pushed the envelope with computer graphics cranked out on their Macintosh computers at home. The lesson was clear. The audience was "bad," but the Fortune 100 corporation of NBC was "badder" still. Even as Kricfalusi confessed disingenuously that "I don't know what hip is" (yet another update of Andy Warhol's "I don't care" aesthetic) NBC was showing that it was now in fact the empire of the hip. No self-doubt was even needed. The imperative to rebrand was fueled in great measure by the growing sense that there now was simply not enough of an audience to go around; that is, not enough to share (profitably) with all of the competition. Branding was the first of many tactics that exploited the instability of the televisual form in the age of digital, and it continues to be the central focus as TV.com initiatives compete above the clutter on the Internet.[20]

Convergent television is also guided by another set of practices: ritualized forms (pitching, writing by committee, executive revolving door). Televisual form has historically been explained in terms of genre, narrative, or modes of reception. I would argue that the social performance of show making—considering TV's creators as industrial actors in an ensemble—must also be considered to fully understand these new forms. Programs on TV are not simply authored "texts," they are also created by "industrial actors" and choreographed through tried-and-proven modes of institutional interaction. The volatility of program forms in the 1990s and after, for example, results in part from the manner in which shows are initiated and developed. With the full-length screenplay as the point of origination for the show/deal now long obsolete, and the detailed prose "treatment" typically used only to sell a producer's optioned idea to a network, producers and screenwriters now rely on the quintessential short-form show starter: the "pitch." Pitching is in many ways a kind of performance art.[21] The ability to effectively reduce a thirty- or sixty-minute narrative to two or three short spoken sentences carries a premium in Hollywood. Some swear by visual aids as part of the process; some vouch for the stand-up dramatization mode as a way to nail down the deal. In whatever guise, writers must hook a produer/buyer/executive's attention in a matter of seconds with the promise of something original. If the buyer is enticed, the writer must be prepared to flesh out additional details of the show's structure, logic, and raison d'être in an incremental narrative process of question and answer and give and take with the buyer.

But it would be wrong to consider the pitch as a simple temporal devolution of the narrative form from screenplay to treatment to premise. Pitches work by hooking the buyer with a short but recognizable convention of some sort, then glomming, spinning, or aggregating it with some other unconventional element in order to create a "just like X but with Y" variant. One result of this logic of juxtaposition and variation is that story sessions are now defined by excessive cross-genre hybridization. And because both short attention span and retorts of "already done" fill the meeting room during pitch sessions, the effective pitcher must have an arsenal of possible show premises to fall back on. This kind of quantity ratchets up both the speed and extent of cross-genre hybridization. The result, arguably, is that shows now must clearly demonstrate originality to get optioned or green-lighted, and to do so quickly with a rapid "just-like-but-very-different" premise. Another result is that the stylistic outcome of this social ritual means that contemporary TV in the multichannel postnetwork era owes more to André Breton and surrealism than it does to an Aristotelian telos and the classic three-act plot.

In industry lore *Miami Vice* (NBC, 1984–1989) stands as the classic example of the pitch-driven show, with creator Michael Mann's two-word pitch used to leverage, launch and update the most stylish of network TV's mid-1980s cable competitors: "MTV cops." Both CBS and critics subsequently pitched the Saturday-morning show *Pee-Wee's Playhouse* (1986–1991) as "*Mister Rogers* on acid," in a way that directly leveraged and then mocked a serious children's program predecessor on PBS. Both examples suggest the extent to which what might be called the "pitch aesthetic" informs TV today, not simply by updating a genre with a new twist but also by positioning the new show over and against a competing network or programming entity. Consider in this regard the wave of denigrating criticism that greeted the implicit pitch and the pitch aesthetic of Fox's reality show *Temptation Island* in 2000–2001: "Take *Survivor* and *Blind Date,* add a dash of *Change of Heart,* top it with a scoop of *Jerry Springer,* and you've got *Temptation Island,* Fox's hit version of *When Good Spouses Go Bad.*" But consider also how such a pitch aesthetic raises the ratings stakes by setting in motion counterpitches and PR spins as well. One rival network executive counterpitched *Temptation Island* in a way intended to hype its own show's alternatives: "It's like Fox swallowed *Survivor* and then crapped it out."[22] The hyperhybridization of the pitched show here (which juxtaposes elements of five previous shows), meets an antagonistic counterpitch that reduces the hit to a meager and binary scatological collage.

The industrial performance art of pitching inculcates the production culture with a clockwork-like dependence on endless variation/replication and a process of generic aggregation. This helps explain the wealth of televisual forms across the multichannel spectrum. But another industrial ritual, "writing by committee," stands as a countervailing performance that works to contain the stylistic volatility of the pitch aesthetic. Most showrunners (producer/creators) in U.S. television have backgrounds as writers, and many others broadly deem such producers the true authors of television.[23] It is the showrunner's defining vision of a series, after all, that stamps the series as distinctive. But the sheer magnitude of the narrative universe needed to support a full season of half-hour or hour-long shows in TV (vs. film) means that actual authorship must fall to a team of writers (sometimes a very large team of writers) over a year of production. Without the relatively leisurely pace allowed in feature film production, television writers must crank out thirty- and sixty-minute scripts at a much faster rate, and they usually do this in teams.

The film industry has traditionally denigrated television for "writing by committee" while assuming ownership for themselves of the traditional creative mythos of quality: sole authorship. Yet the very success of the committee-mode in TV has allowed it to invade the world of feature film production as well. In fall 2000 the industry trades and tabloids often told of the behind-the-scenes creative soap opera that led up to the release of *Charlie's Angels.* The press gagged at the thought that literally scores of teamed and successive screenwriters had been enjoined to write, rewrite, and rewrite the script again.[24] While executives argued that this form of musical chairs helped "punch-up" the scenes, the moral was not lost on many in the industry. Even features had become excessively formulaic, with writers now only needed to fill in the missing chunks and pieces of the narrative blueprint. The big-budget, big-screen action pic had apparently learned the efficiencies of television's network age. Working (significantly) from a television series original, feature films like

Charlie's Angels dutifully mastered TV's stabilizing mode as part of the adaptation by utilizing the large writing committee.

Writing by committee assumes that a show's main story arcs are well known and established, usually in a written document called the show's "bible." Any necessary backstory is thereby codified to ensure continuity in all future scripts. Screenwriters who build a show and script from a bible end up functioning more like "assemblers" punching in a range of possible options—for the joke, punchline, new character, etc.—from a "menu" of possible (but to some, monotonous) range of choices. The anonymity of writing by committee alarms authors, but the actual practice has the more deadly effect of constraining the original volatility of the pitch aesthetic into a fairly rigid matrix of obligatory structural forms. Any variation allowed or required is simply the joke, line, or character that is punched into the established structural slot. Stylistic volatility encouraged by the pitch meets a second ritualized textual force: the rationality, inertia, and redundancy of the menu-driven writing by committee.

Yet another industrial ritual further dulls the pitch mode's tendency to encourage stylish volatility: television's corporate boardroom game of executive musical chairs. The U.S. television networks typically announce their fall schedules in May. As is regularly the practice, a number of television executive heads roll in the months that follow, and new studio/ network chiefs are brought in to clean up the "mess" of those ousted. With their own career moves a concern and with inevitably short tenures to face, the newcomer executives typically let risky shows die on the vine because they will get no credit for the show deals of their predecessors.[25] With the most to lose in the increasingly competitive multichannel market, the majors (CBS, NBC, ABC) are particularly susceptible to the conservative inertia and dulling insecurities of the "executive revolving door" ritual. In many cases management changes like these are commonly couched by spokespersons and the trade press in a binary corporate paradigm of courting, marriage, and divorce. Observers—in remarks such as the "honeymoon is over in [the] alliance of Ovitz, Burkle . . . funny how a little thing can drive a wedge into a match made in heaven"[26]—also reveal the extent to which the industry rationalizes corporate decisions (and exit strategies) in the more emotional language of interpersonal passion and betrayal.

In this ongoing tension between pitch-mode volatility on the one hand, and writing by committee and executive-revolving-door constraints on the other, the newer networks, studios, and upstarts tend to gain the most from the genre-crunching pitch mode. While expensive, star-driven network sitcoms on NBC and ABC encourage generic caution in the writing committees and executive suites, the less traditional generic tastes of UPN, WB, Fox, and Comedy Central place a premium on pitch-glommed story ideas that promise to rise above the programming clutter. Fox's (cheaply made but sensationalist ride-along video) *Cops* gets re-pitched as Fox's (cheaply made but sensationalist videotape carnage collage) *World's Scariest Police Chases,* which gets repitched as *When Animals Attack,* which gets repitched as *When Good Spouses Go Bad.* The (cost-effective) shock-TV success of UPN's *WWF Smackdown* gets repitched as the silicone-enhanced-cleavage-with-SI-like-swimsuit-segment-female-hysteria spectacle *Women in Wrestling,* which then gets repitched as the steroid-enhanced-*Gladiator*-with-goalposts-and-raging-testosterone-masculinity of the newly televised XFL football league. In the programming world of the lower-caste networks (UPN, WB, Fox), the pitch-mode spins out new show concepts with clockwork-like regularity.

Redundancy and stylistic inertia intensify as one moves up the programming food chain to the major networks. Manic genre-hybridization and the reliance on pitch-mode autopilot intensify as one moves down the programming food-chain to lowlier network wannabes (UPN, WB, Fox) and first-run syndicators desperately seeking financing for coproductions and off-prime-time cablecasts. Stylistic permutations are not simply matters "determined" causally either by political economies or by the cadre of mainstream network producers and executives who take redundancy with (a little) variation to the bank. Both ends of the network programming spectrum are managed by divergent socio-professional rituals, now codified in the industrial culture. Televisual form is very much lived. It results, in part, from industrial performances and social relations that precede and follow the televised screen event proper.

Stunting (programming form), the final element in my list of institutional practices, now generates many new formal permutations during a given season, especially during "sweeps" periods.[27] For many viewers, sweeps weeks are now a recognizable, quarterly part of network programming. By setting aside selected weeks in November, February, and May, networks establish advertising rates for the months that follow based on Nielsen ratings calculated during the sweeps. This is a simple enough concept—a consensual way that corporations agree to rationalize both their economic returns and the very ground rules for competition—but it fails to explain the complicated aesthetic processes that sweeps inevitably set in motion. Called "stunts" by critics and networks alike, special episodes of series are frequently aired to attract a higher-than-representative audience and so "spike" ratings. The intended effect of such spikes is that ad rates are set at an artificially higher level. Although spiking is technically prohibited (because it makes a mockery of the premise of "level ground" so essential to accurate ratings analysis among competitors), no one, including the Nielsen corporation, is willing or able to explain how narrative and stylistic stunts jeopardize the rationality of the system.

I have elsewhere described how a range of stunts function for the production culture.[28] This practice includes a number of what might be termed distinct "stunt genres": the masquerade, the production stunt, the docu-stunt, the special "making-of" stunt, the migrating "cross-genre" guest-star stunt, and the cross-network or cross-media stunt. First, beginning in the 1980s a number of prime-time shows systematically began to "masquerade" as entirely different shows, series, or films. *Roseanne* (a *Father Knows Best*-esque fifties domestic sitcom), *Moonlighting* (a Valentino silent film and *Casablanca*-esque drama), *thirtysomething* (a *Dick Van Dyke*-esque melodrama), and *Northern Exposure* (a bohemian western) all had special episodes that completely discarded the standard look of their diegetic worlds and "became" some other look and narrative. A second set of elite prime-time shows like *Moonlighting* (film noir cinematography, Toland-esque deep-focus photography, acute dream-state lighting effects), *The X-Files* (cyberpunk, video-gaming graphics, "live" helicopter footage), *Twin Peaks* (Lynchian altered-state tableaus and set design), *Mad about You* (a live one-take episode pitched as an homage to golden-age live drama and a showcase for the series' award-winning actors who, according to the network, operated "without a net"), *The Drew Carey Show* (music video, *Rocky Horror* stylistics, and choreography in a "musical" episode), and *Freaky Links* (DV-cams, Web sites, downloaded Internet graphics and audio) all used the special episode to stage acutely self-conscious exercises in cinematic production style. For some in the production community, this allowed TV cinematographers, lighting designers, and editors to show off and experiment with cutting-edge looks that standardized genres did not allow and to publicly announce their accomplishment in industry trade convention panels at the NAB convention, SMPTE conferences (Society of Motion Picture and Television Engineers), and Showbiz Expo.

Another favored stunting genre emerged in what I have termed the "docu-stunt," a special episode in which the show becomes a documentary film.[29] *M*A*S*H**, *St. Elsewhere*, *China Beach*, and *Mad about You* all slipped into this mode for sweeps. By doing so, such episodes functioned to foreground the superiority of their actors, who typically deprecated and sluffed their way through verité scenes or confided very "private" and offscreen sentiments directly to viewers. Docu-stunts in these series—and in other very popular shows with large fan bases—allowed actor-now-star-driven ensembles (along with the fans) to muse on the very meaning of the show, but from within a special artificial, diegetic frame that is bracketed off especially for sweeps as "reality." With this diegetic bracketing-off, the special docu-stunt thereby creates for the series not "self-reflexivity" in a Brechtian or Godardian sense, but a self-conscious mutual reflexivity with the fan base.

The next stunt genre—the "making-of" stunt—breaks entirely with the obligation to even protect the integrity of the show's diegetic frame (whether fictional or docu-stunt). First-run syndicated hits like *Xena: Warrior Princess* and *Hercules* have both broken down any notion of discrete diegesis in stunts by allowing actors to appear as "themselves" rather than their screen personas or characters. In one *Xena* episode the fictional characters debate the narratological choices about appropriate character arcs in the series and then slip in and out of temporal incongruities and series roles. In *Hercules,* the archaic myth figures argue over "merchandizing rights" and publicity billing as they cruise down palm-lined streets in Beverly Hills in full myth-era regalia. This stunt genre fulfills the making-of function by providing in-the-know fans with narrative possibilities far too complicated to stage authentically in production.[30] By taking apart the narrative world and reworking it, the studio, in effect, does what Henry Jenkins might call "poaching" and "filking," terms used to describe the deconstruction and remaking of a show or music by fans.[31]

Finally, two stunt genres work by hyping cross-platform or cross-media incursions in special episodes: the cross-genre guest-star stunt and the cross-network stunt.[32] The cross-genre guest star stunt is, of course, among the most common form of stunting, recurrent in series like *Friends* (which, for example, imported *Magnum, P.I.*'s Tom Selleck), *The Simpsons* (which imports practically anyone available in Hollywood's relative directories), *Family Law* (which imported *Matlock*'s Andy Griffith), and *Dharma and Greg* (which imported *Hercules*'s Kevin Sorbo). While this is arguably the most common and recognized form of sweep stunt, it has evolved from its central and almost obligatory place on the comedy/variety shows of the 1950s[33] and occasional use on sitcoms of the 1950s to frequent and excessive movements in contemporary TV. By having film actress Liz Taylor make guest appearances on each and every successive sitcom show aired on one sweeps evening, the host network used the cross-genre guest-star stunt to program the entire evening as an entity. In some ways, this gambit made explicit a process that Raymond Williams theorized as "flow"—the idea that television is not about the kind of individual program that critics tend to isolate but rather about the experience of viewing extended, composite sequences comprised of a succession of texts that include ads, breaks, programs, previews, etc.[34] The Taylor stunt made clear that the network—not an individual show or its creators—had marshalled the star power necessary for this kind of "event television" across an entire evening.

The related but different "cross-network stunt" is certainly more difficult to understand at first than the various guest-star permutations. NBC's sitcom *Jenny* stunted in 1998 by cutting back and forth between a staged episode of MTV/Viacom's *The Real World* and its own *Jenny* diegesis. No real fiduciary interest appeared to guide the intertextual play (NBC and Viacom are wholly distinct corporations), but end-titles betrayed to committed viewers that the sitcom was in fact produced by "MTV productions"—a semiautonomous production entity—which did benefit directly from its contractual relationship as a program supplier across platforms and conglomerates. Many critics and audiences similarly took note of the cross-network stunt engineered by David E. Kelley in 1999. Kelley's hit show *Ally McBeal* had become a flagship leader for Fox Television's programmers, even as Kelley's *The Practice* had earned critical acclaim but little viewership in its first season on ABC. Both competing networks—Fox and ABC—jointly staged a cross-network stunt that brought *Ally McBeal* characters into *The Practice*, and *The Practice* characters into *Ally McBeal*. Although the demeanor of the two legal shows could not be more different (*Ally* had won Emmy awards as a "comedy," while critics regaled *The Practice* as a "serious" ensemble drama), this symbiotic cross-network stunt worked to bring additional viewers to both Fox and ABC. Yet, the symbolic winner was clearly creator/producer David E. Kelley whose "quality" now apparently transcended the proprietary confines of mere network television. With this stunt-derived cultural capital in hand, Kelley went on to land additional deals in following seasons with shows like *Boston Public,* which also cross-stunted with *Ally* during the February sweeps in 2001.

These six recurrent stunt genres all work to do two things. First, they allow the production cadre and the culture that produces TV to come to the foreground on-air (and thus to celebrate and codify their accomplishment in secondary industrial accounts, trades, and professional meetings). Second, the stunts allow members of both the audience and the production culture to articulate, revise, and rearticulate cross-industry relations. In the era of postnetwork instability that defines television in the age of digital, staying immersed inside of a show's lock-tight diegesis is a luxury, one that many new shows simply cannot afford. To stay afloat ratings-wise, to earn critical distinction, to attract Emmy award nods, and to secure and enhance the position of a show and its producers in town—these factors mean that backstory, corporate relations, and self-conscious reflections on critical status and aesthetic hierarchy (of stars, the series, the producers, or the network) will continue to stand as viable onscreen story matters as well. Continuing institutional and cultural instabilities make this so. Stunting is, in some ways, congruent with the pitch-mode of program development. Both practices, that is, encourage stylistic hybridization. Production by committee and executive-revolving-door tendencies, by contrast, tend to constrain formal volatility because both practices work to minimize the economic risk that media corporations face when airing unorthodox programming. Yet these historic constraints have not blunted the popularity of stunt-driven, cross-media permutations. In the multichannel age of digital and conglomeration the formal hybridity of cross-corporate stunting and textual inversion has become even more crucial for newcomer networks with less market share.

A number of the formal and institutional practices described above owe their industrial popularity to the effective (post-vaporware) arrival of digital technologies in the work worlds of convergence TV. These formal elaborations and augmentations include: user aggregation as a countermeasure to meta-browsing; data mining as advertising's response to now-meaningless click-through rates; conglomerating TV/dot-com sites as total marketing antidotes to narrowcasting and unruly user surfing in off-air time; and repurposing as a means to counteract a limited first-run shelf life and to exploit legacy archival holdings in the postnetwork era. These new technology-assisted "innovations" have further broken down the fundamental (even if mythical) wall between the advertising and editorial worlds. The National Association of Program Executives (NATPE) now concurs that the thirty- and sixty-second spots are things of the past, replaced by comprehensive new product placement strategies and programs coproduced by Madison Avenue agencies and their multinational corporate clients like Coca-Cola. Advertising executive Bob Kuperman justifies the loss of the earlier working distinctions and argues that formal permutations will continue: in a panel at the annual NATPE convention titled "When the Advertiser Turns Producer," he claimed that "what we now call interruptive messaging (in advertising), is probably going to be the least efficient way to build a relationship with consumers. In the future, you probably won't know where the commercial stops and the programs begin."[35]

Formal and textual changes in television cannot be viewed as "caused" or "determined" by the technological transition to digital. Rather, what I have referred to as "convergence TV" can be seen, to use Raymond

Williams's term, as "symptomatic"[36] of more fundamental logics and practices in the history of television: syndication, repurposing, branded programming, and conglomeration. That is, digital technologies (and the six types of technologically enabled "textual augmentations" on TV/dot-com sites outlined earlier in the chapter) merely served to accelerate and legitimate these well-practiced industrial strategies. Branding, pitching, and stunting all predated as well as survived and prospered in television's transition to digital. For this reason, they must be seen as more than pre- or protodigital practices that prefigured convergence TV in an art histor-ical sense. Such institutional practices have, in fact, come into their own in the age of convergence television, and are widely deployed in ways that author and inflect digital/televisual forms. TV/dot-com convergence merely provided the technological, economic, and conceptual conditions that allowed branding, syndication, repurposing, and conglomeration to emerge not just as corporate strategies but as viable textual and stylistic practices as well.

FORMS OF DIVERSITY AND DIFFERENCE
IN THE AGE OF CONGLOMERATION

Short-form histories of the rise and fall of network television go some-thing like this: a government-sanctioned and regulated oligopoly in net-work television in the 1960s and 1970s guaranteed the NBC, CBS, and ABC corporations control of well over ninety percent of the television au-dience. The advent of new programming and delivery systems in the 1980s—cable, DBS, pay-per-view, and the VCR and remote—broke this oligopoly and opened American television screens to many more emerg-ing companies. HBO, CNN, MTV, VH1, the Discovery Channel, Cinemax, USA Network, BET, Nickelodeon, American Movie Classics, Lifetime, the Sci-Fi Network, Bravo, ESPN, Fox Sports Net, the History Channel, Home and Garden Television, and many other networks and channels were proof positive that the mass audience had indeed been splintered into niches. Such a splintering and proliferation of networks and chan-nels ostensibly broke down the top-down control of American broadcast-ing in a way that publicly favored the diverse tastes and heterogeneous identities of the American public. This climate of increased diversifica-tion suggested to fiscal conservatives what had long been a mantra of the television industry and the NAB: a free market, not regulation, was the only way to ensure diversity of programming. As a result of this shift (starting in the Reagan/Bush era but continuing through the next two administrations), government regulation effectively dissipated as the

Federal Trade Commission (FTC) and the FCC pulled back in order to let the telecommunications industry and entertainment market work their democratic wonders. Across a broad spectrum of interests, diversity in channel choices was optimistically conflated with cultural, ethnic, and racial diversity per se. The 1934 Radio Act and the 1946 FCC Blue Book's requirements that television must implement measures to guarantee the representation of minority viewpoints, the needs of local communities, and the importance of culturally challenging, noncommercial programming now stood like no-longer-needed archaic remnants of an earlier, less-open era. In contrast to the regulated public service strictures of the earlier era, the open market touted by contemporary television, along with the intensive capitalization deployed by the newer networks and start-ups, would now fulfill the earlier regulatory mandates, even as they made proprietary corporate owners wealthy. The postnetwork era, that is, was to be a "win-win" situation for all concerned—for industry as well as for multicultural diversity.

Yet few looked past the hype to challenge a subsequent trend. After the multichannel market model rose to prominence and regulatory policy withered, merger mania caught up with those in the expanding cable TV entertainment industries. Viacom bought Paramount, who owned the *Star Trek* franchise, which then fueled the launch of UPN, which subsequently lost its Chris-Craft/UPN affiliate station group in a sale to Rupert Murdoch and News Corp., which (ironically) owned and bankrolled UPN's competitor, the Fox Network. Viacom, once a lowly syndication company in the 1950s but now corporate head of MTV, Nickelodeon, and VH1, also had ties to Paramount but took control of venerable broadcaster CBS in 2001. Capital Cities sold ABC to Disney, which further diversified the company by developing ESPN1, ESPN2, and ESPN Classic Sports, the California Angels, and Go.com. Time Warner was merged with CNN, which included the Sports Illustrated programming and print franchise and the massive feature and prime-time production arm of Warner Bros., which developed and fed the nationwide delivery system Time Warner Cable—together creating a massive entertainment conglomerate which successfully realized the mother of all mergers: the AOL Time Warner conglomeration of 2000. While some hand-wringing greeted the implications of a renewed form of "vertical integration" long absent since the 1949 Paramount decrees (where a single corporation was prohibited from owning and controlling each stage of the media cycle—from production, to distribution, to exhibition and broadcast), the new mega-conglomerates like AOL Time Warner reestablished and legitimized vertical integration with a vengeance. And they did so with the blessing of the very same government that had, in the name of public interest, aggressively abolished vertical integration five decades earlier.[37] Why and how did this happen?

In a few short years, a 90-plus share, three-network oligopoly fell to scores of new electronic media competitors promising program diversity. But this diverse pantheon was then reaggregated again into four giant multinational media corporations, which together by fall 2000 had regained and amassed 86 percent of the audience. The present, widespread sanction given entertainment mergers and reconglomeration stems from the fact that these new vertically reintegrated conglomerates have symbolically mastered the very regime of diversity, public service, and democratic taste that regulatory limits were set in place to preserve for the past half century. However, rather than dispersing taste niches and community viewpoints across competing channels, the new conglomerates have mastered the ability to include this diverse pantheon of tastes and perspectives *within* components or "tiers" of the very same conglomerate. Viacom can thereby prove that it meets the needs of the youthful MTV/VH1 demographic, the African American target audience of BET, as well as the mainstream and older demographic tastes of CBS. Viacom proves to its shareholders and to Washington that it is both profitably diverse and inclusive, even as the television industry champions its market-driven diversity.

A recent case underscores the importance of this kind of institutional posture. When the NAACP and others mounted a frontal attack against the networks in 1999 based on the lack of racial diversity in prime-time television, the networks and studios jumped anxiously to "blacken" or "color" many of their existing series and staffs. A subsequent analysis of network programming, however, revealed that prime-time actually represented a higher percentage of blacks than existed in the population as a whole. Yet critics pointed out that this self-congratulatory notion of adequate representational percentages masked a countervailing trend: television had resegregated itself by the very tiering and conglomeration that the new multichannel landscape had legitimized. Yes, images of color existed, but not on the still-very-white worlds of NBC, CBS, and ABC programming, where they were almost nonexistent. African Americans were, however, ever present on the newer networks of WB and UPN, which had adopted the proven start-up strategy that fourth network Fox had exploited so successfully in the late 1980s: both made extensive use of "black-block" programming to reach a young and hip multiracial demographic that the majors no longer needed. Yes, television was diverse, but many critics pointed out that the diversity was based on a caste system of genre and tiering.[38] African Americans, that is, are diverted to the endless ethnic comedies and reality shows so prevalent on UPN, WB, and Fox. Diversity of representation now exists in television, but only because of generic and format "ghettoizations" that the multichannel conglomerates have established and profited from.

Because of this practice the "industry" now regularly deflects criticisms about its lack of public service and diversity by noting that the industry as a whole takes care of providing access to a wide range of groups and perspectives. They seldom point out two factors, however: first, that this ghettoization allows the majors (CBS, ABC, NBC) to be no less appreciably white than they've been for two decades (and to be that way without regulatory pressure); and second, that the new conglomerates actually prosper by internalizing and mastering a regime of difference in the form of corporate affiliate tiering. Thus, the de facto goal of each new conglomerate is to have within the walls of its extended corporate family a programming niche for every taste culture and social identity. Diversity and multiculturalism are now far from abnormal for the industry. While corporate components (specific networks and studios) may become more specialized and homogenous in scope and identity, the larger conglomerates that they comprise today must be tiered and affiliated as multicultural aggregates. This kind of industrial, multicultural aggregation deflects both claims of racism and concerned calls for new regulatory measures to enforce public service, diversity, and democratic representation. The entertainment industries have every reason to internalize and master such ideals: they have done so in practice by instituting multicultural tiering as part of a global, mediated economy of scale.

I began this essay by suggesting that a range of fundamental transformations in industry, economy, and technology have fueled greater volatility and permutation in televisual form. The overdetermined public construction and perpetuation of digital "convergence" as the needed and inevitable outcome of much industrial and cultural activity does two things in this regard: it defines industrial and aesthetic changes in mostly technological terms, even as it conflates and conceals in technology a very different and macroscopic form of convergence—corporate conglomeration and vertical reintegration. The trades hype the wonders of digital multiplexing, high definition, and dot-com start-ups, but the subtext of such hype really concerns new kinds of corporate alignment. Repurposing, content migration, branding, stunting, and conglomerate/multicultural tiering all provide effective, tactical countermeasures in the face of very real anxieties about runaway production, new technologies, and volatile market conditions. Textual practices of aggregation and permutation fit the needs of a post-Fordist industry tied not to standardization and redundancy but to the effective production of flexible semiotic and cultural capital—now requisite industrial competencies in the age of digital.

Declarations of television's imminent demise in the 1990s in the face of the Internet and digital media were greatly exaggerated, including *Wired*'s taunting, precrash cover story about NBC president Bob Wright: "Go ahead, kill your TV. NBC is ready."[39] Such claims were also inevitably offered from some precarious corporate vantage point of vested interest within the high-tech and dot-com euphoria that preceded NASDAQ's precipitous high-tech collapse in spring 2000. A range of institutional players attempting to manage and make sense of the "inevitable" shift to digital—both industrial (the computer and entertainment industries and Hollywood and the film industry) and academic (cultural theory and film studies)—all failed to recognize one persistent and nagging bridge between old media and new media: television. As current initiatives in entertainment and e-commerce show, television brought to the table of technological "revolution" a set of principles that proved to ground the Internet as well: television is electronic, ubiquitous, round the clock, and ostensibly (like the Net) "free." Television, unlike most dot-coms, has also had at its disposal vast amounts of the very material that some argued was the key to maintaining a permanent server-based Net presence in the age of broadband.[40] Tom Rogers, president of NBC Cable and Internet Operations, calms the fears of his anxious shareholders with this very confidence about the network's holdings and deep-storage: "In broadband, you need lots of video material, and it's extremely difficult, if not impossible, to create a rich video library, if you are not already in the business."[41]

The genius of television's persistence as the dominant art form of the second half of the twentieth century was its ability to produce and exploit a set of quantitative and qualitative economic conditions that in turn fueled two fundamental components in the production of a networked, globalized culture: First, the creation of branded entertainment content marked by distinction (through the consolidation and intensification of capital in the entertainment industries); and second, the perpetuation and maintenance of a vast and reliable system of consumerism and global merchandizing. Advertising and commercialism proved to be the keys that linked the efficiencies of capital-intensive content creation (in Hollywood and network television) with the economies of scale required by broadcasting, cablecasting, and satellite distribution. As a nexus between these two worlds, digitalization provided optimal conditions under which a range of existing institutional strategies and new formal permutations could be effectively and profitably deployed.

NOTES

A portion of this chapter was adapted from my essay "Branding" in *Encyclopedia of Television*, 2nd ed., ed. Horace Newcomb (Chicago: Fitzroy-Dearborn Press, 2004).

1. Chris Peacock, "Are You Being Metabrowsed?" *Inside,* December 12, 2000, p. 103.

2. See Horace Newcomb, TV: *The Most Popular Art* (New York: Anchor, 1974); Stuart Kaminsky, *American Television Genres* (Chicago: Nelson-Hall Publishers, 1985); and David Marc, *Demographic Vistas: Television in American Culture* (Philadelphia: University of Pennsylvania Press, 1984).

3. See Beverle Houston, "Viewing Television: The Meta-Psychology of Endless Consumption," *Quarterly Review of Film* 9.3 (1984): 183–95; and Sandy Flitterman, "Psychoanalysis, Film, and Television," in *Channels of Discourse, Reassembled: Television and Contemporary Criticism,* ed. Robert C. Allen (Chapel Hill: University of North Carolina Press, 1987), pp. 203–46.

4. See Allen, *Channels of Discourse;* and Ellen Seiter, "Semiotics and Television," in Allen, ed., *Channels of Discourse,* 31–66.

5. See Sarah Kozloff, "Narrative Form and Television," in Allen, *Channels of Discourse,* 67–100; and Jane Feuer, "Melodrama, Serial Form, and Television Today," in *The Media Reader,* ed. Manuel Alvarado and John O. Thompson (London: British Film Institute, 1990), pp. 253–64.

6. See Horace Newcomb and Robert S. Alley, eds., *The Producer's Medium: Conversations with Creators of American TV* (New York: Oxford University Press, 1983); Nick Browne, "The Political Economy of the Television (Super) Text," *Quarterly Review of Film Studies* 9.3 (1984): 174–82; Robert Vianello, "The Power Politics of Live Television," *Journal of Film and Video* 37 (1984): 26–40; and William Boddy, *Fifties Television: The Industry and Its Critics* (Urbana: University of Illinois Press, 1990).

7. See Lynn Spigel, *Make Room for TV: Television and the Family Ideal in Postwar America* (Chicago: University of Chicago Press, 1992); Herman Gray, *Watching Race: Television and the Struggle for "Blackness"* (Minneapolis: University of Minnesota Press, 1994); Julie D'Acci, *Designing Women* (Chapel Hill: University of North Carolina Press, 1994); John T. Caldwell, *Televisuality: Style, Crisis, and Authority in American Television* (New Brunswick: Rutgers University Press, 1995); and Jostein Gripsrud, *The Dynasty Years* (New York: Routledge, 1995).

8. Clifford Geertz, *Local Knowledge: Further Essays in Interpretive Anthropology* (New York: Basic Books, 1983).

9. The nature of the forms used to work through change and negotiate instability is evident in a variety of socio-professional registers, including the public relations tactics used to integrate the two technical cultures (old media and new media) at markets, conventions, and film festivals: for example, "AtomFilm's Winnebago-mounted, traffic-snarling screening room was one of the most visible symbols of the dot-com invasion" (John Healy, "Humbled Dot-Coms Still Major Presence at Sundance," *Los Angeles Times,* January 22, 2001, p. C1). This case showed how dot-com start-ups worked hard to define themselves as both "cinematic" and "independent" at the Sundance festival. These poses informed their online Web design as well, and spoke to potential "old media" affiliates in a symbolic language they well understood and associated with the festival.

10. Nicholas Negroponte, *Being Digital* (New York: Knopf, 1994).

11. John T. Caldwell, "Hybridity on the Media Superhighway: Techno-Futurism and Historical Agency," *Quarterly Review of Film and Video* 16.1 (1995): 103–111; Caldwell, *Televisuality;* and John T. Caldwell, "Slipping and Programming Televisual Liveness," *Aura: Film Studies Journal* 6.1 (2000): 44–61.

12. Kyle Pope and Scott Collins, "The New Killer App," *Inside,* December 12, 2001, p. 64.

13. Joe Schlosser, "Affils to UPN: Don't Tread on Me," *Broadcasting and Cable,* January 29, 2001, p. 30.

14. Ibid., p. 30.

15. Caldwell, *Televisuality,* pp. 297–301.

16. The trades described the new tactics of Jim Moloshok, president of Warner Bros. Online: "Entertainment companies at first saw the Internet as a promotional tool and used it by giving away their content for free. They are now trying to recapture their brands, their business and their future from the new media companies that at first moved faster and smarter" (Michael A. Hiltzik, "Net Effect: Old Media, New Tech," *Los Angeles Times,* April 12, 1999, p. 14).

17. Caldwell, *Televisuality,* pp. 258–62.

18. It is important to note the distinction between the treatment given to local stations "owned" by network NBC and that given to local "affiliated" stations. The owned stations (such as NBC-4, Burbank) are centered in large cosmopolitan areas, produce significant revenue streams, and were overhauled with explicit changes in name and ID; the affiliates, whose local owners contract to buy and air network offerings (such as KJRH-2), were "wooed" by the network's celebration of a de facto corporate "family."

19. Since the 1950s NBC had started the network programming day with the two-hour talk/news show, *Today,* which was essentially a combination of soft news, happy talk, and short features aimed at the early risers and breakfast viewers of middle America. *Today* was certainly never pitched to the public by programmers as a venue for cutting-edge risk taking.

20. The imperative to brand and rebrand circulates globally as well, as when James Murdoch, CEO of Star TV, with a third of a billion viewers in fifty-three countries, announced that they had revamped their television brand by deleting any explicit reference to TV: "Star TV . . . will be known as STAR, thereby evolving from a television brand to a multi-service, multi-platform brand" (Nyay Bushan, "Star TV Rebrands as STAR," *Hollywood Reporter,* February 2001, pp. A6–12, 65).

21. Consider in this regard the metaphors used to describe this process as an intimate stage that allows screenwriters to spin out story-concept "decorations": "But if Stacey Snider (Universal Pictures chairman) is underwhelmed by pitch, she doesn't show it.

Her job, she explains, is to keep the architecture of the film intact. It's up to the screenwriters to decorate the room" (Patrick Goldstein, "Empire Builders: They Greenlight Big Budget Features and Produce Niche Films. They Schmooze with Julia Roberts and Market the Rugrats. And They're Changing the Course of Hollywood," *Los Angeles Times Magazine,* March 26, 2000, p. 18.

22. Clarissa Cruz, "Havin' a Cheat Wave," *Entertainment Weekly,* January 2001, p. 8.

23. Newcomb and Alley, *Producer's Medium.*

24. Consider the following rather characteristic description of the writing-committee hell that came to be known as *Charlie's Angels:* "But the Murray-Liu screaming matches were only red flag number #1 for *Charlie's Angels.* Red flag #2 was the pink, yellow, and green pages of new scripts that tumbled out of the copying machine daily; [scripts that] bore the names of at least ten writers" (Aljean Harmetz, "They're Rumors, Not Predictions," *Los Angeles Times,* October 29, 2000, p. 87).

25. Brian Lowry, "Innovation Suffers in TV Shuffle," *Los Angeles Times,* August 18, 1998, pp. F1, F8–9.

26. Michael A. Hiltzik, "Honeymoon Is Over in Alliance of Ovitz, Burkle," *Los Angeles Times,* September 19, 2000, p. C1.

27. I am particularly interested in how sweeps and stunting might function in the discourses and practices of the production community, although sweeps are typically seen as a marketing/audience dynamic. Media theorists have latched onto anthropologist Victor Turner's theory of "liminality" as a way of explaining the special-event status of live spectacle programming for the culture of a nation. Daniel Dayan and Elihu Katz, *Media Events* (Cambridge: Harvard University Press, 1992) see the national televised ceremonial events as a liminal space bracketed off from everyday conceptions of time, a symbolic site and event where a people-group can act out alternative identities in imaginative rituals that give culture its meanings. Anthropologists following Turner could find the liminal in things like Mardi Gras or a Papuan sing-sing, and theorists like Dayan and Katz placed it in the macroscopic terms of live broadcasting at the national level. Neither, however, considered how liminality might serve to explain community rituals and events in the cultures of media production.

28. Caldwell, *Televisuality,* pp. 88–92.

29. John T. Caldwell, "Primetime Fiction Theorizes the Docu-Real," in *Reality Squared: Televisual Discourse on the Real,* ed. James Friedman (New Brunswick: Rutgers University Press, 2002), pp. 259–92.

30. Caldwell, "Slipping and Programming Televisual Liveness," 44–61.

31. Henry Jenkins, "Textual Poachers: Television Fans and Participatory Culture (New York: Routledge, 1992).

32. Sometimes these cross-entity stunts work within media entities of the same conglomerate, as when David Hannah, president of UPN's affiliate board of governors, considered the merits of airing shows produced by its corporate partners: "We appreciate the network's efforts to stunt those shows to up the viewership, and ultimately [we] are quite excited to be able to cross-promote when it's appropriate" (Schlosser, "Affils to UPN," p. 30.). While it is easy enough to explain the economic logic of this sort of internal stunting, cross-corporation stunting is more difficult to account for.

33. Denise Mann, "The Spectacularization of Everyday Life: Recycling Hollywood Stars and Fans in Early Television," in *Private Screenings: Television and the Female Consumer,* ed. Lynn Spigel and Denise Mann (Minneapolis: University of Minnesota Press, 1992), pp. 41–69.

34. Raymond Williams, *Television: Technology and Cultural Form* (New York: Schocken, 1974). The Taylor stunt also evokes Browne's notion of the television "super-text"—an extensive text comprised of many programs sequenced by broadcasters according to the logic of "day-parts" (primetime, daytime, near primetime) and targeted demographics.

35. Kuperman, quoted in Joe Schlosser, "Plugging in the TV," *Broadcasting and Cable,* January 29, 2001, p. 34.

36. See Williams, "The Technology and the Society," in *Electronic Media and Technoculture,* ed. John Caldwell (Rutgers University Press, 2000), p. 38.

37. In some cases, the individual components of the new conglomeration evidenced more hand-wringing about the effects of conglomeration than the government. The report that "UPN Executives predicted Friday that their network will continue to operate despite Viacom's new ownership of both CBS and UPN and News Corp.'s (parent of the Fox network) pending purchase of UPN's Chris-Craft–owned affiliate stations" demonstrated how precarious the ownership of content had become and how important it had become to "mark one's turf" in order to maintain one's "brand" in the confusion of conglomeration (Valerie Kuklenski, "UPN Brass See No Course Change Despite New Ownership," *Long Beach Press Telegram,* January 9, 2001, p. c6).

38. I thank Herman Gray for sharing his insights with me on "Black block" programming as a strategy of the new conglomerates. See Herman S. Gray, "Television and the Politics of Difference," in *Cultural Moves* (Berkeley: University of California Press, forthcoming).

39. NBC's boast (or threat) is quoted in Randell Rothenberg, "Go Ahead, Kill Your Television. NBC is Ready," *Wired* 6:12 (December 6–12, 1998).

40. Caldwell, "Hybridity on the Media Superhighway."

41. Hiltzik, "Net Effect," p. 14.

CHARLOTTE BRUNSDON

LIFESTYLING BRITAIN: THE 8–9

SLOT ON BRITISH TELEVISION

There is also the dogma within television, that it is boring to transmit ideas. This is partly to do with the determination on the part of those who work in television to set themselves up as a distinct profession with a quality and a skill and expertise of their own. Therefore, they talk about things being television or not. If someone simply sits in front of a camera and talks and tells you things and points things out with this finger, it is somehow not television. . . . One of the dogmas of the administrative levels of broadcasting is that in some strange way intellectual broadcasting or cultural broadcasting is a strange luxury which we allow ourselves to afford. This seems to me to be a very dangerous and ridiculous idea.—Jonathan Miller (editor of *Monitor* 1964–5, freelance director, Arts Features BBC), interviewed in *The New Priesthood,* 1970

Every time I switch on the television, I see someone stooping with a spoon, then sipping from it, and then turning to someone next to them and going "Aaah." The BBC is becoming a form of kapok, or wall-filling. If it's not broadcasting cookery programmes, it's about decorating your house, or about vets, or *Men Behaving Badly.* Soon there'll be *Vets Behaving Badly.*—Jonathan Miller, in *The Sunday Telegraph,* 1999

British broadcasting has always had a strong impulse to improve its audience. This impulse has, historically, included a rather more "hobbyist" strand than is sometimes recognized in the histories of public service traditions associated with the BBC's first

Director General, John Reith. For example, a rarely remembered period in the output of the Third Programme (the summit of cultural aspiration in the three national radio sevices) involved evening broadcasts in the 1950s to "minorities who are enthusiastically devoted to some form of self-expression . . . the jazz fancier or the pigeon fancier, the man or woman who wants to learn, say, Spanish from scratch, the fisherman or cyclist or collector of LP records . . . the bridge player or the naturalist, the more sophisticated film-goer, the ardent motorist or the enthusiast for amateur dramatics."[1] This is indeed a forgotten history, for in the 1990s, as the second comment from Jonathan Miller in my epigraph indicates, the substantial increase in lifestyle programming in the evening schedules of broadcast terrestrial television proved to be a particularly vibrant symbolic site for the discussion of the state of British television. What I want to do in this essay is to explore the increase in lifestyle programs in terms of British television, and, more generally, television studies. The low critical esteem in which contemporary lifestyle programming is held is echoed in the patchy and meager archiving of its predecessors—the hobbyist and instructional programming of the 1950s, 1960s, and 1970s. When possible, however, I will refer to the archive holdings in an attempt to establish the specificity of contemporary programs.[2]

TV FOR ME

I enjoy cooking and I like food. I'm also interested in most of the domestic arts and, predictably for an Englishwoman of my class and age, I am keen on gardening. However, I am not a housewife, and I find it difficult to pursue these interests, usually arriving home from work between seven and eight in the evening. I think it took me a while, in the early 1990s, to notice that the television programs that I was choosing to watch between eight and nine after I got home were anything more than my own selection from the schedules. Being able to choose programs about cookery, home decorating, clothes, and gardening was something I didn't initially reflect on until there began to be so many that issues of generic variation became insistent. At the end of the decade it was clear that there had been a significant transformation of the British broadcast schedules (particularly on the minority channels BBC2 and Channel 4), and I would agree with Andy Medhurst's "outrageous claim" that lifestyle programs have been the genre of the 1990s.[3] Thus, for example, in a sample week in May 1999 there were in the 8–9 slot, across the five terrestrial channels, two cooking programs, three gardening programs, three home/decorating programs, and various programs on clothes, antiques, holidays, airplanes, and cars. In this same slot six months later (October 9–15, 1999), there were three cooking programs, four on gardening, two on fashion, four on travel, two on house decorating, two on pets and vets, and five on nature. A six-month sample of programs in the slot at the beginning and end of the decade thus shows that the early 1990s boasted no more than a per week total of two or three cooking/gardening and consumer programmes, but by the end of the decade the total is more like seven or eight. The programs that seem to have disappeared from the slot during the decade include "variety" and most types of "serious" documentary.[4] So, what's been happening on the British television schedules, and how can thinking about this contribute to a discussion about the state of television studies?

Both Rachel Moseley in her "Makeover Takeover on British Television"[5] and Medhurst in his "Day for Night" have shown how the transformation of the weekday early evening schedules owe much to daytime television. Both authors point out that this new evening schedule is partly comprised of programs or genres that have been moved to the evening from the daytime schedules, always the domain of the housewife, the mother with children, the retired, and the hobbyist. While the evening programs may have higher production values, many of the formats and concerns have had a daytime life for some years. This sense of generic and televisual origin, though, does not really explain to us why there has been a day-for-night makeover takeover. Thus, before exploring the strand of 8–9 programming in more depth, I want to mention some broader factors that we should note in thinking about these programs.

This programming can firstly be placed within a context of changes in both British society and the television industry. In terms of British society, there are three key factors in considering the growth in lifestyle programming. First is the increase in home ownership (Britain has the highest proportion of homeowners in Europe, and two thirds of the population live as owner-occupiers). This steady increase in home ownership has been accompanied, in the southeast in particular, by the continuing inflation of house prices and the movement of some property areas from a local (national) to an international market price. The last twenty years of the twentieth century saw the consolidation and proliferation of everyday discourses of value and investment associated with the purchase of housing.[6] The second factor is the continuing expansion of female entry into the workforce. In depressed areas, there has been a well-documented increase in female, often part-time, employment in place of male employment, while the more privileged classes are marked by the increasing inroads of women into the professions. In both cases there is a consequent increase in women with control over their own income. Third, despite media hysteria about teenage pregnancies, the most significant statistic about childbirth is the continuing postponement of the first child among the higher social classes.[7] Put together with other factors such as the increase in single-occupancy homes,[8] as well as the much-vaunted privatization of leisure (for example, the garden trade has increased by forty percent in the last ten years),[9] we can hypothesize that it is not lifestyle programming alone that is producing its audience. If the home and person have always been expressive sites, more people are spending more time and money on these pursuits than ever before, and they are doing so in a culture where the gap between rich and poor has continued to accelerate.[10] While the lifestyling of British television has attracted attention as symbolic of the deterioration of that television, it is perhaps more helpful to think of it as one element in the more general lifestyling of the late-twentieth-century British culture.

In terms of the more limited context of British television, we can initially note two key factors. First is that the arrival of satellite, with its premium channel privileging of sport and films and the increase in multiset households, has led to a diminution in family viewing as well as what I would argue to be a discernible feminization of prime-time terrestrial television.[11] Second, with the introduction of the 25 percent rule in 1992 (which specified that the broadcast output of the BBC had to include 25 percent independent productions) there has been a very substantial increase in independent productions appearing on screen. Many of the smaller production companies have much less obviously gendered production hierarchies, and the British Film Institute tracking studies on the television industry suggest that there now are simply more women working in television.[12] Many of the lifestyle shows are made by independents, many are fronted by women, and many have production teams with quite high proportions of women.[13] For our purposes, what is of interest here is both the multilayered feminization of the 8–9 slot and the professionalization of skills previously labeled domestic. For while hobbyism was dominated by men, lifestyle is full of white, educated, middle-class women.[14] The labors of second-wave feminism are beamed back to us in a way as paradoxical as Mrs. Thatcher in the legions of enterprising and rather bossy women earning good money who tell us how to transform the domestic sphere.

Thus the first point about television studies to be noted relative to the changes in the 8–9 slot on British television in the 1990s is that only when we have a sense of these broader determinants can we move on to thinking about the slot itself. That is, television studies cannot hope to illuminate our understanding of television by looking at television alone, but, as I hope to demonstrate here, neither can the textual characteristics of television be explained solely through attention to contextual factors.

The 8–9 slot on British television has had a hard end and a soft beginning. The hard end is nine o'clock, which was for years the time of the main evening news on BBC1, but which also marks "the watershed" before which programs must conform to certain standards of "taste and decency." Thus, on the commercial channels, it is traditionally between nine and ten that crime drama is shown, while on the BBC these shows start after the news at nine-thirty. The early evening is the zone of the local news, U.S. sitcoms, and soap opera, and it is the latter part of this zone, with its traditional gardening programs on Friday evenings, that has been transformed into a cornucopia of cooking, gardening, and decorating programs. Here, the historical hobbyist element in British broadcasting, which ranged from *Blue Peter* to *Barry Bucknell* and *Percy Thrower,* has been transformed through an engagement with consumerism, makeovers, and game shows. The new hybrid formats seek to transform instruction into entertainment through the addition of surprise, excitement, and suspense. As Pawel Pawlikowski, codirector of *Twockers,* a recent bleak drama about car theft by youths, puts it when describing the contrast between his work and other TV, the mass of television "shows aspirational happy Britain where people have a good time."[15]

Pavlikowski's description certainly catches the tone of much of the 8–9 slot, which is relentlessly "up" with its strong sense that not only can things get better but they can get better now for you the viewer if only you paint your garden fences purple, install a water feature, rip out that 1970s carpet, select only the best fresh ingredients, learn that wok cooking is fast and healthy, and treat yourself to a scented bath after clearing your wardrobe of those mistaken impulse bargain buys. If you have a pear-shaped body, don't choose short, boxy jackets, and remember that strong, clear colors work much better than messy patterns while the most unusual plant containers can be made from everyday building materials such as brushed-aluminum central heating flues.

Moseley has pointed out that many of these programs are dependent on the key trope of the "makeover," with its condensed narrative of "before and after."[16] The subject can be a woman, a man, a garden, a room, or a house, but on the television program, a story is told that shows the "before" of the person or place, and then, through the intervention of some kind of expertise, the "after." There is a long history of hobby or enthusiast television programming in Britain, and the gardening, cooking, and do-it-yourself (home improvement) all imply a narrative of transformation. In the older hobby genre, however, the narrative of transformation is generally one of skill acquisition. So, for example, in the 1967 BBC series *Clothes That Count,* each of the ten thirty-minute programs focused on making one garment, interspersing very close camera work on hands and sewing machine with more fashion-show-like segments in which the garment is modeled made up in a range of fabrics. The whole process of making, for example, a piped buttonhole in a coat was shown in real time with framing that mainly excluded the dressmaker's face.

Similarly, in the earliest surviving episode of *Gardener's World,* (aired in April 1972) we are shown appropriate spring pruning techniques, how to divide herbaceous perennials, and the planting out of hardened seedlings in twenty minutes of continuous address by Percy Thrower. The long takes require the concealment of garden tools such as trowels and forks near the appropriate plants so that Thrower does not have to walk laden with tools between his different demonstrations. Here, too, the close-up is on the operation being demonstrated. The programs are didactic; they show how to do or make things and, historically, they deal with the difficulty of doing so on the "now" of television through the device that has become a catchphrase in Britain, "Here's one I made earlier," or else simply through the use of real time. The hobby genre, like the short-lived broadcasts on Network Three in 1957, addressed the amateur enthusiast. By the end of the program, the listener would have learned how to do something. In contrast, the makeover programs offer a different balance between instruction and spectacle that is articulated most clearly through a changing grammar of the close-up, and they most commonly address their audience as a customer or consumer.[17]

While contemporary lifestyle programs retain a didactic element, it is narratively subordinated to an instantaneous display of transformation. Thus while the viewer is shown how to perform certain operations, the emphasis of the program, what the producers call "the reveal," is when the transformed person or place is shown to their nearest and dearest and the audience. The gardening in successful, popular programs such as *Ground Force* is a combination of designing the new garden, clearing the old one, and then planting purchased mature specimens. This is clearly both more televisual (it takes a long time for a seedling to grow into a shrub) and more attuned to many contemporary lifestyles. It is a world away from Percy Thrower's cautious reminder to his viewers in 1972 that "we've talked before about these containerized plants and planting them." The emphasis now is on the result, not the process. Moseley shows how there is frequently a double-audience structure in these programs: an internal audience who knows the person or place being transformed and to whom the transformation is a surprise, and the external television viewing audience, both of which are superintended by the television presenters and experts who have effected the transformation. For without the internal audience to express shock, or joy, or astonishment, how would we, the external audience, understand the emotional significance of what we see? And, further, it is in this double-audience structure that we see the changed grammar of the close-up. Instead of focusing on operations, the camera focuses on reactions: the climax of *Ground Force* is the close-up on the face of the garden owner, not the garden.[18]

This emphasis on affect in the 1990s surprise makeover programs can be contrasted with the moment of revelation in the 1979 BBC series *Design by Five*. This series commissioned five designers to transform rooms for figures in the public eye. Individual programs included "A Kitchen for Magnus Pyke" (aired January 16, 1979), "A Bedroom for Clare Rayner" (aired January 23, 1979), and "A Sitting Room for Alan Coren" (aired February 6, 1979). In these programs the designers were shown discussing their clients' needs and desires, and the viewers were also shown samples of the designers' other work. The clients were in all cases better known than the designers, which meant that the viewer was likely to be familiar with the client and thus have some sense of appropriate surroundings. But the celebrity of the clients, all of whom were articulate and accustomed to being listened to, produced a very different balance of power from that of programs where the transaction is conducted between television people and ordinary people. The design stage was one of negotiation in which potential conflicts became clear. The reveal—in most cases of rooms that seemed grotesquely at odds with the client's persona and wishes—became the opportunity for further negotiation in which the client negotiated good manners, "you've had a marvellous time," with dissatisfaction, "it looks expensive, and I'm ever so practical," as Clare Rayner put it on being confronted with the curtaining of all her walls by Tricia Guild. But the key element here, which allows this negotiation to be conducted without game show affect, in addition to the status and cultural capital of the clients, is that the transformations have been effected on unacknowledged sets. So when Alan Coren observes that "my furniture hasn't really been accommodated" and that "the bits do dominate," he can be critical safe in the knowledge that he does not have to live with what has been done to his home. The project is thus much more obviously educational than entertaining. The clients have participated in part in an effort to collaborate in extending knowledge about what designers can do. Thus we could say that this is realist, rather than melodramatic, television. In contrast, contemporary lifestyle programs in many cases introduce the possibility of humiliation and embarrassment for participants through devices such as having neighbors decorate rooms in each other's homes (*Changing Rooms*) or having partners buy each other's outfits. It is the reaction, not the action, that is significant in this strand of lifestyle programming.

Andy Medhurst suggests that in lifestyle programs as a whole, "our dreamscapes have become domesticated—we now look for fantasy and escape in our back gardens and on our dinner tables." He continues by noting that "these lifestyle shows adhere to a sensibility that's very inward, insular, and small-c conservative, and in this context it's worth noting the non-too-hidden class dimension of such programmes. Despite token gestures elsewhere, all are deeply rooted in white, English suburbia, where the houses and gardens are big enough to warrant makeovers."[19]

While I don't disagree that there is something consummately Blairite about the lifestyle world, I think we can make some useful points about the distinctions between the programming, which we can do in part on the basis of the balance between what I have characterized as "realist" and "melodramatic" modes, and in part on the basis of how these programs characterize their audience, and hence contemporary Britain. For example, *Ground Force,* which is broadcast on Friday evenings on BBC1, has become the BBC's most successful gardening program. Two of its regular presenters have become celebrities, the novel-writing Alan Titchmarsh and the specialist in water features, Charlie Dimmock.[20] The format of this show is the conversion of a garden in collusion with its owners but in concealment from the person seen to care most about the garden. (An indication of the stature of the program is that the special millennium edition converted a garden for Nelson Mandela.) In contrast, *Real Gardens,* also broadcast on Friday evening, is a Channel 4 program hosted by gardener Monty Don. This program focuses on continuity by following the fortunes of six groups of gardeners over the course of the season. The presenters here are relatively low profile and are seen to build up a continuing relationship with "their" gardeners, who are presented in segments every other week to report on progress.

In one episode of *Ground Force* (aired October 15, 1999) a plan is made to revamp the garden of a cricket fan without his knowledge. As is quite often the case in England the weather is rainy, and so the dedicated transformation time is more pressured than normal while ground conditions are extremely muddy. In response the *Ground Force* team become involved in clowning for the camera as water drips down their collars and their boots stick in the mud. In the climax of the program when the owner innocently returns and the *Ground Force* team ostentatiously hide themselves against a wall while the owner's wife and his mother usher him into the garden, it is difficult to be certain about the causes of his emotion, shown in close-ups and juxtaposed with long shots of the transformed garden. Is it, as the program would have us believe, joy at the transformation and moved by the loving concern of his family? Or is it shock at coming home to find the house full of television crew, the cricket run replaced by patio and decking, and incredulity at the family's deception?

Real Gardens offers no reveal. Instead, the selected gardeners are shown over the course of the programs. Although one of the gardeners in this series is the owner of a large middle-class garden, this was not true of the others. I want to comment here briefly on the novice gardeners Jem and Drew, who had only a tiny garden at their home in the south of England. In an early program (aired October 7, 1999) Jem and Drew are taken to the home of an older gardener, Maurice, and his wife, to learn a little about tomato cultivation. This rather charming sequence offers a juxtaposition of the image of a very traditional country gardener with that of a clearly urban gay couple, who all share an interest in organic tomatoes. Jem and Drew were called 'the boys' in a very relaxed way by the presenter, and made a very slightly camp joke about basil being a euphoric when they were in the polytunnel with Maurice. The information about complementary planting as pest control is made clear, but so also is the unfeigned pleasure that all the participants took in the encounter a very different situation than that of the antics before the camera in *Ground Force*.

In both programs there is no comment about the identity of participants. The family in *Ground Force* is of mixed race; the grandmother is black and has a strong Derbyshire accent. Jem and Drew are identified as novice gardeners, not gay men. An interest in gardens and gardening is the key characteristic of the participants, and this shared interest rendered difference ordinary. In effect, then, through their choice of participants these programs make a considerable contribution to changing ideas of what it is to be British (and watching television), and that this may mark changes a little more substantial than what is suggested by Medhurst's "tokenism."

CONTEXTS OF STUDY

I now want to shift away from this 1990s version of the 8–9 slot in order to raise some questions about the constitution of the object of television studies. Apart from my own living room, the place where I have been thinking about this slot has been the Midlands Television Research Group, a group that in 1999 started to work on what we have called "the 8–9 project." With participants Ann Gray, Jason Jacobs, Tim O'Sullivan, and a shifting population of postgraduate students, the group has provided a forum in which we can read new books and articles and present work in progress.[21] Its relevance here is twofold. First, ideas about television, not just television studies, are formed and debated in the group. The group's composition is such that a distinction can be made between the older members (Tim, Ann, and I are all over 45) who have been teaching in higher education for some time, and the younger members, many of whom are graduate students for at least their initial involvement in the group. The television we watch and know is different, and so are the complex pulls of memory and autobiography in our understanding of what television is.[22]

These individual and generational determinations are thrown into greater relief when the television that different group members have and haven't been watching encompasses not only the different viewing times of those engaged in full-time work and those studying, but also the period of massive change in British television, from the arrival of Channel 4 and daytime TV in the early 1980s to the expansion of nonterrestrial services in the 1990s. Not only do the younger members of the group watch different television, but the television that is there to be watched is quite different. In John Ellis's periodization of the three ages of television as scarcity, availability, and abundance, television studies is the discipline of television's "availability," and our viewing in the group encompasses both temporal ends of this era.[23]

But it is not just that the younger members of the group watch different television and that television itself is different, but also that they have a different disposition in relation to television. Television, and the options it offers and the demands it makes, is both more and less significant to the younger members. Herta Herzog, in the early 1940s when she was researching women in the United States who listened to radio soap opera, spent some time puzzling over the issue of whether there were any consistent differences between regular listeners and others.[24] In the end, she suggests that regular listeners could be described as being "more radio-minded" in general. The different disposition that I refer to here could perhaps be thought of as being "more television-minded," in that television is much more readily accommodated with other activities (eating breakfast, doing homework, making phone calls), and is thus both more ordinary and less important. For the group's younger members television is very different from that experienced by someone like Jonathan Miller. In another distinction made by Ellis, Jonathan Miller watches programs while it is more ordinary nowadays to watch television.[25]

This concept is germane to the context of the 8–9 project because of my conceptualization of the 8–9 slot as a lifestyle slot. Initially, I characterized as I watched: I didn't see some of the lifestyle variants in the slot, such as pet and car programs, nor did I notice some nonlifestyle material. The younger members of the group, however, were much clearer about the daytime origins of much of the program and also drew my attention to the "pets and vets" strand.[26] They also pointed out that lifestyle includes programs about cars, which varied widely between diverse topics such as environmental issues and car purchases by women.

Further, it was one of the younger members of the group, Helen Wheatley, who pointed out to us that within this homely aspirant world of lifestyle and makeover there is also an *Unheimlich* strand, a subgenre of programming about security, burglary, and property crimes—that is, the aspirant world under threat. This strand includes emergency-service docudrama programs and closed-circuit television footage programs and offers a chill side to the contemporary drama of the nineteenth-century self-improvement mode of lifestyle.[27] The profile of the slot is transformed when we think of it as offering both "aspirational happy Britain" and a constant minority thread. Self (and home) improvement thus become more ritualistic and propitiary, and the constant "up" tone is a little more like whistling in the dark.

The interaction of the Midlands Television Research Group changed my understanding of what I was studying, and I have relied on work done for and in the group in writing this essay. I suggest that this is symptomatic of the increasing difficulty of addressing contemporary television by oneself. So my second point about television studies is that the well-rehearsed problems about the constitution of the object of television studies (that is, crudely, political economy, production context, text, or audience) have become, and will continue to be, enormously extended with the decline of mono-nation broadcasting systems. At the same time, the issues of generation will become more accentuated. The analytic models of television studies have been developed during times when television is either, in Ellis's terms, "scarce" (the national monopolies of the early days), or still graspably "available" (the extended provision of the later part of the twentieth century). Many established authorities in the field are program, rather than television, watchers. As we move into the age of abundance the scale of the changes to what television is make it increasingly important that we conceptualize what I refer to as television disposition as part of our approach to this protean medium. It is in this context that taking a scheduling period such as 8–9, rather than a program, serial, or genre, can produce an object of study that is specific to television as a broadcast medium and grant appropriate significance to scheduling—even as it decreases, perhaps, in importance. Choosing a time band for a group project permits the productive interplay of different television dispositions and allows us to see how approaches to television are greatly inflected by these.

TV FOR OTHER PEOPLE: THE "DUMBING DOWN" DEBATE AND THE "WALL OF LEISURE"

Jane Root, controller of BBC2 at the time of this writing in 1998, was recruited to the channel from the independent sector, where she had a strong record in "intelligent leisure" programming for the company Wall-to-Wall. In her first years at BBC2 she displayed a scheduling strategy marked by the zoning of programming, introducing the *Art Zone* on Sunday evenings, which was intended to complement the successful *History Zone* on Saturday evenings. She has also been defensive of BBC2's "wall of leisure" and is reported to want BBC2 to "own" leisure subgenres such as travel, cookery, fashion, gardening, and sport.[28] The defense of lifestyle/leisure programming for the BBC is both a historical mission, with continuities between current BBC2 scheduling, the history of the channel, and the hobbyist tradition, and an ethical remit in relation to public service broadcasting. Programs such as *Gardeners' World* are consistently attractive to large (for BBC2) audiences, while the *Ground Force* spin-off, *Charlie's Garden Army* (BBC1), in which Charlie Dimmock enlists a local community in the refurbishment of a neglected space, both appeal to audiences and operate with a quite strong notion of citizenry and the public good.[29] Thus we can see lifestyle and leisure programming as an extension of the democratic remit of public service broadcasting. Peter Bazalgette, recognized throughout the industry as a key mover in this field, has been, as founder of Bazal Productions, responsible for *Changing Rooms, Ready Steady Cook, Ground Force, Pet Rescue,* and the reformatted *Food and Drink*. He offers a much more pragmatic account than does Root, stressing that "it is very important not to just have individual successes but genres," and observing that "we only think up ideas for broadcasters who tell us what they need. We are not a bright ideas company, we provide scheduling solutions."[30] The success of Bazal, which moved into the field by taking over production of the BBC program *Food and Drink,* is founded on deeply anti-Reithian principles, marked perhaps most simply in Bazagette's notion of his product as "scheduling solutions" by the goal of moving programmes from BBC2 to BBC1 (as happened with *Changing Rooms*), and in his own comment: "why have originality when you can have ratings?"[31]

We could say that Root and Bazalgette stake out the field when we attempt to understand the significance of the programs that have figured in recent discussion in Britain about the "dumbing down" of British television. On the one hand, there is an argument that contests the understanding of the public sphere as one solely of citizenry and governmentality. On the other hand there is the search for cheap, ratings-led "scheduling solutions." These notions come together in relation to cost and scheduling, for these are cheap programmes and British television has been for some years clearly moving toward "stripping" in its scheduling.

So here, finally, I want to address my epigraphs, comments about television made thirty years apart by Jonathan Miller, a cultural heavyweight in Britain. Rather than wading through the commentary on this issue in the British press I want to take Miller's comments indicatively. Jonathan Miller (or Dr. Jonathan Miller, as he is normally referred to in the British media) embodies a particular late-twentieth-century idea of an intellectual. As an Oxbridge-educated, trained doctor, who is also an acclaimed opera director and curator, and who is well-known for his highbrow but popular programs, he is liberal, polymathic (polemically committed to arts and sciences), and authoritative. Miller is also modern in that he is one of the generation that embraced television in the 1960s by seeing the new medium as offering a range of intellectual and relative potentialities. His own television work is robustly intellectual, and this in combination with his engaged and impressively broad cultural competences suggests that he can also be seen as an embodiment of a post-1960s public service broadcasting. As indicated in the first quotation above, Miller has never been afraid of "talking heads," and his main interest in television is as a vehicle for ideas. In the 1969 interview above, Miller argues that "intellectual . . . or cultural broadcasting" is not a luxury but a necessity, a key contribution to the body politic.

Thirty years later, in the second quote given above, this veteran of 1960s British television comments on the lifestyle programming that is the subject of this essay. Miller, who also invokes another vigorous strand of British early-evening programming, "pets and vets," as well as the later and very popular comedy *Men Behaving Badly,* makes clear his revulsion at these "wall-filling" programs. It is both cooking and comedy that excite exasperation, and his metaphor of "kapok"—which is actually cushion material, not wall filling—suggests that this exasperation does not discriminate between interior decoration and do-it-yourself activity.

This encounter between Jonathan Miller and kapok is useful in focusing our attention on the concerns—both historical and contemporary—of television studies. For if Miller's anger about wasting airwaves on cookery is symptomatic of an engaged high-cultural concern about the deterioration of British television (and it must be stressed that Miller is engaged; he is not one of the British establishment who pretends never to watch television) then kapok is surely the end through which cultural students of television such as myself have historically entered.

In many ways, the world of lifestyle TV is not dissimilar to the *Nationwide* world we looked at in Birmingham many years ago.[32] It is a world of consumers not citizens, a world of the domestic and the private, a world that has perhaps taken down its net curtains, but only to install a trompe l'oeil "regency" screen. But if this world of private households has moved closer to prime time in the schedules, it is also worth pointing out that it offers a differently contoured public. Medhurst decries tokenism, but I think there is something more positive to be said about the varieties of people that these shows construct as ordinary Britons. Gay couples get to the finals of room-decorating competitions in *Homefront; Looking Good* regularly includes black and Asian viewers in features about foundation, lipstick, and haircare. Mixed-race couples have their gardens transformed on *Ground Force;* cookery programs recognize the wealth of culinary knowledge in the different British populations. These people were not on the screen twenty-five years ago—so if there has been a dumbing down of British television, it seems to me that there has also been a "pluraling" up.

There is, however, a dreadful sense of déjà vu in the contours of this argument. In a context where it is clearly indicated that the traditional "quality" genres of current affairs/documentary and drama are embattled,[33] I'm not sure I want to come out fighting for lifestyle television. Surely I am not still just defending kapok after all these years? No, I think not, but the reason can be found in Miller's use of "kapok." That is, it is precisely the imprecision that points the way: he is saying it is all one undifferentiated load of stuffing. In contrast, I would suggest that perhaps television is now simply more *ordinary,* and that some of it is good and some of it isn't. The 8–9 slot in the 1990s doesn't merely represent the defeat of the investigative journalist by the television cook—although it does do this, and the castigation of television cooks does very little to address the causes of this substitution. It also represents a greater attention paid to the stuff of everyday lives and a broader definition of what "cultural broadcasting" might consist of. For someone like Miller there is a way in which ideas are a hobby, while others have different leisure pursuits. Attention to cooking, home decor, clothing, and gardening is not in itself contemptible. The forms in which this attention is given are various, and the number of programs available allow distinctions to be made. Comparison with earlier instructional and leisure programming has suggested that we might be able to sketch a broad shift in this type of programming from a realist to a melodramatic mode, signified through the shift from close-ups on objects and operations to close-ups on faces. Within that broad shift we can discriminate, in current lifestyle programming, between programs at the more realist end (*Real Gardens*) and those at the more melodramatic (*Ground Force*). I would want to argue for the more realist inflection, and I would go against programmes with a strong stress on "the reveal," which I think often verge on the sadistic.[34]

Against Jonathan Miller, I would want to argue that there is much of value in contemporary British television. Many lifestyle programs should be welcomed as relatively accomplished, contemporary, secular, and socially extensive entertainment texts, or as good, ordinary television for a nation that has changed its disposition toward television but that is also struggling to understand itself as full of difference. The problem is not the presence of lifestyle as such, rather it is the broadcasting regimes and economies that validate Peter Bazalgette's claim that it is always better to have genres than individual programs. Here, I would want to go some way with Miller, for I would not want my enjoyment of a form of programming that is concerned with everyday practices and activities to preclude a recognition of the necessity of producing—and scheduling— programs about a wider world. It is not the presence of lifestyle, an easy and visible target, but the increasing absence of other programming to which we should be attentive.

And so this brings me to my final point about television studies. I have here made a limited defense of lifestyle programming, partly on the grounds that it reflects both a range of everyday pleasures and skills and a greater diversity in the audience. This is a familiar move from what we might call the kapok end of television studies. I want to go on to argue that a text-based television studies (i.e., one that understands itself within arts rather than the social sciences) must engage in evaluation and not restrict itself to this representation or socially extensive paradigm. I have suggested here that in the particular instances I have been discussing, the more explicitly instructive (realist) *Real Gardens* is preferable to the more show biz (melodramatic) *Ground Force*. Lifestyle programs are replete with implicit and explicit aesthetic judgment, and television scholars need to make the case why some are better than others.

NOTES

I have discussed the programs *Clothes That Count* and *Design by Fire* in "Once More on the Insignificant," in C. Brunsdon, C. Johnson, R. Moseley, and H. Wheatley, "Factual Entertainment on British Television: The Midlands TV Research Group's '8–9 Project,'" *European Journal of Cultural Studies* 4.1 (February 2001): 29–62. A version of this article appears in *International Journal of Cultural Studies* 6:1 (2003):5–23.

1. Unsigned article in *Radio Times,* September 29, 1957 (the week that new schedules for the Third Programme were announced). Quoted by Humphrey Carpenter, *The Envy of the World: Fifty Years of the BBC Third Programme and Radio 3* (London: Phoenix, 1996), p. 181.

2. I am very aware of the perils of characterizing genres of programs on the basis of viewing the few remaining editions, and I would welcome correspondence from anyone who can offer more detail.

3. Andy Medhurst, "Day for Night," *Sight and Sound* 9.6 (1999):26–27.

4. Catherine Johnson and Helen Wheatley, "The 8–9 Slot: 1990–92 and 1997–98," paper presented to the Midlands Television Research Group, Warwick University, November 4, 1999.

5. Rachel Moseley, "Makeover Takeover on British Television," *Screen* 41.4 (2000):299–314.

6. The rhetoric surrounding the Conservative government's sale of council (social) housing in the 1980s provides a fine example of this, as do the weekly personal finance supplements of any of the nontabloid newspapers.

7. "Teenage Pregnancy and the Family," *Family Briefing Paper* 9 (September 1999).

8. See Jill Matheson and Carol Summerfield, eds., *Social Trends 2000 Edition* (London: Office for National Statistics/The Stationary Office, 2000), p. 34; Richard Scase, "Britain towards 2010: The Changing Business Environment," University of Kent, October 1999. This report suggests that by 2010 more than half the British population will be living alone. Newspapers reported this information along the lines of Matt Born, "By 2010 Britain Will Be a Giant Singles Bar," *Daily Telegraph,* September 18, 1999, p. 9.

9. The National Farmers Union reported in January 2000 that horticulture is pretty much the only bright spot in British agriculture. The report itself attributes the massive increase (the industry is was worth £640 million at the time of the report) to the popularity of gardening programs and the relief from stress that gardening offers (Greg John and Terri Judd, "Garden Trade Grows 40% in Ten Years," *Independent,* January 1, 2000, p. 5).

10. The 1999 *Wealth of the Nation* report, the first of the triennial reports conducted under the 1997 Labour government, indicates a rise in average income with increasingly marked regional disparities (Cherry Norton, "Inequality Grows in Blair's Britain," *Independent,* October 25, 1999, p. 5).

11. Charlotte Brunsdon, "Not Having It All," in *British Cinema of the 90s,* ed. R. Murphy (London: British Film Institute, 2000).

12. Department of Trade and Industry figures for 1998 quote 88 percent of film and video businesses as employing under nine people (*Cultural Trends,* no. 30 [1999]: 11). BFI Television Industry Tracking Study, *The First Year: An Interim Report* (London: BFI, 1995); *Second Interim Report* (London: BFI, 1997).

13. The jury is still out on whether male and female journalists actually produce different programs, but it is clear that lifestyle programs are themed within the domain of care of the self and home, which are indubitably *still* feminized spheres. For another view, see Frank Mort, *Cultures of Consumption: Masculinities and Social Space in Modern Culture* (London: Routledge, 1996); and Sean Nixon, *Hard Looks: Masculinities, Spectatorship, and Contemporary Consumption* (London: UCL Press, 1996).

14. For example, Channel 4's commissioning editor for features and special projects, Liz Warner, who was appointed in 1999, has spent most of her career in daytime television. A *Broadcast* interview feature on her commented: "She is also the first to admit to commissioning according to personal preferences in her own lifestyle. 'I love eating and shopping,' she says. 'But I also believe in looking at original ways of tackling popular subjects. They have to have human drama, natural narrative, and incredible detail along the way' " (Walé Azeez, "First Lady of Lifestyle," *Broadcast,* November 12, 1999, p. 20).

15. Pawel Pawlikowski, quoted in Jane Robins, " 'Bleak TV' Takes Off in Halifax," *Independent,* September 4, 1999, p. 9.

16. Moseley, "Makeover Takeover."

17. There has been a strong backlash in some hobbyist gardening quarters about the way in which gardening programs encourage the purchase of fully grown shrubs and plants instead of educating audiences about taking cuttings and raising plants from seed. Peter Seabrook, who writes the gardening column in the *Sun,* when commenting on the demise of a year-old fashionable garden magazine, *New Eden,* made clear his disapproval of makeover gardening: "With cooking, if it goes wrong you can do it again in the afternoon. Gardening isn't like that; you only sow one lot of tomatoes a year" (quoted in Jane Robins, "Modernism Spells Trouble in the Garden of Eden," *Independent,* August 1, 2000, p. 8).

18. A 1976 episode of *Gardener's World* used no close-ups of the presenter Peter Seabrook and his hostess, Mrs. Prior, until the final goodbye before the credits. While the program used a great many close-ups, they were all of flowers and plants. The human beings remained in long shot (interspersed with flower close-ups) for the first nine minutes of the programs, after which they were shown in mid-shot from the knees. This was the closest shot until the final sequence (aired May 19, 1976). This is the only programme to survive from 1976.

19. Andy Medhurst, "Day for Night," p. 27.

20. Dimmock, a strong and capable gardener who does not shrink from heavy lifting and other dirty jobs, has shot to tabloid celebrity through much-salacious coverage of the fact that she does not wear a bra—and doesn't see this as a problem. "Of course I'm overexposed, but it's a good laugh. Someone told me 'you've got three years' " (Dimmock interview with Andrew Duncan, *Radio Times,* October 23–29, 1999, pp. 9–13). Dimmock was also on the cover of this issue of *Radio Times,* as she had been in August 1998 as a mock-up of Botticelli's *Venus* (she has long, blonde-auburn tresses).

21. See Midlands Television Research Group, "A Report," *Screen* 40.1 (1999): 88–90, for a short account of the group.

22. On the impact of memory and autobiography, see Karen Lury, "Television Performance: Being, Acting, and 'Corpsing,' " *New Formations* 26 (autumn 1995–96): 114–27.

23. John Ellis, *Seeing Things: Television in the Age of Uncertainty* (London: I. B. Tauris, 2000).

24. Herta Herzog, "What Do We Really Know about Daytime Serial Listeners?" in *Radio Research: 1942–43,* ed. P. Lazarsfeld and F. Stanton (New York: Duell, Sloan, and Pearce, 1944), p. 20.

25. Ellis, *Seeing Things,* p. 5.

26. Catherine Johnson, "Everyday Trauma: Pets, Vets, and Children in the 8–9 Slot," pp. 40–45, in C. Brunsdon, C. Johnson, R. Moseley, and H. Wheatley, "Factual Entertainment on British Television: The Midlands TV Research Group's '8–9 Project,' " *European Journal of Cultural Studies* 4.1 (February 2001):29–62.

27. Helen Wheatley, "Real Crime Television in the 8–9 Slot: Consuming Fear," in ibid., pp. 45–51.

28. Peter Keighron discusses a leaked internal report on BBC factual programming in his article "What Do You Really Want?" *Guardian,* October 25, 1999, p. 3.

29. Katy Elliott, reporting on the audience figures for Friday-night gardening programs, points out that *Gardeners' World* (BBC2) and *Real Gardens* (Channel 4) share a very similar adult demographic. She also states that *Charlie's Garden Army* (BBC1) and *Ground Force* (BBC1) attract a wider spread of viewers (both shows originally appeared on BBC2) (Elliott, "Growing Audiences," *Broadcast* 4 [August 2000]: 20).

30. Peter Bazalgette, in Louise Bishop "A Life of Leisure," *Television,* April 1998, pp. 22–23.

31. Ibid., p. 23.

32. See David Morley and Charlotte Brunsdon, *The Nationwide Television Studies* (London: Routledge, 1999).

33. See S. Barnett and E. Seymour, " 'A Shrinking Iceberg Travelling South . . .'— Changing Trends in British Television: A Case Study of Drama and Current Affairs" (London: Campaign for Quality Television, 1999).

34. See the discussion of the necessity of "informed consent" from "ordinary people" in Stirling Media Research Institute, *Consenting Adults* (London: Broadcasting Standards Commission, 2000).

JEFFREY SCONCE

WHAT IF?: CHARTING TELEVISION'S

NEW TEXTUAL BOUNDARIES

Television art. The very concept remains scandalous, a laughable oxymoron. For the most part, the status of "aesthetics" within the larger field of television studies has changed very little since the appearance of Horace Newcomb's *TV: The Most Popular Art,* one of a very few books to propose a poetics of the medium. Speculating in 1974 on the lack of serious attention given to the narrative art of television, Newcomb writes, "To some extent this is doubtless due to the social stigma attached very early to television by the cultural elite."[1] Gather a roomful of intellectuals of almost any stripe and their one point of agreement will be that television is the sewer of national and global culture. Even today, there is still a great amount of prestige to be mined in claiming that one does not own a television, or if one does, that it is most certainly never turned on (except, perhaps, for state funerals, emergency weather warnings, or the occasional series previewed and cleared by tastemakers in the pages of *Vanity Fair,* the *New Yorker,* or *Rolling Stone*). The situation is little better in the circle of media scholarship itself, where those who would fight to the death arguing over the historical variabilities in Bell and Howell candle strength or debate endlessly the politics of a largely irrelevant phenomenon like "Jenni-cam" will nonetheless dismiss a half century of television history as merely an annoying distraction dividing the celluloid and digital ages. Understanding how gender, sexuality, and identity operate on a *Xena* Web site is somehow a crucial project. Understanding how *Xena* actually negotiates such issues in narrative form remains terra incognito. It is a classic case of the tail wagging the dog.

Despite the isolated efforts of scholars such as Newcomb, John Ellis, Charlotte Brundson, John Caughie, Henry Jenkins, Christopher Anderson, and John Caldwell to initiate debate over the aesthetic properties of the medium, television remains for the most part a technological and cultural "problem" to be solved rather than a textual body to be engaged.[2] One might argue that the only term of aesthetic analysis in TV studies to have achieved any real currency is Raymond Williams's concept of "flow," a term that, despite its initial usefulness, tends to abstract rather than focus issues of televisual form.[3] Even for scholars conversant in televisual textuality, this emphasis on "flow" can, somewhat ironically, render the medium into the very same hallucinatory chaos experienced by Williams himself that night in the Miami hotel room where he first conceptualized the term. For those already hostile to the very concept of television, meanwhile, dipping into this "flow" to better judge its form and texture has the same appeal as sticking one's finger in a bucket of slime to better gauge its viscosity. This emphasis on "flow," moreover, has provided the perfect excuse for many television scholars to write about the medium without actually ever really watching its programming.[4] While most scholars of American literature would be mortified if they misidentified characters or plots in Melville, such inattention to detail is frequent in television studies; indeed, it can be a point of pride. Sadly, this has led to a situation where television itself is often more nuanced and sophisticated than the writing that seeks to theorize it.

Despite this continuing contempt for the medium by the priests of both high tech and high theory, there continues the nagging suspicion or even begrudging recognition that television remains the preeminent information and narrative technology of the world. Perhaps because the attempt to provide a "theory" of televisual spectatorship has proven even more futile than the totalizing drive of apparatus theory in 1970s film studies, academic fashion quickly abandoned its short flirtation with TV in order to occupy a new digital frontier that appeared more accommodating to its desire for techno-social imagineering (and more ripe for institutional funding).[5] And yet, as the digerati predict television's imminent death, the CEOs of various net providers and dot-com companies continue to court mergers with the major players in the TV industry, realizing that for the foreseeable future television will remain the home's primary delivery system for entertainment. Other statistics indicate that while hours spent on the net fluctuate, television viewership remains steady, suggesting that despite the interactive potential of the cyberage most media viewers prefer (for better or worse) to be "captivated" by stories on the tube—all of this even before the dot-com house of cards blew away during the NASDAQ crash of 2000–2001.

Still, there remains very little close analysis of the stylistic and narrative histories of the medium. Addressing this still formidable void in television studies, the following pages examine recent transformations in narrative strategies specific to commercial television in the United States. In particular, I am interested in how U.S. television has devoted increased attention in the past two decades to crafting and maintaining ever more complex narrative universes, a form of "world building" that has allowed for wholly new modes of narration and that suggests new forms of audience engagement. Television, it might be said, has discovered that the cultivation of its story worlds (diegesis) is as crucial an element in its success as is storytelling. What television lacks in spectacle and narrative constraints, it makes up for in depth and duration of character relations, diegetic expansion, and audience investment. A commercial series that succeeds in the U.S. system ends up generating hundreds of hours of programming, allowing for an often quite sophisticated and complex elaboration of character and story world. Much of the transformation in television from an emphasis on plot mechanics to series architecture, I would argue, has developed from this mutual insight by both producers and audiences. It is worth noting that the series to spawn the most involved audience communities in the past two decades, shows like *Northern Exposure, Star Trek, Twin Peaks, Xena, Seinfeld, ER, Buffy, Friends, The X-Files, The Sopranos,* and *The Simpsons,* are those that orchestrate a strong and complex sense of community while also leaving a certain diegetic fringe available for textual elaboration.[6] Whatever their genre or narrative logic, they all create worlds that viewers gradually feel they inhabit along with the characters.[7] Almost all of these shows, in turn, have spawned Web sites and books catering to audience desires to "master" the details and complexities of the story world. Most viewers of *The Simpsons* know who Apu is. True fans also know the names of his wife and eight children.

Although the changes I will address began in the 1970s, they have spread and accelerated in the past decade or so to infiltrate the majority of prime-time series on U.S. television. This will not be a wholly formal survey, however, because I hope to relate these textual developments to larger economic changes in the industry and to an emerging dialogue between the producers and the audiences of television drama. Aesthetics are always interwoven with economic, industrial, and demographic considerations, and the move toward world building in television demonstrates the interdependence of these factors. While I would not want to make any essentialist or teleological claims about what constitutes "true" or "superior" televisual forms, one could argue that television, when forced to compete more aggressively for audiences in the 1980s and 90s, gradually came to recognize and better exploit certain textual strengths it possessed over other media. Cable's fragmentation of the network audience, the growth of "reality television," and the concurrent reduction of more expensive narrative-based programming has created an environment of increasingly specialized narrative vehicles, allowing smaller audience groups the potential for targeted and intensive narrative investment. Although Buffy has endured vampires, demons, and other creatures of the night, for example, she could not have survived the programming practices of the old three-network system—her audience is too specialized, her diegetic realm too complex and bizarre.[8] In this exploration of television's new textual boundaries, finally, I will also address an emerging trend in television narration that raises an entirely new set of questions concerning the relationship among audiences, producers, and the elaboration of televisual worlds—a move toward *conjectural* forms of narration.

EVIL TWINS IN THE MEAT LOCKER

The few histories of television narrative that do exist generally agree that three distinct formats have dominated the medium's history in the United States. The 1950s saw the flourishing of the anthology format, which gave rise to the "golden-age" mythos of the live teleplay as the medium's ideal form. In popular accounts of the medium, this was the era dominated by the genius of Serling, Chayefsky, and other TV playwrights, serious authors who each week created an individual drama on a par with that of the theatrical stage. More recent scholarship in television history has greatly revised this rather idealized fable, demonstrating that the live anthology was a doomed (and often mediocre) genre almost from the moment of its inception. As both Christopher Anderson and William Boddy have argued, mutual transformations in the film and television industries in the early 1950s quickly led to the rise of the second format, the episodic telefilm.[9] Realizing the profound economic and programming advantages of a series featuring standing sets, a continuing cast, and increased durability in syndication, the industry assumed greater control over production by moving its operations from the New York City broadcast studios to the Hollywood soundstages.

In the new episodic telefilm format, viewers revisited a familiar premise each week to watch a continuing group of characters perform a self-contained story. This setup offered the networks distinct programming advantages. Standing sets and long-term contracts with creative personnel both before and behind the camera helped cut production costs, while the ability to slot a recognizable and familiar product into the weekly schedule helped attract and maintain steady viewership. As Boddy demonstrates, however, this transition from live anthology to episodic telefilm was not without its critics. Rehearsing the familiar binaries of art versus entertainment and innovation versus formula, many television critics and cultural pundits of the era bemoaned television's turn toward these more routinized narrative vehicles.[10] Rather than present the fully developed three-act narratives so valued in theatrical and cinematic construction, episodic television presented a world of static exposition, repetitive second-act "complications," and artificial closure. In the battle between the high drama of "The Days of Wine and Roses" and Lucy's "Vitavetavegimen," the latter had emerged victorious.

Television's third narrative format has long coexisted with both the anthology and episodic forms. Serial television, a descendant of the radio soap opera and, before that, nineteenth-century fiction, has been a staple of daytime broadcasting for over fifty years. Here viewers watch in weekly or daily installments an ongoing story that refuses definitive closure, following a group of characters for months, years, even decades. As many writers on soaps have noted, such a format is ideal for the imagined viewership of daytime serials. Posited by broadcasters and theorists as an essentially "distracted" audience, viewers of daytime television require a narrative form marked by glacial emplotment and heavy repetition. Because its viewers are unable to view on a daily basis or with complete attention, serial drama thus accommodates infrequent, sporadic, and new viewers through repetition while also rewarding dedicated viewers through the gradual accumulation and resonance of narrative detail.[11]

Discussing in 1974 a prime-time aesthetic that was almost wholly episodic in form, Newcomb writes: "With the exception of soap operas, television has not realized that regular and repeated appearance of a continuing group of characters is one of its strongest techniques for the development of rich and textured dramatic presentations."[12] This realization came slowly to television over the course of the 1970s and 1980s, leading to a fourth narrative mode that became wholly dominant by the

1990s. This new narrative mode balances episodic treatments of a program's story world with larger arcs of long-term narrative progression. Discussing the emergence of this strategy in *Magnum, P.I.* in the mid-1980s, Newcomb called this mode "cumulative" narrative, referring to the form's ability to "accumulate" nuances of plot and character as a series matures over several seasons.[13] Each installment of *ER,* for example, features a patient or crisis of the week specific to that episode (i.e., bus crash on the turnpike, hospital power outage, liver transplant) interwoven with long-term story lines that may or may not receive attention that week or even that season (Doug and Carol's romance, Peter's deaf son Reese, Weaver's personality conflicts). As in the serial format, these cumulative story lines lead to often-powerful resolutions (frequently promoted and staged during "sweeps" periods). One could certainly quibble about the "origins" of episodic television's move toward orchestrating a more complex sense of serial metatextual history (Lucy was pregnant over several episodes, after all, and the first season of *Lost in Space* brought a mix of episodic and serial forms to prime time in the early 1960s). As a widespread textual strategy, however, this change in series format emerges in such early 1970s programs as *M*A*S*H*, The Mary Tyler Moore Show, All in the Family,* and other "quality" programs of the era. Three of the most influential series in this regard (appearing in the 1980s) would be *Magnum, P.I., Hill Street Blues,* and *St. Elsewhere,* each of which reinvented long-standing television genres (the detective, cop, and medical shows) by focusing less on episodic treatments of crooks and patients and more on the serial development of melodrama involving the private eye, cops, and doctors. This format has become so ubiquitous in U.S. television that purely episodic programs are now almost as rare as live broadcasting and the long-defunct anthology series.[14]

On the one hand, this move to a mixed format might be explained through a wholly economic model of the industry. In the "postnetwork" era of increased competition for viewing audiences, "cumulative" narration provides distinct programming and demographic advantages. By combining the strengths of both the episodic and serials formats, this narrative mode allows new and/or sporadic viewers to enjoy the stand-alone story of a particular episode while also rewarding more dedicated, long-term viewers for their sustained interest in the overall series. As Tania Modleski has noted of the soap opera, the serial aspects encourage all viewers to adopt more consistent viewing habits over time as they become more engaged with a particular series, and yet all viewers can miss episodes and new viewers can find ways of becoming engaged from their very first viewing.[15] Once in syndication and "stripped" across the broadcast schedule five days a week, meanwhile, these episodic elements allow viewers to revisit the series sporadically or even to view episodes transposed in terms of their original running order. Cumulative narrative has not just changed how viewers watch television but also *who* is watching it. In terms of demographics, nestling stand-alone stories within larger story arcs has injected a more convincing "realist" aesthetic into prime time, converting the lowly TV series into what one critic has termed the "prime-time novel."[16] Paradoxically, the very serial elements that have been so long reviled in soaps, pulps, and other "low" genres are now used to increase connotations of "quality" (and thus desirable demographics) in television drama. Consider the example of Fox television's action-espionage series *24*. The single most popular network series for television's most educated and affluent demographic, *24* nestles the lowly "cliffhanger" structure of the old movie serials within a more experimental framework that equates twenty-four hours of screen time with twenty-four hours of "real time." This cumulative device of staging twenty-four episodes over twenty-four consecutive diegetic hours gives the series a "quality" status above and beyond such generic antecedents as *Flash Gordon* and *Commander Cody*.

This cumulative change in narrative sensibility can best be illustrated by comparing the network and postnetwork incarnations of *Star Trek*. Appearing on NBC between 1966 and 1969, the original *Star Trek* series followed the wholly episodic adventures of Kirk, Spock, and McCoy as they guided the USS *Enterprise* on a mission of intergalactic exploration in the twenty-fourth century. As is well known, the program acquired a dedicated audience in reruns, leading to the creation of what remains the largest and most active fan culture in the world. Scholars of *Star Trek* fandom such as Constance Penley and Henry Jenkins have documented how "Trekkers" appropriated the raw materials of the original series and elaborated them into a more extensive narrative universe, cultivating a detailed knowledge of the technology, aliens, and plots of the series while also writing fan fiction that supplemented and expanded the original diegetic boundaries.[17] Borrowing from de Certeau, Jenkins refers to this process as "textual poaching," fans raiding and reworking the series into a textual vehicle more accommodating of their meanings and pleasure.

Looking back at this impulse in early Trek fans, we can see that these viewers were, in essence, converting the often limiting constraints of the episodic narrative format into a more open and boundless serial world— anticipating the dramatic power and pleasure of the cumulative narrative format. Appropriately, then, when the Trek franchise generated its first spin-off in 1987, *Star Trek: The Next Generation*, the series actively accommodated and courted the interests of Trek fandom developed over the previous two decades. *Next Generation* was a model of "cumulative" design, integrating episodic adventures with longer, more character-based arcs of melodrama, the very same transformation that fans had worked on the previous series. The highly rated episode "Relics" is exemplary in this regard. The story begins with the *Next Generation* crew discovering "Scotty," the engineer of the original *Enterprise* from the original series, locked in a state of suspended animation (thus explaining his survival into the time line of the new series). Having introduced a beloved character from the old series into the new one, the story becomes a melodramatic version of "Rip Van Winkle" as Scotty, long in hibernation, cannot find a place in the new *Enterprise*. In one scene, an inebriated Scotty programs the holodeck (a virtual reality machine) to take him back to the bridge of the old *Enterprise*. It is an almost maudlin scene that culminates with the aged engineer toasting his missing comrades and reminiscing with the *Enterprise*'s new captain, Jean-Luc Picard. The power of the scene derives from the viewer/fan's cumulative investment in both the series and the metadiegetic universe to which they both belong. Much of the pleasure here derives not only from seeing Scotty again, but from revisiting the bridge of the old *Enterprise* (lovingly reconstructed in period detail by the series set designers) and seeing that familiar space linked to the new series. Playing to this strength, the corporate architects of the Trek universe have attempted throughout the various sequels and spin-offs of the original series to maintain a sense of logical consistency and interconnection between each individual series. In this respect, *Star Trek's* fans and producers have long made explicit the form of televisual suture implicit in all viewing—audiences stitching together individual episodes into a coherent universe.

Important in terms of television's economics, programming practices, and demographics in the postnetwork age, the medium's move toward cumulative world building also represents a novel solution to an age-old narratological challenge in series production. Producers of long-running television programs have long sought to strike a narrative balance between repetition of premise and differentiation of plot. If a series is to succeed for hundreds of episodes, it must feature an appealingly familiar and yet ultimately repetitive foundation of premise and character relations. No one watched *Seinfeld* because they read *TV Guide* to see what would "happen" that evening in terms of plot; rather, they tuned in to see the four leads enact their typical functions and relationships (George = humiliation, Kramer = physical comedy, Elaine = irritation, Jerry = ironic commentary). On the other hand, too much repetition and familiarity can lead to stagnation, forcing producers to find ways to breathe new life into tired characters and situations. Based almost wholly on repetition, episodic series are particularly vulnerable to this dynamic. Each week viewers of *Gilligan's Island* fully expected that the castaways would look for a possible way to escape the island—only to have the plan thwarted by Gilligan's clumsy antics. Such programs have been called "amnesia television," where characters carry no serial memory of the previous episode's events. Indeed, if the castaways of *Gilligan's Island* had inhabited a cumulative or serial narrative, Gilligan would no doubt have been killed, cooked, and eaten by the fifth episode.

Differentiation within repetition is, of course, a dynamic within all popular, genre-based narratives. A television series, however, faces a unique challenge. Rather than produce potentially infinite variations on a common structure (a "game" theory of genre, as described by Tom Schatz; or pseudo-individualization, to wax Adornoesque), television must produce "parts" that each week embody the whole while also finding, within such repetition, possibilities for novel and diverting variations.[18] This imperative explains the seemingly eternal viability of the "fish out of water" story as a foundation for series architecture. This premise consists of introducing an "eccentric" character or characters into a new and incongruous narrative environment; hillbillies move to Beverly Hills, a witch disrupts suburbia, aliens confront American pop culture, and so on. Such a structure is the essence of the "situation comedy," where the humor is in the situation itself, or as Newcomb notes, in the "confusion" inherent to the situation. "Fish out of water" stories generate endless difference within repetition as writers simply insert the consistently incongruous character(s) into a new "stock plot" each week. What happens when bucolic Jethro decides to imitate James Bond? Can mob boss Tony Soprano successfully negotiate the generation gap with his teenage children? What chaos will ensue when Mork goes skiing? The show, as they say, writes itself.

Considered in this respect, some of television's most notoriously "unoriginal" plots make more sense. Two of the best-known, most-hackneyed, and thus most-parodied television conventions are the amnesia plot and the evil-twin plot. Amnesia, of course, is a godsend to long-running series, allowing characters the temporary freedom to escape their textual prison and engage in activities that violate their character profile, all to the delight of an audience reveling in the characters' aberrant behavior. Amnesia is akin to a narrative "Get Out of Jail Free" card. After all, if character A should sleep with character B during a fit of amnesia, there is no real repercussion once the amnesia fades. The narrative clock returns to zero and the universe returns to normal. The evil-twin plot is somewhat more perverse but serves the same basic function. If character A's evil twin sleeps with character B, or robs a bank, or blows up the town, once again audiences can revel in a familiar character inverted and defamiliarized without consequence, at least to character A himself.

Most contemporary series would no longer employ either of these plots except in parodic form. Instead, other slightly more plausible strategies have replaced them to perform the same textual work. There remains, of course, the dream or fantasy sequence, allowing characters to once again escape diegetic constraint if only for a scene or an episode. Other programs, meanwhile, stage a passing "extraordinary circumstance" to motivate temporary and often quite dramatic character deviation. Hypnosis, misunderstood conversations, peer pressure, overmedication, near-death experiences, and even thematic holiday episodes can give a character license to inject striking difference into usually staid repetition, all without long-term diegetic consequences. In the realm of science fiction, meanwhile, there are unending opportunities for such variations. Transmigration, alien possession, robotic implants, cloning, time travel, and space madness are but a few such pretexts, as is the parallel universe plot, which is essentially the evil-twin story dressed up in the verbiage of quantum physics.

Cumulative narratives, in general, have introduced more sophisticated ways of negotiating this balance, but as a hybrid format they confront the hazards of the episodic and serial modes even as they enjoy their advantages. Early pioneers of the cumulative format (*M*A*S*H*, All in the Family,* and *Magnum, P.I.,* to name a few) gradually turned to serial elements, however limited, as a means of blunting episodic amnesia and allowing more complex story lines to develop. One of the most effective and now ubiquitous conventions to develop from such experimentation was the use of a "reluctant romance" as the serial spine for an otherwise episodic program. Beginning with programs such as *Moonlighting* and *Remington Steele,* flourishing during the multiyear run of *Cheers,* and now central to almost every prime-time program on U.S. television, the "reluctant romance" features an ever-smoldering, on-again/off-again relationship between the series leads. The sexual chemistry and tension generated from such emplotment has proven to be a useful programming hook in maintaining the weekly interest of audiences. Interestingly, while viewers often profess a desire for the characters to consummate their frequently contentious relationship, producers quickly discovered that once characters do indeed become a romantic couple, ratings plummet.

In television as in life, apparently, sexual tension produces interest, sexual satiation produces languor, and too much sexual tension produces frustration. What is a producer to do?

The "reluctant romance" has become such a familiar convention that more recent programs have had to devise innovative strategies to once again inject difference into this now predictable repetition. *Friends,* for example, has approached this convention as almost self-reflexive farce, simultaneously exploiting viewer interest in the Ross and Rachel relationship while also devising almost parodic complications for the couple. After spending many seasons in various degrees of unspoken sexual tension, a brief relationship, a breakup, thwarted reconciliations, and jealousy side-plots, Ross and Rachel eventually were married in an accidental drunken wedding in Las Vegas (and then divorced the next season). Meanwhile, writers found ways to deflect attention from Ross and Rachel by involving Monica with guest-star Tom Selleck, Rachel with Bruce Willis, and then matching and marrying Monica to Chandler over a two-season story arc. Behind all the chicanery, however, viewers know (much as they did with the Doug and Carol relationship on *ER*) that Ross and Rachel are the true center of the cumulative story world, the key narrative issue to resolve before the series comes to an end. Fox's *The X-Files,* meanwhile, took a completely different tactic on the "reluctant romance." For the most part the series ignored it. More accurately, *The X-Files* was for many years very successful at allowing viewers to project a relationship onto Mulder and Scully without ever really making it a central narrative concern (a feat enabled, no doubt, by viewer expectations that all male-female leads must now be romantically linked in television). Fans of the series appeared evenly split on the idea of the relationship, some feeling it inevitable given the history of the two characters, others arguing that the two had always been close friends and professionals but not lovers. In any case, *The X-Files* rather brilliantly was able to indulge the "fantasies" of both groups for many seasons.

As those examples indicate, it may well be that the true art of television writing (as many have argued) is to revisit certain "stock" plots and give them a unique inflection through the specificities of that program's characters and series architecture. David Thorburn has described such inflections on formula and familiarity as the "multiplicity principle," likening it to a form of narrative shorthand that actually enhances rather than diminishes television's dramatic depth.[19] For example, as a classic "fish out of water" story, as well as "reluctant romance," CBS's series *Northern Exposure* was a virtual laboratory for repurposing such television stock plots through its unique architecture. The overall series placed a young,

Jewish, neurotic New York doctor in a small town in Alaska (unhappily exiled there to pay off student loan obligations), where he gradually learns to negotiate and appreciate the various "eccentric" characters who surround him. In the episode "Spring Fever," citizens in the winter-frozen town of Cicely await the symbolic cracking of the ice, a sign that spring has at last arrived. Simmering spring fever allows for a series of character inversions: macho Maurice becomes housemaid for a tough-as-nails female highway trooper; the usually mellow Hollings itches for a fistfight; Joel and Maggie (this show's "reluctant romance") steal a passionate kiss, only to realize in the end it was a "mistake." In another episode, the eternally repressed Joel's rakish twin brother arrives in town, takes advantage of his resemblance to impersonate his usually priggish brother, and sets out to seduce Maggie with no hesitations, neuroses, or apologies (a plot repeated in sci-fi form a few years later on *The X-Files* with Mulder, Scully, and a shape-shifting Mulder look-alike).[20]

This aspect of television art can also be appreciated by examining a single stock plot across a variety of very different series. The "meat locker" plot is as old as *I Love Lucy* (if not older), and involves two characters accidentally locking themselves in a confined space (meat lockers and elevators are the most frequent examples, but any closed room will do). Often, the characters enter as antagonists but emerge with a better understanding of one another. Thus, a couple on the verge of divorce finds themselves trapped in the elevator of the *Love Boat*. After watching a comet from their rooftop, Joey and Ross of *Friends* cannot get back into the building. A shock wave hits the *Enterprise* and Captain Picard finds himself trapped in the turbolift with a group of small children. In the cult-favorite metasitcom *Get a Life,* Chris Peterson and his nemesis Sharon accidentally lock themselves in Sharon's recently and inexplicably installed living room meat locker. The meat locker plot was recycled yet again, on this occasion with derisive contempt, in the Comedy Central series *That's My Bush;* indeed, the one-joke premise of the overall series was to place then recently inaugurated President George W. Bush in a "bad" 1980s sitcom complete with bad sitcom plots ("meat locker," "keeping two dates at the same time," "mistaken identity"). In this instance, Bush's assistant Karl Rove finds himself trapped with White House maid and wisecracking nemesis Maggie (played by ex-*Newhart* receptionist, Marcia Wallace). Assessing their sitcomish predicament, Rove comments on its annoying predictability in biting self-reflexive fashion. In their cynicism, however, writers Stone and Parker see only the repetition here and not the difference. No one is surprised—critics, producers, least of all audiences—that television recycles plots; the true art is in the algebra of such repetition. In the highly conventional *Love Boat* the couple reconciles as expected. Joey and Ross, on the other hand, use their locker premise to motivate a ballet of homoerotic/homophobic physical comedy. The usually forceful Picard must in the end depend on little children to save his life. Finally, true to the arch irony of *Get a Life*, Chris and Sharon emerge hating each other even more than when they entered. The true art in the algebra of televisual repetition is not the formula but the unique integers plugged into the equation.

PURE CONJECTURE

Most of the examples discussed above function within the traditional restraints of a realist aesthetic. No matter how extreme the situation or behavior, the plot remains grounded and motivated by the events and rules of the overall diegetic universe—be it episodic, serial, or cumulative. Picard may turn against his ship, but only because he has been brainwashed by the alien Borg. Someone may transform Xena into a man, put a spell on her, and then have her seduce Gabrielle, but this is because Xena lives in a world of gods and witchraft. The usually kind and caring Dr. Greene of *ER* may become cruel and insensitive, but only because he has a personality-altering brain tumor. In the past few years, however, many high-profile series in U.S. television have begun to feature even more novel strategies for generating difference within cumulative repetition, presenting more experimental modes of narration that reward viewers for their long-term investment in a series (or in television in general).

For example, the final season of NBC's *Seinfeld* featured an episode presented "backwards." Heavily promoted by the network, the episode opened with Jerry, George, Kramer, and Elaine somehow responsible for disrupting a wedding in India. For frequent viewers of the series, the pleasure and anticipation in this particular episode hinged on guessing how the story would regress from this absurdist ending to the typical starting point of small talk in Jerry's Manhattan apartment. *Seinfeld,* of course, was a series propelled by coincidences, cultural minutia, and neurotic obsessions. How, one wondered, would this combination of forces bring the characters to an Indian wedding?

In another example, NBC's top-rated medical drama *ER* staged as its fourth-season premiere a highly promoted and anticipated "live" episode. Performed twice (so that all time zones could participate in the liveness), the episode cleverly played with viewers' expectations and anxieties over the technical execution of the show. How would *ER*, one of the most polished and highly cinematic shows on TV, negotiate the perils, pitfalls, and limitations of live broadcasting? Are the actors up to it? The show's script motivated the live exercise as the product of a PBS documentary team recording (on video, not film) a day in the life of the ER and inserted a number of intentional "mistakes" (spilled coffee, an ambiguous on-air heart attack) to "fool" viewers waiting for disaster. After the show aired, popular magazines compared the two performances. Were they identical? Which was better? What were the "real" mistakes?

Fox's *Malcolm in the Middle* featured an episode with Malcolm and his older brother taking a trip to a bowling alley. From this innocuous premise, the episode employed alternating scenes and split-screen devices to explore two antithetical scenarios. One narrative line followed the boys based on Malcolm's mother taking them to the bowling alley, the other on Malcolm's father making the trip. When Mom is the escort, her overly restrictive manner embarrasses and humiliates the boys in front of their peers. The permissive father, on the other hand, allows for a complete freedom that seems (at least at first) to make for the perfect trip. There is a twist, of course. In the humiliating "mom" scenario Malcolm eventually gets to kiss the girl on which he has a crush, while in the "dad" story, the trip ends in disaster. In the end we are left with an irreconcilable antinomy. Did the boys actually go bowling? What is the status of this "event" in the story world?

On the one hand, such episodes may seem to be little more than garden-variety "self-reflexivity." And yet, it is a form of reflexivity somewhat different from the classical examples drawn from cinema: Daffy Duck under erasure in *Duck Amuck;* Jerry Lewis exiting the set at the end of *The Patsy;* Godard opening *Tout va bien* with the producer signing the necessary checks for the film's completion. Such reflexivity is about "breaking frame," acknowledging the artifice of the overall diegesis. None of the examples above, however, are self-reflexive in terms of violating the "fourth wall"—that is, forcing the viewer into some form of Brechtian distanciation (however mild). Rather, these televisual examples might more appropriately be dubbed "metareflexive," meaning they depend on the long-term viewer's knowledge and appreciation of the modes of narration and emplotment characteristic of the series as a whole. They are, in essence, speculative exercises in form, injecting "difference" into the more repetitive elements of their series architecture by foregrounding, for an episode at least, the audience's appreciation of stylistic and narrational strategies as a vital component of the story world itself.

For example, the backwards *Seinfeld* would be almost indecipherable (or at least not as enjoyable) without a basic knowledge of the series' characteristic modes of emplotment, the character "functions" of the four leads, and the controlling tone of the series' humor. On this one evening, viewers enjoyed not so much a story on *Seinfeld* as they did a state of Seinfeldicity, a particularly precious pleasure in what most fans knew was the final season of the series. John Caldwell, meanwhile, has described the live *ER* as a perfect example of "stunt" television—producers and broadcasters refocusing interest on a series (and inflating its ratings) through a highly promoted deviation from the series profile.[21] As Caldwell argues of the live *ER*, it played on the simultaneous advancement of two stories—the representational drama of *ER* (events in its story world) and the presentational drama of the *ER* cast (as an extratextual construct and pleasure). Perhaps because fans of *ER* are so heavily invested in the cinematic sheen of their melodrama, the episode was not well received by critics and fans as the move from film to video "punctured" the stylistic veneer of the diegesis (Dr. Mark Greene became, simply, Anthony Edwards). *Malcolm in the Middle*, finally, is perhaps the most peculiar of all. Did the boys go bowling or not? Older narrative modes in television would have no doubt grounded this exercise in some form of "realist" frame. Perhaps each brother would have dreamed a different scenario, waking up in the morning to compare notes. Then again, one scenario might really have happened but the other was simply a cautionary dream. In the end, however, some explanation would have been proffered. As it stands, the mom and dad scenarios cancel each other out, and because neither is privileged as "real" the viewer can only surmise that the entire affair exists wholly as a speculative exercise. Television, it would appear, no longer feels compelled to explain narrative variation through the common codes of "realism." Series architecture, viewer sophistication, and the cumulative format have apparently reached the point where television can engage in stories that are wholly conjectural—performative exercises in character, style, and narration.

The series with the most accomplished and innovative history of such "conjectural narrative" is without doubt *The X-Files*. When the series began, writers stuck to a deadly serious cumulative model, vacillating between stand-alone "ghoul of the week" episodes and programs devoted to the ongoing conspiracy arc of alien invasion. This led to an awkward bifurcation in series logic. For one or two episodes, Mulder and Scully confronted an international conspiracy and the prospects of global alien invasion. The next week they matched wits with a swamp monster in New Jersey. In many respects, the series faced the same narrative challenge that confronted its stylistic predecessor, *Twin Peaks:* how to cultivate a central narrative enigma ("Who killed Laura Palmer?" "Is there really an alien infiltration?") while allowing the series to expand in other directions. Both series, in turn, employed a similar strategy to help them escape this dilemma—comedy. Whereas *Twin Peaks* failed miserably (at least with audiences) in its attempts to emphasize humor, *The X-Files* quite successfully began to rearrange its series architecture to allow for humorous commentary on both its episodic "ghoul of the week" stories and its ongoing cumulative search for extraterrestrial life.

Two episodes in particular stand out in this transitional phase. In "War of the Coprophages," Mulder travels to "Miller's Grove" to investigate a series of cockroach attacks. As improbable as this scenario may seem, the episode "plays it straight" for the first two acts, leaving viewers to wonder if the episode can actually be taken seriously. When Mulder hypothesizes that the cockroaches are in fact an alien race of invaders, we realize that we are in the realm of deadpan comedy. The episode's broadcast of *The X-Files*'s signature paranoia culminates with the appearance of what looks to be a real (i.e., nondiegetic) roach scurrying across the screen of the home viewer. "Jose Chung's from Outer Space," meanwhile, takes a page from Kurosawa to present a *Rashomon*-inspired tale of two teens seemingly abducted by aliens. While remaining true to the series' controlling themes of alien invasion and government manipulation, the episode also engages in a sophisticated analysis of the entire "*X-Files/* alien abduction" pop-cult phenomenon. As the various parties involved in the teens' story present their version of events, the narrative indulges a truly postmodern meditation on the status of truth and the place of narrative in popular culture and personal belief.

As the series matured, these one-off "comedy" episodes gradually transformed into fully conjectural narratives. These stand-alone stories appear to have no apparent motivation in, relation to, or impact on the larger universe of the series. They stand as wholly speculative exercises, as ungrounded fantasies that recast, through radical stylistic and narrational deviation, the already well-established series architecture. They allow for elaboration and possibilities unavailable to the "real" story line of the series, especially in terms of Mulder and Scully's relationship. Because they are not framed and/or contained by traditional realist devices for such deviation (mind control, hallucination, alien probes, etc.), they leave viewers wondering about the episode's status in the larger *X-Files* universe. By the end of its run, *The X-Files* balanced all three types of episodes across each season: ghouls of the week, alien conspiracy (cumulative and presented as "real"), and the more conjectural fantasy pieces that are wholly episodic and more indeterminate in status.

Such conjectural episodes have landed the agents in the Bermuda

Triangle; on a movie set watching their own lives under adaptation; and at the center of an episode of *Cops*. Perhaps the most exemplary of such "conjectural" episodes is "The Postmodern Prometheus." The story begins with a pencil drawing of agents Mulder and Scully that morphs into a comic book panel and then finally into live action. Shot in black and white, the episode presents a highly self-reflexive and intertextual retelling of the Frankenstein story, this time centering on a horribly disfigured boy obsessed with Cher and forced into murder. When the sympathetic "monster" is at last caught, Mulder muses that the ending is not right and asks to "speak to the writer" (putatively the comic book–obsessed teen involved in the story). The episode ends with the agents taking the ebullient boy to a Cher concert, where Mulder and Scully dance beneath a disco-ball before once again returning to comic book form. Is this the same Mulder and Scully typically engaged in combating extraterrestrial and governmental experiments on humanity? Yes and no.

WHAT IF?

Mulder and Scully's fade to a comic panel is most appropriate to such a conjectural narrative form, for the precedent of such experimentation comes not from the cinema or modernist literature but from the world of comic books (or graphic novels as aficionados now prefer to call them). For many years, Marvel Comics has featured an intermittent title called *What If?* In these special issues, writers pursue alternative narrative lines from those established in the larger library of comic titles. What if a certain superhero's fiancée had not been killed? What if another hero's archvillain had survived and succeeded in his diabolical plan? Each issue is a road not taken, a purely hypothetical scenario presented strictly for the intellectual and narratological pleasure of the invested reader. While it may seem anticlimactic to argue that television, after a half century of development, has at last achieved the narrative sophistication of the comic book, this does seem to be precisely what is happening across a number of current television genres. Seeing this as a less-than-flattering comparison, however, misunderstands the sophistication of television (and of comic books, for that matter).

Why are TV audiences now amenable to this new conjectural mode? I have suggested some possible economic, demographic, and narratological reasons for this transition, but ultimately the emergence of this narrative form is profoundly overdetermined. While there can be no definitive explanation for this development, I believe that the ability of certain programs to drop realist frames and engage in purely conjectural considerations of form and series mythology is a provocative development that raises a number of interesting issues concerning television's relationship to its changing audience structure, other media technologies, and narrative itself. In this age of audience specialization, for example, it would appear that viewers are willing to watch their favorite shows with greater fidelity and attention. And, as they demand more from TV, TV demands more from them—the story of *Buffy the Vampire Slayer* became so incredibly complex that new viewers needed a roadmap to get their bearings—a single episode would not suffice. This heightened investment spills over into other media as well. As has been generally observed, the number of Web sites devoted to television programs is eclipsed only by the number devoted to pornography (with many others combining both interests!). Despite claims that various new media would lead to revolutionary new entertainment forms, the primary use so far of these media seems to be as a supplement to television (and pornography). Through the proliferation of TV Web sites, chat rooms, videotape, and DVD players, viewers now have the opportunity to "inhabit" a given television show for hours on end. In the network era of limited program choice, even the most dedicated fan of *Ironside* or *Gunsmoke* most likely simply watched each week and then waited for the next episode. (Trekkies are once again the exception, having made audiotapes of each week's episode in the days before VCRs.) As the target of increasingly sophisticated narrowcasting, fans of today's cumulative television often expend great energy both revisiting older episodes of a series and speculating on the future trajectory of the story lines. As Sara Gwenellin-Jones and Roberta Pearson have argued, the "metaverse" of a television series allows for an intensity of investment and depth of immersion well beyond that of any current virtual reality technology.[22] Significantly, this immersion is accomplished more in mental space than electronic, but therein, perhaps, lies its ultimate power. Such immersion, in turn, should make the new textual frontiers of television of central interest in narratological debates, providing active and powerful case studies in the process of making fiction become "real."

This returns us to the opening polemics about the state of inquiry into television aesthetics. So much of the discourse on television and new media has emphasized the fate and futures of the hardware itself. How will future hybrids and applications of these media work? Who will own them? What impact will they have on that eternal Enlightenment dyad of reality and consciousness? These are all important questions, to be sure. But at the heart of all of these questions, it would seem, remains the ability of narrative arts to capture the imagination of audiences, no matter how splintered, self-selected, and interactive they may become in the next century. Whether one ultimately finds this new mode of narrowcasting and intensified viewer involvement the ultimate victory for consumer capitalism or the first step in the demise of its absolute control, such judgments will depend, I imagine, less on issues of hardware and political economy than on the debates so long at the heart of narrative poetics. However dirty, compromised, or implicated in operations of power, television is an art. And if "all art is political" (as Brecht reminds us), it would be foolish to continue ignoring the history, texts, and techniques of what remains the world's most vast, varied, and influential narrative medium.

NOTES

1. Horace Newcomb, *TV: The Most Popular Art* (New York: Anchor, 1974), p. 19.

2. In addition to Newcomb's *TV*, see Horace Newcomb and Paul M. Hirsch, *The Producer's Medium: Conversations with Creators of American TV* (New York: Oxford University Press, 1983); John Ellis, *Visible Fictions: Cinema, Television, Video* (London: Routledge, 1992); Charlotte Brunsdon, "Problems with Quality," *Screen* 31.1 (spring 1990): 67–90; Christopher Anderson, *Hollywood TV* (Austin: University of Texas Press, 1994); Henry Jenkins, *Textual Poachers* (New York: Routledge, 1992); and John T. Caldwell, *Televisuality: Style, Crisis, and Authority in American Television* (New Brunswick: Rutgers University Press, 1995).

3. For a discussion of "flow," see Raymond Williams, *Television: Technology and Cultural Form* (Hanover, N.H.: Wesleyan University Press, 1992), pp. 80–90.

4. This trend has been most pronounced in the attempts to export psychoanalytic film theory into the study of electronic media by constructing an abstract model of televisual spectatorship. Ironically, while psychoanalytic film theory engaged in close textual analysis to generate its claims (Raymond Bellour's work, in particular, comes to mind), psychoanalytic engagements of television favor reducing the entirety of televisual textuality into an undifferentiated mass of textual noise, which is then often annexed to some larger debate about gender, technology, postmodernity, and/or subjectivity.

5. For further discussion of the institutional politics and fate of television studies within the larger academic enthusiasm for new media, see Jeffrey Sconce, "Tulip Theory," in *New Media: Theories and Practices of Digitextuality*, ed. Ana Everett and John T. Caldwell (New York: Routledge, 2003), pp. 179–96.

6. For a discussion of MTM's role in developing the "ensemble" drama, see Thomas G. Schatz, "St. Elsewhere and the Evolution of the Ensemble Series," in *Television: The Critical View*, 4th ed., ed. Horace Newcomb (New York: Oxford University Press, 1987), pp. 85–100.

7. Newcomb (*TV*, pp. 243–64) discusses this quality of television as a function of its "intimacy" and "continuity."

8. Jimmie Reeves, Mark C. Rodgers, and Michael Epstein provide a useful analysis of "cult television" in the network and postnetwork ages in "Rewriting Popularity: The Cult Files," in *Deny All Knowledge: Reading the X-Files,* ed. David Lavery, Angela Hague, and Marla Cartwright (Syracuse: Syracuse University Press, 1996), pp. 22–35.

9. See Anderson, *Hollywood TV*; and William Boddy, *Fifties Television: The Industry and Its Critics* (Urbana: University of Illinois Press, 1990).

10. See Boddy, "Live Television: Program Formats and Critical Hierarchies," in *Fifties Television,* pp. 80–92.

11. Useful discussions of television soap operas can be found in: Tania Modleski, *Loving with a Vengeance: Mass Produced Fantasies for Women* (London: Methuen, 1984); and Robert Allen, *Speaking of Soaps* (Chapel Hill: University of North Carolina Press, 1985). See also Lynn Spigel's "Women's Work," in her *Make Room for TV: Television and the Family Ideal in Postwar America* (Chicago: University of Chicago Press, 1992).

12. Newcomb, *TV,* p. 254.

13. Horace Newcomb, "Champagne of Television," *Channels* 5 (1985): 23. Christopher Anderson elaborates on this in "Reflections on *Magnum, P.I.*" in Newcomb, ed., *Television,* pp. 112–25.

14. Even a program that does follow this format, such as *The Simpsons,* is continually satirizing this mode, as when Homer's boss, Mr. Burns, repeatedly does not recognize Homer despite the fact that the two have crossed paths hundreds of times during the course of the series.

15. Modleski, *Loving with a Vengeance.*

16. Charles McGrath, "The Triumph of the Prime-Time Novel," in Newcomb, ed., *Television,* 6th ed., pp. 242–52.

17. See Jenkins, *Textual Poachers;* and Constance Penley, *NASA/TREK: Popular Science and Sex in America* (London: Verso, 1997).

18. See Thomas G. Schatz, *Hollywood Genres* (New York: Random House, 1981).

19. David Thorburn, "Television Melodrama," in Newcomb, ed., *Television,* 6th ed., pp. 595–608.

20. For a more detailed discussion of *Northern Exposure*'s production history and status as quality television, see Betsy Williams, "North to the Future: *Northern Exposure* and Quality Television," in Newcomb, ed., *Television,* 5th ed., pp. 141–54.

21. John Caldwell, "Slipping and Programming Televisual Liveness," *Aura* 6.1 (2000): 44–61.

22. Sara Gwellian-Jones and Roberta Pearson, "Cult Television, Seriality, and the Rhizomatic Code," paper presented at the "Defining Cult Movies" conference, Institute of Film Studies, University of Nottingham, November 17, 2000.

WILLIAM BODDY **INTERACTIVE**

TELEVISION AND ADVERTISING FORM IN

CONTEMPORARY U.S. TELEVISION

The eventual industrial and textual implications of the current transition from analog to digital formats in U.S. television remain difficult to discern, in spite of the cacophonous promotion of new digital products and services, much overheated media punditry, and extensive journalistic reports from an extremely unsettled television marketplace. Despite the generally weak predictive power and short shelf life of a decade of both apocalyptic and utopian predictions about life in the "post-television era," the effects of technological and industrial realignments on actual viewing practices and the advertising and program forms of American television are still quite uncertain. In this essay I attempt to provide a context for these contemporary disputes through two case studies: first, the long and mostly unhappy commercial history of interactive television over the past thirty years, and, second, the recent controversies over changing program and advertising practices that are seen as one industry response to a new, technologically empowered television viewer.

DREAMS AND NIGHTMARES OF INTERACTIVE TELEVISION

Notwithstanding the current manifest turmoil within the U.S. television industry, it is easy to be skeptical of the self-interested claims for technologically driven fundamental change in the medium, especially in light of decades of unsuccessful business ventures advanced under the banners of technological convergence and viewer interactivity (described by one critic in 1990 as "already the soggy buzzword of the '90s").[1] As early as 1971, a Rand Corporation report on interactive cable television noted that "as is often the case with emerging technologies, . . . the promise of two-way services on cable has at times been oversold," and a nearly unbroken string of failed commercial launches of interactive television, from Time Warner's Qube system in Columbus, Ohio, in 1977 through the same company's costly trial of a state-of-the-art interactive television service in Orlando, Florida, in 1995, suggests the dangers of overestimating consumer interest in interactive television services.[2] Given the unhappy business history of interactive television to date, the skepticism of L. J. Davis's 1998 business history, *The Billionaire Shell Game: How Cable Baron John Malone and Assorted Corporate Titans Invented a Future Nobody Wanted*, does not seem unwarranted.[3] As one journalist concluded in March 2001: "In general, the dream of combining PC technology with America's favorite entertainment medium has been a nightmare."[4]

Similarly, the combined efforts of computer manufacturers, software designers, and Web entrepreneurs to introduce TV program forms and business models into the PC marketplace have also fared poorly over the past decade. These efforts include the failure of an integrated PC-TV apparatus from Compaq, Gateway, and others; slow sales of TV-tuner cards for use in PCs; a range of ill-fated mid-1990s TV-modeled interface designs and delivery systems (including Microsoft's Bob, Windows CE, and a flurry of so-called push technologies); the slower than expected provision of broadband service into the home; the quick court-ordered shutdown of TV-streaming Internet sites like iCraveTV; and the failure of many of the costly efforts by the traditional television networks to establish themselves as Web portals. (ABC-Disney alone spent an estimated $100 million on the Go.com portal before shutting it down.)[5] If the long-heralded convergence of PC and TV indeed ever comes about, it will not be without leaving a formidable number of major corporate casualties and junked business plans in its wake.

Some of the lessons taken from the checkered history of interactive television can be seen in the shifting product and promotional strategies of a single firm, Microsoft, which has repeatedly and unsuccessfully attempted to create a business out of the intersection of the home computer and TV set. After the expensive failure of its early-1990s strategy built around cable television's set-top box as the platform for Microsoft's interactive television software (and the simultaneous failure of the original business model of MSN as an AOL clone providing limited and proprietary Internet access), by 1995 Microsoft responded to the spectacular growth of the Internet by shifting its attention to it as the path for interactive television.[6] The August 1995 initial public offering of Internet-browser maker Netscape, the largest single IPO in history to that date, signaled, in part, the financial market's repudiation of Microsoft's plans for interactive television via cable's set-top box.[7] By the time of Bill Gates's second best seller in 1999, *Business @ the Speed of Thought,* he was willing to admit that Microsoft had taken too long to pull the plug on its mid-1990s interactive television efforts: "As we proceeded, there was a slow realization that the costs were higher and the customer benefits lower than we had all assumed they would be. Interactive television wasn't coming together as soon as we expected or in the way we expected."[8]

Microsoft's April 1997 $425 million acquisition of WebTV, a start-up founded in 1995 by three alumni from Apple Computer, reflected Microsoft's new interest in combining Internet access and television viewing in the same device, as well as an attempt to recoup some of Microsoft's substantial investment in interactive television software.[9] However, WebTV subscriptions quickly stagnated at slightly over a million users, despite price cuts, hardware give-away promotions, and enhanced features. The service was hurt by a history of network outages, an extremely high subscriber cancellation rate, a December 2000 Federal Trade Commission (FTC) settlement over deceptive advertising claims, a March 2001 decision by Sony Pictures Digital Entertainment to withdraw its popular interactive TV game shows, and a general brand image of WebTV as a technologically enfeebled service for technophobes.[10] More fundamentally, as one journalist explained, "selling the Internet on TV meant selling the Internet to consumers who understood the benefits of the Internet but didn't own a PC. And that's a market that is shrinking as PC prices have fallen."[11] Furthermore, by most accounts, relations were strained between the Silicon Valley–based WebTV subsidiary and its corporate parent in Redmond, Washington; according to two CNET reporters in October 2000, the "WebTV transition has been a sometimes-farcical exercise fraught with unclear direction, shameless politics and technological blunders that have already cost both companies untold sums in lost opportunity— if not their assured leadership of the entire interactive TV industry."[12]

Microsoft's TV commercials marking the fall 1999 U.S. relaunch of WebTV, which introduced enhanced interactive television features and was part of a wider repositioning of the brand, tried to redress some of these weaknesses. The campaign from the firm Foote, Cone & Belding, consisting of six thirty-second commercials and one of sixty seconds duration, never displays or demonstrates WebTV in use but offers instead a procession of comic scenarios involving bewildered and sometimes humiliated users of the discredited "Brand X"—in this case, traditional television. The sixty-second commercial that launched the campaign, titled "Chaos Theory," draws on visual elements from the succeeding thirty-second ads, depicting a series of TV viewers reacting with incomprehension to their television sets, which display a jumble of cut-and-pasted program fragments and a chorus of onscreen voices that forms the repeated stuttered phrase, "I . . . could . . . do . . . so . . . much . . . more." Given the commercial's lack of anchoring voice-over narration or obvious narrative structure, the repeated phrase begs the question of subjectivity, evoking both the ventriloquist video hacker of 1980s TV's *Max Headroom* and the authoritarian "control voice" of the opening credits of the 1960s science fiction TV series *The Outer Limits*. The repeated utterance, built from a pastiche of voices from critically disdained genres (confessional talk shows, game shows, financial news programs, South Asian movie musicals, *Baywatch* clones, and sentimental children's melodramas), is shown interrupting and frustrating traditional viewing routines; later the phrase becomes highly directive, apparently commanding a gathering of passersby to a shop window displaying scores of TV sets displaying the same phrase, à la newsman Howard Beale's messianic broadcast voice in the 1975 film *Network*. While the commercial offers a humorous depiction of vaguely pathetic TV viewers who are confused by their "Brand X" television sets, the commercial's own opacity has the effect of leaving actual viewers just as confused about who is speaking and what is on offer in the ad.

Each of the succeeding thirty-second commercials in the WebTV campaign highlights a single feature of the relaunched interactive service (including customized stock reports, intelligent program guides, program-embedded Web links, program schedule reminders, and participatory quiz shows) and each is built around a vignette depicting the inadequacies of the traditional TV-viewing experience and its technologically obsolete viewer. In each vignette, a TV actor onscreen breaks out of the inscribed diegesis to directly confront the startled viewer, and this aggressive and fanciful literalization of "interactive television" evokes the fearful associations of broadcast technology within the home that have been the stuff of innumerable speculative fictions since domestic television was imagined in the 1920s. The interactivity promised here invokes both the familiar advertising trope of a thrilling spectator immersion in the television image and the long tradition of dystopian visions of electronic simulation, from the supposed pathological parasocial interaction of radio soap opera fans of the 1930s to the Orwellian telescreen, the television monitor that performs perfect surveillance of the viewer. The WebTV commercials' refusal to offer an affirmative vision of the new technological capabilities of television, along with the contradictory and highly affective cultural myths the commercials evoke, suggest an ongoing cultural ambivalence about the place of electronic media in the home.

Despite Microsoft's efforts to reposition the WebTV service via its extensive marketing campaign, by October 2000 trade journals were reporting that "the WebTV brand itself has a limited future, its mission confined to the slow business of dial-up Internet access through the TV set."[13] In March 2001 Microsoft announced that WebTV, previously a semiautonomous corporate subsidiary based in Silicon Valley, would be brought into the MSN group and moved to Microsoft's corporate headquarters in Redmond. One columnist remarked that "Microsoft Corp. took the remnants and detritus of Web-TV, screaming and kicking, to Redmond for a decent burial," and most observers saw the move as Microsoft's admission of the failure of WebTV to move beyond a niche market and of the limited appeal of Internet access on television.[14] At the same time, Microsoft folded the existing WebTV technology (and sales staff) into a new product, immodestly called Ultimate TV, which was launched, after several delays, in early 2001.[15] Ultimate TV combined WebTV capabilities with a two-tuner personal video recorder integrated into a DIRECTV satellite TV set-top box, allowing viewers to pause live TV, to digitally record thirty-five hours of programming, and to record two programs simultaneously. Microsoft spent eighteen months and $20 million developing the proprietary Ultimate TV microchip, part of the estimated total of $100 million that its WebTV subsidiary spent developing its interactive television products.[16] As one industry reporter noted, Microsoft's launching of Ultimate TV "sounds a quiet death knell for WebTV."[17]

Microsoft's shifting digital television strategies were part of the company's larger rethinking of its traditional business model. Faced with slower growth in the PC business (one analyst in March 2001 estimated growth in PC sales of only 60 percent over the next five years)[18] and greater resistance among PC users to upgrade to new software releases, Microsoft had little choice but to look beyond the traditional PC platform for its accustomed rate of growth.[19] In January 2001, Bill Gates used a consumer electronics trade show in Las Vegas to introduce Ultimate TV, as well as the company's new video game system, the Xbox. The company's move into the consumer electronics industry reflected a strategic shift from the PC platform alone to six potential software platforms: telephones, handheld computers, television, video games, and the Internet (as well as new partnerships with Starbucks, La-Z-Boy, and Lego). The shift also represents Microsoft's risky move into the highly competitive business of consumer electronics manufacturing, against formidable established firms including Sony.[20] At the same time, Microsoft's launch of Ultimate TV marked an expensive new wager on the general economic prospects for interactive television; one technology analyst noted that "a lot of eyes are watching how well Ultimate TV does. This will be the first indicator of whether this market is real or that there's nothing here and we need to move on. It's a major litmus test for this market genre."[21]

In September 2000, Microsoft CEO Steve Ballmer explained the company's shift in interactive television strategy in terms of the wider repositioning of Web access and television viewing: "I actually think that the current WebTV service is interesting but not overwhelming. What we do today is let you get Internet on TV, as opposed to enhancing the TV experience. . . . Ultimate TV . . . is much more about enhancing the TV experience. . . . You get the Internet on TV, but it's more about enhancing the way you watch TV, recording shows, pausing. I'm bullish on that."[22] *Variety* connected Microsoft's repositioning of its interactive television products to wider changes in the cultural and strategic position of the television set: "While its Web TV service was always aimed at computer users, MS execs say Ultimate TV is aimed squarely at TV watchers. As broadband Internet programming continues to disappoint, the TV that was uncool 18 months ago is once again hip with media execs."[23] In its substantial advertising campaign for the new Ultimate TV service, Microsoft positioned the product more as a personal video recorder than an Internet-access device, thus aligning it in direct competition with the two-year-old TiVo device.

Like personal video recorder pioneers TiVo and ReplayTV, which had been advertising eighteen months before the launch of Ultimate TV, Microsoft faced special challenges, as well as possible rewards, as a pioneer in an entirely new product category. *Advertising Age* quoted Forrester chief analyst, Josh Bernoff, in fall 2000: "You will see an insane amount of brand advertising, especially for TiVo, and probably for Microsoft Ultimate TV, because what's going to happen in the next twelve months is the concept of video recording will be associated in the minds of consumers with a brand name."[24] In July 2001 *Financial Times* estimated that Microsoft was pouring $50 million into marketing Ultimate TV, and one analyst warned in March 2001 that "Ultimate TV will have to do a really good job in marketing this type of enhanced TV product because they are out ahead of everyone else a bit . . . So they'll not only have to define their product but really this entire category. . . . TiVo and ReplayTV had some troubles with this."[25]

The five national television commercials that launched Ultimate TV in March 2001 were produced by the Rodgers Townsend advertising agency in St. Louis (one of three different ad agencies Microsoft hired and fired to market interactive television in the first five months of 2001 alone). Each ad foregrounds a single function of the device's personal video recorder capabilities; at the same time, none of the commercials even mentions Ultimate TV's e-mail or Internet access features.[26] Microsoft's vice president of consumer products addressed the decision to omit Ultimate TV's interactive television features in its advertising by explaining that "the combination of parts is greater than the individual services, but (DVR) will be the selling point."[27] According to the Ultimate TV account supervisor at Rodgers Townsend, Ultimate TV's interactive features were seen by both Microsoft and its advertising agency to be too difficult to explain in a brief commercial spot, and of too little appeal beyond a niche market of potential users.[28] Especially compared to Microsoft's flamboyant WebTV campaign the previous year, the subsequent print (to date only seen in DIRECTV's program guides) and television advertising campaign for Ultimate TV is exceedingly modest and self-effacing in tone, depicting a variety of TV households seamlessly integrating the personal video recorder into their daily routines. These scenes include a couple programming the recording of two different programs while preparing to go out for the evening; a man pausing a live TV broadcast to check on a baby in a crib; a family using the "my shows" feature to distract their dog at dinner time; a man in bed with a cast on his leg appreciating the thirty-five-hour recording capacity; and a housewife watching a soap opera using the instant replay feature to replay lines of dialogue drowned out by her husband's lawn mower outside her window. Despite its ambitious name, the marketing of Ultimate TV suggests Microsoft's lowered expectations for the immediate prospects of PC-like interactivity of the traditional television set.

While Microsoft's overall involvement with interactive television is certain to continue in some form, the first half of 2001 saw intense speculation in the financial press about the company's apparent desire to shed Ultimate TV altogether as part of a proposed deal by News Corp.'s Rupert Murdoch to acquire satellite broadcaster DIRECTV from General Motors' Hughes Electronics subsidiary. Under the complex plan, which emerged after more than a year of negotiations, Microsoft would supply News Corp. $3 billion for the DIRECTV acquisition and transfer Ultimate

TV to Murdoch's new satellite service; Microsoft would in turn become the "preferred supplier" of software for future interactive services on the platform.[29] The *Los Angeles Times* noted that "the deal also would allow Microsoft to exit gracefully from the interactive television business after spinning its wheels for a decade without much success," despite spending an estimated $1.5 billion since its 1997 acquisition of WebTV.[30] For Murdoch, DIRECTV would double the reach of his Sky Global Networks to two hundred million households across the globe, which currently reaches every major population area except China and the United States.[31] While the *Los Angeles Times* reporter noted that "few analysts expect interactive television to be much of a business for years," she also suggested that "some on Wall Street are expecting Murdoch to jump-start the interactive television business if he gains control of DIRECTV by giving away boxes as he has in Britain," where Murdoch's BSkyB reported Interactive revenues for the nine months ending March 31, 2001, of £60 million, of which £55 million related to sports betting via television.[32]

DIGITAL TECHNOLOGIES AND CHANGING TV PROGRAM FORMS

If the experience in interactive television of a company as large and market-shaping as Microsoft suggests the dangers of overestimating the public appetite for enhanced TV services, it is nevertheless clear that at least some of TV's new digital technologies are already having an effect on program forms and advertising practices. In fact, even while the actual number of people who have purchased the new television systems remains relatively small (for example, TiVo reported only 229,000 subscribers by the end of July 2001), industry executives and media pundits alike have been busy predicting winners and losers in the new media environment.[33] In particular, the personal video recorder, launched by TiVo and ReplayTV in 1999, was quickly heralded by several media analysts as a powerfully destabilizing new tool enabling viewers to evade traditional television advertising. The *New York Times Magazine* August 2000 cover article by Michael Lewis about TiVo was subtitled "The End of the Mass Market" and was accompanied by the spectacular cover image of an exploding cereal box.[34] The following summer a *Brandweek* reporter noted that "if there's an antichrist for advertisers, thy name is TiVo," citing the device's potential to "allow viewers to exorcise Madison Avenue's finely focus-grouped and carefully crafted work."[35]

Indeed, the mere threat of the personal video recorder has encouraged a range of new technological and advertising countermeasures to the digital recorder's ability to evade traditional TV commercials. In the first half of 2001, the contracting advertising market for network television brought about by a general economic slowdown (total U.S. advertising expenditures in the first half of 2001 were down 5.9 percent from the previous year) and the September 11, 2001, terrorist attack on New York's World Trade Center caused national advertising revenues to plunge even more steeply (within weeks after the attack, one analyst predicted that total U.S. advertising industry revenues would fall 9 percent for 2001).[36] One much-discussed countermeasure to the personal video recorder is the still rather exotic use of digital imaging technologies to insert virtual "sports enhancements"; that is, graphics or images that are digitally inserted into the live television feed to appear as if they belonged to the space of action. Uses include, for example, providing real-time statistics of the speeds of competitors, highlighting a hockey puck, or providing first-down markers in professional football. Other uses of virtual imaging include inserting virtual billboards at sporting and other live events and placing virtual products into network or syndicated programming.[37] More generally, the advertising and television trade presses over the past few years have been filled with calls for sponsors and broadcasters to develop advertising vehicles that would rebuff the expected assault from digital recorders via what TiVo itself calls inescapable "embedded commerce," including onscreen banner ads, the intensive use of conventional product placement, and the move to single-sponsor infomercials and entertainment programming.[38] The announcement in May 2001 of the first planned use of so-called virtual product placement in dramatic programming was marked by an anticipated agreement between Princeton Video Images and the TBS cable network to offer sponsors the opportunity to digitally insert onscreen virtual products within reruns of *Law and Order*.[39] A Princeton Video Images executive predicted that within two years the majority of its business would involve inserting virtual products into syndicated programming: "We don't call it product placement, we call it product presence, because it's such a seamless way of including the brand."[40] Along similar lines, others in the industry have predicted the development of digital encryption schemes that would limit the personal video recorder's ability to play back specific programs or disable the device's fast-forward function during TV commercials.[41]

In 2001, the deteriorating advertising market and the technological threat of the ad-thwarting personal video recorder had combined to create a climate of increased network accommodation to advertiser wishes in prime-time programming. TiVo has already offered advertisers several areas of branded content, which would evade the commercial-avoiding capabilities of its own device, in the form of TiVo Direct, Network Showcases, TiVolution Magazine, and *TiVo Takes. Broadcasting and Cable* quoted one analyst who saw TiVo's blending of entertainment and advertising content as a sign of the future of advertising: "We've already seen a blurring of the lines between providing information and advertising. . . . Advertisers and programmers are going to have to blur those lines even further in the future."[42] Such so-called embedded commerce had increasingly become the model for network programming as well, especially as the networks faced a rapidly weakening up-front advertising market in spring 2001. With costs-per-thousand viewers expected to fall 12 to 15 percent and the possibility of talent strikes looming, the major television networks themselves undertook new efforts to integrate the marketing and creative ideas of advertisers directly into the fall 2001 prime-time season programs.[43]

At ABC's presentation to advertisers and their agencies in Los Angeles in March 2001, the network announced that it would send every one of its comedy and drama pilot scripts to advertisers, an action that the cochairman of the ABC Entertainment Group characterized as a "little unprecedented."[44] A few months previously, the producer of ABC's daytime series *The View* shrugged off objections to the product placement of Campbell's Soup in the program, telling the press, "we're willing to plug shamelessly, but we have limits. The integrity of the show has to be maintained."[45] In January 2001, the sixth-largest network in the United States, UPN, made a deal with Heineken beer to be the sole sponsor of the evening's prime-time lineup, as well as to provide product placement within the evening's half-hour sitcoms.[46]

At least some in the creative community seemed nonplussed about the growing practice of product placement; the executive producer of *The Drew Carey Show* told the *Christian Science Monitor* in January 2001: "If someone wants to step up and pay for my show, it doesn't bother me to find a way to put their product in my show." The same producer told the paper that he was considering having the show's star make live product pitches in the next TV season's special live broadcast.[47] Another sign of growing network accommodation to the wishes of television advertisers was CBS's August 2001 decision to withdraw several repeat episodes of its prime-time dramatic series *Family Law* after one of the program's major sponsors, Procter and Gamble, threatened to withdraw its advertisements from episodes dealing with what the *New York Times* called "politically or socially charged issues," including handgun regulation, the death penalty, abortion, and interfaith marriage.[48]

The recent spectacular popularity of quiz programs and reality TV shows in U.S. network prime time has also encouraged more intrusive product placement, greater creative roles for sponsors, and increased experimentation with commercial applications of interactive television. In a March 2001 report on interactive television, Jupiter Media Metrix advised clients to continue investing in "interactive-friendly" genres of sports, game shows, and news, while warning that drama and comedy venues would be more challenging.[49] The experience of CBS with the reality TV hit *Survivor,* where a number of sponsors paid $12 million each to place products in the program, was reported to be a very happy one for network and advertisers alike, with one network executive especially proud of arranging for the emaciated contestants to compete for a special prize of Mountain Dew and Doritos: "It's probably the most creative use of product placement in TV," the CBS spokesman boasted.[50]

Concerns over the threat of the personal video recorder, the financial potential of product placement and viewer interactivity, and new levels of network-sponsor accommodation converged in the 2001 trade discussion concerning ABC's reality TV series *The Runner,* which the *New York Times* called "almost surely the most ambitious reality series so far conceived."[51] Although it was pitched to ABC in 2000 by actor-writer-producers Matt Damon and Ben Affleck, in mid-2001 ABC announced that the program would be launched in January 2002. *The Runner* pits an incognito individual contestant who moves across the country fulfilling a series of network-assigned tasks over twenty-eight days, motivated by a reward of up to $1 million if he or she can accomplish the assignments and elude capture by viewers seeking the same prize money. (Viewers sign up as "licensed agents" and track clues and location updates on the program's Internet site.) By July 2001, the show's Web site was already reporting thirty thousand visitors a week, including those seeking to download application forms to become either a runner or one of the agents seeking their capture.[52] *Broadcasting and Cable* called the show "the most expensive and ambitious reality series to hit network television yet," and warned that "it also might be the most dangerous if not executed properly" (conjuring *Fahrenheit 451* visions of telescreen-linked vigilantes pursuing the breathless hero through panopticon streets).[53] The TV critic of New York's *Daily News* noted that "the potential for mob scenes, assaults, mistaken-identity confrontations and other assorted mayhem seemed limitless," and *Daily Variety* reported that "exactly how the runner will be caught—and not harmed in the process—is still being hammered out. But ABC execs are confident they'll be able to work out that detail, as well as find a way to use hidden cameras to track the runner's progress without alerting the public to the runner's whereabouts."[54] After noting that viewers are invited to participate by either helping or hindering the runner, the *Toronto Star*'s TV critic argued that "given that there are cash rewards for the latter, but not the former, I can't see this guy getting more than a mile or so before he gets turned in. Or shot."[55] In response to a press question about what was to stop viewers who think they've spotted the fugitive from attempting a potentially injurious capture, one of the program's executive producers stated, "If you impede the runner, you not only will be prosecuted to the full extent of the law, but you can't win any money."[56] Michael Davies, the producer of *Who Wants to Be a Millionaire?*, was hired by ABC to help run the show, and the job of stage managing what is basically a twenty-eight-day televised national manhunt was turned over to Roger Goodman, a veteran of ABC's sports, news, and special-event programming (including the network's coverage of the 1991 Gulf War and its *ABC 2000* global millennium event). As one ABC executive explained to *Daily Variety*, the network was essentially "creating a gigantic sporting event," to which ABC would enjoy exclusive rights. "It's rife with logistic and liability issues," the executive told the paper.[57]

Beyond the daunting privacy, logistical, and personal safety issues involved in producing *The Runner*, the program also attracted considerable press attention by the unusual lengths to which the network and the show's producers announced they were willing to go to integrate advertising material into the program itself. These efforts were repeatedly justified as responses to the increased ability of TV viewers to escape traditional television commercials through devices like the personal video recorder. ABC's president of program sales told the *New York Times* that such concerns "sent us down the road into evaluation of what kind of programming we might have that could integrate their products into the content. . . . This show does it organically. That's the beauty of it."[58] The cochairman of ABC Entertainment described the show as "one of the best ideas for a television show I have ever heard," in part because of its potential for product placement, which, he told the *Times*, "occurred to us about a nanosecond after we heard Matt and Ben describe the show."[59] The same executive told a group of network advertisers: "Is the runner going to wear Nikes? Is the runner going to wear Reeboks? Is the runner going to wear Adidas? You guys get to decide."[60]

By May 2001, ABC had closed an $8 million deal with Pepsi as *The Runner*'s exclusive soft drink; *Newsweek* reported that "Pepsi was intrigued by ABC's 'open invitation' to actively help create the scenarios for product placements"; and a Pepsi vice president told *Newsweek*, "we are going to work very closely with them to make this different and unusual."[61] The show's producers suggested putting clues to the runner's location in Pepsi's TV commercials, and they were reportedly also pursuing product placement deals with advertisers in eight other product categories, including "a clothes store, a car firm, a fast food chain, a financial services company and a wireless communications brand."[62] In September 2001 *Broadcasting and Cable* reported that ABC had also made a deal with Chrysler for product placement on *The Runner*.[63] An executive for the show's production company told the press, "We don't look at it as product placement, we look at it as product integration."[64] *Newsweek* concluded: "With *The Runner*, ABC is offering advertisers much more [than traditional product placement]—a chance to help decide how the plot of the series will unfold, in some cases on an episode-by-episode or even scene-by-scene basis."[65] Indeed, the network invited advertisers to suggest plot ideas and incidents tailored to their products: "We would absolutely love to hear the advertisers' ideas," ABC's president of sales told the *New York Times*.[66] A Pepsi spokesperson told Britain's *Guardian* newspaper in July 2001: "What really is the most intriguing aspect of the show is how we'll fit in and that Pepsi products can be used as a part of the plot. For example, (the runner) may have to go to a store and purchase a Pepsi."[67] Plans by ABC to promote *The Runner* across its program schedule included onscreen bugs and lower-third crawls updating clues and the current bounty amount throughout the network's programming, as well as allowing advertisers to sponsor branded program updates.[68] In dismissing critics of the show's intensive use of product placement, coproducer Ben Affleck told the *Financial Times* in August 2001: "As if you had some inalienable right to have commercial-free television! What do you think pays for this show?"[69]

Some in the TV industry viewed the unprecedented lengths to which *The Runner*'s producers and network have gone to integrate program and advertising as merely a taste of things to come, as advertisers respond to the increasing ability of viewers to evade the traditional thirty-second commercials and as networks make new business and creative accommodations to advertisers in a weak TV ad market. In addition, several industry executives pointed to the value of product placement at a time when more and more viewers are seen to be increasingly skeptical of conventional advertising forms. As one ad executive told *Brandweek:* "It's far more effective in bypassing the usual alarms that go off; the critical part of the brain shuts down. . . . When you're aware someone's trying to get to you, you're more guarded. When you're not, stuff just seeps in."[70] In support of the practice, the same executive pointed to the recent federally funded efforts by drug czar Barry McCaffrey to place surreptitious antidrug messages in prime-time programs as an alternative to traditional public service ads.[71]

Addressing the new technological and economic climate for television advertising, an NBC executive told *Broadcasting and Cable* in September 2001: 'I think everybody realizes that they have to do business differently and they have to be more open than they were before. . . . Whether it's buying advertiser-supplied programming, whether it's integrating further into a show than you have before, or getting promotional consideration in another media, . . . I just think the whole state of the business is changing.'[72] As an example of the industry's new programming models, the magazine pointed to WB network's mid-season 2002 reality series *No Boundaries,* sponsored by Ford, which was to feature contestants driving and winning Ford Explorer SUVs; the program's title itself echoes the advertising slogan in Ford's ongoing multi-million-dollar marketing campaigns.[73] In August 2001, the *New York Times* reported that UPN, owned by Viacom, was considering offering sponsors the ability to superimpose logos and brand names as onscreen bugs during the network's prime-time programming "as a bonus [to advertisers] for buying large blocks of time to run traditional commercials during regular breaks."[74] While one advertising executive denounced UPN's proposed ad bugs as "shockingly crude and inappropriate . . . a sign of desperation," another industry executive argued that "history has shown that when consumers are exposed to advertising in places where advertising has not been in the past, they initially react negatively—then accept it."[75] Addressing a more general trend, a product placement broker told a British reporter that advertisers' direct involvement in TV programming was likely to increase, with the development "right around the corner" of "single advertising shows" where sponsors produce their own TV programs and integrate their products into the dramatic content.[76]

The prospect of heightened commercial censorship, ad bugs, sponsor-supplied programming, and enhanced product placement, all fueled by both the fearful prospect of the ad-evading personal video recorder and the growing advertiser power in a recessionary TV ad market, has resulted in some misgivings within the television industry, including fear of provoking increased consumer resistance to all advertising. Such contemporary trade anxieties resonate with an older and wider public debate about the limits to commercialization in everyday life. An executive at one product placement firm admitted that its growing use in television programs is "only going to work if there isn't a backlash among consumers," and an editorial in *Brandweek* called the trend toward more product placement "dangerous, for brands, for TV and yes—you and me."[77] Several industry commentators referred to a 2001 Roper-Starch Worldwide survey of TV viewers that pointed to a growing public aversion to advertising. According to the survey, the number of television viewers who switch channels at commercial breaks had roughly tripled to 36 percent since 1985, and the number of viewers who mute commercials had tripled to 23 percent during the same period.[78] The Roper survey also reported that 64 percent of respondents characterize advertising as a "nuisance" that "clutters up" TV (up five points since 1998), and 76 percent felt advertising is "shown in far too many places now, you can't get away from it" (up ten points from 1998).[79] More broadly, according to a September 2000 *Business Week*–Harris poll, 82 percent of consumers think "entertainment and popular culture . . . [are] dominated by corporate money, which seeks mass appeal over quality."[80]

As Raymond Williams noted in 1960, public complaints that advertisers "have gone about as far as they can go" date back at least to the mid-eighteenth century, and there is a poignant déjà vu quality to some of the debates around television's new advertising forms.[81] The two previous periods of sustained business expansion in the twentieth century—the 1920s and the 1950s—coincided not only with advertisers' eager embrace of the new media of radio and television but with the flourishing expression of popular ambivalence about the role of advertising within the context of wider changes in everyday life and cultural forms.[82] Several contemporary observers have noted the ironic echo of earlier broadcast advertising practices in the new world of digital television, including the return of single sponsorship, the integration of commercial and program, and the reprise of the celebrity pitch man.

The sometimes fevered trade and public discussions of the observed and anticipated changes in broadcast television's commercial and program forms in 2000–2001 were linked by many commentators to a wider cultural anxiety about the place of advertising in modern life, ranging from outraged and parodic responses to Fay Weldon's 2001 novel, *The Bulgari Connection*, which pioneered modern literary product placement, to the widely reported attempt by a New York couple to auction the naming rights of their unborn child to corporate marketers.[83] Such wider cultural anxieties suggest that the ultimate fortunes of the various new technological capabilities of digital television will depend on more than questions of technology and market power. In the current fog of marketing hype and economic uncertainty, it is important to note that the response of TV viewers to the increasingly desperate attempts of advertisers and broadcasters to integrate commercial message and program form remains largely untested, and crucial to any outcome.

NOTES

1. Erik Davis, "TV's Fascinating, Frightening Future," *Utne Reader* 48 (July/August 1990): 86–87.

2. Walter S. Baer, *Interactive Television: Prospects for Two-Way Services on Cable* (Santa Monica, Calif.: Rand Corporation, 1971), p. v.

3. L. J. Davis, *The Billionaire Shell Game: How Cable Baron John Malone and Assorted Corporate Titans Invented a Future Nobody Wanted* (New York: Doubleday, 1998).

4. Ian Fried, "Microsoft Shifts WebTV Oversight to Redmond," CNET News.com, March 2, 2001, http://www.news.cnet.com/news/0-1006-200-4997557.html.

5. Harry Berkowitz, "Sparks Fly between Moguls at Conference," *Newsday,* May 4, 2001, p. A62. On the brief history of iCrave, see Samantha Yaffe, "Casters Fighting iCrave," *Playback,* December 17, 1999, p. 1; and Christopher Stern, "Web's iCrave Caves: Settlement Shuts Down Pirate Netcaster," *Daily Variety,* February 29, 2000, p. 7. For a discussion of the legal issues involved in streaming broadcast material on the Web, see Dick Wiley, "Current Legal Issues No Audio (or Video) Hallucination for Webcasters," *Communications Today,* April 6, 2001, n.p.

6. Kathy Rebello, "Inside Microsoft: The Inside Story of How the Internet Forced Bill Gates to Reverse His Corporate Strategy," *Business Week,* July 15, 1996, pp. 56–67.

7. Joshua Quittner and Michelle Slatella, *Speeding the Web* (New York: Atlantic Monthly Press, 1998), p. 249.

8. Bill Gates, *Business @ the Speed of Thought* (New York: Warner Books, 1999), p. 162.

9. Christine MacDonald, "MS Tuned in to Convergence," CNET News.com, April 7, 1997, http://www.news.cnet.com/news/0-1003-200-317912.html.

10. "Free WebTV Promotion," *Consumer Electronics,* September 18, 2000; Lori Enos, "WebTV Settles Deceptive Ad Charges," NewsFactor Network, October 26, 2000, http://www.news.com2100-1040-3_254788.html. Jon Healey, "Company Town: Sony Pulls Interactive Games from WebTV," *Los Angeles Times,* March 1, 2001, p. C4.

11. Richard Shim, "Microsoft's Ultimate Challenge in Interactive TV," CNET News .com, March 27, 2001, http://www.yahoofin.cnet.com/news/0-1006-200-5255384.html ?tag=pt.yahoofin.financefeed.ne.

12. Mike Yamamoto and Stephanie Miles, "Picture Imperfect: WebTV: How Microsoft Lost Its Vision with WebTV," CNET News.com, October 12, 2000, http://www.news .cnet.com/news/0-1006-201-2950148-1.html.

13. Ibid.

14. "A Hitch and a Glitch Leaves Bluetooth No Sales Pitch," *Bangkok Post,* April 5, 2001, n.p.

15. Bill Gates promised an industry group in January 1998 that "you will see a WebTV box that has DSL in the coming year" (Michael Kanellos, "Gates: WebTV, PCs to get DSL," CNET News.com, January 28, 1998, http://www.news.cnet.com/news/0-1003 -200-326014.html; Dominic Gates, "Microsoft's Ultimate Delay," *Industry Standard,* November 13, 2000, http://www.thestandard.com.

16. "Microsoft Designs New WebTV Chip," ZDNet News, August 24, 2000, http:// www.zdnet.com/zdnn/stories/ news/0,4586,2619528,00.html.

17. Shim, "Microsoft's Ultimate Challenge."

18. Alex Pham, "Gates Hopes Xbox Is Key to the Living Room," *Los Angeles Times,* January 8, 2001, p. C1.

19. Microsoft CEO Steve Ballmer told journalists that he expected that most of the firm's revenues would come from Web-based subscriptions and services within four to ten years; see Wylie Wong and Stephen Shankland, "Ballmer Learns from Past Microsoft Missteps," CNET News.com, September 28, 2000, http://www.news.cnet.com/news/0-1003-201-2887282-0.html.

20. Kelly Zito, "Microsoft Branches Out: Software Maker Opens Windows to Video Games, Cellular Phones and More," *San Francisco Chronicle,* January 15, 2001, p. B1; Pham, "Gates Hopes Xbox Is Key," p. C1; Dori Jones Yang, "Why Gates Is Smiling," *U.S. News & World Report,* March 5, 2001, p. 38.

21. Rob Enderle of the Giga Information Group, quoted in Pham, "Gates Hopes Xbox is Key," p. C1.

22. Wong and Shankland, "Balmer Learns from Past Microsoft Missteps."

23. Christopher Grove, "Interactive Tube's Future Looks Hazy," *Daily Variety,* July 21, 2000, p. A2.

24. Tobi Elkin and Hillary Chura, "PVRS Revolutionizing TV Ad Buys," *Advertising Age,* September 18, 2000, p. 16.

25. Paul Abraham, "Television's Revolution Postponed: Digital Video Recorders Were Supposed to Replace Analogue Machines. But They Remain a Cult," *Financial Times,* July 7, 2001, p. 11.; Gartner analyst Mark Snowden, quoted in Shim, "Microsoft's Ultimate Challenge."

26. For Microsoft's controversial moves among ad agencies working on the Ultimate TV account, see "For the Record," *Advertising Age,* March 12, 2001, p. 37; Stuart Elliott, "Stuart Elliott in America," *Campaign,* March 16, 2001, p. 27; Stuart Elliott, "Microsoft Shakes Up Beleaguered San Francisco Agencies by Shifting Its Account for Ultimate TV," *New York Times,* May 11, 2001, p. C5.

27. Shim, "Microsoft's Ultimate Challenge."

28. Telephone interview with Gary Shipping, Ultimate TV account supervisor, Rodgers and Townsend Advertising, St. Louis, Missouri, April 12, 2001.

29. The merger of News Corporation and DIRECTV was complicated by the August 2001 rival bid for DIRECTV from competing satellite sevice Echo Star Communications (Kris Hudson, "EchoStar Drama Gets Complicated, Ergen Has Several Cards Up His Sleeve, Analysts Say," *Denver Post,* August 19, 2001, p. K1).

30. Sallie Hofmeister, "News Corp. to Make New Bid for DIRECTV," *Los Angeles Times,* April 20, 2001, p. C1. See also Jim Rutenberg and Geraldine Fabrikant, "Dream Prize Draws Closer for Murdoch," *New York Times,* May 7, 2001, p. C1.

31. Hofmeister, "News Corp. to Make New Bid," p. C1.

32. Ibid. For a profile on the European interactive television market, see William Echikson, "Europe's I-TV Advantage," *Business Week,* February 19, 2001, 16. The BSkyB results are reported in a May 9, 2001, press release at http://www.corporate-ir.net/ireye/ir_site.zhtml?ticker=bsy.uk&script=410&layout=0&item_id=174017. The fall in News Corp. advertising revenues and share price following the September 11, 2001, World Trade Center attack cast new doubt about the viability of Murdoch's bid for

DIRECTV (see Andrew Clark and John Cassy, "On the Brink of War: Media: Murdoch May Lose DIRECTV Bid," *Guardian,* October 3, 2001, p. 26).

33. TiVo Inc., *Quarterly Report* (SEC form 10-Q), September 14, 2001, http://www .biz.yahoo.comj/e/010914/tivo.html.

34. Michael Lewis, "Boom Box: The End of the Mass Market," *New York Times Magazine,* August 20, 2000, pp. 36–41.

35. Becky Ebenkamp, "Peyton Placement," *Brandweek,* June 4, 2001, p. s10.

36. Claudia Deutsch, "Study Details Decline in Spending on Ads," *New York Times,* September 5, 2001, p. C2; Stuart Elliott, "An Agency Giant Is Expected to Warn of Lower Profits, and Analysts Darken Their Outlook," *New York Times,* October 2, 2001, p. C2. See also Harry Berkowitz, "Media Firms Report Big Losses; Companies Pulled Ads in Tragedy's Wake," *New York Newsday,* October 3, 2001, p. A53.

37. Regarding the nascent virtual advertising business, see William Boddy, " 'Touching Content: Virtual Advertising and Digital Television's Recalcitrant Audience,' " in *Screen Culture: History and Textuality,* ed. John Fullerton (Sydney: John Libbey, 2004) pp. 245–62.

38. TiVo press release; for an account of the increased interest among advertising-supported cable networks in advertiser-supplied programming, see Jim Forkan, "On Some Cable Shows, the Sponsors Take Charge; Advertiser-Supplied Programming Trend Focuses on Outdoorsy and Family Genres," *Multichannel News,* June 4, 2001, p. 53. On the growth of product placement, see Wayne Friedman, "Eagle-Eye Marketers Find Right Spot, Right Time; Product Placements Increase as Part of Syndication Deals," *Advertising Age,* January 22, 2001, p. s2.

39. David Goetzi, "TBS Tries Virtual Advertising," *Advertising Age,* May 21, 2001. Weeks later, there was still confusion about the final status of the *Law and Order* deal, including permission from the show's joint production companies (see Stuart Elliott, "Reruns May Become a Testing Ground for Digital Insertion of Sponsor's Products and Images," *New York Times,* May 23, 2001, p. C6).

40. "Digital Television Advertising," *Financial Times,* June 5, 2001, p. 12.

41. Jon Healey, "Digital Living Room: Copyright Concerns are Creating Static for Digital TV," *Los Angeles Times,* March 22, 2001, p. T7. A TiVo executive told a group of advertisers that disabling the capacity to fast forward through commercials might not be technologically possible, and he warned his audience that they might not want to be the network or sponsor that disabled the viewer's remote control (Ken Ripley, national director, advertising sales, TiVo, at personal video recorder panel, Association of National Advertisers Television Advertising Forum, New York, March 29, 2001). In a chapter titled "Friction-Free Capitalism" in his 1995 best-seller *The Road Ahead,* Bill Gates wrote approvingly about "software that lets the customer fast-forward past everything except for the advertising, which will play at normal speed" when Internet-delivered full-motion video becomes available (Gates, *The Road Ahead* [New York: Penguin, 1995], p. 171).

42. Lee Hall, "Coming Soon to a PVR Near You; TiVo to Provide Uploadable Advertisements, while Giving Customers the Means to Skip Them," *Broadcasting and Cable,* February 26, 2001, p. 40.

43. Michael Freeman, "Networks Ready for Strikes," *Electronic Media,* March 26, 2001, p. 2.

44. Louis Chunovic, "Advertisers Go Deep in New TV Shows," *Electronic Media,* March 26, 2001, p. 3.

45. Ibid.

46. Gloria Goodale, "Ads You Can't Subtract," *Christian Science Monitor,* January 19, 2001, p. 13.

47. Ibid.

48. Bill Carter, "CBS Pulls Show over Concern from P&G," *New York Times,* August 17, 2001, p. C1.

49. Jay Lyman, "Study: Interactive TV to Boom Despite Barriers," *NewsFactor Network,* March 27, 2001, http://www.newsfactor.com/perl/story/8465.html.

50. CBS spokesperson Chris Ender, quoted in Gail Collins, "Public Interests; Elmo Gets Wired," *New York Times,* April 24, 2001, p. A19. See also Bill Carter, "New Reality Show Planning to Put Ads between the Ads," *New York Times,* April 30, 2001, p. A1.

51. Bill Carter, "The New Season: Television and Radio. The Annotated List: France Liberated, Laughs Generated and Reality Revisited," *New York Times,* September 9, 2001, p. B23.

52. David Bloom, "The Digital Dozen," *Variety,* July 23–29, 2001, p. 29.

53. Joe Schlosser, "Safety First for Runner: ABC Being Cautious with Series that Sends Viewers on Manhunt," *Broadcasting and Cable,* April 9, 2001, p. 24; Ray Bradbury, *Fahrenheit 451* (1953; New York: Ballantine, 1976), pp. 138–39.

54. Eric Mink, "Rundown on 'Runner,'" *Daily News,* July 24, 2001, p. 67; Josef Adalian, "ABC's 'Runner' Making Stride," *Daily Variety,* March 21, 2001, p. 1.

55. Rob Salem, "Everyone's Offering a Dose of Reality," *Toronto Star,* August 25, 2001, p. J3.

56. Noel Holston, "On ABC Family, a Different Type of Diversity," *Newsday,* July 25, 2001, p. B35.

57. Adalian, "ABC's 'Runner' Making Stride," p. 1.

58. Carter, "New Reality Show," p. A1.

59. Ibid.

60. Chunovic, "Advertisers Go Deep in New TV Shows," p. 3.

61. Magaret McKegney, "U.S.: Is Reality TV a Survivor?" *Ad Age Global,* June 1, 2001, p. 6; Johnnie L. Roberts, "This Space Available," *Newsweek,* May 7, 2001, p. 42.

62. Wayne Friedman, "ABC Puts Ads on Run: Reality Show 'Runner' Pitches Product Placement," *Advertising Age,* April 30, 2001, p. 3; Gillian Drummond, "Meet TV's Newest Stars," *Guardian,* July 23, 2001, p. 6.

63. Joe Schlosser, "Have We Got a Deal for You: Adjusting to Bear Market, Networks Offer Sponsorships, Product Placements, Other Value-Added Lures this Fall," *Broadcasting and Cable,* September 3, 2001, p. 5.

64. Joanne Weintraub, "Show and Sell: Products a Bigger Part of the Plot," *Milwaukee Journal Sentinel,* June 5, 2001, p. 1E.

65. Roberts, "This Space Available," p. 42.

66. Carter, "New Reality Show," p. A1.

67. Gillian Drummond, "Meet TV's Newest Stars," *Guardian,* July 23, 2001, p. 6. Drummond quotes a LivePlanet executive claiming that "the sponsors are not determining the content of the show, but they are integral to the content. That's a fine point. . . . The runner is not going to go into a store to buy a Pepsi. That would be a gross way of doing this."

68. Roberts, "This Space Available," p. 42.

69. Katja Hofmann, "LivePlanet," *Financial Times,* August 7, 2001, p. 4.

70. Becky Ebenkamp, "Peyton Placement," *Brandweek,* June 4, 2001, p. S10.

71. Ibid. For a discussion of McCaffrey's efforts, see Daniel Forbes, "Prime-Time Propaganda: How the White House Secretly Hooked Network TV on Its Anti-Drug Message," January 13, 2000, http://www.salon.com/news/feature/2000/01/13/drugs/indx.html.

72. Schlosser, "Have We Got a Deal for You," p. 5.

73. Ibid.

74. Stuart Elliott, "UPN Weighs Ad Logos in Prime Time," *New York Times,* August 23, 2001, p. C1.

75. Ibid.

76. Drummond, "Meet TV's Newest Stars," p. 6.

77. Ibid. Karen Benezra, "In Reality, Television Is Overrated," *Brandweek,* June 4, 2001, n.p.

78. Matthew Grimm, "Reality Bites," *American Demographics,* July 2001, p. 56.

79. Ibid.

80. Aaron Bernstein, "Too Much Corporate Power?" *Business Week,* September 11, 2000, p. 144; cited in Matthew Grimm, "Reality Bites," *American Demographics,* July 2001, p. 56.

81. Raymond Williams, "Advertising: The Magic System," in *Problems in Materialism and Culture* (London: Verso, 1980), p. 172.

82. See, for example, Ralph Borsodi, *This Ugly Civilization* (New York: Simon and Schuster, 1929); and Fred Manchee, *The Huckster's Revenge: The Truth about Life on Madison Avenue* (New York: Nelson, 1959).

83. A small sample of the writing on the Weldon controversy includes John Balzar, "Sold! A Literary Soul, Now Mud," *Los Angeles Times,* September 5, 2001, p. B13; "Editorial; Author Should Play by the Book," *Boston Herald,* September 9, 2001, p. 24; Jenny Lyn Bader, "Brand Name Lit: Call Me Tiffany," *New York Times,* September 9, 2001, p. D2; Don Campbell, "For Author, the (GE) Light Dawns," *USA Today,* September 10, 2001, p. A17. For the attempted corporate-naming auction of the unborn child, see Matthew Purdy, "Our Towns: A Boy Named Soup?" *New York Times,* August 1, 2001, p. B1; Arthur Asa Berger, "Sponsor Me: Selling Out or Subverting?" *New York Newsday,* August 17, 2001, p. A49; "Editorial; Ad Mad: The Parents Who Offered Naming Rights for Their Baby Are Not the Problem," *Pittsburgh Post-Gazette,* August 15, 2001, p. A13.

LISA PARKS **FLEXIBLE MICROCASTING:**

GENDER, GENERATION, AND TELEVISION-

INTERNET CONVERGENCE

The April 24, 2000, cover of *Variety* features an image of a blue-eyed baby superimposed on a multitude of Microsoft and WebTV logos repeated across the page. In the understated style of much high-tech advertising, the headline reads: "The next generation of television is here. interactive. personal. internet." The cover announces the birth of a new television era dominated by info-tech giants, and it relies on the metaphor of evolution to do so. This logic of natural development is nothing new in discussions of television. Consider, for instance, the organizational structure of Erik Barnouw's widely read *Tube of Plenty:* the book charts the phases of television's history in terms of its maturation, with chapter titles like "Toddler," "Prime," "Elder," and "Progeny."[1] In the latter Barnouw describes the VCR, cable, and satellite television as network television's "offspring." If we were to add yet another chapter to account for the contemporary moment, it might be called something like "Mutants."

Drawing on the info-tech world's terminology for new generations of innovation, *Variety* calls this phase "Television 2.0," positioning the medium as another software version, upgraded in the latest programming language and thus more efficient and easy to run.[2] I want to question here this logic of evolutionary progress by exploring television's shifting meanings in the context of its convergence with the Internet. Such moments of technological transformation provide rich opportunities for cultural analysis, for they showcase our attempt to reconcile the chaotic indeterminacy of new technologies with existing social and economic structures. The convergence of television and computers is not just about technical mixing; it also activates gendered assumptions about "active" users and "passive" viewers, class-based discourses related to digital access and speed, and broader issues of cultural taste and social distinction. Convergence introduces the necessity of institutional reorganization and shifts in the format of programming as well.

In this essay I examine the emergence of new forms of television in an era of postbroadcasting. I invoke the term postbroadcasting not to refer to a revolutionary moment in the digital age but rather to explore how the historical practices associated with over-the-air, cable, and satellite television have been combined with computer technologies to reconfigure the meanings and practices of television. Postbroadcasting, then, refers to television's current transformations as part of an ongoing set of historical struggles played out over and around the medium rather than as a byproduct of the "digital revolution." Television's previous convergence with cable, satellite, and VCR technologies are just as relevant to contemporary changes in television as are computer technologies. Indeed, over-the-air distribution introduced the possibility of local, national, and international reception, which has influenced the infrastructural model of the World Wide Web; DBS systems introduced early modes of interactivity; and the VCR introduced timeshifting or viewer control over scheduling. All of these practices are now being combined and folded into television's convergence with the Internet and other digital technologies. This is best exemplified by the industry's visions of a new kind of personalized TV, or what I shall call "flexible microcasting."

Convergence is not just about the coming together of technical systems; it involves the shifting meanings of converging technologies as well. Where the "Big Three" television networks have introduced convergent media that tend to reinforce dominant ideologies as part of an effort to maintain hegemony in multimedia environments, online entertainment start-ups such as Oxygen Media and DEN have capitalized on this moment of convergence to target particular niche markets and generate new cultural spaces for women and youth. Because of this we need to explore how technological convergence overlaps with the politics of gender, race, class, and generational differences.

Industry leaders have identified the age of postbroadcasting as the era of "personal television." This concept is coded in titles of new online entertainment services such as MeTV, iCraveTV, and Microcast, and in ads for new digital recording devices like TiVo that encourage potential customers to "teach it what kind of shows you like and it will search out and suggest others."[3] Personal television is a set of industrial and technological practices that work to isolate the individual cultural tastes of the viewer/consumer in order to refine direct marketing in television—that is, the process of delivering specific audiences to advertisers.[4] It is a model of television that promises to tailor packages of content to individual choice, and thus it is ultimately a move toward what might best be described as "the programming of the self." Personal television operates by soliciting and storing the viewer's program preferences and selections within a centralized database. Thus content can be preselected, preordered, "bought on demand," and then pushed or downstreamed to the appropriate users or viewers. This system of personal television technologizes the practice of flipping through *TV Guide* and selecting programs to view or record. It stores in computer memory an individual's preferred modes of television viewing. Because material is "pushed," however, the process of selection—which is often celebrated as expanded viewer choice—is clearly circumscribed by marketers' determinations of "relevant" content. Thus, the industry discourse of personal television has less to do with the viewer's personhood and more to do with new industrial structures of individuation geared toward profit making.

It makes more sense to refer to the personalization of television as a kind of "flexible microcasting," where computer and television technologies are combined to produce the effect of enhanced viewer choice in the form of a stream of programming carefully tailored to the viewer's preferences, tastes, and desires.[5] Flexible microcasting is organized around social distinctions (whether gender, age, race, class, sexuality, or lifestyle) that are arranged to maximize profit for media producers, networks, and advertisers. The personalization of TV is ultimately about developing narrowly defined yet infinitely flexible content that commodifies layers of individual identity, desire, taste, and preference.

This practice of flexible microcasting is being articulated across various sites of television and Internet convergence. Media browsers such as Real.com, for example, allow individuals to fashion their own packages of media content. Media producers license their content to Real, which in turn formats it and makes it available to Web users. Although media browsers duplicate the function of cable and satellite providers, they reconfigure packaging as a personalized process in which the user "cherry picks" select content from a range of channels (including everything from Comedy Central to CNN to Brazilian radio to NPR to MTV). Flexible microcasting involves the digitization of recording and timeshifting practices made possible by the VCR so that scheduling is no longer determined solely by networks, cable, or satellite operators because viewers have a range of options with respect to their content lineups and viewing times.

Moreover, by removing the spontaneity of the practice of channel surfing, this model of flexible microcasting allows programmers to determine more accurately where and when viewers are in the media landscape. In a sense, personal television makes every PC a Nielsen household, assuming the responsibility of "self-packaging" or "self-programming" while being continually scrutinized by marketing systems. As William Boddy details in his essay in this volume, WebTV, another of the current crop of personal television devices, is a set-top box that places a graphic interface on the television screen that offers e-mail and limited Internet access (materials are downstreamed) to viewers with a TV set. Microsoft bought WebTV in 1996 and has since been working on hardware designs that consolidate the television set and the computer monitor. In addition, Microsoft is licensing interactive software to television producers who are trying to incorporate interactive elements, particularly in quiz shows such as *Wheel of Fortune* and *Jeopardy*. So, too, as both Boddy's and William Uricchio's chapters demonstrate—companies such as TiVo and ReplayTV have introduced digital VCRs that allow viewers to store television content on a hard drive and play it back on the television monitor. The digital VCR makes the practice of timeshifting more flexible by allowing the viewer/user to interrupt and resume program flow, randomly access stored material, and archive program preferences. But its limited storage and copy protections constrain users' ability to take control of their viewing preferences. Similarly, media browsers establish a subscriber infrastructure on the Internet. Such services as Real.com emulate cable TV and DBS services that deliver television, radio, and music content to subscribers, but also allow the viewer to customize his or her viewing or listening options out of streams of news, music, entertainment, health, science, and sports. The process of assembling cable television packages, which has been assumed by regional cable operators for nearly two decades, is now being assumed by individual users, thus altering dramatically the concept of network scheduling. Flexible microcasting generates the possibility of greater viewer control over television's temporality, not only in terms of timeshifting content but also by enabling the viewer to determine the schedule and regulate its flow.

Personal television is the most recent articulation of what Raymond Williams calls "mobile privatization."[6] Williams used this term to refer to the way that television institutions reinforced tendencies toward a kind of domesticized individualism set within a complex of abstract public systems. With the portability and miniaturization of television, scholars have begun to consider what Lynn Spigel calls the medium's "privatized mobility" as well.[7] Spigel suggests that privatized mobility emerged with the second wave of television's installation during the 1960s, specifically with the marketing rhetoric surrounding portable TV. Privatized mobility, she claims, became the inverted ideal of mobile privatization and was part of a distinct culture organized around middle-class fantasies of transport, personal freedom, and citizenship. These ideals of transport, freedom, and citizenship have shaped the cultural imagination of television technologies since the 1960s (along with other mobile machines ranging from the Walkman to the GPS receiver to the Palm Pilot). The development of broadband (particularly satellite) delivery systems is likely to extend the places and ways in which we watch television, refiguring the medium as part of a system of "pervasive computing," a kind of naturalized global infrastructure much like the ether itself.[8] If TV viewers will eventually be able to see television anywhere and anytime, we might reexamine the medium's relationship to these ideals of transport, freedom, and citizenship. The industrial model of flexible microcasting blends fantasies of private address and public participation; packages programs that are allegedly fit to one's own tastes and desires; and structures TV viewing as an experience both of physical and social mobility.

Already the politics of class, gender, and cultural taste are forming around television and Internet convergence. Often, importing televisual elements within computer environments is constructed as a contamination or dumbing down of computers' potential. As an AOL-TV interface developer explains to designers, "never forget you're designing for the TV not the computer screen. All of the interfaces have to be straightforward and created with TV in mind."[9] Where interfaces on the computer screen can be complex and challenging, those on the television screen must be made comprehensible to anyone. The discourses surrounding these technologies almost read like *Wired Magazine*'s "Tired/Wired" column, with its contempt for old, slow analog devices in favor of the new techno literati. Where television viewers are perceived as passive couch potatoes, computer users are by comparison seen as active and overworked. Where television viewers often watch hours of programming at a time, computer users are imagined to be multitasking in a highly selective fashion. Where television is massifying, computers are individualized. Where television is slow, computers are fast. On the surface, such claims reek of economic privilege. Those with fast and expensive broadband connections can download more data more efficiently and with the proper hardware can simulate a televisual experience at the computer interface. Those with slow connections, however, are able only to see a tiny and often broken-up image with poor resolution, thus relegating them to second-class content. But perhaps even more important than this explicit issue of access is the gendered assumption that is mapped onto these discourses of speed. In broad terms, the industry's "sophisticated video-seeker" is constructed as an autonomous masculine browser, unlike the passive feminized viewer of analog TV.

THE NETWORKS

To remain viable in the postbroadcasting era, the major TV networks have scrambled to form info-tech alliances. Internet companies with expertise in the digital field are eager to capitalize on the large audiences of the networks—to turn ratings into page views.[10] These partnerships and mergers (i.e., ABC-Go, CBS-AOL, NBC-Snap) have resulted in the redefinition of the Big Three television networks as multimedia portals that direct viewers to media content ranging from Web sites to television programs to films to music and radio shows. Each of the networks has relied on their brand names to "transition" viewers into online domains. Relying on "the power of the peacock," for example, NBC launched its first Internet company, NBCi, in November 1999 as part of a strategy, according to one of its top executives, to keep the network "at the forefront of the convergence of traditional media and the Internet, transitioning TV and radio audiences into Internet users with electronic commerce at the centerpiece of the new strategy."[11] NBC used NBCi to build on its strategies of TV-Internet convergence initiated with the formation of MSNBC in 1996.

Despite these mergers, the networks have not experimented very much with interactive programming. They have used their Web sites primarily as publicity platforms to announce television schedules, promote programs and stars, and direct users to other network-owned Web sites and cable channels.[12] While emergent networks such as UPN and WB have copied Fox's strategy of the 1980s by effectively tailoring content to young adult demographics, the established networks continue to pursue a mass audience. Even though the possibility for interactive narrative structure might seem more conducive to the logic of personalized TV, the networks are so cemented to the current system of magazine sponsorship that they continue to pursue the mass audience—that is, to broadcast rather than microcast. One of their most aggressive, and successful, such efforts has been the recent revival of the quiz show. All three major networks and even Fox have placed programs such as *Who Wants to Be a Millionaire?, Twenty-One,* and *Greed* in prime-time slots. Faced with increasing competition from cable and satellite television and online media providers, the networks have combined this tried-and-true television format with select properties of digital media.

An interesting story about the mutations of network broadcasting has unfolded in the reemergence of the quiz show. As William Boddy reminds us, the quiz shows of the late 1950s were at the center of shifting relations between the networks, advertisers, affiliates, and audiences.[13] The return of this quintessentially televisual genre in the late 1990s was not just part of an economic strategy to reverse fledgling network ratings but also was highly symptomatic of the networks' efforts to simultaneously address a mass audience and redefine themselves in the age of technological convergence. The quiz show is in fact the perfect television format to "transition" network viewers onto the Internet. Fundamentally about testing knowledge, the format can be structured in a way that locates the individual at the intersection of television and computer technologies.[14]

The format of ABC's *Who Wants to Be a Millionaire?*, for example, is organized (both for the contestant and the viewer) as a series of encounters with computer interfaces and telephone connections. The program's very format shares structural similarities with the vision of personal television described earlier. While perched at the interface (which is displayed both in the studio and on the TV screen), the contestant sorts his or her way through a series of multiple-choice questions, attempting to select the proper responses so that he or she will be rewarded with big sums of cash. The program uses flashy spotlights and suspense music to suggest that the very act of being situated at the interface is both exciting and lucrative. These programs not only rely on the appeal of the so-called ordinary man rising into fortune overnight, but they popularize an image of him situated at the computer interface. The show is edited in such a way that it enables viewers to see the contestant's face and interface and play along (especially using new interactive options), and it encourages viewers to visit the program's Web site at a computer interface to further test their knowledge. Like the user of personal television, the contestant's every move is monitored and recorded. The program doesn't applaud his intelligence so much as it celebrates his successful navigation through a series of options displayed simultaneously on computer and television monitors. Because the questions tend to be relatively easy and because there are so many opportunities for assistance from others, the program seems to reward the contestant simply for being there.[15] The "hot seat," then, is also a site of technological convergence—it's a position that is used to instruct viewers about the new structures and interfaces of personal TV.

The use of various screen interfaces and telephony in the quiz show genre is, of course, nothing new. After the FCC passed the Financial Interest and Syndication Rules in the 1970s, syndicated game shows such as *Joker's Wild, Tic Tac Dough, Tattletales, Family Feud, Jeopardy, Hollywood Squares,* and *Love Connection* (just to name a few) used flashy lights and bright colors to create spectacular sets and also integrated screen interfaces to enliven their formats and make them appear more "interactive."[16] This historical pattern of using screens, video playback, and telephony within the quiz/game show genre has extended television's capacity to display and circulate information from outside of the studio, thus enabling the medium to represent itself as a far-reaching center of knowledge. The construction of television in such a way takes on particular importance during this moment of convergence when digital technologies threaten to absorb and forever alter the medium's specificities. The screen interfaces and communication devices embedded within the quiz show's mise-en-scène encourage one to imagine television itself as an information technology that has produced various levels of "interactivity" for decades.

Whereas many syndicated game shows of the 1970s and 1980s were scheduled during the access hour or after the prime-time lineup, ABC placed *Millionaire* in the prime-time schedule. Based on its overwhelming success in the United Kingdom, network executives thought of *Millionaire* as a "blockbuster show" designed to attract the mass audience. Just as earlier shows effectively used handsome male hosts to attract female audiences, the producers of *Millionaire* followed a similar strategy. Executives at ABC anticipated that the widely popular Regis Philbin would bring female fans of his morning talk show to the prime-time slot, potentially attracting their male counterparts as well. *Millionaire*'s sky-high ratings helped ABC become the top-rated network for the first time in more than a decade among male and female and white and African American demographics.

When *Millionaire* first aired in 1999, women and people of color complained to ABC about the relative lack of participation by women and minority contestants. The show's producers responded that season by doing one "ladies' night." By the end of 2000 *Millionaire* had featured less than a dozen African American contestants. Yet, despite the lack of black contestants on the show, it was *Millionaire* that reportedly made ABC the number-one ranked network among black viewers for the first time in ten years.[17] What is unusual about *Millionaire,* then, is that it managed to attract a mass audience (across these different demographics) during its first season, despite the relatively low number of women and people of color appearing on the show. While the range of contestants expanded in seasons that followed, the program's appeal across race and gender demographics suggests that the return of the quiz show is not just about the network's efforts to capitalize on a successful formula; it's also about the current moment of convergence and the ways in which dominant ideologies about gender, race, class, and technology become part of television's efforts to rearticulate itself as a computerized form.

Millionaire evokes, first, the network's shuffling in the era of postbroadcasting, the scandalous history of the quiz show, and the ongoing uncertainty over the future content and form of television, and then negotiates them with computerization. This logic—that television's ideological excess, scandalous history, and technological indeterminacy can be folded into a more ordered, rational, interactive computerized form—is, of course, a gendered one, as feminist television critics such as Lynne Joyrich have suggested.[18] Social discourses imagine television as a feminized and messy form that can be enveloped, reordered, and reactivated by masculine computer technologies. As Ellen Seiter reminds us, we should be skeptical about "laudatory uses of the term 'active' in discussions of media use, and . . . problematize the complex factors involved in attracting both television viewers and computer users to particular contents and genres."[19] In the case of *Millionaire,* perhaps the mass audience's attraction to the genre has as much to do with dominant ideologies that naturalize white middle-class men's position at the helm of information technologies and intelligence as it does with the pleasure of seeing ordinary folk rise to overnight fortune. Despite feminist efforts to claim the computer as a platform for social transformation, the dominant social, economic, and cultural discourses continue to position computer technologies as domains of masculine activity, authority, and control.[20]

The network's use of the quiz show, then, has the effect of staging these technological transitions and convergences in a way that suggests that in the age of postbroadcasting, the network and perhaps only the network can best serve the individualized masculine computer user and the massified feminine TV viewer. The networks' nostalgic and ironic recuperation of the most scandalous genre in American television history (not to mention the turn toward outrageous reality-based series such as *Survivor, Big Brother, Temptation Island, The Mole,* and *Boot Camp*) reveals a kind of desperation in their ongoing efforts to remain viable in the digital age. At the moment when network television could offer innovation in programming and representation, it has resorted to a self-protective discourse grounded in dominant ideologies ranging from masculine control over technology to the "survival of the fittest" reality shows that commercially exploit and culturally recuperate heterosexual romance, surveillance, and militarism.

While *Millionaire* tends to reinforce white, middle-class masculine control over new media, other sites of TV-Internet convergence can be seen as posing a challenge to this logic. In other words, the mixing—or what Marshall McLuhan called "cross-pollenization"—of television and computing might also generate possibilities for social transformation.[21] Both Oxygen Media and the DEN emerged in the late 1990s as online networks that imagined their audiences not only as niche markets but as social communities as well. Despite the DEN's short life, these start-ups sought to capitalize on this moment of convergence in part to produce new cultural spaces for women and youth. I want to turn now to a discussion of these examples in order to better understand the range of practices that defines television and Internet convergence.

OXYGEN MEDIA

Oxygen Media promotes itself as the first "on air and on line network for women, by women."[22] Led by some of the most powerful women in American television (Geraldine Laybourne, Marcy Carsey, Caryn Mandabach, and Oprah Winfrey), the network launched its cable television channel and online media portal on February 2, 2000, just days after its snappy $2 million inaugural ad appeared during the Super Bowl.[23] With imagery not unlike that used in the *Variety* cover discussed at the opening of this essay, the spot featured the clenched fist of a newborn baby girl emerging from a cradle as Helen Reddy's lyrics "I am strong. I am invincible. I am woman" blare in the background. Oxygen used this high-profile ad to announce its own birth as part of a new generation of online and on-air multimedia.

Despite its ambitious marketing campaign, Oxygen had difficulty with distribution during its first year of operations (in part because its executives decided to charge cable providers subscriber fees, which is rare for a new cable channel). By late 2000 Oxygen was only available in limited cable markets (it was kept out of key markets such as New York and Los Angeles) and as part of DIRECT TV's "family package" generating a potential audience of a mere eleven million homes. This relatively small number (Lifetime, for instance, is available in seventy-five million homes) combined with the recent slump in the high-tech economy prompted Oxygen to streamline its operations in early 2001.[24] A year after its launch the network reduced its online offerings from twelve to nineteen Web sites down to four (Oxygen.com, Young Audiences, Oprah, and Thrive). Oxygen also closed its Seattle office, ceased production of several of its original TV programs, and laid off more than seventy of its seven hundred employees.[25] In the meantime, Oxygen's executives have continued to expand their distribution, and they now plan to be in fifty million homes by 2005.[26]

The Oxygen brand works to naturalize the network's presence, suggesting that women's multimedia should be as ubiquitous as the air we breathe. Oxygen is also a pun on the shifting meanings of television distribution in the context of convergence: what does it mean to "air" television in the digital age? These motifs were woven into the titles and themes of programs that appeared in the network's first schedule. *Exhale,* for instance, is a talk show hosted by former *Murphy Brown* star Candice Bergen. *Pure Oxygen* is a variety show that allegedly "informs, entertains, and empowers." *Inhale* is a half hour of yoga training, which reveals the network's shift away from the aerobics culture of the 1980s and 1990s and toward a more cerebral New Age technoculture of mental and physical "balance." Other programs attempt to bring the experiences and cultures of young girls, women of color, single mothers, and female artists to television and computer screens. *Trackers,* for example, is an interactive talk show produced by young girls who use the show's Web site to gather viewers' suggestions for topics of discussion that range from safe sex to suicide. *X-Chromosome* showcases gender-themed work by digital artists working independently or in small studios. Many of Oxygen's TV shows are designed with interactive elements that encourage viewers to visit the network's Web site before or after watching a program, thus addressing the TV viewer as a computer user as well. DIRECT TV subscribers of Oxygen can also access a full range of interactive options provided through a partnership with Wink Communications.

Whereas *Millionaire* reinforces the idea that technology and information are controlled by a privileged class of white men, some of Oxygen's programs encourage viewers to reimagine the television screen as a democratic Internet portal that gives everyone equal access to knowledge about computer technologies and cyberculture. The most interesting contrast to *Millionaire* is *Oprah Goes Online*, a twelve-part series that encourages women to "get websmart in a flash" and teaches them to use computers and surf the Web. The show is set in a TV studio where Oprah and her close friend Gayle King move between two computers as a young African American man and a young white woman show them how to use the computer to go online. Throughout the thirty-minute show Oprah and Gayle move back and forth between two computers in the studio and learn to navigate the World Wide Web. The hosts challenge viewers to follow along or try these techniques later on their own computers. In one episode Oprah and Gayle learn how to buy stamps and clothes, practice their Italian, and find special gifts for family and friends. The studio cameras capture point-of-view shots of the interface over the shoulders of Oprah and Gayle, who invite viewers to take part in a kind of communal Web surfing. This point-of-view framing and shot/reverse-shot editing of interfaces/women's faces sutures the viewer into convergent media spaces, thus blurring the distinction between the televisual and the digital. The show's visual design transforms the act of television viewing into that of cybernavigation and exploits TV's analog signal to offer a digital experience to those who might not otherwise be encouraged to explore computer domains.

In one sense, *Oprah Goes Online* is the antithesis of *Millionaire:* it places an African American woman (who is already a multimillionaire) in the so-called hot seat as she learns how to use a computer. Although the show addresses the viewer as a consumer by encouraging online shopping, it also suggests that viewers/users of television and computers can and should expect to be educated about the very functions and operations of new media technologies. Instead of using the interface to support opportunistic fantasies of individual financial windfall, Oprah's program encourages digital literacy, which is all the more significant given the hegemonic assumptions about gender, technology, and knowledge that structure and circulate invisibly in high-rated network quiz shows like *Millionaire.*

What *Oprah Goes Online* and *Millionaire* share in common is their attempt to position television as integrated with the computer interface. Because the Big Three networks and Oxygen's top executives built their economic success within television, they have a vested interest in ensuring that these successes are not altogether lost with digitization—that is, that the medium of TV is not simply leapfrogged. The quiz show's revival and Oxygen's programs can thus be seen as part of a strategy to develop convergent formats that encourage viewers *to embrace the computer through television* rather than to replace their TVs with new computers.

Advancing this position, Geraldine Laybourne, whom *Wired* calls the "convergence queen," insists that Oxygen's programming is "very contemporary, very in-your-face, as opposed to passive. We're doing everything we can to make this look like a different experience."[27] Oxygen's programs do not look all that "different" from other television shows, but here Laybourne suggests that the new network's version of television will integrate the more edgy elements of a digital aesthetic in order to lend greater social and cultural legitimacy to the medium. There are economic and political motivations for this promotional strategy.

While the Big Three networks have profited as part of a system of commercial broadcasting set up early in the twentieth century, Oxygen emerged only recently as an Internet start-up. It received funding from venture-capital investors ($200 million, for instance, from former Microsoft partner Paul Allen), and $4.5 million from the Markle Foundation, a nonprofit organization trying to democratize the Internet.[28] Thus, while Oxygen is most definitely a high-capital venture, the company is also ostensibly trying to extend women's interest in, access to, and knowledge of multimedia technologies. Its promise to "superserve the needs and interests of women" should not be interpreted only as a consumerist address but also as an insistence that women become players in the production of multimedia and in the information economy. Oxygen's executives have used an already existing and widely available technology—television—as the way into the world of the Internet for digitally disadvantaged groups. Part of Oxygen's agenda has been to connect girls, women of color, digital artists, health activists, working mothers, and media professionals (among others) within new televisual and digital spaces, building gender, class, and race differences into the content and form of multimedia.

Although Oxygen's executives are self-avowed liberal feminists, the press has been reticent to acknowledge their network as such. Articles in *Wired* have undercut Oxygen's feminist potential with belittling headlines such as "Ladies Home Internet" or "A Kinder Gentler Multimedia" or "Sugar Daddy Replenishes Oxygen."[29] Critics complain that Oxygen relentlessly hails women as consumers, and in so doing it overemphasizes personal transformation while failing to deal with "serious" matters. In an article titled "A Wasteland of One's Own," Francine Prose characterizes Oxygen as part of a new "women's culture" (including everything from i-Village to *Bridget Jones' Diary* to *Judging Amy*) that "panders to so-called women's interests—an admittedly narrow range that runs the entire gamut from cosmetics to child care, from personal grooming to personal relationships." She continues by stating that "there's plenty of advice on how to change ourselves—woman by woman, pound by pound, wrinkle by wrinkle—but not a shred of guidance on how to change our situation. Nor is there any suggestion that we might want, or need, to rethink basic issues of power, equity and economics. . . ."[30] Susan Faludi adopts a similar position in a *Newsweek* article by lumping Oxygen Media together with *Sex and the City* and Nike ad campaigns. She critiques these "commercialized feminisms" for "pushing 'happiness'" and claims "the real movement promoted caring, not shopping."[31]

While it is productive for feminists to discuss and evaluate Oxygen in the popular press, it is unfortunate that these high-profile writers overlook recent feminist scholarship on the historical positioning of women as consumers within the public sphere. In some instances, consumer practices such as moviegoing or department-store shopping were an important mechanism of women's socioeconomic mobility and were integral to the formation of female communities and even women's entry into civic/public culture.[32] What is even more disappointing, however, is that this fixation on Oxygen's consumerist address results in a negation of the significance of its technological address—that is, its resourceful use of widely accessible and familiar television technology as a gateway for women and digitally disadvantaged peoples to acquire knowledge of and access to new computer technologies. Oxygen embraces this struggle for technological control as a key dimension of its agenda by plugging itself as "the first and only network to combine advocacy, technology and creativity for a single purpose: releasing the energy of women to do great things."[33] Further, it has partnered with Insight Communications to provide the "young women's technology fellowship" to high school girls in low-income areas. The goal is to "help bridge the digital divide by providing a unique technological education to young women who would not otherwise have the opportunity to participate in such a program."[34] Oxygen's commitment to girls' education in computer technology is further reinforced by its alliance with feminist scholars such as Sherry Turkle, who has examined the gendered dynamics of computer use among girls and boys.[35] These are the untidy byways of what might best be described as corporate feminism: a late capitalist feminism wherein the demand for returns on investments commingles with liberal feminist agendas. Still, we should not entirely overlook the achievements of women's-oriented television networks, even if we remain critical of their corporate logics.

Oxygen Media is only one of several women's-oriented networks to form in the past two decades. Others include the cable channel Lifetime, the Internet start-up iVillage.com, the "omnimedia" venture Martha stewart.com, and most recently WE (Women's Entertainment).[36] The emergence of such networks has resulted in contradictory practices. On the one hand, they mark the possibility of a kind of corporate feminism initiated by liberal feminists who have come into positions of power and authority in the television and high-tech industries during the 1980s and 1990s. Oxygen's executives, for example, grew up in the late 1960s and 1970s in the midst of second-wave feminism. In the 1980s and 1990s they reaped huge financial gains in the television industry as leaders of Carsey Werner Productions (the largest independent television production company and responsible for such shows as *Cosby, Roseanne,* and *Third Rock from the Sun*), Nickelodeon (the first global children's television network), and Harpo Productions (producer of the *Oprah* talk show, films, and television productions, and what was the largest reading club for women in the world). Oxygen's very formation can be seen, then, as the result of strange socioeconomic bedfellows, including the Reagan, Bush, and Clinton administrations' deregulation of the media industries, the growth of family and women's cable television programming, liberal feminist consciousness-raising, nonprofit democratization initiatives, and the emergence of digital technologies.

On the other hand, these women's multimedia networks represent an intensified form of gender commodification as they create distinct brands of femininity and compete for specific women's demographics. Corporate feminism has an ambivalent politics, then, because it involves the production of new technologized spaces for women while (in the vein of flexible microcasting) capitalizing on those spaces as sites of economic exploitation and expansion. A program such as *Oprah Goes Online* may set out to enhance women's computer literacy, but the show, like other commercial programs, is also designed to expand the network's cable and online audience base, attract sponsors, and generate revenue. In this sense Oxygen's convergent formats can be understood as sites where liberal feminism, generational distinctions, and commercial priorities are negotiated to showcase women's mobility at the television/computer interface.

What is perhaps most compelling about Oxygen's version of corporate feminism is its insistence on the possibility of intergenerational practice. Oxygen's baby boomer executives have capitalized (and, of course, want to expand) on their entrepreneurial power in the television industry in order to generate new multimedia spaces and social, cultural, economic, and technological opportunities for women and girls. In pursuing such a strategy, Oxygen has forged economic and social relations among women of different age groups and different social backgrounds as part of the process of building its multimedia network. One reviewer recognizes this intergenerational appeal by noting that "Oxygen offers traditional women's magazine fare, though the titles point toward a younger, hipper demographic. Instead of finance, there's *Ka-ching . . .* For health and fitness, *We Sweat.* Relationship advice comes from *Breakup Girl.*"[37] Although here it is framed in terms of Oxygen's demographic address, the possibility of intergenerational multimedia is especially significant given the tensions that percolated within feminism during the 1990s, which culminated in the need for new terms such as third-wave feminism, postfeminism, and "riot grrrl" feminism.[38] The very emergence of Oxygen can be seen as pushing feminist discourse itself in a variety of new directions, for the network raises key questions about women's access to knowledge about new media technologies, women's corporate power within the entertainment and information economies, and women's intergenerational working partnerships and cultural productions. To be sure, Oxygen's plight to "superserve the needs and interests of women" is certainly worth tracking in the years to come.

Right now, however, executives at Oxygen as well as those at other TV networks have grown increasingly concerned about competition from other online entertainment start-ups, particularly those targeting youth. Companies such as Broadband.com, Heavy.com, Loudtv.com, and Atomfilms.com, for instance, now feature original online audiovisual content and have begun to attract loyal audiences, particularly among Web-savvy and youth demographics. These start-ups tend to position themselves within a framework of cultural reinvention or revolution, rejecting the established institutions of television, seeking new modes of organization, and redefining mediated entertainment. These start-ups challenge network hegemony by claiming to bypass TV altogether and offer quintessentially digital forms of entertainment instead.

THE DEN

Consider, for example, the rise and fall of the Digital Entertainment Network (DEN). While Oxygen was formed through women's success in cable television and syndication, DEN emerged in 1998 as a short-lived Internet start-up spun off of one of the first Internet service providers, Concentric.net. Led by David Neuman, former head of Disney TV, the DEN was one of the first online entertainment companies to design episodic programs for the Web. In 1998 the company launched its Web site as a TV-like network with thirty interactive pilots. Its programs targeted marginalized and underrepresented youth—groups that were rarely (if ever) represented in network television drama. *Tales from the East Side* was a soap opera set in a Hispanic high school in East Los Angeles. *Fear of* a *Punk Planet,* described as the world's first "mosh pit sitcom," focused on a group of punk rock teens trying to keep alive an alternative night club. The *Chang Gang* was described as "an Asian American *X-Files.*" *Redemption High* was a Christian soap opera that explored moral questions faced by teens. Not only did these shows target "fringe" demographics, they openly explored social issues that the Big Three networks tended to avoid, such as hate crime, depression, gang life, gambling, AIDS, transsexuality, eating disorders, and school violence.

Just as gender ideologies inform television's convergence with the Internet, so too do generational distinctions. Neuman went so far as to suggest that the DEN would be "a nurturing force for the self-actualization of Generation Y."[39] The network aggressively pitched its programs to the "Net Generation"—a youth demographic that has grown up with both the Internet and television and is uniquely positioned to contrast and understand the differences between the two mediums. The DEN's executives prided themselves on their radical departure from commercial television. In their mission statement, they defined the online network as "a hip alternative and replacement to the passive, brainkilling experience of watching network and cable television."[40] If MTV revolutionized television during the 1980s, the DEN's executives hoped their network would replace television altogether with a new form they called "infotainment" or "telefusion."[41] As Neuman put it, "Television is where you can't get away with stuff—on the Internet you can." And he continues by stating that "TV is about watering down what's really edgy and cool. The web is the medium of choice for our target demographic."[42] Thus, whereas Oxygen defines itself as ubiquitous as the air, the DEN adopted a quite different strategy, using direct marketing and flexible microcasting to label itself a countercultural space.

While the DEN rejected the "safe" sensibilities of network television, it—like Oxygen—embraced its commercial infrastructure. The DEN Web site was sponsored by such companies as Pepsi, Blockbuster, Microsoft, Ford, and Penzoil, whose tiny animated ads appeared on a banner at the bottom of the splash page. In the "intersodes" (episodes available on the Internet) themselves, users encountered integrated advertisements like those of 1950s TV. Actors in DEN programs occasionally would stop mid-show to endorse a given product, and viewers/users could click on icons to purchase products. In an episode of *Frat Ratz,* for instance, one of the characters is shaving and stops to praise his Schick blade. The programs have also been characterized as "hypermercials" because they were formatted with visual cues that signaled when a product could be purchased.[43] In describing this form of advertising, DEN's CEO Jim Ritts insists, "We can do so much more with product placement in this medium than you could in TV."[44]

One of the distinctions between the DEN and network TV was in scheduling. Rather than creating weekly program schedules like those of the networks, the DEN released six-minute "intersodes" of each series on Sundays at midnight and then made them available on demand at its Web site.[45] Web surfers could watch the DEN's programs whenever they wanted (without ever having to record them) and as often as they liked. The DEN's distribution infrastructure was thus organized according to the "viewing on demand" element of personalized TV. This practice altered television industry practices of licensing and syndication. The online network was conceived of as more of an archive than a schedule, which meant extending viewer access to content. The other primary differences were the short duration of the DEN's shows and their substandard image quality. Because the DEN catered to low bandwidth (56k modem) Web users (which is what most youth were assumed to have had access to), its shows appeared in tiny frames with poor image resolution and sound sync. Although perhaps not ideal, the DEN tried to work within technological and budgetary constraints to create new online entertainment formats that were affordable to produce and accessible to most Web users.

In May 2000, two months after NBC pumped $7 million into the DEN after recognizing its unique potential to reach teens and twenty-somethings, the online network filed bankruptcy and closed down its Web site.[46] There was much speculation in the trade press about the DEN's collapse, especially given its solid financial backing, innovative content, and heavy promotion. For months executives were apparently warned about their hefty payrolls, which included a $1 million salary for President David Neuman and $600,000 for two heads of its music division,[47] and they were also advised to halt lavish spending on their office facilities.[48] Some suggest that it was the DEN's million-dollar mentality (that is, its thoughtless overexpenditures, which were not unique to DEN but rampant in many high-tech companies) that ultimately put the company under. This notion is particularly intriguing given that the DEN's executives insisted that their network was not just another hot high-tech venture but rather one that strived to set a social and cultural agenda.

The DEN constantly tried to distinguish itself by offering alternatives to the "safe" content of network and cable television, but its practices of flexible microcasting represented an intensified form of commercialized media. One review called the DEN an "amazing 21st-century combination of an MTV, a record and video store, QVC, and an entertainment network."[49] Executive David Solomon of DEN claimed that the network's countercultural edge made it qualify as "capitalism with a social conscience."[50] While Oxygen works in part to expand women's access to and knowledge of multimedia, the DEN attempted to address youth in a way that differed from commercial television. It combined practices of direct marketing with the language of a digital counterculture to try to turn a profit and make a social impact. Just as Oxygen participates in the formation of a new kind of corporate feminism and intergenerational women's discourse, the DEN tried to produce a highly commercial yet socially alternative digital youth culture. If the DEN had survived it might have served an important social function, because in the late 1990s and early 2000s American youth seem desperately in need of outlets for sociocultural recognition and expression. This was both exemplified by and resulted from the tragic wave of high school violence in the United States during this period.

Given that the DEN adopted the commercial sponsorship, narrowcasting, and episodic narrative of television, it is ironic that its executives were so quick to condemn the cool medium. What this suggests, however, is that the marketing discourses of online entertainment start-ups are predicated on a critique of television that lay dormant in our culture. The economic viability of the DEN was built on the assumption that youth would want to turn off network and cable TV and turn on the DEN in a search for salient content—that is, content deemed too fringe for broadcast television. This condemnation imagines online entertainment as a more refined practice of microcasting, which becomes a big drawing point for advertisers. But not only did the DEN pinpoint previously ignored niche markets, it seized on a set of broad cultural assumptions about computer and television technologies in its efforts to define itself as "alternative." The DEN contrasted the chaotic indeterminacy of the Web with the rigid conventions of commercial television by reinforcing the myth that the two mediums evolved separately. Rather than recognizing the institutional and textual hybridity of television and the Web, the DEN promoted the notion that television culture is ultimately incompatible with cyberculture.

The DEN's antitelevision rhetoric takes on particular significance in the context of recent high school shootings and the public debates over media violence. Both television and the Internet have been scapegoated as fostering violent behavior. Insofar as television is the more established medium (as well as the more public) it has been the primary target of recent moral panic: instead of contesting discourses of TV violence, the DEN was able to bypass these debates altogether by virtue of its relative invisibility. Because computer technologies are now tied to educational and professional goals, parents often encourage teens to surf the Web while discouraging them from watching television. Quite ironically, then, youth-oriented online portals like the DEN may benefit from the public outcry over TV violence while offering even more explicit representations and direct discussion of teen violence and sexuality.

The DEN might have functioned as a valuable social and cultural space for youth, but its "toss up your hands and walk the other way" attitude toward the medium of television was problematic. It reinforced ideologies that position television as a hopeless and helpless medium, a cultural space of little redeeming value. This is important not only because television is being technologically reconfigured (à la personal TV), but also, and perhaps more important, because television has historically been conceptualized as the culture of housewives and the working classes. Furthermore, just as cable and satellite providers finally begin to package content for ethnic audiences (i.e., BET, Telemundo, etc.), those with class and racial privilege have managed to navigate a path beyond the medium of TV and toward pristine digital pastures. Indeed, television is still imagined as a vast wasteland, especially when contrasted to the tidy labyrinth of the information superhighway. The politics of gender, race, class, and generation are, however, mobilized in various sites of TV-computer convergence ranging from the networks' revival of the quiz show to the programming strategies of Oxygen.com and the DEN. Within each of these instances, cultural assumptions about television and computer technologies emerge. Because of this, it's vital that we understand technological convergence as a set of sociohistorical struggles and economic circumstances rather than as a process of evolution or revolutionary technological progress.

One of the most damaging discourses on television technology has been the "kill your television" bumper sticker displayed since the early 1980s by cultural leftists and environmentalists. One "kill your TV" Web site describes television as "an addictive device which keeps the lower classes subdued," a "perpetuator of violence and materialism," and "a silent destroyer of intellectualism."[51] Although initially intended as a critique and boycott of television's commercial infrastructure, this campaign has discouraged leftist struggles for creative control and social power within the medium of television. The motto "kill your television" plays into the hands of cultural elitists who imagine television, art, and politics as impossible bedfellows. Simply put, we can't afford to kill our televisions. Instead, we need to turn them on, engage with their blue flicker, and talk more about what we want to see. In other words, we need to care enough about television to fight over it, to realize that our creative potential might lay in it. Put another way, if we're really concerned about what the "next generation" of television might look like, we ought to see and imagine ourselves as part of it. Rather than having contempt for the old analog TV set, we should take advantage of this moment of convergence to reevaluate the meanings of television and computers and retool these technologies to satisfy a broader range of democratic impulses.

NOTES

I would like to thank Lynn Spigel, Constance Penley, Anna Everett, Anil de Mello, and Karl Bryant for their critical feedback and helpful suggestions. I also thank Rosi Braidotti, Mischa Peters, Anneke Smelik, and Berteke Waaldjik at the University of Utrecht for helping to catalyze this work as part of our collaborative research on gender, media, and cultural studies.

1. Erik Barnouw, *Tube of Plenty: The Evolution of American Television* (Oxford: Oxford University Press, 1990).

2. Jonathan Taylor, "Television 2.0: Futurecasting the Medium," *Variety,* April 24, 2000, p. 1.

3. TiVo ad, *Wired,* October 1999, pp. 100–101.

4. The model of personalized television intensifies the practice of direct marketing—it enables programmers to deliver accurate counts of audiences to advertisers. Consider, for instance, the merger of Gotcha sportswear, Fox Sports Network, and Broadband Interactive Group. A program called Gotcha TV airs on Fox Sports from 4 to 5 P.M. on weekdays and is projected to have an audience of sixty-eight million viewers. Many companies began transforming their products into mediated forms with the rise of cable television. This not only relates to the increase in infomercials but also to the ways in which the fashion, tourist, food, and home/garden industries have effectively used cable television to transform products into streams of programming and lifestyles on HGTV, Style, the Travel Channel, and the Food Network, among other channels.

5. In industry discussions of personal television, the terms "program diversity" and "expanded viewer choice" frequently emerge. For a thorough discussion of this issue in relation to industry discourses on cable television, see Thomas Streeter's *Selling the Air: A Critique of the Policy of Commercial Broadcasting in the United States* (Chicago: University of Chicago Press, 1996).

6. Raymond Williams, *Television: Technology and Cultural Form* (New York: Schocken, 1974). Also see Joseph Corner, *Critical Ideas in Television Studies* (New York: Oxford University Press, 1999).

7. Lynn Spigel, "Portable TV: Studies in Domestic Space Travels," in *Welcome to the Dreamhouse: Popular Media and Postwar Suburbs* (Durham: Duke University Press, 2001), pp. 60–103.

8. Forrester research projects 34 percent of Internet users will have broadband access by 2002. In 1999 only 6 percent of users had broadband access (Stacy Lawrence, "Streaming Media Numbers Start to Flow," *Industry Standard,* December 21, 1999), http://www.thestandard.com.

9. Marc Graser, "AOL TV Leads Race in Interactive Interfaces," *Variety,* April 24, 2000, p. 9.

10. This strategy of branding has become very important as multimedia mergers try to cultivate specialized audiences for direct marketing. This process did not just emerge with the Internet, however. Cable television has been narrowcasting for over a decade. This strategy was key to the formation and success of the Fox Network during the late 1980s and early 1990s. By 2000, WB (with its prime-time lineup aimed at the echo boomers) and UPN (with its nightly WWF programming to capture the young male demographic) have followed suit. These three newer networks have used narrowcasting to challenge the hegemony of the networks. It is likely that online entertainment companies seeking television viewers will use a similar strategy.

11. "NBC Launches Its First Public Internet Company," NBCi press release, November 30, 1999, http://www.nbcinternet.com/PR113099-1.html.

12. In 1998 NBC experimented with an interactive online version of *Homicide: Life on the Street,* but has since removed it from the network's Web site. To direct viewers to its Web site, ABC has aired Web simulcasts of *The Drew Carey Show* and *Good Morning America.* The latter program conducted a "cave" experiment in which two young adults were asked to live in empty apartments for a week and try to furnish them by ordering everything online. For the most part, however, the networks have not been focused on the development of interactive programming but rather on the acquisition of online domains.

13. William Boddy, *Fifties Television: The Industry and Its Critics* (Urbana: University of Illinois Press, 1990).

14. The genre is also notorious for showing "ordinary people" climbing to success by working through challenging tests of knowledge. As John Fiske suggests, the quiz show uses knowledge to "separate out winners from losers and to ground the classification in individual or natural differences" (Fiske, *Television Culture* [London: Methuen, 1987], pp. 267–68).

15. The questions were so easy, in fact, that one insurance company refused to provide liability insurance.

16. Olaf Hoerschelman, "Quiz and Game Shows," Museum of Broadcasting online, http://www.mbcnet.org/etv/q/htmlq/quizandgame/quizandgame.htm.

17. Lisa de Moraes, "Black and White Viewers Are More in Tune in Top 20," *Washington Post,* February 13, 2001, p. C1.

18. See Lynne Joyrich, *Re-Viewing Reception: Television, Gender, and Postmodern Culture* (Bloomington: Indiana University Press, 1996).

19. Ellen Seiter, "Television and the Internet," in *Electronic Media and Technoculture,* ed. John Thornton Caldwell (New Brunswick: Rutgers University Press, 2000), p. 241.

20. Donna Haraway, "A Cyborg Manifesto: Science, Technology, and Socialist-

Feminism in the Late Twentieth Century," in *Simians, Cyborgs, and Women* (New York: Routledge, 1991), pp. 149–82.

21. Marshall McLuhan, *Understanding Media: The Extensions of Man* (New York: Signet, 1969).

22. See http://www.oxygen.com. This section stems from my work in a collaborative research project with Constance Penley and Anna Everett called the Oxygen Media Research Project, which is headquartered at the Department of Film Studies at the University of California at Santa Barbara and involves reseachers from the University of Utrecht and the University of Southern Denmark. For further information, see the project Web site, http://www.hydrogenmedia.ucsb.edu.

23. Diane Anderson, "Advertising: Girls Play with the Big Boys," *Industry Standard,* February 17, 2000, http://www.thestandard.com.

24. Paula Bernstein, "Cox Will Inhale Oxygen Carriage," *Daily Variety,* March 17, 2000, n.p.; Courtney Macavinta, "Oxygen: Women at Center of Convergence," CNET News .com, April 27, 1999, http://www.news.com/specialfeatures/0.5.35693.00.html.

25. Bill Carter, "Oxygen Media to Eliminate 10% of Its Jobs," *New York Times,* December 6, 2000, p. c6.

26. "First New Series from Oprah Winfrey and 1 Million New Subscribers Mark Oxygen's First Anniversary," *Business Wire,* February 6, 2001; "DIRECT TV Picks Up Oxygen Media TV Network," *Business Wire,* March 20, 2000. All available at http://live.alta vista.com/scripts/editorial.dll?ei =1612018&ern=y.

27. Paula Parisi, "Hollywood 3.0," *Wired,* October 1998, n.p.; Jefferson Graham, "Much-hyped Oxygen Hits Air, Net," *USA Today,* February 21, 2000, n.p.

28. "A Kinder, Gentler Multimedia," *Wired,* July 28, 1999, pp. 22–23. See Markle Foundation mission statement at http://www.markle.org.

29. Judy DeMocker, "Ladies' Home Internet," *Wired News,* August 10, 1999, http://www .wired.com/news/culture/story/15090.html; "A Kinder, Gentler Multimedia," *Wired News* July 28, 1999, http://www.wired.com/news/news/story/20971/html; "Sugar Daddy Replenishes Oxygen," *Industry Standard,* December 11, 2000, http://www .thestandard.com.

30. Francine Prose, "A Wasteland of One's Own," *New York Times Magazine,* February 13, 2000, p. 68.

31. Susan Faludi, "Don't Get the Wrong Message," *Newsweek,* January 8, 2001, p. 56.

32. See, for instance, Kathy Peiss, *Hope in a Jar: The Making of America's Beauty Culture* (New York: Owl Books, 1999); Shelley Stamp, *Move-Struck Girls* (Princeton: Princeton University Press, 2000); Hilary Radner, *Shopping Around: Feminine Culture and the Pursuit of Pleasure* (New York: Routledge, 1995); Rachel Bowlby, *Carried Away: The Invention of Modern Shopping* (New York: Columbia University Press, 2001); and Erika Rappaport, *Shopping for Pleasure* (Princeton: Princeton University Press, 1999).

33. Cited in Prose, "Wasteland," p. 68.

34. Jim Forkan, "Insight, Oxygen Target Digital Divide," *Multichannel News,* January 8, 2001, p. 24. The fellowship will be offered to twelve to fifteen students in Louisville high schools to pay for a two-month after-school program in which girls learn how to use computers and create their own Web pages.

35. Sherry Turkle sits on the advisory board of Oxygen/Pulse, an initiative funded by the Markle Foundation to determine women's opinions about political, social, and technological issues. Turkle is the author of *The Second Self: Computers and the Human Spirit* (New York: Simon and Schuster, 1983) and *Life on the Screen: Identity in the Age of the Internet* (New York: Touchstone Books, 1997).

36. Martha Stewart described her empire in print, on television, and online as an economic strategy called "omnimedia" in a 1999 interview on *Larry King Live*. For a thorough discussion of Lifetime, see *Camera Obscura*, no. 33–34 (Fall 1995). This is a special issue of the journal devoted to Lifetime and edited by Julie D'Acci.

37. Elizabeth Weise, "Oxygenating the Women's Market," *USA Today*, February 3, 2000, http://www.usatoday.com/life/cyber/tech/neto01.htm.

38. For a discussion of these issues, see Leslie Heywood and Jennifer Drake, eds., *Third Wave Agenda: Being Feminist, Doing Feminism* (Minneapolis: University of Minnesota Press, 1997); and Tania Modleski, *Feminism without Women* (New York: Routledge, 1991).

39. Neuman, quoted in David A. Keeps, "Laptop TV," *Details*, September 1999, p. 21.

40. Leslie Walker, "Generation Y Gets the Hard Sell," *Washington Post*, September 30, 1999, http://www.den.net/coolnew/about/pring/1,5817,,00.html?page=washingtonpost.

41. Matt Richtel, "Youthful Web Network Has a Modest Goal: Replacing TV," *New York Times*, June 24, 1999, sec. G, p. 7.

42. Neuman, quoted in Lessley Anderson, "Ex-TV Execs and Animators Turn to the Web," *Industry Standard*, April 6, 1999, http://www4.cnn.com/tech/computing/9904/06/enterweb.idg/.

43. For instance, one can rewind a hip-hop song and order it, or click on a dress and buy it in different colors.

44. Walker, "Generation Y Gets the Hard Sell."

45. The possibility of downloading past episodes radically reconfigures current syndication practices. The DEN produces, distributes, and exhibits its series, suggesting a trend toward vertical integration in online entertainment. By shooting on film rather than digital video, and on location rather than on sets, each show costs about $10,000 to produce and requires fifty-thousand viewers online to make a show financially viable (David A. Keeps, "Laptop TV," *Details*, September 1999, p. 21).

46. Corey Grice, "NBC Takes Stake in Teen Site DEN," *CNET News.com*, March 1, 2000.

47. Ronald Grover, "Digital Entertainment Network: Hard Steps Forward?" *Business Week Online Daily Briefing*, February 11, 2000, http://www.businessweek.com/bwdaily/dnflash/feb2000/nf00211i.htm.

48. "DEN Tells Staff It's Out of Money," CNET News.com, May 18, 2000.

49. Nicole Powers, "WEB: Digital Entertainment Network," *Urb*, September 11, 1999, http://www.den.net/coolnew/about/print/1,5817,,00html?page=urb.

50. Solomon, quoted in Matt Richtel, "Youthful Web Network Has a Modest Goal: Replacing TV," *New York Times*, June 24, 1999, sec. G., p. 7.

51. For a sense of their positions, see the "Kill Your Television.org" Web site at http://www.killyourtelevision.org/html/streets.html, or the "Kill Your TV" Web site at http://othello.localaccess.com/hardebeck/default.htm.

PART TWO

TECHNOLOGY, SOCIETY,

AND CULTURAL FORM

The essays in this section examine how television's traditional cultural form (i.e., national broadcasting transmitted primarily to audiences at home) has changed over the course of the last fifty years. The authors of these essays particularly concentrate on the social contexts for media innovation, reception, and spectatorship, as well as on the way people use television and new media for social contact and communication. Several authors explore how audiences perceive television in the everyday places of late capitalism—including both the digitized domicile and public settings that are increasingly saturated with electronic screens. Other authors concentrate on the prospects of democratic communication in a world where technologies of electronic media (both the traditional forms of broadcasting and the emerging digital media) offer new opportunities and new obstacles.

The first two essays concentrate on the changing cultural forms of television reception with respect to broader changes in the patterns of culture and everyday life. In "Television's Next Generation: Technology/Interface Culture/Flow" William Uricchio reengages Raymond Williams's seminal concept of "flow" to consider three moments of television technology and their preferred styles of audience reception (the living console, the remote control, and the present-day digital, or "smart," TV services like TiVo). Uricchio argues that these different technological forms relate to different relationships between the industry and the audience over the course of time. He questions the degree to which Williams's concept of flow still applies to our present-day sentient TV sets, and he considers how we might better explain television's contemporary technological and cultural forms.

Anna McCarthy's "The Rhythms of the Reception Area: Crisis, Capitalism, and the Waiting Room TV" considers the corporatization of daily life through a case study of television's uses in public spaces, especially spaces of waiting such as doctor's offices, train terminals, and airports. McCarthy argues that while television scholars have focused primarily on domestic reception, we need more fully to consider the public uses of television and what these uses mean for the experience of public life itself. Using insights from sociological studies on waiting, McCarthy demonstrates how the corporate sector (ranging from health care professionals to transportation companies) has produced promotional videos/laser discs for places in which people routinely wait for service. She then considers how television time (TV's temporal/narrative unfolding) helps to produce the spatial experience of "publicness" in contemporary capitalist cultures. She argues that debates over the changing nature of public space might thus benefit greatly from a closer engagement with television studies.

The next two essays consider how new media technologies will or will not affect democratic communication and the creation of an electronic public sphere. Jostein Gripsrud's "Broadcast Television: The Chances of Its Survival in a Digital Age" draws on Raymond Williams's account of broadcasting and its cultural form to evaluate the social impact of new digital communications. A polemical and speculative account, the essay cautions us against the utopian rhetoric of "revolution" that promoters of new media use to describe our digital futures. Instead, he contends that the corporate control of these media will determine their social trajectories. The discourse of choice, interactivity, and individual power surrounding new media, he argues, is mostly hype. He shows instead how corporations are attempting to standardize text/viewer relations within the logic of global capitalism. In the end, he sees television studies as a necessary tool for policy formation that might help to mitigate against the corporate control of media and public culture more generally. For Gripsrud, European models of national public service broadcasting still provide the best hope for democratic communication.

Moving from public service models of broadcasting to the commercial system in the United States, Anna Everett comes to different conclusions. "Double Click: The Million Woman March on Television and the Internet" is a case study of the future of black women's political struggle via new media. Everett shows how the Internet forms a space of alternative community for people who are underrepresented and misrepresented in mainstream media; in this case Everett also demonstrates how the Internet's electronic "imagined communities" are socially mobilized for political protest in the material world of the streets. Specifically, the essay looks at the Million Woman March and the television networks' lack of news coverage on the event. Everett explores the way black women organized the march by strategically deploying the Internet (as well as camcorders) in the face of the disinterest exhibited by traditional broadcast journalists. She argues that black women's use of the Internet as an organizational tool for urban protest demonstrates their understanding of the "racialized hegemony" of traditional news media and their refusal to be reduced to what Paolo Carpignano terms television news' "edited public." In the end, Everett shows that as a cultural form the Internet provides new opportunities for publics to gather, not just online but in offline communities.

WILLIAM URICCHIO

TELEVISION'S NEXT GENERATION:

TECHNOLOGY/INTERFACE CULTURE/FLOW

Like many people in my profession I spend a lot of time traveling and thus in hotels, and for me, at any rate, one of the pleasures of this nomadic life is television. Besides my sense of amazement at the clever disguising of the television set into furniture forms of uncertain stylistic reference, I am fascinated by the many capacities of hotel television systems. During a stay at the Marriott in Cambridge, my television offered such features as interactive messaging, account updates, nearly forty films on demand, and Sony PlayStation, in addition to cable television and both closed-circuit and cable teletext systems. Simply turning on the television provoked a staggering array of decisions regarding language, services, and menu options, all of which had to be dealt with if one wanted to watch television in any of its forms.

The conception of television involved here rubs against the grain of the work I've been doing on early conceptions of the televisual, conceptions that in their nineteenth-century embodiments rendered the appearance of the film medium as something of a disappointment.[1] Simultaneity, I argue, was one of the long-anticipated but ultimately suppressed or bypassed defining characteristics of a medium of "far seeing," a medium more dependent than photography or film on the camera obscura (a metaphor, it should be recalled, with temporal as well as spatial dimensions). This notion of simultaneity was bound up with the idea of connectivity, with extending the boundaries of event and the direct access of the viewing public to it. The idea of the medium, explicitly invoked in terms like "television" and the German word for television, *Fernsehen*, was about the extension of vision in real time.[2] And it is this aspect that in my larger project I've been trying to trace through its many permutations to things like Web-cam sites or Nokia's next generation of mobile telephones.

But hotel television (and the sometimes late nights spent interacting with it) became for me something of a devil's advocate, provoking reconsideration of my research assumptions. The nature of the provocation resonated with images of Raymond Williams, sacked out in his own hotel room in Miami after his long transatlantic crossing, watching a heavy dose of defamiliarized (read American) television.[3] Williams was struck by the seamless flow of American programming, by the strategies that transformed the diverse program elements into a whole. My experience certainly differed from the British broadcasting that Williams had seen, but more significantly it differed dramatically from an earlier generation's ideas of how the medium would function. Having said this, although concepts such as generational distinction offer a heuristic advantage that I will exploit in this essay, it is important to remember that the realities of generational overlap and plurality complicate the lived experiences of television. Williams, for example, commented on the limited persistence of an older notion of programming (in which mix, proportion, and balance still operated), which coexisted along with the more dominant idea of flow.[4] But the heuristic of generational distinction will dominate the pages that follow.

I would like here to explore a particular aspect of television, namely the changing viewer interface with the medium, and pursue some of its implications. The issue is generational in the sense that television's technology, its program access capacities, and its patterns of user interaction have appeared as clustered relationships. These constellations have changed significantly over the years, as evidenced in the space between the idea of direct connectivity so much a part of nineteenth-century television conceptions and the Marriott's elaborate sequence of choices and schedule of movies (or what the trade journals call "near video") on demand. The notion of flow, one of the most developed discursive strands in television studies, touches directly on this point. Flow is obviously a loaded term. Closely associated with Raymond Williams's 1974 groundbreaking contribution to the study of television, the concept has gone on to support very different arguments, and in the process it has helped both to chart shifts in the identity of television as a cultural practice and to map various undulations in the terrain of television studies. It has been deployed perhaps most consistently in the service of defining a televisual "essence" (adhering to Williams's description of flow as "perhaps the defining characteristic of broadcasting, simultaneously as technology and as a cultural form").[5] It has been used to describe the structure of textuality and programming on macro, meso, and micro levels (e.g., Williams's long-range, medium-range, and close-range analyses). It has given form to the viewing experience, serving as a framework within which reception can be understood (variously activated in terms of larger household regimes and the logics of meaning making). And, as Michael Curtin argues in this volume, it can describe the movement of transnational programming.

Williams's formulation and application of the concept is at once evocative and precise, theoretically diffused and carefully (if not completely convincingly) applied and tested. The concept's power and longevity owes as much to this dynamic and shadowy definition as to its descriptive power for the ever-slippery identity of television. Despite its continued (if more muted) invocation, the concept of flow is perhaps most important for the debate and theorization it has provoked. Scholars including John Ellis, Jane Feuer, Rick Altman, John Fiske, John Hartley, Richard Dienst, Klaus Bruhn Jensen, Jostein Gripsrud, and John Corner have all in various ways challenged the operations that Williams sought to describe, in the process contributing to the formation of a discursive field.[6] However, my point in this essay is not to retrace the genealogy of the term, but rather to reposition flow as a means of sketching out a series of fundamental shifts in the interface between viewer and television, and thus in the viewing experience.

A word is perhaps necessary here about the implications of the changes in television's technology, programming, interfaces, expectations, and so forth, some of which this paper will touch on. From its start, television has been a transient and unstable medium, as much for the speed of its technological change as for the process of its cultural transformation, for its ephemeral present, and for its mundane everydayness. While this has always been television's fate, the present day's convergent technologies, economies, and textual networks have not only subverted many of the assumptions that have until now driven the logics of television but have also transformed the medium's context and cultural place.[7] Stephen Heath has put it as follows: "One of the main difficulties in approaching television is the increasing inadequacy of existing terms and standards of analysis, themselves precisely bound up with a specific regime of representation, a certain coherence of object and understanding in a complex of political-social-individual meaning."[8]

Although Heath's observation can arguably be extended to other media systems, television does seem to have more than its share of identity problems. Caught between the "taken-for-granted-ness" associated with a long-domesticated audiovisual delivery system and the recurrent innovation and sometimes radical redefinition that seems emblematic of its technical and expressive capacities, television's identity is a highly unstable affair. This is not to deny that a certain coherence of object and understanding exists, but rather to suggest that it is the coherence of generation, of clustered expectations, technological capacities, and daily practices. While one would want to insist on the fullest sense of Heath's "regime of representation" and within it include technical expectations, institutional systems, and individual practices, the question of how to deal with a dynamic transgenerational medium remains. From this perspective, the relatively little attention directed toward television's history is not only remarkable but ultimately disempowering. It tends to reinforce the "taken-for-granted-ness" of generational coherence and elide the very dynamic that may in the end be a crucial component of the medium's identity and thus the terms and standards of its analysis.

In this sense, flow is a particularly useful term. Not only does the history of its deployment map the development of an academic field, but it also illuminates the clustered experiences of the medium, the generational vision of television. Thus the term will serve as my entry point.

FLOW

Let us return to Williams, dazed after his transatlantic crossing and a strong dose of Miami television. By March 1973, Williams was in San Francisco, where he began a systematic study of his impressions of American television and of flow in particular. What sort of television did he experience? Several measures of the period's television environment offer an insight. In 1973, the United States had a total of 927 VHF and UHF television stations, whereas cable subscriptions were relatively low (the first available data on cable are for 1978 and indicate 13 million cable households, or 17.7 percent of the market).[9] Yet both measures would enjoy rapid development in the years to come, with household cable subscriptions increasing by nearly 350 percent within the next ten years and VHF and UHF stations nearly doubling within the next twenty years. Not only did cable households grow, but so too did the number of channels provided on cable systems. In 1983, 22 percent of cable subscribers had fewer than thirteen channels available—a number that dropped to zero percent within ten years, by which point over 97 percent had over thirty channels. Video cassette recorders also changed the television environment. Four years *after* the publication in 1974 of Williams's *Television: Technology and Cultural Form,* Nielsen estimated a VCR household penetration rate of 0.3 percent with 402,000 VCRs in place. By 1984, 10.6 percent of the market had been penetrated, and by 1994 well over 80 percent had been reached.

Thus in March 1973, Williams would have experienced a form of television largely dependent on limited VHF and UHF transmissions. Although I have not checked the period's broadcast schedules for San Francisco or Miami, we can reasonably assume that he had something like five or possibly six channels available and no cable or VCR. Moreover, it seems unlikely that he had access to a remote control device.[10] Williams experienced a historically specific form of television that included the final days of the "Big Three" hegemony in the United States. In this sense, he was privileged to participate in (and thus write about) a particular generational experience, a distinct clustering of technologies and practices. Months before Williams's arrival, the Federal Communications Commission issued several important guidelines that, while protective of established interests, opened the door for a fundamental reordering of the broadcasting environment that would take place shortly after Williams's departure. New regulations for the diffusion of cable service in urban areas, coupled with guidelines for cable operators as distributors and producers of programming, transformed cable from a community service into a business. Moreover, these developments served as a testament to the cable industry's growing political influence.[11] In 1972, the Domestic Communication Satellite rules allowed private satellite distribution, thereby ending the monopoly of the Communications Satellite Corporation.[12] This change allowed the interconnection of distribution points and linkage with nationwide cable systems without the prohibitive expense of AT&T's land lines or Comsat's service. Time Incorporated's Home Box Office, Ted Turner's Atlanta independent WTCG, and Pat Robertson's Christian Broadcasting Network, to mention but three of the cable operators that would expanded exponentially in the late 1970s and early 1980s, were spawned by these regulatory changes.

Appropriately, the discussion of flow in Williams's *Television* falls within a chapter titled "Programming: Distribution and Flow," attesting to Williams's notion of the term as primarily textual. Flow as programming strategy, as the purposeful linkage of variously scaled textual units in order to avoid ruptures, is what Williams attempts to demonstrate in his long-range, medium-range, and close-range analysis of American and British television. But Williams's ideas need little elaboration here because they are so lucidly presented in his book. Here I wish to situate them and then point to the dynamic of their transformation.

Just as Williams's notion of flow needs to be situated within a particular technological, regulatory, and cultural moment, the changing status of the term, and particularly the criticism it generated, needs to be seen against the changing "regime of representations" of television offered by expanded broadcast channels, cable programming, and the VCR. The growing abundance of televisual material, the ability introduced by the VCR to time shift and zip through advertisements, and the ability through the remote control to zap ads in real-time television all inexorably altered the notion of the televisual, situating to some extent scholarly critiques of Williams's notion of flow. This is neither to trivialize nor undermine the important work of the scholars involved, but rather to situate it within a particular televisual order and to suggest that these perceptions owe something to the ongoing technological redefinition of the medium. This technological transformation, at any rate, is something that I am acutely aware of as I read Williams's words and those of his commentators, because I can attribute many critical insights not only to the accumulated wisdom that is our field but to the very different construction (or generations) of television that I take for granted.

DISRUPTION

If there is any one apparatus that emblematizes the generation of televisual interface that would follow on Williams's heels, it is the remote control device (RCD). As I've indirectly suggested, it stands in synergetic relation to the increase in broadcast channels, the availability of cable service, and the introduction of the VCR by serving to facilitate mobility among the "older" broadcast forms and the "newer" programming sources and by enabling the viewer to move among program forms with considerable ease. Most important, it signals a shift away from the programming-based notion of flow that Williams documented to a viewer-centered notion.

The now ubiquitous RCD device has a history that goes back to late-1920s radio applications, from which point it had a long evolution through cable- and motor-driven connections (Tun-o-Magic, Remot-o-Matic, Zenith's Lazy-Bones) to light-driven models (Zenith's Flash-Matic) to the remarkable wireless and batteryless television RCDs of the 1950s (Zenith's Space Command) to radio-frequency driven and, finally, coded infrared devices.[13] The annals of RCD history are cluttered with anecdotes that help to account for this seemingly endless process of technological innovation. Consider the problem of radio-frequency RCDS inadvertently controlling televisions within a several-hundred-foot radius, or that of RCD-equipped pranksters roaming the streets and wreaking havoc on unsuspecting television viewers by changing their channels or volume level. Each new means of extending the viewer's control seemed to entail unwanted side effects or else whet the appetite for new types of control. There is much to be said about the development of remote control—about the various constructions of interaction of the RCD (from simple on/off commands to GE's "Homenet" device that could control lights, lock doors, and start the oven); about the magic of their names; and about their promotional strategies, promises, and visions of "future" television.

For the purposes of the argument at hand, what I find curious are the recurrent tales of disruption and their status as countertext to the promises of enhanced control that inscribed the RCD in popular discourse and advertisements. Although RCDS had a somewhat marginalized presence in many of the advertisements I've seen, they nevertheless were associated with advances in tuning and control and, of course, with luxury, given their extra cost. Their nominal and visual associations resonated with a larger discourse of remote control systems for warfare, airplanes, garage doors, and various home control systems, and they were positioned somewhere between space-age ambitions and the mundane aspirations expressed by an article in *Family Handyman:* "Let electronic slaves do your bidding."[14]

Control, however, is rarely a widely agreed-on concept: one person's control can be another's disruption. Indeed, a major strand of RCD research considers the implications of the device in collective-viewing situations, most often the family. The data suggest that "even in the mundane, joint, leisure activity of watching television," significant evidence of frustration and stereotypical notions of gender through the exercise of power can be found in RCD control and use.[15] Indeed, some evidence suggests that the frustration levels are sufficiently high such that rituals of domination and power routinely take form around RCD use, leading to predictable discord. Research in this vein resonates well with the previously mentioned notions of disruption to the home viewing environment, as families with radio-controlled RCDS and their neighbors discovered or as gangs of RCD-toting youth and their unwitting victims experienced. The social dynamics in each case differed, but disruption through a technology of control was the same.

But as troubling (or insight-giving) as these domestic cases might have been, the public battle over control and its evil twin, disruption, played out with particular force over a different issue. The ability of the RCD to silence advertising by muting the sound, and ultimately its ability to switch away from it altogether by changing channels or turning off the set, was a site of enormous anxiety for the industry because of the implications for the logics of commercial television. But from the public's perspective, such uses were precisely the point of the new control promised by the RCD. By 1955, articles began to appear in the mainstream press with titles such as "Shoots the TV Commercial: Flashbeam to Turn the Set On or Off," "Don't Just Sit There! Reach for the Switch!," and "TV Commercial Silence."[16] Indeed, in the first half of the 1960s the popular press was as likely to call the RCD a "television silencer" as anything else.[17] Such sentiments, at least in the United States, were nothing new, with *Reader's Digest* offering tips as early as 1953 on non-RCD ways of stopping objectionable television advertisements;[18] but the RCD gave households a semblance of direct control over their viewing experience that terrified advertisers and the broadcasting industry. The result was a series of studies that on the one hand shed light on the particular concerns of the industry but on the other was largely inconclusive, owing to disagreement about standards of RCD activity and research methodology.[19] Despite these extremely interesting attempts to pathologize "disruption" (in this case, viewer control), even before the RCD became a widespread household item it was associated with the strategic interruption of programming, whether "silencing" advertisements, turning the set off, or switching to an alternate channel. Increased programming options only served to throw the weight to this latter option.

The intrusion of the RCD threatened to disrupt more than advertisements. The program-based flow that Williams had experienced and that formed the original meaning of television flow was disrupted as well. Not only was it part of a constellation of technologies and practices that offered extensive program choice, but it also facilitated program change with the mere touch of a button. And, at its most fundamental, it signaled a shift from Williams's idea of flow to flow as a set of choices and actions initiated by the viewer. This shift had implications that went far beyond textual issues. As noted, the ease with which viewers could subvert the programming strategies to which Williams had called attention resulted in something just short of a panic among broadcasters and advertisers because it directly challenged the logic of the ratings system so central to the American industry. Companies such as Nielsen played a major role in studies of RCD distribution and use, but the company was (and continues to be) reluctant to take the "problem" of the zapper into its program ratings calculations, as evidenced by the continued reliance of its evaluation system on viewing numbers organized around programs and fixed-time increments. This framework is the outcome of decades of fine-tuning the balance between the divergent interests of advertisers and broadcasters, and it stands as a remarkable anachronism in an environment characterized by an ever-multiplying array of programming options and the twitchy finger of the zapper. But explicitly acknowledged or not, the RCD was a "subversive technology" that demonstrated from its start that viewers had the ability to disrupt program flow and thus the economic flow so central to commercial television. At the same time, a new conception of viewer-dominated flow took hold.

Curiously, a certain ambivalence pervades descriptions of the audiences who made the transition from programming-centered to viewer-activated notions of flow. Consider the term "couch potato," which, according to the U.S. trademark registration, was first used shortly after America's bicentennial, on July 15, 1976.[20] Deployed three years after Williams's visit to America, the term originally seemed to describe that segment of the population that regularly shared his Miami viewing experience, a public caught up in the program flow that the Big Three had refined to an art. But despite the date of its introduction, the term only entered widespread currency ten years later, between 1985 and 1986, by which point nearly half the U.S. households used cable, 30 percent were equipped with VCRs and up to half with RCDs.[21] This crucial span of ten years attests to the ambivalence between programming-centered and viewer-centered notions of flow, both covered by the term. On one hand seemingly passive, drawn from one time block to the next, the consummate *television* viewer, the couch potato seemed to be the perfect target of the program-driven notion of flow. On the other hand, armed with a television RCD, a VCR, a VCR RCD, a stack of tapes, and a cable television guide, the couch potato as active zapper and zipper engaged in viewing activities that were highly mobile and unpredictable, thus embodying a viewer-side notion of flow. The term thus seems to have fallen out of contemporary use, perhaps because of this ambivalence. Or perhaps it is due to a change in metaphors (the distinction between "sit back" technologies such as television and "lean forward" technologies such as the computer). Or perhaps it relates in some way to the penetration for the broader public of the active audience theories associated with cultural studies (theories themselves to an extent coincidental with the increase of RCD use). Or perhaps it is due to the qualitative increase in options for control that are characteristic of the late 1980s. Whatever the reason, the larger point is about the subtle but important shift in the concept of flow away from programming strategies toward viewer-determined experience.

THE PRESENT AS INTERMEZZO

Over the past decade, the televisual landscape has been gradually changing in ways that bear on the medium's textuality and viewers' interface with it. Yet the most evident of these changes—for example, the interactivity introduced by video games or the explosion of television channels and services promised by digital compression technologies—may not be the most interesting or determining in terms of viewer-medium relations. I will argue, in fact, that the most fundamental transformation of that relationship can be found with the application of metadata systems and filtering technologies to the process of program selection. But first, the obvious developments.

Consider the dramatic changes to the idea of television—at least for a certain age cohort—introduced by Nintendo, Sony PlayStation, Microsoft, and other providers of video games. These program systems have established new patterns of interaction with the "device formerly known as television" along with a new constellation of cultural icons. While many of us might beg the question, pointing to divergent uses of video display (surveillance, medical applications) and distinguishing them from television, it's not clear that the users of home video games are so scrupulous or theoretically consequent. Indeed, the point is precisely that increasing user-side familiarity with "television" as a platform for interactive gaming necessarily transforms the same users' notions of "ordinary" television programming. As the game-playing cohort comes of age and enters the sights of mainstream program marketers, we will surely see the results in both technological and textual realms. And while the implications of this are bound to be profound (on the levels of program interactivity and textual uniqueness, thus posing new threats to the collective experience once entailed by the term "broadcasting"),[22] the interface they provide remains conceptually linked to the RCD in the sense that both rely on viewer-steered interactions. Viewers will continue to make conscious choices within certain fixed program parameters, and some sort of manual interface, be it a joystick or control module, will continue to provide the means for those choices.

Digital television services will almost certainly include interactive games in their program packages (something readily available in many hotel television services). But continued advances on the compression front and the increasing presence of optical fiber in the cable infrastructure have combined to open the way for a widely hyped environment of five hundred to two thousand channels. What precisely this environment will look like is uncertain, but as early as 1993 television executives like Ajit Davi (Cox Cable), who had a rather conservative six-hundred-channel scenario, suggested a process of segmentation that would include:

- A 100-channel grazing zone made up of present-day broadcast and cable feeds;
- A 200-channel quality zone offering two extra channels in support of the grazing zone and including the possibility for replays;
- A 50-channel pay-per-view (PPV) event zone;
- And a 250-channel near-video-on-demand (VOD) zone.[23]

While at least in Davi's forecast personal messaging and billing were not part of television, his vision was simply a quantitative extension of currently existing hotel television. To be sure, the quantitative enhancement of programming choices will intensify a series of strategies that analysts have already described in the medium's present-day organization under the rubric of "survival strategies." Especially at this historical moment, when the industry is embedded in a particular televisual order and seems to be about to break out of it in various ways, thinking about how best to cope with the new possibilities (and still maximize profits) seems to be conflicted. (Indeed, such discursive conflict is the allure of media in transition.)

In terms of programming strategies, the starting point is that increased program availability will only intensify the choices of the active zapper, and thus a battery of weapons have been developed to stabilize her or his viewing habits.[24] Producers, advertisers, and programmers seem to be redoubling their efforts to maximize something like Williams's notion of flow in its most literal sense, linking program units in such a way as to maximize continued viewing. Time-tested programming techniques such as a strong lead-in with a highly rated program at the start of a time block, or the hammock (packaging of a new or weak entry between two strong ones), or stacking series of the same or similar genre to minimize disruptions can all be expected to intensify. Indeed, stacking has become the channel identity strategy of many cable outlets, as evidenced by Animal Planet, the History Channel, and the Cartoon Network. Perhaps more interesting are the continuity strategies evident in techniques such as reworking end or opening credits (dropping theme songs, superimposing credits over the opening of the narrative, using outtakes or an epilogue to hold viewers to the end of the slot); using "hot starts" (where a new program begins without an advertising buffer between it and the preceding program); sharpening program hooks before ad breaks by showing previews of the following sequence; using pre-grazed programs (sports summaries, for example); and local fine-tuning of the program mix.

Of course, larger issues such as a reworking of program economics through low-cost programming (reality television and game shows) and economic convergence (permitting a greater number of channels to fall under the interest of a smaller number of organizations) have obviously also been responses to the new television environment (and the perceived threats that it entails). In this latter case, the threats posed by an ever-more fragmented array of channel choices are countered by systematic investment in multiple channels (as embodied by Ted Turner's empire, ranging from various news channels to classic film channels to an array of highly specialized niche-market channels for airport lounges and doctors' waiting rooms), and in cross-media ownership (for example, the recent merger of Time Warner–CNN and AOL). The point throughout is that these broadcast strategies are intensifying as the competition for steady viewers heats up.

The pressures of increased program availability seem likely to intensify the use of these strategies, and although textual transformations will doubtless continue to evolve, as suggested by the video game sector, the fundamental tensions we have thus far seen between program-based and viewer-based notions of flow remain unchanged. The present as intermezzo? At least regarding the well-hyped developments in interactivity and greatly increased program access, the interface between program and viewer remains conceptually within the horizon of expectations established by mid-1980s RCD culture. The next act is about to follow.

THE TELEVISION FAIRY AND ITS RELATIVES

A black-box technology for the family television set managed to spark controversy in several European countries thanks to its ability to perceive specific program forms (advertisements) and textual elements (sex and violence). The box, marketed under the name of the Television Fairy (the *Fernsehfee* in Germany and the *Televisiefee* in the Netherlands), automatically "zaps" to the next channel when coded to block offending elements. Despite the objections of the advertising industry, the Dutch courts found that the Television Fairy simply automated what the RCD-equipped viewer already had the capacity to do—zap.[25] Although I do not wish to challenge the wisdom of the courts, I would like to argue that the technological family of which the Television Fairy is a member in fact operates on a very different conceptual principle. It speaks directly to a new type of interface between program and viewer, and in its more developed technological embodiments it points to a concept of flow that is fundamentally different from the two generations thus far considered here. At its core is a radical displacement of control. Control—which was once seen as the domain of the television programmer and, following the widespread use of the RCD, as the domain of the viewer—is now shifting to an independent sector composed of metadata programmers and filtering technology (variously constructed as search engines and adaptive interfaces).

Before going on, it may be useful to take a quick look at the position of this new development. Technological innovation has long had the effect of destabilizing the status quo, as television's own developmental history in the late 1930s and 1940s amply demonstrates. Seen variously as a form of radio, film, and telephone, television provoked a series of mini-ontological crises in existing media before finding its own identity, and in the process delimiting the identities of its fellow media. Today's digital technologies have had much the same effect, although their radical potential has tended to be masked by the "taken-for-granted-ness" of existing media forms.[26] One of the few overt contestations of media identity has been taking place between the computer and television, with each industry showing interest in the other's expressive forms and markets. Thanks to intensified convergence and the television medium's own shift from broadcasting to a variety of alternate carriers (cable, satellite, and video-on-demand systems), content has been loosened from any particular distribution form, thereby giving the Internet access to once-exclusive televisual domains. Digitalization technologies have also encouraged television providers to offer services that look very much like those associated with the Internet, showing that the knife cuts both ways. The results (from the television side of the equation) can be seen in relatively fast-growing developments that take advantage of computer technology and the Internet such as the Television Fairy, TiVo, and WebTV—systems that offer new kinds of interfaces between viewer and program.

TiVo offers its subscribers a far more elaborate set of options than does the Television Fairy, yet the underlying principles are related. Among its selling points are an extensive guide to programming, near effortless recording possibilities, time shifting even within "live" programs, and perhaps most important, the ability to code the television to search for one's favorite programs.[27] This last feature not only means that coded programs are faithfully recorded and displayed, but also that programs considered "related" by TiVo will also be recorded. Like the Television Fairy, TiVo relies on an invisible part of each television program—an encoded information track with metadata on program genre, start and stop times, etc. The television technology in these cases is little more than a set of filters that receives certain types of data and triggers a certain type of response: ignore, recommend, record.

But TiVo is only the beginning. TiVo's parent company, Philips, has developed an advanced technology, now in the laboratory under the working title of Double Agent. Here, the management problem of the two-thousand-channel, fifteen-thousand program environment of the future is squarely on the agenda. Designed for a digital television environment, Double Agent essentially offers the same features as TiVo. Like TiVo, although with even more sophisticated adaptive agent learning capabilities, Double Agent learns about its user's program interests through its "observations" of viewing habits and, on the basis of these observations, makes predictive selections for the viewer. The technology involved draws first on the metadata accompanying each program, then processes it through several different filters (known as jurors) that test the program according to various taste criteria, at which point an "umpire" decides which combination of the jurors' reports is relevant for the viewer and then makes program suggestions accordingly. Both the jurors and the umpire are adaptive, learning from the viewer's response to predictions by factoring in such elements as time of day and day of the week and self-correcting with each session.[28] To its credit, Philips has taken pains to protect the user profiles thus generated, placing them on the local server (for the record, the project is currently aimed not so much at developing a marketable product as testing concepts).[29]

Double Agent's principles are familiar. Users of search engines are doubtless accustomed to interacting with metadata and filtering agents, and frequent customers of Amazon.com have probably experienced the uncanny accuracy of adaptive agents that learn from purchasing patterns and recommend books that are most likely of interest (or already read). Double Agent's main advance reflects the previously mentioned intensification of convergence, and it may be found in the extension of these computer-only technologies to the television selection process. Of relevance to the argument at hand, this technology signals a fundamental shift in viewer-program relations. Neither the viewer nor the television programmer dominate the notion of flow. Instead, a new factor enters the equation: the combination of applied metadata protocols (which code the program within certain limited parameters) and filters (search engines or adaptive agent systems that selectively respond to the metadata). Neither of these factors are neutral. Metadata protocols, much like a catalog in an archive or index in a book, determine how we conceptualize program categories and what texts we will be able to locate. Consequently, there is a great deal at stake for both producers and viewers in terms of precisely what will be labeled and how, and thus what will be seen.[30] And as users of the various Internet search engines know all too well, filters have very different sensitivities and capacities. Here, too, system requirements have great bearing on what links will be made and thus what will be seen.

The pas de deux between these two intermediaries, each partial and in its own way deforming, is thus designed to result in something approximating our individual taste formation. The task will not be easy, but the envisioned result would seem to be a prime case for flow—a steady stream of programming designed to stay in touch with our changing rhythms and moods, selected and accessible with no effort on our part, anticipating our every interest (thanks to extensive digital video backup), and nearly infinite in its capacities.

BEYOND FLOW

As we have seen, changes in television's technology and cultural form have brought with them changes to the idea of flow. Although it is fair to question the appropriateness of maintaining and reworking the concept from Williams's original meaning, failing to do this would seem to deprive our thinking about the medium of a vital element (as Williams himself suggests) and an element of discursive continuity. In order to see where we have reached in this regard, with the latest technological and cultural developments in the medium, it is useful to recall Williams's own language. Williams defined flow as "the replacement of a programme series of timed sequential units by a flow series of differently related units in which the timing, though real, is undeclared, and in which the real internal organization is something other than the declared organization."[31] This definition, particularly in retrospect, resonates with the notion of ideology as false consciousness still in circulation in the early 1970s: the timing of program elements and their organization are something other than they are declared to be, just as the world of appearances belies its real material contradictions.

Locating Williams's notion within the period's leftist discourse helps to deepen the implications of flow. The choice of the term may have been linked with the period's dominant (capitalist) cultural insistence on "the free flow of goods" or "the flow of ideas" associated with Western democracies. Seen on a global level, such patterns of flow were anything but free or reciprocal. And the resonance with the notion of false consciousness was almost certainly inspired by Williams's reading of television's economies of time and sequence, as well as by his understanding of the medium's evocation of liveness and pseudo-liveness. But what are we to make in this light of the development of interfaces such as metadata and adaptive agents?

Experientially, the new technologies promise to scan huge amounts of programming and in the process package relevant programs into a never-ending stream of custom-tailored pleasure. Never has the prospect of flow been rendered so effortless for viewers and programmers alike. But to what extent do the three main components of Williams's definition of flow—differently related units; timing that is real but undeclared; and internal organization that is other than the declared organization— relate to this vision of the medium? As should by now by clear, all three conditions are met and indeed intensified by the new technological and cultural organization of the medium. Near-future scenarios promise that our televisions will be programmed from a potential pool of fifteen-thousand programs per day and will be capable of storing weeks' worth of material. Program diversity, limited only by our taste profiles, is guaranteed, as is complete program availability in a virtual present. The status of internal organization can only be other than what it is declared to be to the extent that it does not accurately mirror and predict our individual interests, tastes, and lifestyles (raising powerful questions about the interplay of structure, agency, and the formation of identity). Williams's conditions are certainly fulfilled, but they are also fundamentally transformed.

My brief look here at viewer-television interfaces has sketched a narrative of shifting agency. The agency of the television programmer has been displaced by that of the RCD-equipped viewer, which in turn has been displaced by metadata programmers and adaptive agent designers. Although by no means as concrete in the popular imaginary as traditional television programmers and zapper-equipped viewers, this new interface industry will quickly make itself felt (consider Google's success in the Internet market as simply the tip of the iceberg). As agency shifts to this new constellation in the television/computer world, we can expect a rapid growth in the power and presence of as-yet unheard of industries.[32] And concomitant with this shift, we can perhaps expect a displacement of the perceived need for overt viewer control, much as the endeavors of television programmers have themselves been displaced.

Although crystal gazing is not the point of this paper, the transformation of the viewer-television interface entails other sorts of change that merit mention. The disruption, which characterizes contemporary commercial television in the form of advertising, breaks, and viewer-zapping activity will most likely be minimized by economic strategies more appropriate for a fragmented channel environment and by new selection mechanisms (the possibilities are many: product placement, pay-per-view, near-video-on-demand). And the diverse appeals and programs currently associated with broadcasting will inevitably be exchanged for the logics of taste profiles and the continuities of the familiar, both of which will be guaranteed by adaptive agent technologies. In the process, the textures of televisual flow will likely be more homogenized than not. One might also reasonably expect that the liveness and pseudo-liveness that Williams described as a characteristic of the medium will be dropped for the virtuality and omnipresence offered by filters and adaptive agents in combination with digital video recorders (as can be seen in the examples of TiVo and Double Agent). Again, such changes have centrally to do with this new, technologically ordered concept of flow.

And the consequences? These developments will obviously draw on television's continued convergence with the computer and will empower new commercial sectors specializing in viewer-program interfaces. As this happens, the importance of discursive control over television programming will be a central issue: Who will determine metadata protocols? How will program forms be conceptualized, categorized, and articulated? How will information and access be structured? Related concerns apply as well to filtering devices. The ability to locate and sort particular types of programming, the capacity to respond to certain adaptive cues, and the position of promoting certain program choices all suggest a powerful alliance of attributes. While we can expect public concerns about the privacy and use of the lifestyle/consumer profiles that will be gathered by television's adaptive agents, the less visible issue of what constitutes our "personalized" program package has the power to be far more determining and far less central to the public agenda.

Raymond Williams's notion of flow as both an instance of and a metaphor for ideology was primarily concerned with the "undeclared," with the deceptive presentation of program timing and organization, and with false consciousness. Over the intervening years, particularly in the context of cultural developments that have for better or worse been labeled postmodern, the understanding of ideology has changed. In the place of epistemological theories like those deployed by Williams, a more sociological and in some senses more "neutral" notion of ideology has taken hold, one more concerned with beliefs, values, and ideas.[33] Along the way, the various metaphors used for ideology have also changed. "Filters," for example, have been invoked as appropriate metaphors for ideology because they suggest not so much distortion and false consciousness as they do the partiality and selection implicit in any encounter with reality. But as I have argued above, other metaphors—such as flow—have maintained their relevance by changing their meaning. In the case of flow, we have seen the process by which this occurred by looking at the interaction of changes in television's infrastructure and at the transformation of the viewer-television interface. We have seen a shift in the televisual environment from broadcasting as an activity associated with the public sphere to narrowcasting via metadata and adaptive agent mediations of individual tastes. And we have seen a shift in the form of the viewer-television interface—particularly in the notion of flow—that has slowly transformed from being centered on programming to active audience to adaptive agent.

From its start, the concept of flow has been centrally concerned with content management and with viewer attraction. It has been used to describe economies of time and consciousness in the form of the viewer's encounter with programming. As we have seen, generational clusters of television technology and cultural practice have each been bound up in particular power dynamics and discursive strategies. Thanks to Williams, the concept of flow, as a repository for thinking about changing strategies for content management, can also serve as a metaphor for our changing notions of ideology. Although its meaning is different, this metaphor remains vital to a critical understanding and evaluation of our interface with the television medium.

NOTES

1. William Uricchio, "Cinema als Omweg: Een nieuwe kijk op de geschiedenis van het bewegende beeld," *Skrien* 199 (1994): 54–57; and most recently, "Technologies of Time," in *Allegories of Communication,* ed. John Fullerton and Jan Olsson (London: John Libbey Ltd., 2004).

2. Indeed, the term *Fernseher* originally referred to the telescope that in a sense literalizes the meaning of the medium that I have been investigating.

3. Raymond Williams, *Television: Technology and Cultural Form* (1974; Hanover, N.H.: Wesleyan University Press, 1992), chapter 4.

4. Ibid., 83.

5. Ibid., Williams, 80.

6. John Ellis, *Visible Fictions: Cinema, Television, Video* (London: Routledge and Kegan Paul, 1982); Jane Feuer, "The Concept of Live Television: Ontology as Ideology," in *Regarding Television: Cultural Approaches—An Anthology,* ed. E. Ann Kaplan (Los

Angeles: American Film Institute, 1983), pp. 12–22; Rick Altman, "Television/Sound," in *Studies in Entertainment: Critical Approaches to Mass Culture,* ed. Tania Modleski (Bloomington: Indiana University Press, 1986), pp. 39–54; John Fiske, *Television Culture* (London: Methuen, 1987); John Hartley, *Teleology: Studies in Television* (London: Routledge, 1992); Richard Dienst, *Still Life in Real Time: Theory after Television* (Durham, NC: Duke University Press, 1994); Klaus Bruhn Jensen, *The Social Semiotics of Mass Communication* (London: Sage, 1995); Jostein Gripsrud, "Television, Broadcasting, Flow: Key Metaphors in TV Theory," in *The Television Studies Book,* ed. Christine Geraghty and David Lusted (London: Arnold, 1998), pp. 1998; John Corner, *Critical Ideas in Television Studies* (London: Oxford, 1999).

7. For more on this transformation, see William Uricchio, "The Trouble with Television," *Screening the Past: An International Electronic Journal of Visual Media and History* 4 (1998), http://www.latrobe.edu.au/www/screeningthepast/.

8. Stephen Heath, "Representing Television," in *The Logics of Television,* ed. Patricia Mellencamp (Bloomington: Indiana University Press, 1990), p. 268.

9. The data in this section are drawn from various editions of the Electronics Industries Association's *Electronic Market Data Book* (Washington, D.C.: EIA, 1973–79), and from the *Television and Cable Factbook* (Washington, D.C.: Television Digest, 1978–80). See also Bruce C. Klopfenstein, "From Gadget to Necessity: The Diffusion of Remote Control Technology," in *The Remote Control in the New Age of Television,* ed. James Walker and Robert Bellamy Jr. (Westport, Conn.: Praeger, 1993), pp. 23–40.

10. Contram/SRI's estimate of remote control market penetration begins 8 years later [1981] and puts remote control device (RCD) penetration rates at 16 percent of the market, a percentage that is possibly inflated. Nielsen, which included RCDs for the first time in its studies in 1985, found that only 29 percent of American households had the device, compared with Contram/SRI's finding of 38 percent for the same year (*Broadcasting,* May 11, 1992, p. 52).

11. *Cable Television Report and Order,* 36 FCC2d 143 (1971). For a broader discussion of this point in the context of remote control devices, see *Television and the Remote Control: Grazing on a Vast Wasteland,* ed. Robert Bellamy Jr. and James Walker (New York: Guilford Press, 1996), pp. 20–21.

12. *Domestic Communication Satellite Facilities,* 35 FCC2d 844 (1972).

13. For an overview of this fascinating chapter in technological history, see Louise Benjamin, "At the Touch of a Button: A Brief History of Remote Control Devices," in Walker and Bellamy, eds., *Remote Control,* pp. 15–22. For design implications, see Janet Abrams, "Hot Buttons," *ID: The Magazine of International Design* 42 (1995): 56–59.

14. J. Stanley, "Let Electronic Slaves Do Your Bidding," *Family Handyman* 32 (1982): 86. See also D. T. Friendly, "But Can This Thing Walk the Dog?" *Newsweek,* April 28, 1980, pp. 71–72.

15. Alexis J. Walker, "Couples Watching Television: Gender, Power, and the Remote Control," *Journal of Marriage and the Family* 58 (1996): 813–23. These findings are supported by studies ranging from David Morley, *Family Television: Cultural Power and Domestic Leisure* (London: Comedia, 1986) to Gary Copeland and Karla Schweitzer, "Domination of the Remote Control during Family Viewing," in Walker and

Bellamy, eds., *Remote Control*, pp. 155–68. Walker and Bellamy's book contains several other studies and overviews relating to domestic RCD interactions.

16. Titles from, respectively, *Science Digest* 38 (1955): 94; *Reader's Digest* 80 (1962): 197–98; and *Electronics World* 65 (1961): 48–49.

17. Typical is "Refinement for TV Silencers: Remote Control Devices," *Consumer Reports* 30 (1965): 475.

18. C. L. Walker, "Blab-Off: How to Stop Objectionable TV Commercials," *Reader's Digest* 63 (1953): 71–72.

19. For a summary of trends in RCD research, see Nancy Cornwell et al., "Measuring RCD Use: Method Matters," in Walker and Bellamy, eds., *Remote Control*, pp. 43–56.

20. J. E. Lighter, ed., *Random House Historical Dictionary of American Slang* (New York: Random House, 1994), p. 492.

21. The data in this section is drawn from various editions of the *Electronic Market Data Book* and *The Television and Cable Fact Book*.

22. The most profound implications may be those faced by the theorist, because interactive games pose fundamental questions about the ontological status of the text.

23. K. Maddox, "The Big Picture," *Electronic Media*, November 9, 1993, pp. 1, 23, 31.

24. Not all advertising and broadcasting executives agree on this point, and some evidence suggests that increased program supply encourages viewers to fall back to restricted program encounters. For more on changes in the industry's antizapping strategies, see Bellamy and Walker, "A Tool for the Second Generation: Changing Patterns of Television Programming and Promotion" in Bellamy and Walker, eds., *Remote Control*.

25. "Commerciele tv-zenders vrezen censuurkastje," *Volkskrant*, October 27, 1997, p. 7.

26. Consider, for instance, the increasing reliance of the film medium on digital special effects and color correction, video editing, exhibition using CD sound tracks, and distribution in the form of video and DVD. Through it all, the medium remains unproblematically regarded as film.

27. For more on TiVo, see the company site at www.tivo.com.

28. Adaptive agents have also been applied to interactive narratives, doing away with the "need" for active choice and instead appearing as a seamless narrative that happens to be differently configured for different viewer profiles.

29. "Help! The Couch Potato Is Drowning!" *Philips Research Password* 1 (1999): 10–13.

30. Among other issues, current prototypes fail to distinguish between the horror genre and science fiction, a Western bias fails to account for non-Western program genres, and it is unclear if information regarding the production staff will be included.

31. Williams, *Television*, p. 87.

32. The merger of AOL with Time Warner demonstrates the vitality of this sector, as does the fact that Yahoo, after a mere ten years of existence but before the dot-com collapse, attained greater value than the Disney empire.

33. Foucault's notion of discourse is but one instance of the change. For an overview of this developmental view of ideology, see Terry Eagleton, *Ideology: An Introduction* (London: Verso, 1991).

ANNA MCCARTHY **THE RHYTHMS OF THE**

RECEPTION AREA: CRISIS, CAPITALISM,

AND THE WAITING ROOM TV

For several years I took photographs of TV screens in public settings, using a slow-shutter 35mm camera and some 1000 ASA film, in order to document how the screen is installed, decorated, and integrated from place to place. I visited a variety of institutional and not-so-institutional places of commerce and transit and labor and leisure that define everyday life outside the home: delicatessens, theme restaurants, railway stations, bars, shops, malls, and waiting rooms, to name just a few. Some were establishments I visited or passed by regularly; others were places I had read about and visited for the express purpose of photographing and observing their TV activity. Still others were places I happened to encounter once, by chance, while passing through a town or visiting a highway rest stop. The process made me look very closely and carefully at how the material practices of using (or neglecting) and viewing (or ignoring) TV sets change from place to place. During the same period, I read all the articles I could find in the press and in more specialized publications that provided some clues to the significance of TV's flickering, blurting presence in such places. Articles on topics as diverse as the legal load-bearing requirements for overhead TV mounts on walls and the relationship between traffic flow and viewer attentiveness at the airport gate can be found in a vast array of professional and popular literatures. Trade journals as unrelated as *Medical Economics* and *Foot-*

wear News, Progressive Architect and *Progressive Grocer* describe potential uses of television as a sales tool, a companion for waiting clients, and many other things, and in the process they detail to an amazingly explicit degree their institutional theories of spectatorship outside the home.

Press articles provided details of an even broader selection of televisual phenomena in specific places. Some were mostly descriptive, as in the plethora of *USA Today* articles describing the decor of sports bars. A number registered opposition to the phenomenon of ambient television, as in the numerous op-ed pieces expressing editorial outrage at CNN's noise pollution in hotel elevators. And occasionally genres of out-of-home TV came to my attention through press coverage that remains to this day amusingly inexplicable: most noticeably the surprisingly frequent occasions that hard-core porn "accidentally" appeared on the closed-circuit TV screens of airports and other transit sites.

As an archive these pictures and the professional and popular discourses on TV outside the home that annotate them bear witness to continuities in screen practices and rhetorics across locations and communicate the wide diversity in and among these conventions. Compare, say, a TV screen in a small grocery store (figure 1) and a large-screen news channel display in Penn Station (figure 2). The former, encased in the walnut veneer of the cast-off domestic receiver, is part of the public area of the store. Yet at the same time it is integrated into the workspace. A sheet of newspaper covers it, no doubt to protect it from the damp floral goods sold around it. Presumably, its snowy broadcasts from local stations make the slow wait between flower sales less onerous for the store worker. The giant Penn station video wall, in contrast, is designed for viewing by an anonymous public, more specifically for the professional-managerial demographic interested in continuous news and stock quotes. As a looming moving-image monument, it spectacularizes the mobile networks of travelers and workers in the space and punctuates the routines of the commute with the urgent liveness of televised financial information.

Both of these TV screens are commercial devices and both use video technology, but on the phenomenal level of experience perhaps the only thing they have in common is the fact that they are *site specific,* reflecting in their material and sensorial form the social and physical arrangements of the environments in which they sit. And when an institutional rhetoric (usually commercial) emerges around the presence of screens like these, it is usually supremely concerned with adapting the TV screen and its image to the requirements of its site. This is certainly the case with the video wall, a form of TV extensively discussed in journals for technicians.

But what does it mean to call television site specific, transferring to an

1. TV in shop. Photo by Anna McCarthy.

2. TV in Penn Station. Photo by Anna McCarthy.

entire medium a term generally reserved to describe a particular category of modern art—the installation?[1] The term is useful even when, or especially when, it is taken out of its art context and applied to the discourses and practices of TV's installation in everyday places, because it captures some of the flexibility and adaptability of the medium and its microlevel uses. Rather than characterizing the TV set's relation to, or impact on, its environment as one unvarying way of experiencing relations between public and private, site specificity is a conceptual tool that allows for plural characterizations. Rather than seeing TV as a singular way of demarcating and engendering social space, site specificity focuses attention on a more complicated field of use and misuse values for the console. The processes that blend the audiovisual and material forms of the TV screen with the social conventions and power structures of its locale are myriad. Indeed, although we might initially treat our encounters with TV sets outside the home as a disruption, and thus echo the outrage against the mediatization of public space that appears periodically on newspaper editorial pages,[2] TV sets in public places more often than not adapt to the flow of activity within their environment, so well that they are barely noticed. (Just for the sake of argument, imagine how disruptive a 16mm film projector would be in the innumerable places, from the airport to the food court, where TV screens broadcast their images unattended.)[3] Outside the home as within it, TV is often domesticated as furniture, decorated with a doily, a vase of plastic flowers, or some family photographs.[4] And as at home, the TV set is also often used as an object in local communication; it is a thing that people use to make statements to each other in a social space.[5]

These and other material practices of the television set or video screen conform closely to the physical requirements and social protocols of the respective worlds they inhabit—so much so, indeed, that even though there is clearly a standard repertoire of placement techniques for TV sets (such as the pervasive convention in public places of placing the monitor overhead and out of reach) the significance of such techniques as *statements* can vary greatly from site to site. The seemingly trivial practice of placing plastic flowers beside TV sets, for example, has very different meanings in the Brazilian homes documented by media ethnographer Ondina Fachel Leal than in the downtown New York knish bakery shown in figure 3. In the former case, according to Leal, plastic flowers reinforce the sense of upward mobility signified in the TV set.[6] Although such interpretations are not beyond the realm of possibility in the case of the TV installation in the bakery, the plastic flower–adorned TV, along with the microwave it sits near, serve the more direct and pragmatic pur-

3. TV in knish bakery. Photo by Anna McCarthy.

pose of demarcating the dining area for customers and shielding the workspace behind the counter from the customer's direct view. If there is a clear and consistent difference between domestic and nondomestic conventions of TV set placement (and it is important to recognize that the distinction is limited by its broadness and asymmetry) then it seems to have a lot to do with the presence of institutions other than the family in social space outside the home. The objectives of commerce, of governmental and other authorities in public spaces, shape the gestures and speech acts that are performed by and through television. Thus, for example, in public places the TV set often serves as a site for institutional interdictions—through the conventional practice of placing no-smoking signs on or near the TV set or, more reflexively, through the injunctions instructing the viewer not to touch that are often glued to the screen. (Of course, this does not mean that the mastery over space imagined in these institutional repertoires of rhetoric and practices for site-specific TV is actually realized.)

The implications of television's adaptive, site-specific qualities lie in the way we think of the medium's relationship to the politics of everyday life and experience. Historical and ethnographic studies of the domestic screen, such as Lynn Spigel's *Make Room for TV* and David Morley's *Family Television* have shown that the site-specific operations of the TV set extend beyond simply adapting to the conventional spatial or sensorial arrangements of places like the family living room.[7] Rather, when TV enters an environment it also enters into, and takes up a position within, the immaterial networks of power that characterize the site. Such studies, scrutinizing how domestic conflicts play out in both representations and acts of TV viewing, forcefully demonstrate how TV activates and embodies the gendered struggles that lie beneath the surface of domestic life. Moreover, in addition to producing a microlevel politics of viewing (revolving around seating arrangements, lighting, authority over program choice, etc.), television images play out a broader cultural ideology of space in particular places. Thus, as Morley and others examining European broadcast and reception spheres note, by appearing to make "elsewhere" present in the home, the screen serves as a discursive and material figure for the ways in which family life is integrated into macrolevel issues of the nation, international politics, and the global marketplace.[8]

Again, it is important to note that although the material processes that make TV both an object in an environment and a window to elsewhere may indeed make "global" issues palpable within social space, this does not signal a state of hegemony over viewers. Far from it. In public as at home, TV is an object around which a number of everyday human activities are focused: not only viewing but also eating, drinking, reading, talking, and many other routine aspects of daily life. Indeed, one of the benefits of photographing TV settings is the way the camera exposes the inapplicability of Orwellian imaginings of the public TV screen as a technology of control that standardizes places and subjects. Such absolutist and alarmist images of TV—often promoted in the media and in Hollywood films—are swept away by the flow of everyday life and by the quite visible collection of uses and misuses to which TV is put within it.

The remainder of this essay probes the cultural politics and political economy of site-specific television in one particular type of place: the waiting area. Of all the public uses of television, the idea of TV as a way of passing time while waiting is perhaps the most pervasive one, second only to point-of-purchase video advertising in stores. Indeed, according to retail-display consultant Paco Underhill, the two often overlap.[9] Several commercial TV networks especially designed for waiting areas have emerged in recent years in the United States: the CNN Airport Network, the Commuter Channel, the Food Court Entertainment Network, and CNN's Accent Health Network for physicians' offices are some major ones. Although sociologist Barry Schwartz claims, in his classic study of queues, that "in waiting, usable time becomes a resource that is typically non-usable," place-based advertising professionals offer the opposite proposition.[10] Far from understanding waiting as an interruption in the flow of supply and demand, they propose that it can be a moment when the flow of goods and services may be replenished and refreshed through brand reinforcement. In the complex web of scientistic rhetoric through which place-based advertising practices acquire institutional legitimation, waiting areas provide a stationary and focused group of viewers of advertising as a natural resource out of which an "audience commodity" may be extracted and sold to advertisers. And unlike the home audience, made unknowable by its privacy, the waiting room's audience is predictable and, by extension, more focused. As a brochure for the CNN Airport Network boasts, commercial display at the airport gate "allows your message to break through the barriers that reduce television advertising effectiveness: Zapping, Clutter, and Lack of Competitive Separation. In many of the busier airport gate areas in the United States, the CNN Airport Network is the only channel to watch."[11]

Many of these "place-based media" companies, like the Airport Network, are owned in full or in part by Turner Private Networks. This division of Turner's global news corporation provides CNN-branded closed-circuit programming to public and private institutions, in some instances paying a usage fee to the site (e.g., the Airport Network) and in other instances merely providing the host institution with a certain amount of airtime for its own messages (as in the case of the Food Court Entertainment Network). But although they are "branded" with CNN logos both onscreen and on the sturdy cases that house these networks' monitors, the relationship between their programming and the ideals of journalistic inquiry are more ambivalent than those of the flagship CNN network. There are no battlefields, no national crises, and no political scandals in the resolutely cheerful canned programming that often emanates from the screens of TV networks specially designed for stores, hospital waiting areas, and airport gates. More often than not, waiting-area networks present consumer news and information, trivia questions, top-ten lists, and factoids. Yet although they may seem trivial as a result, these networks—and particularly CNN's Accent Health Network for doctor's offices, on which I will focus here—offer us a revealing glimpse into the kinds of everyday struggles that the TV set can make visible in social space outside the home. The politics of waiting room TV go beyond the not-insignificant fact that such screens transform waiting populations into audiences that may be sold to advertisers. It may seem difficult to imagine that these canned broadcasts trace out wider social faultlines in the same way that, as many have argued, major national news crises reported on TV or radio constitute the "imagined community" of viewers as a public sphere. But, as I will suggest, TV networks for waiting places must nevertheless be seen as site-specific mediations of "larger" issues of the nation and of the gendered and racialized positions it assigns to its subjects. Struggles over citizenship in television are as tangible in the cycles of the waiting room as they are in the spectacularized "live" space of the broadcast image.

The mediation of waiting through the unspectacular and banal presence of TV narrates the relationship between people waiting and the larger institutions with which they are enmeshed—and it does so *through* the very mundaneness of the programming it presents. Networks for waiting rooms link the "leisure technology" of TV with the temporal organization of modern bureaucracy and with the particular experiences that modern topoi of waiting rooms contain. Cycling cheerfully for hours at a time, these site-specific networks program our everyday itineraries with cheerfully busy consumer, health, and business news. By making waiting a form of relaxing, or learning, or catching up on the world, they may or may not synchronize with the rather more ambivalent affects of waiting, poetically described by Patricia Mellencamp as "the mission and desire of being 'on time' while feeling timeless, contextless, unmoored, noplace, in an anonymity of suspended time."[12] In waiting areas, commercial TV networks must interweave their cyclical flows into institutional settings (like the for-profit health care organization) where emotions and attitudes as mixed as boredom, anxiety, and grief meet rigid state and corporate forms of social management. The process of synchronizing and acclimating commercial TV program flows to their sites is therefore necessarily a fraught procedure, as likely to expose the inequities of host institutions as it is to entertain, or inform, or manage a waiting audience of patients.

The tensions activated by the presence of tailor-made television networks in the waiting room are largely problems of time and timing. Waiting is an activity that marks time, and the waiting room is a space designed to contain, order, and perhaps defuse this (in)activity. As Mellencamp notes, waiting and viewing are comparable in that both can be forms of temporal suspension. The fact that the passage of time is a basic reason for TV's presence links the waiting room screen to more enduring ideologies of broadcasting—perhaps not only the powerful simultaneity produced by liveness (although later I will argue for such a link) but certainly also the more subtle operations of TV time, such as the demarcation of work and leisure in the home and, as Morley and Robins argue, entire regions via the imposition of predictable, repetitive news and entertainment cycles.[13] TV's ability to mark time in its environment is a key to its site specificity; TV networks for waiting rooms, one industry audience researcher explained, "must reflect the length of time people spend at the site. If video is used where people are actively moving around, the program segments should be very short. . . . On the other hand, video in areas where people are in a waiting mode can use longer, more traditional television-length segments such as those shown in gatefold waiting areas and on planes."[14]

To get a sense of how the market research process targets and defines the waiting room population as an audience commodity, it is helpful to compare the construction of viewership in place-based media with institutional beliefs about the home. The most notable difference is a temporal one; unlike the twenty-four-hour cycle of the broadcast day segmented into its gendered parts, the waiting room's program cycle exhausts its entire run of programs in a few hours.[15] However, the absence of temporal delineations of audience does not mean that waiting room TV networks do not gender their spectator nor that time is irrelevant to this procedure. Rather, place-based media professionals invoke a site-specific space-time framework in the speculative process of defining the audience's social—and physical—characteristics. They place a premium on the fact that the location of the spectator is itself a piece of marketing information. John McMenamin of Turner Private Networks explained the basic principles of consumer motivation in place-based media to a *Tampa Tribune* reporter with a rhetorical question: "How much good can that commercial for Tylenol be in the middle of a *Seinfeld* episode when the viewer has no headache? . . . If you're sitting in a medical waiting room it has a much greater impact on your thought process and your staying power."[16] In the advertising system of waiting room networks, both the health status and the commercial receptiveness of the spectator are thus directly correlated with the location of the screen.

Yet this concern with space in the construction of an audience commodity is not at the expense of time; waiting room networks remain deeply invested in synchronizing programming with the passage of daytime hours. Temporality, indeed, is what differentiates them from standard "geo-marketing" forms. For while the latter base consumer profiles on the postal codes of people's homes—a spatial "identifier" that remains fairly stable in time—place-based media construct demographic profiles from the succession of spaces through which consumers move over the course of the day. The audience commodity of place-based media thus emerges from a time-based geography of the consumer's movements, its value extracted from the mobility of the viewing market. Like outdoor advertising, a commercial category under which such networks are occasionally subsumed, TV programming for specific places attempts to put a price tag on our more momentary and illegible spatial profiles—our erratic flight paths from waiting room to pharmacy to home—with advertisements that might influence purchasing decisions we make along the way.

This keen awareness of the mobility of modern consumer markets and of how people spend their time in daily errands foregrounds a point of connection between "in-home" and "out-of-home" TV. In each institutional sphere, knowledge of the subject's movements in space and time is given gendered values. Although site-specific TV networks are located outside the home—historically the arena in and toward which corporate marketers believe acts of female consumption take place—their ways of framing and knowing consumers perpetuate the logic of consumption as female domestic labor. Women's *actual* movements in public are, of course, reflections of an infinitely diverse number of motivations between and within work and leisure. But in place-based media's map of the world, the places that count are those somehow attached to the itineraries of domestic, particularly maternal, work. A 1990 audience study performed by Lifetime Medical Television, a physician TV network owned by cable's Lifetime network, found that the majority of the medical waiting room population is female. And these waiting women (especially in the waiting rooms of pediatricians) are very likely to visit the pharmacy after their visit.[17] In describing the network's research techniques to an audience of electronic-media advertising professionals, the company president stated: "We can follow them out of the office. In our early research at pediatric sites we saw that many times the office visit was followed by a trip to a supermarket, drugstore, or other retail venue."[18] This statement, noteworthy for its unnerving voyeurism, exploits the contiguities between everyday spaces—in this case, the waiting room and the drugstore. It does so in order to synchronize the routines of the waiting room with the routines of the point of purchase. TV's presence in the waiting room, in this gendered geography of sickness, becomes the linchpin in an institutional fantasy of female consumer movement along a virtual, economized pathway from waiting room screen to pharmacy cash register.

Thus, although they are temporally tailored to fit their sites, waiting room networks perpetuate a rather less site-specific sense of women consumers as subjects whose itineraries and activities are peculiarly available for molding with commercial television. The on-site network's targeted waiting mother is not that different from the female spectator imagined for decades in network TV—both are busy workers for whom the TV image designates moments of labor and leisure in and outside the home. (And, indeed, because physicians' offices are open only during business hours, the waiting room screen can be seen as an alternative, "consumer educating" version of daytime TV.) Domestic and nondomestic advertising platforms may be site specific in the way they track their imagined daytime spectator, at home and outside it, but in each site, TV, time, and gender intertwine.[19] From home to doctor's office, cyclical program flows, regardless of length, enact a particular sense of what Modleski has called the "rhythms of reception" that makes dwelling in, and passing through, particular places an imperceptibly sponsored experience.[20] Diverse and flexible, yet consistently gendered, site-specific patterns of habit and interruption are thus staged in the rhythms of TV program cycles that air all across the landscape of everyday life.

To understand the political tensions that can be activated alongside such gendered models of the female spectator in waiting room TV, it helps to start by specifying exactly what the habitual rhythms of the waiting room *are*. What does the flow of everyday action in such places feel like? Certainly, particular affects are associated with the act of waiting— routine, boredom, repetition, *deadness*. William James described waiting as a "little dungeon of time," although perhaps a better carceral spatial metaphor than the dungeon is the oubliette. Literally "the place of forgetting," the oubliette was a room in the basement of the medieval castle, a place where prisoners were neither tortured nor executed but simply left to die.[21] The comparison touches on a key anxiety of bureaucratic waiting, one in which we imagine we have been forgotten, that others are being served in our place. And it touches on the imperceptible deathliness, rather than the traumatic violent death, that waiting can feel like. It is an act defined by inaction, a happening in which nothing happens.

Perhaps the symbolic intensity of waiting derives most strongly, however, not from the medieval period but from the modern era, when the act and representation of waiting articulates the alienation of the contemporary subject. Bracketed from our lives yet part of the everyday, waiting and the waiting room stage people's encounters with administrative power. The bureaucratic zone of the reception area and the uncertainties of waiting serve as a key mise-en-scène in popular and elite narratives of alienation, from Terry Gilliam's *Brazil* to Beckett's *Godot*.

Such narratives often work to foreground the quantitative organization of people that waiting implies, to call attention to the consequences of systemic attempts to rationalize waiting as a purely mathematical problem, an instrumental hiatus in the flow of goods and services.

While the modern affect of boredom may have an erotic political charge on occasion (Walter Benjamin called it "a warm gray fabric lined on the inside with the most lustrous and colorful of silks")[22] it is hard to have political fantasies about the act of waiting. The boring scenarios of the waiting room that play out in modern institutions are generally far from pleasurable. Indeed, waiting signifies inequalities and disruptions in the underlying systems of everyday life.[23] After all, although it might be described as a state of inactivity, waiting—along with the queues and traffic jams it engenders—is a situation we often find ourselves in at times of urgency, emergency, and crisis.[24]

In some instances, waiting can mark the fact that one's everyday life is always in crisis. For many people—women, the poor, and others who occupy particularly disadvantaged positions within systems of social administration—the long wait is a time-consuming and inevitable requirement of basic access to goods and services in modern life. The fact that waiting areas are anonymous spaces not meant for dwelling only underscores the disempowerment of their waiting populations. Photographer Anna Norris has documented how the recent welfare reform bill in the United States, which limits the number of years one may collect unemployment benefits and receive family assistance, has led to a decor change in social services waiting areas. Large posters now adorn the walls, announcing to the waiting client that "the clock is ticking" and "your time is running out." Environments designed for waiting thus materialize a set of ergonomic directives and compromises that reflect ideas about efficiency, not comfort or habitability, and that assist in the transfer and administration of bureaucratic power essential to the operations of the state and its management of disempowered classes.[25]

Where does television fit in this everyday politics of tedium and trauma, distraction and dispossession? When considered as a televisual affect, waiting seems to be the opposite of the liveness so often ascribed to television—and in fact is closer to deadness. Prison metaphors of the dungeon or oubliette attached to waiting seem apt enough when one considers that viewers of waiting room TV networks are often described in industry and popular print media as "captive audiences" (as if this means that they are captivated ones). But such phrases are significant also because they link the waiting room to a wider cultural condition—what Michel Foucault called the carceral, a set of tutelary bodily techniques and mental discipline performed by institutions and their subjects by the modern state in hospitals, alms houses, and other welfare places. The educational aims of carceral institutional cultures can certainly be discerned in the use of waiting room videotapes in public health contexts; video is a primary form of patient education in sexually transmitted disease clinics, where those present in the waiting room are presumed to constitute an "at risk" population.[26]

Carceral codes, and the idea of the audience as a collectivity that needs to be disciplined, also pervade discussions of waiting room TV in more corporate sectors of the health care professions. In the discursive arena of the American health industry's trade press, health information and target marketing intertwine. A 1998 article in the journal *Medical Economics* reviewed for its managerial readers the costs and benefits of TV in the waiting room, focusing particularly on questions of what patients should and shouldn't watch. Certain physicians were dismayed, the article reported, by the fact that their patients were watching "soap-opera couples in heat, and often bizarre daytime talk show fare" while waiting for appointments.[27] The solution, the article suggested, was informational, health-education-oriented television, provided as an alternative way of passing the time in medical contexts. It also suggested that doctors might use the TV set to promote their practices, citing the example of a New Orleans urologist who "transform[ed] the waiting-room television into a marketing tool by producing—and starring in—simple videotaped programs."[28]

The approach to waiting room TV that the article ultimately espouses is one that intertwines commercial promotion, health information, and entertainment—an approach embodied in CNN's Accent Health Network (AH). The network's package of health-related programming, distributed, at the time of this writing, via laser disk to six thousand high-volume physicians' offices, is both informational and consumer oriented. Program segments promoting over-the-counter health care and nutrition products are linked by image material typical of the small-budget network: trivia questions, top-ten lists, and recipe ideas. Such low-intensity, cheaply produced text-based programming that is easy to recycle is common in waiting areas. It suits the space's purposes by producing not an absorbed spectator but rather a temporarily occupied one. The "lite" information and trivia featured on waiting room screens, like the factoid teasers that appear on broadcast channels prior to a break in order to hold viewers, orient the viewer in consumer culture. In the case of AH, they do so by naming brand-name products like M&M's candy (figure 4) to go along with the brand-name products sponsoring the network.

4. Mind Bender. Photo by Anna McCarthy.

I took photographs of the AH screen on one of several visits to an outpatient center attached to an urban hospital in the northeast United States. The center consists of a large array of office suites devoted to general and specialized medicine in a multistory atrium building. In this particular installation site I photographed the AH screens in different rooms and tracked the amount of time people seemed to be waiting.[29] Serving Medicaid clients, members of several different managed care systems, and, presumably, some percentage of the fortunate few who still have independent health insurance, this facility is populated by a large, highly diverse patient base. Patients and staff move constantly between the suites on each floor—from the office of a specialist to the radiology department to the examining table of a "primary care" physician—with much waiting in the patient's case along the way.[30] In each suite, a monitor sits nestled in its beige branded casing, occasionally supplemented with magazines "borrowed" (perhaps by one of the staff) from American Airlines. Printed signs attached to the casing encourage spectator interaction in a cheery first-person address: "Can't hear me? Turn me up!" (the opposite would be unthinkable: "Don't want to listen to me? Turn me off!"). The sound is loud but not too intrusive—most people had no problem talking or reading rather than watching the screen. I wondered, though, what it would be like to work day after day within earshot of the same cycling programs and announcements.

Like all so-called place-based media, AH extracts hypothetical demographic information from location and attempts an alteration in the itinerary of the viewer. Its economy rests on the fact that it knows something important about its viewer: that is, it knows that he or she is unwell. It knows other things, too, such as the high probability that the viewer is a woman who might stop at a pharmacy after leaving the waiting room—hence the predominance of ads for brand-name cough syrup and children's formula over-the-counter medications.[31] If the sociological axiom that "the distribution of waiting time coincides with the distribution of power" is correct,[32] then AH presents us with a corollary, namely, that these differential power relations are reflected not only in the question of who has to wait but also in the question of who has the option of not watching television and who is able to isolate himself or herself from television advertising in a waiting environment—not the staff and certainly not the patients. Freedom from television advertising is apparently a prerogative of the doctors alone.

Yet it would be a big mistake to assume that the people who must sit and wait with the TV screen are indeed the passive "dupes" of targeted advertising that network rhetoric describes. My own righteous indignation at the hegemonic practices of AH's brand-name commercials for generic drugs was tempered, after a while, by the realization that the people waiting for their appointments approached the screen's promotional conceits with a healthy skepticism. Because there was little to do other than watch AH, people tended to observe me with interest as I photographed. When they saw that my subject was the TV screen they would often communicate—verbally, or with a wry expression and a shake of the head—their amusement at the irritatingly cheery discourse emanating from the screen. One woman held up three fingers and grimaced, implying, I think, that this was her third viewing of a particular segment. In light of this obvious annoyance, it is intolerable that the network promotes its branded consumer information to physicians as an aid to waiting. *Medical Economics* reported that the presence of CNN could ameliorate the increasingly inevitable long wait that patients must endure: one physician's testimony claims that patients "really like it . . . Some even take notes. Best of all, they don't complain about their wait as much."[33]

This kind of proposition about television's relation to waiting—the idea that it transforms the experience by providing an edifying distraction—ignores the possibility that the program's perpetual cycle introduces a jarring sense of conflicting temporalities into the waiting room. The network's cyclical, rhythmic programming can be seen as a compressed and speeded up analog of the cyclical returns and repetitions that make up the broadcast day or week. One feels as if one has been waiting an entire day when the cycle starts anew. As a bubble of machinelike, unvarying time, the waiting area's programming loop foregrounds the structure of access, duration, and delay in the waiting environment, *heightening*, rather than diminishing, awareness of the duration of the wait for those who sit in its presence.[34] According to Schwartz, the everyday phenomenon of the queue is a masked arena of economic exchange and social contest: the long wait calls attention to disruptions in flows of supply and demand and exposes the structural fault lines in modern forms of economic exchange, welfare, and leisure.[35] The articulation by AH of a parallel, though asymmetrical, temporality in the waiting room, highly indicative of these fault lines, narrates the kinds of rupture in access to information, goods, and services that constitute crisis in modernity.[36]

The sense of crisis often embedded in waiting situations links them to live television coverage of natural and technological disaster, coverage that is haunted, as several critics have noted, by the specter of social breakdown and economic disorder.[37] Mary Anne Doane suggests that broadcast TV's repetitive cycles of crisis and interruption harness the dialectic power of banality and shock as a legitimizing mechanism that is "crucial to television because it . . . corroborates television's access to the momentary, the discontinuous, the real."[38] However, Patricia Mellencamp offers a different sense of TV's crisis, one that takes the act of waiting into account, particularly the sense of waiting for information that is so integral to such broadcast events. She points out that "like passengers and their families, TV waits, counting time against death threats. Waiting by/with TV for the resolution of the Iranian 'hostage crisis' metamorphosed into a late-night television show, *Nightline,* and the making of a TV news star, Ted Koppel, whose topics are often the management of crises . . . However fraught with anxiety and potential shock, this is not dialectic time—this is what Walter Benjamin might call homogenous time, empty time."[39]

One could argue, initially, that AH disarms even the potential for dialectical negotiation of shock through the TV broadcast, enacting instead a prerecorded scene of watching and waiting in which no unanticipated textual resolution is possible; indeed, if a large-scale catastrophe were to happen while I wait for my doctor's appointment, I would only find out on leaving the building. By isolating televisual routine from televisual interruption and instantaneity, AH might at first seem to be the final evacuation of the cultural specter of crisis that haunts, and is revived by, network TV, replacing unpredictability with the semipermanent and endlessly repeating technology of the laser disk. From this perspective, TV's ideological image as a news technology of urgency and immediacy recedes in favor of the image of television as the ultimate ossification of habit. In managing the spectator not through liveness but through deadness, AH projects its comforting, uninterrupted bedside manner into the social space of bureaucracy.

But if the political act performed by the waiting room TV sets of AH is this separation of crisis from "televisuality," then it is an act that must be understood in the context of a wider political economy. The breezy commercial address of AH is entering the medical environment at a moment when, in fact, there actually *is* a crisis going on in the United States—a crisis in health care, not only in health insurance but in basic access, as more and more people find it impossible to get insurance or find themselves with health plans that limit the amount of care they can receive. Indeed, rather than evacuating crisis from the experience of waiting AH marks its existence. It calls attention to the probabilistic, "just-in-time" economy of scale that leads many facilities to double book and over-schedule rooms. Although in 1997 a trade publication reported that "a national poll of 1,014 Americans found that about half spend 20 minutes or more in the waiting room," such statistical data on waiting time should be taken with a grain of salt, as research on this issue is conducted primarily by health care organizations themselves.[40] During one ninety-minute site visit I observed numerous people whose wait exceeded the entire duration of my time there. Although this kind of duration was no doubt due in part to the fact that the city was in the midst of a flu epidemic, the fact that waiting time could be dramatically increased during the relatively minor crisis of a seasonal, predictable epidemic does indicate a definite shortcoming in this "just in time" model of health service management. Indeed, according to one source HMOs are acknowledging such problems—not by reducing the wait but by hiring consultants to redesign waiting rooms.[41] And it is worth adding that for managed care "clients" the CNN-branded wait in the physical premises of the medical facility is often merely the end point of a far longer waiting period. In many companies, one must pass the dual gatekeeping examination of the primary care physician and the health care corporation's case managers before seeing a specialist.

This advanced institutional network of waiting suggests that crisis is still attached to the television screen—not through the spectacular, interruptive iterations of shock that Doane describes in network broadcasting but rather through the resolute, unchanging banality of programming cycles unable to adjust to the cycles of the health care institutions in which they play. It is apparently easier for CNN to synchronize with high-volume aviation networks moving millions of people thirty thousand feet in the air at hundreds of miles per hour than with the terrestrial bureaucracy of health care "networks."[42] The result is a situation that feels something like the conventional comedic representation of "technical difficulties" in TV broadcasting: CNN's programming cycles, never changing, seem like the health care system's version of a transmission asking the viewer to "please stand by" while "Theme from a Summer Place" plays in the background.[43]

In the late 1990s, when I conducted this research, AH executives were aware of the network's difficulty synchronizing its program flows with the reality of waiting for the doctor. Their first proposed solution was to change the length of programming to two hours so that fewer people would experience the cycle more than once.[44] This change would surely have reinforced the comparison to a "stand by" notice. Given the significant increase in production costs that come with adding news and other live-action program forms (especially in light of the research requirements and the legal restrictions on content that medical marketing faces in particular), the new material would likely have consisted of the kinds of trivia texts—quizzes, recipe substitutions, and "did-you-know" segments—that already make up a large proportion of the programming on AH. Although this change would have made AH's program duration correspond more closely to the rhythms and routines of its environment, it would also have undoubtedly led to a different kind of relationship between screen and space; in audio terms, for instance, the introduction of more text-based programming would replace the intrusive direct-audio address of the network's "news and views" segments with the kind of benign contemporary "muzak" that plays in the background of the local forecasts on the Weather Channel. Not surprisingly, the network pursued other options.

The fact that the kind of "lite," time-filling programming aesthetic that AH embodies is found on broadcast TV as well as TV for waiting areas raises a larger, more speculative question, namely, how much is the experience of waiting built into the format of TV programming and images in general—that is, when we are watching are we always waiting in some way or another as well? There are several possible ways to pursue affirmative answers to these questions. Noting the presence of screens in other sites, such as at health clubs, solo-dining restaurants in cities, or on airplanes, we might wonder whether video makes potentially difficult or anxiety-provoking experiences seem like a routine, everyday reality, as mundane as the act of waiting. This idea of watching and waiting as material for "coping" is certainly a possibility in other medical contexts. One Beverly Hills dentist who offers his patients a headset and video of movies like

Die Hard and *Braveheart* to watch while he drills makes precisely this claim: "Watching television relieves a tremendous amount of anxiety for them."[45] Perhaps TV screens in commercial aircraft help translate a space potentially fraught with anxiety into nothing more scary than a waiting room. And passing the monotonous time of exercise is certainly (well, for me at least) the appeal of health club TV networks. By broadcasting their sound over separate AM frequencies for exercisers with portable radios, they provide a means to retreat from the here and now of the gym to another audio zone.

Waiting is in some ways central to the everyday experiential structure of TV's flow. Waiting translates into pleasurable anticipation in the case of cliffhanging serial drama, and less pleasurably in the interruptions and returns that constitute the succession of broadcast segments. Watching always means waiting in some way or another—waiting for an upcoming program, a better music video, the resumption of a narrative interrupted by commercials. And, for that matter, anyone who has ever been a member of a studio audience at a TV show taped live knows only too well how much waiting that experience involves. But on a deeper, structural level waiting and viewing are bound together in the everyday experience of TV as a technology that mediates the experience of the passage between distinct spheres of social life, most notably, as Paddy Scannell argues, work and leisure.[46] The prevalence of TV sets in work spaces certainly calls attention to the ways in which the passage of time at work may be experienced as a form of waiting—usually of waiting for work to end, a possibility signified in the predominance of temporal references in the titles of films about the experience of the corporate workspace—for example, *Nine to Five* or *Clockwatchers.* If TV does, as Scannell suggests, manage and blur the distinctions between work and leisure in everyday life, then perhaps this ambiguity makes the completion of routine tasks and activities more tolerable in places where we work or wait, as well as at home.[47]

Waiting, from this vantage point, beomes a "deep structure" of television spectatorship, regardless of where we watch TV. But there is a problem in relying too heavily on such theoretical premises, for they lead us toward a rather stark understanding of the politics of leisure, one in which time off is no more than a mystification of the real organization of industrial culture. From such a perspective we may think we're having fun or relaxing, but actually our leisure is just another way of waiting to go back to work. In this view, the hard-won leisure hours of the twentieth-century labor movements are merely a stage in capital's reproduction of everyday life; leisure appears as the opposite of work and is thus integral to the latter's continued existence insofar as it manages the passage of time from one work day to the next.[48] Within such an overly schematized rubric, TV is just an epiphenomenal distraction from the process of waiting for work to resume. The argument may hold water in terms of orthodox Marxism, but it takes us down a rather worn path back to the question of free will or determinism among media audiences, and it says very little about the more dialectical and site-specific work that television's presence performs within the diverse institutions that house it.

If there is any value to such large-scale explanations it is in the way they remind us of the broader political resonances of everyday, ordinary structures of feeling. But we must look elsewhere for more lasting insight on the more complex systems of empowerment and disempowerment that waiting might actually make visible in social space on the microlevel. Alice Kaplan and Kristin Ross propose in their influential essay on the legacy of situationism that "the political . . . is hidden in the everyday, exactly where it is most obvious: in the contradictions of lived experience, in the most banal and repetitive gestures—the commute, the errand, the appointment."[49] The omnipresent screen in transit stations, banks, and waiting rooms—the precise arenas in which these "banal and repetitive gestures" take place—suggests that TV might be a crucial phenomenon for assessing the nature and direction of a politics of everyday places. As I discovered photographing the Accent Health Network, local and environmental processes often interrupt and defuse the kinds of temporal suspension and commodification that idealist institutional visions of the waiting spectator project. If waiting is indeed central to the general organization of TV time, this should not obscure the fact that televisual waiting is also a grounded activity that takes on different meanings from place to place.

To affirm the quantum operations of the screen in its immediate environment need not be a romance of the local as much as a recognition of the particular kinds of spatial systems that TV networks—all networks—are. If, as Bruno Latour proposes, the network is a spatial system that is "local at all points,"[50] then the value of distinctions like work versus leisure for the study of television and its settings lies not so much in their overarching, never-failing applicability as in their local adaptability. This is the axiom that has informed my own multiscale approach, spanning from the discursive arenas of trade journals like *Medical Economics* to the local experience of actual sites.

By way of conclusion I move laterally to examine the potential for performing rather more aggressive interventionist actions through the TV set in another local site where TV images and ads brand the process of waiting—that is, the transit station, where looped cycles of trivia, institutional announcements, and advertising play on the Commuter Channel (or at least they did until the network went out of business in 1999). Like AH, the channel's temporal relation to its space marks a particular point in the cycle of work-leisure relations—the commute. If AH addresses a viewer for whom normal routines are to some degree in suspension because they are pushed aside by the necessity of a doctor's visit, the Commuter Channel addresses the waiting person as a spectator who is literally in transit between these two spheres. Like much transit advertising the channel presents leisure products and job retraining programs as alternatives to the daily cycle of the commute. Not only is the commercial management and branding of waiting via television different on the platform than it is in the living room and the doctor's office, so too are the possibilities for challenging the commercial construction of captive, waiting audiences—at least in the case of low-budget, fly-by-night networks like the Commuter Channel.

I want to close with a small but suggestive example of one such intervention, in which activist artists used the Commuter Channel's cycles of advertising and information as the basis of political play, directing their critique of everyday life not at the TV screen—as Henri Lefebvre or Guy deBord might have—but more brazenly at the dialectical force that the Commuter Channel might be said to materialize: that is, *capital*. The group, a San Francisco collective named Together We Can Defeat Capitalism, bought airtime on the Commuter Channel last summer to broadcast a simple message to waiting rapid-transit passengers: "Capitalism stops at nothing" (figures 5 and 6).

This anticommercial generated some controversies for the network and municipal authorities. After the transit system received some calls inquiring or complaining about the ad, the Commuter Channel inserted a disclaimer card in front of the slogan announcing that the message was a paid advertisement, thus adding a layer of autocritique to the group's message. This disclaimer also called attention, however, to some of the more subversive aspects of the advertisement. The visual style of Together We Can Defeat Capitalism's commercial message plagiarized the visual style of the transit system's announcements, adopting exactly the same font and format as the electronic text informing passengers about the next train to arrive (figure 7). Appearing at the same rate as an advertisement but looking a lot like train information, this ad would perhaps solicit a sense of irony in the attentive observer, revealing that the cycle of advertisements is faster than that of train arrival.

It would be an act of brave political optimism to attribute huge revolu-

5. "Advertise your business." Photo by Andy Cox.

6. "Capitalism Stops at Nothing." Photo by Andy Cox.

7. "Daly City." Photo by Andy Cox.

tionary potential to such a local and site-specific television practice. No doubt what made this intervention possible was the fact that the Commuter Channel needed the business as it was teetering on the verge of bankruptcy. "Blue chip" place-based networks like the Airport Network would likely not have accepted the advertising.[51] But the value of such small-scale activities for critical thinking about TV is not the revolutionary potential that they may or may not contain but rather the resourcefulness with which they mark the politics of the waiting room TV. They are designed not to interrupt the routines of a space but to foreground those routines by locating large-scale social power—in this case, the largest: capitalism's annihilation of space with time, on a continuum with the daily frustrations of waiting. As both interruptions in and continuations of the rhythms of the reception area, they are a good reminder of the way that the routineness of television and its cycles can materialize and not simply obscure the politics of time, access, and commerce in social space. In public contexts—whether the airport, Planet Hollywood, or the doctor's waiting room—the placement of the television set and its images in relation to the overall space is a dialectical relationship, one that gives expression not only to managerial goals for organizing a space via TV but also to the contests for power that such goals anticipate and that may yet take place.

NOTES

This chapter presents condensed and revised material from the introduction and chapters 3, 6, and 7 of my book *Ambient Television: Visual Culture and Public Space* (Durham: Duke University Press, 2001).

1. On the concept of site specificity, see Pamela M. Lee, *Object to Be Destroyed: The Work of Gordon Matta-Clark* (Cambridge: MIT Press, 2000); and Thomas Crow, "Site-Specific Art: The Strong and the Weak," in his book *Modern Art in the Common Culture* (New Haven: Yale University Press, 1996), pp. 131–50. I invoke the concept of site specificity in full awareness and acknowledgment of the somewhat ambiguous position it occupies within the practices and categories of contemporary art criticism. Specifically, as Crow points out, site-specific art is a problematic category of "intervention" because, at least in its "weak" form, it is a form of conceptual art that does not so much break from a canonically modernist metaphysics of presence as displace the latter's utopian characterization of spectatorship as "voluntary introspection and self-awareness" onto the principles of phenomenological investigation (135).

2. See, for example, Adam Hochschild, "Taken Hostage at the Airport," *New York Times,* October 26, 1996, p. 25; Cheryl Jackson, "Firms Can't Wait to Make Their Pitch," *Tampa Tribune,* January 4, 1997, p. C1; Colin Campbell, "Changes Afoot in TV Babble at Hartsfield," *Atlanta Journal and Constitution,* April 3, 1997, p. 1B; and "Why Monopoly on Cacophony?" *Atlanta Journal and Constitution,* March 18, 1997, p. C1.

3. This is not to say that 16mm TV has not served similar purposes as TV in public places, particularly in stores at point of purchase. But TV technology's adaptability makes it particularly appealing in the world of commerce. For example, the CNN Airport Network's speakers can be calibrated to adjust, automatically, to the ambient sound levels of the surrounding area so the program's sound is supposedly less intrusive.

4. See John Hartley, *The Politics of Pictures* (New York: Routledge, 1992), 110; and Ondina Fachel Leal, "Popular Taste and Erudite Repertoire: The Place and Space of Television in Brazil," *Cultural Studies* 4.1 (1990): 19–39.

5. Herman Bausinger, "Media, Technology, and Daily Life," *Media, Culture, and Society* 6.4 (1984): 343–51; Ien Ang, *Living Room Wars: Rethinking Media Audiences for a Postmodern World* (New York: Routledge, 1996); and David Morley, *Family Television: Cultural Power and Domestic Leisure* (New York: Routledge, 1990).

6. Leal, "Popular Taste," p. 21.

7. Lynn Spigel, *Make Room for TV: Television and the Family Ideal in Postwar America* (Chicago: University of Chicago Press, 1992).

8. For a history of this discourse, see Spigel, *Make Room for TV.* For its role in contemporary constructions of (inter)national community, see David Morley and Kevin Robins, *Spaces of Identity: Global Media, Electronic Landscapes, and Cultural Boundaries* (New York: Routledge, 1995).

9. Paco Underhill, *Why We Buy: The Science of Shopping* (New York: Simon and Schuster, 1999), pp. 45–52.

10. Barry Schwartz, *Queuing and Waiting: Studies in the Organization of Access and Delay* (Chicago: University of Chicago Press, 1975), p. 16.

11. "CNN Airport Network" (brochure) (Atlanta: Turner Broadcasting System, Inc., 1994). For more on zapping, see David Barboza, "With Consumers Surfing around TV Commercials at Home, Some Companies Take the Ads on the Road," *New York Times,* July 14, 1995, p. D4.

12. Patricia Mellencamp, *High Anxiety: Catastrophe, Scandal, Age, and Comedy* (Bloomington: Indiana University Press, 1992), p. xi.

13. Morley and Robins, *Spaces of Identity.* See also Paddy Scannell, "Radio Times," in *Television and Its Audience,* ed. Philip Drummond and Rob Paterson (London: British Film Institute, 1988), pp. 15–31; and Tania Modleski, "The Search for Tomorrow in Today's Soap Operas," *Film Quarterly,* 33.1 (1979): 12–21.

14. Beth Corbett, "Place Based Media Research: Doing It Right the First Time," in *ARF Fourteenth Annual Electronic Media Research Workshop* (New York: Advertising Research Foundation, 1995), p. 147.

15. The exception here is Turner's short-lived Checkout Channel, designed for viewing in grocery-store queues, which varied its programming with the time of day in a familiarly gendered mix: its daytime programming featured fashion tips while the evening programming consisted of "stock prices and economic news" (Eben Shapiro, "TV Commercials Chase Supermarket Shoppers," *New York Times,* May 25, 1992, p. 35). On seasonal changes in the Airport Network, see Tammi Wark, "Business Travel Today," *USA Today,* December 26, 1996, 1B.

16. Quoted in Cheryl Jackson, "Firms Can't Wait," p. C1.

17. David J. Moore, "Just What the Doctor Ordered," in *ARF Ninth Annual Electronic Media Workshop: Ratings at a Crossroads* (New York: Advertising Research Foundation, 1990), p. 303.

18. Ibid., p. 304.

19. See Mellencamp, *High Anxiety,* for a full analysis of these key terms.

20. Tania Modleski, "The Rhythms of Reception: Daytime Viewing and Women's World," in *Regarding Television,* ed. E. Ann Kaplan (Los Angeles: AFI Press, 1983), pp. 67–75.

21. Thanks to Toby Miller for telling me about this historical architecture of waiting.

22. Walter Benjamin, *The Arcades Project,* trans. Howard Eiland and Kevin McLaughlin (Cambridge: Harvard University, 1999), p. 881.

23. Schwartz, *Queuing and Waiting.*

24. Anthropologist Vincent Crapanzano describes the hidden crisis in waiting as a dialectical play between anticipation and deadness: "Waiting means to be oriented in time in a special way. It is directed towards the future—not an expansive future, however, but a constructed one that closes in on the present. . . . Its only meaning lies in the future—in the arrival or the non-arrival of the object of waiting" (Crapanzano, *Waiting: The Whites of South Africa* ([New York: Random House, 1985] p. 44).

25. Roy P. Fairfield, "Humanizing the Waiting Space," *Humanist* 37.4 (1977): 43.

26. For a public health perspective on waiting room TV, see L. O'Donnell, A. San Doval, R. Duran, and C. R. O'Donnell, "The Effectiveness of Video-Based Interventions in Promoting Condom Acquisition among STD Clinic Patients," *Sexually Transmitted Diseases* 22.2 (1995): 97–103.

27. "TV in the Waiting Room: There's More to Watch than Soap Operas," *Medical Economics,* July 13, 1998, p. 140.

28. Ibid., p. 141.

29. It is a testament to the anonymous public qualities of the space that not once was my presence questioned by the staff present in the reception area, despite the fact that I carried a camera and spent in one instance over ninety minutes in one waiting room. Being a "participant observer" in an anonymous public setting is an interesting form of social experience. My research was conducted largely in silence, although on every occasion I left the building feeling as if I had had a great many interactions with other waiting people. However, these interactions were largely nonverbal—involving smiles, gestures, and other expressive ways of forging a sense of commonality within a place. For a detailed description of the sociological characteristics of public space, see Erving Goffman, *Relations in Public: Microstudies of the Public Order* (New York: Harper and Row, 1972); and Lyn H. Lofland, *A World of Strangers: Order and Action in Urban Public Space* (New York: Basic Books, 1973).

30. This kind of multisite structure is what Charles Goodsell describes as a "dog kennel" in "Welfare Waiting Rooms," *Urban Life* 12:4 (1984): 467–77.

31. This profile was developed by market researchers investigating the potential audience of Lifetime Medical Television, a short-lived place-based media venture of the Lifetime network. See Moore, "Just What the Doctor Ordered," p. 304.

32. Schwartz, *Queuing and Waiting,* pp. 14, 16.

33. "TV in the Waiting Room," p. 140.

34. Browsing through health pamphlets to distract from the experience of waiting can provide analogous moments of wait consciousness. The author of an article about waiting alone in the examining room for the doctor to arrive described her experience in these terms: "I don't know precisely how long I waited, but I do know that I had time to read the complimentary brochures on chlamydia and Kegel exercises, time to notice the strip of hair I'd missed when shaving my legs, time to watch my skin turn to gooseflesh under my gown as I pondered the Latin derivation of the word speculum" (Laura Billings, "Ladies in Waiting," *American Health for Women*, April 1998, p. 104).

35. Schwartz, *Queuing and Waiting*, p. 16. Schwartz's hypothesis is born out in the spatial contexts of welfare reform in the late 1990s.

36. See Jürgen Habermas, *Legitimation Crisis* (Boston: Beacon, 1975); and James R. O'Connor, *The Fiscal Crisis of the State* (New York: St. Martin's Press, 1973).

37. Doane, "Information, Crisis, Catastrophe," p. 237. See also Mellencamp, "TV Time and Catastrophe: Beyond the Pleasure Principle of Television," in Mellencamp, ed., *Logics of Television*, 240–66.

38. Doane, "Information, Crisis, Catastrophe," p. 238.

39. Mellencamp, *High Anxiety*, p. xii.

40. *Hospitals and Health Networks*, September 5, 1997, p. 26.

41. Billings, "Ladies in Waiting," p. 104.

42. The frequent use of the term "network" to describe health maintenance organizations harnesses diverse connotations, ranging from the television industry to the speed, efficiency, and instantaneity of newer technologies. Considered in this light, the emergent technology of telemedicine is a materialization of the network model of managed care.

43. "Waiting for Edward," a recent episode of the Cartoon Network talk show *Space Ghost: Coast to Coast*, referenced this convention in very apropos terms: for several minutes, the show consisted simply of a character-generated title card bearing the word "waiting," accompanied by a light Latin jazz song played for its duration, followed by half of a second musical recording.

44. "TV in the Waiting Room," p. 141. According to this article, network officials claim that repetitiveness leads 4 percent of subscribing practices to remove the network each year.

45. The idea that TV viewing is a way of distracting people from anxieties or other painful sensations is at the root of health club TV systems. See Dana Connor, "That's Entertainment," *Club Industry*, June 1995, pp. 24–27.

46. Scannell, "Radio Times."

47. Scannell, "Radio Times."

48. On broadcasting's role here, see ibid., p. 28.

49. Alice Kaplan and Kristen Ross, "Introduction," *Yale French Studies* 73 (1987): 3.

50. Bruno Latour, *We Have Never Been Modern*, trans. Catherine Porter (Cambridge, Mass.: Harvard University Press, 1993), p. 117.

51. This does not mean that "interventions" are not possible in more policed on-site TV environments like the airport. In summer 1999, an apparently disgruntled employee of the Bangkok airport's internal television system interrupted the broadcast of the championship soccer match between Thailand and Vietnam with a twenty-second clip from a hard-core pornographic film. Following the incident, the *Bangkok Post* reported, the firm announced that it would "air an apology on the airport's video screens every hour for seven consecutive days." Moreover, the article noted, Charnchai Issarasenarak, assistant secretary to the transport minister, said that the ministry "had the right to sue Media Networks [the closed-circuit company] for allegedly tarnishing the country's reputation" ("TV Screens Turn Blue at Don Muang," *Bangkok Post*, August 17, 1999, n.p.). My thanks to Israel Burshatin for alerting me to this event. This example of an institutional blanketing of a space with television momentarily disrupted by an unruly, tactical action is instructive in the way it demonstrates how the consequences of this action can resonate over a long temporal duration and along networks wider than the immediate space of the screen. Indeed, the hourly apologies directed at spectators in transit who are unlikely to have seen or even heard of the initial affront only amplify its effects in social space. A twenty-second clip becomes, in the sensitive multinational environment of the international airport, a rupture in the position of the nation in wider international relations. For another report on a hard-core porn interruption of a place-based TV system, this one in Cairo, Egypt, see Peter Warg, "Commuters Red over Blue Flicks," *Variety*, February 22–28, 1999, p. 168.

JOSTEIN GRIPSRUD

BROADCAST TELEVISION: THE CHANCES

OF ITS SURVIVAL IN A DIGITAL AGE

Television as we know it is a form of broadcasting, constructed as a social institution on the model of broadcast radio. The present technological shift from analog to digital forms of production, storage, and distribution of signals raises important questions concerning the very fundamentals of broadcasting as a social institution and cultural form. In several ways, digitalization may be said to represent a particular challenge to traditional European notions of public service broadcasting. In this essay I attempt to briefly outline and discuss these issues both as problems for scholarly television theory and as problems for media political practices.

Theoretically, the problematic in question may be said to concern the relations between media technologies and social and cultural conditions at large. Such relations have been studied in different ways with a view to several media. I am here thinking of work about, for instance, the social and cultural preconditions for and impact of printing, the telegraph, the telephone, and so forth.[1] Raymond Williams's founding contribution to critical television theory was in a sense written within such a tradition—it was not titled *Television: Technology and Cultural Form* by accident.[2] Williams's idea is that a plurality of technical advances and a particular set of social conditions together produce both the need for broadcasting and the technology required for its realization. He argues in favor of a dialectic view of the relationship between social structures and processes on the one hand and technical and scientific developments on the other, against both technological determinism and a view of technology as a pure "effect" of social circumstances.

The transition from an analog to a digital technological base for broadcast media is obviously related to significant social changes. Digitalization, understood as the expansion of computer technology, is both one of the causes of what seems to be a major restructuring of social life, including, not least, the phenomenon referred to as "globalization," and one of the effects of this ongoing process. The question I want to look into here is, then, whether or to which extent "broadcasting as we know it," and its public service version in particular, will survive in the new "information society" that Manuel Castells calls "the network society."[3] And I might as well say at the outset that my main point is that there is a strong tendency to overlook or underestimate the continued importance of the social structures and needs to which broadcasting as a social and cultural form has been tied. I think it is necessary, not least from a political point of view, to balance the present hype of a digital revolution by pointing to social and cultural forces that are generally disregarded by the engineers, technology fans, and commercial interests that now dominate the public discourses on digitalization, convergence, and so on.

WHAT IS BROADCASTING?

The word "broadcasting" is an agricultural metaphor. It originally referred to the sowing of seeds by hand, in as wide (half) circles as possible.[4] The metaphor, in other words, relies on the existence of a bucket of seeds—that is, centralized resources of information, knowledge, creative and technical competence, and the like—that is to be distributed as widely as possible in a certain "field" or territory. "Broadcasting" is thus an optimistic, modernist metaphor: successful sowing will, given the right conditions of growth, yield a rich harvest some time in the future when universally distributed information, education, and entertainment (the classic formula for John Reith's public service broadcasting at the BBC) results in an enlightened, socially and culturally empowered, and presumably quite happy, population.

According to Raymond Williams, broadcasting as a cultural form reflected, first, a pronounced centralization of resources and power in general, and, second, what he termed the "mobile privatization" of people's lives, that is, the increased social and geographical mobility of individuals and nuclear families at the expense of the stability of older, traditional social communities. Both of these processes are still fundamental characteristics of all modern, capitalist societies. Broadcasting's two main functions in this situation are, according to Williams, the efficient distribution of essential information to all citizens and the production of a shared, primarily national but also regional identity.

This is in a sense a perspective that emphasizes how broadcasting is adequate to the needs of government in nation-states. One could say that it particularly highlights broadcasting's potential as a useful instrument for those who hold political, social, and cultural power. There is, however, another side to this, namely the needs and rights of citizens. Broadcasting is also a—or probably *the*—central institution within the public sphere, making essential information, knowledge, and cultural experiences available at the same time to all members of a particular society. This is evidently of great importance to a functioning modern democracy, and it means that broadcasting may serve the interests of the governed as much as those of the government and other centers of power.

Raymond Williams wrote his book on television in the first half of the 1970s. Even if his experience and knowledge of multichannel, commercial television in the United States were an important factor in his thinking at the time, and in particular for his concept of "flow" as a defining characteristic of broadcast texts, it seems clear that today's television, with its multitude of satellite and cable channels available to large sections of the population in every developed country, is drastically different from the sorts of television landscapes Williams had in mind. His final chapter (titled "Alternative Technology, Alternative Uses?") is wonderfully perceptive and even prophetic in its discussion of, for instance, cable systems and satellite television, but it does not really relate these developments to the fundamental social functions of broadcast television he had pointed out earlier in the book. This task is for us to do, some twenty-five years later, as digitalization is about to realize and radicalize much of what Williams could only treat as possibilities.

The key question, however, is whether or to which extent the fundamental features of the society in which broadcasting was constructed as a social institution and cultural form are still in existence. While the modernist optimism implied by the broadcasting metaphor may have paled (and one may suspect that there is no longer a single bucket of seeds but many), it also seems impossible to deny that power and knowledge are still concentrated or centralized, in some fields possibly more than ever. Moreover, if mobile privatization characterized people's lives in the early-to mid-twentieth century, it certainly is no less adequate as a description of today's situation. Consequently, broadcasting's provision of a more or less shared cultural menu is still a highly important element in people's construction of their social identities, their sense of selfhood, and their experience of community. Broadcast media relate to fundamental, elementary social and psychological needs (or wishes or desires) that are not likely to go away in the foreseeable future. The end of broadcasting would presuppose a radical change in what historians mean by mentalities, and they belong, according to the influential conception of Fernand Braudel, to the inert phenomena of *la longue durée*.[5]

WHAT IS DIGITALIZATION?

Digitalization means, first of all, and very simply put, that the information that ends up as sounds and images in people's homes (or elsewhere) is produced, stored, and transmitted in the form of digits—that is, in the form originally associated with computers. Besides the improved quality of sound and images, I see three major consequences of this technology:

1. *Convergence.* It will, some say, become increasingly difficult to tell the difference between a TV set, a computer, and a mobile phone, because they can all be used for finding and using the same material. The Internet will merge with traditional and new forms of broadcasting, especially when it can be accessed from anyone's TV set.

2. *Radically increased capacity of transmission.* Because digital signals take up so much less bandwidth space than analog ones, the number of channels will increase enormously. As I understand it, there is already a technical capacity for over fifteen hundred digital TV channels via satellites over Europe. The number of specialized or "thematic" channels serving a multitude of differently segmented audiences (from ethnicities to hobbies) may, in principle, grow almost beyond anyone's imagination.

3. *Interactivity.* The number of channels available will be so great that there will be ample space also for various kinds of response. Previously passive audiences are enabled to become much more active participants in the hitherto mostly unidirectional process of broadcasting. Interactivity will take a multiplicity of forms, from video-on-demand to feedback to ongoing broadcast programs and, not least, the individual viewer's chances to choose which of several available camera angles they prefer on, for instance, an ongoing soccer match.

And there will be channels exclusively devoted to what we now know as video or computer games—the Nintendo and Sega channels are close at hand.

All of these prospects are, of course, in many ways exciting. It is not my intention to deny this, and I do not believe it is possible to stop the transition to such an advanced and integrated digital system of communication. Some of its possibilities are obviously interesting and also positive from political, social, and cultural points of view. It is, for example, highly relevant in relation to the construction and development of various "micro" or "particularistic" public spheres for diasporic communities or cultures.[6] Generally, a number of special interest groups, hitherto dispersed in time and space, will now experience new possibilities for community and identity.

But what concerns me here are the ways in which digitalization will affect traditional broadcast TV, and European public service TV in particular. It has, for instance, been argued that our traditional notions of "channels" of broadcasting will become obsolete because viewers will be able to compose their own personalized schedules from a large number of suppliers—what has been termed "MeTV" in Britain.[7] Audiences are expected to make full use of the possibility of watching the six o'clock news at twenty past nine—after first watching their favorite shows from the Golf Channel and the History Channel—and then ending the evening's viewing with a feature film ordered from a video-on-demand supplier. Supposedly, almost no one will continue to use a few traditional broadcast channels with a mixed menu of programs. I heard this view expressed seven years ago by an executive at the Norwegian Broadcasting Corporation, the old public service broadcaster in my country, and it seemed that in Norway this was, at least at that time, the dominant way of thinking about the future. The corporation was to become primarily a producer of good programs, its role as a distributor and composer of a schedule of a certain mix of programs was expected to lose importance in what has been termed the postbroadcasting age.[8] With the new technology, according to British consultant Pam Mills, "the consumer, the viewer, the receiver will be king."[9] In this perspective it seems that the end of broadcasting means the end of powerful centers in the system of communication; endlessly fragmented audiences entail the fragmentation and redistribution of social and cultural power to the benefit of the consumer. For my part I have several kinds of problems with such prophecies. First, I don't believe they will be fully realized and, second, I find them at least in part politically dubitable.

When we talk about a "digital revolution" it may be worth reminding ourselves that digitalization in many ways could rather be described as a technological renewal that to some extent enhances the use of already existing possibilities. This is true for a variety of reasons, the first of which is that analog satellite TV already offers a vast number of channels. Terrestrial digital TV, which will, it seems, be developed in many or possibly most European countries, will not provide a great increase in the number of over-the-air channels. It can carry, according to one source, a maximum of eight additional full-quality channels with some interactive services included.[10] The fifteen hundred or so digital channels delivered via satellite to, for example, my digital satellite dish is something else. But as early as 1992 I could get around one hundred channels on my analog dish.

The ways in which I made use of those one hundred channels may indicate why another fourteen hundred actually are of very limited interest to me. I had about a dozen channels in Scandinavian languages, another dozen or so in English, and approximately a dozen more in German. I also received one or two channels in French, three in Italian, and several in Spanish. The rest were in languages totally incomprehensible to me: Polish, Bulgarian, Turkish, Arabic, Japanese, Chinese, and so on. I did occasionally tune in for a small dose of Turkish music or Middle Eastern folk comedy or take a quick look at some spectacularly sexist Italian talk shows; a bit more often I would watch some German or French talk shows. But most of the time I stayed with the Norwegian channels. When I left them, it was most often to enjoy a movie channel, watch some Scandinavian or American shows on Scandinavian channels, or check out English-language news channels such as CNN, Sky News, and BBC World.

This pattern did not really change with my transition to digital television, which was forced on me by the duopoly satellite companies. In my experience the only major advantage of digital television is that movie channels transmit the same movies three times in the same evening (i.e., one channel has become three, showing the same movies in the same sequence with starting points one hour apart). The general viewing pattern I just described is quite normal, I suspect, for the somewhat cosmopolitan, well-educated, and bilingual or multilingual viewer of satellite TV, be it analog or digital. The lesser-educated and less-linguistically competent will make even less use of the channels that are not in their own language. Other than using a movie channel with subtitles and sports channels, the latter group will tend to stick to channels that not only are in their own language but also that are about or constantly refer to the nationally and regionally defined world they inhabit. It is hard to see why digitalization in itself would bring drastic changes here. Even if the number of so-called thematic channels in more or less understandable languages increases, traditional broadcast channels in the viewers' own languages, with a mixed menu of quite expensive so-called quality programming, will most likely continue to be people's first priority.

Another reason that digitalization is not as revolutionary as expressed by proponents is that possibilities for time shifting have existed for decades. Since the explosive spread of vcrs in the 1980s it is possible to watch a tv program at a time determined by the viewer. This has, of course, been used quite frequently for catching a particular sports event or episodes of a soap opera, but such use of vcrs has in many European countries been much less frequent than their use for playing rented or purchased videotapes, primarily movies. The reasons for variance are highly interesting and concern some of the primary aspects and functions of broadcast television: simultaneity, liveness, and ritualization of everyday life. Several anecdotes here can illustrate some of the ways in which broadcast tv and the temporal structures of everyday life are intertwined.

The first anecdote dates from the early 1980s, when the bbc rescheduled the popular and long-running drama series *Doctor Who.* The response to this change is well expressed in the liberal-intellectual British newspaper the *Guardian:* "All those who have grown up or grown old with *Doctor Who* . . . know it to be as essential a part of a winter Saturday as coming in from heath, forest, or football, warm crumpets . . . before the fire, the signature tune of *Sports Report,* and that sense of liberation and escapist surrender which can only come about when tomorrow is a day off too. These conditions cannot be created on Mondays and Tuesdays. Saturday will be smitten by the destruction of an essential ingredient, and *Doctor Who* will be destroyed by this violent wrenching from its natural context."[11] After the arrival of vcrs, one could imagine nostalgic *Doctor Who* fans taping the Tuesday episode and then playing it on Saturday afternoon. Yet this practice never became widespread, simply because it would not be the same thing, as my second anecdote illustrates.

In the late 1980s a well-known Norwegian composer of serious music was asked to make an engagement on a Wednesday evening. "No," he said, "I can't, I've got to watch *Dynasty.*" The person inviting him out asked, "But can't you tape it?" But the composer answered, "No, I gotta get it live." The remark was intended as a joke, but it was also meant to be taken seriously. That particular evening at about nine o'clock was the first time this particular episode was available to Norwegians, and if the composer postponed viewing until the next evening, he would not the next day be able to talk to others about it or understand what TV critics might have to say about the episode in Thursday morning's papers. Indeed, Wednesdays were simply defined as *Dynasty* nights: the weekly episode of this show was central among the things that made Wednesdays different from Thursdays and Tuesdays.

In other, more general, terms, digital TV may offer greater possibilities for time shifting, but it is not at all certain that these will be particularly successful. One of broadcast media's basic functions has been, and will almost certainly continue to be, that of marking the rhythms of time during the day, the week, and throughout the year. This concerns a fundamental social-psychological human need. Even if working hours are becoming more flexible and some of the culturally based markers of time may be in decline, there is little chance, I think, that such a basic need will go away in a decade or two.[12]

Another factor lessening the impact of the digital revolution is simply that video-on-demand is no big deal. Every day, a number of feature films are playing on a number of the traditional mixed channels. Satellite and cable TV have also offered subscription movie channels for many years, often with deals such as "two for the price of one" and thus at a relatively low monthly price (e.g., the price of two or three rented videos). Most people in urban areas also have quite a short walk or drive to the nearest video rental store. Most of the video-on-demand systems via digital TV are actually near-video-on-demand. This means that, for instance, twelve movies will be running continually on forty-eight channels, so viewers will have to wait for up to thirty minutes before they get the film they ordered with their remote controls.[13] If you can walk to your local video store and back in fifteen minutes, and there choose from hundreds of movies, one would think that may still be the more interesting option to people who are not happy with the offers on all their available channels.

The final factor I'd like to mention is that watching TV on a computer or a mobile phone is not a significant issue. Using the computer or other electronic equipment as a TV set may just mean not having to buy an extra TV. It is hard to see a major impact in watching, for instance, a breakfast show on a microwave instead of an ordinary TV set. For my part, I would hate to watch a soccer game or a feature film on my mobile phone, and I am actually glad to get a chance to move away from my computer when I want to watch TV. Opposite the TV set I have furniture designed for relaxation, not work. When I occasionally watch TV news on my computer, I move to a very comfortable chair in a corner of my study and use the PC screen as a TV set. The flip side of this aspect of convergence is that the TV set can be used to access the Internet. This factor will most probably open the Net to the many sorts of people who have hitherto demonstrated little interest in it, but the point is that there will still be an experiential and social difference between using the Internet and watching television. The fact that daytime gradually fades into nighttime does not mean we cannot tell the difference between day and night. A key to understanding broadcast TV's chances of survival is precisely to be found in a somewhat closer look at what "watching TV" means in practice, that is, what sort of practice it is most of the time for most people.

BROADCASTING'S CONTINUED ROLE IN THE EMERGING INFORMATION SOCIETY

The Internet is largely a space for purposeful activity. It is a space to search for specific sorts of information, join chat groups or, for that matter, play games. Watching broadcast television is quite different from using the Internet, especially for those who have access to only a few more or less solidly programmed channels. What generally happens in such a situation is that a viewer will flip through two to five favorite mixed channels to look for anything of interest—a practice that probably is widespread. But viewers may also be aware that a favorite program is on at a particular time, on a particular channel, as usual, or they will know from newspapers or friends that a one-off program or event is to be broadcast just then. Such viewing is very common, and is in a sense more purposeful or intentional than merely sitting down and turning on the set. Viewers are acting on information they cannot possibly have about one hundred, five hundred, or fifteen hundred channels. And they know that their actions are more or less the norm, so if they want to take part in tomorrow's conversations at work or in the local bar, they need to concentrate on what goes on in the handful of central broadcast channels.

Results from marketing research may also help to elucidate why people tend to watch a rather limited set of channels even if given many alternatives. If consumers are considering a purchase—for example, a car or a household appliance—they tend to restrict their search and evaluation to a very limited set of brands. According to research presented in the volume *Marketing Models*, "many empirical studies show that consumers do not search and evaluate (consider) all the brands of which they are aware. The consideration set may be defined to be all those brands that the consumer will evaluate or search for a given purchase."[14] The numbers of brands included in such consideration sets have in various empirical studies been reported to vary between 2.0 and 8.1, with the typical size being between 3 and 5.[15] The reasons for this may be many and may also vary between various product categories, but it seems likely that cognitive psychology is involved in some way; that is, there may simply be limits to the number of (partially similar) alternatives that people can handle or to which they can relate.

The relatively "passive" viewers who let themselves be informed and entertained by broadcast television along these lines cannot be expected to be replaced by "active" interactors who are busily planning their viewing "freely" as isolated individuals, and are constantly talking back to producers and/or distributors. There is something very utopian and even silly about these images of future viewers as individuals wholly outside their geographically determined communities, actively enjoying an imagined total "freedom" from the powerful programmers of broadcast TV. One might suspect that such ideas have been cooked up by socially isolated and alienated computer nerds, mostly young men who much too often still live at their parents' houses, and then subsequently are turned into fancy theoretical constructs by socially isolated and alienated academics with a penchant for simple-minded liberalist anarchism.

While the number of channels continues to grow, in Europe the time spent watching TV is mostly stagnating or even dropping. It seems to be hard to get Europeans to spend more than between two and four hours per day on TV, even if just having the set on is included in those figures. In 1997, Greece had the highest average viewing time per day in Europe, with 229 minutes. Spain and the United Kingdom came second, each with 219 minutes, followed by Italy at 214 and Turkey at 207. The United Kingdom thus appears to be the most Mediterranean country in northern Europe. At the lower end we find, for instance, the Netherlands with 136 minutes and Sweden and Norway with 141 and 144 minutes, respectively.[16] These northern European countries have a much higher penetration of cable and satellite TV than does the United Kingdom. In 1997, cable alone reached 96 percent of households in the Netherlands, while cable and satellite combined covered 63 percent of households in Norway and 62 percent of households in Sweden.[17] In the United Kingdom, 10 percent of households were cabled and 18 percent had satellite TV. In Greece the combined cable and satellite coverage was 2 percent, and in Italy it was 6 percent and in Spain 18 percent. Whatever else these figures can be taken to mean, they indicate that an expanded choice in channels does not necessarily lead to expansion of total viewing time. Other social and cultural factors seem to be much more important in determining how much time is spent on TV, and, as mentioned, this time seems to be finite. If we suppose that viewers are just minimally rational, they will try to make the most of their viewing time. They will certainly not want to spend it flipping through fifteen hundred channels to see what's on— flipping through a mere five hundred channels has been estimated to take about forty-five minutes.[18] And they do not want to spend it on program material that is linguistically incomprehensible, socially and culturally strange or irrelevant, or of low quality.

The more channels on offer, the tougher the competition over viewers' time. It is quite common to regard this situation as one that will encourage "tabloid" or "trash" program formats. I agree that this is one possible trend, but I would also like to emphasize that the greater the number of channels, the more valuable to viewers are those channels that experience has taught them can largely be trusted as suppliers of reliable information and genuinely high-quality engaging, relevant, and entertaining material. Both traditional public service channels and commercial channels with public service obligations will consequently in a number of countries have a very strong position from which to fence off much of the new competition that digitalization might bring. Even if their share of any day's or evening's viewers may drop a bit more from the approximately 30 to 40 percent that each of the major channels generally attracts, I feel that in most countries three to six channels with a mixed menu of more or less well-done programs is adequate to serve most viewers well into the so-called digital age.

Another reason I believe this is because of the continued existence of political measures intended to ensure proper funding and other forms of support for the maintenance of public service television's ability to compete with the bundle of socially irresponsible and financially extremely resourceful alternatives that will appear. In the 1990s, public service broadcasting enjoyed almost surprisingly strong political support both in the Council of Europe and in the European Union. Even if there are reasons to worry over some of the consequences of liberalist policies within the European Union, it seems clear that the present ways of organizing broadcasting services in western Europe can count on relatively energetic support for quite some time. Other forms of support include, for instance, the sort of regulation now agreed on within the European Union that is meant to guarantee that major national and international sporting events are to be available without extra cost to anyone in possession of a TV set. It remains to be seen, of course, how the conflicts between principles and interests in this area develop, but so far public service broadcasting, especially if it is financed by license fees only, is in no immediate danger of losing its necessary political support.

Importantly, even the end of public service television will not mean the end of broadcast TV. A striking feature of the developments in U.S. television since the mid-1980s that is often overlooked is the establishment of new national, terrestrial networks. It was once thought improbable that ABC, CBS, and NBC would ever have serious competition from newcomers. However, Rupert Murdoch proved the skeptics wrong with the success of Fox, and others have followed in his footsteps. I trust these investors to be careful when they estimate that the chances for profit are good in old-fashioned broadcast TV. Although audience figures on any given night may have reduced over the years, it is in itself remarkable that they have all survived and made lots of money in markets that have had between fifty and a hundred alternatives available on cable and, in the last half of the 1990s, the option of the Internet.

I believe the reasons for this staying power are to be found not least in the fundamental social and cultural functions of broadcasting, which are tied to the continued importance of geographical space and regional and national communities. As digital technology continues to expand and provide new forms of communication, broadcasting will remain, just as other media have continued to exist even when challenged by new forms. The book, for example, has been around for quite some time, and I believe that broadcast radio and television will also survive the addition of related digital services.

CONCLUSION

I would like to end here by briefly summarizing some of the social and cultural factors that support my optimism on behalf of traditional, if also renewed, broadcast TV, of the European public service variety at least. We are still in a social situation that very much resembles what was described by Raymond Williams as a set of preconditions for broadcasting as a cultural form: that is, concentrations of power and essential forms of information and knowledge on the one hand, and mobile privatization on the other. The possibility of reaching all citizens with important information remains valuable to nation-states, and the need for institutions that can provide some sort of social cohesion has not lessened. There is still a need for a limited set of central arenas in any functioning, democratic public sphere. And so, I think, there is still an important role to be played by a few central broadcast TV channels in each country. Even though the importance of geography may be reduced and the nation-state may similarly be reduced in importance, nations and regions will continue to exist—supported, for instance, by the elementary boundaries of languages. So too will the various communities located at these levels, and the need for shared experiences. Broadcasting is not going to go away in the foreseeable future, and more or less solid public service television will, if properly supported, have particularly good chances of survival.

The role of broadcasting is even more important as the overwhelming mass of information available in general increases the need for trustworthy editorial services. For ordinary people, the delegation of editorial responsibilities to ethically qualified, professionally competent, full-time employees is a simple necessity in today's situation. The need for editorial support or aid is already obvious on the Internet. Broadcast TV will benefit from this, and also from our basic need to have available at the press of a button relevant, carefully selected and produced, engaging, and entertaining audiovisual signs of our place in a larger, more broadly composed community.

NOTES

I was in 1997 to 1999 involved in the politics of public service broadcasting in Norway as chair of a new advisory body, the Public Service Broadcasting Council. The task of this council is to oversee and evaluate the performance of all radio and television channels in Norway that are obliged by license agreements to adhere to public service principles. The council presents a report to the Ministry of Culture every year, which is also distributed to all members of parliament and the public at large. In our report for 1998, we also tried to formulate some thoughts on the implications of digitalization. This essay in part draws on this report, of which I was the principal author.

1. See, for example, Marshall McLuhan, *The Gutenberg Galaxy: The Making of Typographic Man* (Toronto: University of Toronto Press, 1962); Marshall McLuhan, *Understanding Media: The Extensions of Man* (New York: McGraw-Hill, 1964); Elizabeth Eisenstein, *The Printing Press as an Agent of Change* (Cambridge: Cambridge University Press, 1980); Walter J. Ong, *Orality and Literacy: The Technologizing of the Word* (London: Methuen, 1982); and Daniel J. Czitrom, *Media and the American Mind: From Morse to McLuhan* (Chapel Hill: University of North Carolina Press, 1982).

2. Raymond Williams, *Television: Technology and Cultural Form* (New York: Shocken, 1974).

3. Manuel Castells, *The Information Age: Economy, Society, and Culture,* vols. 1–3 (Oxford: Blackwell, 1996).

4. I am in this section basically repeating an argument previously presented in my essay "Television, Broadcasting, Flow: Key Metaphors in TV Theory," in *The Television Studies Book,* ed. Christine Geraghty and David Lusted (London: Arnold, 1998), pp. 17–32.

5. Fernand Braudel, *On History,* trans. Sarah Matthews (Chicago: University of Chicago Press, 1982).

6. For more on this see, for example, Daniel Dayan, "Media and Diasporas," in *Television and Common Knowledge,* ed. Jostein Gripsrud (London: Routledge, 1999), pp. 18–33.

7. See, for example, Roger Silverstone, "Future Imperfect: Media, Information, and the Millennium," in *The Post-Broadcasting Age: New Technologies, New Communities,* ed. Nod Miller and Rod Allen (Luton: John Libbey Media/University of Luton Press, 1995), pp. 2–16.

8. Miller and Allen, *The Post-Broadcasting Age,* pp. vii–xii.

9. Mills, cited in ibid., p. 22.

10. Rolf Brandrud, *Public Service selskapenes stilling i den digitale framtid* (Copenhagen: Nordisk Ministerråd, 1997), p. 41.

11. Cited in Paddy Scannell, *Radio, Television, and Modern Life: A Phenomenological Approach* (Oxford: Blackwell Publishers, 1996), p. 155.

12. See, for example, Scannell, *Radio, Television, and Modern Life* (especially chapter 7), for further arguments.

13. Brandrud, *Public Service,* p. 44.

14. Gary Lilien, Philip Kotler, and K. Sridhar Moorthy, *Marketing Models* (London: Prentice Hall International, 1992), p. 66.

15. See, for example, John R. Hauser and Birger Wernerfelt, "An Evaluation Cost Model of Consideration Sets," *Journal of Consumer Research* 16 (March 1990): 393–408.

16. Nordic Information Centre for Media and Communication Research, "TV i Norden, Europa och Världen," *MedieNotiser,* no. 2 (1999): 18.

17. Ibid., p. 15.

18. Miller and Allen, *The Post-Broadcasting Age,* p. 24.

ANNA EVERETT **DOUBLE CLICK:**

THE MILLION WOMAN MARCH ON

TELEVISION AND THE INTERNET

The Internet was definitely a factor in helping to get the word out to Sisters about the [Million Woman] March. From August 10th, 1997, to 12:01 A.M., October 25, 1997, the official Web site took 1,010,000 hits from around the world. . . . This doesn't take into account the number of hits or e-mail at the regional MWM Web sites across the country.—Ken Anderson, "I Speak Today," Million Woman March Web site manager

I speak today because I'm fearless, and I even speak because of my fear. . . . I speak today because I really have no choice.—Congresswoman Maxine Waters

It was a beautiful day, wasn't it? I've rarely been as proud as I was on Oct. 25th, and I think most of us felt the same. We also found that we don't need the mainstream media to publicize or endorse our events/ourselves.—Sis. Mickey, Million Woman March participant

There was now more of a risk that the women and their skills would become entangled with each other and wander off on their own. . . . They weren't only processing data for the boss. If they were pooled with their colleagues, their working environment was a hive of activity . . . a multiplicity of informal networks, grapevine gossip riding on the back of formal working life.—Sadie Plant, *Zeroes + Ones*

 The failure of television networks to recognize the existence and significance of black women's technolust was evident in the anemic coverage of the phenomenally successful Million

Woman March in Philadelphia on October 25, 1997. Due to an apparent disinterest in the yearlong planning efforts of march organizers and supporters,[1] the mainstream broadcast media were ill prepared for the magnitude of the event transpiring before their collective televisual gaze. The spectacle of a massive stream of orderly black female (and supportive male) bodies, detached from the familiar frame of a newsworthy urban riot or rap-music concert run amok, clearly left mainstream journalists scrambling for explanations for this latest manifestation of black-white cultural disconnect, while betraying traditional media myopia. As the *Los Angeles Sentinel* asserted in its critique of television and the Million Man March two years earlier, "One may rest assured [that] coverage would have been extensive and comprehensive if the March had erupted in violence."[2]

Despite the lack of television coverage, the Million Woman March was planned and staged with the hopes of gaining public visibility for a series of contemporary social injustices. Adhering to what Elsa Barkley Brown describes as a tradition of "negotiating and transforming the public sphere" in ways that advance "African American political life in the transition from slavery to freedom," march organizers hoped to generate support for multiple concerns.[3] Key among these concerns were education, job training, and job opportunities for black women; the increasing incarceration of black women; the quality of life for black seniors; and drug traffic in the black community (in particular, to call for an investigation of alleged CIA involvement in the drug trade in communities of poor people of color).

The march was conceived and orchestrated by two Philadelphia locals. Phile Chionesu, a small business entrepreneur, was its visionary and founder. Aiding in the realization of Chionesu's vision was march co-chair Asia Coney, a longtime public housing activist.[4] That the Million Woman March drew its inspiration from the Million Man March is apparent and widely acknowledged. While Chionesu acknowledged her debt to her male counterparts, she also clearly distinguished the women's agenda from that of the men's: "The Million Man March, for many of us, showed in a very magnificent way that the coming together of a body of men brought about some very positive aspects. We saw brothers come back and immediately become responsible for family and community. . . . We were going to be in step with our brothers. We say, once again, that the brothers atoned; we are now stating clearly that we will assist in setting the tone."[5]

Although the choice to stage the march in Philadelphia obviously had to do with the fact that the organizers lived there, the locale was not chosen merely for convenience. It was also a strategic choice based on the history—and historical memories—of that city. In an interview that ran in *Final Call* (the weekly publication of the Nation of Islam) Coney makes this clear. Responding to *Final Call*'s question of "Why have the March in Philadelphia?" Coney replied: "We recognized initially that Philadelphia was the first capital (of America). We understand that many historical events and programs were started here. The Benjamin Franklin Parkway was designed by a Black man. We watched as a bomb was dropped on Osage Avenue and acted like it happened in another country. One of the major primes of this march is to go back to the root. In a sense, this being the first capital, we had to bring it home. We had to bring it to Philadelphia. As you well know, the brothers went to Washington. The following year they went to New York. There was no need to continue to highlight those particular locations. But, to make folks understand that there is a clear connection, we didn't just pick it out of the sky. Philadelphia is where it started. So, it is clear there was no place else to go." Further explaining their purpose, Chionesu added: "Black women have made achievements for many years and now is the time that we must take another step forward. Now, we must put it all together and prepare something we can give to our daughters and to our entire race as a people. This is a timely situation because we see all the changes that are occurring in the world, and we must make the preparation to be a vital part of what is getting ready to occur."[6]

Key among the "changes that are occurring in the world" is, of course, the increasing use of computers. By all accounts, the march's phenomenal success owed much to the Internet. In fact, one of the most remarkable aspects of the Million Woman March was black women's strategic use of the Internet to orchestrate a massive grassroots movement, even in the face of disinterest from the mainstream channels of broadcast journalism.[7] Moreover, because of their persistence through the Internet and other alternative means of communication, these low-profile urban women drew large numbers of women to the streets. This in turn compelled the racially biased mainstream media to recognize the march as "newsworthy" and to cover in fact (the event's success) what they ignored in theory (its very possibility).[8] Indeed, despite initial disinterest, a few mainstream print media outlets, c-span, and Philadelphia's local stations did in the end cover the event.

Given the historical disinclination of patriarchal structures, including media institutions, to accord women their rightful places in the annals of technological advancement, this deliberate avoidance of the Million Woman March until it was well underway is hardly surprising.[9] As Laura

Miller observes in her article on the problematic rhetorics of "cyberbabe harrassment," no matter "how revolutionary the technologized interactions of on-line communities may seem," gender roles still provide a foundation for the intensification of social controls that "proscribe the freedoms of men as well as women." Because, as Miller asserts, the media accept "the idea that women, like children, constitute a peculiarly vulnerable class of people who require special protection from the elements of society [that] men are expected to confront alone," the fact of black women's sophisticated engagement with cyberactivism is likely to be unfathomable.[10]

Nonetheless, the significance of the Internet's role in the success of the Million Woman March testifies to the marginalized black masses' refusal to be reduced to what Paolo Carpignano and others term television news' "edited public," or to what I call the inevitable road kill on the fast-moving information superhighway.[11] In this essay I look at the relationship between television and emerging forms of digital reproduction along two discursive tracks. The first is the issue of television's response, or lack thereof, to black people's revolutionary assemblies at the Million Man March in 1995 and Million Woman March in 1997. The second is the issue of black women's particular engagement with the Internet. I am interested in how black women use the Internet in the glaring absence of television to foreground black people's unabated and unabashed liberation struggles for self-determination and social change by any means necessary.

MEDIATING BLACK WOMEN'S HISTORIC INTERVENTIONS IN THE PUBLIC SPHERE

What was so striking about the near-absence of network television cameras in the history-making Million Woman and Million Man marches was their remarkable contrast to the ubiquitous television presence during the epochal events of the 1950s and 1960s civil rights movement. During that era, the spectacle of such black women as Fannie Lou Hamer and Rosa Parks transgressing the "accepted bounds" of domestic spaces to make their voices heard in the public sphere clearly made for riveting television.[12] At the same time, Lynn Spigel reminds us of the failure of 1950s TV to reconcile its idealized depictions of rigidly masculinized public and feminized domestic spaces with the reality of women's increased roles in the workplace. Spigel states: "The housewife image might have had the unplanned paradoxical effect of sending married women into the labor force in order to obtain the money necessary to live the ideal [pictured in 1950s era sitcoms]." For, as Spigel adds, "both the advertising and the homes themselves were built on the shaky foundations of social upheaval and cultural conflict which never were completely resolved."[13] Indeed, Fannie Lou Hamer's televised "Is This America?" speech at the 1964 Democratic National Convention in Atlantic City signaled a pivotal moment in the history of television's relationship to the civil rights campaign. Despite President Johnson's directive that the networks kill the live feed of her speech, all of them aired Hamer's powerful speech in its entirety later that night.[14] Perhaps the anomaly of seeing these resolute black women foregrounded in a confrontation with authority was compelling because, as Kay Mills observes, "black women were able to play such an active role in areas where leadership was foreclosed for men because the black women were invisible to white eyes."[15]

The march recalls even earlier instances in the mediation of black women's efforts at social and political liberation struggles, which bear recounting here. In the nineteenth century, black women freedom fighters such as Harriet Tubman and Sojourner Truth established a formidable tradition of breaking through the idealized public sphere's ossified gender divide. Indeed, Congresswoman Maxine Waters's "I Speak Today" address at the Million Woman March so evokes historical accounts of Sojourner Truth's 1851 "Ain't I a Woman?" speech that a brief revisitation of it is warranted here even though the scope of this essay precludes a full discussion of this impressive black herstory and its obvious lessons for our own time.

One of the earliest mediated instances of a black woman "speaking truth to power," to borrow Anita Hill's terminology, was Sojourner Truth's famed 'Ain't I a Woman?' speech at the 1851 Women's Rights Convention in Akron, Ohio.[16] Due to conflicting accounts of Truth's extemporaneous talk, it is impossible to extricate the legend that springs from Frances Gage's 1863 report and the contemporaneous newspaper claims to carry her exact words. Regardless of the enduring debates and our inability to ever know the speech's textual specifics, at issue here are the indices of the significant continuities and ruptures that characterize nineteenth-century mediations of black women's public speech acts and those of our own time. In the former, print media's representation of black women's entry into modernity is muted; in the latter, black women's self-presentation through digital media heralds their postmodern arrival. Whereas the limits of nineteenth-century race and gender identity politics dictated that Truth, a former slave, could address only the all-white assembly (gathered to discuss women's suffrage) on the sufferance and authority of white abolitionists, the simultaneously public and clandestine communicative possibilities of late-twentieth-century Internet technology enabled organizers of the Million Woman March to authorize their own addresses to a global assembly, and to do so on their own terms through computer-mediated communications. For these women (to use McLuhanesque terms) "the medium was the message" to a large extent.

Clearly, the decentralizing communicative force of the Internet marks a significant rupture in television's historic containment and co-optation of black women's "sass." In her significant book *Black Women Writing Autobiography: A Tradition within a Tradition*, Joanne Braxton historicizes "sass" as a survivalist speech act utilized by black women during and after slavery. Sass, for slave women, Braxton notes, employes verbal warfare and defensive verbal posturing as tools of liberation. This impertinent speech also denotes self-esteem and self-defense. Braxton also alerts us to this potent term's African etymology: "Sass is a word of West African derivation that is associated with the female aspect of the trickster. The *Oxford English Dictionary* attributes the word's origin to the poisonous 'sassy tree.' A decoction of the bark of this tree was used in West Africa as an ordeal poison in the trial of accused witches, women spoken of as being wives of Exu, the trickster god."[17]

To be sure, it is the sass contained in both Sojourner Truth's "Ain't I a Woman?" and Maxine Waters's "I Speak Today" speeches that are reflexive of notable continuities in black women's ongoing and relentless public and personal strategies for negotiating political and sociocultural autonomy. Consider Truth's sassy utterances. For example: Frances Gage's excerpted eyewitness account of Truth's speech reads: " 'That man over there says that women need to be helped into carriages, and lifted over ditches, and to have the best place everywhere. Nobody helps *me* any best place. *And ain't I a woman?* . . . I could work as much, and eat as much as a man—when I could get it—and bear the lash as well! *And ain't I a woman?* I have borne children and seen most of them sold into slavery, and when I cried out with a mother's grief, none but Jesus heard me. *And ain't I a woman?* "[18] Now, hear the rhetorical resonance in this excerpt from Maxine Waters's address to the march's throng: "I speak today because I'm so very happy. . . . I speak today because I'm vulnerable. I speak today because I'm strong. I speak today because I'm fearless. . . . I speak today because I am a woman, a black woman bonded with other black women, determined to love, to be loved, to grow, to create, to live. I speak today because I really have no choice. I speak because my very soul is stirred, inspired, and excited. We the women hailing from this nation, [in] all shapes, sizes, and views have something to say today. I speak today because I am determined that we will all be free, we must be free, as a black woman, a mother, a wife, a grandmother, a sister. I am you, and you are me."[19]

Besides the masterful rhetorical refrains ("Ain't I a Woman?" and "I Speak Today") punctuating their historically situated societal reprimands, these speeches are also yoked by their skillful deployment of sass as a means of resistance to the double repression of race and gender most identified with the black woman's experience in the West. It is true that the sassy, unruly black woman image is a familiar and romanticized media archetype, particularly in her signifying economy as the mammy. Think of Hattie McDaniel's 1939 Academy Award–winning portrayal of a sassy slave mammy in *Gone with the Wind,* and of all her television progeny (Beulah, in the show of the same name, and Florence in *The Jeffersons*). As a means of countering mainstream culture's co-optation and commodification through Hollywood's fictional black sass put in the service of privileging whiteness, Truth's and Waters's real sass foreground its enduring emancipatory allure.

UPLOADING SASS TO THE ONLINE AGORA AND DOWNLOADING INFORMATION TECHNOLOGIES TO THE STREETS

The march's Web site manager Ken Anderson's 1997 revelation that the march's official Web site tallied more than one million hits (visitors to the site) in a two-month period does much to collapse the bipolar base on which our racialized technological superstructures frequently rest, both comfortably and too predictably. Of late there has been much discussion in the popular media about bridging the digital divide.[20] These belated mainstream calls for universal access to new media are certainly necessary. However, it is equally necessary to acknowledge the sass of black women who have already begun to bridge the divide. Rather than decry the disproportionate rate of computer technology diffusion within the black diasporic community, these everyday African American women in 1997 found an ingenious remedy, or tactic of cultural intervention, via the Internet.

In Michel de Certeau's *The Practice of Everyday Life*—an homage to "a common hero, an ubiquitous character, walking in countless thousands on the streets"—the unpacking of certain postmodern practices of bricolage, or "making-do," is instructive.[21] For example, when we learn that black women office workers downloaded from the official Web site directives provided by march organizers and then made photocopies for their computerless counterparts, we are reminded of de Certeau's discussion of

French workers' "diversionary practice of '*la perruque*,'" which, according to de Certeau, "is the worker's own work disguised as work for his employer . . . Accused of stealing or turning material to his own ends and using the machines for his own profit, the worker who indulges in *la perruque* actually diverts time (not goods, since he uses only scraps) from the factory. . . . In the very place where the machine he must serve reigns supreme, he cunningly takes pleasure in finding a way to create gratuitous products whose sole purpose is . . . solidarity with other workers."[22] Web site manager Anderson reports how black women workers' use of this worker-unity tactic galvanized hundreds of thousands: "While I was at the march, Sisters walked up to me (I was at a vending booth with another Brother) and told me that they would not have heard about the march without the Web site. I have heard from at least 30 Sisters who printed out the entire Web site and shared it with friends, neighbors, and co-workers who weren't online yet. This is very flattering, and I appreciate every Sister's attention to and use of the Web site."[23]

There is a significant issue underlying Anderson's account. In addition to his optimism regarding black women's guerrilla tactics and instances of la perruque in their embrace of the Internet, Anderson makes us privy to something truly amazing in black women's tactics of "making do." By making virtual computers available to black women who "weren't online yet," march supporters with access to actual Internet technology, either through their jobs or their computers at home, effectively transformed low-tech, 1960s-era mimeograph activism into high-tech digital news and information flows. Out of necessity and through the economy of computer-mediated communication, these black women subverted their marginal status as technology consumers and laborers into that of technology innovators and producers. Through their clandestine cultural production of sassy online discourses, these women, in effect, downloaded the digital agora and took information technologies to their offline sisters, to the streets of Philadelphia, and to cable and local television airwaves.

SELF-AUTHENTICATING NARRATIVES
AND "TEMPORARY AUTONOMOUS ZONES"

Once it became apparent that network television would not assist in the efforts by march organizers to get media coverage, the organizers set about the task of formulating alternative modes of self-authenticating narratives. Refusing racialized invisibility, organizers utilized instead a number of alternative media options. Using consumer-grade camcorder technology to document their mass mobilization feat, the organizers created a composite video ethnography by combining local and national broadcasts with cable television coverage of the march. In this way, they temporarily made cable and local TV realize their potential as "citizen technologies."[24]

The camcorder videotape recodes the logic of technological determinism for the resistance arsenal of these contemporary freedom fighters. The tape reads as a reply of late 1960s counterculture video practices that, according to Patricia Mellencamp, were "founded on a belief in liberation via the democratic pluralism of television—anyone could control the means of production, anyone could and should be an artist."[25] The production values of this compilation tape testify to the audiovisual proficiency of this "colonized class" to not only represent, but also to present these black women's "oppositional cyborg politics," a grassroots politics facilitated by march organizers' emergent technomastery.[26] The video is framed at its beginning and end with an artistically rendered computer-generated title page announcing the Million Woman March and its historic date of October 25, 1997. The ensuing documentary footage is contextualized within an audiovisual representational field comprised of a voice-over excerpt from Maxine Waters's "I Speak Today" speech that enlivens a sepia-tone snapshot image taken from the march's crowd. This is followed by a transition wipe into slow-motion footage of a teenage girls' marching band leading the march's throngs. Conspicuous is the absence of national television coverage except that of one segment from NBC's *Today* show combined with that network's local affiliate coverage in Philadelphia and C-SPAN's full—if delayed—cablecast. It is the small, iconic text-box image that alternated between identifying the day, "Sat.," and its show schedule that suggests C-SPAN's coverage was not live."[27]

My own channel surfing on the day of the march failed to locate anything but cursory mentions of it in network and cable news programs. Although the next day the story did make the front page of the *New York Times,* replete with a three-column-wide color photo of marchers, it remains perplexing that event-driven TV news bureaus would ignore the rousing speeches of such iconic figures as Maxine Waters, Winnie Mandela, Dick Gregory, and the daughters of Malcolm X and Betty Shabazz, as well as the phenomenal pictures of the unprecedented crowds in Philadelphia captured by the "mass-cam" and sky-cams of local Philadelphia news organization helicopters. Marking the convergence of new and traditional media, the video ethnography produced by march organizers concludes with end credits highlighting their Internet address, which loops back to diegetic footage of several marchers stressing their excitement about returning to their communities and sharing their wonderful experiences in online chat sessions and through their own video diaries. Apparently, the repressed zeitgeist of sixties-era counterculture video art and activism, promulgated by the activist groups TVTV, Ant Farm, Video Theater, Videofreex, Global Village, and others, has returned with a new media vengeance.[28] Video vans have been displaced by the digitized mobility of the Internet's streaming video functionality. In fact, march organizers posted to their Web site calls "to gather copies of video and photos taken at the Million Woman March," as well as requests "to have you record your experiences coming to, being at, and returning home from the March . . . We are compiling an international record of the Million Woman March. We really need your help."[29] In some ways, this cyberactivism approach marks a new media redux of the agit prop trains used by the Soviet constructivist filmmakers who, to paraphrase Patricia Mellencamp, would have loved the speed of the Internet and its amazing ideological use value.[30]

In their attempt to recode and circumvent the logic of network news gathering, the march organizers' use of the camcorder and Internet embodies the spirit of what Hakim Bey refers to as the "temporary autonomous zone." Echoing de Certeau and Sadie Plant's sentiments about the efficacious "data piracy" strategies of women and working-class groups to use the master's tools in subversive maneuvers, Bey describes temporary autonomous zones as enclaves of "intentional communities, whole mini-societies living consciously outside the law and determined to keep it [so], even if only for a short but merry life." Although Bey acknowledges that the temporary autonomous zone is a failed romantic notion from another time that "remains precisely science fiction—pure speculation," he nonetheless recommends it conceptually today "because it can provide the quality of enhancement associated with the uprising without necessarily leading to violence and martyrdom."[31] The fact that black women and their supporters used the march to construct their own very real and apparently necessary temporary autonomous zone cannot be minimized nor dismissed. For this reason, it is useful to consider the march as a documented enactment of what Chela Sadoval terms "cyborg feminism and the methodology of the oppressed," a cyborg consciousness "developed out of a set of technologies that together comprise . . . a methodology that can provide the guides for survival and resistance under First World transnational cultural conditions."[32]

As these examples of black women's technolust clearly illustrate, any fair assessment of black computer literacy confounds the dominant culture's techno rhetoric that reifies black people unproblematically as poster children for the digital divide discourse. Underscoring the incongruence of the image of black technophobia and a black technophilic reality is Anderson's account of the revolutionary usage of the Internet. As Ken Anderson, the self-proclaimed "humble servant to the cause," aptly puts it: "There is a complete strategy around the issue of using this medium to spread the word, increase activism, increase the number of Sisters on the Net, increase networking opportunities for Sisters worldwide, and to provide real-time communications utilizing chat sessions and email. . . . These are indeed exciting times. Just when no one thought women of African descent were paying attention, along come[s] the MWM and its Internet presence."[33]

Anderson's remarks, then, seem to confirm the beliefs of Sadie Plant and others that subordinate classes of women and blacks are able to use the master's tools to dismantle his house of racial domination and masculinist privilege, to rephrase Audre Lorde's famous saying. In Plant's discussion of Alan Turing's ideas about the subversive potential of machines' *détournement* on the slave-master relationship, Plant provides us with a particularly useful analogy for considering the march organizers' tactical use of the Internet for their own unedited global publicity and promotion. In her important book *Zeroes + Ones,* Plant gives us a sense of Turing's prescience regarding man's inability to restrict machine power or subordinated groups' use of that power. For Turing, man's presumed dominion over the "rest of creation" does not necessarily translate into an assured superiority over his own machine creations. Plant quotes Turing's statement, "We like to believe that Man is in some subtle way superior to the rest of creation. . . . It is best if he can be shown to be *necessarily* superior, for then there is no danger of him losing his commanding position."[34] But as Plant reminds us, "Turing's words were laced with irony. He relished the possibility that machines would undo this necessity. . . . Turing knew that this attempt to produce highly programmed slave machines would backfire. It is [in Turing's words] the 'masters who are liable to get replaced' by the new generation of machines." Through their masterful use of the new generation of computer machinery, march organizers effectively bore out Turing's late 1940s prophecy. Indeed, as a result of their unanticipated usage and mastery of the Internet, black women, in this instance, succeeded in upsetting "the old distinctions between the user and the used," the master and the slave.[35]

Through the Internet, the march's digerati were able, albeit temporarily, to undo their representational enslavement in the racialized agenda-setting economy of broadcast television's master class. Moreover, they mobilized their virtual community online to disrupt and reveal broadcast television's denial (at that time) of the Internet as a viable, real-world broadcast alternative. Viewed in this way, the political, social, and economic achievement of the Million Woman March cannot help but reaffirm one's cautious optimism about the much-hyped democratizing potential of the Internet, despite its increasing Wall Street corporatization. While mainstream television remained indifferent to the march's sociopolitical agenda, its economic impact was not ignored by online reporting. The *Philadelphia Inquirer*'s online venue, along with AFAMNET, reported that an astounding $21.7 million windfall was generated by the march for the local Philadelphia economy. According to Tom Muldoon, president of the Philadelphia Convention and Visitors Bureau, "The impact [of the march] was felt as far away as Dover, Del. (88 miles from Philadelphia), where the Sheraton was sold out."[36] Tanya Hall, executive director of the Multicultural Affairs Division, stated that "we were delighted that this historic event was held in Philadelphia. . . . The incredible economic impact of the march emphasizes the tremendous economic strength of African-American women in this country."[37]

In the afterglow of the Million Woman March's success, event organizers posted a note of thanks to their groundbreaking global constituency. "What is important," organizers proclaimed, "is that Sistahs from around the nation and the world came together. . . . A great deal was done with very little. The power of Sisterhood is amazing. This was a day for Sisters to come together for repentance, resurrection, and restoration. Thank you for being involved and connected."[38]

MODERN MAMAS: MIDWIVES TO THE BIRTH OF A DIGITAL NATION

As early as July 1997, regional march organizers in Philadelphia instructed visitors to their Web sites to "feel free to make copies of this webpage and share it with other Afrikan women." Among the agenda items for march organizers in the midwestern states was the solicitation of computer needs and expertise.[39] In fact, from the outset these women were demonstrably adept at enlisting the Web to promote their pre-march conference, the organizing and fundraising activities that became pivotal to the success of the main event. Indeed, these women's profound optimism against incredible odds is particularly well conveyed in *The Final Call*'s interview with march co-chairs Chionesu and Coney. By their comments we understand their self-perceptions as midwives to a new movement. Undergirding their faith in the power of sisterhood were the efforts and tremendous sacrifices of regional organizers and lay supporters of the march. In expressing their thoughts in *Final Call* just two weeks prior to the big day, the women were striking in their confidence and self-possession. In response to the question, "You are two weeks now from the event, how do you feel?" Chionesu replied: "Mixed emotions. Excited, obviously elated because we are really beginning to see the manifestation of our works. . . . It's a feeling that is almost indescribable. But the flip side is that we also know that the work is really just beginning. Now the birthing process is about to come to its point of fruition. The child, in a sense, is about to be brought forth. Now we have to raise this child. Raising a nation is a lot of work. Raising a people is a lot of work. So, although we see how wonderful October 25th is going to be, we know that on October 26th the work will have just begun."[40]

What Chionesu could not know at this point was how truly difficult it would be to maintain the success of the march. For accompanying the post-march accolades were a number of detractions (ironically, from several vociferous sources in digital spaces online) and a host of other problems. Shortly after the march event, organizers posted an "international scam alert" on their Web site to advise supporters of the flood of counterfeit march memorabilia: "A number of individuals and groups are . . . using familiar sounding names and images to make money for themselves only. . . . A poster being circulated by Michael Brown is not the official poster sanctioned by the National Organizers and Founders of the Million Woman March."[41] In an effort to foreclose disinformation circulation, organizers also posted requests that supporters check the Web site for updates "before interviews are given in order to reduce the misuse or misinterpretation of information."[42] In addition to policing their new proprietary information and commodity rights boundaries, organizers encountered a plethora of post-march criticisms and diatribes, congealing coincidentally in the online ether that had nurtured their grand vision.

One of the most vitriolic condemnations of the march was an editorial produced by Gary Hull for the Ayn Rand Institute's MediaLink department. Hull's online article, titled "The Pied Pipers of Tribalism: The 'Million Woman March' Should Have Promoted Individualism Not Tribalism," seeks to discredit both the march and progressive educational practices in higher education. Hull writes: "Lurking behind the rally's love of all things African was the insidious message to every listener: Ditch your brain; subordinate your will; accept the notion that your life has no reality except as an appendage of the tribal organism. These ideas are not originated by the leaders of the march. They come from the humanities departments at our colleges and universities. The organizers merely spread in the culture what college professors now teach in class. . . . Travelers on the Million Woman March will find that this tribalist road leads only to poverty, dictatorship, and slavery."[43]

It is highly improbable that march organizers were wounded by this particular reception from a nonmainstream think tank, especially considering organizers' attitudes of strength and triumph against the odds. At the same time, however, the *Philadelphia Inquirer* tallied via its Web site a host of mixed reviews of the march from several online editorial forums, including the "letters to the editor" pages at both the *Inquirer* and the *Daily News*. From the *Daily News*, Ken Wyllie of Philadelphia wrote, "In a time [when] we preach equality, the news media showed gross disrespect for our women. It is sexist, disgusting and dead wrong. . . . The American media owe our sisters an apology."[44] A less affirming response was posted by Della Rucker of Philadelphia, who wrote, "Women who feel it is just an African-American problem should have referred to it as just that. Instead, they are being racist, trying to justify themselves."[45] On November 2, 1997, Donna White of Claymont, Delaware, wrote into the *Inquirer* stating, "The essence of the cluster was that of strength unknown. . . . Some of us can even testify to the rewards of the march and will extend the knowledge to others. . . . My sisters, remember not only who you are, but all that is yours."[46] J. Collison, identifying himself to the *Inquirer* as "King of Prussia," wrote, "Do we get a turn now to have a march for whites only? No, of course not. That would be racist."[47] Despite a diversity of views from the public, the majority of commentary posted to the Web site was supportive of the march. As time passed, however, the difficulty of sustaining the march's coalition became evident as the organization imploded under the weight of its phenomenal success. In October 1998 *Inquirer* reporter Karen E. Quinones Miller wrote several articles on the organizational split that occurred after the march. At the heart of the split, Quinones Miller found, was the statement by co-chairs Chionesu and Coney that "we both decided that we had to move forward, but we did not necessarily agree on the direction." In fact, the women announced at a town meeting that "one organization is now two," the Million Woman Universal Movement and Sisters of the Million Woman March.[48] Cognizant of how the split could negate the march's unifying effect, Coney insisted that, "you will not see Phile and I attacking each other, and you can be clear that if she needs me, I will be there, and vice-versa."[49] Indeed, Coney and Chionesu reaffirmed their mutual commitment to the cause when they both participated in the April 2001 "Race in Digital Space" conference at the Massachusetts Institute of Technology. Notwithstanding their remarkable ability to organize the march in Philadelphia in 1997, the organization's implosion may be most exemplary of Hakim Bey's observation that the temporary autonomous zone's "greatest strength lies in its invisibility." Because, he goes on to say, "As soon as the [zone] is named (represented, mediated), it must vanish, it *will* vanish, leaving behind it an empty husk, only to spring up again somewhere else, once again invisible because undefinable in terms of the Spectacle."[50] As if confirming Bey's thesis, the spirit of the Million Woman March influenced another iteration of the zone as the predominately white-women-led Million Mom March was called to push forward a revived gun control campaign after the 1999 Columbine High School shootings.

CONCLUSION

Although commercial imperatives of network systems' ratings television invariably disregards black women as both citizens and consumers, black women have used the Internet's logic of decentralization to reposition themselves, if only briefly, at the center of public life in America.[51] Surely, the role of the Internet (as well as camcorders) in constructing a temporary autonomous zone enabled march organizers to disabuse the nation momentarily of the view that women required special protection both *from* and *in* the public sphere. Having said that, one point must be made. We are well advised to adopt Herman Gray's suspicions of "uncritical celebrations of the practices of collective and individual subjects (the working class, women, people of color) as resistance."[52] Thus, to remain vigilant in our efforts to scrutinize both the hyperbole of new media deification and demonization we must strain to situate our knowledges of new and traditional media production and consumption in actual cases of the often unanticipated use of media. In that vein, I have demonstrated here that television's power to "edit" its publics is equally matched by black women's determination not to be ignored as they take their historic grievances to the streets, with or without the televisual panopticon. In the 1980s a short-lived maverick television news and information program called *South Africa Now* began each show emphasizing television's then unparalleled influence with the adage, "If it's not on TV, it doesn't exist." The arrival of the Internet, however, has modified this once widely held truism; perhaps the new adage should be, "If it's not on TV, it probably *does* exist on the Internet."

NOTES

1. See, for example, Michael Janofsky's report on the Million Woman March in his article "At Million Woman March, Focus Is on Family," *New York Times*, October 26, 1997, p. A1.

2. For a thorough discussion of this and other ongoing concerns, see, for example, the editorial "Million Man March: Almost a Blackout," *Los Angeles Sentinel*, October 26, 1995, p. A6.

3. Elsa Barkley Brown, "Negotiating and Transforming the Public Sphere: African American Political Life in the Transition from Slavery to Freedom," in *The Black Public Sphere*, ed. Black Public Sphere Collective (Chicago: University of Chicago Press, 1995), p. 111.

4. For background on the organizers, see Karen E. Quinones Miller, "One Year Later, Marching Apart," *Philadelphia Inquirer*, October 25, 1998, http://www.philly.com/package/wmill/Inq/mill102598.asp.

5. Chionesu, quoted in ibid.

6. See the *Final Call* interview with Phile Chionesu and Asia Coney at http://www.netset.com/~kandi/index8.html/guests.html/intrvw1.html.

7. The significance of the Internet in the success of the Million Woman March was relayed to me in an e-mail from the march's Web site manager, Ken Anderson, on October 30, 1997.

8. A similar charge of whiting out matters of concern within the black community by television broadcasters was made with respect to the noncoverage of the Million Man March two years earlier; see the editorial "Million Man March: Almost a Blackout," *Los Angeles Sentinel*, October 26, 1995, p. A6. Despite the avoidance of this story by the national TV media, some mainstream print media outlets, C-SPAN, and Philadelphia's local stations were compelled to cover the event as it unfolded because the unprecedented numbers made the event newsworthy.

9. For a creatively insightful look at women's underacknowledged participation in computer science, see Sadie Plant, *Zeroes + Ones: Digital Women and the New Technoculture* (London: Fourth Estate, 1997).

10. Laura Miller, "Women and Children First: Gender and the Settling of the Electronic Frontier," in *Resisting the Virtual Life: The Culture and Politics of Information*, ed. James Brook and Iain A. Boal (San Francisco: City Lights, 1995), pp. 50–53.

11. Paolo Carpignano et al. discuss the shifting construction of the mass media as today's problematic public sphere in "Chatter in the Age of Electronic Reproduction: Talk Television and the 'Public Mind,'" *Social Text* 25/26 (1990): 33–55.

12. The quoted term is borrowed from Sohnya Sayres, "Accepted Bounds," *Social Text* 25/26 (1990): 119–28.

13. Lynn Spigel, "Television in the Family Circle: The Popular Reception of a New Medium," in *Logics of Television: Essays in Cultural Criticism*, ed. Patricia Mellencamp (Bloomington: Indiana University Press, 1990), p. 78.

14. See my essay, "Civil Rights Movement and Television," in *The Television Encyclopedia*, ed. Horace Newcomb (Chicago: Dearborn-Fitzroy, 1997), pp. 370–73.

15. For a complete discussion of Fannie Lou Hamer's pivotal role in the civil rights movement, see the biography by Kay Mills, *This Little Light of Mine: The Life of Fannie Lou Hamer* (New York: Plume, 1993).

16. A more complete account of the contested history of Truth's legendary utterance can be found at http://www.britannica.com/women/pri/q00160.html.

17. Joanne M. Braxton, *Black Women Writing Autobiography: A Tradition within a Tradition* (Philadelphia: Temple University Press, 1989), p. 30.

18. Ibid.

19. The text of the speech here is taken from my transcription of a videotape of the event sent to me by march Web site manager Ken Anderson. I hasten to add that Waters's tag line, "I am you, and you are me," was delivered prior to another utterance of that phrase that seared it forever into our public consciousness. Waters's phrase, however, must be understood as circulating before Linda Tripp of the Clinton-Lewinsky scandal used it.

20. The issue of the digital divide has captured the public imagination and has been, and continues to be, debated at length. See, for example, the PBS documentary *The Digital Divide,* which aired in January 2000; Jube Shiver Jr., "Racial Divide Is Growing in Internet Use," *Los Angeles Times,* July 9, 1999, p. A10; and "More Blacks Are Using Internet, Survey Finds," *New York Times,* October 23, 2000, p. A21.

21. See Michel de Certeau's dedication page in *The Practice of Everyday Life,* trans. Steven Rendall (Berkeley: University of California Press, 1984); and Eric Auchard's "World Leaders Take Fresh Look at Digital Divide," http://dailynews.yahoo.com/h/nm/20010717/wr/column_pluggedin_dc_2.html.

22. de Certeau, *Practice of Everyday Life,* pp. 24–25.

23. Ken Anderson, e-mail to author, October 30, 1997.

24. Kenneth C. Laudon, "Promise versus Performance of Cable," in *Wired Cities: Shaping the Future of Communications,* ed. William H. Dutton et al. (Boston: G. K. Hall, 1987), p. 36.

25. Patricia Mellencamp, "Video and the Counterculture," in *Global Television,* ed. Cynthia Schneider and Brian Wallis (Cambridge: MIT Press, 1988), p. 200.

26. The quoted term is from Chela Sandoval, "New Sciences: Cyborg Feminism and the Methodology of the Oppressed," in the *Cybercultures Reader,* ed. David Bell and Barbara Kennedy (London and New York: Routledge, 2000), pp. 374–87.

27. Granted, the march's extensive C-SPAN excerpts might be a result of the participation of videographers in the march, which likely precluded the taping of this and other live television coverage.

28. For a description of these groups, see Mellencamp, "Video and the Counterculture," pp. 198–223.

29. Marchers were instructed to mail their materials to the Philadelphia headquarters; see "Video, Photos, Experiences at the Million Woman March," at http://timesx2.com/mem/page39.html.

30. Mellencamp, "Video and the Counterculture," p. 201.

31. Hakim Bey, "The Temporary Autonomous Zone," http://www.to.or.at/hakimbey/taz/taz3a.html.

32. Chela Sadoval, p. 375.

33. Anderson, e-mail to author, October 30, 1997.

34. Turing, quoted in Plant, *Zeroes + Ones,* pp. 88.

35. Plant, *Zeroes + Ones,* pp. 88–89.

36. See "Successful Million Woman March Generates $21.7 Million," June 3, 1998, http://www.afamnet.com/nationalpage/frontpage/110597_million.htm.

37. Ibid.

38. This quote is from the original 1997 Million Woman March Web site (now defunct), which outlined the march's twelve "platform issues."

39. More information on the pre-march convention held in Philadelphia on July 16–19, 1997, can be found on http://www.netset.com/~khandi/index8.html/guests.html/milsis.html.

40. Chionesu, quoted in ibid.

41. Million Woman March, international scam alert, at http://timesx2.com/mwm/page42.html.

42. Ibid.

43. See the full text of Hull's article at http://www.aynrand.org/medialink/tribalism.html.

44. The complete text of this letter can be found at "Letters to the Editor," "Missteps on Women's March," *Daily News,* October 31, 1997, http://www.philly.com/packages/wmill/opin/dn/lmar31.asp.

45. Ibid.

46. See Letters to the Editor, "The Million Woman March," *Philadelphia Inquirer* November 2, 1997, http://www.philly.com/packages/wmill/opin/inq/corn02.asp.

47. Ibid.

48. Chionesu and Coney cited in Karen E. Quinones Miller, "Million Woman March Organizers Split Group," *Philadelphia Inquirer,* October 12, 1998, http://www.philly.com/packages/wmill/inq/mrch12.asp. See also her article "One Year Later, Marching Apart," *Philadelphia Inquirer,* October 25, 1998, http://www.philly.com/packages/wmill/inq/mill102598.asp.

49. Coney cited in Quinones Miller, "Million Woman March."

50. Bey, "Temporary Autonomous Zone." In his discussion of the concept of the temporary autonomous zone as a more viable approach to world change, Bey writes: "I distrust the word revolution. . . . Even if we replace the revolutionary approach with a concept of insurrection blossoming spontaneously into anarchist culture, our own particular historical situation is not propitious for such a vast undertaking. Absolutely nothing but a futile martyrdom could possibly result now from a head-on collision with the terminal State, the megacorporate information State, the empire of Spectacle and Simulation."

51. In part, this disregard is connected to the larger issue of how audiences are imagined and measured by market research companies. On this issue of audience measurement and its "illogics," see Eileen Meehan, "Why We Don't Count," in Mellencamp, ed., *Logics of Television,* p. 126.

52. Herman Gray, *Watching Race: Television and the Struggle for "Blackness,"* (Minneapolis: University of Minnesota Press, 1995), p. 3.

This group of essays addresses electronic media's relationship to nationalism, globalization, and what might be called the politics of dislocation that mobile communication systems both introduce and redress. Dealing both with broad issues of political economy and with the more "local" issues of text, context, and reception, this section demonstrates the way television travels simultaneously within global, local, national, and diasporic contexts. In the process, the authors collectively show how television and new forms of electronic media contribute to our sense of place, nation, community, borders, and cultural contact with distant others.

The first two essays are historical in nature, and both attempt to reconsider how the history of national media industries should be conceptualized and written. Jan Olsson's "One Commercial Week: Television in Sweden Prior to Public Service" is a detailed historical account of Sweden's early attempts to install the new technology of television into its national culture. The essay explores both commercial and government agendas, showing how the early convergence among media industries of film, radio, and television became a site of national struggle. Olsson argues that "convergence" is not simply a contemporary phenomenon caused by new media mergers but rather should also be understood as a historical phenomenon, common to previous moments in television's innovation. Olsson reframes the focus of television history, in this case by demonstrating that the typically assumed divisions between the American commercial system and European public service models were not so distinct in practice. With this framework in mind, Olsson details the case of a week-long Swedish initiative in 1954 to promote television through public displays of TV in commercial venues. In the process, he shows how the early commercial model was eclipsed by state-controlled public service broadcasting yet in many ways was also a foundation for it. He additionally demonstrates how Sweden's national public service model both defined itself against and yet actively sought to emulate U.S. commercial programming.

Michael Curtin's "Media Capitals: Cultural Geographies of Global TV" traces the history of three "media capitals" and reflects on their changing fortunes during the last fifty years of television. Curtin refocuses the object of television history—in this case by demonstrating that the rise of any national television system should be studied not simply via the standard "national media" model that traces the development of television in one national state. Instead, he argues that the history of national television systems must be examined cross-culturally and through methods that allow us to understand the convergence between media distribution systems across national space. To this effect, Curtin considers the broad cultural geography of the television age by drawing comparisons among three cities (Chicago, Los Angeles, and Hong Kong), and he looks at changing patterns of production, distribution, and exhibition. Considering the different fates of the three production centers since the 1950s, Curtain ends by examining the contemporary global connections between Hollywood and Hong Kong. More speculatively, he questions how these mergers relate to changing concepts of the nation-state.

David Morley's "At Home with Television" explores the role of broadcasting and new media in the construction of a symbolic sense of home— or *Heimat*—for national and diaspora populations. Following the work of critical geographers, he argues that the postmodern universe is one that stresses phenomena such as mobility, placelessness, and various forms of "homelessness." Morley considers such theorizations of placelessness in relation to the spatial disembedding and space-time compression that are held to be the consequence of new technologies of communication. In the process he also explores the possibilities for the development of a strand of television studies that reintegrates traditional geographical concerns with patterns of residence, mobility, and transportation systems alongside the focus on systems of symbolic communications, which is now more conventional within the field.

Priscilla Peña Ovalle ends this section with a case study of the digital diaspora and the identity politics of TV/digital convergence. Like Anna Everett, Ovalle is interested in how publics that were historically disenfranchised by television use the Internet to gather; but her essay "Pocho.com: Reimaging Television on the Internet" specifically links this to issues of diaspora and national identity by showing how diaspora/border communities use the Internet to critique mainstream U.S. media culture. Ovalle's essay focuses on Pocho.com, a Web site that engages a particular identity formation of Latino publics. Forged both in distinction to Chicano/a and Mexican Americaness, Pocho.com recuperates the pejorative term "Pocho" for purposes of political satire, and, Ovalle argues, the Web site directly critiques mainstream television's marginalization and denigration of Mexican Americans by poking fun at mainstream news, sitcoms, and other genres. In a more serious way, the site also provides opportunities for media activism and political activism more generally, and for rethinking the history of the Chicano/a movement for a newer generation.

JAN OLSSON **ONE COMMERCIAL**

WEEK: TELEVISION IN SWEDEN

PRIOR TO PUBLIC SERVICE

In Europe, television was predominantly introduced as a national public service institution, while American television from the outset came to the fore as a commercial undertaking. In this essay I deal with the inception of television in Sweden, belatedly introduced in the mid-1950s after a research and experiment phase that started in 1947. Sweden's geography, in combination with its limited and dispersed population, complicated television's introduction. Even more of a complication factor was the political vacillations concerning whether to adopt a mode of production that was strictly public service, and thus part of the corporate structure of the national radio, or to accept some form of commercial input. By focusing on one specific media event and its reception, the so-called Sandrew Television Week in May 1954, I will take a closer look at the discursive frames vis-à-vis commercial television in the Swedish context. After the alluring success of this weeklong preamble to commercial television, produced by the Sandrew film company, the Swedish audience had to wait decades for the next commercial opportunity—or onslaught. The Sandrew Week coincided with and even exacerbated a volatile spurt leading up to a formal parliamentary decision on the future of the medium, which then eventually halted the vacillations.

In the 1986 study *Kampen om TV* (The television feud), Karl-Hugo Wirén meticulously maps the power play between interest groups ranging from the inception of a small research body in 1947 to the formal decision in Parliament in May 1956 to award the concession for the new medium to the Swedish Radio Corporation (Radiotjänst).[1] Overall, the political-economic level of television in Sweden has inspired much more scholarly attention than has the history of televisual representations, the establishing of program formats, and the interplay in the "flow" between domestic and syndicated programs.[2] Even the peculiarities of audience formations and viewing spaces—that is, beyond the cornucopia of statistical information—have largely gone unnoticed. Besides the structural gambits in the lofty spheres of political economy, issues concerning media effects have dominated the research agenda, with, in the last decade, somewhat of an ethnographic slant.[3] The lack of competition and program choices for the audience positioned the television medium at center stage of a national frame of experiences for more than a decade. The formation of a Swedish television audience is thus riveted to a single channel, initially with few broadcasting hours per day, without options for zapping or channel surfing. The production and distribution of television in Sweden thus represent activities within one and only one institution framing all radio and television undertakings from the mid-1950s up until cables and satellites eventually introduced scores of channels of all stripes. One would expect that such a monolithic viewing environment would prompt research on formats, modes of address, and representational matters, and that these aspects of the televisual landscape would be situated in relation to issues of "suburbanization," family life, and the overall political framework of the late 1950s and early 1960s. This is not, however, the case.

To be sure, this lack of research has to do in part with the absence of a proper institutional framework for television studies in Swedish academia. Scholars have primarily been preoccupied with the institution and the politics of public service and have focused on certain program types—news, documentaries, and social affairs—or the balance between high-art undertakings and entertainment, and have yet to confront questions concerning spectatorship and narrative. Scholars have predominately emulated a mass-media inflected perspective informed by critical stances from communication studies, sociology, and political science. During the 1990s, however, a major research undertaking devoted to "ether media" in Sweden has generated several valuable studies. Overall, the perspective is centered on program production within the public service company, and the scholars deploy a systematic frame of reference for both radio and television. The focus on both media, which more or less inform all the studies, provides a first survey of the contours of the field, however without an outlook on the international television history and with few references to the disciplinary horizons of television studies. It might be that as an institutionalized viewing habitat, public service television engenders a televisual avenue of research framed by the social sciences, while clear-cut commercial-television habitats inspire scholarly agendas informed by discursive analysis, issues of spectatorship, and a theoretical vocabulary affiliated with cinema studies and/or cultural studies.

In spite of the monopoly structure, introduced as a so-called quality alternative to commercial programming, a host of commercial formats were picked up from American models and inserted into the Swedish monopoly "flow." And, even more interesting, many American shows—for example, *The Perry Como Show, Perry Mason, I Love Lucy,* and *Bonanza*—were brought to Sweden and aired for many years but, of course, without breaks for commercials. Paradoxically, the Swedish audience for these shows was larger than the American audience and had more viewing options across the schedule. When *Bonanza* was rerun and repackaged in the early 1980s as "vintage" television, over 60 percent of the Swedish audience turned on the sets.

The competition, detailed by Wirén, between interest groups prior to Parliament's decision to award a television monopoly to the Swedish Radio Corporation provides the backdrop for my discussion here of the Sandrew Television Week.[4] In retrospect, the Sandrew Week of commercial television—spearheaded by the Board of Telecommunications, the radio industry, and Philips and others in the hardware business—represents a matter of radical difference in relation to the story of television in Sweden, otherwise strictly public service. The Sandrew Week marks the overture to television, in a highly ambitious fashion, showing the medium's possibilities and illustrating various program formats. The Sandrew Week also marks a televisual avenue not further explored, or rather, an unwanted model aborted by the authorities.

Television spectatorship in Sweden thus started in public spaces as a major media event during a time when there were only around three hundred sets owned by an exclusive group of households in Stockholm, households that in most cases were affiliated with the industry. The Sandrew Week was primarily a local affair, given the transmitter's limited coverage. Broadcasting to only a few hundred homes does not in itself constitute a media event, but together with a structure for reaching a wider nonhome audience, the Sandrew Week became precisely such an occurrence. In order to avoid a Stockholm-centered perspective, it is important to stress that parts of southern Sweden enjoyed access to Danish television starting in 1952; that part of the country could eventually zap between two national channels. An enterprising group of local television enthusiasts in the northwest part of Sweden's most southern province, Scania (Skåne), even organized public shows in a barn in a hilly village at a time when they could offer only Danish programming.

Before discussing the Sandrew Week, I will first provide a brief overview of the struggle for control over television broadcasting, based largely on Wirén's research, in order to situate the Sandrew Week in its genealogical context of political economy and discursive framing. Television found its first home at the Royal Institute of Technology as the Agency for Television Research, founded and managed by the institute, the National Board of Telecommunications, the Ericsson Telecommunication Company, and the Defense Research Establishment. In 1949, Radiotjänst (the Swedish Radio Corporation) and the radio industry became partners in the so-called interest group controlling the Agency for Television Research. Five companies represented the radio industry: four domestic groups (AB Aga Baltic, AB Gylling & Co, Luxor Radio AB, and Svenska Radio AB) and the Swedish branch of Philips. After initially focusing on technical standards for broadcasting, the agency's next step was to build an experimental transmitter for local broadcasting in Stockholm. It was ready in 1949 and housed at the Royal Institute of Technology. Eventually actual transmission became an issue, but only during a few hours per week and strictly for research purposes. Prior to this limited and highly local broadcasting that started in 1950, at a time when television sets were not offered on the market, the agency was extremely discreet about its activities and the technical state of affairs. In particular, the radio industry adamantly demanded maximum silence; that is, the market should not suspect that television was in the pipeline. Such an expectation, the industry worried, would negatively affect the sale of radio receivers—a fear openly acknowledged in the records. The press was therefore not regularly updated on the agency's activities. Behind the scene lurked the truly crucial issue of how to organize program production once the medium became a reality. There were basically two competing models with some overlap between them. The first operated on a domestic radio analogy vying for a national television monopoly and hoping to offer the same line of "quality" programming as radio. Consequently, according to this plan, television was to be organized within the framework of the Swedish Radio Corporation. At that time, the radio monopoly still transmitted over only one national channel. This noncommercial, radio-inflected model for television sought financing via license fees from owners of television sets. Initially, before the medium had leverage enough to collect a substantial level of license income, the proponents for the model expected the government to allocate resources.

After a series of proposals and shifting alliances (to which I will return), the second model for television eventually emerged as a spin-off from the film industry and was based on commercial financing. It came to be embodied by the Sandrew Week. Advertising and business interests, particularly the radio industry, then on the verge of taking on the hardware market for television, were intrigued by the prospects of rapid market penetration offered by an already functioning production structure for moving images. The film industry could mobilize considerable production resources, while the Swedish Radio Corporation had only limited camera experience within the agency and at that time no production capacity. After a previous attempt from the radio industry at achieving concession for experimental broadcasting in 1953, the agency eventually hooked up with the film industry for the Sandrew Week. Thus an alternative to radio-controlled television emerged, offering a model for commercial broadcasting and a program constellation that could produce a sufficient number of attractive program hours per day.

The film industry, and particularly theater owners, otherwise showed little if no enthusiasm for television. It is telling that the Sandrew Week emanated from the division at Sandrew studios that produced commercials and films commissioned by clients. The studio head himself, Mr. Sandrew, expressed no interest in the new medium and framed his negative response from the perspective of film exhibition. The prime mover was, instead, Bo Löfberg, head of the division for client-commissioned films. The Sandrew Week came about after a series of earlier initiatives originating from the radio industry.

Tensions within the interest group for the Agency for Television Research had resulted in a transfer of mandate to a government commission appointed in 1951. At this stage the radio industry wanted the agency to expand its broadcasting agenda, but the board was not ready for this move and therefore was instrumental in blocking the proposal and bringing about a government commission with a new set of players. The commission was instructed, as a basis for a government bill, to investigate all aspects of televisual possibilities and come up with a proposal on how to organize broadcasting in Sweden. Both the Board of Telecommunications and the Swedish Radio Corporation were represented in the commission, while the radio industry had less influence, with only one representative who did not come from the radio industry proper. The formation of the commission to a certain extent marked the board's victory over the radio industry in terms of control of the future transmission of signals. As a government authority, the board could not, however, act independently of the political leadership and the ministry of communication, nor could the board escape their logic. At a critical juncture, the board actually pushed too hard in a direction that the social-democratic government did not want to endorse, and that push resulted in the concession for the Sandrew Week. At that time the commission had been in place for almost three years. Prompted by the Sandrew Week in May, it seems, the commission finally managed to come up with its findings, conclusions, and recommendations a few months later. At one stage of its work, in a tentative report from 1952, the commission itself sought a more active broadcasting role by requesting money from the government to conduct transmission, under its own auspices, from the Royal Institute of Technology. The government turned down the commission's proposal, so the scope of the weekly experimental broadcasting stayed the same and organization continued through the obsolete agency along with the technical division of the Swedish Radio Corporation.

By refusing to grant resources for broadcasting to the commission, the government repositioned it as a purely investigative body. The board, confident in terms of control over the distribution of television, at this stage wanted to pave the way for regular broadcasting without losing more time. From its perspective, commission-organized broadcasting represented a first bet at boosting the televisual activities. In the next round, the board and its representative in the commission, Erik Esping, backed a proposal dated 1953 from a consortium representing the radio industry, together with a mix of popular movements and commercial organizations. The consortium outlined plans for broadcasting eight to ten hours a week during 1954 and fifteen hours in 1955 through 1957. After 1957, the consortium expected that a state-sponsored network would take over. Sponsors were to finance 75 percent of the program time. After long deliberations, and after referring the proposal for consideration to an array of interest groups and organizations, the government turned it down in February 1954. Several weeks before the government's formal decision, the Sandrew studios sought a concession for commercial broadcasting for two hours a day.

Sandrew's initiative was embraced by the radio industry and supported by the board, particularly by Erik Esping, one of the more high-profile commissioners. In fact, Esping was instrumental in piloting the application to a favorable outcome that eventually granted a concession for broadcasting. In the wake of the process, the board lost its right to issue such concessions. The board's privilege was revoked by the government on June 4, 1954, less than two weeks after the conclusion of the Sandrew Week. Not surprisingly, given the government's hesitation that Esping and the board had encountered, and bypassed, concerning the first Sandrew application, the government later turned down a second application from the Sandrew studios for broadcasting during fall 1954 and into 1955. This second, more extensive, application was filed in March—that is, prior to the Sandrew Week in May. By chance or design, the very day that Sandrew filed its second application the Swedish Radio Corporation also sought a concession and a small budget for a more intense experimental phase of broadcasting. At this highly critical juncture the government, now on the verge of taking over the right to issue concessions after reprimanding the board, had two radically different alternatives to review. One of them was in the process of achieving a track record, the commercial one, after a couplike intervention by the board. The Swedish Radio Corporation indeed had some technical know-how via the agency, but it also had limited production experience. The Radio Corporation did, however, host an informal Television Club organized by employees, a group that had so far enjoyed little support from the corporate level. The outcome of the equation was that the government decided to award a test concession to the Radio Corporation and then allocate the modest sum of money requested—about $870,000—for training a television crew within the framework instituted by the agency.

At this point, the commission had yet to present its findings and recommendations. The board's strategic alliance with the commercial model not only provoked the government but also Erik Esping's colleagues in the commission, and not least the representatives from the Swedish Radio Corporation. The latter body had been if not an active partner in the commission's proposal from 1952 then at least a silent one acknowledged as the "natural" program provider within the framework of the proposal. The tables turned when the radio industry, after initially backing the commission's initiative, repositioned itself as partner together with a film studio in a scheme for commercial television. With a concession issued by the board, and backing from the radio industry, the Sandrew studios at that stage represented a full-fledged television alternative that also appealed to advertising agencies and business interests. The radio model was still strongly supported by newspaper interests, who by chance also controlled 75 percent of the stocks in the Swedish Radio Corporation. Furthermore, the newspapers were not keen on a competition for advertisements from a new medium. The newspaper organization was allied with several popular movements, many with a conservative outlook on cultural change. More important, the social-democratic government, particularly the secretary of communications, who was responsible for telecommunication matters, shared the anti-commercial bias.

When the board had propelled the commercial alternative spear-headed by the film industry, the majority in the government commission decided to increase the tempo and deliver its recommendation in late 1954. The commission's majority eventually favored the radio model. The Swedish Radio Corporation had by then already regained the initiative when the government turned down the Sandrew studios' second appli-cation. In the commission, only Esping militated against awarding a monopoly concession to the Radio Corporation. Esping had, however, one partner in arguing for a financing model that included revenues from sponsored programs and commercials: Mr. Nyström, the representative from the electronics industry. Along this line, Esping and Nyström pro-posed an alternative to the majority's recommendation by arguing for a combined model including commercial interests, particularly the Sand-rew studios, as partners in the production structure. The Sandrew Week had by then successfully demonstrated the viability of a commercial television concept. Commercial financing was, of course, possible even within a monopoly structure controlled by the Radio Corporation. If the commercial capacity and competence were bypassed, the minority claimed, the development would be too slow and would translate to a very limited amount of broadcasting hours per week. It goes without saying that the radio industry wanted as much broadcasting as possible to stimulate the sale of sets. And from such a perspective the film industry was, if nothing else, an important program provider.

During 1955, before presenting a bill to Parliament, the Ministry of Communication was active behind the scenes, and the commercial inter-ests had not yet given up hope of being partners within a national mo-nopoly. The government bill was presented in Parliament in 1956 and won a majority on May 24 of that year. The monopoly concession was thereby formally awarded to the Radio Corporation. There were to be no commercial or sponsored programs. Television was to be financed by licenses paid by owners of television sets and by subsidies from the government.

Thus, television in Sweden came to be developed within a media configuration free from market considerations and was based on a pro-gram concept envisioned as educational, culturally uplifting, and inter-spersed with quality entertainment along with a centralized, semiofficial voice for news. Objectivity and diversity were part of the instruction. In the debate leading up to the concession, American television represented both a model to shun, according to those inclined toward public service, and one to emulate with a local slant for those vying for commercial television. The agency had, in fact, been instituted after field trips to the United States in the mid-1940s by two young engineers from the Royal Institute of Technology, Hans Werthén and Björn Nilsson. They returned very enthusiastic about what they had seen. Over the years a host of delegations crossed the Atlantic to get a firsthand impression of U.S. models for television. Even prior to the establishment of the agency, Swedish newspapers reported with some regularity on the television situation in the United States. Particularly for those with a limited interest in the medium, the American commercial structure allegedly evidenced how superficial television was in the hands of the market.[5] The concession given to the Swedish Radio Corporation, devised as an alternative to such models, did not, however, preclude the import of some of the most popular American program formats and series.

One can, of course, dismiss the relevance of such a monolithic construction of American television. In the Swedish discourse, it hovered in the background as the undesirable other in campaigns for a public model. As Michael Curtin's research on early television in Chicago demonstrates, there were several production centers in the United States recruiting local talents from stage, radio, and other venues and testing different types of program formats prior to the gradual relocation of production to Hollywood.[6] The latter process and the shifting strategies deployed vis-à-vis television by the film industry have been analyzed in depth by Christopher Anderson.[7] And although Swedish critics often denounced American TV commercials, Sandrew studios aired sponsored programs that resembled early U.S. programs like *Texaco Star Theater*, which were sponsored by and named for single corporations.

The Television Week was launched at a time when both the Sandrew studios' second application and the one from the Swedish Radio Corporation were awaiting government decision—and the commission had yet to present its recommendations. In fact, the targeted audience for the Television Week was foremost the members of Parliament, a group that eventually would determine the faith of the new medium. Sandrew's ambition vividly illustrated what could be expected from a commercial television model, and the industry wanted the politicians to have a firsthand experience of a Swedish commercial alternative rather than only a vague impression of American commercial television. The hardware industry, represented by Philips, wrote to the speaker of Parliament asking for permission to place sets in the building to enable decision makers to acquaint themselves with this particular form of television during the week. The request was granted and a handful of sets were placed in Parliament, with one in the office of the secretary of communications. In addition, consoles were placed in the press union's headquarters to propel press coverage.

Predictably, those less enthusiastic about commercial television claimed that one showcase week would not give an accurate impression of what regular run-of-the-mill programming would offer; the leading social-democratic newspaper, for instance, represented this line of reasoning. From the perspectives of press coverage and audience penetration, the Sandrew Week most certainly fulfilled its ambitions, even if neither the commission nor the government was won over. What made the week a major media event was the widespread introduction of television in different types of public spaces, with an array of sets placed in radio retailers' windows, department stores, restaurants, film theater lobbies, and so on. It was mandatory to apply for police permission for public outdoor exhibitions of this kind, and some venues had done so. However, the police had turned down a handful of such applications on the grounds that the expected throng outside the shop windows would block traffic. Some shops had not applied for permission and were apparently unaware that permission was required. A few of the negligent shops were reported by police patrols, but the district attorney wisely refrained from taking the perpetrators to court. Needless to say, the police records are helpful in locating where sets were available to the public. Predictably, the concentration was high along the popular downtown thoroughfares. Some of the week's key venues had in fact offered television during demonstrations arranged even prior to the establishment of the agency, for instance the department store NK (Nordiska Kompaniet). One movie theater, the Royal, owned by Sandrew, offered big-screen projection during the broadcasting hours, between four and six in the afternoon.

The very first demonstration in Sweden of the new medium took place at the Röda Kvarn movie theater in December 1930, where the system presented was by John Loggie Baird, the Scottish television pioneer. Local entertainers were presented from a studio, while the sound component was delivered by way of telephone, in an interesting media constellation. In 1935, Svenska Radiobolaget hosted a more academic and technical demonstration by broadcasting from the company's offices to the Royal Institute of Technology. In 1938, Philips and one of the morning newspapers, *Stockholms-Tidningen,* gave a week-long demonstration featuring domestic actors and international celebrities like Josephine Baker. And the same newspaper, *Stockholms-Tidningen,* along with the British company Pye Limited, transmitted from a movie theater, the China, to the department store NK in 1948. An amusement park in Gothenburg hosted another experiment in 1950, again with Pye. Further, the agency had organized a handful of demonstrations in addition to the test broadcast on most Wednesday afternoons. Department stores, amusement parks, and more academic arenas thus represented the first venues for this new technological attraction. The montage of exhibition spaces is almost identical to the sites favored for the introduction of moving pictures at the turn of the century.

For the Television Week in 1954, the permissions issued by police came with four conditions: somebody responsible had to be inside the shop during broadcasting; the set had to be turned off if a throng should form and block the sidewalk or street traffic; the loudspeaker volume had to be regulated so as not to cause disturbances; and all instructions from police officers had to be followed without delay. All in all, seventy-seven applications for public broadcasting reached the police authorities (five of which were not granted due to expected traffic problems).[8] In addition, the police reported six shops for broadcasting without permission. One can surmise that many more had failed to secure permission, but that their locations were less conspicuous or less prone to attract traffic-blocking crowds, and hence not deemed problematic by the police. Indeed, the six offenders, five radio retailers and one bookstore, all had very central downtown addresses.[9] Radio retailers dominated the group with permits, but it also included tailors, men's shops, candy stores, bookstores, paint shops, a travel agency, a group of food stores belonging to the cooperative Konsum group, a bank, a printer, and a publisher. The majority of businesses were located downtown, but several were in the suburbs or in remote city districts.

The total number of sets available for public audiences, then including indoor broadcasting not requiring permission, was estimated to be between one thousand and twelve hundred. It is virtually impossible in retrospect to track down more than a few of the indoor venues. The well-known ones were, apart from Parliament (six sets) and the press center at Rosenbad (five sets), the department stores NK and Pub (around ten each), and lobbies in the movie theaters Rigoletto, Palladium, Röda Kvarn, and Park. As mentioned above, the Royal theater offered big-screen projection and donated the entrance fees to a charity organization for children. Ostermans Marble Halls hosted seven Radiola sets and, just like the Royal, they charged an entrance fee, about 10¢, that was donated to charity. It was, apparently, important not to make money on commercial television at this stage. A legitimate theater owned by Sandrew, Intima Teatern, had installed five sets in the lobby. Several restaurants showed television, for instance, Solliden at the Skansen outdoor museum. And one of the public baths, Centralbadet, allegedly offered broadcasting.

A veritable media hype during spring 1954 mobilized an enormous interest for the Sandrew Week in May. Newspapers and weekly magazines of all stripes propelled a frenzied expectation of something truly exceptional, irrespective of the previous small-scale demonstrations of the medium. The Sandrew Week was marketed as the real thing and nothing less than a full-scale model of television proper ready to proceed to the next level within months if the politicians so wished. The medium's future was envisioned as a form of family-based home entertainment, which would translate into nice sales figures for the hardware companies. As Lynn Spigel's research vividly illustrates, home-based television puts in motion an imaginary, multilayered mobility via the representational frames offered.[10] The Sandrew Week, however, offered a radically different experience of mobility by situating the medium in a complex montage of public terrains embracing an array of venues offering shifting spatial constellations and spectatorial interfaces. There were both indoor and outdoor sites; places for entertainment or dining as well as places of commerce; commerce-related venues dedicated to radio or television hardware as well as businesses offering totally different types of goods; and spaces inspiring either thoughtful flânerie or brisker activities. Overall, television was situated either in a metropolitan constellation of spaces, defined by a regulated flow of traffic and pedestrian distractions, or in inside places with well-defined agendas in terms of commerce or culture or exhibition.

Pedestrian traffic nodes and hubs were particularly attractive sites for television owing to the sheer number of people normally intersecting there. The police permits explicitly underscored the importance of maintaining an uninterrupted flow around such hubs by turning down applications targeting these places. Televisual spectatorship thus was expected to mobilize a potential, and paradoxical, threat to metropolitan normality by putting forward a media attraction designed to temporarily transform areas devised for passage to sites for congregation in front of screens displaying TV entertainment. Such a formation of audiences brought sidewalk flow to a standstill by causing pedestrians to stop to gaze at the screen instead of casting passing glances at the shop window. The riveting attention solicited by the window display did not trigger anything beyond the visual pleasure itself; there was nothing to buy in the aftermath of the viewing experience, except perhaps the goods or services marketed by the program sponsors. The display launched an attraction that commanded a longer attention span than the distractions otherwise offered in the shop windows. Television thereby transformed the shop windows into theatrical exhibition spaces. As evidenced from manuals for window display, the trick was to devise an arrangement or constellation of display items that caught the prospective shopper's attention. What was being marketed was, instead, a media blueprint, a set of program formats, a virtual competition or duel between two televisual regimes—one on display, the other still only a horizon of expectations.

Thus, prior to relegating television spectatorship to its "natural" site, the home, the audience for the then nonexistent broadcast medium was temporarily constituted on the streets by leaving the homes to experience the televisual thrill in public venues or on the sidewalks. In this respect, the introduction of television was framed as a major publicity campaign engineered to ensure both a concession for future broadcasting and an audience excited enough to eventually, by buying consoles, take the medium off the streets and into their homes. Such a future state of affairs with a fragmented and family-based model for spectatorship would give the Board of Telecommunications the opportunity to distribute the signals; it would promote a longstanding structure for program production spearheaded by the film industry; and it would transform the hardware interest into a television industry. In the end, the hype that preceded the actual event effectively placed the Stockholm population in front of the sets and, in the process, temporarily shifted the metropolitan traffic to another, nonmoving gear. The sets transformed the sidewalks to spectator stands by their sheer attraction power. The sets installed in restaurants, cafes, and other public venues offered a middle ground and a mode of spectatorship with a lasting currency, particularly during television's first years. This mode of spectatorship is still a fixture in bars, lobbies, and airports. Moreover, for particular types of programs—for instance, major sport events with fan appeal—public viewing seems to be highly rewarding, as noted by Anna McCarthy in her analysis of the historical background for this type of spectatorship.[11]

The Board of Telecommunications' cooperation with Sandrew was highly visible during the week—the director-general, Håkan Sterky, delivered the opening address, and commissioner Esping gave a round-off speech on the final day. These program slots were sent live from the studio; the soundtracks were recorded if not aired by the Swedish Radio Corporation.[12] A substantial number of the Sandrew programs were filmed in advance at their studio at Lästmakargatan, which was used for all live broadcasts during the week. The signals were radio linked from the studio to the Royal Institute of Technology and transmitted from the institute. The technical team had access to two experienced experts from

Marconi, and the cameras came from the same company. The directors consisted of a handful of young Swedes under the apprenticeship of the more seasoned Andrew Osborne, who was semiaffiliated with the BBC. The filmed program slots used 35mm stock, with 16 mm for the news items. Overall, the technical aspects of the work earned praise in the press.

In the application for a Television Week, the studio outlined a program model based on a mix of live material and films. Thus, performance-driven modes were interspersed with consumer-oriented information, news, weather, sports, and educational matters. The performance section included jazz, operetta, opera, ballet, modern dance, and even the Salvation Army band. Program sponsorship was an integral aspect of the model, but the commercials were not allowed to interrupt the program flow. A sponsor who paid for a filmed program slot was awarded a one-minute commercial at the opening or closing of the program. Some of the sponsors built the entire program around their own product: Philips presented a tongue-in-cheek lecture on television; Svenska Radiobolaget presented a program devoted to a police car equipped with radio; the department store NK staged a fashion show on their own premises; a car importer showcased Volkswagen. The Radio Company Luxor was responsible for the operetta, or rather a string of duets performed by two young stars. The performers could, of course, also be enjoyed on record, which provided a link to the company's gramophone players. The link between a dance program—featuring both classical ballet and modern dance—and beauty products was less obvious and failed to convince the reviewers in the press. Other sponsors included the army (two programs), the Civil Defense Agency, a tire company, a cooperative food retailer chain, a private food retailer, Scandinavian Airlines, a shoe retailer, two banks, two petroleum companies (British Petroleum and Shell), an insurance company, a chocolate manufacturer, a sewing machine manufacturer, a research institute for consumer issues, a coffee roasting house, and a magazine for the clothing industry. In order to insure high program standards, an advisory board consisting of renowned pillars of society was appointed. The advisory board's selection of sponsors—many prospective ones were turned down—represented a cross-section of Swedish society, resulting in a commercial television model with a public service agenda.

The news section was presented by an anchorman who had been a radio correspondent in the United States for a decade. The news segment was in fact quasi independent of Sandrew and was turned over to a weekly magazine called *Se*, which was literally an emulation of *Look* magazine. The news photographer Svenolow Olsson had access to a car, helicopter, and all kinds of resources to capture on the fly more or less breaking news material. The news section was, however, the most complex aspect of the broadcasting undertaking, and the stress factor involved led to several mishaps during the first days. Needless to say, the films and studio-based live slots were much easier to handle. One aspect of the news, the weather forecast, presented by two meteorologists, from the Scandinavian Airlines System and the national weather service, respectively, turned out very well according to all accounts.

The magazine *Se* was published, in addition to a host of other weekly magazines, by Åhlén & Åkerlund. The publishing house then expanded its undertakings by the timely launching of a new magazine, *TV-Journalen* (The television journal), devoted to the upcoming week of broadcasting. Most of the advertisements in the journal came from program sponsors for the Sandrew Week. However, only one issue was published: when the televisual initiative was transferred to the Swedish Radio Corporation, their weekly radio magazine expanded its focus and added television to its line of publishing, and thus Åhlén & Åkerlund's magazine was liquidated in the wake of the demise of the commercial alternative.

Much to my surprise, when I began looking for material related to the Sandrew initiative, I found practically all of the sponsored films produced for the Television Week in the vaults of the Swedish Film Institute. Very few of these programs have been shown since the event, in spite of the fact that they feature an array of very popular Swedish entertainers.

The Sandrew Television Week commenced Monday, May 17. On the first day, broadcasting started at 4 P.M. with a male announcer, Mr. von Strauss (a new face was introduced every day). The announcement was followed by an opening address, delivered by Håkan Sterky, director-general from the board. Lars Sellergren then played two classical piano pieces, by Schubert and Chopin. The live programs predominantly offered high art, social issues, or educational matters, program material with a decidedly public service penchant. The first sponsored slot came from NK and was composed of a fashion show introduced by a frame story focused on a family shopping at the store for the summer season. The next program provided light entertainment featuring Latin American performers, conveniently available from one of Sandrew's theatrical venues.

After the light entertainment from the show world, the program returned to high art: Eva-Lisa Lennartsson read two poems (by Nils Ferlin and Artur Lundkvist, respectively) and a short story, *The Kiss*, by Hjalmar Söderberg. The next hour started off with Philips's metatelevisual show, *We're Watching Television*, presented by Robert Brandt and assisted by a ballerina, Gerd Andersson. The program offered a witty account of the history of televisuality, which then led to issues related to home-based spectatorship: where to place the console; appropriate viewing distances; light sources in relation to the screen, and so on. The news section then followed and included a segment from the king's visit to the province of Småland; refugees arriving at Bromma airport; and an interview with a secret guest—the Swedish Hollywood actor Alf Kjellin. The weather forecast concluded the news. The next program, sponsored by a distributor of beauty products, offered ballet and modern dance, featuring stars from each area. The three dance segments were each introduced by a mini-lecture delivered by the director of the Dance Museum, Bengt Häger. An operetta cavalcade, sponsored by Luxor Radio, wrapped up the first day of broadcasting.

The introduction of television, like other new media, is often described as a privileged moment, as well as a moment of profound fascination. To track down the moment of inception, even if the criteria tend to shift in various national contexts, seems to be a worthy historiographical endeavor. In a Swedish context the first Sandrew day is indeed a plausible candidate for "a first," even though experimental broadcasting had been going on for several years, and even though transmissions to temporary venues had occurred on several occasions from 1935 onward. Prior to the Sandrew Week it was virtually impossible to buy a television set in Stockholm. Those who had a set were affiliated with the industry, and therefore very few individuals outside the trade had been able to see the material transmitted via the agency. Then again, the intense debate around televisual matters and the string of public exposures of the medium prior to the Sandrew initiative seems to have exhausted the fascination factor and precluded more speculative readings concerning the possibilities of television in the reception material in the press. Overall, the paramount issue on the televisual agenda informed the response: Should Sweden adopt commercial or noncommercial television, or, perhaps, form a Swedish compromise?

Generally, the reception material displays a tone of sobriety, critically analyzing the pros and cons in relation to longtime considerations. The fascination factor, otherwise a standard trope in the historiographical discourse on television inception, was hence somewhat bracketed. The Stockholm daily *Svenska Dagbladet* phrases this succinctly: "At the restaurants, where sets were also placed, the guests initially showed much interest, but after the first wave of curiosity they resumed conversation and eating and drinking, paying little attention to the new visual gadget. With some exaggeration, it seems as if television turned unfashionable in two hours." The same newspaper claimed that city life was little affected by the event, with no crowds or stampeding and "very little enthusiasm outside the shop windows."[13] *Dagens Nyheter* reported a different state of affairs—that broadcasting was on the verge of causing traffic chaos when thousands of viewers congregated outside shop windows.[14] These differences in views might, however, be a result of the respective cultural outlook of each newspaper—conservative versus liberal.

Overall, the press coverage focused on the technical quality of the broadcasting and on program content, in addition to reporting from various viewing spots. Almost one hundred thousand spectators seem to have acquainted themselves with the first day's program, which was transmitted over about twelve hundred sets (the figures fluctuate from one thousand to fifteen hundred, the latter of which probably includes sets in private homes). *Kvällsposten* reported that most spectators watched only one or two programs before leaving, few watched the entire two-hour broadcast.[15] Other newspapers reported that people were trapped in the throng and had to stay for the entire program span.

One of the recurring complaints was that the size of the screen was too small for public viewing. Even more problematic was the fact that some patrons apparently had forgot to place loudspeakers outside their shop windows and therefore the television audio could not be heard. Thus it seems as if the size of the screen and the public viewing situation did not inspire actual fascination but rather a distracted, somewhat critical mode, although clearly viewers were interested enough to turn the sidewalks into audience stands. The only news item in the press alluding to a more engaged level of spectatorship was a report from a domestic viewing context. Börje Heed in *Aftonbladet* wrote: The kids have not been so quiet for years, silent and with eyes full of amazement."[16] Indeed, underpinning this contention were several illustrations in the press material that showed children absorbed in watching television.

The press coverage mainly addressed how personalities came across; what kind of program types were appealing or unappealing; what the medium might do differently or even better than radio and cinema; how elegant or inelegant the commercials were inserted (those opposed to commercial television suspected that cruder methods would be used later); how attractive the weather forecast was; and, finally, how difficult it was to handle news, even if that type of program was regarded as the most worthy to pursue.

The new magazine TV-*Journalen* in its first and only issue featured the poet/artist/song composer Evert Taube on its cover and pronounced him as the first Swedish television star. His program opened the second day of the Sandrew event and received rave reviews. In addition to his success, a new star was launched prior to broadcasting, the young singer May Thomson, who sang a tune in the jazz program slot shot late in March. Long before her program was aired she recorded the song for the Columbia label, made her debut on radio, and shot a screen test. The rest of the performers had star status from the outset.

The department store NK documented all stages of their involvement in the Sandrew Week. In their photographic collection are stills of production at the Sandrew studios, but even more interesting are the photos of television viewing at the department store. That series of photos belongs to a genre of photographs documenting spectators in front of sets, which were published in most newspapers and weekly magazines. At times, the photos show only a group of people trying to get a glimpse of a set invisible in the photo, but another frequent image is a form of shot/reverse shot captured first from behind an outdoor crowd then cut to a photo from inside a shop over the shoulder of the set, so to speak, focusing on the spectators. In addition to documenting public viewing, resourceful reporters visited some of the prominent domestic sites. Erik Esping and his family were presented in front of their television set in a feature article in an upscale weekly magazine.[17] And Bo Löfberg, the man behind it all, had invited the chairman of the advisory board to his living room.[18] Both Löfberg and Esping hoped for a future for the Sandrew project. In his closing address on air, Esping elaborated on this theme on behalf of the production crew:

> Everybody is tired and happy, but in unison say: "How sad that this is all over, now we know so much more about television, now we could go on." And if I can add a personal reflection, I would be highly pleased if there were a future opportunity for this line of television at least on this level.
>
> I want to emphasize that I think the scope of this week's broadcasting represents an absolute minimum, and that it would be nice if all of us that have promoted and hoped for Swedish television would get resources to continue. Given what we have seen here, and I restrict myself to the technical aspects, I claim that the picture quality in the main has been on par with the highest international standards. Furthermore, many have criticized us for not having been able to start regular broadcasting earlier, and that we're lagging behind, and that we can't handle the technical aspects. . . . Today we command the necessary resources to compete with television elsewhere, but it's necessary to assemble all the resources, to utilize them properly so that Swedish television can become what we believe and hope it can be.[19]

Esping here takes on the role of an unabashed spokesperson for commercial television, rehearsing a line of argument that he presented more fully as a dissenting voice within the commission.

The secretary of communications, Sven Andersson, had little to say about the Sandrew Week. In a small story in *Sverige Nytt* he was quoted as saying the event was "technically enchanting [with] surprisingly few mishaps. The general audience has been appreciative, but one wonders if this evidences a genuine interest or only curiosity."[20] When the government had turned down Sandrew's second application and awarded a test concession to the Swedish Radio Corporation, the secretary was more optimistic about the televisual prospects when interviewed in the social-democratic morning paper: "The secretary of communications is convinced that television will be an immediate hit in Sweden. I believe that the television set will become a household item much faster than the telephone."[21] In fact, the number of issued licenses—that is, the number of sets sold—surpassed all predictions and the license revenues were much higher than expected, which eventually paved the way for a second channel.

Irrespective of the success of the experiment with a socially responsible model for commercial television, neither the commission nor Parliament could be convinced that the new medium had a future outside a radio-inflected public service structure. The subsequent formation of a public service approach from scratch led to a very slow start for television in Sweden when the Radio Corporation built up its production structure. The domestic film industry, already hard pressed by gradually decreasing ticket sales, had temporarily curtailed film production in 1951 as a protest against the level of taxation imposed on the industry. Production for television could have changed the film industry's prospects, just like it did in Hollywood for some of the studios. The crisis became imminent around 1960, and in 1963, a state-subsidized production structure within a new body, the Swedish Film Institute, more or less picked up the remnants of the industry's production resources. The industry survived but the bulk of the film produced presupposed institute financing.

The television fare offered to the Swedish audience relied heavily on American and British programs, demonstrating that the division between the commercial and public service sectors is not distinct, a state of affairs still very much alive in the current discussion about the future of public service. Nowadays public service represents just two channels out of a cornucopia of available options.

Although the Sandrew experiment was short-lived, by the end of the 1950s the Swedish Radio Corporation found other ways to encourage sales of TV sets to consumers in the name of public service. The 1958 soccer World Cup, hosted by Sweden, boosted the national sale of television sets in addition to pulling together a hitherto unprecedented national audience for a major sports event. In many respects, in terms of home viewing the televised World Cup represents a counterpart to the Sandrew Week's audience formation on the sidewalks four years earlier. The company had consolidated its resources and the soccer event offered an attraction spectacular enough to generate interest in participation via television. The local team's triumphs (Sweden played until the finals, where they lost to Brazil) further exacerbated the hype. Not long ago, the government tried to persuade Parliament to support a short list of sport events of alleged national interest that theretofore had been aired by either public service or via the only commercial channel accessible without cable subscription. The bill was turned down. The idea to use television as a vehicle for positioning a national audience in relation to important events (sports seem to be the only type of affairs with a national currency these days) apparently still has resonance enough to generate government intervention, but not leverage enough to be carried all the way through in the new televisual terrain. In the current era of commercial cable and satellite competition, the curious tensions between public service and consumer-oriented models are more than ever on the agenda. The still-unresolved structural uncertainties as to the role of public service television in a nonmonopoly market have led to crisis after crisis within the Swedish Television Corporation. The firing and hiring of CEOs and chairpersons for a while took on dimensions contrary to the nature of public service, blurring the boundaries between news and soap. The structural gambits have turned the vicissitudes of postmonopoly television and its key players almost as newsworthy as the premonopoly initiative during that crucial week in May 1954.

NOTES

All translations are mine unless indicated otherwise.

1. Karl-Hugo Wirén, *Kampen om TV: Svensk TV-politik, 1946–66* (Stockholm: Gidlunds, 1986).

2. I am, of course, using Raymond Williams's concept in a metaphorical sense. Discontinuity between programs is the governing principle in the public service context. Announcers mark the gaps in the "flow" and situate each program slot as different from what precedes and succeeds it.

3. During the 1990s, a major research project devoted to ether media in Sweden resulted in several valuable studies. The perspective is, however, overall centered on the program company responsible for both radio and television in Sweden. Surveying both media as all the studies do from various perspectives, of course, provides a preliminary overview but not much more.

4. Sandrew was and is one of the leading film companies in Sweden. Anders Sandrew (1885–1957), né Andersson, appropriated his new name from a brand of port wine, Sandrew, but he chose to pronounce his new name as if it were Swedish. His business career started with a humble grocery store, which he and his brother turned into a very successful venture in their late teens. Out of his grocery fortune Sandrew began to acquire movie theaters in the late 1920s as a sideline to real estate investments, and then he gradually developed a vertically integrated film company.

5. The American hardware interest RCA had promoted the new medium already in the late 1940s by donating a set to the Swedish king, perhaps the first set given to a "private household" in Sweden.

6. See Michael Curtin's essay in this collection.

7. Christopher Anderson, *Hollywood TV: The Studio System in the Fifties* (Austin: University of Texas Press, 1994).

8. The following shops were denied a permit: AB Cloetta, Norrmalmstorg 1; AB Gylling, for the Marabou confection shop at Stureplan 6; Svenska Siemens, Kungsgatan 34; Luxor Radio, Dufva at Stureplan 4; LM Ericsson, Kungsgatan 33.

9. Namely Nimbus Radio at Hamngatan 13–15; Eterton Radio at Malmskillnadsgatan 38; Royal Radio at Kungsgatan 32; Kungsbokhandeln at Kungsgatan 26; Sporres Radio at Kungsgatan 12–14; Franks Radio Vasagatan 10.

10. Lynn Spigel, *Make Room for TV: Television and the Family Ideal in Postwar America*, (Chicago: University of Chicago Press, 1992).

11. Anna McCarthy, *Ambient Television: Visual Culture and Public Space* (Durham: Duke University Press, 2001).

12. The two addresses are reprinted in Arne Sanfridsson's useful book *Min Svenska TV-historia*. Sanfridsson was part of the technological division with the Swedish Radio Corporation during the days of the agency. Arne Sanfridsson, *Min svenska TV-historia* (Stockholm: Arne Sanfridsson, 1981).

13. *Svenska Dagbladet*, May 18, 1954.

14. Article signed Bert in *Dagens Nyheter*, May 18, 1954, p. 1.

15. Kvällsposten, May 18, 1954.

16. Article by Carro Bergkvist and Börje Heed in *Aftonbladet*, May 18, 1954, p. 4.

17. Article by Brita af Ornäs in *Vecko-Journalen* 1954, no. 2, p. 25.

18. Article by Sonja Magnusson and Len Waernberg in *Husmodern* 1954, no. 14, pp. 21 and 36.

19. Esping quoted in Sanfridsson, *Min svenska TV-historia*, p. 75.

20. "Från vårt redaktionsfönster," *Sverige Nytt*, 1954, no. 20. p. 5.

21. *Morgon-Tidningen*, June 15, 1954.

MICHAEL CURTIN

MEDIA CAPITALS: CULTURAL

GEOGRAPHIES OF GLOBAL TV

Although Hollywood exports continue to dominate global entertainment markets, debates about transnational flows of television have moved beyond the media imperialism thesis to focus on deliberations about globalization.[1] The complexity of the word "globalization" is perhaps suggested by the fact that TVB, Hong Kong's dominant local broadcaster, is now busy concocting a global satellite service in collaboration with MEASAT, a Malaysian media corporation. Meanwhile, the Hong Kong office of Sony Pictures Entertainment (led by a Hollywood executive in charge of a Chinese staff that reports to the Los Angeles division of a Japanese conglomerate) is diligently producing close to four thousand hours of TV programming each year that is specifically targeted at local Asian audiences. These unprecedented initiatives point to new patterns of television flow. As the local goes global and the global tries to become local, or perhaps regional, one is struck by disjunctures very much like those observed by Arjun Appadurai more than a decade ago when he contended that contemporary culture is fundamentally fractal, "possessing no Euclidean boundaries, structures, or regularities."[2] Political, economic, and cultural phenomena overlap, converge, and collide, disrupting our prior confidence in holistic approaches to culture and society. When I returned to Hong Kong on a research trip in 1999, the most popular TV programs on the summer schedule were two "imported" historical dramas—a remarkable development given that both series were transnational coproductions of media organizations from Taiwan and the People's Republic of China. During a period of rapidly escalating military threats across the Taiwan Straits, Hong Kong— and much of East Asia—was nevertheless grooving to the adventures of Princess Huanzhu and Emperor Yongzheng. Indeed, the latter series was a reputed favorite of China's premier, Taiwan's president, and Hong Kong's chief executive, a shared TV diet that was reportedly one of the few things that all three could agree on.

Meanwhile, the very same summer Richard Li, the son of Hong Kong's most influential tycoon, was hard at work assembling the elements for Asia's first regional, interactive, digital satellite service. With little more than a pocket full of change, a big family name, and an exceedingly sharp executive staff, Li won a bidding war for British-owned Hong Kong Telecom, iced a cable deal with the richest man in Taiwan, and pulled on board various creative allies hoping to assemble enough TV content to make his digital snake oil sing. By comparison, Li's erstwhile partner, Rupert Murdoch, was in league with a former official of the Chinese propaganda ministry, forming a joint-venture company that had taken charge of STAR TV's northern satellite beam. The world's reputedly most powerful media mogul thus relinquished operational control to local executives who, so far, have put together the most successful commercial satellite service in China and are now in the process of taking over Hong Kong's number-two local broadcaster, ATV.

In short, the rate of deal making is dizzying and the creative activity is frenetic. This comes only a few years after the Asian economic crisis and the near collapse of the Hong Kong film and TV industries. As television scholars, we are challenged to make sense of this increasingly complex environment, which is now commonly characterized by transnational and transmedia alliances. But the most pressing question confronting us may not be "What?" or "Who?" but rather "How?" How do we study these complex patterns of flow? How do we deploy our limited research resources? How do we invest our time? The challenges scholars now confront are as deeply methodological as they are conceptual.

Traditionally, television studies has been resolutely national, focusing on a medium contained within the regulatory, political, and economic environs of a nation-state. International media studies maintained a similar respect for state sovereignty attending to the exchange of cultural products between nations or producing comparative studies of national media systems. More recently, however, scholars are relinquishing the metaphor of national containers, choosing instead to examine the ways in which contemporary television is transcending frontiers and disrupting conventional structures of domination. Studies that emphasize the one-way flow of U.S. programming to the periphery of the world system are being reassessed in light of increasing multidirectional flows of media imagery.[3] These new patterns of flow should not be construed as multilateral in the conventional sense because they do not involve the exchange of programming between sovereign states. Instead, these flows emanate from particular cities that have become centers for the finance, production, and distribution of television programs: cities like Bombay, Cairo, and Hong Kong. One might refer to these cities as media capitals because they represent centers of media activity that have specific logics of their own; ones that do not necessarily correspond to the geography, interests, or policies of particular nation-states. For example, Hong Kong television is produced and consumed in Taipei, Beijing, Amsterdam, Vancouver, Bangkok, and Kuala Lumpur. The central node of all this activity is Hong Kong, but the logics that motivate the development of the medium are not primarily governed by the interests of the Chinese state or even the Special Administrative Region.

Given that such media capitals have grown in importance and that new logics seem to be governing the development of transnational television, this essay suggests that it might be time to trade one unit of scholarly analysis for another. That is, we commonly study television as a national phenomenon. What if, instead, we were to begin to study *media capitals,* seeing them as bound up in a web of relations that exist at the local, regional, and global levels, as well as the national level? Such a suggestion is anticipated in recent research—for example, David Morley and Kevin Robins's analysis of the electronic landscapes of Europe, Joseph Straubhaar's approach to multicentric media flows, and Marie Gillespie's explorations of audience uses of Bombay film videos in Punjabi neighborhoods of London.[4] These and other studies urge us to see the nation as an important but not sufficient site of media analysis. Yet despite this growing body of work, the residual attractions of nation-based research are still strong. Most television histories and most global communication textbooks exhibit this tendency. Even some of the best volumes, such as *New Patterns in Global Television,* nevertheless portray the medium as primarily connected to particular states.[5] In large part, this bias is due to the fact that it is difficult to find a locus for talking about television flows without falling back on methodologies and narratives that direct our attention to national boundaries.

On the other hand, the concept of media capitals portrays cities like Hong Kong as positioned at the intersection of complex patterns of economic, social, and cultural flows. A media capital is a nexus or switching point, rather than a container. In some ways, this approach compares to Saskia Sassen's notion of global cities. In her estimation, urban locales that once served as national centers of industrial production have now been superseded by global financial and service centers. Sassen contends that since the 1980s, as marketing and manufacturing operations dispersed, the functions of finance, planning, and design have congregated in transnational centers of the global economy. Yet she points out that "the maintenance of centralized control and management over a geographically dispersed array of plants, offices, and service outlets cannot be taken for granted or seen as an inevitable outcome of a 'world system.' The possibility of such centralized control needs to be produced."[6] That is, scholars need to understand the historical processes and the specific institutional practices by which some cities rise to the status of global centers and others do not. Sassen focuses her analysis primarily on the financial and producer service sectors (such as accounting and law), showing how patterns of economic exchange and institutional organization were dramatically transformed during the 1970s and 1980s. Yet the question remains: How have such patterns of globalization affected other important industries, especially the culture industries? Economic analysis can certainly tell us a great deal about the emergence of global media capitals but, as I demonstrate below, social and cultural forces are tremendously influential as well. How, then, does one write the history of media capitals without either characterizing them as epiphenomena of capitalist development or as mere extensions of the nation-state?

In his assessment of Latin American media, Jesus Martin-Barbero contends that "historians of the mass media have studied only the economic structure and the ideological content of the mass media; few have given close attention to the mediations through which the media have acquired a concrete institutional form and become a reflection of the culture."[7] By invoking the concept of mediations, Martin-Barbero points to the complex ways in which quotidian experiences of human migration, social change, and popular memory in Latin America have found expression in the cultural output of media institutions during the twentieth century. Rather than merely acting as instruments of elite control, he suggests that these institutions mediated a complex array of historical forces. By extension, in this essay I will show how the future as well as the past history of media capitals most crucially hinges on their ability to register and articulate the social experiences of their audiences.

Media capitals, then, are sites of mediation, locations where complex forces and flows interact. They are neither bounded nor self-contained entities. Rather we should understand them in the manner that geographers like Doreen Massey and Kevin Robins understand cities, as meeting places where local specificity arises out of migration, interaction, and exchange.[8] As such, media capital is a relational concept, not simply an acknowledgment of dominance. For example, Hong Kong's claim to such status is crucially dependent on its historical, cultural, and institutional relations with such places as Guangzhou, Singapore, and Taipei. Moreover, the city's status as a media capital is an ongoing matter of negotiation, contention, and even competition. Singapore, for example, officially touts itself as the "media hub" of Southeast Asia, and Taipei eagerly attempted to take advantage of Hong Kong's seeming vulnerability when sovereignty over the territory was transferred to Beijing in 1997. Thus capital status can be won and lost, and the term itself evokes both senses of the word: capital as a center of activity and capital as a concentration of resources, reputation, and talent. Media capitals are places where things come together and, consequently, where the generation and circulation of new mass culture forms become possible.

My aim in this essay, then, is to suggest how scholars might use media capital as a concept that would foster empirically grounded analysis of the temporal dynamism and spatial complexity of a global media environment. Such an approach does not seek to diminish the importance of economic or national forces but rather to elaborate more fully the complex logics of contemporary television. It poses such questions as: On what basis does a particular locale deserve to be called a media capital? How did it emerge as such? Why does it succeed? How does it operate in relationship to various states, markets, and audiences? What is its relationship to other media capitals? And, perhaps most important: What does the history of a particular media capital tell us about processes of globalization?[9] In other words, in this essay I advocate historically informed *cultural geographies* of television and I speculate about the viability of such an approach by comparing the history and fortunes of three media capitals—one currently in an ascendant phase (Hollywood); another in a state of disarray (Hong Kong); and a third eclipsed by more powerful rivals despite showing early potential as a significant site of cultural production (Chicago). Although this preliminary study is limited by its focus on television, in it I nevertheless attempt to discuss the medium's relations to other cultural forms (film, radio, music) and social forces (migration, geopolitics, capitalism). Hopefully, the comparisons elicited from this inquiry will yield some productive insights and point toward potential avenues for future research, even if I can't—within the scope of a single essay—account for all factors and influences that shape a media capital.

HOLLYWOOD AND CHICAGO: REGIONAL AND NATIONAL ORIGINS

The competition to become the acknowledged media capital in North America begins with the early history of radio during the 1920s. At that time, the cornerstone of U.S. broadcast regulation was the concept of *localism,* which designated licensees as trustees of the airwaves, operating on behalf of a local community. Localism is a concept that refers back to the New England village green of the early republic, where it was intended that political decisions should grow out of interpersonal deliberation among the assembled population of any given town or borough. When it was first adopted as a centerpiece of broadcast policy during the late 1920s the concept was already an anachronism because radio, and later television, was largely dominated by major corporations based in New York City. Nevertheless, the concept of localism was enshrined in key pieces of legislation, no doubt partially due to public nostalgia for small-group communication along with the widespread criticism of monopoly corporations, such as RCA.[10] This combination made New York corporations cautious about their national network aspirations and alerted them to the potential benefits of limited autonomy for some of their local and regional operations.[11]

Besides government policy and public opinion, other forces militated for the dispersion of creative activity during the radio era. For example, production costs were somewhat modest, making the differences between network and local programming less consequential. Those cities with a substantial pool of creative talent in related art forms could develop music, variety, drama, and public affairs programs of relatively high quality. Such was the case with Chicago and Hollywood, both of which became important centers of program production.[12] The national networks understood the fairly obvious advantages of Hollywood radio. As historian Michele Hilmes has pointed out, major broadcasters turned to Hollywood in an attempt to tap an existing pool of cinema stars and to realize cross-promotional strategies between the two media.[13] Film stars would draw viewers to a radio show and the radio show would help promote the performer's next movie. Yet outside of the Hollywood film community Los Angeles itself offered few incentives as a base of network operations. At the time, the population in the far western part of the United States was relatively sparse and manufacturing output remained comparatively insignificant until World War II. Los Angeles had a modest social infrastructure, a diminutive regional economy, and (besides Hollywood) relatively thin cultural resources. Consequently, when the networks looked westward, they were not tapping existing regional or local circulations of capital, talent, or audiences so much as they were tapping the assets of the relatively self-contained creative enclave of the national film industry.[14]

Chicago, on the other hand, offered the advantages of a major *regional* center of manufacturing, transportation, and communication. Located at the heart of a vast interior railroad network, Chicago was the premiere locale for the processing and transshipment of agricultural commodities from the American heartland to the urban markets of the East Coast, and it was an important center for the manufacture and marketing of consumer goods. It became the central node of a powerful agro-industrial complex during the nineteenth century; in the twentieth century it continued to play an important role despite the increasing synchronization of the national economy. Chicago mediated between rural and urban, between local and regional, and between midwestern and national contexts. It brought agricultural goods to the national market in processed form and it returned finished products to the prosperous towns and cities of the Midwest.[15]

As a consequence of this mediating role, Chicago became an important base of operations for advertising firms that wanted to be close to the headquarters of their clients, such as meat processing companies, household products manufacturers, and grocery store chains.[16] Just as Chicago-based catalog sales corporations—such as Montgomery Ward, Spiegel, and Sears and Roebuck—played a mediating role in the emerging consumer culture of the pre-radio era, Chicago-based ad agencies became leaders in the development of radio programming and promotion. In part this had to do with the proximity of these agencies to the corporate headquarters of their clients, and in part it was a result of the fact that Chicago agencies also promoted themselves as particularly responsive to the complexities of marketing to audiences in small towns as well as major urban locales. They claimed the unique advantage of being able to tell a manufacturer that a particular sales approach was designed to "play in Peoria," a small midwestern city close to Chicago that was portrayed as harboring the epitome of mainstream values and tastes. Peoria was to Fordist mass culture what Los Angeles is perhaps to neo-Fordist niche cultures today. It was emblematic of the terrain that many advertisers wished to navigate in the pursuit of responsive consumers. Between the 1930s and 1950s, Chicago ad agencies touted themselves as standing at the nexus of national and local sentiments. They operated in a huge city with a substantial immigrant population that came both from overseas and from the rural heartland. Radio signals from Chicago stations traversed ethnically diverse urban neighborhoods as well as many towns and small cities across the Midwest. At such, Chicago supposedly provided an assimilationist laboratory where foreign and domestic, urban and rural, would hopefully come together as a mass American market. Major corporate sponsors specifically commissioned these agencies to produce promotional messages that were less governed by the logic of big-time show business than by the worldviews of middle-American listeners.[17]

Because at the time the actual production of radio programming was primarily in the hands of sponsoring advertisers, the New York–based networks shared managerial control over broadcasting content with program producers in Chicago and Los Angeles. Sponsors in search of expensive star power turned to Los Angeles, while those plying the cultural terrain of the heartland sought out the talents of the Chicago creative community, which for its part offered innovative contributions to such narrative genres as the soap opera, drama, and domestic comedy, as well as information formats such as home improvement and farm programming. Famous programs included *Ma Perkins, Jack Armstrong, Vic and Sade, The Story of Mary Marlin, Amos 'n' Andy, Lum 'n' Abner,* and *Fibber McGee and Molly.* Although lower wages were paid to Chicago scriptwriters and performers, the city nevertheless became a vibrant center of radio production, offering opportunities to a broad range of creative personnel.

Later, with the emergence of television, Chicago seemed poised to continue its mediating role in U.S. popular culture. Radio dramas were adapted to television and broadcasters pioneered innovative formats for children's programming and variety/talk shows. The national networks welcomed these ventures and even adopted some Chicago programming for regional and national distribution.[18] Network responsiveness to local initiative was largely due to the economic, creative, and technical challenges confronting national broadcast services during the late 1940s and early 1950s. National TV program production and distribution was far more expensive than network radio.[19] Furthermore, the major networks were unsure about the popularity and commercial viability of various forms of programming. Local experimentation complemented development efforts at network headquarters in New York. Finally, national broadcasters were receptive to such initiatives because they needed to convince local television station personnel and government regulators that network affiliation was advantageous to viewers in local communities. Regardless of their ultimate intentions, the network executives needed to appear committed to the concept of localism if they were to entice stations to affiliate and if they were to convince regulators that television networking would serve local as well as national interests.[20] For all of these reasons, the Chicago School of television flourished during the first decade of the new medium.

Yet by the middle of the 1950s, network infrastructures were solidly in place and television was emerging as the preeminent form of national media. Demand for network advertising time grew dramatically, although supply was limited by regulatory design to two, and later three, national services. Given these oligopoly conditions, the networks now seemed confident that they had consolidated their dominant position in the industry. Consequently, they then sought to "rationalize" and centralize their operations. One of the key sites in this process was to pry loose the creative control that sponsors and advertising agencies enjoyed in the field of program production. Whereas networks previously offered entire blocks of broadcast time to a sponsor who would then develop program content under the guidance of an advertising agency, networks now began to produce more of their own programming. Instead of the *Texaco Star Theatre* or the *Kraft Music Hall,* networks developed programs like *Ben Casey* or the *Beverly Hillbillies,* programs over which they enjoyed creative and operational control. As for actual program production, the networks increasingly turned to Hollywood film producers and commissioned them to develop telefilm series under network guidance rather than continuing the New York– and Chicago–based practice of broadcasting live performances. Whereas during the early television era New York, Chicago, and Los Angeles all served as major production centers, the New York–based networks chose to consolidate studio operations on the West Coast during the late 1950s, shutting down production in their own city as well as in Chicago. This new network partnership with Hollywood supposedly made it easier to contain costs and retain creative control. It furthermore took advantage of new distribution opportunities, as telefilm programming could now be marketed to local stations as inexpensive reruns of prime-time hits as well as sold to newly emerging markets overseas.[21]

As Christopher Anderson and I have argued, this centralization of creative activity took place during a period of lax federal oversight, and by the time regulators began to respond, local television production was a shambles. Government hearings in 1962 only testified to how thoroughly the networks had altered the conditions of production and transformed the discourse of television.[22] During these sessions it was virtually impossible for critics to mount a coherent attack on network policy, and consequently the Federal Communications Commission buried the findings without taking action. Indeed, the FCC during the early 1960s seemed more preoccupied with the potential uses of television as an instrument of international diplomacy. Under the aegis of President Kennedy's "New Frontier," FCC Chair Newton Minow promoted the export of U.S. telefilm and negotiated the rapid deployment of the world's first communications satellites.[23] In these ventures, government partnership with the major networks was seen as more important than principles of localism or antitrust.

The government therefore tacitly endorsed the consolidation of network operations, heralding both the high network era of U.S. television and the apogee of a Fordist regime of accumulation in the United States. Television became a vital complement to national systems of mass production, distribution, and consumption. The role of regional economies diminished as a result, and the mediating function of regional cultural centers such as Chicago, Cincinnati, and New York diminished as well. Television became so widely perceived as a national medium that many viewers saw local programming as little more than an occasional nuisance. American TV had become Hollywood TV, financed and managed on the East Coast and produced on the West Coast, a binary relationship that belied the centralization of media power at the national level.

As for the global context, Hollywood television embraced an international rather than a transnational logic. As was the case with most industrial behavior under Fordism, program export policies and technology development were largely predicated on the projection of national power. Rather than a cooperative transcultural venture, the main objective of industry executives and government policy makers was to sustain U.S. leadership among an alliance of nations. Prime-time programming was exported intact, as if the modern, consumerist qualities of Hollywood fare would invariably draw the allegiance of populations around the world. Consequently, series development and production remained focused on U.S. audiences and advertisers.[24] The tastes of overseas viewers were rarely taken into account, except by syndicators as they attempted to hawk the programs in diverse cultural contexts. Moreover, the infrastructure of American television remained resolutely national—foreign ownership of media enterprises, transnational coproductions, and the conscious design and marketing of transnational programming were all virtually unheard of. During the high network era of the 1960s and 1970s, U.S. television was Hollywood television, which had an international afterlife but was nevertheless an emphatically national phenomenon.

The cultural logic of American television today remains largely the same. Producers primarily focus on national audiences, thinking little about viewers at the local or global levels, which in large part is due to the economics of the industry. The U.S. national networks still provide the broadest promotion and exposure for new programs and they pay hefty license fees that help to defray much of the initial production cost. Moreover, program popularity at the national network level is still considered the most important signifier of syndication potential, and syndication is where most programs begin to turn a profit. Accordingly, success in U.S. network television rarely means financial disaster, but failure on the U.S. networks can rarely be turned into success in the syndication market.

Exceptions exist, of course, and they begin to portray the ways in which Hollywood is changing. *Baywatch* is perhaps the most famous example. Despite its disastrous initial run in the United States, some estimates claim it to be the most heavily viewed program in the world.[25] Heavy viewing is no doubt the operative concept explaining *Baywatch*'s success, because like much of Hollywood's export fare the program reportedly draws the attention of global audiences due to its visual appeal. But the old maxims of the international syndication market may be giving way to new calculations regarding audience tastes and behaviors. Increasingly, overseas viewers are being defined by demographic factors other than citizenship. Syndicators often strategize about program marketing on a regional basis, by thinking about similarities among viewers in Taipei, Seoul, and Tokyo rather than automatically presuming differences between Chinese, Korean, and Japanese audiences. Despite the many national influences that continue to exist, syndicators and satellite broadcasters are now alert to the opportunities engendered by the emergence of a pan-European business class, a South Asian youth culture, and a Greater China media market.

These changing patterns in TV syndication are attributable to a number of factors, among them the growth of transnational media conglomerates, the proliferation of new distribution vehicles (cable, satellite, video), the reregulation of electronic media, and the emergence of new production arrangements—all of which might collectively be referred to as marking the transition from a "high network" to a "neo-network" era of television.[26] Program distribution was once constrained by government regulation of technology so as to minimize the number of network competitors at the national level and to control the flow of international programming. Now, however, conditions have changed dramatically, not only in the United States but also in countries around the globe. Audiences that were once interpellated by the monopoly institutions of national broadcasting are now hailed by media products that flow through a wide variety of channels. What was once organized as television for all citizens of a nation is now organized according to niche demographics and consumption patterns. The number of services and programming choices is multiplying rapidly in countries as diverse as India, China, and Italy. In Taiwan, for example, television in the late 1980s was dominated by three terrestrial broadcasters affiliated with the government, the military, and the ruling political party. In the decade that ensued, television channels and video materials proliferated at a fantastic rate. Today, prime-time shows on the terrestrial stations average only a three to five rating, while more than eighty cable channels vie for the remainder, most of them averaging ratings of one or less. In this environment, media producers find that the branding of products is often more important than futile attempts to control the mode of distribution. Unlike the network era when the control of a few national channels was the key to profitability, neo-network television firms focus on marketing, promotion, and the control of intellectual property.[27] *Star Trek, Star Wars,* and Disney animation all are powerful brands in markets around the globe. Given a greater range of choices, audiences are drawn to the products by textual elements—characters, story lines, special effects—rather than by the technological and regulatory constraints formerly imposed on the delivery system.

One would think that under such conditions Hollywood would only feel more confident about its future prospects. Yet we need only consider the example of *The X-Files* to identify some of Hollywood's most recent sources of anxiety. The program initially achieved notoriety on Fox Television, the first new network to dislodge the traditional broadcast monopolies in the United States and the first North American network to become part of a transnational conglomerate with origins outside the United States. Just as remarkable, *The X-Files* was produced on location in British Columbia during its first five seasons largely because a favorable currency exchange rate, a cooperative local government, and lower costs for labor and materials made the northern location especially attractive to the program's producers.[28] *The X-Files* is not alone in making the decision to migrate its creative operations. Over the past few years, industry representatives and local government officials in Southern California have been ranting about the flight of television and film productions to such locations as Vancouver, Toronto, London, Melbourne, Orlando, and, interestingly enough, Chicago and New York. Although these productions still bear the markings of Hollywood's generic conventions, stylistic devices, and financing arrangements, and although they feature well-known stars, Hollywood representatives nevertheless sense a dispersion of activity that begins to question the necessity of locating production in Southern California. Hollywood remains an important node for the "face work" of the industry, but new circuits of transportation and communication may be rendering the material location of a production less consequential.[29] Even the vaunted advantages of Hollywood's technological sophistication are no longer so palpable. As the case of *The X-Files* suggests, high-tech effects are becoming available at a lower cost in more dispersed locations. Indeed, one of the most visually elaborate science fiction films of recent years, *The Matrix,* was filmed at a studio in Australia with a producer from Hollywood, directors from Chicago, a stunt coordinator from Hong Kong, and a digital special effects team from the San Francisco Bay Area. All of which raises the question: Is Hollywood really necessary as anything other than a meeting point for industry personnel, as a place to do the necessary face work to get a production online? Moreover, will this dispersion of program production engender the development of collateral creative activity in distant localities that may, in turn, begin to compete with Hollywood? In British Columbia, for example, runaway Hollywood productions have helped to revive the television production industry in western Canada, which now generates programs for global, national, and local markets.[30]

Another issue that generates tremendous anxiety in Hollywood these days has to do with the control of copyright. During the high network era, television producers controlled the exposure of their programs by technological and regulatory means. One could only gain access to a program at a certain time in a certain locale. Today, anxieties about the unauthorized circulation of product has motivated Hollywood to think more transnationally. International release windows for films and television programs have been tightened so that pirates have a tougher time getting product to market before the exhibition of the copyrighted version. This makes the transnational viewing of Hollywood television more synchronous and it encourages the development of more integrated distribution strategies.

Indeed, transnational copyright enforcement has also become a major preoccupation of the Hollywood establishment. After the intensive lobbying that began during the Reagan years, intellectual property issues have risen to become one of the leading foreign policy concerns of the American government. In most U.S. embassies around the globe, one can find at least one foreign service officer specializing in intellectual property issues. President Reagan was especially renowned for raising the topic during consultations with other heads of state, and the Clinton administration was only slightly less vigorous in its pursuit of the issue.[31] All of which helps to explain why two former presidents of the United States were so fulsomely supported by the Hollywood community during their campaign fundraising drives.

Such anxieties suggest how the geography of television is changing and how Hollywood's status as a global media capital remains, but the conditions of its dominance have been altered dramatically. Its hegemony is neither stable nor inevitable. Even though producers and directors in Hollywood may continue to fix their attention primarily on U.S. audiences during the creative process, they nevertheless are working in an environment that is rapidly changing around them. Besides the challenges posed by new competitors, runaway production, and intellectual property, Hollywood is also facing competition from regional television services that are connected to the specific patterns of circulation in different parts of the world. One of the media capitals that has proven most durable and resilient in generating such challenges is Hong Kong.

HONG KONG TELEVISION

When broadcast television first came to Hong Kong in 1967, the local society was only beginning to experience the emergence of a broad-based consumer culture. Throughout much of the 1940s and 1950s waves of immigrants from mainland China and from overseas Chinese communities flooded into the city, dramatically altering the quality and tempo of everyday life in the colony. Previously, Hong Kong had been a transit point for Chinese trade, culture, and human migration, but only a relatively small population made the territory their home. Located on the south coast of China at the mouth of the Pearl River, Hong Kong was an entrepôt for a lucrative flow of goods between Europe and Guangdong Province.[32] Yet Hong Kong itself was not the center of economic or cultural activity in southern China. One hundred miles inland, the city of Guangzhou (Canton) was the main nexus of a lucrative network of agricultural and cottage manufacturing industries. It was also the cultural and intellectual capital of Cantonese society. In the mid-1800s, Hong Kong was by comparison a sparsely populated stretch of rocky headlands that was seized by British traders in order to establish a base for their commercial operations in East Asia. Most Chinese who traveled to the colony to find work or to do business planned to return to their homeland as soon as possible.

Cataclysmic events of the twentieth century would forever alter the character of Britain's farthest imperial outpost. During World War II, the Chinese civil war, and periods of economic reversal, hundreds of thousands of people of all political stripes sought sanctuary in the colony. Most imagined the city as a temporary home, seeing their fortunes as ultimately tied to the villages where they had grown up and where their ancestors had lived for centuries. Yet the political tides of the era forced many to remain in the territory, where they found work, started businesses, and raised families. A city of little more than a million at the end of World War II, the population in Hong Kong tripled before cold war tensions and government regulations began to restrict the flow of newcomers during the 1960s.[33] Despite these political constraints—and because of its central position in the Chinese diaspora—the city continued to prosper as a nexus for financial and trade relations between mainland China and the rest of the world, serving as the conduit for well over two-thirds of all international trade and investment during the last four decades of the twentieth century. Just as important, Hong Kong has become the central locus of banking and investment for the extensive transnational business activities of overseas Chinese communities around the world. Moreover, the city's growing wealth and influence during the 1960s and 1970s in turn fostered its status as a regional trade and finance center for all of East Asia. Like Chicago, Hong Kong mediates a vast and complex field of material and economic flows.[34]

The city's emergence as a media capital must furthermore take into account the influences exerted by migrations of cultural institutions and creative talent. Prior to World War II, Chinese performers and audiences looked to Guangzhou for leadership in matters of art and culture, with Cantonese opera serving as one of the most popular forms of entertainment. During the 1930s, nascent film studios happily appropriated the songs, narratives, and performance styles of the art form. Indeed, many filmmakers simply recorded and exhibited opera performances via the new cinema technology. Thus during this formative period Guangzhou became both the center of Cantonese opera and Cantonese film production. But as the fortunes of war disrupted cultural activities on the mainland, many creative personnel sought refuge in Hong Kong. Likewise, filmmakers and artists in northern China, especially Shanghai (then known as the Hollywood of China), fled south during the Japanese invasion and the civil war between Nationalist and Communist factions. Hong Kong offered sanctuary to members of these creative communities and therefore emerged during the postwar period as the most prolific producer of popular Chinese cinema.[35]

Yet despite Hong Kong's ascendant status, Guangzhou, Shanghai, and mainland culture had tremendous influence on the creative styles of this powerful new center of cinema production. Although the influx of refugees enhanced the creative resources of the Hong Kong film industry, it nevertheless diminished the medium's ability to express local concerns. Moreover, refugee filmmakers commonly addressed audiences that reached far beyond the territory and consequently featured themes, stars, and topics that appealed to those far-flung audiences. Until the border was sealed after the revolution, the mainland was a major market for such filmmakers, as also were overseas Chinese communities in places such as Taiwan, Singapore, Bangkok, and London.[36] In a sense, films produced in Hong Kong were powerfully influenced by external economic, political, and cultural forces and therefore were not particularly expressive of life within the colony. Narratives were often set in mythical locales or distant Chinese cities. Indeed, the urban landscape of the territory was rarely recognizable to viewers. Similarly, the dilemmas that onscreen characters faced were only allegorically linked to the complex challenges confronting immigrants to the city. Although widely popular with audiences during the 1950s, many critics and historians contend that this diasporic Chinese cinema became increasingly irrelevant to local Hong Kong audiences during the 1960s, as the city experienced a period of dramatic social and economic change. By mid-decade, filmmakers began to offer more contemporary topics and treatments that responded to these changes, but it happened too late, as attendance at Chinese films, particularly Cantonese films, began a serious period of decline.[37]

One of the key causes of declining attendance was a significant population shift in the colony. During the 1960s, immigrants were beginning to accept the fact that their stay in Hong Kong might be longer than they expected and many were beginning to enjoy unrivaled prosperity. As incomes rose, so did the size of families, and young people came to comprise a larger percentage of the population. The youth culture that subsequently emerged in Hong Kong exhibited distinctive tastes, values, and life experiences. Many young people had absolutely no contact with life on the mainland and therefore did not share their parents' nostalgia for home. This cultural amnesia was compounded by the fact that the colonial school system sought to neutralize political tensions between the pro- and anti-Communist factions of Hong Kong society by eliminating twentieth-century Chinese history and civics from the school curriculum. Although the refugee generation had fixed its attention on the fortunes of mainland society and politics, members of the younger generation harbored no such proclivities.[38] In many cases, they had more experience with Western popular culture than they did with traditional Chinese culture and politics. Hollywood movies and U.S. music became extremely popular in Hong Kong during the 1960s. Nevertheless, young people also seemed to be searching for cultural forms that were more proximate and more relevant.[39]

It was at this juncture, after extensive government deliberation, that broadcast television was first introduced to Hong Kong.[40] The first license, TVB, was allocated to a consortium of local business leaders, among them Sir Run Run Shaw, head of Hong Kong's most powerful film studio, Shaw Brothers, which had dominated the world of Chinese cinema for much of the post–World War II era.[41] Shaw's success emanated from the fact that he and his brothers built a vertically integrated media empire that operated throughout East and Southeast Asia. In virtually every major city with a substantial Chinese population, Shaw owned theaters and film distributorships. In Bangkok, Singapore, and Kuala Lumpur, as well as a host of other cities throughout the region, Shaw had a dominant position in the market, both for Chinese and Hollywood film exhibition. Based in the Clearwater Bay section of Hong Kong, Shaw Brothers established the largest studios in Asia, with elaborate sets and thousands of artists under contract. Yet Shaw noticed the slackening of cinema attendance during the late 1960s and consequently began to shift his attention from film to television. Within a decade he took control of TVB and—in part because of pressure from government regulators who were concerned about media cross-ownership—he relinquished his active involvement in cinema in favor of the new medium. Although no longer able to access transnational Chinese film audiences, Shaw was able to address a rapidly growing and increasingly prosperous local television audience.

The popularity of local television grew with fantastic speed. By 1973, some eighty percent of Hong Kong homes owned receivers that enabled them to pick up two local Chinese-language stations, which produced most of their own programming. Wildly popular, television quickly became the dominant advertising medium, with TVB reportedly attracting more than 50 percent of total ad revenues for all media in the territory. The station then used its leverage to put pressure on advertisers and creative personnel in order to forge long-term contracts that insured the continued dominance of TVB. Although many criticized Shaw's vertically integrated monopoly, TVB was nevertheless a hotbed of creative endeavor during the early years of the medium. Revenues were high, budgets were big, and the station served as a magnet for writers, performers, and directors from theater, film, publishing, and other realms of creative endeavor.[42]

Consequently, television became the primary site of public deliberation regarding the emergence of a distinctive Hong Kong identity. Local news programming was extremely popular during this period, especially stories about the work of an independent commission set up to investigate business and government corruption.[43] As the first public examination of malfeasance in the colonial power structure, the inquest had a transformative impact on Hong Kong society, generating widespread discussion about tradition, ethics, and the rule of law. Television producers furthermore tapped this popular fascination by crafting prime-time crime series that were among the first dramas produced in the colony. Variety shows were also an important genre during the early years of television, with singing stars fashioning a local musical style that merged U.S., Japanese, and Chinese influences into a distinctive pop form featuring contemporary lyrics by local songwriters. Out of this milieu emerged Cantopop, a style that still dominates the Hong Kong music scene today and has a powerful influence on entertainment industries throughout Asia. Finally, domestic dramas about the dilemmas of everyday life in the territory produced legions of loyal fans that tuned in on a nightly basis. Among the most popular was a serial narrative about the fortunes of a local family that is unexpectedly reunited with a long-lost son from the mainland. The mainland son, Ah Chian, is not able to adapt to modern Hong Kong society, however, and it is this issue that explicitly foregrounded distinctions between the values and attitudes of the societies on either side of the border. Viewed by more than 90 percent of TV households, the series provided a pretext for wide-ranging discussions regarding identity, migration, and popular values.[44]

In sum, Hong Kong's rapid embrace of television was connected to the fact that it mediated complex relations between East and West, between tradition and modernity, and between immigrant and indigenous populations. Television both responded to and shaped the social transformations then taking place in the colony. Furthermore, the medium is credited with sparking the revival of the film industry and with fostering the growth of the local pop music industry.[45] Thus locality and identity were important factors during this period of cultural ferment, but interestingly the output of these local culture industries also proved popular when circulated in overseas Chinese communities where similar social dynamics were at work. Younger generations of overseas Chinese seemed to share the interests and enthusiasms of Hong Kong residents, and the city became widely recognized as the capital of Chinese popular culture.[46] No longer seen as a colonial enclave inhabited by immigrants, Hong Kong shed its reputation as a conduit for cultural influences from afar and instead became recognized as a cosmopolitan center of East Asia.

NEO-NETWORK HONG KONG

Even though Hong Kong television emerged at the juncture of complex transnational flows of people, goods, and culture, the circulation of its television programming—as opposed to its film and music texts—was largely restricted to the confines of the territory due to regulatory and technological constraints. In neighboring mainland China, television receivers were not widely available until the 1980s, and governments in Taiwan, Singapore, and other East Asian countries placed restrictions on program imports. Moreover, telefilm copies of Hong Kong programs were difficult to syndicate in other overseas locales because broadcasters there were loathe to give up airtime for programming that seemed targeted at Chinese minority communities. During the 1970s, programmers in London and even Bangkok (home to a large Thai-Chinese community) commonly saw TVB programs as niche products, ill suited to the needs of British or Thai mass audiences.

Such obstacles were not immediately problematic for Shaw because TVB profits from local operations grew annually at a fantastic rate during the first two decades of the medium. Yet by the late 1980s growth rates began to plateau and consequently TVB and ATV, its key competitor, began to show significant interest in international markets. Thanks to the increasing diffusion of cable television and videocassette technology, Shaw and his management team began to turn their attention to overseas Chinese communities, the very same audiences that had fostered the first incarnation of Shaw's media empire. Beginning first with videocassette rentals, TVB established outlets and franchises in cities as diverse as Amsterdam, Penang, and Vancouver. Then, culling information from its rental database, TVB began to invest in cable services in places like Canada and Taiwan, where its video rentals had proven especially attractive to local viewers. More recently, TVB expanded its operations into mainland China, where it markets videos, syndicates programming, and pursues investments in joint broadcast ventures. Touting itself as having the world's largest library of Chinese telefilm programming—with over seventy-five thousand hours of domestic dramas, kung fu epics, musicals, and films—TVB imagines a Greater China audience as the key to its future growth. Indeed, Managing Director Louis Page expects net income derived from international operations to rise from under 3 percent to some 30 percent of overall profits.[47]

The scope of these aspirations is suggested by the diverse nature of TVB's media ventures. In Amsterdam and other cities around the world, one can walk into a TVB video shop that is stocked from floor to ceiling with television series available for sale or rent. In Toronto, TVB's main broadcast feed is available on cable TV in virtually the same form as that found in Hong Kong. The broadcaster's signature is also recognizable at one of its most profitable overseas operations, TVBS, a joint venture with Taiwan's ERA Communications that is one of the top four channels in Taiwan. More recently, Shaw's company announced a joint venture with INTELSAT, the world's oldest global television service, to develop the infrastructure for a global satellite service with interactive capabilities. Finally, these and other ventures have reminded TVB management of the importance of feature films as the anchor of any successful cable/satellite programming platform. Thus, Shaw's company is actively exploring the expansion of its film operations, which have languished for more than twenty years.[48]

Some critics have commented that the intensity of TVB's initial attachment to local politics and popular culture in Hong Kong has diminished since the 1980s. In part, this may be attributable to the ossification of program formats, the increasing attention to budgetary controls, the shifting political winds since the restoration of Chinese sovereignty, and a desire to play it safe as the dominant advertising outlet in the territory. In another sense, however, TVB's attachment to the territory may be changing because the future prosperity and growth of the company no longer depend on Hong Kong. Instead, TVB is becoming a transnational television service with an eclectic set of commitments. The company is at the same time a niche service for expatriates in Canada, a highly conventionalized medium in prosperous Hong Kong, a popular source of pirated entertainment in mainland China, and an innovative agitator in the competitive and highly politicized media environment of Taiwan. As its audiences become more dispersed, many observers wonder how much longer TVB will remain a locally owned venture. Investors from Singapore and London have at times taken substantial ownership positions in the firm, and merger talks have been reported over the past decade with such media giants as News Corp. and Time Warner. For now, a very elderly Run Run Shaw remains in charge, but his management cadre has taken over much of the daily operation of the firm and has publicly delineated the importance of overseas ventures to the future health of TVB. Managers claim that TVB's survival ultimately relies on its ability to expand transnationally, offering a host of television services that highlight distinctions between Chinese popular culture and Hollywood popular culture. The history of Shaw Brothers and TVB is instructive because it tracks the social and cultural changes in the territory in the latter part of the twentieth century. During an extended period of political strife in mainland China, Hong Kong served as a haven for a diasporic Chinese film industry and only later discovered a distinctive local identity during the age of television. It now faces the challenge of adapting to the transnational and transmedia environs of the neo-network era, while at the same time it is pressed to maintain a cultural voice that is distinctive from Hollywood.

TOWARD THE STUDY OF MEDIA CAPITALS

Although an unlikely combination, these brief cultural geographies of Hollywood, Hong Kong, and Chicago suggest new ways of thinking about patterns of flow and articulation within the realm of television and popular culture. They also stimulate our consideration of the historical trajectory of television's development within a global—as well as national, regional, and local—context. But perhaps most important, the cultural geographies of these three cities invite close comparison in hopes that such an exercise might yield fresh insights regarding the current circumstances of each and the future prospects of Hollywood and Hong Kong as global media capitals. Toward that end I will revisit key elements of the discussion above, with particular attention to the role that cultural difference plays in the constitution and maintenance of a media capital.

As noted, national integration in the United States under a Fordist regime of accumulation proceeded throughout the radio era, but this tendency was tempered by residual circulations of goods, capital, and people at the midwestern regional level. Thus, subnational tendencies continued to exert a strong influence over institutions of culture at the very moment when radio and cinema provided new possibilities for the national and even international circulation of cultural forms. Chicago broadcasting rose to prominence because it mediated between both regional and national economic forces and between urban immigrant groups and rural Anglo populations. It tapped the imagery of small-town America in order to legitimate its role in the radio era and it fabricated a midwestern sensibility that seemed a popular and culturally distinctive response to the ravages of Fordist economic transformation.

Yet as television took hold, the differences that distinguished Chicago broadcasting became more difficult to sustain. During the 1950s, the full flowering of mass culture and mass production altered the fundamental institutional arrangements of broadcasting, while the emergence of cold war geopolitics further facilitated the process of nationalization. By extending the logic of World War II homefront mobilizaion into the 1950s and 1960s, the federal government actively nurtured the consolidation of national values and attitudes as well as institutions. Calls for a united response to Communist expansionism provided a pretext for the marginalization of local and regional perspectives. This integrationist discourse was not only pitched at races, classes, and ethnicities but also at regions and localities, making it difficult to articulate the value of subnational differences.[49] Consequently, economic and political forces profoundly altered the terms of cultural production, while at the same time Hollywood TV thoroughly absorbed the cultural capital of a midwestern perspective and transformed it into a national suburban ethos of middle-class diligence, prosperity, and progress. For example, *Father Knows Best, My Three Sons,* and *The Beverly Hillbillies* all bear the markings of earlier radio domestic comedies out of the Midwest. Consequently, Chicago's demise as a media capital was as much a product of semiotic as economic or political forces. By the end of the 1950s, the cultural differences that originally constituted Chicago broadcasting were no longer salient enough to maintain its mediating role. What did Chicago have to offer that Hollywood did not? In such a context, the logic of Fordist consolidation proceeded without serious challenge.

Today, however, the situation has changed dramatically. The end of the cold war makes it difficult for the U.S. government to mount sustained effort behind a national cultural agenda. Moreover, new patterns of transnational corporate activity, along with innovations in transportation and communication technologies, herald the transition to a globalized neo-Fordist economic order of flexible production and niche marketing. In this new era, the cost of entry-level television production has decreased dramatically, while at the same time the number of communication channels has proliferated, not only on cable and the Internet but also on videotape and disc. Even in relatively impoverished parts of the world, the number of information and entertainment options has exploded. In the face of this plenitude, national officials and industry strategists find it difficult to regulate the flow of popular imagery. No longer are national television systems so easily dominated by a few centralized, state-sanctioned institutions. Further exacerbating this trend are changes in U.S. foreign policy, which has shifted from attempting to dominate a cold war international system to the active promotion of trade liberalization. This aggressive policy initiative has, on the one hand, extended the reach of Hollywood programming while unexpectedly, on the other hand, it has facilitated a dispersion of creative activity to locations outside of Southern California. Not only does Hollywood face the problem of runaway production but it also confronts competition from media services around the world that are now pressed to expand beyond their own national contexts.

Herein lies the irony of Hollywood's current condition. Certainly, Hollywood has succeeded as the media capital par excellence by absorbing elements from around the world and transforming them into a distinctive style that has broad global appeal. Hollywood fare is especially successful in transnational markets when it competes against poorly financed local productions (e.g., Latin America in the 1960s) or when it is used to flush out programming schedules in markets with rapidly expanding airtime (e.g., Europe in the 1980s). Indeed, Hollywood television is still riding high on the sale of its programming to new cable and satellite services that have emerged recently in countries undergoing trade liberalization and policy deregulation. Yet in many other places local and regional services are maturing, and Hollywood faces growing competition from producers in places like Beirut, Madras, and Mexico City. Just as Hollywood throughout its history absorbed elements and artists borrowed from afar, so too are other media capitals adapting the genres, visual conventions, technologies, and institutional practices of Hollywood to local conditions. Like Detroit in the 1960s, Hollywood today produces big, bloated vehicles that command the fascination of audiences around the world. Yet at the same time it increasingly must take account of competitors who fashion products for more specific markets, using local labor, materials, and perspectives. Such programs are not only cheaper to produce but also more attractive to target audiences because they are more culturally relevant.[50]

Hong Kong is one such competitor. Its central position in the economic flows of East Asia marks one very important reason for its emergence as a global media capital, but patterns of human migration provide other reasons as to why Hong Kong has risen to such prominence. Tumultuous political developments on the mainland from the 1930s to the 1960s turned the colony into one of the most important nodes of the Chinese diaspora. During the late 1960s, the city emerged as a distinctive center of media production when television began to hail a rapidly growing resident population instead of the sojourner generations of earlier times. Reflections on an emerging Hong Kong identity became reflections on the everyday tensions between East and West as well as tradition and modernity. Interestingly, such reflections resonated with overseas Chinese audiences and, more recently, audiences in post-Mao China.

In her study of Shanghai media use during the mid-1990s, Mayfair Mei-hui Yang found that Hong Kong and Taiwanese television and music are far more popular and influential with mainland audiences than is Hollywood fare. As state influence over everyday life recedes, audiences seem to be searching for cultural resources that reflect on the quotidian challenges they confront. Yang observes that such media products "have enabled the detaching of Chinese subjectivity from the state and its mobilization across imaginary space to link up with alternative Chinese subjectivities far away."[51] These new linkages and subjectivities result from interactions among Chinese societies as they experience processes of modernization and geopolitical realignment. Moreover, they represent something quite different from common characterizations of Hollywood hegemony or the McDonaldization of Chinese culture. Instead, Yang observes, "The binary constructions of center versus periphery and West versus the rest prove inadequate, as the outside 'center' that is having the most impact on China today is not the West but the modernized and commercialized Chinese societies of Taiwan, Hong Kong, and overseas Chinese."[52]

Circulations among these societies do not, of course, preclude interactions with the West, but those interactions are often mediated via the popular texts and institutional practices of Hong Kong media. The city serves as a nexus for flows within a Chinese cultural sphere. It also serves as a site where media practitioners from all over cultural China congregate to do the face work necessary for mass media production. Furthermore, the city sits at the very apex of career pilgrimages by successful performers and impresarios. Run Run Shaw's life is perhaps emblematic of this tendency. Born and raised near Shanghai, Shaw began his career working with his brothers producing and exhibiting martial arts films in 1930s Shanghai. He then migrated to Singapore in order to set up a prosperous chain of theaters throughout Southeast Asia. Later, during the 1950s, when the demand for Chinese movies was growing rapidly, Shaw moved to Hong Kong, where he took charge of production at Shaw Brothers and established one of the largest film and TV studios in Asia. It would have been far more difficult to set up such a studio in Singapore or Shanghai, because by the late 1950s Hong Kong had become the nodal point for the migrations of creative talent within the Chinese culture industries.[53] Like Shaw, others have made their way to the territory over the past several decades for the very same reason: director Peter Chan hails from Bangkok, actress Michelle Yeoh from Malaysia, singer/actress Faye Wong from Beijing, actor/veejay David Wu from Seattle, director Sylvia Chang from Taipei, and TV executive Robert Chua from Singapore.[54]

Thus capital, expertise, and cultural resources from Chinese societies around the world all flow through Hong Kong. Yet the city's fortune as a media capital rests not only on its centrality, but also on its marginality. Hong Kong is very Chinese and also remarkably Western, and yet it's not really either, nor can we simply say that it is both. It exists at the center of flows among Chinese communities, yet it is also on the periphery of both China and the West. One might say that its power and its vulnerability derive from its "marginal centrality." The recent restoration of Beijing's political control over the city highlights these ambiguities by significantly altering the intentions, strategies, and behaviors of media organizations based in the former British colony. On the one hand, Hong Kong broadcasters must now acknowledge the influence of Beijing's political elite and must find a place in the national order. On the other hand, however, these broadcasters seem determined to carve out transnational strategies that offer them some hope of maintaining a modicum of independence and prosperity.[55] Ironically, Hong Kong is both threatened by Beijing and dependent on the historical and cultural legacies that the two cities share. It therefore must mark its distance from Beijing and from Hollywood if it is to survive as a media capital. For the attraction of Hong Kong TV, as Yang suggests, resides in its perceived distance from the disciplinary logic of the Chinese state and the cultural logic of Hollywood.

This peculiar dilemma bears consideration in light of Chicago's experience as a media capital. Part of Chicago's demise as a broadcasting center can be explained by its diminishing identity as a site of mediation between national and regional, urban and rural, Anglo and other. By the 1950s the city lacked a political, economic, or cultural rationale for its existence as a major media production locale, therefore making it difficult for Chicago broadcasters to mount substantial resistance to the consolidation of national network television. Now, in the neo-network era, Hong Kong faces a similarly complex challenge of repositioning its television institutions in relation to Beijing and Hollywood. At the center of current debates over the future of Hong Kong media floats the illusory visage of a Greater China audience—the Asian counterpart to aspirations for a pan-European "television without frontiers" or a Latin "audiovisual space."[56] At its economic core, this Greater China audience is composed of Hong Kong residents and close to 50 million overseas Chinese with per capita incomes that rank among the highest in the industrialized world. Add to this total the roughly 250 million urban inhabitants of mainland China—almost all of whom have access to television in their homes—and we begin to discern why this potential audience has generated so much discussion. Hong Kong plays a key part in this speculation because it is widely acknowledged for its central role in trade, investment, migration, and cultural flows among Chinese communities around the world. In other words, like Chicago of a prior era, Hong Kong plays a distinctive mediational role for a vast and enormously complex economic and cultural formation. But this mediational role is crucially dependent on its position at both the center and the margins of Greater China. It furthermore depends on the useful fiction of Greater China, when in fact the concept lacks both boundaries and coherence. It is perhaps more appropriate to suggest that Hong Kong mediates a useful fiction rather than a coherent entity.

In his controversial 1993 essay, Samuel Huntington argues that geo-politics in the post–cold war world will be shaped by civilizational conflicts rather than economic or political tensions.[57] Huntington identifies seven great civilizations—among them, Islam, India, China, the West—that are based on underlying religious, linguistic, and cultural affinities. In an attempt to chart new patterns of transnational media flow, Joseph Straubhaar appropriates Huntington's approach in order to explain the emergence of what he refers to as geo-cultural television markets. Straubhaar writes: "If [Huntington's] analysis extends to culture as represented on television, then we might expect to see the Chinese market broaden to a 'Confucian' cultural influence area market, the Arabic language market broaden to an Islamic market, and a Slavic-Orthodox market emerging out of the ex-USSR and Eastern Europe." Straubhaar refers to these as geo-cultural markets that are often spatially dispersed but nevertheless held together by historical, religious, linguistic, and cultural affinities.[58] Straubhaar's suggestion is enormously productive when cast in relation to the concept of media capitals. Hong Kong media are perhaps best understood as both responding to flows within a Chinese—or Confucian—geo-cultural sphere and as participating in the maintenance of an infrastructure that sustains that very sphere of interaction.

Great care must be taken, however, to appropriate this insight without bringing on board the cultural essentialism that informs Huntington's analysis. One danger is that his approach reifies an orientalist opposition between East and West. It creates unities where none may exist and it suggests that such unities are "facts of nature" rather than products of power. Another problem with Huntington's approach is that it recenters "authentic" Chinese culture as emanating from the Middle Kingdom, when in fact some of the most dynamic centers of this sphere are to be found in places like Singapore, Taipei, and Hong Kong.[59] But perhaps most worrisome is that Huntington's essentialism refocuses our attention on boundaries and containers rather than on complex patterns of flow. And here is where we might find particular advantages to the study of media capitals, for the concept asks us to think in terms of patterned change rather than essential qualities. It furthermore directs our attention to the uneven and often conflict-ridden development of contemporary media, focusing our attention on difference as well as similarity.

Thus, media capital—as a concept—allows us to speak of Hong Kong's marginality as well as its centrality, and to consider the implications of Greater China without falling prey to this powerful fiction. It furthermore invites us to acknowledge the attractions of Hollywood media without presuming their inevitable dominance in all corners of the globe. And, finally, it encourages us to remember the history of Chicago broadcasting in anticipation of the inevitable changes that await Hong Kong and Hollywood in the not-too-distant future.

NOTES

I would like to thank the Taiwan National Endowment for Culture and Art and the U.S. Fulbright Commission for providing research support during the 1999–2000 academic year. I also want to express my appreciation to colleagues at the Institute of Ethnology, Academic Sinica, and the Foundation for Scholarly Exchange, who graciously hosted my sabbatical in Taipei, and to colleagues and students in the School of Journalism and Mass Communication at the Chinese University of Hong Kong, where I served as a visiting professor during the 1996–1997 academic year. I would also like to thank Herman Gray and Mayfair Yang for comments on earlier drafts of this essay.

1. See, for example, David Barker, *Global Television: An Introduction* (Malden, Mass.: Blackwell, 1997); Colin Hoskins, Stuart McFadyen, and Adam Finn, *Global Television and Film: An Introduction to the Economics of the Business* (New York: Oxford University Press, 1997); John Tomlinson, *Cultural Imperialism: A Critical Introduction* (Baltimore: Johns Hopkins University Press, 1991); John Tomlinson, *Globalization and Culture* (Chicago: University of Chicago Press, 1999); McKenzie Wark, *Virtual Geography: Living with Global Media Events* (Bloomington: Indiana University Press, 1994); and in a related but contrary vein, see James Curran and Myung-Jin Park, eds., *De-Westernizing Media Studies* (London: Routledge, 2000).

2. Arjun Appadurai, *Modernity at Large: Cultural Dimensions of Globalization* (Minneapolis: University of Minnesota Press, 1996), p. 46.

3. Joseph Straubhaar, "Beyond Media Imperialism: Asymmetrical Interdependence and Cultural Proximity," *Critical Studies in Mass Communication* 8 (1991): 1–11.

4. David Morley and Kevin Robins, *Spaces of Identity: Global Media, Electronic Landscapes, and Cultural Boundaries* (London: Routledge, 1995); Joseph Straubhaar, "Distinguishing the Global, Regional, and National Levels of World Television," in Annabelle Sreberny-Mohammadi, Dwayne Winseck, Jim McKenna, and Oliver Boyd-Barrett, eds., *Media in Global Context: A Reader* (London: Arnold, 1997), pp. 284–98; Marie Gillespie, *Television, Ethnicity, and Cultural Change* (London: Routledge, 1995).

5. John Sinclair, Elizabeth Jacka, and Stuart Cunningham, eds., *New Patterns in Global Television: Peripheral Vision* (New York: Oxford University Press, 1996).

6. Saskia Sassen, *The Global City: New York, London, Tokyo* (Princeton: Princeton University Press, 1991), p. 325.

7. Jesus Martin-Barbero, *Communication, Culture, and Hegemony: From the Media to Mediations*, trans. Elizabeth Fox and Robert A. White (Newbury Park, N.J.: Sage, 1993), p. 163.

8. Doreen Massey, "A Place Called Home?" *New Formations* 17 (1992): 3–15; Kevin Robins, "Prisoners of the City: Whatever Could a Postmodern City Be?" *New Formations* 15 (1991): 1–22. See also Janet Lippman Abu Lughod, "Communication and the Metropolis: Spatial Drift and the Reconstitution of Control," *Asian Journal of Communication* 2.3 (1992): 13–30; and James Hay, "Invisible Cities/Visible Geographies: Toward a Cultural Geography of Italian Television in the 1990s," in *Television: The Critical View,* 5th ed., ed. Horace Newcomb (New York: Oxford University Press, 1994), pp. 602–15.

9. Globalization is understood here as a process that operates at the local, national, regional, and worldwide levels, as opposed to a process that emphasizes the latter. Furthermore, this essay does not recommend that media research exclusively focus on media capitals to the exclusion of more localized media institutions, nor am I suggesting that these capitals exist in splendid isolation. Rather, their existence is fundamentally relational, and they draw on a complex array of resources from actors, institutions, and cultural forms within their geographic spheres of influence. For example, Hollywood media crucially rely on New York financial and distribution resources, and Hong Kong media are closely linked to capital and creative talent in Taipei. Indeed, one of the purposes of emphasizing the study of media capitals is to uncover the elaborate linkages between these centers of creative production and the extranational (transnational and subnational) resources on which they rely.

10. For example, see the texts of the 1927 Radio Act and the David Amendment in *Documents of American Broadcasting,* 4th ed., ed. Frank J. Kahn (Englewood Cliffs: N.J.: Prentice-Hall, 1984).

11. The early history of struggles over the control of radio broadcasting can be found in Erik Barnouw, *A History of Broadcasting in the United States* (New York: Oxford University Press, 1966); Susan Smulyan, *Selling Radio: The Commercialization of American Broadcasting, 1920–1934* (Washington, D.C.: Smithsonian Press, 1994); and Robert McChesney, *Telecommunications, Mass Media, and Democracy: The Battle for the Control of U.S. Broadcasting, 1928–1935* (New York: Oxford University Press, 1993).

12. Other active producers of local, regional, and national radio programming were located in Cincinnatti, the home of Proctor & Gamble household products, the largest daytime advertiser in U.S. broadcasting, and in Detroit, home of the major automobile manufacturers.

13. Michele Hilmes, *Hollywood and Broadcasting: From Radio to Cable* (Urbana: University of Illinois Press, 1990).

14. Space limitations do not allow a full discussion here of the rise of Hollywood and the decline of other film-producing centers around the United States, such as Chicago, New York, and Florida. For a discussion of the move to Hollywood during the first decade of the twentieth century, see David Bordwell, Janet Staiger, and Kristin Thompson, *The Classical Hollywood Cinema: Film Style and Mode of Production to 1960* (London: Routledge and Kegan Paul, 1985), pp. 121–23. For a discussion of the international operations of Hollywood distributors during this early period, see Kristin Thompson, *Exporting Entertainment: America in the World Film Market, 1907–1934* (London: British Film Institute, 1985). As a national media capital, Hollywood, of course, played a role in the commercial and ideological operations that facilitated the United States' rise to power in the twentieth century. In many ways, Hollywood's operations—distributing film internationally and absorbing talent from abroad—prefigures its eventual emergence as a global media capital.

15. William Cronon provides the best account of Chicago's material mediations of the agro-industrial complex of the American heartland in *Nature's Metropolis: Chicago and the Great West* (New York: Norton, 1991); and James Carey discusses Chicago's role as a communication and transportation hub in *Communication as Culture: Essays on Media and Society* (Boston: Unwin Hyman, 1989). Other useful histories of Chicago include James B. Gilbert, *Perfect Cities: Chicago's Utopias of 1893* (Chicago: University of Chicago Press, 1991); and Lizabeth Cohen, *Making a New Deal: Industrial Workers in Chicago, 1919–1939* (New York: Cambridge University Press, 1990).

16. Ad firms like Benton and Bowles; McCann-Erickson; Leo Burnett; and Foote, Cone, and Belding got their start in Chicago servicing such clients as Swift & Co., Oscar Meyer, Colgate-Palmolive, Johnson & Johnson, General Foods, and A&P grocery stores.

17. Robert C. Allen, *Speaking of Soap Operas* (Chapel Hill: University of North Carolina Press, 1985); Roland Marchand, *Advertising the American Dream: Making Way for Modernity, 1920–1940* (Berkeley: University of California Press, 1985); Melvin Patrick Ely, *The Adventures of Amos 'n' Andy: A Social History of an American Phenomenon* (New York: Maxwell McMillan, 1991). See also biographies of Chicago ad executives, such as Fairfax M. Cone, *With All Its Faults: A Candid Account of Forty Years in Advertising* (Boston: Little, Brown, 1969); and John Gunther, *Taken from the Flood: The Story of Albert D. Lasker* (New York: Harper, 1960).

18. See Joel Sternberg, "A Descriptive History and Critical Analysis of the Chicago School of Television, 1948–1954," Ph.D. diss., Northwestern University, 1973; and Sternberg, "Television Town," *Chicago History* 4 (summer 1975): 108–17.

19. This involved a system of landlines for the interconnection of stations with the broadcast headquarters in New York, as well as the construction of studio space specifically designed for television production. Initially, radio studios were converted into cramped, makeshift television facilities until more suitable, and far more expensive, facilities could be developed.

20. Vance Kepley Jr., "From 'Frontal Lobes' to the 'Bob and Bob Show,'" in *Hollywood in the Age of Television*, ed. Tino Balio (Boston: Unwin Hyman, 1990); William Boddy, *Fifties Television: The Industry and Its Critics* (Urbana: University of Illinois Press, 1990).

21. Histories of these transitions in the television industry can be found in Christopher Anderson, *Hollywood TV: The Studio System in the Fifties* (Austin: University of Texas Press, 1994); Balio, *Hollywood in the Age of Television;* Boddy, *Fifties Television;*

and Michael Curtin, *Redeeming the Wasteland: Documentary Television and Cold War Politics* (New Brunswick: Rutgers University Press, 1995).

22. Christopher Anderson and Michael Curtin, "Mapping the Ethereal City: Chicago Television, the FCC, and the Politics of Place," *Quarterly Review of Film and Video* 16.3–4 (1999): 289–305.

23. Herbert I. Schiller, *Mass Communication and American Empire* (1969; Boulder: Westview Press, 1992); Michael Curtin, "Dynasty in Drag: Imagining Global Television," in *The Revolution Wasn't Televised: Sixties Television and Social Conflict*, ed. Lynn Spigel and Michael Curtin (New York: Routledge, 1997), pp. 245–62.

24. See, for example, the comments of TV producer David Kendall, interviewed in Richard Ohmann, Gage Averill, Michael Curtin, David Shumway, and Elizabeth Traube, eds., *Making and Selling Culture* (Hanover, N.H.: Wesleyan University Press, 1996), pp. 69–70.

25. Joseph R. Dominick, *The Dynamics of Mass Communication*, 5th ed. (New York: McGraw-Hill, 1996).

26. See my "On Edge: Culture Industries in the Neo-Network Era," in Ohmann et al., eds., *Making and Selling Culture*, pp. 181–202; and "Gatekeepers of the Neo-Network Era," in *Advocacy Groups and Prime-Time Television*, ed. Michael Suman and Gabriel Rossman (Greenwich, Conn.: Praeger, 2000), pp. 65–76. Other analyses of these changes can be found in John Thornton Caldwell, *Televisuality: Style, Crisis, and Authority in American Television* (New Brunswick: Rutgers University Press, 1994); J. Fred MacDonald, *One Nation under Television* (New York: Pantheon, 1990); and Janet Wasko, *Hollywood in the Information Age: Beyond the Silver Screen* (London: Polity, 1994).

27. Michael Curtin and Thomas Streeter, "Media," in *Culture Works: Essays on the Political Economy of Culture,* ed. Richard Maxwell (Minneapolis: University of Minnesota Press, 2001), pp. 225–49.

28. In 1999, after several seasons, the producers of *The X-Files* decided to return to Southern California because they were seeking a new look for the long-running series and because of contractual arrangements with some of the show's stars.

29. See Anthony Giddens's discussion of "face work" and trust in *The Consequences of Modernity* (Stanford: Stanford University Press, 1990), pp. 83–88.

30. Serra Tinic, "Imagining Canada in Hollywood North: National Identity and the Globalization of the Vancouver Television Industry" (Ph.D. diss., Indiana University, 1999).

31. See Bernard Tavernier's account of the heavy pressure exerted by Ronald Reagan on the visiting president of Turkey, in John Walker, *Distress Signals: An Investigation of Global Television* (New York: First Run Icarus Films, 1991).

32. The opium, tea, and silk trades have received much attention, but the porcelain trade was perhaps even more important from the Chinese perspective. Land reclamation projects in the Pearl River Delta during the seventeenth and eighteenth centuries yielded lush farmland that enriched the local gentry, who then turned their resources to the expansion of cottage industry production of porcelain servingware to be shipped around the world. The demand for inexpensive "China" grew fantastically

throughout the West, which in turn helped to solidify relations with the outside world, foster urban growth, and establish a cosmopolitan merchant class. Guangzhou (Canton) was the center of these lucrative activities, but it was only accessible to foreigners during a limited trading season. Avaricious British merchants concocted the seizure of Hong Kong to establish a year-round base of operations that would solidify their access to the Pearl River Delta.

33. See, for example, Benjamin K. P. Leung, *Perspectives on Hong Kong Society* (Hong Kong: Oxford University Press, 1996).

34. See Claudia Cragg, *The New Taipans: A Vital Sourcebook on the People and Business of the Pacific Rim* (London: Arrow Books, 1996); and Sterling Seagrave, *Lords of the Rim* (London: Bantam Press, 1995).

35. See Choi Po-king, "From Dependence to Self-Sufficiency: Rise of the Indigenous Culture of Hong Kong, 1945–1989," *Asian Culture* 14 (1990): 161–76; Paul Fonoroff, "A Brief History of Hong Kong Cinema," *Renditions* 29/30 (1988): 293–308; Ian C. Jarvie, *Window on Hong Kong: A Sociological Study of the Hong Kong Film Industry and Its Audience* (Hong Kong: University of Hong Kong Press, 1977); and Stephen Teo, *Hong Kong Cinema: The Extra Dimension* (London: BFI Publishing, 1997).

36. Grace L. K. Leung and Joseph M. Chan, "The Hong Kong Cinema and Its Overseas Markets: A Historical Review, 1950–1995," in *Fifty Years of Electric Shadows: Hong Kong Cinema Retrospective,* ed. Law Kar (Hong Kong: Hong Kong Urban Council, 1997), pp. 136–51.

37. See Po-king, "From Dependence to Self-Sufficiency"; Fonoroff, "A Brief History of Hong Kong Cinema"; and Teo, *Hong Kong Cinema: The Extra Dimension.*

38. Poshek Fu, "Decade of Turbulence: Modernity, Youth Culture, and Cantonese Filmmaking in Hong Kong," in Kar, ed., *Fifty Years of Electric Shadows,* pp. 34–62.

39. Paul S. N. Lee, "The Absorption and Indigenization of Foreign Media Cultures: A Study on a Cultural Meeting Point of the East and West: Hong Kong," *Asian Journal of Communication* 1.2 (1991): 52–72.

40. A cable TV system had existed since 1958 but was connected to a very small number of Hong Kong households.

41. For the sake of clarity, I focus on Shaw in this essay. A fuller discussion of the Hong Kong film and TV industries can be found in my "Industry on Fire: The Cultural Economy of Hong Kong Media," *Post Script* 19.1 (fall 1999): 20–43; and my "Hong Kong Meets Hollywood in the Extranational Arena of the Culture Industries," in *Sites of Contestation: Localism, Globalism and Cultural Production in Asia and the Pacific,* ed. Kwok-Kan Tam and Wimal Dissanayake (Hong Kong: Chinese University of Hong Kong Press, 2001), pp. 79–109.

42. Cheuk Pak-Tong, "The Beginning of the Hong Kong New Wave: The Interactive Relationship Between Television and the Film Industry," *Post Script* 19.1 (fall 1999): 10–27; Choi Po-king, "From Dependence"; James Kung and Zhang Yueai, "Hong Kong Cinema and Television in the 1970s: A Perspective," in *A Study of Hong Kong Cinema in the Seventies,* ed. Li Cheuk-to (Hong Kong: Hong Kong Urban Council, 1984), pp. 14–17; and Terence Lo and Chung-bong Ng, "The Evolution of Prime-Time Television

Scheduling in Hong Kong," in *Contemporary Television: Eastern Perspectives,* ed. David French and Michael Richards (New Delhi: Sage, 1996), pp. 202–20.

43. Joseph Man Chan, "Mass Media and Socio-Political Formation in Hong Kong, 1949–1992," *Asian Journal of Communication* 2.3 (1992): 106–29.

44. Eric Kit-wai Ma, *Culture, Politics, and Television in Hong Kong* (London: Routledge, 1999).

45. See Kung and Yueai, "Hong Kong Cinema and Television."

46. It should be pointed out that even though the tastes of younger viewers may have sparked the production of texts that addressed distinctive local concerns, television programming was nevertheless targeted at a mass audience, and family viewing was most common. Similarly, until approximately 1990 Hong Kong cinemas catered to family audiences.

47. Yiu-ming To and Tuen-yu Lau, "Global Export of Hong Kong Television: Television Broadcasts Limited," *Asian Journal of Communication* 5.2 (1995): 112.

48. In addition to information gleaned from the business and trade press, this history of TVB's strategy is based on personal interviews with Michael K. W. Chan, deputy general manager of TVB International, April 25, 2000, and Helena K. F. Lee, marketing communications manager of TVB International, June 26, 1997.

49. Herman Gray discussed this in a talk at Stockholm University, Film Department, 1999.

50. We already see major media conglomerates like Sony and Viacom responding to these emerging market conditions by basing new production operations outside of Hollywood. For example, Sony has an Asian film and television production unit based in Hong Kong, and Viacom's Asian MTV satellite channels are programmed and produced in Asian locales. As with the Detroit auto companies of a prior era, the place-based managerial culture of Hollywood will ultimately have to acknowledge that those who control the capital resources in the media industries don't really care where programs are produced as long as they prove profitable. Regarding the appeal of more local programming, see Straubhaar, "Beyond Media"; and Hoskins, McFayden, and Finn, *Global Television and Film.*

51. Mayfair Mei-hui Yang, "Mass Media and Transnational Subjectivity in Shanghai: Notes on (Re)Cosmopolitanism in a Chinese Metropolis," in *Ungrounded Empires: The Cultural Politics of Modern Chinese Transnationalism,* ed. Aihwa Ong and Donald Nonini (New York: Routledge, 1997), p. 311. For related and similar findings, see Thomas B. Gold, "Go with Your Feelings: Hong Kong and Taiwan Popular Culture in Greater China," *China Quarterly* 136 (1993): 907–25; James Lull, *China Turned On: Television, Reform, and Resistance* (New York: Routledge, 1991); and Jianying Zha, *China Pop: How Soap Operas, Tabloids, and Bestsellers are Transforming a Culture* (New York: Free Press, 1995).

52. Yang, "Mass Media," p. 311.

53. It is interesting to think of these migrations in relation to Benedict Anderson's discussion of professional "pilgrimages" among local elites during the colonial era, in *Imagined Communities: Reflections on the Origins and Spread of Nationalism* (London: Verso, 1983), pp. 104–28.

54. Interestingly, top creative talent began migrating to Hollywood during a period of uncertainty surrounding the return of Hong Kong to Chinese rule. Yet several years later many of these performers and directors returned to the territory, and even though some of them have maintained connections to Hollywood, Hong Kong once again has become the center of their professional activity. Regarding the migration of talent to Hollywood, see Steve Fore, "Home, Migration, Identity: Hong Kong Film Workers Join the Chinese Diaspora," in Kar Law, ed., *Fifty Years of Electric Shadows*, pp. 126–35.

55. Outside the United States, I focus on Hong Kong as one example that emerged out of a particular cultural milieu and a particular transnational pattern of circulations. Other media capitals will have other histories, often tied during their early phases to the politics, culture, and economy of a nation-state. But places like Cairo, Bombay, and Mexico City merit special attention because they point to the increasingly transnational logic of their media environments.

56. "Television without frontiers" refers to a series of policy initiatives in the European Union aimed at bringing into being a pan-European media market. Similarly, Armand Mattelart has advanced the idea of developing media products based on linguistic and cultural affinities that might tie together Spanish, Portuguese, and Italian media with counterparts in Latin America. See Armand Mattelart, Xavier Delcourt, and Michele Mattelart, *International Image Markets: In Search of an Alternative Perspective* (London: Comedia, 1984).

57. Samuel Huntington, "The Clash of Civilizations," *Foreign Affairs* 72.3 (1993): 22–29.

58. Straubhaar, "Distinguishing the Global," p. 291.

59. See Aihwa Ong and Donald Nonini, "Chinese Transnationalism as an Alternative Modernity," in Ong and Nonini, eds., *Ungrounded Empires*, p. 9.

DAVID MORLEY

AT HOME WITH TELEVISION

In recent years much has been made of the idea of postmodernity. Images abound of our deterritorialized culture of "homelessness": images of exile, diaspora, time-space compression,
migrancy, and "nomadology." The concept of home often remains the
uninterrogated alterego of all this hypermobility. Certainly, traditional
ideas of home, homeland, and nation have been destabilized, both by new
patterns of physical mobility and by new communication technologies
that routinely transgress the symbolic boundaries around both the private
household and the nation-state. The electronic landscapes in which we
now dwell are haunted by all manner of cultural anxieties that arise from
this destabilizing flux.

My argument here draws on insights from contemporary work in
the field of cultural geography that insists on the necessity of rethinking
our sense of place in the context of the transformations and destabilizations wrought both by the forces of economic globalization and by the
global media industries. However, I am also concerned with articulating
these issues of "virtual geography" relative to some older debates about
the conceptualization of alterity and of the foreign (the unfamiliar, or
Fremde, which is the negative of *Heimat*) by reference to its significance
in the mediated rituals of exclusion by means of which the home and
Heimat are purified.

In part, the question for me also concerns the need to articulate, more effectively than is often done, different levels of abstraction in these debates. In particular, I want to advocate what could perhaps be described as a grounded theory approach, which places particular emphasis on the integration of micro and macro levels of analysis. I attempt to offer an approach to the analysis of micro structures of the home, the family, and the domestic realm that can be effectively integrated with contemporary macro debates about the nation, community, and cultural identities. The key concepts deployed in this analysis are those of boundary maintenance and boundary transgression. My focus is thus on the mutually dependent processes of exclusion and identity construction at both micro and macro levels of analysis. In my attempt to develop this analysis I draw on work in media studies (including some of my own earlier research) on the role of various communications technologies in the maintenance and disruption of the symbolic boundaries of both home and *Heimat*. My ambition is to broaden the theoretical frame within which they have this far been set. My further aim, at least implicitly, is to advocate what might perhaps be described as a materialist television studies that does not abstract the text from its material conditions of consumption by audiences who live in, or move through, a world whose geography continues to have determining effects on their lives.

AT HOME IN POSTMODERNITY?

The modern home can itself be said to be a phantasmagoric place to the extent that electronic media of various kinds allow the radical intrusion of distant events into the space of domesticity: in Zygmunt Bauman's terms, this represents the deeply problematic "invasion" of the "realm of the far" (that which is strange and potentially troubling) into the "realm of the near" (the traditional arena of ontological security).[1]

In the traditional vision of things, cultures were understood as being rooted in time and space, embodying genealogies of "blood, property, and frontiers." However, as Nigel Rapport and Andrew Dawson observe, the world "can no longer be easily divided up into units, territorial segments . . . each of which shares a distinctive, exclusive culture," so that there are no longer such "traditionally fixed, spatially and temporally bounded cultural worlds" from which to depart and return—precisely because the "migration of information, myths, languages and above all, persons . . . brings even the most isolated areas into a cosmopolitan global framework of interaction."[2]

In the founding statement of the journal *Public Culture,* Arjun Appadurai and Carol Breckenridge declared that their starting point in developing their mode of analysis was the recognition that "the world of the late twentieth century is increasingly a cosmopolitan world. More people are widely travelled, are catholic in their tastes, are more inclusive in the range of cuisines they consume, are attentive to global media-covered events and are influenced by universal trends in fashion."[3] In a similar spirit, James Clifford writes of the "cosmopolitical contact zones" in which we live today, commonly being traversed by "new social movements and global corporations, tribal activists and cultural tourists, migrants workers' remittances and email."[4] Bruce Robbins argues that "we are connected to all sorts of places, causally if not always consciously, including those that we have never travelled to, that we have perhaps only seen on television—including the place where the television itself was manufactured."[5]

This is the world of Ulf Hannerz's "global ecumene," where rather than seeing cultures as a global mosaic of separate entities rooted in space we see a complex system of long-distance cultural flows of images, goods, and people interweaving to form a kaleidoscope of unstable identities and transpositions.[6] In Jacques Derrida's terminology the effect of the "techno-tele-media apparatus" is to destabilize what he calls the national ontopology—that sense of the naturalness and givenness of territorialized "national belonging."[7] In this context, as Sandra Wallman observes, "even homogenous populations now come up against otherness as soon as they have access to modern media of communication." Thus, she argues, alongside increasing rates of actual physical mobility, there is for many people an increasing awareness of the *possibility* of movement as "mass media images, no doubt reflecting the mixture of people in many cities, sharpen ordinary citizens' awareness of cultural forms which are not primarily theirs."[8] As Doreen Massey puts it, the consequence is that "few people's . . . daily lives can be described as simply local. Even the most 'local' . . . people . . . have their lives touched by wider events [and] are linked into a broader geographical field. . . . Nobody in the First World these days lives their daily lives completely locally, entirely untouched by events elsewhere."[9] In today's world the distribution of the familiar and the strange is a complex one, in which, in Clifford's words, "difference is encountered in the adjoining neighbourhood, [and] the familiar turns up at the end of the earth."[10]

In this connection Appadurai poses the question of what "locality" can mean, in a world where "spatial localisation, quotidian interaction and social scale are not always isomorphic."[11] In noting the influence of the electronic media in eroding the relationship between spatial and virtual neighborhoods, which are increasingly in disjuncture from each other, Appadurai argues that we should understand neighborhoods as the "actually existing social forms in which locality . . . is realised," where this realization may equally well take spatial or virtual form. In the logic of these arguments, a virtual neighborhood can easily extend across transnational space.[12]

For Appadurai cultural spaces of connection such as this, in the form of diasporic public spheres, are increasingly part of many people's everyday lives. The engines of these diasporic public spheres are both symbolic "mediascapes" and actual patterns, or "ethnoscapes," of geographical mobility. The combined effect of these factors, he claims, is the incapacity of states to prevent their minority populations from linking themselves to wider constituencies of religious or ethnic affiliations," with the result that the era is over when "we could assume that . . . public spheres were typically, exclusively or necessarily national."[13]

If we take mobility to be a defining characteristic of the contemporary world, however, we must simultaneously pose the question of why (and with what degrees of freedom) particular people stay at home, and ask how, in a world of flux, forms of collective dwelling are sustained and reinvented.[14] It would be pointless, as Clifford observes, to simply reverse the traditional anthropological figures of the sedentary native and that of the intercultural traveler, so as to turn the old margin into the conceptual pivot of a generalized nomadology that claims that "we" are all now equally travelers. Rather, he argues, we need to develop a more nuanced analysis of the specific tensions in particular historical situations between dwelling and traveling.[15] What is required then is a "comparative cultural studies approach to specific histories, tactics and everyday practices of dwelling and travelling," and Clifford suggests that "we need to think comparatively about the distinct routes/roots of tribes, barrios, favelas, immigrant neighbourhoods—embattled histories with crucial community 'insiders' and regulated travelling 'outsiders.' What does it take to define and defend a homeland? What are the political stakes in claiming (or sometimes being relegated to) a 'home'?"[16]

The transformations in communications and transport networks characteristic of our time, involving various forms of mediation, displacement, and deterritorialization, are generally held to have transformed our sense of place, but their theorization often proceeds at a highly abstract level toward a generalized account of nomadology.[17] Recent critiques of the Euro-American–centered nature of most postmodern theory point to the dangers of such inappropriately universalized frameworks of analysis. My aim here is to open up the analysis of the varieties of rootedness, exile, diaspora, displacement, connectedness, and/or mobility experienced by members of different (class, gender, ethnic) groups in a range of socio-geographical positions.

It has been claimed that the paradigmatic modern experience is that of rapid mobility over long distances. However, against this paradigm John Tomlinson argues that the model of contemporary life as characterized centrally by voluntary forms of mobility is, in fact, strictly applicable only to a relatively small number of highly privileged people. Tomlinson rightly argues that it is "important not to exaggerate the way long-distance travel figures either in the lives of the majority of people in the world today or in the overall process of globalisation." Indeed, as he insists, despite the increasing ubiquity of various forms of travel, "local life . . . is the vast order of human social existence. . . . Local life [still] occupies the majority of time and space," and mobility "is ultimately subordinate to—indeed derivative of—the order of location in time and space which we grasp as 'home.' "[18] To this extent, the paradigm of mobile deterritorialization is only applicable to, according to Tomlinson, the "experiences of the affluent . . . information rich sectors of the most economically developed parts of the world" rather than being a truly global experience.[19]

Of course, many poor people are also highly mobile, but their enforced migrancy, whether for economic or political reasons, is quite another matter. This same point, concerning what Massey calls the "power geometry" of postmodern spatiality, is also well made both by Hannerz in his insistence on the need to distinguish "voluntary" from "involuntary cosmopolitans" and by Bauman in his distinction between those he calls the "tourists" and the "vagabonds" of the postmodern era.[20] The question is one of who has the access to which forms of mobility and "connexity," and, crucially, who has the power to choose whether, when, and where to move.

Despite all the talk of global flows, fluidity, hybridity, and mobility it is worth observing that, in the United Kingdom at least, there is evidence that points to continued geographical sedentarism on the part of the majority of the population. Thus Peter Dickens argues that despite widespread assumptions to the contrary, geographical mobility in the United Kingdom actually declined in the 1970s and 1980s as compared with the so-called stable times of the 1950s and 1960s.[21] Similarly, Diane Warburton argues that the "mobility of people in the UK has been overplayed," and she quotes MORI opinion poll research that suggests that "overall, there is a clear focus of attachment on the most local area." She goes on to argue that notwithstanding considerations of global connexity, "most people have an environmental horizon which is very local—the end of the street or the top of the next hill."[22] While these gross statistics evidently conceal important variations (not least by class, ethnicity, and gender) the evidence indicates that sedentarism is far from finished. Thus, while one recent report noted that people in the United Kingdom now often live farther away from their relatives than they did in the past, it seems that the majority still live within one hour's journey time of relatives, and that 72 percent of grandparents still see their grandchildren at least once a week, which indicates a fairly low radius of intergenerational mobility. At its simplest, as John Gray has noted, "over half of British adults live within five miles of where they were born."[23] It would seem that for the majority of the U.K. population, at least, David Sibley is still right when he observes baldly that, globalization notwithstanding, "many people live in one place for a long time."[24] As Ken Worpole put it in a study of urban life in the United Kingdom: "Still, for a significant proportion of any population, the town or city they are born in is the one that will shape their lives and become the stage-set of their hopes and aspirations."[25]

While many people remain local, however, and while many are kept in place by structures of oppression of various forms, the experience that is most truly global is perhaps that of locality being undercut by the penetration of global forces and networks. To this extent, almost everywhere in the world experience is increasingly disembedded from locality, and the ties of culture to place are progressively weakened by new patterns of connexity. It is, as Tomlinson argues, in the transformation of localities rather than in the increase of physical mobility (significant though that may be for some groups) that the process of globalization perhaps has its most important expression.[26] This is to suggest that although increased physical mobility is an important aspect of globalization for some categories of people, "for most people, most of the time the impact of globalisation is felt not in travel but in staying at home." However, their experience of locality is transformed by the now banal and routinized process of "consumption of images of distant places," which paradoxically become familiar in their generic forms (the streets of New York, the American West, etc.) even to those who have never visited them, as they are normalized in the mediated life world of the television viewer. This is to argue that, as Tomlinson further states, the "paradigmatic experience of global modernity for most people . . . is that of staying in one place but experiencing the 'dis-placement' that global modernity brings to them."[27]

HOME, COMMUNITY, AND NATION

One key question in understanding the process of displacement is how the various media transgress the boundaries of the "sacred space" of both the home and the *Heimat,* and how that transgression is regulated by various "rituals of purification." A further question concerns the way in which conflict is generated in the process of identity formation, by the attempt to expel alterity beyond the boundaries of the ethnically, culturally, or civilizationally "purified" homogenous enclave—at whatever level of social or geographical scale. In these processes the crucial issue in defining who or what "belongs" is, of course, also that of defining who (or what) is to be excluded as "matter out of place," and whether that "matter" is represented by "impure" or "foreign" material objects, persons, or cultural products. My own principal interest here lies in making links between patterns of residence or mobility and patterns of cultural consumption, as factors in the construction of identities. This is to argue, following Scott Lash and Jonathan Friedman, for a perspective that can deal with two simultaneous modes of circulation: first the "one in which goods, such as TV broadcastings, records, videos, [and] magazines circulate among the audiences," and second, "that of the built environment, in which the population circulates among the symbolic goods."[28]

In some cases, global media flows are consumed by audiences who are themselves highly mobile. Thus, developing his earlier argument, Appadurai writes of the need to pay attention to what he calls the mutual contextualizing of electronic mediation and mass migration in situations where moving images meet deterritorialized viewers. As he puts it, when "Turkish guest workers in Germany watch Turkish films in their German flats . . . and Pakistani cabdrivers in Chicago listen to cassettes of sermons recorded in the mosques of Iran," this gives rise to "a new order of instability in the production of modern subjectivities" precisely because both messages and audiences are in simultaneous circulation.[29]

This is, however, only one side of the story. If hypermobility is one of the tropes of postmodernity, then another of its key emblems is perhaps the gated community. We see a rather different picture if we consider Sibley's work on the growing tendencies toward residential segregation throughout the affluent societies of the West, alongside Roger Silverstone's comments on television itself as a suburbanizing medium (which through its repetitive patterns serves to consolidate the ontological security of those who choose to live behind the walls of these gated communities).[30] Here the "rituals of purification" and "geographies of exclusion" of which Sibley writes generate not new forms of instability or hybridity but rather new forms of consolidation of established patterns of social and cultural segregation.

Given my earlier involvement in studies of domestic media consumption, my interest here is in articulating the micro and macro dimensions of these questions. In the work I did with Roger Silverstone and Eric Hirsch on the household uses of information and communication technology, part of our focus was on the symbolic meanings that household technologies had for their users, especially the symbolic meaning of the television as a material object, as well as a relayer of messages.[31]

By the same token, as broadcasting connects the private home to the public world it also simultaneously transgresses the boundaries of the household and is thus often felt to stand in need of some form of regulation. All households regulate these matters in some way or another: in my earlier project with Silverstone and Hirsch our interest was in the variety of ways in which households of different types enacted their regulatory strategies. To give one small example of where these concerns led us, we were initially puzzled, in one household, by the particularly systematic way in which not only the television set but all the communications technologies and their wiring were carefully hidden away inside decorative cabinets and panels so as to be quite invisible. As we came later to understand, this was not simply an aesthetic choice: the husband in this family worked a complex shift system as a policeman and was often called out from home to work. These interruptions made it very difficult for the husband and wife to sustain what they felt was a satisfactory sense of family time with their children, and in this context it seemed that the very presence of communications technologies, which symbolized the further possible interruption of their domestic life, had to be hidden away.[32]

If we shift from the micro to the macro, however, and from the home to the *Heimat,* we see that if the television set is often both physically and symbolically central to the domestic home, then it (or its predecessor, the radio) has often been equally central to the construction of the imagined community of the nation as a symbolic home for its citizens. In Britain Paddy Scannell, and in Sweden Orvar Löfgren, have both analyzed broadcasting's ritual role in bringing together the dispersed households of the nation into symbolic union as a "national family."[33]

Löfgren's central concern is with the question of how people have come to feel at home in the nation and with the educative role of broadcast media in the everyday process of what he calls the "cultural thickening" of the nation-state. Löfgren calls this the "micro-physics of learn-ing to belong" to "the nation-as-home, through which the nation-state makes itself visible and tangible . . . in the lives of its citizens." In this analysis these media are seen to supply "the fragments of cultural mem-ory" that compose "the invisible information structure" which consti-tutes a person's sense of their homeland as a virtual community.[34] Löf-gren observes that in Sweden by the 1930s national radio had constructed a new *Gemeinschaft* of listeners tied together by the contents and myths of national radio broadcasting. This synchronized experience of radio came to provide a stable national frame of understanding for local events and topics in an educative process that turned the nation into something resembling a vast schoolroom. This broadcast national rhetoric took many forms—not in the least ritual ones, such as familiarizing people with the national anthem and inscribing it at key moments in their own domestic practices. Even the weather was nationalized, and its national limits were clearly demarcated so that "in the daily shipping forecast, the names of the coastal observation posts of Sweden were read like a magic chant, as outposts encircling the nation."[35]

In a similar vein, in his introduction to the catalog of Mark Power's photographic project on the shipping forecast in the United Kingdom David Chandler notes that while the information on weather conditions at sea around the nation is plainly of practical use only to seafarers, the size of the listenership of the BBC radio's shipping forecast (broadcast four times a day since 1926) and the affection in which the broadcast is held by many who never go to sea, indicates that "its mesmeric voice and timeless rhythms are buried deep in the public consciousness. . . . For those of us safely ashore, its messages from 'out there' [and] its warnings from a dan-gerous peripheral world of extremes and uncertainty are reassuring."[36]

Nikos Papastergiadis has argued that "the symbols and narratives of the nation can only resonate if they are admitted to the chamber of the home."[37] Radio often achieves, as Chandler notes, exactly this kind of intimacy. His argument is that if the shipping forecast enhances our sense of comfort in being safe at home, this sense is also a matter of national belonging in the profoundest sense: "The shipping forecast is both na-tional narrative and symbol; for seventy years it has given reports on an unstable, volatile 'exterior' against which the ideas of 'home' and 'nation' as places of safety, order and even divine protection are reinforced. In those brief moments, when its alien language of the sea interrupts the day, the forecast offers to complete the enveloping circle and rekindle a picture of Britain glowing with a sense of wholeness and unity."[38]

National broadcasting can thus create a sense of unity and of corresponding boundaries around the nation. It can link the peripheral to the center; turn previously exclusive social events into mass experiences; and, above all, penetrate the domestic sphere by linking the national public into the private lives of its citizens through the creation of both sacred and quotidian moments of national communion. Not that this process is always smooth and without tension or resistance, however. Löfgren notes that, historically, what was at stake was both the nationalization of the domestic and the domestication of the national, so that "the radio turned the sitting room into a public room, the voices from the ether spoke from the capital and united us with our rulers, but also with all other radio listeners around the country." Nonetheless, this socialization of the private sphere, in the service of the "civilisation of the peripheries" of the nation, could also give rise to resentment. Löfgren notes that one Swedish listener recalls, "When the radio was on, the room wasn't really ours, the sonorous voices with their Stockholm (accents) . . . pushed our own thick (regional) voices into a corner where we commented in whispers on the cocksure statements from the radio."[39] Similarly, in the United Kingdom only some categories of listeners feel that the shipping forecast symbolizes the boundaries of a nation with which they identify very much, not least because the radio station on which it is broadcast itself fails to achieve a popular appeal beyond the realms of the older, more middle-class sections of the British radio audience. If national broadcasting systems play a central role in the construction of the "national symbolic,"[40] the public spheres that they construct do not feel equally *Heimlich* (home-like) to all of the nation's citizens.[41] Historically, in the United Kingdom if the public sphere has felt like a *Heimlich* place for metropolitan middle-class white men, it has not seemed so to people who are outside those categories, whether by virtue of class, gender, race, or ethnicity.[42]

Let me now return to the micro level and take another example from the Brunel research project of how households deal with the media's capacities to transgress their boundaries. In another of the households we studied, the parents were particularly concerned by the prospect of deregulated television broadcasting bringing pornographic or violent programming within their children's grasp (much as many parents are today concerned about what their children may find on the Internet). The father expressed his anxiety about their children's viewing habits thus: "[They] have sets in their rooms and [we] can't know what they are watching all the time"; his particular concern was that they might watch "foreign" programs of a sexual nature.[43]

For this family, the fear was that the household's microboundaries would be transgressed directly by unwanted "foreign" elements and by bringing "matter out of place" into the home, particularly into the private space of the children's bedrooms. However, this concern can readily be seen to have parallels at other geographical scales. Thus in recent years many national governments have attempted to control the consumption of "foreign" media on their national territories by outlawing satellite dishes. Not long ago, in an uncannily exact mirror-image of the other's policies, while the Iranian government was attempting to ban satellite dishes on the grounds that foreign programs were part of a Western cultural offensive against Islam, the mayor of Courcouronnes (a poor, mainly North African immigrant area south of Paris) also banned the dishes from the high-rise blocks in which many of his constituents live, at the instigation of the French National Front, in whose eyes the dishes represented the threat of a population that resides physically in France but inhabits (via satellite) a world of virtual Islam.

If in the United Kingdom the appearance of a satellite dish on the walls of a house was often taken to signify its inhabitants' abandonment of the space of national public broadcasting and citizenship in favor of the pleasures of international consumerism, in France, as we have seen, these dishes have "become the symbol of . . . immigrants as an alien cultural presence, threatening the integrity of French national identity."[44] In a pun on the term for a satellite dish, *antenne parabolique,* these dishes are now often referred to as *antenne paradiabolique*—signifiers of trouble, if not evil. In the words of a French Ministry of Social Affairs report: "There are risks of the people concerned [i.e., those with satellite receivers] being manipulated by foreign powers, all the more so in that the number of DBS dishes is constantly growing, particularly in the *banlieues.* . . . In addition, the various channels are broadcast in Arabic, which could undermine years of literacy classes and other efforts at Gallicising these people. Moreover, the religious content of certain programmes will probably increase the Islamisation of the *banlieues.*"[45] Increasingly it seems that the people of the *banlieues* are considered by mainstream French society as a threat, insofar as they are seen as living in "their own Muslim world . . . courtesy of local mosques and satellite television beamed in from North Africa and Saudi Arabia."[46] These migrants' inhabitation of a transnational or diasporic public sphere of the type that Appadurai describes is thus presented as in effect a form of cultural treason.[47]

Just as in France, in Germany there has also been considerable anxiety in recent years about the perceived cultural withdrawal of immigrant populations into satellite television, in this case into the separate audio-visual space offered by Turkish-language satellite television stations. This withdrawal has, in some cases, been taken to constitute an index of the essential foreignness of these immigrants and to constitute evidence of a culpable lack of willingness on their part to integrate into German culture and society. However, Kevin Robins, based on his research on the media and cultural practices of the Turkish diaspora population in Europe, argues that the question is not an either/or of whether immigrants have withdrawn into their own cultural space or are assimilated into the host culture. Rather, he claims, the question is one of how these migrants are not so much caught between two worlds as engaged in constructing various forms of hybrid identities that enable them to participate simultaneously in both.[48] From this perspective the question is how, for different members of different parts of these migrant communities, it is possible for them to engage in a new kind of "commuting migration" (between German and Turkish virtual and geographical spaces) that allows them to be both assimilated *and* withdrawn at different times in relation to different topics and issues.

Long ago, Raymond Williams spoke of the media as enabling forms of "mobile privatization" that supply an experience of "simultaneously staying at home and imaginatively . . . going places."[49] However, Shaun Moores in his study of satellite broadcasting notes that "if broadcasting is able to 'transport' viewers and listeners to previously distant or unknown sites . . . then we need to specify the kind of 'journeys' that are made. Who chooses to go where, with whom, and why? . . . Who stays 'at home'? . . . Who feels the need to escape its confines?"[50] Moores's main concern is with why, particularly among working-class and ethnic minority communities in the United Kingdom, satellite television has come to symbolize a desirable form of freedom of viewing in contrast to staid, old broadcasting institutions such as the BBC.[51] The issue is why, for some citizens of the nation, forms of broadcasting that transcend the boundaries of narrow British culture are felt to be both more desirable and more *Heimlich*. The question of what is foreign to whom is perhaps best posed empirically. Foreignness can sometimes be a matter of nationality but in other cases also a matter of class, of gender, of race, or of ethnicity.[52] Certainly Marie Gillespie found that in Britain the migrant Asian community she studied had a particular interest in video, cable, and satellite media precisely to the extent that they felt ill served by the existing British national broadcasting media.[53] For exactly these reasons, rates of subscription to satellite and cable services in both the United Kingdom and in France are now at their highest among ethnic minority groups.[54]

A whole series of critics have supplied us with images of our (supposedly) new disembedded status within the virtual geography of postmodernity. Mackenzie Wark (following Joshua Meyrowitz)[55] has alerted us to the transformations of time and space brought about by electronic technologies. In his version of this argument, Wark announces that nowadays in the emerging "virtual communities" unanchored in locality, which are made possible by the "ever more flexible matrix of media vectors crossing the globe, we no longer have roots, we have aerials," and "we no longer have origins, we have terminals" insofar as we live in a new virtual geography—the terrain of telesthesia (or perception at a distance) "created by the TV, the telephone, and the telecommunications networks crisscrossing the globe."[56] However, while it must be acknowledged that satellite media technologies are producing new definitions of time, space, and community, it is not a question of physical geography somehow ceasing to matter but rather a question of how physical and symbolic networks become entwined and come to exercise mutual determinations on each other.

In his analysis of the dynamics of the "purification of space" Sibley is centrally concerned with what he calls the geography of exclusion as enacted through the policing of boundaries of various sorts.[57] This applies at both micro and macro levels: just as the home may be seen as profaned by the presence of matter out of place, the neighborhood may be seen as profaned by the presence of "strangers," or the national culture seen as profaned by the presence of foreign cultural products. Sibley observes that if the home, the neighborhood, and the nation are all potential spaces of belonging, this is no simple matter of disconnected, parallel processes. His interest is in demonstrating how each of these spaces conditions the others—"how the locality and the nation invade the home . . . providing cues for behaviour in families, as they relate to their domestic environment." As he puts it, "spaces are simultaneously tied together by media messages, by things like the local rules about the appropriate uses of suburban gardens, and by macro factors such as the immigration policies of the state."[58]

Thus, as in George Revill's commentary on Carol Lake's fictionalized portrait of her district of a British city in the mid-1980s, while media of various sorts transverse the urban community of which Lake writes, it is still a world of "backdoor gossip, chance encounters and casual meetings" where "national and international events are always articulated through local channels of communication, events half-heard on the radio or television." In this world, events such as the nuclear fallout at Chernobyl or riots in another British city "become local as they are mixed into conversations bound into the day-to-day problems of the community."[59] To understand these processes we need to interconnect these different cultural events, occurring simultaneously at different geographical scales.

In this connection Sibley observes that "residential space in the modern city can be seen as one area where purification rituals are enacted and where group antagonisms are manifested in the erection of territorial boundaries which accentuate difference or Otherness."[60] This argument provides a close parallel to Mike Davis's analysis of the processes of social segregation involved in the retreat of the affluent into gated communities in parts of the United States and, increasingly, elsewhere, whereby those who can afford it retreat from what they perceive as the threat of alterity in the world of public space.[61]

Threatening encounters with those defined as alien—those responsible for "cultural miscegenation"—can, of course, take place not only in physical but also in virtual or symbolic space. Here we return to the role of the media. Insofar as the television set is usually placed totemicly within the symbolic center of the (family) home, it can serve either to enhance or disturb viewers' symbolic sense of community. In some cases, television can serve to bring unwanted strangers into the home. Thus, in her analysis of viewers' letters written to the producers of the black sitcom *Julia*, produced in the 1970s by NBC in the United States, Aniko Bodroghkozy discovers a letter from a white viewer pleased with his continuing success in keeping black people out of the physical neighborhoods in which he lives, who is outraged at their symbolic invasion of his living room via their representation on television.[62] In a parallel fashion, although the power relations in the two cases are different in crucial ways, Phillip Batty quotes from a member of the Ernabella aboriginal community in Australia who complained that the arrival of "unimpeded satellite television transmission in our communities will be like having hundreds of whitefellas visit, without permits, every day."[63]

In a world where many people live in multiethnic cities, for some viewers unhappy with this hybridity, and with what Kobena Mercer has called the sheer difficulty of living with difference,[64] the television set can also sometimes offer majority viewers the solace of symbolic immersion in a lost world of settled homogeneity. Thus Bruce Gyngell, former head of TV-AM in Britain and now returned to work in television in his native Australia, has claimed that Australian soap operas such as *Neighbours* and *Home and Away*, which receive far higher ratings in Britain than in Australia, appeal to many within the British audience precisely because they are, in effect, "racial programmes" depicting an all-white society for which some Britons still pine. Gyngell trenchantly claims that *"Neighbours* and *Home and Away* represent a society which existed in Britain . . . before people began arriving from the Caribbean and Africa. The Poms delve into it to get their quiet little racism fix."[65] The exclusion of ethnic minorities from these programs is a matter of resentment among black and Asian viewers. As one such viewer notes, "things like *Neighbours* and *Home and Away* . . . show absolutely no ethnic minorities in the cast at all."[66] Conversely, it has also been argued that the particular popularity of the British soap opera *Coronation Street* among British expatriates in Australasia and elsewhere is evidence of their nostalgia for a lost white past. Indeed, although other British soap operas such as the BBC's *Eastenders* have at times featured Asian and Afro-Caribbean characters, it was only in 1998, thirty-eight years into its run, that *Coronation Street* got its first Asian family when the "Desais" took over the street's corner shop. Even now on the whole, as Sallie Westwood and John Williams argue, the United Kingdom's television soap operas "are suffused with notions of Englishness and belonging which exclude . . . the Other British—the myriad and diverse peoples who are part of the nation."[67]

The destabilizations of the postmodern period have certainly given rise to a variety of defensive and reactionary responses—witness the rise of various forms of born-again nationalism accompanied both by sentimentalized reconstructions of a variety of "authentic" localized "heritages" and by xenophobia directed at newcomers, foreigners, or outsiders. Certainly, in the face of these developments, it has come to seem to many critics that any search for a sense of place must of necessity be reactionary. However, Massey rejects the notion that a sense of place must necessarily be constructed out of "an introverted, inward-looking history, based on delving into the past for internalised origins." That way of thinking about space and identity is premised on the association of spatial penetration with impurity; against any such inward-looking definition of place and identity Massey argues for "a sense of place which is extroverted," where what gives a place its identity is not its separate or "pure" internalized history, constructed in antagonism to all that is outside (the threatening otherness of externality), but "an understanding of its 'character' " where it is the "particularity of its linkage to the 'outside' which is . . . part of what *constitutes* the place."[68]

Today, the equation of the desire for "roots" or "belonging" with a politically regressive form of reactionary nostalgia is widespread. Against this, Wendy Wheeler argues that it is in fact politically crucial for us to come to terms with this desire, rather than simply to dismiss it. Thus, she argues that we badly need to develop a better political response to the nostalgic desire for community by "articulating a politics capable of constituting a 'we' which is not essentialist, fixed, separatist, defensive or exclusive."[69] This would be, in Massey's terms, an "extroverted" politics of place.[70]

In conclusion it is perhaps worth noting the findings of Nora Rathzel's empirical study of attitudes to *Heimat* and *Ausländer* (foreigner) in Germany. Rathzel investigated the relationship between these two terms with reference to the question of whether people holding particular concepts of homeland were more inclined to perceive outsiders as threatening. Her empirical material, while based on a small sample, goes some way in demonstrating that people who hold a reified, harmonious image of *Heimat* as something necessarily stable and unchanging are, of course, particularly likely to be hostile to newcomers, who are then held to be the cause of all manner of disorienting forms of change. For these people, what makes these images of *Ausländer* threatening is precisely that they "make 'our' taken-for-granted identities visible and deprive them of their assumed naturalness," so that "once 'we' start becoming aware of 'them,' 'we' cannot feel 'at home' any more."[71] It may be that, as Phil Cohen argues, "if immigrants put down roots, if ethnic minorities make a home from home, then they are perceived to threaten the privileged link between habit and habitat upon which the myth of indigenous origins rests."[72]

In this spirit Azouz Begag argues that an immigrant "is a person designated as such by someone living in a particular place who sees the presence of the other as a threat to his own sense of being within that territory."[73] Thus, Marc Augé notes that "perhaps the reason why immigrants worry settled people so much is that they expose the relative nature of certainties inscribed in the soil."[74] Elsewhere Augé remarks that now that the other "of postcards and tourist trips" is on the move and can no longer "be assigned to a specific place," it seems that "in the eyes of those who cling to the ideal of having 'their' land and 'their' village" the example of successful immigration is perhaps more terrifying than that of illegal immigration, insofar as "what's frightening in the immigrant is the fact that he is also an emigrant."[75] In a similar vein, Iain Chambers, drawing on the work of Emmanuel Levinas, writes of the difficulty created by the question of the Other, the outsider who "comes from elsewhere and . . . inevitably bears the message of a movement that threatens to disrupt the stability of the domestic scene."[76] In Levinas's terms, this threat is represented by "the stranger who disturbs the [sense of] being at home with oneself."[77]

More recently, with the development of computing technologies and the Internet, debates that previously were conducted with reference to traditional broadcasting media have been transposed into cyberspace, even if much of this debate has displayed what Kevin Robins has characterized as a naive "politics of optimism."[78] Against tendencies to take a utopian view of the possibilities of transcending social division in cyberspace, the Net can still reasonably be described as overwhelmingly, if with important exceptions, a "Whitezone," a "Boyzone," and a "YanquiNet." There are some categories of people that are completely missing from cyberspace, and as such it displays little diversity: its citizens include few old people, few poor people, and few from poor countries (except a small minority of Third World elites). In this connection, what is true of geographical mobility in physical space is also true of the structure of access to cyberspace. We are not all nomadic fragmented subjectivities living in the same postmodern universe. For some categories of people (differentiated by gender, race, and ethnicity as much as by class), the new technologies of symbolic and physical communications (from airplanes to faxes) offer significant opportunities for interconnectedness. For these people there may well be a new sense of postmodern opportunities. At the same time, however, for other categories of people without access to such forms of communication and transport, horizons may simultaneously be narrowing. And for yet others, their journeys (and encounters with alterity) are not chosen but imposed on them by economic or political necessity.

It does seem that there can be, for us, "no place like *Heimat*." Or at least that the traditional backward-looking concept of *Heimat* as a sacred and secure place (from which all threatening forms of Otherness have been excluded) can only be a recipe for disaster. The virtual geography in which we live is, of course, in many ways quite new: communications technologies have had a profound transformative effect in disarticulating communities from any necessary foundation in physical contiguity. However, as we travel the new electronic highways of cyberspace, we should beware the reduplication, if in new forms, of some of the very oldest and most regressive structures of purification and exclusion.

NOTES

Some sections of this essay previously appeared in my "Bounded Realms: Household, Family, Community, and Nation," in *Home, Homeland, Exile,* ed. Hamid Naficy (London: Routledge, 1999); other sections appear in my *Home Territories: Media, Mobility, and Identity* (London: Routledge, 2000).

1. See, for example, Zygmunt Bauman, *Globalization* (Cambridge, Eng.: Polity, 1998).

2. Nigel Rapport and Andrew Dawson, eds., *Migrants of Identity: Perceptions of Home in a World in Movement* (Oxford: Berg, 1998), p. 81.

3. Arjun Appadurai and Carol Breckenridge, "Why Public Culture?" *Public Culture* 1 (1988): 5.

4. James Clifford, "Mixed Feelings," in *Cosmopolitics: Thinking and Feeling Beyond the Nation*, ed. Pheng Cheah and Bruce Robbins (Minneapolis: University of Minnesota Press, 1998), p. 369.

5. Bruce Robbins, ed., *The Phantom Public Sphere* (Minneapolis: University of Minnesota Press, 1993), p. 3.

6. Ulf Hannerz, *Transnational Connections: Culture, People, Places* (London: Routledge, 1996), chapter 4.

7. See, for example, Jacques Derrida, *Spectres of Marx* (London: Routledge, 1994).

8. Sandra Wallman, "New Identities and the Local Factor," in Rapport and Dawson, eds., *Migrants of Identity*, pp. 195, 201.

9. Doreen Massey, *Space, Place, and Gender* (Cambridge, Eng.: Polity, 1994), p. 60.

10. James Clifford, *The Predicament of Culture: Twentieth-Century Ethnography, Literature, and Art* (Cambridge: Harvard University Press, 1988), p. 14.

11. Arjun Appadurai, *Modernity at Large: Cultural Dimensions of Globalization* (Minneapolis, University of Minnesota Press, 1996), p. 179.

12. Ibid., p. 22.

13. Ibid.

14. See, for example, James Clifford, *Routes: Travel and Translation in the Late Twentieth Century* (Cambridge: Harvard University Press, 1997).

15. Ibid., p. 24.

16. Ibid., p. 36.

17. See, for example, Joshua Meyrowitz, *No Sense of Place: The Impact of Electronic Media on Social Behavior* (Oxford: Oxford University Press, 1985); and Alberto Melucci, John Keane, and Paul Mier, eds., *Nomads of the Present: Social Movements and Individual Needs in Contemporary Society* (London: Hutchinson, 1989).

18. John Tomlinson, *Globalisation and Culture* (Cambridge: Polity, 1999), p. 9.

19. Ibid., p. 132.

20. Massey, *Space, Place, and Gender;* Hannerz, *Transnational Connections;* and Bauman, *Globalisation.*

21. Peter Dickens, *One Nation? Social Change and the Politics of Locality* (London: Pluto, 1988).

22. Dianne Warburton, "A Passionate Dialogue," in *Community and Sustainable Development*, ed. Dianne Warburton (London: Earthscan Books, 1988).

23. John Gray, "Do We Really Want More U.S. Decadence?" *Guardian*, January 27, 1997, online version at www.guardian.com.uk.

24. David Sibley, *Geographies of Exclusion: Society and Difference in the West* (London: Routledge, 1995), p. 29.

25. Ken Worpole, *Towns for People* (Milton Keynes: Open University Press, 1992), p. 26.

26. Tomlinson, *Globalisation and Culture.* See also, for example, Anthony Giddens,

The Consequences of Modernity (Cambridge, Eng.: Polity, 1990); and Geoff Mulgan, *Connexity* (London: Chatto and Windus, 1997).

27. Tomlinson, *Globalisation and Culture*, pp. 9, 119, 150.

28. Scott Lash and Jonathan Friedman, eds., "Introduction," in *Modernity and Identity* (Oxford: Blackwell, 1992), p. 20.

29. Appadurai, *Modernity at Large*, p. 4.

30. Sibley, *Geographics of Exclusion;* Roger Silverstone, ed., *Visions of Suburbia* (London: Routledge, 1997).

31. See David Morley and Roger Silverstone, "Domestic Communications," *Media, Culture, and Society* 12.2 (1990): 31–55; Roger Silverstone, Eric Hirsch, and David Morley, "Information and Communication Technologies and the Moral Economy of the Household," in *Consuming Technologies,* Roger Silverstone and Eric Hirsch, eds. (London: Routledge, 1992). The set of concerns mentioned here is linked closely to that of Lynn Spigel on the domestication of television in the United States (see her *Make Room for TV: Television and the Family Ideal in Postwar America* [Chicago: University of Chicago Press, 1992]).

32. See Eric Hirsch, "New Technologies and Domestic Consumption," in *The Television Studies Book,* ed. Christine Geraghty and David Lusted (London: Arnold, 1998), pp. 158–74; and Eric Hirsch, "Domestic Appropriations," in Rapport and Dawson, eds., *Migrants of Identity,* pp. 161–80.

33. Paddy Scannell, *Radio, Television, and Modern Life* (Oxford: Blackwell, 1996); Orvar Löfgren, "The Nation as Home or Motel?" Department of European Ethnology, University of Lund, 1995; and Orvar Löfgren, "In Transit: On the Social and Cultural Organisation of Mobility," working papers, Department of European Ethnology, University of Lund, 1996.

34. Löfgren, "The Nation as Home or Motel?" pp. 12, 14.

35. Ibid.

36. David Chandler, "Postcards from the Edge," in Mark Power, *The Shipping Forecast* (London: Zelda Cheatle Press, 1996), p. i.

37. Nikos Papastergiadis, *Dialogues in the Diaporas: Essays and Conversations on Cultural Identity* (London: Rivers Oram Press, 1998), p. 4.

38. Chandler, "Postcards from the Edge," p. ii.

39. Löfgren, "The Nation as Home or Motel?" pp. 26–27.

40. See, Lauren Berlant, "The Theory of Infantile Citizenship," in *Becoming National: A Reader,* ed. Geoff Eley and Ronald Grigor Suny (Oxford: Oxford University Press, 1996), pp. 495–508.

41. See, for example, Bruce Robbins, ed., *The Phantom Public Sphere* (Minneapolis University of Minnesota Press, 1993); Nancy Fraser, "Rethinking the Public Sphere," in Robbins, ed., *The Phantom Public Sphere,* pp. 1–33; Joke Hermes, "Gender and Media Studies: No Woman, No Cry," in *International Media Research,* ed. John Corner, Philip Schlesinger, and Roger Silverstone (London: Routledge, 1997), p. 73.

42. See Annabelle Sreberny, *Include Me In: Rethinking Ethnicity on Television* (London: Broadcasting Standards Commission, 1999); and Arun Kundnani, "Stumbling On: Race, Class, and England," *Race and Class* 41.4 (spring 2000): 1–18.

43. See, for example, Roger Silverstone and David Morley, "Families and Their Technologies," in *Household Choices,* ed. Tim Putnam and Charles Newton (London: Futures Publications, 1990).

44. Alec Hargreaves, "Satellite Television Viewing among Ethnic Minorities in France," *European Journal of Communication* 12.4 (1997): 460.

45. Cited in ibid., p. 461.

46. Mary Dejevsky, "The Angry Sound of the Suburbs," *Independent,* October 26, 1995, online version at www.independent.co.uk.

47. Alec Hargreaves and Antonio Perotti, "The Representation on French Television of Immigrants and Ethnic Minorities of Third World Origin," *New Community* 19:2 (January 1993), pp. 251–61.

48. Kevin Robins, "Negotiating Spaces: Turkish Transnational Media," in *Media and Migration,* Russell King and Nancy Wood, eds. (London: Routledge, 2001).

49. Raymond Williams, *Television: Technology and Cultural Form* (London: Fontana, 1976), p. 26.

50. Shaun Moores, "Television Geography and Mobile Privatisation," *European Journal of Communication Studies* 8.3 (1993): 336, 365.

51. Shaun Moores, "Satellite TV as a Cultural Sign," *Media, Culture, and Society* 15.4 (1993): 621–39.

52. Regarding class, Dick Hebdige, "Towards a Cartography of Taste," in *Hiding in the Light: On Images and Things* (London: Routledge, 1988), pp. 45–76; and Ken Worpole, *Dockers and Detectives: Popular Reading, Popular Novels* (London: Verso, 1983).

53. Marie Gillespie, *Television, Ethnicity, and Cultural Change* (London: Routledge, 1995).

54. See Sreberny, *Include Me In;* and Hargreaves, "Satellite Television."

55. Meyrowitz, *No Sense of Place.*

56. Mackenzie Wark, *Virtual Geographies: Living with Global Media Events* (Minneapolis: University of Minnesota Press, 1994), pp. x, xiv.

57. Sibley, *Geographics of Exclusion.*

58. Ibid., p. 90.

59. George Revill, "Reading Rosehill," in *Place and the Politics of Identity,* ed. Steve Pile and Michael Keith (London: Routledge, 1989), p. 127.

60. David Sibley, "The Purification of Space," *Environment and Planning (D): Society and Space* 6:4 (1998): 409–421.

61. Mike Davis, *City of Quartz* (London: Verso, 1990).

62. Aniko Bodroghkozy, "Is This What You Mean by Color TV?" in *Private Screenings: Television and the Female Consumer,* ed. Lynn Spigel and Denise Mann (Minneapolis: University of Minnesota Press, 1992), pp. 143–67.

63. Phillip Batty, "Singing the Electric," in *Channels of Resistance: Global Television and Local Empowerment,* ed. Tony Dowmunt (London: British Film Institute, 1993), p. 110.

64. Kobena Mercer, *Welcome to the Jungle* (London: Routledge, 1994).

65. Gyngell, quoted in Andrew Culf, "Popularity of Australian Soaps Based on British Racism Fix?" *Guardian,* November 2, 1993, online version at guardian.co.uk.

66. Quoted in Sreberny, *Include Me In,* p. 27.

67. Sallie Westwood and John Williams, eds., "Introduction," in *Imagining Cities: Scripts, Signs, Memories* (London: Routledge, 1997).

68. Doreen Massey, "A Global Sense of Place," *Marxism Today* (June 1991): 27, 29.

69. Wendy Wheeler, "Nostalgia Isn't Nasty," in *Altered States*, ed. Marc Perryman (London: Lawrence and Wishart, 1994), p. 108.

70. Massey, *Space, Place, and Gender.*

71. Nora Rathzel, "Harmonious *Heimat* and Disturbing *Ausländer*," in *Shifting Identities and Shifting Racisms*, ed. Ann Phoenix and Kum-Kum Bhavnani (London: Sage, 1994), p. 91.

72. Phil Cohen, "Homing Devices," in *Re-situating Identities*, ed. V. Amit-Talai and C. Knowles (Petersborough, Ontario: Broadview Press, 1996), p. 75.

73. Azouz Begag, "North African Immigrants in France" (Loughborough: European Research Centre, Loughborough University, 1989), p. 9.

74. Marc Augé, *Non-Places: Introduction to an Anthropology of Supermodernity*, trans. John Howe (London: Verso, 1995), p. 119.

75. Marc Augé, *A Sense for the Other: The Timeliness and Relevance of Anthropology*, trans. Amy Jacobs (Stanford: Stanford University Press, 1998), pp. 108–9.

76. Iain Chambers, "A Stranger in the House," *Continuum* 6.1 (1998): 35.

77. Emmanuel Levinas, *Totality and Infinity: An Essay on Exteriority* (Pittsburgh: Duquesne University Press, 1969), p. 39.

78. Kevin Robins, "The New Communications Geography and the Politics of Optimism," *Soundings* 5 (1997): 191–202.

PRISCILLA PEÑA OVALLE

POCHO.COM: REIMAGING TELEVISION

ON THE INTERNET

Image: a reproduction or imitation of the form of a person or thing; especially: an imitation in solid form . . . a mental picture of something not actually present.

Imagine: to form a mental image of (something not present).

Imagery: the product of image makers.—Merriam-Webster online

Mexican Americans have long been the subject of political discourse in America. Issues such as Proposition 187b and bilingual education have created intense opinions on all sides of the (televised) political spectrum, particularly in California. The desire of the United States to culturally and economically separate itself from Mexico is at the heart of both of these issues. By re-creating a physical "border" in 1848—consuming the Mexican land now called New Mexico, Utah, Nevada, Arizona, California, Texas, and western Colorado—the United States effectively divided a people geographically and, more important, culturally. Since then, Mexican Americans have struggled with issues of identity and "belonging" in a way unlike any other "immigrants." They are culturally separated by two worlds (as in those labeled "First" and "Third"), while ancestrally living in their own backyards. The United States has succeeded in subordinating yet another native population by ignoring, denying, and persecuting its heritage and cultural autonomy—an occupation via impregnation and bastardization. How have Mexican Americans as a people survived this history?

It is my belief that Mexican Americans have persevered through timely rearticulations of "identity" while reorganizing a core cultural heritage. In this essay I will attempt to explore such a reidentification through examining an engagement with cyberspace. I will show how one Web site, Pocho.com, illustrates a re-presentation of Chicano cultural icons and stereotypes in an effort to "place" or "imagine" the self in the mass media imagery on the northern side of the border, as well as the historical significance of the iconic depictions chosen. Although the Internet is known for its communal possibilities, I focus here on the particular ways that one site has cultivated an "identity" while it simultaneously per- petuated a tradition of activism through subversion, humor, and iconic revision in a mass media form. Pocho.com has succeeded in creating a unique subversive political community in cyberspace, and, further, it has provided opportunities for education, activism, and solidarity through humor.

What is Pocho.com? What is a Pocho? To answer this, we must go back in the history of Mexican American identity. Identification of Mexican Americans by the government is often termed "Hispanic." This label, popularized by the Nixon administration, was coined as a convenience; that is, "Hispanic" is for census purposes a generic term including any- one of Mexican, Cuban, or Puerto Rican descent. Around the time of this coinage, however, a reidentification movement began in the Mexi- can American community. The 1960s and 1970s witnessed a rebirth of the term "Chicano." Until this time, "Chicano" or "Chicana" essentially meant the "lowliest, tackiest, most uncultured border crossin' Mexican," but it was transformed into a chosen title of "pride and defiance."[1] The appropriation of this negative label can be defined as a first wave of identity. "Pocho" then replaced "Chicano" as a pure insult until the 1990s. "Pocho" did not reference recent immigration but rather a growing di- vergence (both culturally and generationally) from the homeland (Mex- ico). A "Pocho" is thus one who lacks certain signifiers of his or her own Mexican culture, sometimes to the point of not knowing the Spanish language. By adopting this title, the Pocho/a community has reclaimed a subordinated identity for its cultural evolution. A Pocho/a, as I use the term, is described as a Mexican/American hybrid.

One's identification as Chicano/a is intrinsically politicized. The difference between a Mexican American and a Chicano/a lies in self- identification. To be of Mexican descent and simply reside in America makes one Mexican American; to declare one's self Chicano/a is to align with a political state of being. To say "I am Chicano/a" is to negotiate the internal relationship between the Mexican and American cultures and thus articulate a distinct crossbreed consciousness. To be Chicano/a is to be outside the "national imaginary" of both Mexico and the United States; it is to balance on a cultural and political fence.[2] While it is possible to be Mexican American and not Chicano/a, one cannot be Chicano/a without being Mexican American. In this case, it is not solely the geographical location, but the political and ideological affiliations that demarcate these identities. What then of a Pocho/a? A Pocho/a is a Chicano/a and therefore Mexican American, yet many Chicano/as would not claim Pochismo/a (the act of being a Pocho/a). In the case of a Pocho/a, identity goes beyond geography and ideology. To put it plainly: "Pochismo is Chicanismo with a sick sense of humor."[3]

Political consciousness and activism are a tradition of the Chicano/a identity. This is particularly clear in the case of the arts. Chicano/a theater, songs, and murals tell tales of family, unity, uprising, and vindication. In her article "Teatro Chicano and the Seduction of Nostalgia," Catherine Wiley explores *teatro* (Chicano/a theater) as a "conflict of nostalgia" created by confrontations between Chicano/as, Mexico, and the United States. She finds this nostalgia a problem because it "clouds its subject's relationship with his or her own history, by imposing the idealized space and time of 'long ago and far away' on the present."[4] Although Wiley does acknowledge the paradoxical balance of the Chicano/a identity as expressed through teatro, she defines it exclusively in terms of geographical longing. While such longing may be hereditarily articulated in teatro, I believe that the Pocho/a identity, as experienced on the Internet, seeks a different goal: the pursuit of a new, humorous, and subversively political identity. In short, the Internet houses the continuation of an "identity movement," defined here as the evolution of a cultural and political autonomy rather than as an imagined reunification with a homeland.

In "Virtual Commonality: Looking for India on the Internet," Ananda Mitra discusses the way a community or nation might be imagined on the World Wide Web. Following Benedict Anderson's assertion that any community or nation is "imagined" because of its reliance on mediated ritual (language, print media, etc.) as a measure of national identity, Mitra looks to online news groups as a means of identifying a virtual, national imaginary, and she cites the textual productions of these news groups as a means of self-imaging. That is, the way a person articulates an argument in cross-posted messages (extending to other, less-related news groups) redefines or reorganizes the national image of the originating news group (nationality).[5] Whereas Mitra discusses an (imagined) image as produced from textual postings, I focus here on the literal imagery of Pocho.com and the way in which it imagines and places itself in the American mass media national imaginary.

The imaging of an online racial identity is relatively new to discussions of online representations. When the goal of an online identity has traditionally been to shed the offline persona, if only for a small amount of time, what can be said about a site that represents its community as a racial image, such as Pocho.com? In their book *Race in Cyberspace,* editors Beth Kolko, Lisa Nakamura, and Gilbert Rodman shed light on the lack of racial discussion in Internet dialogues. In their collection, contributor Jennifer González mentions two sites that explore the idea of a digitally created body as a "physical" online entity. This new trend marks the importance of an online imagined self, however limited the use or exposure. What is key about González's findings is that the bodily representations, however ideologically or intentionally created otherwise, manage to mirror the ideal or fetishized image of a "body."[6] In this way, we can see the once-imagined image of an online community now moving toward a chosen or created iconic imaging of the self.

What is the importance of this imagery? In the case of Mitra's work, this self-imaging is the result of discursively negotiating a cultural identity due to geographical relocation. With "a majority of these users . . . in the United States . . . and still fewer in India," this "image" is an "amalgam" of the immigrant and the homeland.[7] In the case of Chicano/as, however, the "image" is different. Chicano/as have been born into that binary position. Chon Noriega articulates this best when he states: "As U.S. citizens of Mexican descent, both [Mexican Americans and Chicano/as] were *outside* the nation, whether in terms of its social imaginary or its legal rights, while they were *inside* the administrative control and incorporation of the state. It is within this ambivalent context that the state compelled Chicanos and other racial groups to adopt and construct minority identities as the sine qua non of political recognition. Thus, the paradox of incorporation involved exchanging difference for identity."[8] For Chicano/as, self-imaging is a means of infiltrating the "social imaginary" and reconciling a place inside the "official" (media) state. However, Noriega further identifies a "cultural nationalism" at work to "define difference"; Chicano is defined "against the backdrop of the 'non-Chicano.' "[9] It seems that the Chicano/a imaginary has been self-identified, if not widely distributed: cultural icons such as the zoot suit might come to mind at the mention of the word "Chicano." How, then, might the Pocho/a fit into this practice of self-imaging?

As the identity has evolved—from Chicano/a to Pocho/a—so has the political medium. *Pocho* magazine began in 1989 as a zine, yet it soon occupied a space on the World Wide Web. This switch was originally only in platform; the content largely remained the same as the print version. The black-and-white photocopied format suited the written material, lending a grittiness to the text and images. With time, the Web site known as Pocho.com became its own community, moving beyond the simple political satire format of the zine. Although the content remained the same from zine to Web, its online organization was an imagined neighborhood—literally depicted as a cartoon barrio image with hotspots for links—a telling sign of what was to come. This early incarnation of Pocho.com was introduced as a "Virtual Varrio" (barrio translated as neighborhood and pronounced with a "v"). While the site has since changed layouts multiple times, it continues to create a dialogic space where political issues are raised and critiqued through satire. Issues that pertain to the Pocho/a community (especially the mainstream media channels that neglect to address this community) are rewritten as comedic commentaries. In this way, the community "can textually produce itself, thus imagine itself—as well as present itself to the outside world."[10] This process is important for a group that has traditionally been denied a place by mainstream media. Television, radio, newspapers, and film—unless specifically targeting Chicano/as—do not include Chicano/as in the fictional English narrative. This fact has become a focus of Pocho.com, which features a criqitue of the Chicano/a presence (or lack thereof) on network television.

September 1999 marked the "brownout," a nationwide response to the lack of Latino characters on prime-time network television.[11] A coalition of Latino groups declared a two-week period, September 12–26, as the official date to flex the muscles of the Latino viewing public.[12] The launch of this tactic was planned to coincide with the beginning of National Hispanic Heritage Month and was aimed at increasing both roles and job opportunities for Latinos in mass media.[13] The brownout was not the success its proponents intended, which underscored the Latino/a English viewing public's pessimistic lack of interest. Why did such a large community neglect to voice a desire for greater representation? Could it be that a lack of previous exposure to active, fictional media representation has left a void, even in our imaginary? Where *do* we imagine ourselves? As Ella Shohat suggests, "communities invisible in the 'old media' have begun to relocate their struggles over land and resources to online technologies."[14]

While Shohat focuses her investigation on the naturalized colonialist rhetoric often used in discussing the Internet, she also explores the way some minority and diasporic communities have managed to cultivate online "spaces" of relation. In the case of the Pocho/a, such "struggles" do not simply pertain to "resources"; along with presenting a comedic discourse and social critique, Pocho.com champions an emerging political identity as well. By taking advantage of the brownout, Pocho.com managed to exemplify these qualities, critiquing the "old media" as well as effectively and visibly "relocating . . . to online technologies."

Unfortunately, it is that presentation to the outside world that has caused some criticism of Pocho.com. Remarkably, the greatest opposition has come from the Chicano/a community itself. To understand this, we can look to the Pocho/a history and philosophy. Lalo López and Esteban Zul created *Pocho* magazine in an attempt to "convert . . . anger into satirical drive-bys over white (and brown) picket fences."[15] To effectively battle hegemony, a close inspection of the dominant Chicano/a ideology was necessary: self-critique was essential in reviving the spirit of the Chicano/a movement. López, in his writings on Pochismo entitled "Generation Mex," states: "We both realized that we had to knock down some Chicano icons to see if they could get back up by themselves. Also, the Anglo icons had to be torn down and *destroyed*."[16] Needless to say, some of those "Chicano icons" were not pleased with being "knock[ed] down" or having other cultural idols deconstructed. The elder Chicano/a community has "attempt[ed] to establish a particular dominant image," perceiving homogenous unity as the key to recognition and respect.[17] Noriega's comments about cultural nationalism help to illuminate these sentiments. If "Chicano" was defined against "non-Chicano,"[18] then what can we make of a non-Chicano Chicano? It seems that the Chicano/a movement was now experiencing the same anxiety they caused their Mexican American ancestors. Likewise, Pocho.com's reaction was instrumental in creating an entryway for the new generation into the political arena. Without identifying and reworking (satirizing) the traditions and foundations of the Chicano/a movement, self-discovery and progress could not be possible. A political new wave might be less able to identify with any "movement" without such revisions. López continues: "Our honorable ancestors want us to believe that they already took care of all the problems we face."[19] Those problems still exist, and Pocho.com is eager to pulverize them.

It is understandable that the application of satire to a minority movement can be seen as ignorance of the past or sheer disrespect. If Pocho/as can now laugh at elements of the Chicano/a movement, does this depreciate the importance of that history? No, it celebrates it. Laughter corrodes the barriers that formality erects. As Mikhail Bakhtin in *Rabelais and His World* eloquently states, "Certain essential aspects of the world are accessible only to laughter." Bakhtin cites Rabelais's style of excess (the "grotesque") as a form of celebration. This celebration was a means of "uncrown[ing] and renew[ing] the established power and official truth," initiating a "new awareness" that "had found its most radical expression in laughter."[20] Like the carnivals Rabelais describes, celebration—laughter—is a means of conveying a public sentiment, developing a sense of community, and reinvigorating the people. Using satirical tactics, Pocho.com has managed to re-invigorate a political consciousness. The seriousness of the Chicano/a movement, however beneficial or necessary, was in danger of becoming an official entity, one that by way of its seriousness "pretended to be absolute." Laughter, according to Bakhtin, is a relative of "the people's unofficial truth."[21]

Still, this satirical humor must be held to some standard in order to be deemed progressive enough for an "identity movement." In *Watching Race*, Herman Gray suggests an excellent model for this test. Investigating the television program *In Living Color,* Gray proposes that we should use satire and parody strategically in order to successfully criticize racism and class inequality. While Gray finds *In Living Color* to "settle around a position of ambivalence," he could not easily state the same of Pocho.com.[22] *In Living Color* was required to broaden its appeal to attract white, middle-class audiences—one of the many constraints of television. Pocho.com has instead customized its content; the target Pocho/a audience possesses the cultural knowledge necessary for the humor as visitors to the site are often directed from other Chicano/a Web site links. However, this does not prevent "others" from accessing and appreciating the humor: most satirical subjects are public personalities and political officials. What is most powerful in Pocho.com is that, while entertaining, the site also informs the audience of pertinent issues in the news and community. Most effectively, it accomplishes this with political and satirical bite.

Of course, this method is not entirely new to Chicano media discourse. Satiric traditions can be seen in films such as *Born in East L.A.* and with performance groups such as Culture Clash.[23] What is unique about Pocho.com is its continued presence. Unrestrained by the extreme financial commitments of 35mm film production or network television's political queasiness, Pocho.com is able routinely to update its content and presentation; as an occupant of the Internet, Pocho.com has the added luxury of a consistent "time slot," "location," and "distribution." None of these elements are in real danger of demotion, thereby achieving a longer-term cultivation of audience than is ever granted network or public television arenas. This, however, does not mean Pocho.com should or will remain satisfied with simply an Internet presence. Like *Born in East L.A.* and Culture Clash, Pocho.com continues to make its racial and cultural identity known online. This, in itself, is a rather large leap toward a colorful online community.

THE POCHO WEB SITE

On entry the Pocho Web site, at this particular point in time, reads like a network television site.[24] Familiar TV images pepper the page, including celebrity faces and prime-time television show logos. A banner announces "Pocho TV Network," beneath which resides the site features (which I have numbered here for ease of reference). On the left side of the Pocho home page is the customary panel (1) with navigational options: "Home," "Primetime," "Telenovelas," "Links," "Pocho store," and "Contact the Networks!" Directly below this (2) is the snide white male associated with the (now-defunct network) television program *Action*. Over his image flash the phrases: "Latinos, Schmatinos. Diversity, Schmiversity. Tell 'em I'm out to lunch." Below this are two ads (3) for Pocho-related T-shirts. To the far right is a smaller panel (4) with the additional options of "Showtimes"—that is, links set to look like a programming schedule. These links read "La Cucaracha," "GenMex," "Pocho Magazine," "Cholo Chatroom," and "In News: Buchanan Seeks to Switch Parties."

The bulk of the site announces a new fall show lineup. On closer inspection it becomes clear that familiar network icons have been altered. The home page centerpiece (5) is an image of the actors associated with the television program *Everybody Loves Raymond*. However, this version reads (in the sitcom logo font and format), "Everybody Hates Ramón." Beneath this are the following "program" links/options, including images and captions, in a horizontal panel:

[6] *Third Rock from José:* Hollywood loves aliens from Outer Space, Not From Outta the State!

[7] *Emmy Ribbon Campaign:* Latino group declares victory after the Emmys.

[8] *Just Shoot Him:* This happenin' whitecom adds a young Latino male. Target: Laughs!

[9] *Touched by an Anglo:* The office heats up once again as Mr. Jameson offers mandatory free massages to the girls in the secretarial pool.

In its initial presentation, Pocho.com succeeds in fulfilling Gray's call to "disturb and interrupt television's own discourse."[25] Network television sites are familiar to the average Internet "surfer"; the Internet's capacity for entertainment-related URLs knows no bounds. Pocho.com arrests this typical visual discourse by subtly rewriting the images while radically revising the narrative text in both captions and articles. To explore this further, we can take the larger home-page fragments and identify each subversive, educative/advocative, and identity-oriented element at work.

The link "News" is a prime example of Pocho.com's brand of education through humor. "News" presents a satire of political reports regarding right-wing presidential candidate (for election 2000) Pat Buchanan. By imagining Buchanan as a member of the smaller, more progressive Mexican political parties Partido de la Revolución Democrática (PRD) and Partido Acción Nacional (PAN), the text simultaneously deflates the ultraconservative North American candidate while recognizing the emerging Mexican political parties and their opposition to the long-ruling Partido Revolucionario Institucional (PRI). While moments of humorous exaggeration do exist (such as the framing of Buchanan as a "little Nazi"), nuggets of truth are nestled in the text for further inspection by Pocho/a readers. Consider the following paragraph:

> Political analysts say Buchanan's announcement will likely hurt the Republican party, since all the right-wing nutzos will follow Buchanan wherever he goes, but the candidate's decision could deal a death blow to Mexico's opposition, *which have been trying like heck for about 70 years to win an election against the Institutional Revolutionary Party, PRI.* "Sure, Buchanan has name recognition. But everybody in Mexico hates the guy's guts! If he comes down here, he'll screw everything up! What an asshole!" said Lalo de la Garza, president of El Partido Revolucionario de Gente Humilde Sin Possibilidad de Ganar un Elección Contra El PRI en 2000. "*Somehow I still think the opposition would be better off with Cuautemoc Cardenas as our candidate, though I'm not quite sure. At least he's Mexican. Not to mention he's got a cool Aztec name.*"[26]

Acknowledgement of the PRI's long unrivaled rule is framed by fictionalized situations (Buchanan in Mexico? The fiction is not so subtle). The mention of Cuautemoc Cardenas offers a Pocho/a reader just enough truth to research the then PRD presidential candidate elsewhere. Yet, to keep this information delectable, Pocho.com manages to poke fun at Cardenas's name and smaller political parties within the same paragraph.[27]

In balancing fact and fiction, Pocho.com exemplifies the delicate cultural equanimity maintained by Pocho/as.

Pocho.com at its informative and critical best is reflected in items 7 and 8. Item 7 is titled "Latino Media Diversity Group Declares Victory in Emmy Ribbon Campaign" and is formatted like the "News" item. Unlike the Buchanan piece, item 7 directly targets the Chicano/a community, its notion of activism, and its overall representation on the "small screen." Centering on the semifictitious "Latino Media Coalition,"[28] this item focuses on ineffective attempts to change the media industry and the long history of Chicano/a media activist organizations.[29] Commenting on the superfluous ribbon campaigns, an invisible ribbon is created by the Latin Media Coalition and "worn" by every celebrity at the Emmy Awards. Pocho.com thus critiques the ignorance and screen power of the "star" industry while ridiculing Latinos for expecting action from outside the community. In itself, the invisible ribbon symbolizes the Chicano/a televisual media presence.

In item 8 an acute switch in mode articulates the injustice of the shooting of Javier Ovando and his subsequent paralysis. Framed as the television sitcom *Just Shoot Me,* this narrative rewrite is simply an excuse to expose this quickly forgotten news story and police injustice. It reads: "Just Shoot Him! Set in the New York editorial offices of the fictional 'Blush' magazine, LAPD Rampart Division framing victim Javier Ovando joins the snappy ensemble cast of *Just Shoot Me.* He'll be the first Latino paraplegic to costar in a sitcom, thanks to the LAPD's CRASH anti-gang unit who first handcuffed him, shot him in the head and planted a weapon on his crumpled body!" The tonal shift occurs abruptly after the setting is established, and it ceases to be a simple comedic tale. The revival of the long-dead news piece alerts the reader to another overlooked act of violence against Chicano/as performed by the Los Angeles Police Department. Further, the use of "Javier's" mug shot, darker in contrast to *Just Shoot Me*'s well-lit publicity photo, foregrounds the program's ultra-white cast as they hold their hands in a mock "gun" position. The image of "Chicano" in this case reflects the more common news coverage of gang violence while using that very image to solicit political unrest regarding police abuse.

These elements are only the tip of the Pocho.com iceberg. Each successive visit to the Web site produces many more texts for the purposes of entertainment and gleaning information. As a target of Pocho.com, Chicano/a political enemy Bob Dornan has been awarded a separate site devoted to his political campaign and attempted recruitment of Chicano/a voters.[30] Lalo López and Esteban Zul have managed to deflate another political figure with a dose of Pochismo. Still, how much impact can these sites really have? That is, what is the use of this political satire site to an individual Pocho/a on the Internet? What could make a functionally subversive political community capable, according to Mitra, of "producing a new computer 'reality' . . . the sum of the various opinions, ideas and practices, and ideologies represented by the texts"?[31] What is needed, and what Pocho.com has, is a "Cholo Chatroom."

Some cultural critics warn that online communities can sometimes excite ethnic and nationalist sentiments that ultimately re-create dominant, colonialist tropes. For example, Ella Shohat argues that "cybertravel across national borders becomes a travel of recuperation." She further claims that the excitement of forging new paths online, both culturally and representatively, largely rearticulates the colonialist rhetoric of Western civilization onto a hyperreality.[32] Shohat's critique rightfully acknowledges the importance of minority presence online (especially in contrast to the lack of minority representation in larger media formats—CNN, the Associated Press, Reuters, ABC, BBC, and Hollywood) but she neglects *why* such images are necessary.[33] Further, she does not explain how communities striving for visibility in their own language, inside their "own" borders, and within (to a large degree) their native-born culture. What does it mean when the "recuperation" is one of personal and cultural identity and the "cybertravel" occurs within one nation/al border? Pocho/as maintain a unique position in relation to American cultures; this position—this identity—has only begun to be realized in the past fifty years (beginning with Chicano/a). As a result, the Pocho/a community has emerged to further test cultural waters. As López explains: "Many older Chicanos can't understand that their successes have freed us up from the narrow definitions that once constrained them. . . . We give our Chicano culture flexibility never achieved before—we can bend it, fold it, slice it and dice it."[34]

This desire to reshape cultural identity is simultaneously a fractal and an expansive goal. Perhaps being placed in such a broad category as "Hispanic" has incited a desire to imagine and/or reclaim subsets of identity: Mexicano/a to Chicano/a to Pocho/a. In order to work through these issues, Pocho.com has provided the traditional Internet space for talk. In this chat room members can enjoy the diverse company of this intranational diaspora. Reasons for entering this community vary; however, most members are affiliated with Chicanismo/a and Pochismo/a. Although topics span all popular cultural phenomenons, it is arguable that the strongest responses are those related to self-identification. One posting requested opinions on the best environment in which to raise a daughter as a proud Chicana: Michigan or Texas?[35] Another posting stated: "A semester of Mexican-American studies/Mexican-American history/Spanish classes didn't give me the sense of race that I was looking for. So what did it take? One hour of Pocho.com!"[36] What might have offered such an accessible understanding to this student? Perhaps the image-oriented nature of the site, especially combined with the cultural and political criticisms, allowed an identification process based not only on image but on contradiction as well.

Both Mitra and Shohat discuss electronic communications in terms of communities displaced across national borders (particularly those separated by oceans). While most elements of these arguments apply to the "Cholo Chatroom," what makes this community unique is its emerging cultural identification within a singular nation. Further, members of this community seek not only identification with one another but also re identification with a larger "imagined [imaging/image] community,"[37] in this specific case, network television. Pocho.com has provided a space for exploration of identity, culture, and community, all the while exploiting the satiric potential of each element. With such a sophisticated communal base, recognition and respect by the dominant media cannot be far behind; for now, however, it will strictly be on the Pocho/a's terms.

The television narrative rewritings note this well. Items 2 and 5 through 9 all continue to critique the media and its treatment of Chicano/as. Item 2 (*Action*) taunts the viewer and results in the punchline: "*Inaction:* A show about Diversity in Hollywood." "Everybody Hates Ramón" parodies the television family "united in hatred for [the] undocumented Mexican immigrant" hired "to do a little laborin'. " The impact of this joke is enhanced with the knowledge of day laborer abuse and its consistent neglect by the news media. The "character image" used here calls to mind the undocumented worker—a mental image used by California and elsewhere in the United States to reinforce the "importance" of a border. Adding (self-inflicted) insult to injury, the role of Ramón is played by "Carmine Petrocelli," an Italian surname. Item 6 features the predominant Latino portrayal on television: the Colombian drug lord. This show, "Third Rock from José," plays on the fascination in the United States with extraterrestrial aliens and the distaste for "illegal" ones. A "cameo by George W. Bush" is the highlight of this episode.

If the Web site's underlying goal is to assert a new identity, what then do we make of the stereotypical images inserted into the Pocho.com revision/critique? In light of its call for fair media portrayal, it is curious that Pocho.com would choose to insert such recycled stereotypes when rewriting the network image-text. Both "Third Rock from José" and

"Everybody Hates Ramón" feature Latino stereotypes; if the underscored point of these satirizations is to criticize the media's lack of brown representation, then why do these models perpetuate the images that have historically been so fiercely rejected by the Chicano/a community?

First, such images are a better comedy tool because they serve as "in-jokes." Second, these in-jokes are a valuable means of enhancing a sense of community. Third, while this may initially appear hypocritical, the re-creation of these network-favored depictions might be read in the context of early Chicano political struggles against stereotypes. In *Shot in America*, Chon Noriega looks at the original motivator for Chicano/a presence in and on television: a movement against stereotypical representation, particularly the infamous Frito Bandito.[38] By "mimicking the very stereotypes that secure their exclusion," Pocho.com might be seen as paying homage to early Chicano/a works like *Los Vendidos* (The Sellouts) and taking it one step further. In *Los Vendidos,* an anglicized Mexican American woman seeks to purchase a " 'Mexican-type' " robot to "add a 'brown face in the crowd' to the governor's luncheon." The punchline of this sketch is that the stereotypes presented for purchase—a "Frito Bandito-style revolutionary," a zoot-suiter, farmworkers, etc.—are all human while the salesman is revealed as the real robot. The televised version of this play frames the motive as political infiltration.[39] While *Los Vendidos*'s narrative ends before the Chicano/a infiltration can be witnessed, Pocho.com completes the sentence and punctuates the revised image with a scolding text.

Despite the parodied images, Pocho.com does not let its visitors remain passive in the struggle for positive media representation. The text accompanying the images states this case, but there are more obvious elements. For example, "Links" (item 1) points visitors to information on the "brownout" television protest. Although the event ended and the link is no longer active, it does illustrate the importance placed on activism in the Pocho site. Visitors were encouraged to resist the networks denying Chicano/as a mass media presence and to directly e-mail petition notices via the site-provided addresses. In this way, Pocho.com offers an accessible method of declaring dissatisfaction and requesting more Chicano/a characters on television. In effect, Pocho.com provides a platform for the Pocho/a advocative "voice." To immediately fill the void and provide site content, Pocho.com features its own creative rewriting of television programming. It is my belief that this version of the ever-changing site provides much more than a simple act of humor; Pocho.com succeeds in re-presenting itself to the public as multimedia icons while criticizing the portrayals historically presented to and rejected by the Chicano/a community. In addition, these images represent the past (stereotypes) and the present (new programming) to emphasize a struggle continuing since the 1960s. By organizing these elements around humor, Pocho.com looks to the future and, in Bakhtin's words, "clear[s] the way for them."[40]

Posting to the "Cholo Chatroom" is in itself a form of activism (or at the very least, action) as suggested by the animated head of "Subcommandante Marcos" (an indication that one has entered the chat room). The Internet is the cyberfrontier utilized by the Zapatistas; likewise, it is a method for educating and organizing members of the Pocho/a community. Although controversies are occasionally sparked (sometimes intentionally), an overall concern for one another persists; it is understood that this is a community not simply in cyberspace but a space within the tangible walls of the United States. As "Riri" expressed in response to the Michigan/Texas debate: "Please don't be afraid to ask for help or suggestions. We are all here because we're interested in what the others have to say. This is not a homogenous group by any means, but there is a sense of unity."

Finally, the "Pocho Store" offers the visitor an opportunity to declare "Pochismo" to the physical world. Issues of *Pocho* magazine, T-Shirts (as seen in item 3), and videos are also available through this URL. Of course, Pocho.com does not miss a comedic opportunity: "Be the pride of your Barrio and suburb and/or Suburban Barrio! Only the finest in Pocho paraphernalia in Aztlan or the Outer Territories is available to you from the Pocho Products Catalog! Buy these items before they are declared "illegal and highly deportable" by the frightened Gringo authorities and populace! Get yours today—and get Aztlan mañana!"[41] The threat "illegal and highly deportable" mimics the current and standard news media framing of Chicano/as. By coining the term "suburban barrio," the site recognizes and reconciles the dichotomized domiciles of Pocho/as; in relating this back to "Aztlan," the text successfully regroups this diaspora into a simultaneously physical and imagined collective yet again. Aztlan— the elusive Aztec homeland and physical space known to the United States as the Southwest (namely, all of Mexico that has been conquered)— serves as a simplified metaphor for Chicano communities online: a unification/representation in a space/site that does not physically exist. While many Chicano sites profess a strict nostalgia for this "homeland," Pocho.com points to this endless search as a cultural marker in itself ("get Aztlan mañana!"). If one accepts Aztlan as the allegorical place of union for a bordered people, then it is fitting that Pocho.com's host service would be named Azteca.net, as the Aztecs were the original inhabitants of Aztlan.

Noriega notes that "during the Chicano movement . . . the major spatial metaphor—Aztlan—became increasingly tied to an identity rather than a space."[42] If traditionally the notion of nationality has been linked to physical space, then what of a cultural identity that has manifested itself in a nonphysical hyperreality, although often occupying the literal, physical space of what was once Aztlan (as in the case of a Pocha residing in Texas)? Returning to the blanket identification "Hispanic" and its popularization during the Nixon years, we might find a general example of national refusal. In rejecting the proscripted label "Hispanic," Chicanos began an evolution of terms/categories as self-reification. By refusing to accept a term cultivated for U.S. national ease (the census), Chicano/as and Pocho/as opposed the cultural herding by self-fractalization. In continuing to adopt and redress slanderous terms as points of identification, Chicano/as and Pocho/as placed themselves outside of the assigned national spaces and labels. However, both Chicano/as and Pocho/as have sought and claimed an alternative "space" as their own point of origination: theater (performance) and cyberspace, both serving as a surrogate Aztlan. By directing this movement of identity in/through these "spaces," Chicano/as and Pocho/as have sought to exist beyond the physical borders of nation—cultivating, in hyperreality, a *spatial identity*. The search for representation in mass media (from film to television to new media) points to a desire for both self-recognition and recognition by others inside and (potentially) outside the national borders—a presence unique to mass media, particularly the Internet—to further, in Shohat's words, "facilitate a discussion of community identities—not in isolation, but in relation."[43]

Like the hybrid notion of "netizen," the Pocho/a community is not and cannot simply be limited to Chicano/as. Although I write this essay with Pocho/as as a closed union of Chicano/as, Pochismo/a actually aims beyond notions of (physical) national and cultural boundaries. Instead, it is the progressive fusion of all cultures. Esteban Zul notes that "Pochismo is more inclusive than Chicano." In his mind, Pochismo/a is a temporary identity meant to evolve. Just as Chicano/a begat Pocho/a, so must this identity produce the next. Zul continues, "Someday some kid's going to tell me Pochismo's full of it. When he comes, I hope I can say, 'I've been waiting for you. Let's destroy it.' "[44]

In the meantime Pocho.com has succeeded in creating its own system of representative channels. The "Pocho Network," the site title originating as a spoof of the television giants denying access and representation, has since become a truth. In the time since the "Pocho Network" first "aired" online, Pocho.com has expanded its own borders, creating affiliates or channels. The "Pocho.com Network Sites" have since grown to include, among others, Cartoonista.com, a site focusing on the political cartoon stylings of Lalo Alcaraz; Smokinmirrors.net, an agitprop artist collective online gallery; Generationmex.com, featuring the writings of Lalo López; InvisibleAmerica.com, featuring news articles about the "invisible majority" of both North and South America; and—as an extension of InvisibleAmerica.com—Cybracero.com, a site that solves the "problem" of labor immigration by allowing immigrants to work in "First-World" countries cybernetically as opposed to physically. In the end, Pocho.com and its network sites continue to re-present and re-imagine the Chicano/a and Pocho/a identity in the mass media imagery on this side of the border. Although this presentation may currently occupy only cyberspace, it is the beginning of a realized infiltration of images into the mainstream American imaginary, continuing what *Los Vendidos* began. This time, it is being transmitted to the world.

While at the core the case I have presented may apply to other minorities, I feel that this specific argument needs to be made as a means of placing the Chicano/a and Pocho/a identity within the discussion of online identity and imagery. While this site (or any other minority-specific site, for that matter) may be criticized for largely playing to its own audience, I do not think this is a negative point at this very moment and time. Instead, it is a means of accomplishing what the brownout intended: to flex the muscles of the (Latino/a, Chicano/a, and Pocho/a) viewing public. What is happening online in sites such as Pocho.com and Cybracero.com is a revision of mainstream media representation. Further, this is happening in a space where the audience must seek out the programming, providing the necessary first step in any media reform scheme: community support.[45] I do not see this phase of Pocho.com as an end in and of itself, but instead as a media rebirth, a chance to recapture the momentum once practiced in Chicano public television programming in the 1960s and 1970s. The World Wide Web is an open door, a chance for ideas to gain audience recognition and a necessary training ground for writers and image makers. This is a new version of local, public access programming opportunities, but with international exposure. If this activity becomes stagnant, if there is no move toward other media forms, then perhaps it is all for naught. But the Internet is a newly image-oriented medium and race is still making itself known in this proclaimed "color blind" online state. The fact that Pocho.com is thriving and the fact that community support is only a click away (visitors can and do help fund the site via online contributions) are testament to the wider media potential these sites provide. By way of satirical, political material and discussions of race, a larger American audience is inevitable yet not necessarily the point or a necessary point at this stage. A wider media uprising is simply a matter of time, resources, and gradual mainstream accreditation.

NOTES

1. Lalo López, "Generation Mex," 1994, www.generationmex.com/genmex2.html.

2. Chon Noriega, *Shot in America: Television, the State, and the Rise of Chicano Cinema* (Minneapolis: University of Minnesota Press, 2000), p. xxiv.

3. López, "Generation Mex."

4. Catherine Wiley, "Teatro Chicano and the Seduction of Nostalgia," *MELUS* (spring 1998): 99.

5. Ananda Mitra, "Virtual Commonality: Looking for India on the Internet," in *Virtual Culture: Identity and Communication in Cybersociety,* ed. Steven Jones (London: Sage, 1997), pp. 55–79.

6. Jennifer González, "The Appended Subject: Race and Identity as Digital Assemblage," in *Race in Cyberspace,* ed. Beth E. Kolko, Lisa Nakamura, and Gibert B. Rodman (New York: Routledge, 2000), p. 36.

7. Mitra, "Virtual Commonality," pp. 63–64.

8. Noriega, *Shot in America,* p. xxviii.

9. Ibid., p. xxxi.

10. Mitra, "Virtual Commonality," p. 55.

11. "Latino Groups Seek Boycott of 4 Major TV Networks; Protest in September Would Aim to Get More Hispanics on Programs," *St. Louis Post,* July 28, 1999, p. A5.

12. "Despite the Link between the Audience and Commercials, the Brownout Was Not Planning to Boycott Sponsors," *Dayton Daily News,* July 28, 1999, n.p.

13. It seems odd that a term so self-consciously "inclusive" as Hispanic originally only warranted a week of national recognition, despite the many ethnicities the term is meant to include. National Hispanic Heritage Week was eventually expanded to a month in 1988.

14. Ella Shohat, "By the Bitstream of Babylon: Cyberfrontiers and Diasporic Vistas," in *Home, Exile, Homeland: Film, Media, and the Politics of Place,* ed. Hamid Naficy (New York: Routledge, 1999), p. 223.

15. Lalo López, "Generation Mex," http://www.generationmex.com/genmex5.html.

16. Ibid.

17. I am borrowing this phrase from Mitra, "Virtual Commonality," p. 68.

18. Noriega, *Shot in America,* p. xxxi.

19. López, "Generation Mex."

20. Mikhail Bakhtin, *Rabelais and His World* (Bloomington: Indiana University Press, 1984), pp. 66, 99.

21. Ibid., pp. 212, 90.

22. Herman Gray, *Watching Race: Television and the Struggle for Blackness* (Minneapolis: University of Minnesota Press, 1995), pp. 144, 130.

23. See Rosa Linda Fregoso, "Humor as Subversive De-Construction in *Born in East L.A.*," in *The Bronze Screen: Chicano and Chicana Film Culture* (Minneapolis: University of Minnesota Press, 1993), pp. 49–64. Incidentally, Culture Clash had a thirty-show run on Fox TV; Lalo Alcaraz was a staff writer for the program.

24. The description here is based on the Pocho Web site circa September to November 1999.

25. Gray, *Watching Race,* p. 145.

26. See http://www.pocho.com/noticias.html, emphasis added.

27. *El Partido Revolucionario de Gente Humilde Sin Possibilidad de Ganar un Eleccion Contra El PRI en 2000* (The revolutionary party of humble people [people that work the land] without the possibility of winning the election against the PRI in 2000).

28. The National Latino Media Coalition was "an umbrella organization for major national Latino organizations during the Brownout," http://205.253.75.10/hispanic/arts/brownout1999.html.

29. Noriega, *Shot in America,* p. 25.

30. See http://www.members.tripod.com/~vivabob98/index.html.

31. Mitra, "Virtual Commonality," p. 58.

32. Shohat, "By the Bitstream of Babylon," pp. 229, 216.

33. Ibid., p. 228. However, Shohat does make mention (p. 226) of a desire for the "home imaginary"; in my case, it is the regular and realistic representation of a culture/ ethnicity on network media.

34. López, "Generation Mex."

35. "I don't want to start a war with this one. . . ."; posted by Rosa on November 22, 1999.

36. "Soy Pocha," posted by Krystylbaby on December 4, 1999.

37. Mitra, "Virtual Commonality," p. 56.

38. Noriega, *Shot in America,* pp. 28–50.

39. Ibid., pp. 121–23.

40. Bakhtin, *Rabelais and His World,* p. 95.

41. Products are currently on www.latinoshirts.com.

42. Noriega, *Shot in America,* p. 129.

43. Shohat, "By the Bitstream of Babylon," p. 230.

44. Zul, quoted in Peter Hong, "They Were Chicanos but Now Proudly Say They're Pochos," *Los Angeles Times,* March 16, 1999, posted on http://www.pocho.com/about/latimes2699.html.

45. Noriega, *Shot in America,* p. 132.

PART FOUR

TELEVISION

TEACHERS

This section takes up the well-rehearsed debate about the educational potential of television and its ability to provide forms of democratic communication and citizenship. The essays in this section variously consider the institutional and "disciplinary" contexts in which television has been studied and/or used as an instrument for education, and they also question the degree to which education (and television studies in particular) has ever operated outside of commercial imperatives. In other words, these essays reexamine the "ivory tower" idealism that has historically structured debates on the educational versus commercial nature of television. The authors of these essays collectively illustrate that in actually existing democracies education has (for better or worse) itself become a "culture industry."

In "Television, the Housewife, and the Museum of Modern Art" Lynn Spigel examines efforts made by the museum in the 1950s to affiliate with the new medium of television. Like other historical essays in this book, Spigel's article rethinks some of the central assumptions of television history—in this case by reexamining the presumed antipathies between commercial and educational television, between entertainment and art, and between women's "low" genres and "high" culture. The case of MoMA demonstrates that educational/public institutions for the arts did not always imagine themselves as separate from commercial television. In fact, in the early 1950s MoMA purposefully distanced itself from the newly allocated educational channels and instead established liaisons with the major networks and attempted to attract a mass audience (especially housewives). In so doing, the museum displayed modern art to viewers through television's vernacular conventions of liveness and participatory address while also using popular women's genres. Showcasing "high" art on a "low" medium, however, presented significant challenges for the museum, which ultimately brought an end to these early endeavors. Spigel analyzes MoMA's conflicting aesthete and popular ideals, and she considers some of the more general issues this case poses concerning the perceived (gendered) divisions between "high" art and "low" media.

John Hartley and Julie D'Acci end this volume by considering the field of academic television studies itself, especially its relationship to the entertainment industries and commerce. In "From Republic of Letters to Television Republic: Citizen Readers in the Era of Broadcast Television," Hartley traces the history of television studies (and in particular its anti-TV, ideological critique) through a broader perspective on the history of reading and citizenship. He argues that critics have tended to approach television and television audiences as unruly forces in need of discipline. In response he claims that the foundational theorists of cultural studies (in particular Richard Hoggart) imagined television in more positive ways as a form of democratic teaching. Hartley returns to this discussion of television as a teacher and a source of cultural citizenship in the increasingly fragmented, narrowcast, and suburbanized cultures of postmodernity, and he concludes that television studies—with its focus on power, ideology, and hegemony—has approached television with undue anxiety and has tended to overlook its "democratic" potential as a teacher and space for citizenship. In his view the discipline is overly disciplined and fails to confront the kinds of "ordinary" lessons in media literacy and cultural citizenship that television teaches audiences every day.

Julie D'Acci reaches a different conclusion in "Cultural Studies, Television Studies, and the Crisis in the Humanities." Focusing on the way U.S. universities have used cultural studies as a remedy for a fiscal crisis, D'Acci argues that the relatively new and loosely constituted field of television studies has suffered under the sway of this fiscal remedy. Claiming that cultural studies is often used as a way to generate revenue in the U.S. academy (largely through the consolidation of disciplines and enrollment numbers), D'Acci argues that television studies has become a prime target of opportunity for fields in the humanities (especially English departments), most of which have historically reviled television (and as a result have not paid attention to developments in television scholarship and the television industry itself). She further argues that studying television under the umbrella term "cultural studies" has largely resulted in "ideological readings" that divorce television from its industrial, institutional, historical, and aesthetic bases. Hoping to guard against this purely textual/literary approach to television—as well as what she sees as a related strand of "neo-liberalism" that fosters a kind of "anything goes" methodological morass in the commerce-oriented contemporary academy—she claims that television studies needs to establish disciplinary criteria and then map out a clearly defined model of study. D'Acci turns to the British cultural studies "circuit model" of culture, and she revises it for what she calls the "media circuit" model of television studies. In the end, D'Acci aims to convince us that a renewed focus on disciplinary rigor, within what she nevertheless admits is the necessarily interdisciplinary field of television studies, is in fact a necessary and welcome goal for media scholars today.

LYNN SPIGEL

TELEVISION, THE HOUSEWIFE,

AND THE MUSEUM OF MODERN ART

In 1964 David Wolper produced a pilot for *Miss Television USA*. Hosted by Byron Palmer, the program presented local beauty queens, all from California, who competed for the coveted award. In the talent sequence featuring Miss Santa Barbara, Palmer drags an easel on stage and promises viewers that the performance will be "rather unique." Miss Santa Barbara then floats onto the runway stage, where she begins a heartfelt dialogue about the meaning of art while also gesturing to some of her handiwork hung in a gallerylike setting. After several moments of artful revelry backed by somber violins, the tone changes. A whimsical flute pipes up, and Miss Santa Barbara redirects our attention to the easel in the center of the stage. "Inspiration," she tells us, also comes from the "fun things in life." Then, at rapid speed, she begins to draw the image of Linus, the popular character from Charles Schulz's *Peanuts*. After finishing her cartoon, she looks into the camera and warmly intones, "Linus and I hope you've enjoyed our presentation here tonight." Finally, after a musical crescendo and much (canned) applause, she takes a bow and Palmer hurries the next contestant onto the stage.

Although Miss Santa Barbara was not crowned Miss Television, her strange talent segment is nevertheless historically significant for television studies. It highlights a much more general set of cultural dynamics between television and the visual arts in the early decades of the medium's meteoric rise. This program (and, as we shall see, many like it) presents art through the conventions of American vernacular entertainment forms—notably vaudeville and female pageantry. In addressing popular tastes, it scandalizes divisions between high and low by moving from the staid art appreciation lecture to Miss Santa Barbara's rather frantic attempt to get Linus drawn in two seconds flat while maintaining her own corporeal grace. The program foregrounds new ways of looking at art—ways of looking that are not bound to passive gallery observation but are instead communicated through conventions of televisuality itself—especially television's aesthetics of "liveness," its performative and intimate styles of communication, and its use of women's genres.

To be sure, *Miss Television USA* was not alone in its efforts to present art through vernacular women's genres and live "boffo" entertainment styles. In fact, this quirky pilot should be seen in the context of a much larger cultural initiative—waged by traditional institutions of the arts—to make art appealing to the growing ranks of television watchers, especially to housewives. During the late 1940s and early 1950s museums in New York, San Francisco, Detroit, Dallas, Boston, Buffalo, St. Louis, Los Angeles, Toledo, and other cities tried to use television as a form of popular pedagogy, hoping to teach viewers about their collections and thus encourage museum patronage. In the face of suburban expansion, these urban institutions of the arts saw television as a key tool in reaching the suburban family audience. And like David Wolper's extravagant display of female spectacle, these institutions also tried to increase their "fem" appeal by using entertainment formats aimed at women.

In this essay I consider how the worlds of museum art and commercial television collided in the 1950s, at the time when television rose to prominence as the dominant form of entertainment and information in the United States. I focus especially on New York's Museum of Modern Art (MoMA), which had a sustained and developed interest in using television to communicate the visual experience of looking at gallery art. In 1939, the year MoMA opened its West 53rd Street building (a starkly modern structure that Alan Wallach calls a "utopian" engagement with the technological future),[1] MoMA officials also began to consider television a technological marvel that might extend the museum's reach past its newly built doors. Consequently, in this same year MoMA became the first museum in the United States to appear on television.[2] By the late 1940s, when television began to enter American homes, the museum was among the most enthusiastic players in the new field.

Most crucial in all its endeavors were the museum's assumptions about the new suburban television culture and the domestic environment of reception. In attempting to use television as a forum for painting, MoMA officials continually stressed the need to reach the typical TV viewer at home. And rather than using educational broadcasting as their inspiration, they sought liaisons with commercial networks. By presenting art in the language of entertainment—especially through televisual conventions of liveness and women's genres—the museum hoped to establish itself as a commercial success in its own right. While now a forgotten chapter in television history, MoMA's early interest in television and its struggles with the medium suggest something of the complex relationship between fine art and commercial media in the postwar period. Indeed, the case of MoMA asks us to rethink the binary logic that pits television against art, domesticity against publicness, and entertainment against education.

As the bastion of the urbane world of modern art, and as a central institution promoting the male centered canon of European modernism, MoMA nevertheless courted television audiences, especially housewives, in order to maintain its dominance as the leading museum of modern art (not only in the United States but increasingly abroad). However, while recognizing the need to woo home audiences with entertaining programs, MoMA officials also expressed a great deal of anxiety about the effects that their use of television might have on the museum's reputation and prestige among its traditional art patrons.

Certainly, this conflict was not new.[3] The case of MoMA's "Television Project" is part of a much longer set of historical relationships among modern art, women, domesticity, and consumerism. As Christopher Reed argues, since the nineteenth century, modernist movements have depended on women, domesticity, and consumer culture for their patronage and cultural hegemony. Department stores, haute couture, and calendar art were among the greatest popularizers of modern art. But, at the same time, modern art and architecture have tended to "assert their accomplishments through contrast with domesticity," and artists, curators, and the artworks themselves have expressed a great deal of anxiety about consumer culture, domesticity, and all things feminine.[4] This simultaneous embrace and "othering" of femininity, domesticity, and commercial culture was at the heart of the cultural struggle waged by MoMA as the museum attempted to juggle the cultural fields of popular media and modern art.

FROM PROP HOUSE TO IN-HOUSE

While television historians have focused on the networks' interest in Broadway theater and vaudeville as sources and inspirations for early programming, we know very little about the role other cultural institutions have played in the development of television as an institutional and cultural form. We know even less about the way television might have influenced the broader field of visual culture and traditional modes of gallery exhibition and reception. Despite the fact that cultural theorists have generally hailed the postwar period for its postmodern blurring of high and low culture, and despite the fact that many cultural theorists see television as the postmodern medium par excellence, the actual historical links between television and the traditional cultural institutions of modernity are barely understood.

When it came to art museums, at least, these links were strong. In the early 1950s, museums across the nation took an interest in using television as a kind of second gallery, hoping both to educate viewers and to advertise the museum itself.[5] For their part, the networks encouraged these ties. The NBC records are full of letters from museums, artists, and other groups in the visual arts. Meanwhile, CBS Chairman William S. Paley sat on the Board of Directors at MoMA and was instrumental in forming various partnerships between that museum and his network. As early as 1948, Paley attended meetings of the Television Committee of the citywide Museum Council, where he expressed CBS's interest in collaborating with art museums.[6] In short, the worlds of museum art and television joined together in mutual relations of support. As the assistant curator at the San Francisco Museum of Art claimed in 1952, "television programs presented during an eight month period reached approximately 1,500,000 people, or ten times the annual attendance at the museum."[7]

MoMA played a central role within this context. In 1948, at a time when only about 2 percent of American homes had a television set, MoMA aired programs in conjunction with NBC, CBS, and local New York broadcasters.[8] By 1949, the museum had increased its activities, participating in a television production about every other week (or every ten days). An internal report stated: "At the present rate of requests from telestations we will have participation in twice as many shows, or one a week during 1950."[9] As this report suggests, MoMA's early participation in television was greatly facilitated by the fact that local broadcasters and national networks were hungry for anything that could catch the visual attention of the viewer. So, too, as a center for production, and as one of the first areas of the country with multiple television stations, New York City was filled with production companies hoping to capitalize on the new medium. As MoMA's public relations director, Betty Chamberlain, claimed: "The tele situation here in New York seems to be going in all directions at once. Practically everyone in television has simultaneously and suddenly decided that there is great disgust on the part of the public at seeing nothing on television except sports. So they are all at once trying to discover uses for culture—or Kultur. Some new tele outfit, usually starting in someone's apartment, is springing up at least every week, and all these budding hopefuls came around to talk to me about the possibilities of art on television. But none of them have any ideas."[10]

In Chamberlain's view, the problem was that commercial broadcasters approached the museum as a prop house, an attitude that was perhaps best summed up by CBS's William S. Paley, who reportedly told a museum official, "just give us the material . . . and we'll put it on the air."[11] In contrast, Chamberlain and her colleagues at MoMA wanted to play an active role in program production by developing techniques through which to convey the importance of art to the public (and hence the importance of the museum itself). To that effect, one in-house report stated in 1949: "Although television may not reach huge audiences at present, it seems worthwhile for the museum to familiarize itself with the medium and to come to know what makes a good tele art program. This should put the Museum in a position of a certain amount of authority in the field, which may be valuable particularly when reproduction on television is improved and when color is introduced."[12] As this report suggests, MoMA saw television not simply as a venue for publicity or education, but as central to the maintenance of its own cultural power.

The museum's interest in television was part of its more long-term democratic mission, since the 1930s, to court the general public, especially women (a mission that had previously led to complaints by critics that the museum had "vulgarized" art).[13] During World War II, MoMA and the Metropolitan Museum of Art both gained respect by linking their institutions to the war effort. The same period witnessed a boom in art's popular appeal, which was inspired by the media's increased attention to art, government-sponsored campaigns like "Buy American Art Week," and the sale (through credit financing) of famous paintings at Macy's and Gimbles (two of New York City's largest middle-class department stores). In this context, museum patronage increased significantly; the number of art galleries in New York grew from 40 at the beginning of the war to 150 by 1946, and both public and private gallery sales skyrocketed.[14] These trends continued after the war. In 1962, the Stanford Research Institute estimated that "120 million people attend art-oriented events" and that "attendance at galleries and museums almost doubled during the 1950s." Tourism at MoMA was "only outnumbered by the Empire State Building."[15]

While museum officials welcomed and certainly promoted this surge in museum patronage, they nevertheless were nervous about the tastes and decorum of their new museum publics. Continuing with the historical ambivalence (or outright antagonism) between modern art movements and women (which has been discussed by scholars such as Christopher Reed, Griselda Pollack, and Andreas Huyssen),[16] this postwar boom in patronage at art museums left some museum officials anxious about what they perceived to be the unruly practices of their new female patrons. In 1961, an executive at New York's Metropolitan Museum of Art noted that the rise in museum-going had resulted in groups of "young mothers who don't understand why they can't wheel their baby coaches through the galleries." Met director James J. Rorimer further complained that the upsurge in museum attendance "presents us with very many problems," and he especially singled out women's spike heels as "my bête noire."[17] MoMA officials also thought that this tourist class of patrons was "a curious cat to skin."[18] Consequently, the museum studied their tastes and motives, and curators prepared exhibits with their interests in mind.[19]

In attempting to attract these wider publics, MoMA officials knew that their specialization in modern art posed special challenges. In the postwar period, modern art—with its links to Europe, communism, and internationalism—was often viewed with skepticism. At its most extreme, government officials (including congressmen and senators) saw modern art movements (especially abstract expressionism) as subversive to American values (or even communist) and they sought to stop the promotion of American modernism abroad.[20] More generally, popular media often poked fun at modern art's incomprehensibility and also often associated it with "subversive" foreign influences and un-American values. Television programs from sitcoms to documentaries often engaged in this populist rejection of modern art movements.[21]

At the same time, however, television and other popular media provided the public with opportunities to learn about the arts, and at times the media promoted a more positive interest, or at least curiosity, in modern art and abstraction. Striking here, for example, is a 1957 issue of TV Guide (at that point, already the leading national magazine for television). The front cover showed popular variety-show host Ed Sullivan and star Judy Taylor; the back cover displayed an abstract rendering with a short informational blurb about nonobjective art, which then dovetailed into a promotional advertisement for subscriptions to the magazine.[22] Thus, while some cultural venues and government officials represented modern art as a threat to America, or just plain "bad," this TV Guide issue is exemplary of a contradictory trend that was more accepting of modern art and even made it consistent with the values and goals of corporations.

In non-objective art, there is no attempt made
to interpret anything specific.
By using color, line, mass and texture,
ideas in pure design are created.
    Above is a perfect example—just as
TV GUIDE is a perfect example of creating
with a specific objective in mind—your
TV pleasure and convenience.
    Return the coupon inside, today,
to subscribe at really money-saving rates.

non-objective

TV's Ed Sullivan and non-objective art share the bill on this front and back cover of
TV *Guide.*

More broadly, as Serge Guilbaut argues, modern art and the American avant-garde were nourished by the postwar ethos of corporate liberalism, an ideology that he suggests embraced modern art (specifically, abstract expressionism) as an example of freedom of expression and individuality in American life.[23] To be sure, MoMA (under the auspices of Nelson Rockefeller, whose family founded MoMA and who dominated the museum's direction in the 1940s and 1950s) was centrally instrumental in the effort to embrace modernism. During the cold war, MoMA's international program championed the cause of modern art. According to Russell Lynes, MoMA's numerous activities abroad were directly political, intended as an antidote to the idea (widely held overseas) that America, while an economic superpower, was nevertheless a cultural wasteland.[24] Eva Cockroft has further detailed MoMA's efforts to spread American modern art abroad by showing how these efforts dovetailed with similar strategies by the USIA and CIA (which also wanted to promote American art in the name of freedom), and especially with Nelson Rockefeller's financial and political support.[25]

Outside of these directly political cold war initiatives, the idea that modern art represented freedom and individual expression permeated much of its promotion to ordinary citizens. In this regard, it is not surprising that the appetite for modern art was especially associated with youth and progressive lifestyles. In 1958, the *New York Times* reported that there was a growing demand for reproductions of "modern master-works" among young couples who were buying good-quality reproductions of European artists such as Braque, Picasso, Feinger, Roualt, and Mondrian.[26] So, too, modern art—especially modern design in furniture—was often promoted as the signature style for a progressive housewife. In 1949, a number of New York City art museums (including MoMA) collectively mounted a series of lectures called "Home Fashion Time" with speakers on everything from furniture to textiles, while the Detroit Institute of Arts mounted a show it called "For Modern Living."[27] Meanwhile, in 1952 MoMA began to allow museum members to borrow paintings, prints, and sculptures for their homes. Most of the borrowers were young people eager to try out modern abstractions and nonobjective art.[28] This trend continued through the 1960s as art and industry increasingly were wed. By 1966, the fibers division of the Allied Chemical Corporation sponsored a gallery exhibition billed as "color happenings," which exhibited psychedelic art for the home and showcased a housewife who, like a performance artist, used slide projectors to change her decor so that she might "change her home as often as she changes her dress."[29]

In all of these ways, museums made bridges between the world of art, everyday life, and consumerism, and modern art itself was increasingly promoted within a vernacular mode that spoke the language of "ordinary" people—particularly the housewife. For museum curators, television (as the ultimate bridge to both everyday life and acts of consumption) seemed an obvious tool for the development and promotion of the arts.

Within this context, MoMA pursued television with four related aims. First, it attempted to intervene in policy debates regarding the future of commercial and educational channels. Second, it attempted to create its own programs for commercial distribution (albeit within the confines of its nonprofit status as a public museum). Third, it tried to devise television production techniques that would maximize audience pleasure. And fourth, it attempted to establish a television archive consistent with its efforts in the film library. Funding for these ambitious aims came in 1952 when MoMA received a three-year grant from the Rockefeller Brothers Fund to study the museum's relationship to television. Conducted under the auspices of avant-garde filmmaker Sidney Peterson and MoMA consultant Douglas Macagy, the "Television Project," as it was called, became especially active in the area of in-house productions. Peterson spearheaded a series of what the museum called "experimental" telefilms and oversaw the museum production of various series on the arts. At a time when television's future was unclear, Peterson imagined the medium as an egalitarian art form, and he wrote a lengthy dissertation on its prospects—even likening the television image to the mannerist movement in painting. In addition to, and often at odds with, Peterson's more aesthete, if populist, vision, other participants in the Television Project also participated in the museum's more general interests in using television for education and publicity, interests that were taken up by the education, design, architecture, and painting departments. In fact, the only people who openly opposed television were the people in the Film Library, who were reputed to "hate TV"; but even they eventually were active in archival projects.[30] In all of these efforts, MoMA explored TV's role in teaching the public how to appreciate, consume, and look at art in the age of television.

Given these institutional ties, it seems especially curious that broadcast historians have generally ignored the connections between commercial TV and fine art.[31] In part, the reason for this is that our first major broadcast histories were written in the 1960s, at a moment when the reigning national discourse on television imagined commercial TV as art's opposite. I am referring, of course, to the Federal Communications Commission (FCC) and Chair Newton Minow's "Vast Wasteland" speech in 1961 that carved out a fundamental schism between commercial TV and the arts, a schism that focused debates on the medium throughout the decade.[32] Indeed, despite Minow's intentions (he sought to raise standards in the industry and embellish educational TV), the term "vast wasteland" came to have a life of its own, and even today the term is synonymous with an outright rejection of TV as the enemy of art. In this discursive context, broadcast historians (most notably Erik Barnouw) presented romantic tropes in which educators, journalists, and people in the arts assumed the part of disenfranchised heroes fighting the crass commercial industrialists.[33]

Yet, when we look at the historical record there is really no evidence that people in the arts a priori resisted commercialism, nor did they necessarily refuse to associate with popular cultural forms and practices. And why should they? Museums had previously accepted commercial sponsorship, and they were well acquainted with techniques of theatrical showmanship and department store display.[34] For example, MoMA had a long history in trafficking with New York City's commercial culture. In the 1930s, the museum built a patronage for European modernism through tie-ins with department stores.[35] From this point of view, television seemed more a logical extension of the shop window than the classroom.[36] The museum felt aptly suited to the medium because of its historical commitment to industrial design and the display of everyday objects. A report in the museum files boasts, "MoMA . . . can always put something on TV due to its policy of interpreting the field of art to include household things as well as paintings, etc."[37]

The early efforts of MoMA in television also challenge our present-day taste hierarchies and implicit cultural assumptions about the relative value of educational/public TV versus commercial channels. In fact, rather than embracing educational TV and public funding, notes in MoMA's files indicate that, with varying degrees of enthusiasm, museum officials had a clear preference for commercial broadcasting over educational channels, and museum officials even organized against state control of television in this regard. The museum saw a clear economic advantage to commercial broadcasting. While educational programs required considerable subsidies, commercial TV would allow the museum to operate on a "self-supporting basis."[38] Certainly, in the first four years of broadcasting, the FCC "freeze" on station allocation made the possibility of educational broadcast stations remote. But even when the FCC lifted the freeze and allocated 252 educational UHF channels, people in the arts were often more interested in commercial stations and network delivery than they were in the prospects of educational channels. This was certainly the case with MoMA. When the freeze ended in 1952, Chamberlain (who attended policy-related meetings) sent a memo to Museum Director Rene d'Harnoncourt, advising him that "the lifting of the freeze will make news. My feeling is that we should not release our TV plans in conjunction with this, or get tied up with it at any time, because we should not let it be thought that we are planning our programs just for the educational channels only."[39]

What MoMA resisted was not educational channels per se, but rather state-run educational television. Thus, although the museum did support educational television under the banner of a New York City station, it opposed the New York State Board of Regents's plan to build and control stations. Chamberlain kept vigilant notes on the meetings of the Board of Regents in which she spoke constantly of her antagonism toward their plans for educational stations—an antagonism that d'Harnoncourt apparently shared. In Chamberlain's view, state-run channels posed the threat of censorship or, at best, bureaucratic governance of art education. In particular, she focused on the inferior level and indoctrinating effects of art education in the school curriculum, noting that the state had not "always been progressive." Moreover, she noted that the Board of Regents did not further the goals of MoMA's Education Department and had not been "receptive to our school's teaching methods."[40] With their zeal to provide the public with their own brand of art education, MoMA officials also knew that educational channels would not provide the large audiences that commercial television promised.

Given all this, MoMA officials thought commercialism was the way to go. As one internal report of 1953 noted, we need "to discover the value of the institution as a commodity in the commercial field. Either we have such a value or we don't."[41] A few months later, Macagy wrote a self-congratulatory memo to d'Harnoncourt in which he spoke of a meeting with CBS that he had attended. In that memo he proudly claimed that MoMA was "in the position to talk the language of the network boys."[42] Clearly, the museum conceived of its educational function completely within the logic of commercial public relations.

THE HOUSEWIFE AND THE CONNOISSEUR

In seeking bridges with commercial broadcasters, the museum made assumptions about its audiences and their tastes. Although the MoMA archive for the Television Project contains almost no concrete information on ratings and demographics, internal memos and reports continually hypothesized about audiences and what they wanted. In his 1955 report, *The Museum Looks in on TV* (a book-length manuscript written for the Rockefeller Brothers Fund), Macagy saw the TV audience as a special challenge for the traditional museum. His first chapter, "The Connoisseur and the Viewer," detailed broad differences between the traditional aesthete of centuries past and the contemporary TV audience. While the art connoisseur is "contemplative," the television viewer is "distracted." If the connoisseur submerges himself in the artwork, the television viewer is "inattentive to the visual quality of the image" and instead responds to "movement and the story." While the connoisseur is "elite" and part of a minority culture, the television viewer "is less catholic" in his tastes. While the connoisseur is a solitary "gentleman," the TV viewer is a family (he spoke of the "suburban" setting) where women play a key role.[43] Calling television viewers "restless hermits," he argued that there was a "great difference between the person who goes to the trouble of visiting a museum and the one who may choose to go elsewhere without moving from his living room."[44]

If Macagy imagined the traditional art connoisseur as male and described (in clearly loaded terms) art's fate in the new suburban family context, Sydney Peterson had an even more explicitly gendered— and contrived—theory. In 1953, in a report written for the Rockefeller Brothers Fund, Peterson drew a sketch of the TV audience that portrayed the average viewer as both feminine (if not biologically, then at least in spirit) and divorced from city life. Borrowing sociologist David Riesman's famous characterization of suburbanites as "the lonely crowd," Peterson argued that the audience for TV art programs was the "lonelier crowd"—a group of atomized isolated viewers who lived in suburban exile.[45] In this psychological profile of the average member of this lonelier crowd, Peterson argued that programs on the arts misunderstand suburbanites because they assume the audience is the "monstrously simplified figure of . . . a housewife" who is "profoundly uninterested in learning." While he agreed that "men are not a significant audience for art programming," he attempted to come up with a less condescending attitude toward the viewer.[46]

In so doing, Peterson theorized, in a somewhat inexplicable move, that the audience for art programs was a "hermaphroditic family group with or without a child."[47] In describing this "androgynous adult" viewer, Peterson claimed that "the relative proportion of feminine to masculine attributes in the figure of the adult would be roughly two to one." To illustrate his position, he drew a picture of the housewife's brain. Outlined in pink crayon, the head was apparently feminine. Various regions of the brain were designated by different TV genres. In what looked like a coloring-book version of phrenology-style "brow" charts, Peterson put the masculine-defined genres of news and public issues at the top of the head while the female-oriented "domestic issues" were positioned at the low end of the neck. By and large, however, the housewife's brain was colonized by commercials that were scattered throughout.[48]

To be sure, Peterson and Macagy formulated their views about the family audience for art within the broader context of the era's fascination with "taste," in particular the association of taste with "vernacular" everyday arts and domesticity. This fascination was famously instigated by Russell Lynes's article "Highbrow, Middlebrow, Lowbrow." Originally published in *Harper's* in February 1949 and then popularized in *Life* (in summary form) in April of that year, the article argued that while tied to economic class and profession, taste had replaced class to become the new mode of social distinction in America. "The old structure of the upper class, the middle class, and the lower class is on the wane," Lynes argued. "It isn't wealth of family that makes prestige these days. It's high thinking."[49]

When *Life* presented its summary of Lynes's views, it included a two-page picture chart outlining the various taste levels.[50] The chart depicted everyday, vernacular objects. For example, while the highbrow coveted Eames chairs, the middlebrow liked Chippendales; while the highbrow wanted industrial objects like ashtrays from chemical supply companies, the lower middlebrows wanted his-and-hers towels; while highbrows went in for Calder, the lower middlebrows bought lawn ornaments; while the upper middlebrows sported quiet tweed jackets, the lowbrows wore old army clothes. In this way, the chart associated taste with the domestic and traditionally gendered objects of fashion and home decor. In fact, for Lynes, the mark of a true highbrow was that he had completely aestheticized everyday life. As he wrote, "it is this association of culture with every aspect of daily life, from the design of his razor to the shape of the bottle that holds his sleeping pills, that distinguishes the highbrow from the middlebrow or lowbrow."[51]

The sexually charged aspect of this highbrow fascination with the everyday was nowhere better stated than in Lynes's quotation of Edgar Wallace, who, when asked by a journalist, "What is a highbrow?" answered, "A highbrow is a man who has found something more interesting than women."[52] Here, as elsewhere, the gender of the highbrow was male, even while his tastes seemed to be in the traditionally feminine realm of domesticity. This contradiction went beyond the stereotypical association of taste for decor and fashion with "dandyism" or gay sensibilities and into a more unstable and contradictory set of cultural vexations around what exactly constituted masculine and feminine dispositions in relation to the modern "vernacular" arts of postwar culture.

This enigma of the gendered nature of taste—coupled with more traditional class-based concepts of "brow" sensibilities—haunted the directors of the Television Project as they searched for ways to appeal to broad publics while nevertheless maintaining their legitimacy among their own traditional highbrow "art" publics. On this, Peterson and Macagy took clearly different views. While Macagy spoke with what Lynes would have called a highbrow's disdain for both the middlebrow patron (the "weekend throngs") and TV's "restless hermits," Peterson hoped to use television for the cause of art, and in particular he sought ways to address housewives (or at least his hermaphodite viewer with a female brain) living in suburbia U.S.A.

Although Peterson's views were quirky, his basic assumptions about the female nature of the television audience also informed MoMA's more general attempts to promote modern art. A museum report stated that as early as 1948 MoMA had "participated in many daytime programs aimed primarily at housewives."[53] By speaking directly to housewives about homemaking concerns, the museum hoped to "educate" women about art's relevance to their daily lives. Yet, at the same time, given their views on the nontraditional, distracted, and feminized TV art publics out in the suburban hinterlands, both Peterson and Macagy deliberated on the most effective ways in which television should speak to these viewers, and in this regard they considered the kinds of programming formats and modes of narration that might keep audiences tuned to art programs.

In Macagy's clearly pessimistic view, the fate of art on television was compromised by at least three obstacles: the audience, the technology, and the commercial imperatives of the medium. In a somewhat theoretical treatise, Macagy speculated that TV viewers were averse to artistic contemplation. "Television's restless hermits," he argued, are "not content to meditate with the mind's eye."[54] Instead, he argued, they have a "practical outlook" toward art.[55] Although couched in clear disdain, Macagy's notion of the "practical outlook" seems somewhat of a precursor to Pierre Bourdieu's concept of the "popular aesthetic": the attitude toward art that expects it to have a useful function, an immediate application to everyday life.[56] In Macagy's view, the audience's practical orientation toward art was aggravated by the fact that the technological/reproductive quality of the TV image was so low that TV could never offer a true aesthetic experience. Moreover, commercial broadcasters fostered a "practical outlook" because, above all else, they wanted to turn aesthetic experiences into acts of shopping.[57]

In light of all this, Macagy felt that rather than think of television as a substitute for firsthand aesthetic experience, at best the museum could use television to fulfill its democratic responsibility to educate the public and lead them toward the virtues of art appreciation.[58] Nevertheless, just as they dismissed state-run educational channels, both Macagy and Peterson were particularly weary about what Macagy called "kindergarten classes of the air."[59] Macagy argued that while art critics should avoid conforming to broadcasting modes of personality and performance that are "embarrassing" to them, they nevertheless must leave their "museum manners" behind and find an appropriate way to perform their roles as experts for their new TV publics.[60] Peterson was especially adamant on this topic. He argued that the use of experts lecturing an audience was a "dangerous game." "The connoisseurship of the mass audience," he claimed, "has a very different basis from that of the expert."[61] Peterson felt the art program should organize itself around popular entertainment genres, showmanship, and participatory modes of address. As an example he noted that the "most successful cookbook of the day is the *Joy of Cooking* and probably the most popular approach to painting is one of joy through looking."[62]

To be sure, some of these communicative styles had already been played out on radio. As Paddy Scannell argues in his work on BBC radio, "the communicative task that broadcasters faced was to find forms of talk that spoke *to* listeners, modes of address which disclosed that listeners were taken into account in the form of the utterance itself." "What this came to down to," he suggests, "was that broadcasters discovered that existing forms of talk [the lecture, the sermon, the political speech] were inappropriate for the new medium of radio." Instead of rhetorical forms designed for publics constituted as crowds, the BBC devised more informal modes of address that spoke to "each listener as someone in particular" in a vernacular language and with subject matter to which this ordinary listener could relate.[63] In a similar way, MoMA had to find a new visual vernacular so that art might speak to individual viewers watching TV in their homes. In the process, museum officials discovered that existing modes of art education—the classroom lecture, the gallery tour, the slide show—did not interest the audiences to whom they now spoke.[64]

In their quest to find a popular format for art education, MoMA officials had examples to emulate. Among these was television's most popular artist, John Gnagy, a self-taught "doodler" from Pretty Prairie, Kansas, who started in television as early as 1946. By 1952 (when MoMA began the Television Project) Gnagy had gained a wide following for his fifteen-minute shoestring-budget show *Draw with Me.* In a 1952 interview with the *New York Times,* Gnagy admitted, "Let's not call my program art. . . . It's a fence-straddling combination of entertainment and education." The show featured Gnagy showing viewers step by step how to draw owls, flowers, and other such realistic subjects. According to the *New York Times,* "the only things [about the show] that could be called arty are the plaid shirt and the Vandyke beard. This, however, is considered to be part of the showmanship."[65]

On the face of it, Gnagy's program seemed to be exactly what the people at MoMA had in mind—entertaining showmanship that encouraged the viewer to learn via participation. But, in fact, the people at MoMA thought Gnagy a bane to art education. The same *New York Times* article cited a resolution adopted by the Committee on Art Education, a national group of twelve hundred educators chaired by Victor D'Amico, education director at MoMA. The resolution, which was mailed to WNBT (a station that aired *Draw with Me*) proclaimed: "Television programs of the John Gnagy type are destructive to the creative and mental growth of children and perpetuate outmoded and authoritarian concepts of education."[66] Thus, although MoMA officials sought to educate via entertainment, they nevertheless distanced themselves from the likes of the midwestern doodler. Once again, the problem was that MoMA had to perform its assumed role as a democratic cultural institution that engaged a broad public while still appeasing the aesthete and urbane dispositions of patrons and museum officials who had a considerable degree of antagonism toward popular modes of expression.

In order to balance these competing aims and publics, MoMA devised strategies by which to represent intellectuals in nonthreatening ways. As early as 1947 MoMA produced a film (in conjunction with Princeton University), titled *What Is Modern Art?*, which depicts an artist giving a lecture on modern art to a rather skeptical woman, who in many ways serves as a kind of relay with whom equally skeptical audiences might identify.[67] Peterson took this tactic and embellished it for television. In art programs, he argued, "the audience should be represented in the person of an innocent bystander able to ask questions which might embarrass the emcee, who has, after all, his personality, his public persona . . . to protect."[68] In other words, Peterson assumed that audiences would enjoy knocking the experts off their museum pedestals.

A good example of the host-humiliation technique came on October 16, 1954, when MoMA televised its twenty-fifth anniversary show. Hosted by d'Harnoncourt and the director of museum collections, Alfred Barr, the anniversary show appeared as an episode of the CBS public affairs program *Dimension*. It was broadcast live and used "liveness" in strategic ways. In the opening sequence d'Harnoncourt presents a Legér painting, whereupon he is joined on stage by a professor from NYU's art history department. When the professor decides to show Stuart Davis's abstract painting *The Flying Carpet*, he suddenly realizes the painting is not in the room. With a look of puzzled embarrassment, he asks the cameraman to move to another gallery space, where the painting hangs. But, unfortunately for the professor, more mayhem is in store. When the camera moves to the next gallery, it reveals a rather disheveled-looking TV floor manager hanging out in front of the painting, smoking a cigarette—so close to the canvas, in fact, that it appears he is going to burn a hole in it. When the floor manager realizes that he is on live TV, he runs out of the frame. The befuddled professor then tries to make the best out of a bad situation and calls the floor manager back, asking him whether he likes the painting. The floor manager replies, "Uh huh, it's nice, it's big," to which the professor remarks, "You can tell us what you really think. Because if you don't like it, you won't be the first person who didn't respond favorably to modern art."[69]

If you haven't already guessed, this entire broadcast—mistakes and all—was scripted from the start. The floor manager is an actor. The shot of the floor manager running from the frame is listed as an "accident shot." The stage directions read: "Camera is seemingly bumped and viewer now sees part of the 'Flying Carpet' and Floor Manager, well to the left, [is] perplexed." After the "accident shot," the professor is supposed to "laugh" and then call the floor manager back to the scene, reminding him (and, of course, viewers) that "this is a very casual program."[70] The script is based on the assumption that the viewing audience did not like to be lectured by intellectuals, and as one report stated, the show ideally would give viewers the sense that the "audience [was] eavesdropping on the conversation."[71] The program also anticipated what MoMA officials more generally assumed about the television audience's disposition toward modern art, as well as toward professors. The floor manager character takes the role of the skeptic, airing the then widespread populist distrust of modern art. Meanwhile, the professor is knocked down a few pegs because he has made such a terrible mess of things on live TV. Thus, the seemingly earnest dialogue between the professor and the floor manager is nothing other than a staged act, more like a vaudeville routine than a classroom lecture. (Perhaps not coincidentally, Peterson later recommended that the art program's emcee should "be able to play straight man to the other straight men.")[72]

Insofar as Peterson and other officials at MoMA especially targeted the housewife, they used similar scenarios of staged spontaneity in art programs aimed specifically at women. Moreover, rather than simply simulate casual talk (as in Scannell's radio examples) MoMA officials tried to simulate "girl talk." In these programs the housewife trumped the expert, becoming a kind of everyday critic whose homemaking experience and feminine nature gave her a kind of arty "horse" sense that the educated (mostly male) experts lacked.

The television publicity surrounding MoMA's "Good Design" exhibit is a perfect case in point. A 1953 museum proposal called for thirteen half-hour programs directed by Edgar Kaufmann Jr., director of Good Design at MoMA. The budget submitted by the production company contracted to make the films stated that "the films are to stimulate, as far as possible, the intimacy and spontaneity of a 'live' TV show."[73] Kaufmann's treatment for the series sheds further light on the way this sense of intimacy and spontaneity were used to simulate casual conversation among the hosts and female audiences at home. According to the treatment, the "introduction" to the series would be filmed at MoMA and would present the selection committee (composed of artists, designers, and museum experts) "sitting on a lounge with six superb objects." Just after this, the "female influence [would be] brought in" by a character who was a "homey type."[74] This attempt to create a sense of dialogue between the expert and the housewife was key to the rhetoric of MoMA's TV efforts.

Although the films for the show never materialized, the "Good Design" exhibit was publicized in 1954 on a two-week series of live spots that appeared on Margaret Arlen's CBS morning show. The show was "addressed to [the] morning housewife audience."[75] Once again, the spots were scripted, even while they had the feel of spontaneous conversation. The proposal for the morning spots called for a "cast" that included a "bright housewife (amateur?)" character who would ask Kaufmann questions.[76] Like the floor manager in the twenty-fifth anniversary show, this character was probably intended as a stand-in for the naive viewer. But unlike the rather déclassé floor manager—and as the parenthetical "amateur?" phrasing indicates—she was probably designed to flatter the audience by being a little more art-wise than the average housewife. When they went to air, the "Good Design" spots used a more pared-down interview format with Kaufmann, Arlen, and a "guest" designer, but they retained their homey appeal. The script for the March 17, 1954, broadcast text called for a "living room type set" where Kaufmann appeared as Arlen's guest. It was probably no accident that the program (and others like it) included women designers. The "Good Design" spots further encouraged viewer identification and participation by informing the audience that the objects on display were, as Arlen pointed out, "available to everybody—at every price."[77]

In programs like this, MoMA's weekly ventures on morning and daytime TV were part of a more general set of cultural strategies that linked fine art with homemaking practices. As discussed earlier, these strategies were common to museum and gallery exhibitions on modern design, but they also resonated across popular magazines, newspaper articles, and books on interior decor.[78] So, too, network television shows (both fiction and documentary) typically represented art as a specifically female concern, associating art with middle-class domesticity, shopping, and the everyday life of the white middle-class homemaker.[79]

For instance, in a 1953 episode of *Omnibus* featuring Thomas Hart Benton, host Alistair Cooke visits the artist's home where viewers not only see Benton's paintings but also share in a night of poetry recitals and music performed live by the entire Benton family. Similarly, a 1959 episode of Edward R. Murrow's *Person to Person* goes "live" to the home of Norman Rockwell, where viewers meet the artist's wife, children, and little dog Lolita. Addressing Mrs. Rockwell, Murrow asks, "You must have quite a decorating problem. Do you keep many of Norman's original paintings on the wall?" Such visits to the artists' homes thus provided viewers with a sense of "dropping in," not only on the artists and their families, but also on the artwork itself. Like the "eavesdropping" theme in the anniversary show, this was a nondidactic form of documentary; any lessons learned about art seemed more coincidental than planned. In fact, by the early 1960s, the nondidactic imperative led to the presence of women art connoisseurs and critics turned "fem-cees." Aline Saarinen of NBC was the first art critic to be hired for regular appearances on a network daytime program (she appeared in short segments of *Today*). Like the people at MoMA, she also understood that intellectuals did not go over well on television and instead called herself an "entertainer" rather than a "stuffy" critic.[80]

In 1962, this association of women, domesticity, and the arts reached the status of media event when CBS *Reports* aired "A Tour of the White House with Mrs. John F. Kennedy." Under attack for spending national taxes on the frivolous goal of redecoration, the Kennedys welcomed TV audiences into their home in order to convince the nation that Jackie's pursuit of antique decor (much of which came from Europe) was a patriotic attempt to restore American heritage to the White House. The live-on-tape program used Jackie's female narration to teach the nation about the importance of visual design—not just for private pleasure but for public service. With one out of every three homes tuned to the program, the *Tour* (which aired simultaneously on CBS and NBC) was viewed as a huge popular success.[81] The critics doted on Jackie's performance (especially her "ease" and "warmth" in front of live TV cameras) as much as they spoke of the art and antiques she presented. As the nation's premiere housewife, Jackie turned out to be the ideal art "expert"—the darling of the critics and a great TV personality.[82] Not surprisingly, when Lady Bird Johnson took over as first lady, she too starred in a TV art show. The program, titled "Paintings in the White House: A Close-Up," was a history of the White House as shown through forty-seven paintings on display there.[83]

If these White House art tours mostly served the goals of the Kennedy and Johnson administrations, the networks had their own reason for exploiting the arts. At a time when the industry was trying to convince the public to purchase color receivers, paintings had a new use-value. As early as 1950, the networks used both MoMA and the Metropolitan Museum of Art to test their color systems. Broadcast in 1954, NBC's first nationwide color-compatible show was titled "A Visit to the Metropolitan Museum of Art."[84] Later, in the 1960s, under the auspices of its "In Living Color" campaign, NBC aired documentaries on national art museums, including the Louvre and the Kremlin. Still other color broadcasts relied on entertainment genres, an appeal to women, and a sense of live showmanship.

The 1967 program *Color Me Barbra* is perhaps the most extreme example in this regard. "Act I" is set in the Philadelphia Museum of Art, where

Barbra Streisand takes the role of a French chambermaid who cleans the museum at night. As she stops to contemplate the artwork, the paintings come to life, and Barbra (seemingly a victim of Stendahl Syndrome) projects herself into the canvas. For example, when she arrives in a gallery full of abstract art, she sheds her black-and-white French maid outfit and reappears in a colorful halter gown that mimics the abstract patterns in the paintings. Dressed as a canvas, she then performs a modern dance routine. In another sequence, Barbra takes a more somber tone. After looking a little too long at a Modigliani painting, she becomes the girl in the picture and enters a set made to look like a Parisian café, where she drinks a glass of wine and belts out the French lyrics to "Non, C'est Rien." Obviously recalling the famous "painting come to life" sequence in the 1951 film *An American in Paris,* the program served as a not-too-subtle ad for color TV. While set in the staid space of an art museum, the "art into life" conceit not only provided a stage for colorful performance but also a reason for constant costume changes. In effect, the program doubled as a fashion show in which paintings and haute couture shared the stage.

Interestingly, as well, given MoMA's and the networks' early attempts to use the popular vernacular to appeal to audiences, "Act II" of *Color Me Barbra* is set in a circus. In other words, just in case the museum's largely European collection was a "turnoff" for the nonart crowd, the producers provided a true form of Americana. In fact, the program is quite self-reflexive about this. In the opening part of the circus segment Barbra greets the audience in French, and English subtitles appear on the screen. However, her "Frenchness" turns out to be a vaudeville gag as she breaks out of French to return to her Jewish American persona. Then, as she switches back to English, the subtitles turn to French. The circus act, then, neatly undoes all the pretensions of her previous visit with European art. As a whole, *Color Me Barbra* is a perfect example of both the museum's and the network's aim to present art through vernacular genres, a sense of live performance, and a special appeal to the female viewer.

FROM PROP HOUSE TO FLOP HOUSE

By the time *Color Me Barbra* made its way into American living rooms, art (like everything else on TV) had become a network-controlled affair. In fact, MoMA ended its entrepreneurial efforts in the mid-1950s, leaving behind barely a trace of its once grand designs for in-house productions. Indeed, despite MoMA's early interest in television, the new medium posed obstacles to the museum's traditional function as a bastion of

Color Me Barbra. Barbra's dress matches the paintings as she sings and dances in the Philadelphia Museum of Art.

Museum officials worried about theft when loaning artworks to broadcasters. Here, armed guards stand watch over the Cellini Cup as it appears on TV. Illustration in Macagy, *The Museum Looks in on TV*, 1955.

modern art. While MoMA (and other museums) often complained of practical problems (such as television's inferior reproduction techniques or the fear that artworks would be damaged or even stolen by production crews), these were considered stumbling blocks that might be overcome. But the one problem that seemed insurmountable was, ironically, the very thing that the Television Project was designed to master: commercialism. Despite MoMA's rigorous efforts to establish links with the industry, the commercialism of the medium and the widely held prejudices about its audiences made people at the museum nervous.

As early as 1948, officials at MoMA spoke of the need to counteract the "tendency [in the industry] to relate the museum or the works of art . . . with the advertised product," and they also refused to appear in programs that "seemed totally undignified" or "ridiculed" art in some way.[85] A good example came in 1951, when d'Harnoncourt received a letter from CBS executive Fred Rickey asking him to lend Picasso's *Girl before a Mirror* for a local afternoon program that would test the network's color TV system. The color broadcast would feature popular TV entertainers Arthur Godfrey, Ed Sullivan, and Faye Emerson as well as more high-art fare. (The Metropolitan Museum of Art had already loaned Renoir's *By the Seashore* to CBS.)[86] Apparently d'Harnoncourt found the request of great importance because he turned the letter over to Alfred Barr (who, as director of museum collections, typically was not involved in issues of TV publicity). Barr agreed to loan the painting with strict provisions. First, he stipulated that because Faye Emerson was "not herself well informed about pictures" the museum would require her to consult with a representative from MoMA. Second, Barr insisted that the artwork should "not appear in the same image with the advertising material, which I believe is a Pepsi-Cola bottle, and that there would be no direct connection made between the museum's loans and the advertising commercial."[87]

The tensions expressed in this incident permeated the entire atmosphere of MoMA's Television Project in the next three years. The most serious problems arose around the production of the in-house experimental programs. While MoMA's education department enjoyed both popular and critical success with its 1952 children's series titled *Through the Enchanted Gate,* the series that Peterson produced with the Rockefeller monies led to heated disputes. More hopeful than Macagy about television's possibilities for the museum, Peterson thought that television had much in common with painting, and he hoped that these commonalities might be used strategically to bridge the art world with consumer culture.[88]

Peterson's first venture was an animated children's series he called *They Became Artists*. Above all, it was an attempt to explore the marketability factor. To produce the series, Peterson orchestrated a four-way deal between the museum, NBC, the artist Marc Chagall, and United Productions of America (UPA)—an independent Hollywood animation company that produced, among other things, the cartoon *Mr. MaGoo*. However, legal complications with Marc Chagall and the difficulties of coordinating agreements among the numerous parties involved doomed this project to failure. Although a film about artist Raoul Dufy was completed, in the end, as one report put it, "the museum directors felt that it did not further the cause of modern art, and though Dufy transparencies were used they could not see that there was enough art in it to warrant giving it a museum label."[89] Consequently, the museum returned the film to UPA and stipulated that MoMA's name never be used in connection with it. Despite the fact that NBC offered to continue with the UPA series (as well as to collaborate on two other museum projects), MoMA declined the offer.[90]

The second project, a series of telefilms titled *Point of View*, was similarly disappointing. Conceived as a series of fifty-two or more programs, each fifteen minutes in length, the programs were to be "filmed for either network broadcast or syndication."[91] Although commercial in nature, the series experimented with the expressive aspects of the medium in ways Peterson thought would combine aesthete sensibilities with television's popular vernacular and commercial logic. The basic goal of the *Point of View* series was to "present the city itself as a work of art" (and in this regard, the series echoed previous documentary/avant-garde city films). In addition, it was designed "to cope with the problem of using TV, as in effect, an additional gallery . . . with the programming requirements of the commercial medium."[92] In 1955, the project was further described as an attempt to use André Malraux's dream of a "'museum without walls' . . . in the interest of getting closer to a hypothetical TV audience."[93] As these descriptions suggest, Peterson seems to have assumed that because commercial television privileged a sense of liveness and focused on everyday subjects it was fundamentally hospitable to his (and his colleagues) wish to make the public see the "spirit of art" in the objects of everyday life. He thought he could create experimental documentaries that would run on commercial stations while also fulfilling the museum's aesthetic disposition. By trying to bridge the two domains, Peterson wound up pleasing no one.

The seven-minute pilot, "Architectural Millinery," was "a study of hats and roofs in New York and elsewhere."[94] The film made visual comparisons between skyscrapers and headgear, forcing the spectator to see the city from an aerial perspective. Museum staff and directors regarded

A still from a television commercial crafted by MoMA's one-time production partner, the animation company United Productions of America. The still was reprinted in Macagy's *The Museum Looks in on TV*.

it as a failure, but its basic goals were considered promising and Peterson resumed production on the series. The second film in the series, "Manhole Covers," took the opposite point of view, picturing New York City from the underground perspective of the sewers.[95] The film opens on a shot of MoMA's exterior, after which it cuts to a camera that emerges out of a manhole. The narrator tells us, "And there is another museum, which is the city of New York itself."[96] In many ways, the film reads as an experiment with form, using exaggerated camera angles and montage to produce something of the "shifting planes of reality" that Peterson thought mannerist painting and television had in common. But, despite his interest in formal experimentation, Peterson was hoping to achieve popular appeal by taking a "light and witty approach to the props of everyday life."[97] Attempting to "arrive at a kink of commentary somewhat less didactic than is the case with the usual documentary," he used the radio and TV comic Henry Morgan as the narrator.[98] In addition, he intercut the film with silent footage from Charlie Chaplin shorts and the *Pumpkin Race,* and added ragtime piano music on the soundtrack.

Peterson's divided sensibility was immediately rejected by the museum. An internal museum report on the *Point of View* series states: "The series brings up for the nine millionth time the question of the audience. Whom are we trying to attract? . . . The great majority of people who come to the museum can be figured to have a reasonable amount of education. The audience cannot be supposed to have the same."[99] But, it was not just that the museum thought the films were too "difficult" for the TV crowd. Instead, MoMA officials seem also to have feared for their own reputation. According to the report: "The Museum . . . seemed to feel . . . that by affixing its signature to either of the films the Museum would be thought to be endorsing the architecture of the buildings or lowering its intellectual level by inducing people to look at manholes."[100] In March 1955, MoMA sold the films to the Mavro Television Company with the proviso that the company "agrees to make no reference to, nor use the name of the Museum of Modern Art in the films themselves, nor in any advertising, selling, or promotion of these films nor in any other manner whatsoever."[101]

While it is obvious that Peterson seems to have been somewhat misguided, or at least out of touch with the tastes of MoMA's directors, the situation more generally highlights the complex tensions that existed between the museum's commercial goals and its desire to maintain cultural legitimacy. As Peterson himself admitted, "Every time a museum of art appears on the air . . . it takes its prestige with it. Its neck is out.[102] The case also suggests that while both commercial TV and the art world wanted to make art more relevant to life, art and commerce still distinguished themselves in important ways. The liveness of TV and the industry's focus on everyday domesticity was simply not the same as the art world's desire to make patrons understand the relevance of modern art in their lives. While at times the two institutions cooperated in mutual relations of support, at other times the goals of the art museum and those of the television industry were completely different in nature. At still other times, the two institutions feared that such collaborations would weaken their legitimacy within their respective cultural fields. As Pierre Bourdieu has taught us, the journey from one cultural field to another can sometimes result in a loss of prestige and power for the person who dares to cross the line.[103]

ART LESSONS

The museum's short-lived romance with television, along with its fears about its own cultural devaluation, attest to the difficulties that traditional institutions of culture had when attempting to adjust to the demands of television. While the museum initially saw itself as part of a TV avant-garde, it eventually threw in the towel and accepted a more backstage role. Macagy's 1955 report declared that MoMA had shut down in-house production indefinitely.

To be sure, it was not just that MoMA shied away from television. As network production moved from New York to Hollywood and as the major Hollywood film studios solidified contracts with the networks, MoMA's chances to compete in the commercial arena were fading fast. Macagy's 1955 report admitted that art programs were typically sustaining unsponsored programs that lost money for commercial broadcasters. The ratings were characteristically low.[104] Television remained an inferior means of reproduction and, like Macagy, many felt that it did not promote an aesthete sensibility in the observer. In addition, as the museum fully realized the legal difficulties involving copyright and the privacy of artists (problems that Peterson specifically addressed in an appendix to Macagy's 1955 report), the prospects for the Television Project seemed dim.

But even while MoMA did not come out the victor, its early participation in television provides clues about the broader historical relationships between modern art and commercial media culture in postwar America. First, as the evidence here suggests, the "postmodern" blurring of high and low was not simply achieved through some general postwar condition of late capitalist production that was then expressed in cultural styles. Too often, I would argue, discussions of postmodern visuality lose all sense of historical agency and events that might explain the circumstances under which high and low came into cultural contact. At least in this case, the evidence suggests that any mergers that took place were part of concrete historical struggles. The art world maintained its distinction from the world of commercial television, even as it momentarily merged with the industry in vested interests. In fact, the maintenance of this distinction in the face of a booming media culture was one of MoMA's central concerns.

Beyond this, however, this case also raises questions about the ways in which the visual arts themselves changed in relationship to new forms of expression on television. Television's kinetic liveness and participatory modes of audience address dovetailed with movements in the art world including action painting, performance art, and happenings—all of which variously foregrounded liveness, intimacy, and participation. So, too, TV's presentation of amateur art and its address to housewives as amateur designers dovetailed with the art world's increasing problematization of the relationship between amateurism and professionalism. Its presentation of domesticity and commercial imagery is consistent with Pop art's and assemblage art's fascination with household products and industrial production (and, of course, these artists used television as subject matter in their work).[105] Finally, although in complex ways, its address to women is in sync with women's own increased participation in the art world. While I am certainly not suggesting a direct causal relationship between television and postwar art movements, it does seem important to consider how television's ways of looking at art—especially its use of liveness, participatory modes of address, and vernacular women's genres—might be related to changes in the public perception of art, the artist's own perception of her or his craft, and the physical spaces of gallery display.

After 1955, MoMA was less interested in using television as an electronic extension of the gallery than it was in collecting television as an art object in and of itself. In 1962, one year after Minow's "Vast Wasteland" speech, MoMA's Film Library (now apparently over its disdain for TV) held a "retrospective" of "Golden Age" programs it called "Television U.S.A.: 13 Seasons."[106] Given the museum's "live from New York" bias, it is perhaps no surprise that most of the programs chosen for the exhibit were New York-productions of live anthology dramas, live variety shows, news and documentary series, fine art performances, and other programs on the arts. *Gunsmoke* was the only Hollywood series included in the show.

The program book for "Television U.S.A." suggests some of the fundamental ambivalence MoMA officials had toward commercial television by this point. The book stated that television was divided into "two camps": the industry that is concerned with money and "artists and journalists whose standard of 'success' is the degree to which television realized its potentialities as an art form."[107] Given this statement, it is most paradoxical that "Television U.S.A." also included commercials in the exhibit. In fact, the program book also stated, "Almost everything has been tried to create original commercials. As a result, radical avant-garde experiments which would be frowned upon in other areas of television are encouraged in this field."[108] Consequently, "Television U.S.A." exhibited everything from Brewer's beer to Rival dog food ads as proof of television's potential avant-garde status. Five years after the retrospective, in 1967, MoMA opened its television archive. But the museum's attempts to save TV as art also quickly vanished.[109]

Instead, by the early 1970s MoMA embraced the emerging world of video art, engaging a more narrowly defined "art" public and leaving behind its dream to reach large audiences with commercial TV. Moreover, in 1972, when MoMA held its famous "Open Circuits" conference on the future of television and video, video was established as art (with a capital "A") largely through assertions of its difference not just from television's commercialism, but also from television's domestic, everyday, feminine status. Indeed, MoMA's embrace of video art degraded television by aligning it with femininity and the home. In his essay for the book that came out of the conference, Gregory Battcock spoke of early television as part of the "mother form" of architecture. Noting new developments in both portable cameras and video aesthetics, he stated: "By moving the television set away from the wall one moved it away from its mother." And this move away from the mother ushers in an "era of visual video communication of importance equal to that of the sculptural communication begun in ancient Greece."[110]

It is no small irony that this trivialization and feminization of television should take place at MoMA, a museum that had previously attempted with great rigor to further the cause of modern art by courting the commercial television audience, especially the housewife. Indeed, as the case of the Television Project shows, the great divide between television and art was in no way inevitable nor conceived as such from the start. If we now widely regard TV as art's opposite, this isn't a natural conclusion nor is it based solely on social distinctions of "taste."[111] Instead, these commonsense taste distinctions are also the product of concrete historical struggles among institutions and industries that fought for power over visual culture and its publics. As television enabled more people to see painting in new ways, MoMA officials tried to form links with commercial broadcasters and networks. By pursuing this commercial path, they hoped to bypass the demands and biases of the state-run education system. They also attempted to appeal to families, especially housewives, by presenting art in entertaining "women's" genres. Despite MoMA's failures, the Television Project demonstrates that there were significant links between the private sphere of suburban domesticity and the public/ urbane world of art. To think of these worlds as binary opposites is in fact to misunderstand the cultural logic of late capitalism. Indeed, for cultural critics, this case suggests a need to reconceptualize the historical relations among entertainment and education, domesticity and public culture, femininity and modernism, and television and art.

NOTES

This essay is based on my "Live from New York: Television at the Museum of Modern Art, 1948–1955," which appears in the conference proceedings for the University of

Stockholm journal *Aura* 6.1 (spring 2000): pp. 1–23. My thanks to Michelle Elligott and Charles Silver at the Museum of Modern Art and to Jeffrey Sconce for his editorial suggestions.

1. Alan Wallach, "The Museum of Modern Art: The Past's Future," in *Art in Modern Culture: An Anthology of Critical Texts,* ed. Francis Frascina and Jonathan Harris (New York: Harper Collins, 1992), pp. 282–91. Note, as well, this was the same year RCA debuted its commercial television system at the New York World's Fair.

2. Betty Chamberlain, draft of letter to Federal Communications Commission, ca. 1951, Series III. Box 19: Folder 12.d., Museum of Modern Art Library, New York, New York (hereafter referred to as MoMA Library).

3. As I discuss further on, MoMA had since the 1930s tried to woo the general public—especially women—and in this endeavor the museum was at times ridiculed for making art vulgar.

4. Christopher Reed further argues that the "domestic . . . remains throughout the course of modernism a crucial site of anxiety and subversion." See Reed, ed., *Not at Home: The Supression of Domesticity in Modern Art and Architecture* (London: Thames and Hudson, 1996), pp. 7 and 15–16. For other books on modern art/design, women, and domesticity, see Cecile Whiting, *A Taste for Pop: Pop Art, Gender, and Consumer Culture* (Cambridge: Cambridge University Press, 1997); Penny Sparke, *As Long as It's Pink: The Sexual Politics of Taste* (London: Pandora, 1995); and Lucy R. Lippard, *The Pink Glass Swan: Selected Feminist Essays on Art* (New York: New Press, 1995).

5. These included museums in Buffalo, Los Angeles, Milwaukee, Manhattan, St. Louis, San Francisco, Seattle, Dallas, Minneapolis, Detroit, Chicago, and Toledo. In 1954, the Museum of Fine Arts in Boston wired its building to televise programs (on station WGBH) from all exhibition floors. See Walter Muir Whitehill, *Museum of Fine Arts, Boston: A Centennial History* (Cambridge: Harvard University Press, 1970), pp. 614–15.

6. Tom Braden, letter to Nelson A. Rockefeller, June 29, 1948, Series III. Box 18: Folder 3, MoMA Library. Braden was secretary at MoMA at this time as well as chair of the TV committee of the Museum Council.

7. Allon Schoenor, "Television, an Important New Instrument of Mass Education for Museums" (speech presented at "The Role of Museums in Education," seminar at the United Nations Educational, Scientific, and Cultural Organization, September 27, 1952, Brooklyn, New York), p. 1. A transcription of the speech is in the NBC Records, Papers of Davidson Taylor, Box 278: Folder 10, Wisconsin Center Historical Archives, State Historical Society, Madison (hereafter referred to as Wisconsin Center Historical Archives).

8. The bulk of programming consisted of "a few photos, particularly views of the Museum, of the garden with people eating in it, of the movie hall. These are used in programs about what to do on the weekend if it rains and if it doesn't and you have to stay in the city" (Betty Chamberlain, letter to Miss Ethel Hoffman, July 30, 1948, Series III. Box 19: Folder 12.d., MoMA Library).

9. Untitled report, n.d., Series III. Box 19: Folder 12.d., MoMA Library.

10. Betty Chamberlain, letter to Miss Ethel Hoffman, July 30, 1948, Series III. Box 19: Folder 12.d, MoMA Library.

11. William S. Paley, cited in Douglas Macagy, *The Museum Looks in on TV*, 1955, p. 196, Series III. Box 14, MoMA Library.

12. *The Museum and Television,* May 1949, p. 2, Series III. Box 19: Folder 12.d., MoMA Library.

13. See Russell Lynes, *Good Old Modern: An Intimate Portrait of the Museum of Modern Art* (New York: Scribner, 1973), p. 233; and Amy Marver, "Introduction," in "New York Eyeline," Ph.D. diss., University of California—Irvine, 2001.

14. Serge Guilbaut, *How New York Stole the Idea of Modern Art: Abstract Expressionism, Freedom, and the Cold War,* trans. Λ. Goldhammer (Chicago: University of Chicago Press, 1983), p. 91.

15. Stanford Research Institute, Report from Long Range Planning Service, 1962, p. 2, White House Staff Files, 1962–63, John Fitzgerald Kennedy Library, Boston, Massachusetts.

16. Reed, *Not at Home;* Griselda Pollack, "Modernity and the Spaces of Femininity," in Frascina and Harris, eds., *Art in Modern Culture,* pp. 121–35 (Pollock's essay begins by considering the antagonism to femininity in the context of MoMA's "great man" historical canon); Andreas Huyssen, *After the Great Divide: Modernism, Mass Culture, and Postmodernism* (Bloomington: Indiana University Press, 1986).

17. Both citations are in McCandlish Phillips, "Attendance Sours at Museums Here," *New York Times,* November 27, 1961, sec. 1, p. 3.

18. This phrase was used by Douglas Macagy (who, as described in the text, was the consultant for MoMA's TV Project); see his *The Museum Looks in on TV*, p. 6.

19. For example, a 1952 study of museum attendance at MoMA showed that "only 40.3 percent of the total people attending from March 31 through April 22 entered the galleries without also patronizing its movies and/or restaurant" (Macagy, *The Museum Looks in on TV*, p. 6).

20. For example, Representative George A. Dondero of Michigan regularly denounced abstract art and "brainwashed artists in the uniform of the Red art brigade" (cited in Eva Cockcroft, "Abstract Expression, Weapon of the Cold War," in *Pollack and After: The Critical Debate,* ed. Francis Frascina [New York: Harper and Row, 1985], p. 130). For more on the responses to and popularization of art and modern art in particular, see Gilbaut, *How New York Stole the Idea of Modern Art;* Karal Ann Marling, *As Seen on TV: The Visual Culture of Everyday Life in the 1950s* (Cambridge: Harvard University Press, 1994), chapter 2; and Michael Kammen, *American Culture, American Tastes: Social Change and the Twentieth Century* (New York: Knopf, 1999).

21. See my "High Culture in Low Places: Television and Modern Art, 1950–1970," in *Disciplinarity and Dissent in Cultural Studies,* ed. Carey Nelson and Dilip Parameshwar Gaonkar (New York: Routledge, 1996), pp. 313–46. See also my forthcoming *High and Low TV: Modern Art and Commercial Television in Postwar America* (Chicago: University of Chicago Press); and Gilbault, *How New York Stole the Idea of Modern Art,* chapter 2. Guilbaut discusses how mass media such as radio and magazines popularized ideas about modern art in the 1940s. For more discussion of debates about modern art on network news programs, see Naomi Sawelson-Gorse, "Sound Bites and

Spin Doctors," in *The New Frontier: Art and Television, 1960–1965,* museum catalog, curated by John Alan Farmer (Austin: Austin Museum of Art, 2000), pp. 69–87.

22. *TV Guide,* February 4–10, 1957. The back cover stated, "In non-objective art, there is no attempt made to interpret anything specific. By using color, line, mass and texture, ideas in pure design are created. Above [a reproduction of non-objective painting] is a perfect example—just as *TV Guide* is a perfect example of creating with a specific objective in mind—your TV pleasure and convenience. Return the coupon inside, today, to subscribe at really money saving rates."

23. Guilbaut, *How New York Stole the Idea of Modern Art.*

24. Lynes, *Good Old Modern,* p. 233.

25. In the interest of his international and particularly Latin American investments, Rockefeller expanded MoMA's international program and reconstituted it as the International Council of MoMA in 1956. Cockcroft, "Abstract Expression," pp. 125–33.

26. Dore Asiton, "From Chromos to Masterpieces," *New York Times,* March 30, 1958, sec. 2, p. 3.

27. Edward J. Wormley, "The Year in Design," *New York Times,* September 25, 1949, sec. 20, p. 3. MoMA's 1949 show was titled "Modern Art in Your Life." See *The Museum of Modern Art Bulletin* 17:1 (1949). It included Magritte's painting *The False Mirror* (1928), on which CBS's original "eye" logo was based (p. 36).

28. Betty Pepis, "Art in the Home," *New York Times,* September 20, 1953, sec. 6, pp. 52–53.

29. Judy Klemesrud, "Instant Redecorating (If a Fuse Doesn't Blow)," *New York Times,* November 5, 1966, p. 24.

30. Betty Chamberlain claimed that "Dick Griffith [curator of the Film Library] says the film people, much as they hate TV, could not possibly raise any serious objection to our operating such a TV department as long as it is not the same department as the film library" (Chamberlain memo to Rene d'Harnoncourt, April 11, 1952, Series III. Box 18: Folder 3, MoMA Library). However, by 1954 the Film Library did cooperate with a producer at NBC because the network put film librarian Iris Barry on the "NBC payroll as official agent and coordinator in Europe" (Richard Griffith, memo to the Coordinating Committee, October 22, 1954, Series III: Box 18: Folder 7, MoMA Library).

31. In the United States, scholars have devoted some attention to performance arts such as ballet, the symphony, and theater. See, for example, Brian G. Rose, *Television and the Performing Arts: A Handbook and Reference Guide to American Cultural Programming* (New York: Greenwood Press, 1986). In the British context, John Walker has considered the translation of fine art to television. See his *Arts TV: A History of Arts Television in Britain* (London: Arts Council of Great Britain: 1993). There have also been several museum exhibitions on the relation between television and visual art. For example, in 1986 the Queens Museum in New York mounted "Television's Impact on Contemporary Art," and in 2000, the Austin Museum of Fine Art mounted "The New Frontier: Art and Television, 1960–1965."

32. Newton N. Minow, "The Vast Wasteland," address to the Thirty-Ninth Annual Convention of the National Association of Broadcasters, Washington, D.C., May 9, 1961.

33. In the Barnouw model, industry workers like NBC's Sylvester "Pat" Weaver and CBS journalist Edward R. Murrow are presented as exceptions to the rule. While these people often did act with great courage against commercial trends, such "exceptionalist" histories fail to explore the larger cultural conditions under which their actions were possible. As opposed to this model, by looking more broadly at the relationships between the networks and traditional institutions of the arts, we can see that such people operated in a cultural field where the arts and television were not diametrically opposed. In addition, we can see that their actions were generated not in spite of but rather because of the relationships among different cultural institutions. See Erik Barnouw, *Tube of Plenty: The Evolution of American Television* (New York: Oxford University Press, 1975). Note that this book was a condensed version of Barnouw's three-volume *History of Broadcasting in the United States* (New York: Oxford 1966, 1968, 1970), which he wrote over the course of the 1960s.

34. Numerous scholars have demonstrated the historical links between modern art and commerce, and some have specifically detailed these links in relation to museums. See, for example, Neil Harris, *Cultural Excursions: Marketing Appetites and Cultural Tastes in Modern America* (Chicago: University of Chicago Press, 1990); T. J. Jackson Lears, *Fables of Abundance: A Cultural History of Advertising in America* (New York: Basic Books, 1994); Andreas Huyssen, "Escape from Amnesia: The Museum as Mass Medium," in *Twilight Memories: Marking Time in a Culture of Amnesia* (New York: Routledge, 1995), pp. 13–35; Daniel J. Sherman and I. Rogoff, eds., *Museum Culture: Histories, Discourses, Spectacles* (Minneapolis: University of Minnesota Press, 1994); Terry Smith, *Making the Modern: Industry, Art, and Design in America* (Chicago: University of Chicago Press, 1993); and Michelle Bogart, *Artists, Advertising, and the Borders of Art* (Chicago: University of Chicago Press, 1995).

35. For example, in 1936, when MoMA held its Van Gogh exhibit, the Saks Fifth Avenue department store promoted the show with a Van Gogh–inspired display in its window, called "Van Gogh Colors" (Marver, "Buying into Modernism," chapter 1. Marver also discusses more downtown/downscale store tie-ins with MoMA).

36. The Detroit Art Institute was so keen on the link between art appreciation and consumerism that its education department hosted a show called "Let's Go Shopping" on a local commercial station.

37. Untitled notes on the "Good Design" show, ca. 1953, Series III. Box 18: Folder 3, MoMA Library.

38. "Projects," ca. fall 1953, Series III. Box 18: Folder 4.b., MoMA Library.

39. Betty Chamberlain, memo to Rene d'Harnoncourt, July 25, 1951, Series III. Box 19: Folder 2.d., MoMA Library.

40. See, for example, her memo to Rene d'Harnoncourt, in ibid.

41. Untitled notes, ca. 1954, Series III. Box 18: Folder 4.b., MoMA Library. My guess is that either Peterson or Macagy wrote these notes with respect to the *They Became Artists* series that I discuss further on.

42. Douglas Macagy, memo to Rene d"Harnoncourt, September 23, 1953, Series III.

Box 18: Folder 8.c., MoMA Library. It should be noted that even while they embraced commercial television, Macagy and his colleagues at MoMA knew that, despite some common interests, commercial broadcasters often held museum people in contempt, and vise versa.

43. Macagy, *The Museum Looks in on TV*, pp. 1–17.

44. Ibid., p. 400.

45. Peterson, *The Medium*, 1955, p. 2, Series III. Box 14: Folder 14, MoMA Library.

46. Ibid., pp. 5–6.

47. Ibid., p. 6.

48. Ibid., pp. 15–16.

49. Russell Lynes, "Highbrow, Lowbrow, Middlebrow," *Harper's*, February 1949, p. 19. It should be noted that while Macagy clearly spoke the language of "brows" he specifically resisted placing the television audience into any brow level. He wrote, "Reasonably accurate calipers for gauging brow heights in the American television audience still have to be formed" (*The Museum Look in on TV*, p. 43).

50. Tom Funk drew the taste-level chart for *Life*, April 11, 1949, pp. 100–1.

51. Lynes, "Highbrow, Lowbrow, Middlebrow," p. 20.

52. Cited in ibid.

53. Untitled report, ca. 1950, Series III. Box 19: Folder 12.d., MoMA Library.

54. Macagy, *The Museum Looks in on TV*, p. 40.

55. Macagy, "The Practical Outlook," in *The Museum Looks in on TV*, pp. 53–70. Part of Macagy's thinking here was that television was more utilitarian than aesthetic. He claimed that the viewers' "doll-house window on the world is a functional piece of furniture," and that the TV was a "labor saving device" that substituted for actual activities in the outside world (p. 40).

56. Pierre Bourdieu, *Distinction: A Social Critique of the Judgement of Taste,* trans. Richard Dice (Cambridge: Harvard University Press, 1984).

57. Macagy directly tied this practical outlook—and the commercialism of the medium—to the industry's promotion of the live aesthetic and its forms of intimate address that made the viewer feel "there" on the scene of presentation. "The whole tendency," he speculated, "is in the direction of reducing . . . 'psychical distance.' It is a concerted effort to identify what appears on the screen with the phenomenal scene of the living room. The viewer must be made to believe that he is the object of personal address . . . part of the studio group. And the studio group, it may be recalled, is a unit in the elaborate economic machinery of commercial production for mass consumption" (Macagy, *The Museum Looks in on TV*, p. 56).

58. Ibid., p. 18.

59. Macagy, however, pointed out that "asking too much" of the TV audience was also a mistake (*The Museum Looks in on TV*, p. 24).

60. Ibid., p. 63.

61. Peterson, *The Medium*, p. 101.

62. Ibid. Note that television critics of the era also preferred art programs with participatory, entertaining formats (and they also had a general disdain for "arty pretensions" and were disappointed with the inferior quality of the television image).

For example, Jack Gould, the influential *New York Times* critic, applauded MoMA's thirteen-part series for children, *Through the Enchanted Gate,* because it made the child a "doer, not a viewer," but he added that the program should have had more stress on the "participation" and a "brisker pace" (Gould, "Modern Art Museum's 'Through the Enchanted Gate' Encourages Children at Home to Display Talent," *New York Times,* May 14, 1952, p. 37).

63. Paddy Scannell, *Radio, Television, and Modern Life: A Phenomenological Approach* (Oxford: Blackwell, 1996), p. 24. For a study of pedagogical discourse on U.S. radio of the late 1920s–1950s see Joan Shelley Rubin, *The Making of Middlebrow Culture* (Chapel Hill: University of North Carolina Press, 1992), chapter 6.

64. Certainly, MoMA wasn't alone in its search for a new visual vernacular. Allon Schoener (assistant curator at the San Francisco Museum of Art) noted that "lectures and gallery talks do not belong in television" and that museums should instead exploit the "intimacy of the medium." To that effect, Schoener (who produced a series called *Art in Your Life*) decided to include an audience-participation segment in which viewers "will be encouraged to telephone questions that may arise in their minds during the course of the program" (Schoenor, "Television, an Important New Instrument of Mass Education for Museums"). Davidson Taylor of NBC spoke with Schoener about the possibility of producing an art program for his network (see Allon Schoener, letter to Davidson Taylor, October 5, 1952, NBC Records, Papers of Davidson Taylor, Box 278, Folder 10, Wisconsin Center Historical Archives). Two years later, NBC considered producing a show with Salvador Dali in which "Mr. Dali of the waxed mustaches and frantic manner would paint a picture for NBC audiences while they watched." As the program proposal noted, this would result in "Bravura showmanship and a decent work of art" (Robert D. Graff, memo to Davidson Taylor, June 9, 1954, NBC Records, Papers of Davidson Taylor, Box 279: Folder 69, Wisconsin Center Historical Archives). While the show never came to fruition, both NBC and CBS were interested in art as subject material, and MoMA made ties with both networks for somewhat more sober pursuits.

65. Val Adams, "Art Instruction for the Masses," *New York Times,* January 20, 1952, sec. II, p. 3.

66. Ibid., p. 3.

67. This film is housed at the UCLA Film and Television Archives, Los Angeles, California.

68. Peterson, *The Medium,* p. 103. Chamberlain also noted the importance of including this layman character. She wrote, "In general there is an attempt to have discussion, probably with laymen present such as taxi drivers, etc., to keep the program lively. No one wants to see a program resembling a college lecture with slides" (Chamberlain, letter to Miss Ethel Hoffman, July 30, 1948, Series III. Box 19: Folder 12.d. MoMA Library). As these examples suggest, in programs and films of this type, the "skeptic" was usually a woman or a working-class man, while the expert was a white man.

69. Note that the actual program is slightly different from the script. I transcribed this dialogue from the kinescope that is housed at the Museum of Television and Radio, New York City.

70. *Dimension,* script, air date: October 16, 1954, Series III. Box 18: Folder 3, MoMA Library.

71. Untitled notes, ca. 1954, p. 2, Series III: Box 18: Folder 3, MoMA Library.

72. Peterson, *The Medium,* p. 103.

73. See "Budget for Proposed Series of TV Films on the Subject of Good Design," ca. 1953, Series III. Box 18: Folder 3, MoMA Library.

74. "Proposal for TV: Good Design," spring 1953, p. 2, Series III. Box 18: Folder 3, MoMA Library.

75. "Report on TV Activities," ca. 1953, Series III. Box 18: Folder 3, MoMA Library.

76. "TV Proposal—Good Design at the Table," ca. 1953, Series III. Box 18: Folder 3, MoMA Library. The proposal included plans for a viewer contest.

77. "Broadcast Text: Margaret Arlen at 8:55 over WCBS-TV (NY)," air date: March 17, 1954, p. 2., Series III., Box 18, Folder 3, MoMA Library.

78. See, for example, T. H. Robsjohn-Gibbings, "American Idiom," *New York Times,* September 24, 1950, p. 4; Betty Pepis, "Decorating the Walls," *New York Times,* May 31, 1953, p. 39; Betty Pepis, "Art in the Home," *New York Times,* September 20, 1953, sec. 6, pp. 52–53; J. C. Furnas, "You, Too, Can Have Art Treasures," *Saturday Evening Post,* November 3, 1957, pp. 28, 83–84; and Cynthia Kellog, "Home Furnishing Report: Background Story," *New York Times,* sec. 6, pp. 9, 52.

79. See my essay "High Culture in Low Places: Television and Modern Art, 1950–1970," and my forthcoming book *High and Low TV: Modern Art and Commercial Television in Postwar America.*

80. "Frank Views on Art (Including 'Sacred Cows') are Offered by Critic Aline Saarinen on NBC-TV's 'Today' " and "Aline in Wonderland," NBC news releases, February 13 and 27, 1963 (Eero and Aline Saarinen Papers, Archives of American Art, Smithsonian Institution, Washington, D.C.). Sawelson-Gorse ("Sound Bites," p. 72) observes that some fan mail for these *Today* segments contained voyeuristic comments on Saarinen's sex appeal. This was, of course, consistent with other responses to female hostesses—as well as network thinking about them—on early TV and specifically on the *Today* show. See my *Make Room for TV: Television and the Family Ideal in Postwar America* (Chicago: University of Chicago Press, 1992).

81. The *Tour* did not run on ABC, which opted instead to feature its police show, *Naked City.* See Jack Gould, "Mrs. Kennedy TV Hostess to the Nation," *New York Times,* February 15, 1962), p. 18.

82. See ibid.; and "That TV Tour," *Newsweek,* February 26, 1962, pp. 23–24.

83. See "First Lady in Film," *New York Times,* May 4, 1965, p. 87; and Val Adams, "TV Role Accepted by Mrs. Johnson," *New York Times,* February 3, 1965, p. 71.

84. The museum used the color broadcast to promote its newly "modernized" building and to court a national audience. See "A Visit to the Metropolitan Museum of Art: NBC," script, air date: May 8, 1954, NBC Records, Papers of Davidson Taylor, Box 279: Folder 69, Wisconsin Center Historical Archives.

85. See *The Museum and Television,* May 1949.

86. Fred Rickey, letter to Rene d'Harnoncourt, June 19, 1951, Series III. Box 19: Folder 12.d., MoMA Library.

87. Alfred H. Barr Jr., letter to Mr. Rickey, June 20, 1951, Series III. Box 19: Folder 12.d., MoMA Library.

88. Peterson especially likened television to mannerism (Peterson, *The Medium*, pp. 45–47).

89. Report on *They Became Artists* series, ca. 1954, Series III. Box 18: Folder 3, p. 2. Another report stated that "although precautions had been taken to avoid a stylistic resemblance to Dufy's drawings in the animated sequences, it was felt that a slight sense of parody had crept in" (Macagy, The *Museum Looks in on TV*, p. 202).

90. See Elizabeth Tillet, "Case Studies," appendix to Macagy, *The Museum Looks in on TV*, p. 225. MoMA, however, did mount an exhibit of UPA's animation in 1956 and also placed UPA prints in its Film Library.

91. Ibid., p. 266. Prints of the films are in the MoMA Library.

92. "Committee on Art Education—TV Seminar (Text for Introductory Speech)," ca. 1954, Series III. Box 18: Folder 3, MoMA Library.

93. Tillet, "Case Studies," p. 267.

94. "*Description of Series,*" n.d., p. 1, Series III. Box 20: Folder 16.b., MoMA Library.

95. As one report said, Peterson "was hoping to open the eyes of the audience to things they looked at every day without seeing" ("Description of Series," p. 2).

96. The film is now in the MoMA Archive. It was conceived by Peterson but directed by Ruth Cade.

97. "Description of Series," p. 1.

98. "Committee on Art Education."

99. "Point of View," report, n.d., Series III. Box 20: Folder 16.b., MoMA Library.

100. Ibid.

101. Assistant secretary at MoMA (no name given), letter to Mavro Television Company, March 18, 1955, Series III. Box 20: Folder 16.b., MoMA Library. The museum also stipulated that the narration would be pulled from the film. Macagy stated that "the narration was brash; the effect could be too closely associated with the aesthetically inhibitive outlook encouraged by commercial broadcasting" (*The Museum Looks in on TV*, p. 205).

102. Peterson, *The Medium*, p. 124. In a similar vein, Macagy suggested, "some [curators] fear the stigma of the popularizer" See (*The Museum Looks in on TV*, p. 21).

103. See especially his *The Field of Cultural Production* (New York: Columbia University Press, 1993).

104. Macagy, *The Museum Looks in on TV*, p. 19.

105. For early examples, see Richard Hamilton's *Just What Is It That Makes Today's Homes So Different, So Appealing?* (1956); Andy Warhol's *$199 Television* (1960); Tom Wesselmann's *Great American Nude* (1962); and Robert Rauschenberg's *Dante's Inferno* (1964). Working in numerous media and traditions, artists have continued to use television as a subject in their work. For interesting discussions, see the Queens Museum, *Television's Impact on Contemporary Art,* exhibition catalog (New York: The Queens County Art and Cultural Center, 1986) and Farmer's catalog for the Austin Museum of Art, *The New Frontier.*

106. As far back as the early 1950s, both Nelson Rockefeller and Rene d'Harnoncourt wanted to establish a canon for TV as an art form. See "Untitled Report," ca. 1953, Series III. Box 18: Folder 3, MoMA Library; and Davidson Taylor, memo to Sylvester L. Weaver Jr., November 12, 1953, NBC Records, Papers of Davidson Taylor, Box 278: Folder 10. Wisconsin Center Historical Archives.

107. Jac Venza, ed., *Television USA: 13 Seasons* (New York: Museum of Modern Art Film Library; Doubleday, 1962), p. 15.

108. Abe Liss in ibid., p. 38.

109. For a discussion of the history of TV archives and the attempt to collect TV as an art form, see my "The Making of a TV Literate Elite," in *The Television Studies Book,* ed. Christine Geraghty and David Lusted (London: Arnold, 1997), pp. 63–85.

110. Gregory Battcock, "The Sociology of the Set," in *The New Television: A Public/Private Art,* ed. Douglas Davis and Allison Simmons (Cambridge: MIT Press, 1978), p. 21. For a more detailed discussion of this, see my "High Culture in Low Places," p. 301.

111. It should be noted that I am not suggesting that everyone accepted television from the start. Instead, by the time television became a commercial reality, there were already well established antimass-culture sentiments established in the United States and Europe, and these sentiments were applied by some to television even before it became an everyday reality. My point here is that despite this legacy of taste wars and hostile attitudes toward mass culture, at the dawn of television many cultural institutions hoped the medium would be different. We might compare this to our present-day discourse on new media and its potential as a form of electronic art.

JOHN HARTLEY **FROM REPUBLIC OF LETTERS**

TO TELEVISION REPUBLIC? CITIZEN READERS

IN THE ERA OF BROADCAST TELEVISION

The era of popular broadcast television, which has lasted fifty or so years from the mid-1950s, was also the period when television studies budded off from an already hybrid knowledge tree. Treated as part of mass society, television was routinely analyzed as a bad object and blamed for social, political, cultural, and behavioral outcomes that were, a priori it seemed, negative. Very little progressive optimism was applied to television in a systematic way in formal academic, intellectual, and critical writing. This was in large part a symptom of twentieth-century intellectual politics, with television as merely the latest in a long line of miscreant media stretching back through movies, radio, and music to the gutter press, yellow press, and penny dreadfuls of previous centuries. Cultural elites were habituated to "assailing" media that in their view failed to "uplift" the masses.[1]

Television studies branched off from existing branches of social theory, social science, psychology, cultural criticism, and other academic disciplines. Its immediate purpose was not to understand but to discipline television. The term "discipline" here invoked two senses at once: first, to put TV into the supposedly orderly context of disciplinary taxonomies of knowledge; and second, to discipline TV via rhetorics of control, prohibition, and pejorative labeling. The disdainful mood was not confined to academics. Scholarly analysis and popular journalistic accounts seemed to agree that the right way to take television seriously as an object of study was to treat it as a pathology of some sort. The successful titles were by professional critical pessimists such as Jerry Mander and Neil Postman, who used arguments that had hardly changed since the 1950s.[2] Even Pierre Bourdieu weighed in from left field, but with the same old story.[3] Few influential voices took television as a force for good. Little commonsense rhetoric or media discussion had a good word to say for it either, even among the very people for whom television was and remained the most popular pastime in history. People got used to thinking that watching television was a behavior, of interest to psychologists. It was not, in other words, taken to be emancipatory or literate communication, of interest to democrats.

Metonymically, TV was routinely made to stand for society as a whole. Following from scientific method, analysis was insistently present tense, generalizing and universal, not historical and contingent. Indeed, TV was not taken as a thing in itself. "Freedom to think of things in themselves" had been Virginia Woolf's touchstone for intellectual emancipation.[4] But television was persistently treated as a symptom of something other than itself—power, usually—that was thought to be threatening to social or moral well-being.[5] This mental default setting not only missed the opportunity to understand television in itself, but also inhibited the freedom to think among critics. "Television rots your brain" became normal science. Thus any new investigation was confronted not by TV in itself but by a thick encrustation of prejudicial, pejorative, and pathological language that sometimes seemed to hide the thing itself entirely from view. Television studies therefore needed not to add to the store of research in this familiar mode, but to rethink its own assumptions, rhetoric, and purposes. It risked becoming the very thing it purported to criticize. It was commonplace to assume that television was an ideological discourse dedicated to producing preferred readings about moral or political issues in its viewers. But television studies was doing the same thing to its own readers. Especially in critical pedagogy, whether formal in schools or informal in journalism, a narrow range of negative opinions about television was successfully established, becoming so naturalized and widespread as to seem unarguable.

Certainly a major component of television studies was an attempt by social and cultural critics, themselves working outside and against the grain of contemporary popular media, to critique, contest, and control the media's productive capacity, to limit its sociocultural and ideological reach and curtail its politico-commercial power. Not much work in television studies was devoted to arguing for the expansion of the productive capacity of television, whether that capacity was understood in semiotic, social, democratic, or industrial terms.

MEDIA REPUBLICANISM

In spite of the early view of television studies, an alternative way of thinking was already at hand. For several centuries thinkers in various fields had written of such imaginary domains as the "republic of letters," the "republic of taste," even a "republic of the fine arts."[6] This republican terminology had seemed to fizzle out with the advent of screen and electronic media; it was confined to print and painting (i.e., to political philosophy and the philosophy of art—disciplines of collection rather than diffusion). But if print and preindustrial visual media had democratizing tendencies and were useful in both constituting and tutoring cultural citizenship, then it seemed appropriate to ask if the contemporary mass media might be thought of in the same way.[7]

That is my present purpose. In this essay I seek to restore republican terminology to television by comparing it with the republic of letters. Did broadcast television, the thing in itself, constitute a republic in these terms? The most important question at stake in this thought experiment is that of the status of the audience. The republic of letters was and remains characterized by the interaction between authorial voices on the one hand, and a readership, often vast, on the other. Within the textual system of print literacy, the most important product was not the commodity form as such—books, newspapers, magazines, etc.—but the readership that long before television had been formed at one and the same time into market, public, and nation. Did the television audience amount to a cultural commons in the same way? Television could be understood historically in comparison with print literacy and its order of reading.[8] From this perspective, the TV audience could be seen as an extension and reformulation of the reading public rather than representing its demise.

In the U.S. context the term "republican" referred to a political party; in the Australian context to a constitutional reform movement; in the British context, perversely, to Irish nationalism. Its source predated but informed each of these applications of the term. An early *Dictionary of Quotations* gave the term "respublica" as "Lat.—'The common weal.'—The general interest."[9] This early modern usage was part lawyer's jargon, part literary. A telling instance of this use of the notion of a republic of letters came from Thomas Paine. In *Rights of Man* (1792) he praised the "representative system" of government over hereditary ones, writing as follows:

Experience, in all ages and in all countries, has demonstrated that it is impossible to control nature in her distribution of mental powers. She gives them as she pleases. Whatever is the rule by which she, apparently to us, scatters them among mankind, that rule remains a secret to man. It would be as ridiculous to attempt to fix the hereditaryship of human beauty as of wisdom. Whatever wisdom constituently is, it is like a seedless plant; it may be reared when it appears, but it cannot be voluntarily produced. There is always a sufficiency somewhere in the general mass of society for all purposes; but with respect to the parts of society, it is always changing its place. It rises in one to-day, in another to-morrow, and has probably visited in rotation every family of the earth, and again withdrawn.

As this is in the order of nature, the order of government must necessarily follow it, or government will, as we see it does, degenerate into ignorance. . . .

As the republic of letters brings forward the best literary productions, by giving to genius a fair and universal chance; so the representative system of government is calculated to produce the wisest laws, by collecting wisdom from the place where it can be found. I smile to myself when I contemplate the ridiculous insignificance into which literature and all the sciences would sink, were they made hereditary; and I carry the same idea into governments. An hereditary governor is as inconsistent as an hereditary author.[10]

Paine united the three elements of a republican approach by bringing together: textuality (republic of letters); nation ("respublica," the common weal); and citizenship (representative government). Paine actually modeled his favored system of government on publication—on the republic of letters itself. He put his model into practice, too. He was one of the founders of the United States of America, which, in an early and unsurpassed act of branding, he named. And he was a founder of the République française, where he was an elected Girondist deputy in the National Assembly (and imprisoned for opposing the execution of the ex-king). He had a go at reforming Britain, too, via *Rights of Man* and *The Age of Reason,* but to less immediate effect.

Paine's model of republicanism could assist television studies. It was significant that the bringing together of textuality and citizenship in the common good or general interest was done in *Rights of Man,* one of the founding texts of political modernity in the West. The combination of textuality and citizenship has often been mistaken for a recent, postmodern gesture, and frequently condemned for being antimodern and apolitical, even antireal. The idea that it might be at the heart of modern political theory and practice was anathema to some of the very modernists who practiced that theory.[11] However, the republic of letters had a fully documented historical basis. The reading public was literally, historically, the model for the public.[12]

TEXTUALITY AND CITIZENSHIP

For a comparison between television and the republic of letters to make sense, the television audience needs to be understood as a public in the same way that the readership of (commercially produced) newspapers has been understood since the nineteenth century. There were, of course, many technical and social differences between print and screen media and between reading publics and media audiences.[13] But public communication was central to any polity organized along democratic lines, where a sovereign but anonymous population governed itself via representative intermediaries. A two-way flow of information was needed to link the imagined community together, with public affairs and decisions heading one way and public opinion and feedback heading the other. Polities adopted different mechanisms to channel this public communication, but in all cases both a literate population and a truly ubiquitous media were required. Such media literally constituted the public in the act of mutually informing them and their representatives from day to day.

Ever since the advent of modernity in the West, there has been a noticeable tendency for publics to place their trust in the fastest and (compared with existing forms) least mediated medium, which often was also the newest and most obviously technological. In the Reformation, print was trusted more than sermons and homilies. There was a good reason for the public to distrust public preaching as opposed to private reading. Sermons and homilies were not, as they may intuitively have appeared to be, oral, face-to-face communication between an individual cleric and his lay congregation. With the Reformation they became a fully constituted mass medium, with a centralized, uniform message, political surveillance, and legally enforceable delivery to "the simple people." In England and Wales, for example, a manual was issued that standardized Protestant propaganda throughout the realm. Its full title proclaimed its purpose: *The Book of Homilies. Certain Sermons Appointed by the Queen's Majesty to be declared and read by all Parsons, Vicars and Curates, every Sunday and Holiday in their Churches; and by Her Grace's advice perused and overseen for the better understanding of the simple people.*[14]

In the Industrial Revolution the popular daily press (both commercial and radical) was trusted more than official government information channels.[15] In the twentieth century the public information content of cinema, which via newsreels, documentary, and hybrid genres such as biopics was for decades a significant competitor with newsprint, was more or less completely abandoned to television following World War II. By the 1970s television news was trusted more than print sources—a major milestone in semiotic history. By the turn of the twenty-first century, the instantaneousness and decentralized provenance of Internet information was beginning to win trust in its turn.[16]

In other words, the platform of the medium—print, screen, or interactive—was less crucial for the purposes of citizenship than its speed, ubiquity, and the perceived trustworthiness of its information. Of course, reading such media differed experientially depending on the nature of the platform—watching TV was not like sitting at a computer, which was not like reading a book. But at the fundamental level of constituting publics for democratic polities, this was irrelevant. Reading itself migrated across platforms, from sermon to print to newspaper to cinema/radio to television to interactivity, and each successive platform supplemented rather than supplanted its predecessor. Reading *as a public* persisted, even though the mode of literacy required changed and the readership for a given platform was most likely to be taken as "the" public during its initial ascendancy and popularity.

Reading itself was always a multiskilled activity: reading print was never just that. Print literacy involved visual (design) and pictorial (image) elements, not to mention sound (reading aloud). Similarly, both screen and interactive media, even cinema, retained major commitments to printed text, from credits, subtitles, and intertitles to product placement and all sorts of signage within the fictional world en scène. Reading thus was a varied activity at different periods and in relation to different media forms. It was sustained by graphic, aural, and visual codes that were more or less naturalistic and hence less or more difficult to learn, but never entirely separated from each other. Watching television was also always hearing—in fact television was as much a talking medium as a visual one, and sound was often the dominant element of the television text. Soon, assisted by technology, viewers could remotely mute irritating or offensive sound content but leave the pictures up. Like cinema, television also involved written graphics of various kinds both on-screen and off—from maps and charts in news shows to *TV Guide* on the armchair.

The idea of the republic of letters had egalitarian and utopian resonance in the eighteenth century because involvement in it was not based on property or inheritance and could not therefore be controlled by traditional aristocratic governance. It was understood as inherently more *transparent* than previous modes of communication.[17] Talent in authorship was not heritable. The ability to read was not socially exclusive. It was therefore a shadow republic used by polemicists such as Thomas Paine to harry the inequities of the actually existing formal constitution. But in principle, the republic of letters was no more nor less than the reading public of print literacy constituted as a modern political public and cultural consumer all at once.

THE ORDER OF READING

At the turn of the twenty-first century, a book was published that provides a glimpse into the state of the republic of letters and of scholarship about it. *A History of Reading in the West* showcases an important strand of European thinking about publishing, the book trade, literacy, and reading publics.[18] The concluding chapter by Armando Petrucci considers the future of reading.[19] Petrucci is a leading authority on writing and the social history of books in the Italian paleographic tradition, an expert in the very crucible of the republic of letters.[20] He describes the "chaos" resulting from overcapacity in that realm: it was "irrational" on both the supply (addresser) and demand (addressee) sides.

On the supply side, publishers are "dominated by the terror of a market crisis continually perceived as imminent." The market has "gone mad." Publishers offer: "*Triviallitteratur* and classics with parallel translations, journalistic 'instant books' of the worst sort, books for hobbyists, philosophical or linguistic essays, collections of jokes, volumes of poetry, mysteries, science fiction, books on politics, histories of customs or of sex, and lightweight romances. Neither the publisher's imprint nor the way a book is marketed nor the price discriminates among them, or brings any sort of order to the mass of texts that are produced every day."[21] Publishers are hardly failing to produce books, which are appearing in alarming numbers, but they are, Petrucci argues, failing to discriminate within an "order of reading" shared by themselves and their readership: "For some time now, what the major publishers have been doing . . . [is] obliterating every criterion of selection. It might be considered a genuine fraud perpetrated on the reader-consumer."[22]

Petrucci sees the same indiscriminate tendencies on the demand side: "The reader-consumer reacts in an equally irrational manner." He goes on: "The reader behaves in a highly disorganized and unpredictable way within the market. He or she buys or does not buy, chooses or refuses to choose, prefers one type of book today and another tomorrow, is seduced on one occasion by a reduced price, on another by the graphic presentation of a book, on still another by a passing interest or by a publicity blitz. In short, the reader too begins to lose all criteria of selection, which makes it hard to programme production rationally on the basis of predictable public tastes." Petrucci contrasts the distracted, irrational, seduced consumer of this imagining with the "so-called strong readers" who had "solidly consistent tastes" but "declining numbers"; and who "in every society make up the most conservative (and hence most stable) portion of the universe of readers." Petrucci paints a picture of what he calls "reading disorders" in the republic of letters. He laments the inauguration of an age of purposeless reading—of "reading to read." This he contrasts with reading for improvement, or for induction into a Foucauldian "order of reading," characterized by discrimination, classification, a canon, and the reduction of discursive multiplicity, authorial fertility, and potential infinity of meanings to a system with constraints, controls, and restrictions—and thereby, of course, productivity.[23]

Petrucci suggests that the republic of letters is in a period of decline and fall, comparable to that of another, ancient republican empire, but this time the barbarians at the gate are electronic. Literacy itself had remained unbroken since Pharaonic Egypt and Sumerian Mesopotamia (3100 B.C.E. or thereabouts), but during that time there had been crises of reading, almost amounting to mass extinctions, notably in the Dark Ages after the fall of the Roman Empire and in the Renaissance during the fall of the Roman Church. In both periods established canons were overturned and abandoned and new literacies put in their place (both were Romano-Latin canons giving way to Germanic and Anglo-Saxon vernaculars). It seems that at the end of the twentieth century the same fate awaits another Roman imperium—that of letters. Roman script itself is feared to be giving way to visual media, its order reduced to chaos, its practice preserved in barbarous hypertext at best. But in fact the "decline and fall" scenario is evidence less of an actual historical event than of a certain historiographical attitude. Just as the actual Roman Empire did not decline and fall until Edward Gibbon said it did, for eighteenth-century reasons,[24] so, too, did television not cause the decline and fall of the order of reading, even if it was associated with changes in literacy.

Critics, intellectuals, and academics are Petrucci's "strong readers" with established tastes and commitment to a stable canon, and therefore they are the most conservative in relation to changes in reading practices. They are most likely to dismiss everything on TV as worthless and to see in its indiscriminate publishing and reading practices the annihilation of their own order of reading. A republican TV studies needs to investigate the scenario, without assuming in advance that television is the death of knowledge, that purposeless reading is the end of history, and that non-canonical texts are the end of truth as we know it.

Indeed, does Petrucci's excellent concept of an order of reading—the imposition of discipline in the taxonomical sense, of classification and the reduction of meaning to a system with controls and restrictions that enables productivity—apply to broadcast television? Does television establish its own internal, systemic "governmental" apparatus—an order of viewing amounting to a republic of television? If so, does that have anything to teach those for whom the crisis in the established, modernist order of reading is seen as a decline or disaster? Is "reading television" an extension of the republic of letters or its doom?[25]

If the foundation of modern citizenship occurred somewhere in the interactions between the "two Rs" of reading and rioting, between journalism and politics in the streets of Paris, for instance, then how might transformations in the order of reading have produced changes in citizenship? How did textuality influence citizenship in, if one can be recovered for analysis, a republic of television?

TELEVISION AND THE REPUBLIC OF LETTERS

Historically, television viewing displays characteristics that are directly comparable to developments in the history of print literacy. To the extent that this is so, television can be seen as an extension of the republic of letters, even if both letters and the republic are somewhat transformed in the process.[26] The chaotic and irrational disorder that Petrucci describes in both publishing (supply) and reading (demand) applies directly both to television programming (supply) and viewing (demand). Broadcast TV appears to be a very weakly disciplined medium compared with letters.

However, this is not so different from early print. In the sixteenth-century book publishing was still organized around a practical presumption that knowledge and the knowing person were in principle coterminous, and that therefore no system of generic classification was necessary because one person could "know everything." This was the period of "universal" histories, for instance, in which authors attempted or purported to write the entire history of the world—from creation to the present—often in one volume (Sir Walter Raleigh, while imprisoned in the Tower, was among the last to attempt this feat in 1614 with his own *History of the World*). If knowledge was understood as universal and comprehensive, it didn't need to be divided into specialist branches. This was certainly the case for early television content—there is almost no evidence of specialization of audience. Even where different demographics are targeted they remain aspects of a universal "normal family"—mom, dad, teens, children. Television content and its consumer are assumed to be in principle coterminous. Both literate reading and television viewing were in principle available to everyone who shared the code, and once inside virtually everything was on offer to virtually everyone. This is why broadcasters tended to conceptualize their regime as a "paedocracy"[27] rather than a republic—they addressed a universal, prespecialist subject, of which the best commonsense model was not the citizen but the gratification-seeking child.

As far as content is concerned, an order of television discourse based on genre, scheduling, and channel was quickly established and widely understood. The classification of early print content in the sixteenth and seventeenth centuries was not radically different:

- Publishing required *genre:* for instance, books on household or enterprise management, religion, narrative entertainment, etc.
- Reading (like TV viewing) was time sensitive, requiring *scheduling.* Reading for different purposes—action, reflection, or passing time—would be done at different times of the day or year. Different kinds of books were produced to fulfill such various needs.
- Publisher-booksellers were the equivalent of *channels.* It was important for readers to know which supplier could be trusted—to be, for instance, Protestant. But equally, choice among a limited bundle of differentiated but nearby outlets was important. The earliest retail bookseller-publishers congregated around St. Paul's churchyard in the City of London, for instance. Readers could channel change by walking next door.

Print literacy took several centuries to evolve the complexity, scale, and professionalization that resulted in such important taxonomic innovations as the Dewey system of library classification, and thus to render its repertoire more productive for knowledge-seeking readers. Television did not evolve an equivalent system in its broadcast era (it remained, as it were, consumptive, wasting itself away as it lived on its own tissue). Despite the brief ascendancy of commercial video libraries there was little systematic public archiving of television. This strange failure was hardly noticed in television studies, which was silent while television companies taped over master copies of classic series, even while expensive attempts were being made at the same time to archive cinema, provoked by the chemical crisis that threatened nitrate film. Meanwhile, knowledge-seeking viewers and television researchers had to rely on their own resources to gather and archive television content. Real libraries continued to obsess about books, gathering and classifying television content only fitfully and unsystematically, as ephemera not knowledge.

Television literacy was gained informally. Especially in relation to television's most popular forms, there was no school, no tutoring, no orderly progression through levels of difficulty, no homework and no canon of required reading. Here television differed from print literacy, which depended from the start on specialist institutions to promote the skill of reading. (Such institutions included the church, state, and "dame schools"—that is, private schooling in Early Modern England typically offered by women in their homes.) Only the word "waste" described the relationship between knowledge and the untutored watching of television.[28] Masses of information were there, but there was no search engine to help self-motivated viewers to find their way to and through it.

Despite the large number of help shows, ranging from cooking and house makeovers to gardening and sex, little effort was made to render broadcast television itself into useful knowledge. Schools used television as they had already accommodated film. As entertainment it was banned and denigrated, but like film it was accepted into the classroom in the form of improvement-oriented documentaries (often somewhat older than the students who watched them). In some U.S. colleges television content that had been produced for the broadcast audience could be watched for course credits as early as the 1970s, with series like Jacob Bronowski's *The Ascent of Man* on PBS. In the same period, the Open University in the United Kingdom began to use broadcast TV as well as correspondence for direct teaching. In the same vein, but on a potentially much larger scale, the Shanghai Television University was founded in China in the 1990s, with a promise of universal postschool education via broadcasting.

Television entertainment aimed at popular audiences also started trying to be helpful, and not just with daytime shows aimed at busy housewives. Some began to offer fact sheets (later Web sites) to extend their utility. Others gave the phone numbers of helplines offering further information on stories covered, from natural disasters on the news to teenage pregnancy in the TV version of *Clueless*. But television as a popular pastime remained most heavily committed to a chaotic disorder of programming in which a massive repertoire of incommensurate material was broadcast under the banners of variety, entertainment, and purposelessness. Watching TV was just that, not *for* anything, and in principle everything was meant to be legible to all viewers.

Whether viewers wanted a more productive, purposeful, disciplined order of viewing was never tested, although public service broadcasting in Europe came closer to recognizing that possibility than did commercial network television in the United States. The capital intensity of television production and the need for audience maximization to achieve profit meant that viewers were encouraged to be noncanonical, purposeless, and undisciplined—watching to watch, as it were. This is exactly as Petrucci characterizes contemporary readers, especially younger ones. He writes of the emergence of the "anarchical reader," quoting Hans Magnus Enzensberger on the "liberty of the reader": "This freedom [to make whatever use of the text suits the reader] also includes the right to leaf back and forward, to skip whole passages, to read sentences against the grain, to misunderstand them, to reshape them, to spin sentences out and embroider them with every possible association, to draw conclusions from the text of which the text knows nothing, to be annoyed at it, to be happy because of it, to forget it, to plagiarize it and to throw the book in which it is printed into the corner any time s/he likes."[29] Enzensberger is evidently promoting the freedom of readers rather than describing in any scientific detail what actually existing readers may have done in statistically significant numbers.

There was a similar debate in media studies about whether audiences had rights: "semiotics" said yes; "power" said no.[30] Whatever the case, in both literary reading and television viewing, there were essentially similar possibilities for readers and audiences. The anarchic potential of the republic of letters was also one of the most frequently noted characteristics of television usage. But what Petrucci lamented as anarchy Enzensberger proclaimed as freedom. That freedom consisted in the openness of text to being used in ways that were aberrant from the point of view of producer institutions. Print shared this productive capacity with television. Indeed, at the very dawn of television studies Umberto Eco had identified "aberrant decoding" as one of the defining characteristics of the "television message."[31] Following Eco and Enzensberger, a republican media studies perhaps might promote more self-conscious and adventurous exploitation of that basic "right" than currently prevails.

IRONCLAD ORDER TO DISCIPLINED ORDER?

The stages in the establishment of television's regime of viewing could be compared with similar stages in the history of reading. Television's history as a mass medium began not with anarchy but, on the contrary, with what Petrucci calls "an ironclad 'order of video.'"[32] This is a highly ideological form of programming, backed by both cultural control (it was produced by elites) and political regulation. It was designed to impart specific meanings from a trustworthy center to a powerless lay populace. To the limited extent that this is so (and notwithstanding the viewer freedom noted above), TV is doing no more than following in the footsteps of reading.

Reading was established in the early modern West as a tool of government, or governmentality more widely.[33] Within ruling circles themselves, full literacy (i.e., writing as well as reading) was used as an autonomous means of communication. Beyond such circles, reading but not writing was promoted for highly ideological purposes within the most controlled environment. This work was first undertaken by religious authorities (sixteenth to seventeenth centuries). Later, state schools and public libraries (nineteenth and twentieth centuries) took over as bearers of what Petrucci calls the "democratic ideology of public reading."[34]

The publishing industry accommodated its output to ideological requirements. For instance, popular nonfiction, especially travel and exploration, natural history, and popular science, was used for directly counterrevolutionary purposes in the nineteenth century. Organizations like the Society for the Diffusion of Useful Knowledge (1826) were designed "to undermine political radicalism with rational information"; the aim being, as some working-class readers reportedly complained, "to stop our mouths with *kangaroos*"—to silence dissent with nature study.[35] Or as Petrucci puts it: "Before the advent of television, reading was the best means for diffusing values and ideologies and the one easiest to regulate, once controls had been established for the processes of production and, above all, the distribution of texts."[36]

If the early regime of broadcast viewing was ironclad, there were longstanding and sometimes brutally enforced regulations about the content of print, with prohibitions extending from science and politics to religion and sex. People were burned alive for what they published. The initial ironclad order of reading was loosened if not unhinged by the effects of growth, fragmentation, competition, internal opposition, and deregulation over a long period. However, the liberty of readers was never complete. It remained confined to Enzensbergian freedom in the act of reading itself. Property and defamation laws, and restrictions relating to obscenity, national security, and community values, continued to govern what could and could not be read and by whom. Even in countries like the United States, with its fully modernized First Amendment constitution guaranteeing freedom of speech (i.e., publication), both formal regulation and informal cultural policing ensured that the much-vaunted freedoms of print literacy were constantly chaperoned, the more so in the most popular media.

The will to govern applied equally to print, television, and successor media. It was driven by the popularity of a medium not by its platform. This was evident internationally once again as new computer-based interactive media matured into popular or mass media. The early anarchic regime of reading/viewing on the Internet and the World Wide Web (e.g., open source) was brought progressively under the control of various national legal and corporate (copyright) systems. Landmark decisions imposed governmental control over content in countries as varied as France (Nazi content on Yahoo), the United States (intellectual property law, e.g., Napster), Malaysia (Asian values), and China (national self-determination).

International cooperation in content policing was evident, too, especially in the areas of security (hacking the Pentagon), finance (secure credit cards), and Western family values (child pornography). As well as national and moral considerations, commercial imperatives were at work. Massive investment in interactive technologies required equally massive numbers of users—scale was still the key to financial return. An orchestrated campaign to suburbanize the Internet—to assure middle-of-the-road users that the pleasures and dangers of ungoverned street life were not "just a click away"—focused on stories about pedophiles. These almost mythical figures took over the traditional role of ogres and footpads (figures of fear of communication in its physical mode, at least until *Shrek*). They were in direct line of succession of all the weird and wonderful corruptors of youth that were said to lurk within each new medium, from popular fiction in print through cinema and radio to television itself. Making the highways and byways of hypermedia safe for suburban pilgrims was the moral of these stories.

Television was not ideologically ironclad as opposed to print literacy; it was simply and briefly a successor, and any ironcladding had already been thoroughly battle hardened in previous media from print to radio. Unwittingly or otherwise, the first generation of highly literate TV producers, regulators, and critics (but not audiences, Enzensberger would argue) organized broadcasting's regime of viewing around the imposition of control, not the encouragement of innovation; it was compliance before performance. Perhaps it was inevitable that those schooled in the disciplinary apparatus of print literacy should seek both government over the new medium and the maintenance of strictly enforced distinctions between it and the established order of reading. But the eventual and inevitable failure of those controls and distinctions did not have to be seen as disaster or decline. It was just history repeating itself.

READING, WRITING, AND REDACTION

Just as there had been in print, in early television there were very general and extensive forms of prohibition, from banning to bowdlerization, designed to make television knowledge unharmful. There was a radical separation of reading from writing TV. There was a regulatory presumption of television's disorderliness and its potentially disruptive effect on viewers and cultures. Television was praised only when it was being used to teach the most conservative or law-affirming cultural and political values associated with patriotism and wise consumption. But it was prevented from trying to stimulate viewers too much, in fictional as well as factual output. The only effect television was allowed to have without questions being asked by populist politicians in Parliament or Congress was on sales of toothpaste, and only then if they increased.

The curious (or perhaps merely Foucauldian) situation arose where print reading was widely praised because it seemed orderly and well governed (schools, libraries, disciplines) but its value was said to reside in the freedom it bestowed on readers. Meanwhile television watching was criticised for disorderliness, even though TV's regime of viewing could not be satisfactorily controlled. Governmentality was inevitable. Regulation of any textual system is necessary for its productive capacity to develop, but nevertheless the early history of television regulation was governmental in an oppressive, not a fully productive, sense. It was characterized by general and uncomprehending attempts to discipline its potential unruliness; that is, not to develop its own regime of viewing, or semiotic and informational productiveness, so much as to minimize its effect on *other* people, print, and politics. There were voices that promoted the educative and enlarging potential of television in democratic countries.[37] But the prevailing discourse was dedicated to keeping the new medium as distinct as possible from the existing order of reading, not to welcome it as an extension and democratization of the same.

Meanwhile, even under such ironclad regulatory pressure, television did in thirty years what the republic of letters took three hundred to achieve: it established its own transnational and societywide "order of viewing." That order displayed features that seemed contradictory when considered from the point of view of contemporary book reading. Anarchic freedoms coexisted with ironclad ideologies. What was the relation between addresser (text) and addressee (citizen) in this context—was it more anarchic or more ironclad? Television studies explored this relation almost exclusively in terms of power; that is, presuming that the order of viewing was ironclad. But two concepts derived from the republic of letters were available to help to identify how the order of television operated, and how comparable it was with the order of reading. One of these concepts was authorship; the other was writing.

Much has been written about the nature of authorship, from its omniscience to its death. But as a central component of the republic of letters authorship has rarely been associated with television and other electronic media (although it achieved limited purchase in cinema studies via auteur theory). Conversely, the characteristic modes of text production in television have rarely been applied to print. Television was from the start a team sport. Authorship was diffused among many individuals and may more properly have been claimed by a studio, company, or channel than by a person, as creative intellectual property increasingly was. In television, authorial originality of imagination or expression, or of research and information gathering, or of a shaping artistic vision, emerged as much from direction as from scripting, from producers as much as from performers, and more from the corporate resources of giant organizations (Fox, Viacom, BBC) than from individual creative genius (which nevertheless was both valued and necessary throughout the whole enterprise). Did this suggest that television authorship and literary authorship had nothing in common? Did corporate authorship entail more ironclad control as opposed to anarchic individual talent? Not really.

Apart from the banal fact that literary authors often worked in TV, and vice versa, there was more to authorship in practice than the ideology of the creative individual allowed. Within the republic of letters itself, for instance, according to Petrucci, "there is another anomalous and potentially 'anarchical' figure who corresponds to the new readers and their innovative reading practices. It is the consumeristic writer who produces texts of para-literature, rewrites other people's texts, churns out lightweight romantic fiction and mysteries, or patches together articles for second-tier periodicals, often anonymously or as a member of an editorial team."[38] This very interesting figure, Petrucci suggests, had "surfaced" in previous "times of crisis in book production, of a suddenly expanded reading public, or of widely divergent levels in the product."[39] But Petrucci's historical observation is clouded by his prejudicial language, noted in terms such as consumeristic, para-literature, churns out, lightweight, patches together, and second-tier.

A more neutral term to identify this type of writer is required in order to advance understanding of the interconnectedness of corporate authorship, popular media, and servicing the needs of users, whether readers or viewers. Corporate authorship in the context of public communication was first established in journalism. It is in this context that I have identified the emergent figure of the redactor: one who produced new material by a process of editing existing content.[40] Redaction is a form of production not reduction of text (which is why the more familiar term "editing" is not adequate). Indeed, the present day could be characterized as a redactional society, indicating a time when there is too much instantly available information for anyone to see the world whole, thus resulting in a society that is characterized by its editorial practices, by how it uses the processes of corporate and governmental shaping of existing materials to make sense of the world. Individual authorship itself is increasingly redactional in mode. The most trusted and most visited sources of truth are not individuals but organizations, from CNN to the *Guardian Unlimited* Web site, depending on your preferences. It is redaction, not original writing (authorship) as such, that determines what is taken to be true, and what policies and beliefs should follow from that.

The republic of letters and the television republic are both represented by redactors. It is no longer accurate to draw a distinction between print and media literacy, or between literary authorship and media production. In any textual system undergoing massive expansion, a major priority is for someone to sort out order from chaos. This is what the redactor does. Everywhere in the republic of letters, from Dorling Kindersley to textbooks, pulp fiction to journalism, there was a diffusion of authorship into redaction. Petrucci's separation between original and "para" literature is untenable. In television, the redactional form of authorship has been standard practice. There was major overlap between the most popular and expansive parts of the republic of letters and that of television. The redactor brought together information, images, "matter of reasoning," and discourse not only within but also between the apparently distinct republics of letters and television.

The anonymous and unknown population—the reading public—that has gathered together into some sort of relationship with all this material has made some use of it. Attention needed to shift from studying TV's impact on individuals and societies and toward the use made of it by such. Watching television needed to be thought of more as a literacy than as a behavior. If, however, television were ever to claim literate status then it would have to include writing as well as reading. The stakes in shifting the conception of TV literacy from read-only to read-and-write were, as it transpired, high. Petrucci writes: "Writing is instead [of reading] an individual skill and is totally free; it can be done in any fashion, anywhere and to produce anything the writer wants; it is beyond the reach of any control or, at the limit, of any censorship."[41] Petrucci contrasts the individual freedom of writing with his ironclad order of video: "In the electronic mass media, television in particular . . . a 'canon' of programmes is rapidly becoming uniform throughout the world, and . . . the viewing public (of all cultural traditions) is just as rapidly being levelled."[42]

In fact, such a radical distinction between the freedom of writing and the constraint of reading could not be sustained even within the republic of letters, where written literacy was routinely conventional, instrumental, coercive, and dull. But even so, writing was evidently more active and individuated than watching TV purposelessly as part of a "leveled" public was reputed to be. So, did TV literacy begin to extend writing to those who were formerly restricted to reading? The evidence suggests that it did:

– At the most basic level, viewers with remote control devices could countermand the flow of television sequence by zapping, slaloming and muting. This demotic form of redaction apparently has been highly valued in some contexts (competitive zapping in U.S. fraternity-house TV lounges), and highly irritating in others (homes where Dad controls the control).

– Much more sophisticated forms of writing and rewriting of television textuality are evident in the fan cultures that have been extensively studied by Henry Jenkins and others.

– Extending slowly from art college, avant-garde, and political advocacy groups, the redactional skills of scratch video and image/sound manipulation were extended to those who could do clever things with computers. These included Web sites that make cult TV characters participate in viewer-created narratives, dance routines, or even other worlds.[43]

– Even within the TV industry as established, the distinction between viewer and maker has been dissolving: weakly in various audience participation shows; strongly in such "access" series as the wonderful *Video Nation,* broadcast by the BBC.

– The public became star of reality TV formats, from *Popstars* to *Big Brother.* Audience interaction is central to such formats and extended to non-TV platforms including the Internet, telephone, and SMS (short message service). Successful broadcast shows like *Dawson's Creek* began to introduce interactive elements on the Web such as Sony's *Dawson's Desk* and *Rachel's Room* sites, thereby encouraging audiences literally to write themselves into the narrative.

– The invidious distinctions between amateur, connoisseur, and professional remained forceful but blurred. Home video was used for an increasingly sophisticated range of activities—from cannily faked accidents for submission to *Funniest Home Video*–type shows to the "Jenni-cam" phenomenon where private individuals set up Web cams in their domestic space and shared their lives with up to millions of fellow netizens. Various TV channels experimented with shows that resulted from giving young people cheap digital cameras and an arduous, amusing, or audacious task.

– Social groups ranging from indigenous peoples to migrants and expatriates, including advocates for movements arising from various identities based on gender, ethnicity, sexual orientation, region, or age, increasingly have used both broadcast TV and nonbroadcast video to communicate to their own communities and to communicate about themselves to larger publics.

– Home video, community video, corporate video, promotional video, and music video all extended television "writing" beyond broadcasting and across the spectrum from amateur to avant-garde.

After decades of patiently taking their turn as receivers of television discourse, viewers are being transformed and are transforming themselves into transmitters in increasing numbers, well beyond the control of any ironclad videologues.

POLITICAL AND SEMIOTIC ECONOMY: WHO RULES?

A republican television studies would be interested in ordinariness and "suburbanality," in the extension of cultural and semiotic resources into everyday life.[44] It follows that the primary object of study need not be the ownership and control of television stations. The ownership of publishing houses has had an important bearing on book production but does not explain the republic of letters. Similarly, media ownership does not explain the semiotic, social, or even political productivity of the textual system of television—only how it could be exploited by certain state or commercial forces.

A republic of television, if there were one, would not be sustainable if it were a feudal monarchy, at the whim and disposal of interlocking royal families of big corporations like News International, Viacom, and Disney. Some of these groups did in fact display monarchical tendencies, including a desire for hereditary succession. Despite the best efforts of long-serving CEOs like Rupert Murdoch and Kerry Packer on behalf of their offspring, they were rarely successful in that aim. Thomas Paine can rest easy. Television as a textual system is an invention of commercial culture and cannot exist without corporate organization. Part of the project of republican television studies thus would be to investigate the extent to which any potential television republic could be realized in that corporate, baronial context.

The viewing public of ordinary viewers had very little direct financial or managerial stake in TV production, but viewers did make a high semiotic or cultural (and temporal) investment in television's textual and social form. In other words, the familiar feudal language of media moguls, press barons, and literary lords was at odds with the much more modern structure of the television republic as it developed into a textual system on a societywide scale. The growth, diversification, and use of media textuality was not in the control of the feudalists; nor were viewers ever mere serfs of the semiotic economy.

The political economy approach to television focused on ownership, control, finance, and regulation and often had very little to say about, and no way of measuring, the productivity of the system in terms of meaning, knowledge, communication, information, and culture. This approach is associated with writers like Herbert Schiller, Nick Garnham, Peter Golding, and Graham Murdock, even Naomi Klein.[45] But that cultural, noninstrumental use of the media, human rather than economic, was its use value for the viewing public that television called into being (and that was the extent of its purposelessness). The interests of commercial producers did not extend very much further than enlarging the potential viewing public and stimulating reconsumption, which of course explains why TV encouraged reading over writing for so long.

But the viewing public could not be confined to such a subsistence economy. The system was too large, complex, and diverse to remain under the control of any one power, no matter how powerful some individuals appeared to be. A republican television studies would be interested in the relations between different powers within its commonwealth, but it would not need to assume a priori that only one of those powers could explain everything else in the system.[46] The golden eggs gathered so spectacularly by farmer-Rupert and his feudal cousins were actually laid by the rather unglamorous goose of the viewing public. Each needed the other in a commercial democracy. And as Richard Caves argues in his economic analysis of the creative industries, innovation— the very use value that made these industries viable—is in the gift of the consumer not the producer: "It is almost appropriate to say that innovation in creative industries need involve nothing more than consumers changing their minds about what they like."[47]

But as television studies grew, the agenda of the political economists of the media failed to keep an imaginative grasp on the semiotic productivity of the system they analyzed. They used popular media largely to promote their own agendas of leftist critique or policy regulation. But meanwhile it was increasingly evident that the existing representative apparatuses of old democracies allowed little room for direct self-representation by media citizens, except as such relationships were already heavily mediated via the marketplace and government offices. A republican television studies would be useful, therefore, to identify ways in which the ordinary public could be better represented within a developing television republic.

MEDIA CITIZENSHIP

The concept of citizenship was the subject of widespread reflection during the era of broadcast television, and not only in the field of political science. Citizenship was no longer simply a matter of civic rights and duties: the concept shifted from law to history. Following the classic work of T. H. Marshall, it could be argued that the history of citizenship in modernizing countries was one of the extension of rights and reduction of duties. But, more important, citizenship evolved increasingly from the political toward the cultural domain, and from obligations to a state toward self-determination by individuals.

In that context it was important to understand what form "media citizenship" might take. Marshall suggested that from its Enlightenment base in civil or individual rights, citizenship extended from there to political (voting) rights during the nineteenth century, thence to social (welfare, employment) rights up to 1950.[48] In advanced modern countries during the second half of the twentieth century it extended to cultural (identity) rights and, most recently, to do-it-yourself ("DIY") citizenship.[49]

With extension came also dissolution. As James Holston and Arjun Appadurai pointed out, the rights of citizens were increasingly claimed by noncitizens (welfare rights, for instance), while the duties (jury and military service, taxation) seemed increasingly onerous and apt to be evaded.[50] Attempts to revive citizenship led to "perverse outcomes." Attempts to make it more exclusive and local led to xenophobic violence; the alternative attempt to make it more inclusive and transnational "tends to preclude active participation in the business of rule."[51] Holston and Appadurai wrote of the "replacement" of the "civic ideal with a more passive sense of entitlement to benefits which seem to derive from remote sources. Far from renewing citizenship, violence and passivity further erode its foundations."[52]

Violence and passivity as an outcome of evolving senses of citizenship? Violence and passivity were the very effects that watching a lot of television was said to produce. Once again, although here in a negative form, the connection between textuality and citizenship needed investigation. Television may have added to xenophobia, remoteness, violence, and passivity, but its textuality may also have been a site for new forms of cultural engagement and even civic participation through which emergent forms of citizenship could be discerned.[53]

In the modern era no citizenship evolved anywhere without citizen readers. The evolution of citizenship began with the inauguration of civil and individual rights, followed by political rights; both of these were achieved among communities, such as the Parisian poor, whose civic and political emancipation followed their mobilization as readers of, for example, scandalous journalism, political pamphlets, and revolutionary philosophy. The Enlightenment, in short, was written down, diffused by reading, and established by those who made up the reading public. As Holston and Appadurai argue: "The extension of the shared beyond the local and homogenous is, of course, an essential part of citizenship's revolutionary and democratic promise. This extension of citizenship is corrosive of other notions of the shared precisely because its concept of allegiance is, ultimately, volitional and consensual rather than natural."[54] Writing, specifically journalism, was the medium by means of which "the shared" was extended in an ultimately volitional, consensual way. The "democratic ideals of commonwealth, participation and equality"[55] were the core values of the republic of letters.

Holston and Appadurai discuss the politics of identity in the context of citizenship. Noting that feminism had taken a lead in critiquing a liberal notion of citizenship that relegated prior differences of gender, for instance, or race, to the private sphere, they pointed to a current problem of democracy: "The politics of difference becomes more important and potentially incompatible with that of universal equality as the real basis for citizenship. For example, this politics argues that although different treatment (e.g., with regard to gender) can produce inequality, equal treatment, when it means sameness, can discriminate against just the kinds of values and identities people find most meaningful."[56]

A polity that was "indifferent" in both senses, with the indifference of impartial law (and impartial media) and the indifference of uncaring inequality, fueled criticisms of what became known as the "democratic deficit" of otherwise egalitarian, modern, secular countries. The demand for cultural citizenship based on identity, and for recognition and respect for identity based on authenticity or essential qualities such as ethnicity or sex, extended (perhaps to the breaking point) conceptualizations of equal citizenship based on civil, political, and welfare/employment rights. Holston and Appadurai argue that: "The argument from authenticity leads to a politics of difference rather than to a politics of universalism or equalization of rights. . . . Although this kind of demand would seem contradictory and incompatible with citizenship as an ideology of equality, there is nevertheless a growing sense that it changes the meaning of equality itself. . . . Thus, it would define citizenship on the basis of rights to different treatment with equal opportunity."[57]

In the context of growing demands for difference within universalizing polities, what was the role of television? One version of its history, which I offered in *Uses of Television,* was that the population gathering and popularizing imperatives of commercial television had a part to play in this process. As communities became more virtualized, and consent more volitional, television was able to provide a means of "cross-demographic communication" unrivaled by any other means in history. Within that context, it was one mechanism for the actual process of sharing difference. It was possible to extend the notion of the shared without that entailing the erasure of difference. Thus while television was routinely accused of provoking violence or encouraging passivity among its vast audiences, the possibility that it played a role in reconstituting citizenship on the site of virtualized identities of various kinds needed to be further explored.

CITIZENSHIP AND IDENTITY

Holston and Appadurai sought to relocate citizenship in the world's major cities, and of course they were right to do that. But citizenship was never a spatial belonging alone. Increasingly media critics and commentators have looked for ways in which the symbolic if not the juridical element of citizenship might be shared through media that were not available when citizenship first extended from urban centers to the vast and virtual imagined communities of nations. Cities were of course the strategic site for the early development of citizenship, but the new media, including television, played a part in "virtualizing" what had already been "nationalized" and thereby abstracted.

The possibility that television was a component of communicative democracy has not gone unnoticed by other critics. Writing from a feminist perspective, for instance, Joke Hermes argues that: "Popular culture is typically unorderly and unattractive from a modernist point of view; creative and inspiring, however, seen from a post-modern orientation— especially when democratic government and community-building are seen as endeavours that benefit by, nay, even need central fictions. Thus, even though popular culture is never the domain of administrative politics, of voting and decision-making, it may provide the grounding for a citizen identity."[58] From this perspective, Hermes concludes that "women's crime writing offers elements of a feminist utopia and ongoing criticism of the hurdles women face in their march towards full social and civic participation." These popular books "contribute to building a sense of what is needed where sex, justice, humour, and professionality are concerned."[59] Such cultural citizenship—a community of readers in this case, gathered in the name of pleasure, fiction, commitment, and engagement—needed to be understood in new ways: "Citizenship also needs to be understood as intrinsically mediated practices . . . Because citizenship cannot be defined as the membership of one community only, there is room for a broad orientation and inclusion of core democratic values, without necessarily excluding other views and ideas, coming from other (interpretive) communities. Individuals can be competent participants in different communities fully aware that codes or ideologies clash but not particularly concerned about this—since we are all adept to 'do in Rome as the Romans do.' "[60]

Hermes is at pains to point out that the participation she describes is not reading only but extends to writing: "The women's movement is a case in point. Many types of media content have been generated by feminists, ranging from flyers and political tracts to songs, autobiographies and literary novels. . . . The felicitous combination of tradition, technology and distribution may make a media form especially suitable for specific social groups—whether we are talking books when it comes to the women's movement, music genres for the black movement or videotapes for migrant groups."[61] In short, popular media in general (not just books) not only produced a reading public that used them to ground its own commitment to citizenship but also existed as modes of writing available to groups who wished to share their identity or difference among their own or wider communities, as Rita Felski first pointed out about the "feminist public sphere."[62]

Not just for individual citizens themselves but for specific social groups based on identity and difference, it was increasingly the case that membership was no longer of the public but of many different publics at once; public spheres became public "sphericules."[63] Groups and movements pursuing goals related to identity via cultural politics needed internal communication for the adherents to the cause, and external communication to address wider publics.[64] One place where such group-based communicative practices jostled and coexisted was, of course, television, which remained the cultural forum that Horace Newcomb and Paul M. Hirsch said it was many years ago,[65] the more so as it moved into the postbroadcast era of subscription-based viewing.

In relation to ethnic communities this could produce what Herman Gray called "complexity in an age of racial and cultural politics where the sign of blackness labors in the service of many different interests at once." Gray identifies three kinds of discursive practice on American television that anchored contemporary images of African Americans, including assimilationist (invisibility); pluralist (separate but equal); and multiculturalist (diversity). Of these coexistent forms the multiculturalist one is the most interesting, certainly for Gray, who reported that "in shows that engage cultural politics of difference within the sign of blackness, black life and culture are constantly made, remade, modified, and extended. . . . In these shows, differences that originate from within African American social and cultural experiences have been not just acknowledged, but interrogated, even parodied as subjects of television."[66] Gray shows in detail how textuality and citizenship intersect in such "multiculturalist" black television: *In Living Color* and *A Different World*, for instance, have used drama, humor, parody, and satire to examine subjects as diverse as Caribbean immigrants, black fraternities, beauty contests, gay black men, the Nation of Islam, Louis Farrakhan, Jesse Jackson, Marion Barry, racial attitudes, hip-hop culture, and white guilt. The richness of African American cultural and social life as well as the experience of otherness that derives from subordinate status and social inequality are recognized, critiqued, and commented on. The racial politics that helps to structure and define U.S. society is never far from the surface."[67] Such shows, in short, addressed African American viewers as part of a "complex and diverse" culture marked by internal difference, rather than addressing the "hegemonic gaze of whiteness." But of course those same images were available for anyone to see, "creating a space for this slice of black life in the weekly clutter of network television."[68]

While Herman Gray cheerfully admits (unusually for a media scholar) that some of the appeal of the shows he analyzed was that as a TV viewer he liked them, he is also trying to draw more impersonal lessons from thinking about blackness in the context of television: "Cultural struggles, including those over the representation of blackness in our *present*, help us to prepare the groundwork, to create spaces for how we think about our highly charged racial *past* and possibilities for our different and yet contested future. Commercial television is central to this cultural struggle. In the 1980s, claims and representations of African Americans were waged in the glare of television. Those representations and the cultural struggles that produced them will, no doubt, continue to shape the democratic and multiracial future of the United States."[69]

Cultural struggles went on within television, between it and its audiences, and between TV and critics from various complicit but more or less hostile groups. One such struggle was about the effort to have representatives from significant identity groups develop as writers, not simply as readers, or at best as on-screen symbols. Gray makes a point of naming the black professionals and production companies working in the industry who were having a material impact on the representation of African American culture on American TV—as writers. This was still a struggle because half a century of audience maximization and an obsession with promoting reconsumption had not done much to encourage diverse writers, least of all from minorities. But Gray demonstrates that things were changing historically.

TELEVISION: TEACHING GOOD CITIZENSHIP

As the market matured, and as new communication technologies began to allow "television" to be studied in the past tense, some of the gains and losses of the early strategy of audience maximization and reconsumption could be assessed. It was, of course, conventional to criticize broadcast television for universalising the viewing subject and for making too little allowance for difference. Television was also frequently criticized for ideology, populism, dumbing down, and all that. The losses involved were obsessively cataloged in TV studies.

Have there been any gains? Chief among them surely is the creation of the viewing public. Just as the popular press of the nineteenth century was responsible for the creation of the mass reading public, and hence the public, so TV became the place where and the means by which, a century later, most people got to know about most other people and about publicly important events or issues. Located in the heart of civil society, private life, and everyday culture, television occupied the very place from where the most important new political movements of the current period arose, from feminism to the green movement. Even the most sober critics believed it could promote new forms of citizenship. For instance, according to Peter Dahlgren, "Television can also engage and mobilize. . . . The question is whether television can . . . make a social difference. I would maintain that the medium has not yet lost this potential, limited though it may be. Television is a tricky medium and can do many things, including, perhaps—given the right circumstances—generating societal involvement and conveying a sense of citizenship."[70]

Here television is being recognized, albeit cautiously and belatedly, as part of the public sphere. Such recognition implies that television can engage and mobilize its vast cross-cultural audiences in ways that modernist critics were reluctant to admit. I argue in *Uses of Television* that broadcast television did indeed function to generate societal involvement and a sense of citizenship. The means by which it achieved this were not, as Dahlgren suggests, at the margins, with a well-meaning charity appeal here or consumer campaign there, but rather in its very structure as a popular medium of communicative entertainment. Television not only created the largest imagined community the world has ever seen (the TV audience), but it functioned as a teacher of cultural citizenship over several decades. That was the outcome or productivity of its literacy.

More recently, and as the medium itself evolved into postbroadcast forms with fragmented programming and user-choice options, television began to contribute to a "DIY" citizenship. But the routine form of analysis of the relation between TV and its audiences—that is, via concepts of power, hegemony, ideology, and populism—contrived to dismiss, downplay, or set aside the role of television as a teacher, along with the creative and autonomous uses to which those who are literate in its order of viewing could put it.

A rereading of some of the founding theorists of cultural studies, especially Richard Hoggart, suggests that popular television was understood from the start at least partly in terms of a pedagogic or teaching role.[71] The positive potential of such a role has been somewhat forgotten in subsequent work in cultural studies. But television continued into the postmodern period various teaching functions inherited both from modernity and from premodern (medieval) cultural formations. It behaved anthropologically in this respect, not like a pedagogical institution. It taught in a transmodern mode by promoting, among audiences who were not instrumentally purposeful in their learning, the construction of selves, semiotic self-determination, and a sophisticated understanding of (literacy in) the mediasphere.[72] I apologize for the neologism, but I call this function of television "democratainment."[73]

During the broadcast era television was busy creating the viewing public and teaching new forms of citizenship based on population gathering within a recognition of different identities. Meanwhile, what were the uses of academic criticism of television? TV studies as a disciplinary discourse had one direct effect on television itself that was not helpful. The new medium was launched into a hostile critical climate in the period between the 1930s and 1950s. Subsequently, TV studies evolved during the hyperpoliticized and adversarialist intellectual environment in the 1970s. Throughout, academic and a good deal of journalistic criticism of television was dedicated to disciplining the new medium as if it were a disorderly child. The response of TV was to make itself as safe as possible, not to be too adventurous, to be disciplined in the way that a boarding school is supposed to be disciplined—by prohibition and uniformity.

Such discipline produced a characteristically peculiar action in TV's body politic. It ended up looking like an Irish dancer—all buttoned up, stiff, and straight-faced at the top, legs going like the clappers underneath, control and creativity copresent but not on speaking terms, the rational part held impassively aloft by the wildly energetic but skillfully choreographed emotional part (the legs) that were studiously ignored even as they skipped between the athletic and the erotic. A suitably republican image, perhaps, to suggest that television was working, indeed dancing, on the ground of democratization throughout its broadcast history. During the same period, for many intellectual critics, the extension and celebration of democracy was seen not as a desirable goal but as a defeat of more revolutionary-utopian aims.

Television became old when the desires and fears it used to evoke as the latest, most popular, all-singing, all-dancing attraction were transferred to newer media such as the Internet. This is perhaps a good time to reassess the legacy of both television and television studies. One possible judgment is that TV itself had less to be embarrassed about than its critics. The teacher's report on TV studies itself might read "must try harder"; for instance to help make TV more varied, publics more literate, and the relations between the established republic of letters and the emerging media republic less hostile. The technology is there, thanks to postbroadcast media providers and a media-literate population, but the software— the critical discourse itself—is very conservative, prejudicial, and nostalgic. Television studies has much to learn, not least from the citizens of media, as it explores the next phase of development of the republic of television.

NOTES

1. John Carey, *The Intellectuals and the Masses* (London: Faber, 1992), pp. 6, 214–15; see also Richard Butsch, *The Making of American Audiences: From Stage to Television, 1750–1990* (Cambridge: Cambridge University Press, 2000), chapters 10 and 15.

2. See, for instance, Bernard Rosenberg and David Manning White, eds., *Mass Culture: The Popular Arts in America* (Glencoe, Ill.: Free Press, 1957); Jerry Mander, *Four Arguments for the Elimination of Television* (New York: William Morrow, 1978); Neil Postman, *Amusing Ourselves to Death: Public Discourse in the Age of Show Business* (New York: Penguin, 1986).

3. Pierre Bourdieu, *On Television*, trans. Priscilla Parkhurst Ferguson (New York: New Press, 1998).

4. Virginia Woolf, *A Room of One's Own* (1929; Harmondsworth: Penguin, 1945), p. 34.

5. Butsch, *Making of American Audiences*, pp. 231–34.

6. John Barrell, *The Political Theory of Painting from Reynolds to Hazlitt: "The Body of the Public"* (New Haven: Yale University Press, 1986).

7. Mark Gibson, *Monday Morning and the Millennium* (Ph.D. diss., Edith Cowan University, Perth Australia, 2001); McKenzie Wark, *The Virtual Republic: Australia's Culture Wars of the 1990s* (Sydney: Allen and Unwin, 1997); Catharine Lumby, *Gotcha! Living in a Tabloid World* (Sydney: Allen and Unwin, 1999).

8. John Hartley, *Uses of Television* (London: Routledge, 1999).

9. D. E. MacDonnel, *A Dictionary of Quotations, in most frequent use, taken chiefly from the Latin and French, but comprising many from the Greek, Spanish and Italian languages, translated into English; with illustrations historical and idiomatic* (London: G. and W. B. Whittaker, 1822), p. 337.

10. Thomas Paine, *Rights of Man: Being an Answer to Mr. Burke's Attack on the French Revolution,* ed. Hypatia Bradlaugh Bonner (1792; London: Watts and Co., 1937), p. 148.

11. For example, Greg Philo and David Miller, *Cultural Compliance* (London: Longman, 1999).

12. See Richard D. Altick, *The English Common Reader: A Social History of the Mass Reading Public, 1800–1900* (Chicago: University of Chicago Press, 1957); Jon P. Klancher, *The Making of English Reading Audiences, 1790–1832* (Madison: University of Wisconsin Press, 1987); Thomas Richards, *The Imperial Archive: Knowledge and the Fantasy of Empire* (London: Verso, 1993); Martyn Lyons, "New Readers in the Nineteenth Century: Women, Children, Workers," in *A History of Reading in the West,* ed. Guglielmo Cavallo and Roger Chartier, trans. Lydia Cochrane (Cambridge, Eng.: Polity, 1999), pp. 313–44; John Hartley, *The Politics of Pictures: The Creation of the Public in the Age of Popular Media* (London: Routledge, 1992), chapters 5–8; and John Hartley, *Popular Reality: Journalism, Modernity, Popular Culture* (London: Arnold, 1996).

13. Hartley, *The Politics of Pictures;* Hartley, *Popular Reality.*

14. *The Book of Homilies. Certain Sermons Appointed by the Queen's Majesty to be declared and read by all Parsons, Vicars and Curates, every Sunday and Holiday in their Churches; and by Her Grace's advice perused and overseen for the better understanding of the simple people* (1574; Cambridge: Cambridge University Press, 1850), p. 157.

15. Klancher, *Making of English Reading Audiences;* James Secord, "Progress in Print," in *Books and the Sciences in History,* ed. Marina Frasca-Spada and Nick Jardine (Cambridge: Cambridge University Press), pp. 369–89. See also works by Jürgen Habermas; e.g., *The Structural Transformation of the Public Sphere: An Inquiry into a Category of Bourgeois Society,* trans. Thomas Burger with the assistance of Frederick Lawrence (Cambrige: Cambridge University Press, 1989).

16. John Hartley, "The Frequencies of Public Writing: Tomb, Tome, and Time as Technologies of the Public," *Democracy and New Media,* ed. David Thorburn and Henry Jenkins (Cambridge, MA: MIT Press, 2003), pp. 247–69.

17. Scott Robert Olson, *Hollywood Planet: Global Media and the Competitive Advantage of Narrative Transparency* (Mahwah, N.J.: Lawrence Erlbaum Associates, 1999), pp. 5–6.

18. Guglielmo Cavallo and Roger Chartier, eds., *A History of Reading in the West,* trans. Lydia Cochrane (Cambridge: Polity Press; Amherst: University of Massachusetts Press, 1999).

19. Armando Petrucci, "Reading to Read: A Future for Reading," in Cavallo and Chartier, eds., *A History of Reading,* pp. 345–67.

20. Armando Petrucci, *Writers and Readers in Medieval Italy: Studies in the History of Written Culture,* trans. and ed. Charles M. Radding (New Haven: Yale University Press, 1995).

21. Petrucci, "Reading to Read," p. 356.

22. Ibid.

23. Ibid. pp. 349–50, 356.

24. Edward Gibbon, *The History of the Decline and Fall of the Roman Empire.* New edition, with an introduction by David Womersley (London: Penguin Books, 1995).

25. To coin a phrase; see John Fiske and John Hartley, *Reading Television,* 25th Anniversary Edition with new foreword by John Hartley (London: Routledge, 2003).

26. Lumby, *Gotcha!;* Wark, *Virtual Republic;* and Gibson, *Monday Morning,* chapter 6.

27. Hartley, *The Politics of Pictures.*

28. Ibid., pp. 143–44.

29. Hans Magnus Enzensberger, "A Modest Proposal for the Protection of Young People from the Products of Poetry," in *Mediocrity and Delusion: Collected Diversions,* trans. Martin Chalmers (London: Verso, 1992), p. 11; quoted in Petrucci, "Reading to Read," p. 365.

30. For the "semiotic" side, see John Fiske, "Moments of Television: Neither the Text nor the Audience," in *Remote Control: Television Audiences and Cultural Power,* ed. Ellen Seiter, H. Borchers, G. Kreutzner, and E. Warth (London: Routledge, 1989). For the "power" side, see David Morley, *Television Audiences and Cultural Studies* (London: Routledge, 1992), p. 29. See also Nicholas Abercrombie and Brian Longhurst, *Audiences: A Sociological Theory of Performance and Imagination* (London: Sage, 1998), p. 31.

31. Umberto Eco, "Towards a Semiotic Enquiry into the Television Message" (1966), trans. Paola Splendore, *Working Papers in Cultural Studies* 3 (1972): 103–21.

32. Petrucci, "Reading to Read," p. 367.

33. For this term and its application to media citizenship, see Toby Miller, *The Well-Tempered Self: Citizenship, Culture, and the Postmodern Subject* (Baltimore: Johns Hopkins University Press, 1993); and Toby Miller, *Technologies of Truth: Cultural Citizenship and the Popular Media* (Minneapolis: University of Minnesota Press, 1998).

34. Petrucci, "Reading to Read," p. 349.

35. Cited in Secord, "Progress in Print," pp. 377–78.

36. Petrucci, "Reading to Read," p. 349.

37. Some were discussed in Hartley, *Uses of Television.*

38. Petrucci, "Reading to Read," p. 366.

39. Ibid., p. 366.

40. John Hartley, "Communicational Democracy in a Redactional Society: the Future of Journalism Studies," *Journalism: Theory, Practice, Criticism 1.1* (2000): 39–47.

41. Petrucci, "Reading to Read," p. 349.

42. Ibid.

43. For instance "Jezmond's Portal to Xena Video Odyssey—Remixed Xena Flicks!" http://www.jezmond.com/portal.html.

44. "Suburbanality" is from Hartley, *Uses of Television,* chapter 15.

45. Herbert Schiller, *Culture, Inc.: The Corporate Takeover of Public Expression* (New York: Oxford University Press, 1989); Nicholas Garnham, *Capitalism and Communication: Global Culture and the Economics of Information* (London: Sage, 1990); Peter Golding and Graham Murdock, eds., *The Political Economy of the Media* (Cheltenham, Eng.: Edward Elgar, 1997); Naomi Klein, *No Logo: Taking Aim at the Brand Bullies* (Toronto: Vintage Canada, 2000).

46. Gibson, *Monday Morning.*

47. Richard Caves, *Creative Industries* (Cambridge: Harvard University Press, 2000), p. 202.

48. T. H. Marshall, *Class, Citizenship and Social Development* (1949; Chicago: University of Chicago Press, 1977). See also Hartley, *Uses of Television,* pp. 162–63.

49. Hartley, *Uses of Television,* pp. 177–88.

50. James Holston and Arjun Appadurai, "Cities and Citizenship," *Public Culture* 8:2 (1996), p. 190.

51. Ibid., p. 191.

52. Ibid.

53. Hartley, *Uses of Television.*

54. Holsten and Appadurai, "Cities and Citizenship," pp. 191–92.

55. Ibid., p. 192.

56. Ibid., pp. 193, 194.

57. Ibid., pp. 194–95.

58. Joke Hermes, "Cultural Citizenship and Popular Fiction," in *The Media in Question: Popular Cultures and Public Interests,* ed. Kees Brants, Joke Hermes, and Liesbet van Zoonen (London: Sage, 1998), p. 160.

59. Ibid., p. 164.

60. Ibid., p. 160.

61. Ibid., p. 166.

62. Rita Felski, *Beyond Feminist Aesthetics* (Cambridge: Harvard University Press, 1989); "The Feminist Public Sphere" is a chapter in this book.

63. Stuart Cunningham, "Popular Media as Public 'Sphericules' for Diasporic Communities," *International Journal of Cultural Studies* 4.2 (2001): 131–47.

64. Felski, *Beyond Feminist Aesthetics.*

65. Horace Newcomb and Paul M. Hirsch, "Television as a Cultural Forum" (1983), in *American Cultural Studies: A Reader,* ed. John Hartley and Roberta E. Pearson (Oxford: Oxford University Press, 2000), pp. 162–73.

66. Herman Gray, *Watching Race: Television and the Struggle for "Blackness"* (Minneapolis: University of Minnesota Press, 1995), p. 84.

67. Ibid., p. 91.

68. Ibid., pp. 111, 112.

69. Ibid., p. 173.

70. Peter Dahlgren, "Enchancing the Civic Ideal in Television Journalism," in Brants, Hermes, and van Zoonen, eds., *The Media in Question,* p. 93. See also Peter Dahlgren, *Television and the Public Sphere* (London: Sage, 1995), p. 146.

71. Hartley, *Uses of Television,* chapters 10 and 11.

72. Hartley, *Popular Reality.*

73. Hartley, *Uses of Television,* chapters 12 and 14.

JULIE D'ACCI **CULTURAL**

STUDIES, TELEVISION STUDIES,

AND THE CRISIS IN THE HUMANITIES

▬▬▬ Much has been written in the last few years about the crisis in
▬▬▬ the humanities, especially in the United States and the United
▬▬▬ Kingdom. But it is clear that variations of this crisis are surfac-
ing in many areas of the globe. The ever-increasing domination of instrumental reason, the sovereignty of the sciences, and the growth of the
technocratic university all pose dangers to the teaching of the humanities
(as well as the arts), and the funding of programs and teachers. Multiple
things can be said, of course, about the language of crisis, which for many
in the field of media studies, is embarrassingly close to the unabashed
tabloid. But as Bill Livant pointed out, and Patrick Brantlinger reiterated,
the word "crisis" in Chinese is a combination of the characters meaning
"danger" and "opportunity."[1] For this essay the crisis offers me an opportunity to reflect on the current state of television studies in the United
States; and to champion a particular approach. But it also opens onto a
pit of dangers—primarily those of reacting, policing, and universalizing.
Given the specific historical conjuncture I'm addressing, I hope to make
plain why and how these dangers need to be risked.[2]

Let me begin by quickly summarizing the three predominant ways the
crisis in the humanities has been figured. First, as a crisis involving the
1970s "invasion of the others" (women's studies, African American and
ethnic studies, and queer studies) into the academy, and the subsequent

"culture wars" in the 1980s over literary and cultural canons. Second, as a crisis over instrumental knowledge and practical education in the new corporate university where students are consumers and nonapplied knowledge is ever more devalued, suspect, or defended as the hand-maiden to the sciences.[3] And third, as a crisis surrounding Western hegemony over knowledge, specifically over philosophy and theory. Of course, in this aspect of the crisis, with the West losing domination, the question becomes exactly *whose* crisis is it anyway?[4] A number of people have written extensively about these issues, including Patrick Brantlinger, Stuart Hall, Herman Gray, Bill Readings, Lawrence Grossberg, and Patrick Furey and Nick Mansfield.[5]

CULTURAL STUDIES AND THE HUMANITIES IN CRISIS

Cultural studies, especially in the U.S. academy, is thoroughly imbricated in all three conceptions of the crisis. In many ways, of course, this attests to the victory of those who pioneered the study of culture and those who fought for the inclusion of cultural inquiry into more traditional canons and curricula. In other ways, it underscores the dangers and historical perversities involved in the victory.

Turning to the first conception of the crisis, cultural studies (although initially linked with the invading others) has recently been used to integrate the others and quell their assaults on traditional canons by providing bridges between Asian American, Latino/a American, African American, queer studies, women's studies, subaltern studies, and other so-called area studies and more traditional disciplines like literature and languages, art, music, history, sociology, and communications.[6] All of this is achieved by means of cultural studies' most institutionally utilitarian and flexible concept—interdisciplinarity—a concept that has given it the dexterity both to provoke and now ameliorate the culture wars. The recent ameliorative function is abetted by issues involving the second conception of the crisis—the burgeoning of the corporate university. In this instance, cultural studies' interdisciplinarity shows up as a part of university streamlining and downsizing in a number of administrative maneuvers ranging from calculated management strategies to scattershot and naive attempts at reform to genuine commitments to educational change. In the process, cultural studies is used to refurbish and refresh traditional departments by integrating scholars who are part of the cultural studies publishing boom, and thus lure more students/consumers with hipper subject matter. (Problems for media studies may arise when the subject matter involves media—as a good deal of work in cultural studies does—but the scholars have little or no training in its history, methods, or scholarship.) Cultural studies animates the third conception of the crisis because its theoretical and methodological openness and its resistance to defining its project allow it to counter the notion of Western philosophical hegemony and figure as a flashpoint for a new intellectual globalism. On the other hand, it also becomes a lightening rod for criticisms of an openness that is seen as a veiled neoliberalism and a mask for Western capitalist hegemony.[7]

As this state of affairs attests, cultural studies, as a catchphrase and a scholarly approach, may be seen to function in the United States as an all-out performative—bringing into being whatever it happens to stand for, or whatever it is brought in to do, in any specific situation.[8] Bill Readings, in *University in Ruins,* argues along these lines when he says that "the culture" in cultural studies "has achieved a place similar to the word excellence" in American higher education—ubiquitous and miraculous precisely because it signifies everything and nothing at the same time.[9] Not everyone agrees, however. Ted Striphas, for example, has contended that we need not look at how cultural studies is incessantly and multiply invoked and written about (not at its metadiscourse) but rather at how it is actually taught and practiced at various universities, and he documents numerous discrepancies between the metadiscourses and the pedagogy.[10] But when a phrase, and a tradition of research, teaching, and practice, generate such contradictions and when these undergo perpetual resignification for a variety of utilitarian ends, it seems absolutely imperative that at every turn we ask the question "in whose interest?"

In the course of this essay I will suggest that it is not only possible but propitious (in the historical context I'm outlining) to delineate what cultural studies generally is and what it is not, what it sanctions and what it does not, how it can be taught and practiced, and what might even constitute some of its research protocols.[11] I concentrate, however, on delineating these things primarily for television studies, which has been shaped within a cultural studies tradition.

CULTURAL STUDIES AND TELEVISION STUDIES IN THE UNITED STATES

In the United States, cultural studies and television studies came together during the late 1970s and early 1980s, with 1978–1982 forming the turning-point years. This history and its multifold versions are familiar, but as I reconstruct it, Todd Gitlin's influential "Dominant Paradigm" article of 1978 played a major part in priming the American pump for a flood of scholarship from England and Australia that would channel the energies of critical U.S. scholars desperate for an alternative to the administrative/effects model, and for a critical approach that would deal with television programs and viewers as well as television industries.[12] The impact of Curran, Gurevitch, and Woollacott's *Mass Communication and Society* (among the first of this scholarship published in a collected volume) cannot be overstated. Grouping together, as it did, political economists such as Graham Murdock and Peter Golding from Leicester, cultural critics such as Stuart Hall and Dick Hebdige from Birmingham, and media scholar James Carey from the United States, the book influenced a particular brand of American cultural studies—a brand dedicated to analyzing the interworkings of industries, programming, and everyday life. Brunsdon and Morley's *Everyday Television: Nationwide,* and Fiske and Hartley's *Reading Television* (both published in 1978, and then hitting the United States with force in the following two years), along with the 1980 *Culture, Media, Language,* edited by Hall, Hobson, Lowe, and Willis, provided empirical and theoretical models for a ready generation of American scholars. (Hall's field-defining and much-debated encoding/decoding article, which was published in *Culture, Media, Language,* had already been circulating via tattered photocopies in communication departments throughout the country.) By the late 1980s and early 1990s, cultural studies (now heavily influenced and reshaped by feminism, poststructuralism, postcolonial theory, and race theory) was evolving into a new, although loosely construed, dominant paradigm in many communication departments. It seemed like a hard-fought struggle would grant it the power to shape the future of the field.[13]

At this moment of perhaps fantasized utopian possibility, when a redefined and invigorated critical television practice had secured the institutional space and legitimacy needed to delineate all the specificities of its objects, its methods, and theoretical confluences, it was hit with a spate of developments from several fronts at once. Each development captured scholarly attention, sometimes (and necessarily) stealing the focus from television per se, sometimes shaking the belief in television as a specific object of study, sometimes causing television to be treated as an undifferentiated cultural text, and most of the time inducing confusion involving theories, methods, objects, and disciplines.

From the front of U.S. television, the impact of new technologies, especially the Internet, signaled an undreamed-of future and cried out for academic investigation; the unequivocal fact of a global media environment mandated a new focus on broad rather than narrow questions concerning electronic media; and the fragmentation of cable and satellite services and the birth of niche narrowcasting sounded the death knell for network hegemony and, consequently, any easy claims about a dominant mass broadcasting and its influences. On the cultural studies front, Grossberg, Nelson, and Treichler's infamous *Cultural Studies* volume delivered a version of the approach to a host of other disciplines in the United States, notably English, having enormous ramifications for American cultural studies and media studies alike, ramifications that shuttled media studies (including film as well as television) ever more swiftly in a text-centered direction.[14] Although the publication of cultural studies–based analyses that explored the interworkings of industries, programs, audiences, and contexts had been building steam (and in many instances continued to forge ahead), other cultural studies work on television began to seize on general ideological interpretations of texts or programs. There developed, in other words, a tendency in some analyses to overlook the conditions and specific shaping forces of production; the conditions and intricacies of reception; and, ironically, because much of this was considered to be text-based work, the specificities of the televisual form (from narrative structure to genre to the operations of televisual techniques).[15] Some of this text-centered work began to branch out to incorporate loosely conceived "ethnographies" (mostly to demonstrate the multiplicity of viewer interpretations) but with little attention to the histories and complexities of these methods or the status of the evidence and the conclusions involved.[16] John Fiske's 1987 *Television Culture*, advocating textual polysemy and variegated audience readings, has been excoriated for abetting this interpretive trend and for conceiving of popular culture as a repository of pleasure and audiences as powerfully resistant (although initially, the book garnered praise for reinvigorating a critical approach that was seen to flirt with ideological determinism).[17] On the sociohistorical front, the formation of a global economy, the erosion of world communism, and the shrinking of viable challenges to capitalism and the status quo posed widespread challenges to the critical study of American television; while in the U.S. academy renegotiations of Marxist and neo-Marxist approaches, as well as economic and legitimacy crises, taxed the fledgling field. All of this is to reiterate that a cultural studies–based approach to television, on the verge of honing and delineating its objects and methods, on the verge of systematically confronting theories of Althusserian ideology, structuralism, and semiotics with theories of hegemony, discourse, and postcolonialism and poststructuralism in general, was besieged all at once by a group of powerful forces that shook it soundly.

Within the specific institutional and historical contexts described above, the study of television from a cultural studies perspective has been criticized from many different positions both within and outside the approach itself. Some of the most persistent critics are media scholars from a political economy tradition (hailing from the United States, England, and Glasgow) who, among useful assertions, have incessantly and erroneously charged that cultural studies bears the blame for an erosion of U.S. television studies by churning out nothing but scholarship that celebrates and shores up the culture industries. What they vilify, however, is a caricature of the approach—a caricature that accentuates and distorts the interpretive and pleasure-oriented trends I have alluded to; that effaces the enormous amount of other work in the tradition; and that fosters unnecessary and unproductive divisions in critical media studies and university departments. As indicated by the factors listed above, the state of affairs is far more complex than such a univocal response would suggest.[18]

Recently, cultural studies in general, and media-centered cultural studies by implication, have also been taken to task by a number of Latin American scholars within their overall critiques of American scholarship and globalism. A presumed correlation between U.S. cultural studies and a radical postmodernism that's equivalent to neoliberalism runs through much of this criticism. Postcolonial writer Roman de la Campa, in summarizing a good deal of this work, particularly that of Chilean theorist Martin Hopenhayn, outlines features of the neoliberalism that these scholars see coursing through U.S. cultural studies. Some of these features reverberate with cultural studies' call to investigate industrially produced cultural products, its wholesale critique of the state, its interest in utopian dimensions of consumption, and its fascination with variegated instances of reception and general resistance and resilience. "The market," writes de la Campa, "is understood as the only social institution that provides order without coercion; politics and the state lose their transformational capacity . . . consumerism becomes inherently emancipatory in the absence of liberationist discourses . . . and the blanket deconstruction of modernizing schemes transforms structural underdevelopment into healthy examples of diversity and localized heterogeneity."[19]

Much of the other criticism from this perspective is equally daunting, although it is different from that by the U.S. and U.K. political economists because it doesn't urge a return to a unidimensional political economy or the subordination or minimization of cultural analysis. Moreover, it forces a focus on a social context that spawns both the U.S.

political economy and cultural studies scholars—a context in which a long-term booming economy (despite the vicissitudes of market slumps, crashes, and recessions) has conditioned all academic responses in ways that may be obscured by diatribes, from elite social positions, against capitalist culture industries (which, it goes without saying, need severe and constant criticism, as well as radical change).

THE CIRCUIT MODEL

I want to argue here that each of these criticisms, and a host of other dangers currently faced by a cultural studies approach to television in the United States, may be confronted by a robust reassertion of a revised circuit model as a matrix for defining the field's object of inquiry and a guide for its methodological study. The model needs revision to function not as communications—not as a circuit of meaning (which is not to say that it couldn't function that way among others)—but as a heuristic model for scholarly analysis and teaching, a model for how to approach and conceive of the object of inquiry that the field of television studies wants to contribute. I argue this for a number of reasons. Such a model, however provisional, ensures a common framework within which work may be conducted, understood, and assessed; and within which an object of inquiry may be elaborated over a wide span of time. It affords the unparalleled benefits of building systematically on previous scholarship and of deploying, debating, debunking, and redesigning analytical methods for investigating that object. I hasten to add, however, as I alluded to above, that I'm not implying that applications of the model (whether explicit or implicit) have withered away. We have seen various incarnations in recent years in several books and many articles about television.[20] In fact, my contentions about the value of a revised model are best seen as the results of an ethnographic-like trolling through the writing of those scholars I see as performing the diverse, imaginative, yet coherent cultural studies work I am advocating. It is simply my intention here to make the framework more overt, and, although I propose a variation of the model, I hope not to inscribe more boundaries than intended or to imply or encourage a freezing of the sites, or a flattening of them into a schema that works to favor the synchronic and obscure the diachronic (which I very much want to promote).[21] A diagrammatic model may seem to engrave limits and confines with blatancy and abandon, casting a cold eye on the fact that limitations and confines are what any critical approach continuously struggles to uncover, reflect on, and negotiate. But as with any prose account of a critical paradigm that tries to incorporate the insights of poststructuralism, such a model may be seen as furnishing time-bound guidelines of ever-evolving methods, objects, and theoretical conceptions. I'm convinced that such a model is open and flexible enough, as well as based on enough years of input from scholars the world over to make the myriad dangers worth risking.

A Tour of Models

The model I'm espousing may, of course, be traced from Stuart Hall's "encoding/decoding" (1980) to Richard Johnson's "circuit of production, circulation, and consumption of cultural products" (1986) to the Open University's "circuit of culture" (1997) to the variation I want to propose in this essay—a "circuit of media study." Stuart Hall's encoding/decoding (figure 1) was widely publicized in the 1980 book *Culture, Media, Language*.[22] It has been central in the theoretical literature of the field, in historical retrospectives, and in pedagogical practice, but it may have had less of an effect on the field's actual research than might be assumed. Designed to be specifically homologous to Marx's sketch of commodity production in *Grundrisse* and in *Capital* (drawing particularly on the 1857 *Introduction to the Grundrisse*), and deriving an elegance and staying power from this homology, "encoding/decoding" diagrams the various phases of the television phenomenon, stressing the "linked but distinctive moments of connected practices"—a continuous circuit through a "passage of forms." Essentially, Hall argues that this circuit of three moments or phases (encoding, the TV program as meaningful discourse, and decoding) elucidates how the forms that coalesce in encoding (social relations, practices, and the means of production) get transformed, in the TV program, into discourse and transformed again, at the level of decoding, into forms of social relations and practices.

There is no doubt that Hall meant "encoding/decoding" to be a reflection on television specifically and not a model for cultural studies in general. There is also no doubt that he centers on the discursive form of the television message—that TV meanings and messages in the form of "sign vehicles" are the heart of the model. It is odd and interesting, however, that each moment of Hall's model has been singled out (and criticized) for being afforded undue primacy; Hall himself says that both encoding and the TV program as meaningful discourse are necessarily privileged. But many scholars have noted that when it comes to encoding/decoding it is the moment of decoding that seems to carry the day (and David Morley's work has greatly contributed to this fact). The dominant (preferred), negotiated, and oppositional positions from which a TV message may be decoded are well-ingrained truisms, not only for

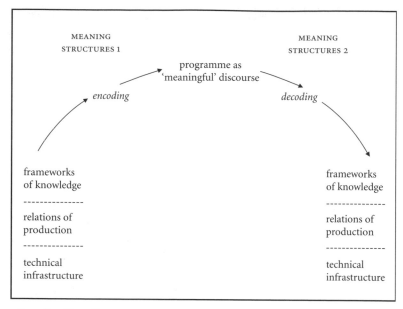

MEANING STRUCTURES 1

MEANING STRUCTURES 2

programme as 'meaningful' discourse

encoding

decoding

frameworks of knowledge

----

relations of production

----

technical infrastructure

frameworks of knowledge

----

relations of production

----

technical infrastructure

1. Encoding/Decoding.

television scholars but for media students the world over. A main observation I want to make here is that there is a clear "circulant" in Hall's model and it is the discursive message that is transformed from social relations, practices, and economic means of production (encoding) into a moment of signification (program/discourse) and back again to forms of social relations and practices (decoding). The elegance and clarity of the model is thus its Achilles' heel, pointing as it does to the circulation of messages and meanings, and implying that it is the meanings of the TV program (those encoded into them and decoded from them) that are the natural objects of study in this thing called television studies.

Hall himself has criticized aspects of the model, by commenting that its focus on meaning is too cognitive and thereby inscribes no space for pleasure or the operations of the unconscious; that the encoding site is too homogenous and is linked too directly to a purported dominant ideology, and thus does not reveal encoding's contestatory character; that the division into three distinct analytic moments (although defensible) has been complicated by the insights of poststructuralism; and finally that the model lacks and needs a bottom half that would depict decoding as linked back to encoding, and make plain that it is not the "real world" down at the bottom of the model (out of which encoding emerges and into which decoding returns) but a continuous loop involving the "real world" in discourse.[23]

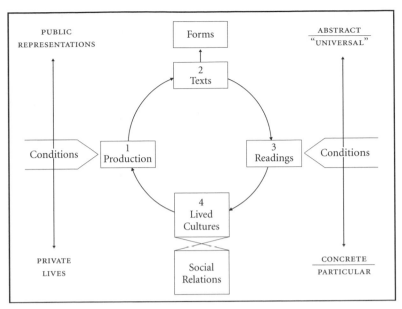

PUBLIC
REPRESENTATIONS

Forms

ABSTRACT
"UNIVERSAL"

2
Texts

Conditions

1
Production

3
Readings

Conditions

4
Lived
Cultures

PRIVATE
LIVES

Social
Relations

CONCRETE
PARTICULAR

2. Circuit of Production, Circulation, and Consumption of Cultural Products.

Richard Johnson's circuit model (figure 2) appeared in his 1986 essay "What Is Cultural Studies Anyway?" (although it was first introduced in 1983 as a paper for the Centre for Contemporary Cultural Studies). Because the 1986 essay was published in the literary-oriented *Social Text* it was one of the first systematic and wide-reaching introductions of cultural studies to language and literature departments in the United States. Johnson, who succeeded Stuart Hall as the director of the Centre, revises and widens the encoding/decoding model to deal with cultural studies as a whole rather than simply the topic of TV. Needless to say, this article remains one of the most useful and perceptive reflections on the objects and methods of cultural studies. To a great degree, Johnson maintains Hall's connections to Marx's circuit of production and consumption, as well as the notion of forms. However, Johnson's diagram, unlike Hall's, does not depict a circuit of meaning but rather a circuit of the production, circulation, and consumption of cultural products, with each of the boxes in the diagram (production, texts/forms, readings, and lived cultures/social relations) representing a moment in the circuit. What circulates around this circuit seems to be "the cultural product" itself. But Johnson hastens to tell us (and this is important given that his circulant is a product) that there is (or when applied in a capitalist context, most often is) a dual aspect to the circuit: it is both a circuit of capital (that is, a product produced by a capitalist system travels around the loop) and a circuit of the production and circulation of subjective forms (the cultural, or subjective, side or form of the product also travels around the loop). It is these subjective forms that concern Johnson the most because for him cultural studies tracks the "historical forms of consciousness or subjectivity, or the subjective forms we live by, or . . . the subjective side of social relations." He attempts to clarify what he means by subjective forms by saying that while Marx was concerned with those social forms through which human beings produce and reproduce their material life (forms figured in the circuit-of-capital aspect of the loop), cultural studies "looks at social processes from another complimentary [sic] point of view. [Its] project is to abstract, describe and reconstitute in concrete studies the social forms through which human beings 'live,' become conscious, sustain themselves subjectively" (which is figured in the circuit-of-subjective-forms aspects of the loop).[24]

Cultural studies, then, is the study of cultural products from their subjective and consciousness-oriented points of view. Johnson, in fact, eschews using the word "culture" in favor of consciousness and subjectivity, describing consciousness as involving cognition, knowledge, and active mental and moral self-production, and describing subjectivity as involving affect, aesthetics, and individual and collective identities. "*All social practices*," he says "can be looked at from a cultural point of view, for the work they do, subjectively."[25] While his exact take on the categories of consciousness and subjectivity, and the precise meanings of the "subjective forms we live by" or the "subjective side of social relations" are never, I think, completely clear or concrete, the diagram and Johnson's subsequent explication of the ways the various moments have and could be analyzed methodologically provided an extremely productive jumping-off point for general cultural studies research as well as for specific research into television studies. I have been surprised that as the years have gone forward the model has not garnered a good deal more systematic critique, amplification, and application.

Some facets of Johnson's model are troublesome and need enumeration here, and several others will be enlarged on in my discussion of the model I want to propose. First, as is evident in Johnson's diagram, the arrows in the circuit are curiously and counterproductively one-way; second, the designation of a cultural product as the circulant (even when seen in its "subjective form" dimension) acts to constrain other possible conceptions of the object of study or the types of research questions that the model could encourage, promote, and sustain; third, the inscription in the diagram of the contrasting forms of public/abstract/universal and private/concrete/particular, while provocative, seem too binary and con-

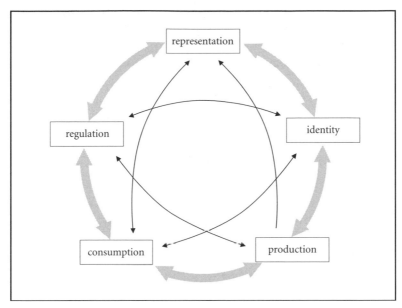

3. Circuit of Culture.

sequently too limiting for a general model; fourth, and particularly salient for the model I'll offer, it is the imbrication of the cultural with the
economic and the material, and the material dimensions of the cultural
(or of consciousness and subjectivity), that need to be stressed rather
than stressing, as Johnson tends to do, their separation.

The Open University's 1997 model (figure 3) is very similar to the one I
have been working on, and has also further influenced my own. Called
the "circuit of culture," its inheritance from Johnson's model is apparent
and acknowledged. In this model, what the authors call five "cultural
processes" are identified: representation, identity, production, consumption, and regulation. These are the processes through which any analysis
of "a cultural text or artifact" must pass if it is to be fully studied.[26] In this
model, then, it appears that the analysis is what travels around the circuit
(represented by the exterior arrows). The interior arrows depict articulations—the linkages among and between the processes that are forged
both in the history of the processes themselves and by the researchers
who study them. It is immediately obvious that the Open University
diagram corrects the one-way arrows in Johnson's model by making
them go in both directions, and it also adds new processes—representation, regulation, and identity—into the mix. Production here involves
not only understanding how an artifact (the authors use the Sony Walkman as their example) is produced technically but how it is produced

culturally—how it is made meaningful. From production, the authors move directly into their consideration of representation—how the production of the artifact is represented in various ways. They then move into a consideration of identity/identification—how the representations of the artifact are aimed at creating an identity for the artifact that would aid in establishing an identification with a group of consumers. They move next to consumption, focusing on how the phase of production (which in this example includes not only production per se but also representation and identity) is strategically oriented toward creating consumption. In their scrutiny of consumption, the authors show that no matter how strategic and concerted the designs are at the level of production in order to foster consumption, consumers and their uses of products are unpredictable. The process of regulation is, finally, examined to reveal the ways that cultural regulation (in this instance, policing the boundaries between public and private by ensuring that the Walkman's sound doesn't penetrate public space) further influences production, representation, identity, and consumption. I'll return to some criticisms of this model later.

THE CIRCUIT MODEL UNDER FIRE

Before delving into my own model, it is crucial here to understand the concerns of the general circuit model's most outspoken critic, Lawrence Grossberg, who in several articles over the years rails against such a model (most often against encoding/decoding).[27] Although he seems primarily to chafe at the circuit model's use for cultural studies generally, he also decries it as a model of a cultural studies approach to television per se. His main objections are, first, that cultural studies has been submerged under a model of communication, with culture and communication seen as fallaciously and reductively equivalent; and, second, that the Centre for Contemporary Cultural Studies has, in fact, (he says quoting Hall) been equated with the Centre for Television Studies. The singling out of the sites of production, text, and consumption is similarly erroneous and reductive because it predefines those domains and their contents by abandoning the radical contextualization of cultural studies and reifying the encoding/decoding model. Grossberg also contends that within a "communicational cultural studies" based on such a model, only consumption is really relevant; and culture is reduced to a notion of meaning (a distinctly nonmaterial conception of meaning, at that), with an occasional nod to pleasure and desire. Furthermore, he believes that we must abandon the model because "the problematic of one cultural studies investigation is not the same as that of another"; that is, no two cultural studies projects are alike.[28]

Grossberg ultimately argues that we need to shift our analytic focus away from texts, audiences, and industries to an examination of research questions ("what's happening" sorts of questions) and their relationships or articulations to contexts. While I could not agree more with the need to turn away from an overemphasis on textual interpretations or textual meanings (whether ascribed to the researcher or to the real or imagined audience member) and turn to research questions and their articulations, I do not believe that a jettisoning of the circuit model is the way to go. I especially don't believe it in the face of such slim (to date) delineations of the notion of context, nor in the face of the fact that meaning (when conceived under the aegis of discursive practices, as I'll discuss below) is quite specifically understood as material and, furthermore, need not be divorced from affect or the unconscious.[29] Also, such a circuit model seems to me to imply everything but a privileging of consumption; and like any scholarly work it need not suggest that its designation of particular domains or their "contents" is conceived of as fixed or even valid as analytic domains for all time. Grossberg's defense of the uniqueness and specificity of each cultural studies project is important (as are all of his forebodings), but it must be balanced by an acknowledgment of the commonalities, the accumulations, and the understandings based on previous work. A circuit model doesn't hawk a formulaic approach to TV studies; rather, it underscores that we cannot start from ground zero each time we embark on a new project, and that explicitly working from the scholarship of the past (scholarship that has contingently delineated and analyzed various dimensions of production, reception, cultural artifacts, and sociohistorical contexts) is the best way to structure our current inquiries and our pedagogical practice.[30]

A CIRCUIT OF MEDIA STUDY

The diagram I present here (figure 4) is similar to that of the Open University.[31] I call it a "circuit of media study," but in other places I have referred to it as the integrated approach to media studies.[32] The main differences between my model and that of the Open University's are that mine includes four rather than five sites— production, cultural artifact, reception, and sociohistorical context—which are figured as spheres with broken lines in order to represent porous and analytical rather than self-contained and fully constituted domains. My model also inscribes the process of articulation (the thinner arrows in the interior) operating

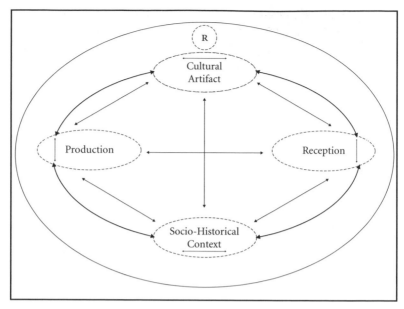

4. Circuit of Media Study.

within as well as between and among the sites (for reasons that will become clear below); and it inscribes the researcher or the receiver (the "R" at the top) within the model itself, because it is the researcher (or receiver) who produces his or her version of the object and the articulations.[33] The thicker outer arrows represent the specific research question and its analysis that travels around the loop (going in either direction and starting from any point) and is the model's circulant; but, unlike that described by the Open University group, the analysis traveling around this loop is not limited to that of a cultural artifact or text.

In contrast to the Open University model, my model subsumes regulation under the site of production, which I conceive of as encompassing all phases of the production moment or the industry or the overall institutional context from which programming emerges and is regulated (programming, however, as we will see below, is not the only artifact designated under the heading cultural artifact, nor is the industry studied only as a producer of programming). I also don't designate representation or identity as separate sites in my model. Representation and identity are complicated moments for the Open University group, with identity seemingly added in order to incorporate the wealth of scholarly work that argues (correctly, in my opinion) that it is notions of identity that are an essential domain of culture—much in the way Richard Johnson argued that subjectivity is culture's proper domain.[34] The Open University model uses identity to deal with both the identity of the product and that of its consumers, thereby making the point that it is the task of culture industries to establish an identification between the two. In my model, rather than create a separate category for these processes, I deal with issues of product identity in each of the sites, depending on the project in question, and I deal with consumer identity primarily under the rubric of reception, where I grapple with most aspects of subjectivity, although subjectivity may be dealt with under the rubric of the sociohistorical context or under production (when, for example, examining the social relations of production in, let's say, a study of the writers' strike that threatened Hollywood in 2001). I also haven't found it necessary to establish representation as a separate site, but, again, I deal with issues involving representation under all four of my designated sites, specifically claiming that representations or texts emerge and can be studied at all four sites (even though some analyses may concentrate a lot of effort in this regard at the level of the site I dub cultural artifact).

The sites themselves, let alone their interactions, have innumerable dimensions that systematic research can more fully construct and elucidate. But let me just suggest a couple of points here. I see each site as marking out a convergence of discursive practices, which as the phrase indicates are themselves convergences of meaning and matter (including people, environments, and money). They also involve (as do all discursive practices, even though they have been inadequately analyzed and theorized in this regard) the subjective dimensions of affect and unconscious processes.

THE SITES AS CONJUNCTURAL

Conceiving the sites as convergences of discursive practices facilitates a number of analytical claims and moves. First, it allows the conjunctural character of the sites to be brought to the fore. In other words, each site or moment of the circuit (seen as distinct for analytical purpose) mobilizes conjunctures of economic, cultural, social, and subjective discourses. In contradistinction to the beliefs of some of the political economy–oriented scholars referred to above, critical scholarship does not need to look only or even primarily to the site of production (the industry or producing institution) to analyze economic implications or the operations of money, even when analyzing television produced by capitalist culture industries. A cultural studies analysis, for example, could concentrate on the site of the cultural artifact and examine the high-budget or low-budget production values—capital transformed into style—evident in the formal dimensions of particular programs; or it might focus on reception and investigate the various in-home technologies—capital as domestic goods—of viewers from different socioeconomic strata. Conceiving the sites in this way can illuminate the reasons why more in-depth work on aspects of the individual sites (in addition to their interrelationships) needs to go forward under the cultural studies banner. For example, work on a specific aspect of the cultural artifact, industry, reception, or sociohistorical context may be conceived of and designed within the parameters of the four-part model but be undertaken as a precise examination of a micro-instance, and such work can open onto descriptive elaboration without being considered either purely formalistic or sociological.[35]

Having said this, cultural studies work on television (and this is one of the main things missed by the political economists) should in no way be, and in numerous instances has not been, what John Caldwell calls "de-industrialized cultural studies."[36] To the contrary, the four-site model not only precisely points to seeing the conjunctural aspects of each individual site but also to seeing industries and their specific economic imperatives in relation to the other three areas; at the same time the model makes clear that cultural artifacts, reception, and sociohistorical context cannot truly be conceived or understood apart from the specific conditions of television production that are operative for the specific project in question. (It needs to be stressed at this point, however, that a four-site model does not mandate that each site be examined fully for each and every analysis or research question; rather, it simply illustrates the point that the operations and effects of each should be considered when designing any project, fashioning any research question, evaluating any claims, or making any conclusions.)

HEGEMONY, ARTICULATION, AND THE SITES

Foregrounding the notion of discursive practices also emphasizes the model's lineage in a theory of hegemony and a reliance on the analytical notion and practice of articulation. Hegemony is the process by which various discourses in a social formation come to achieve positions of relative power in negotiations and struggles with other discourses. Cultural studies, for its part, is dedicated to analyzing the operations of power; and in the 1980s, scholars within the tradition began incorporating Gramsci's work on hegemony to modify the structuralist determinism of Althusser's ideological model. Hegemony was also more compatible with the discourse approach that much of cultural studies similarly gravitated toward in the 1980s. Although Ernesto Laclau and Chantal

Mouffe have endeavored to weave together hegemony and a version of discourse theory, much detailed theoretical work that would equally carefully weave together cultural studies, discourse theory, hegemony, and television studies, as I mentioned earlier, is still needed.[37] Drawing on Laclau and Mouffe, however, we may see that the hegemonic status of any discourse is, by its very nature, always open to change, negotiation, and displacement; and it is the process of articulation that is both responsible for the flux and the provisional (hegemonic) fixity.

Articulation, in Laclau and Mouffe's account, is the process by which an "element" gets linked into a particular discourse to become a "moment" in that discourse—to take up its meaning in that particular discursive practice.[38] By way of example, in the sociohistorical context of the 1960s and 1970s in the United States, "gay" was an element that became unlinked from its quasi fixity in particular discourses like religion (in which it was a moment articulated to "sin") and like psychiatry (in which it was a moment linked to "sickness" and "deviance"), and then became rearticulated in civil rights discourse to "equality" and in activist discourse to "pride." These various discourses and their articulations of gay then battled over what could become the hegemonic meanings of gay in the social formation at the time. This example might imply a type of cultural studies analysis that, when applied to television, would necessarily be centered on the meanings of gay in particular television programs (whether they be news, documentaries, sports, or entertainment forms); it also might seem (along the lines of the encoding/decoding model) to conceive of these TV-generated meanings as the natural object of inquiry of something called television studies. Although such analyses are important, particularly if they focus on the material and affective dimensions of these meanings, there are also many other ways of demonstrating the work of hegemony and articulation in the model I discuss here.

Speaking first to the issue of meaning—meaning must be studied in each site, not simply that of the cultural artifact or even the sociohistorical context. The meanings and articulations of gay, for example, have countless ramifications at the level of production; first, for workers in all aspects of the industry, including specific employment benefits, job security, general workplace climate, and physical and psychological safety; and, second, for the industry's target audience imperatives, such as the 1990s pursuit by the networks of a socially liberal urban professional market with gay-themed programming, as demonstrated in the work of Ron Becker.[39] At the level of reception, those same meanings have equally countless ramifications that could be pursued in studies similar to those conducted on other audiences by David Morley, Ann Gray, Ellen Seiter,

Christine Geraghty, Jacqueline Bobo, and Marie Gillespie, among others.[40] What must be stressed here is that cultural studies analyses, based in hegemony and articulation, are not simply about the meanings generated in TV programs or about meanings in the sense of ideas about things, but about meanings in the material sense of discursive practices that involve physical bodies, physical workplaces, the materiality of households or other viewing spaces, and the subjective feelings generated (as well as the more idea-oriented aspects involved).

Much excellent cultural studies work on television has analyzed (both implicitly and explicitly) the workings of hegemony and articulation and, in the process, the material dimensions of discursive struggles, making plain that television as an object of inquiry has innumerable dimensions in addition to what might be the meaning-oriented and ideological ones of particular programs. Let me offer a few examples from the rich array of this work to illustrate some ways (sometimes tacit and sometimes overt) of putting into motion the different phases of a cultural studies circuit model.[41]

John Caldwell's compelling book on U.S. television programming in the 1980s and 1990s concentrates on a woefully underexamined domain in cultural studies work—the formal and stylistic dimensions (the material dimensions) of television programs as cultural artifacts. Here, therefore, is a study that focuses quite intensively on TV programs, not to perform ideological readings or interpretations of their meanings but rather to conduct analyses of their style. In surveying 1980s and 1990s programs, Caldwell identifies what, in the terms of the circuit of media study I'm advocating, might be called a "hegemonic discourse" of excessive visual style. He labels this "televisuality" and detects two incarnations of it. Within the site the model marks off as the cultural artifact, he articulates one incarnation (involving high production values and film-feature-style cinematography) to a stylistic history he dubs "the cinematic," and the other incarnation (involving an obsession with effects such as image/text combinations and hyperactivity) to a stylistic history he calls "the videographic." Moving his articulatory practice from the site of the cultural artifact to the interconnections with the other sites, Caldwell argues that televisuality achieved hegemony because at the levels of production and reception, respectively, the networks (spurred by competition from cable) and the audience (based on new cable-induced expectations) had themselves articulated cinematic programs to a discourse of distinction (involving quality, art, and the filmic) and videographic programs to the new MTV discourse (involving youth, energy, and nowness), both of which were deemed preeminently desirable at the time. Caldwell himself further articulates televisuality to a general and hegemonic discourse of stylistic excess and consumerism in the sociohistorical context of all American mass culture.[42]

If Caldwell's book focuses on the stylistic dimensions of programs as cultural artifacts with linkages to production, reception, and the sociohistorical context, Lynn Spigel's work on the installation of television in the United States focuses on TV itself as a cultural artifact (a new, weakly articulated technological, social, and cultural element) that in 1950s America was articulated to numerous discourses (including romance, family, gender, health, public/private space, and interior decor), thus becoming a moment in those discourses and achieving intelligibility within their terms. These discourses emerged from multiple sites: from various aspects of production in forms such as advertisements and network documents; and from various aspects of the sociohistorical context in forms such as women's magazines, popular books, and books on interior design. Although TV was articulated in these discourses to both utopian and dystopian dimensions (viewing, for instance, could be a boon for the romantic life of the fifties couple or it could spur either spouse to be more interested in onscreen activities and objects of desire; it could promote healthy family relaxation or give viewers the dreaded disorder of "telebugeye"), Spigel demonstrates that ultimately these articulations tried to maximize the pleasurable and minimize the displeasurable aspects of the new technology. The material and affective dimensions of television's discursive domestication are demonstrated in the site of reception, where Spigel discusses the concomitant fashioning of living rooms as home theaters, the new floor plans of houses in which dining room and living room combinations and general open spaces could facilitate viewing (especially by the housewife who was occupied with such chores as food preparation), the installation of dishwashers to hasten cleanup and allow the housewife to join the family viewing circle, the continual negotiation of family power revolving around the new technology, and the engendering of feelings such as pleasure, displeasure, horror, and desire.[43]

Taking another tack, Yeidy Rivero's work on Puerto Rican television, particularly on the program *Mi Familia* (the first program in Puerto Rican television history to feature a black family), attends to the site of production. Rivero interviews *Mi Familia*'s production staff and the media professionals at the channel Telemundo, and reveals how the production personnel insisted on articulating "blackness" to a historical discourse called "la gran familia puertorriquena." This was a discourse generated by Puerto Rican elites in the nineteenth century to forge class and racial solidarity against the Spanish colonialist government, but one that in current times, Rivero argues, prevents racial issues and hierarchies from being confronted. According to Rivero, such an articulation, and the TV-buttressed hegemony of la gran familia puertorriquena, has numerous material and affective effects on the full examination of Puerto Rico's racial dynamics and the everyday lives of its populations, keeping alive, as it does, the idea that Puerto Rico is one big family with no race-based stratification, and repressing the differences of blacks in the social formation.[44]

Meanwhile, Purnima Mankekar, in *Screening Culture, Viewing Politics: An Ethnography of Television, Womanhood, and Nation in Postcolonial India,* turns her attention to the site of reception, using ethnography (here, a combination of participant observation and interviews) to work with twenty-five Indian families (half of whom are Hindu, a quarter Muslims, and a quarter Sikhs) to investigate the place of Doordashan (Indian national television) in the reconstitution of postcolonial "Indian Womanhood" in the 1980s and 1990s. Among many other things, Mankekar demonstrates how Doordashan articulates Indianness and Indian Womanhood to discourses of Hindu preeminence, in the process othering Muslims and Sikhs and portraying postcolonial India as a Hindu nation and Hindu women as the nation's spiritual core. She shows, however, the ways that women viewers disentangled the intertwining of gender and this specific form of nationalism by rearticulating Indian Womanhood to the various discourses that constituted their local lives and using the televised tales to help them interpret and understand their actual felt vulnerabilities and rage.[45]

Finally, Szu-ping Lin, in *On Prime Time: Television Drama and Taiwanese Women,* zeroes in on the sociohistorical context (and ultimately its relationships to programming, production, and reception). She shows how particular elements in the Taiwanese social formation have come to be understood and experienced by their incorporation as moments in various competing discourses. By way of example, she details how the element of "broken palms" (occurring when the top line of the palm cuts across the entire surface of the hand) had traditionally been articulated, as a moment in the discourse of fortune telling, to bad luck when occurring in women, but good luck in men. She profiles the many adverse effects this articulation produced in the historical lives of women—difficulties getting married, abandonment and persecution by families, blame for the misfortune of those around them, and so forth; and she describes how in recent years the Taiwanese government and various

Taiwanese social groups have actively tried to break the old fortune telling myth by promoting the discourse of rationality and science in which a broken palm is articulated to nature and fortune telling's myths to superstition. She then investigates one of the popular prime-time serials (from the genre called Hsian-Tu Hsi) on the topic, looking at the sites of production, cultural artifact, and reception, and carefully researching how the program deals with broken palms in the course of its run—how the producers and writers wanted to foster the dissolution of the myth and how some viewers and social action groups wanted the program taken off the air because they felt it contributed to reviving and sensationalizing the residual superstition in some facets of the population.[46]

In spite of the different research questions, emphasis on different sites, and involvement of different types of hegemony, each investigation analyzes the object of study (television) as an interaction among the various sites, and each shows ways that intensive examinations of the hegemonic process and its sundry articulations reveal the historical configurations of discourses and power; configurations that are further illuminated by the articulation practices of cultural analysis and thus laid open to intervention and change.

INTERDISCIPLINARITY/DISCIPLINARITY AND THE MODEL

As may be confirmed from the examples given above, conceiving the model as involving discursive practices foregrounds the fact that cultural studies and cultural-studies-oriented work on television is of necessity interdisciplinary. It also points to the fact that the sites have been constituted and analyzed by (among others) discourses of various disciplines and fields such as those delineated by John Frow and Meaghan Morris in their introduction to *Australian Cultural Studies,* including aesthetic discourses, economic discourses, theoretical discourses about commodity production and circulation, discourses of gender, discourses of politics, and ethnographic discourses,[47] as well as discourses of race, religion, nation, housing and urban planning, and so forth. It furthermore points to the fact that the various discipline-based discourses involve specific methodologies, such as specific schools of stylistic analysis; narrative analysis; industry and economic analysis; analysis of human and cultural geography; postcolonial analyses; and qualitative sociological analysis including participant observation, interviewing, survey research, specific schools of ethnography—especially the postcolonial critiques and approaches that have reshaped the field—and so forth. While John Corner, among others, has warned against an unexamined, untheorized con-glomeration of methods from a conglomeration of disciplines, others such as Richard Johnson have urged that what we actually need to do is perform the careful work necessary to integrate fully the various methods in the particular analysis we are conducting.[48] Reasserting the usefulness of a circuit model, particularly as a heuristic and teaching tool, makes a number of points regarding methods, the discipline-based discourses, and their analyses of the sites in question—primarily that they have histo-ries of trial and error, debate, and revision; and that while we shouldn't accept any bodies of knowledge as foundational, we'll surely come to understand our objects and methods more satisfactorily by vigorously and systematically confronting all the work that has gone before.

The crisis in the humanities needs to be addressed by a kind of inter-disciplinarity that wholeheartedly engages the methods and subject mat-ter of various fields of study. As is obvious, TV studies must grapple with specific aspects of fields such as literary and film studies, economics and business, sociology and anthropology, history, political science, geogra-phy, and psychology, among others. Such a grappling allows for precise analyses of the articulations that build hegemony and for the ways to uncouple and recouple them. Such an interdisciplinarity is a far cry from the assumption that the "in-between" work of cultural studies takes place at the most obvious and accessible edges of the disciplines in question and simply involves the general demonstration of ideology or resistance at work. A revised circuit model allows us to systematically constitute (in whatever contingent and open-ended ways) the specificities of all the interconnections that form television studies. And it is these specificities that will serve to stave off a dissolution of television studies in the United States into a faux cultural studies media scholarship that is indeed syn-chronous with neoliberalism and in danger of becoming so attenuated that it simply fades away.

I see the revised model as an analytical tool that is aimed at under-standing how, in a given time and circumstance, a particular approach proceeds. It is also aimed at elaborating the principles that guide it and that can be passed on to future generations to handle as they will. Instead of seeing the model as a policing of the field, I see it as a reaction against a policing that is out of view and far less obvious, a policing that occurs because of the ways the openness and flight from definition in some cultural studies has been taken up in the U.S. academy. Such openness can be misread as freedom and a clear analytical model as a constraint. But, in fact, it just might be the other way around.

1. Bill Livant, "The Imperial Cannibal," in *Cultural Politics in Contemporary America,* ed. Ian Angus and Sut Jhally (New York: Routledge, 1989), p. 35. Patrick Brantlinger, *Crusoe's Footprints: Cultural Studies in Britain and America* (New York: Routledge, 1990), p. 12.

2. I want to thank the participants of the conference "Images of Femininity in East Asian Media," City University of Hong Kong, September 1999, for their comments on these issues.

3. For example, art as teaching the design and graphics skills that may be used to create new biological and technological models; philosophy as furnishing the ethics for biotechnology; music, art, literature, and other humanities as triggering the creative juices for imaginative scientific thought and breakthroughs, and so forth.

4. See Brantlinger, *Crusoe's Footprints,* for another look at these points.

5. Brantlinger, *Crusoe's Footprints;* Stuart Hall, "The Emergence of Cultural Studies and the Crisis of the Humanities," *October* 53 (summer 1990): 11–25; Herman Gray, "Is Cultural Studies Inflated?" in *Disciplinarity and Dissent in Cultural Studies,* ed. Cary Nelson and Dilip Parameshwar Gaonkar (New York: Routledge, 1996), pp. 203–16; Bill Readings, *The University in Ruins* (Cambridge: Harvard University Press, 1996); Lawrence Grossberg, "Toward a Genealogy of the State of Cultural Studies," in Nelson and Gaonkar, eds., *Disciplinarity and Dissent in Cultural Studies,* pp. 131–47; Patrick Furey and Nick Mansfield, *Cultural Studies and the New Humanities* (Oxford: Oxford University Press, 1997).

6. For another look at these issues, see Herman Gray, "Is Cultural Studies Inflated?" in Nelson and Gaonkar, eds., *Disciplinarity and Dissent in Cultural Studies,* pp. 204–16.

7. For example, see Roman de la Campa, "Cultural Studies, Globalization, Neoliberalism," in *The Politics of Research,* ed. E. Ann Kaplan and George Levine (New Brunswick: Rutgers University Press, 1997), pp. 69–89.

8. Cultural studies, too, could be described as in crisis, especially the kind of "organic crisis" discussed in the work of Antonio Gramsci, Ernesto Laclau, and Chantal Mouffe. See Ernesto Laclau and Chantal Mouffe, *Hegemony and Socialist Strategy: Towards a Radical Democratic Politics* (London: Verso, 1985), p. 136.

9. Readings, *The University in Ruins,* pp. 89–118.

10. Ted Striphas, "Introduction: The Long March: Cultural Studies and Its Institutionalization," *Cultural Studies* 12.4 (1998): 453–75.

11. Contrary to many people in the field at the time, Cary Nelson thought it important and possible, and not in violation of the spirit of cultural studies, to articulate some of its premises and protocols. See Cary Nelson, "Two Conferences and a Manifesto," *Journal of the Midwest Modern Language Association* 24.1 (spring 1991): 24–38.

12. Much of the critical and Marxist work in the United States at the time was focused on industry-based analysis, a lot of it involving media ownership. James Carey's work had begun to direct U.S. scholars to a type of cultural analysis, but it was the British and Australian scholarship that, in my opinion, fully ignited a widespread cultural studies approach.

13. Todd Gitlin, "Media Sociology: The Dominant Paradigm," *Theory and Society* 6 (1978): 205–53; James Curran, Michael Gurevitch, and Janet Woollacott, eds., *Mass Communication and Society* (Beverly Hills: Sage, 1979); Charlotte Brunsdon and David Morley, *Everyday Television: "Nationwide"* (London: British Film Institute, 1978); John Fiske and John Hartley, *Reading Television* (London: Methuen, 1978); and Stuart Hall, Dorothy Hobson, Andrew Lowe, and Paul Willis, eds., *Culture, Media, Language* (London: Hutchinson, 1980). For another look at the place of communications in early U.S. cultural studies, see Lawrence Grossberg, "Can Cultural Studies Find Happiness in Communication Studies?" *Journal of Communication* 43.4 (autumn 1993): 89–96.

14. These are ramifications that I'm not attributing to the volume itself but perhaps to the ways the volume and the approach were taken up. Lawrence Grossberg, Cary Nelson, and Paula Treichler, eds., *Cultural Studies* (New York: Routledge, 1992). Richard Johnson had introduced another version of cultural studies to U.S. English departments via his "What Is Cultural Studies Anyway?" *Social Text* 16 (winter 1986/ 87): 38–80. See David Bordwell, *Making Meaning: Inference and Rhetoric in the Interpretation of Cinema* (Cambridge: Harvard University Press, 1989) for his argument about film criticism's emphasis on interpretation and meaning at the time.

15. Here I am referring to the techniques of camera work; editing; sound; and mise-en-scène, including makeup, lighting, sets, props, and the movement of figures in the frame. See David Bordwell and Kristin Thompson, *Film Art: An Introduction,* 5th ed. (New York: McGraw-Hill, 1997).

16. Here, to cite simply a few pioneering examples, I am expressly *not* referring to the pathbreaking work on romance reading by Janice Radway, *Reading the Romance: Women, Patriarchy, and Popular Literature* (Chapel Hill: University of North Carolina Press, 1984); or the work of Ellen Seiter et al. on audiences in "Introduction," and " 'Don't Treat Us Like We're So Stupid and Naive': Towards an Ethnography of Soap Opera Viewers," in *Remote Control: Television, Audiences, and Cultural Power,* ed. Ellen Seiter, Hans Borchers, Gabriele Kreutzner, and Eva-Maria Warth (London: Routledge, 1989); or Ien Ang's *Watching* Dallas: *Soap Opera and the Melodramatic Imagination* (London: Methuen, 1985).

17. John Fiske, *Television Culture* (London: Methuen, 1987). A closer reading of *Television Culture* will demonstrate that Fiske situates programming more within its industrial context, deals more with its formal dimensions, and consequently points more toward television's constraints than has been typically reported.

18. The invaluable contributions of this group of critical scholars, however, should not be minimized. I am simply and specifically reacting to their diatribes (all of which are not uniformly dismissive) against a cartoon version of cultural studies. See, for example, Mike Budd, Steve Craig, and Clay Steinman, *Consuming Environments: Television and Commercial Culture* (New Brunswick: Rutgers University Press, 1999); Greg Philo and David Miller, "Cultural Compliance: Dead Ends or Media/Cultural Studies and Social Science," Glasgow Media Group paper, June 1998; Robert McChesney, "Is There Any Hope for Cultural Studies?" *Monthly Review* 47.10 (March 1996): 1–18; Mike Budd, Steve Craig, and Clay Steinman, "The Affirmative Character of U.S. Cultural Studies," *Critical Studies in Mass Communication* 7 (1990): 169–84; Nicholas Garnham,

"Political Economy and Cultural Studies: Reconciliation or Divorce?" *Critical Studies in Mass Communication* (March 1995): 62–71; and Graham Murdock, "Across the Great Divide: Cultural Analysis and the Condition of Democracy," *Critical Studies in Mass Communication* 12 (March 1995): 89–94.

19. Roman de la Campa, "Cultural Studies, Globalization, Neoliberalism," in Kaplan and Levine, eds., *The Politics of Research*, pp. 69–89.

20. To give a few examples: Horace Newcomb, *Television: The Critical View*, 6th ed. (New York: Oxford University Press, 2000); John Corner, *Critical Ideas in Television Studies* (Oxford: Oxford University Press, 1999); John Hartley, *Uses of Television* (London: Routledge, 1999); Nicholas Abercrombie, *Television and Society* (Cambridge, Eng.: Polity, 1996); Lynn Spigel, *Welcome to the Dreamhouse: Popular Media and Post-war Suburbs* (Durham: Duke University Press, 2001); Herman Gray, *Watching Race: Television and the Struggle for Blackness* (Minneapolis: University of Minnesota Press, 1996); Michael Curtin, *Playing to the World's Biggest Audience: The Globalization of Chinese Film and TV*, forthcoming; and Anna McCarthy, *Ambient Television: Visual Culture and Public Space* (Durham: Duke University Press, 2001).

21. Thanks to the participants of the conference "Images of Femininity in East Asian Media," City University of Hong Kong, September 1999, and my "Debates in Cultural Studies" seminar in fall 1999 at the University of Wisconsin—Madison.

22. Stuart Hall, "Encoding/Decoding," in Hall et al., eds., *Culture, Media, Language*, pp. 128–38. A longer form of the essay had previously circulated as a paper of the Centre for Contemporary Cultural Studies, titled "Encoding and Decoding in Television Discourse."

23. Stuart Hall, Ian Angus, Jon Cruz, James Der Derian, Sut Jhally, Justin Lewis, and Cathy Schwichtenberg, "Reflections upon the Encoding/Decoding Model: An Interview with Stuart Hall," in *Viewing, Reading, Listening: Audiences and Cultural Reception*, ed. Jon Cruz and Justin Lewis (Boulder, Colo.: Westview Press, 1994), pp. 253–74.

24. Richard Johnson, "What Is Cultural Studies Anyway?" *Social Text* 16 (winter 1986/87): 43, 45.

25. Ibid., p. 45.

26. Paul du Gay, Stuart Hall, Linda Janes, Hugh Mackay, and Keith Negus, *Doing Cultural Studies: The Story of the Sony Walkman* (London: Sage, 1997), p. 3.

27. Grossberg, "Can Cultural Studies Find Happiness," pp. 89–96; "Cultural Studies: What's in a Name?" (pp. 243–71), and "Toward a Genealogy of the State of Cultural Studies" (pp. 272–86), along with other articles, in *Bringing It All Back Home* (Durham: Duke University Press, 1997).

28. Grossberg, "Can Cultural Studies Find True Happiness," pp. 92–95. See also the article mentioned in note 27; Grossberg, "Cultural Studies: What's in a Name?" p. 256.

29. In a note for the article "Cultural Studies: What's in a Name?" Grossberg defines context as "specific bits of daily life, positioned between culture (as a specific body of practices) and social forces/institutions/apparatuses," p. 399. See Grossberg, "Toward a Genealogy of the State of Cultural Studies," pp. 131–47; "Cultural Studies: What's in a Name?" pp. 253–54; and "The Formations of Cultural Studies: An American in Birmingham," in *Relocating Cultural Studies*, ed. Valda Blundell, John Sheperd, and Ian

Taylor (New York: Routledge, 1993), pp. 21–64. See Laclau and Mouffe on discursive practices in *Hegemony and Socialist Strategy,* pp. 104–14.

30. By way of some examples, for production one would acknowledge the elaborations involving the general structural level of the corporate capitalist enterprise-ownership structures, corporate hierarchies, job distributions, and so forth; and those at the level of the overall production process such as the production of formulaic programs, the rationalization and streamlining of the production process, the fashioning of target audiences, and so forth. One would also need to draw on previous work and conduct a good deal more research on noncommercial (public, community, amateur, etc.) production sites and institutions. For reception, one would draw on and conduct further research into the overall institution of viewing: the social and environmental factors that comprise viewing situations, such as traditional family hierarchies; and the myriad dimensions of the actual viewer/program interactions, including how meaning, pleasure, and other forms of affect may actually get produced; how audience members may absorb, reject, or negotiate norms offered up by programs; how particular groups choose programs and use representations; how fans become avidly involved, and so forth.

31. Many thanks to Fran Breit and Aaron Cohen for their help in rendering the model.

32. See my "Television Genres," in *International Encyclopedia of Social and Behavioral Sciences* (Oxford: Elsevier, 2001), pp. 15574–78; "Gender, Representation and Television," in *The Television Studies Book,* ed. Toby Miller (London: BFI, 2002), pp. 91–94; and "Television, Representation, and Gender," in *The TV Studies Reader,* ed. Robert Allen and Annette Hill (London: Routledge, 2003), pp. 373–88.

33. The researcher should be conceived of as emerging from a very similar diagram to the one presented here. In the case of the researcher, however, the cultural artifact would be seen as academic scholarship; production, the specific institutional conditions of academic writing; reception, the specific reception conditions (conferences, journals, and so forth); and the sociohistorical context, the overall social conditions of the times in question. I use this "R" also to designate a general receiver to make the point that TV audience members may perform operations similar to both the ones spelled out here and those associated with more formal media analyses by media researchers.

34. See, for example, Paul Gilroy, "British Cultural Studies and the Pitfalls of Identity," in *Black British Cultural Studies,* ed. Houston A. Baker, Jr., Manthia Diawara, and Ruth H. Lindeborg (Chicago: University of Chicago Press, 1996), pp. 223–39.

35. Jostein Gripsrud in his *The Dynasty Years* (London: Routledge, 1995), p. 64, discusses something close to this when describing the difference between "explanation" and "interpretation." Here, I am thinking about work on television forms, aesthetics, and genres; and on television collectors, audience testing, and the myriad other underexamined aspects of programming, texts, cultural history, industries, and reception. Of course, not every site needs to be examined for every project.

36. Caldwell, *Televisuality,* p. 24.

37. Cultural studies scholars such as Stuart Hall, David Morley, Lawrence Grossberg, Graham Turner, and John Hartley, among others, have addressed these issues. I am simply arguing that more detailed theoretical work (along the lines of Laclau and Mouffe's yoking together of hegemony and discourse theory) still seems necessary for cultural studies.

38. Laclau and Mouffe, *Hegemony and Socialist Strategy,* pp. 105–7.

39. Ron Becker, "Prime Time Television in the Gay Nineties: Network Television, Quality Audiences, and Gay Politics," *Velvet Light Trap* (fall 1998): 36–47.

40. See David Morley, *Family Television: Cultural Power and Domestic Leisure* (London: Comedia, 1986); Ann Gray, *Video Playtime: The Gendering of a Leisure Technology* (London: Routledge, 1992); Ellen Seiter, *Television and New Media Audiences* (London: Oxford University Press, 1999); Christine Geraghty, *Women and Soap Opera: A Study of Prime Time Soaps* (Cambridge, Eng.: Polity, 1991); Jacqueline Bobo, *Black Women as Cultural Readers* (New York: Columbia University Press, 1995); and Marie Gillespie, *Television, Ethnicity, and Cultural Change* (London: Routledge, 1995).

41. In the following section I read the work of various cultural studies television scholars through the specific lens of the circuit model I'm discussing here.

42. Caldwell, *Televisuality.*

43. Lynn Spigel, *Make Room for TV: Television and the Family Ideal in Postwar America* (Chicago: University of Chicago Press, 1992).

44. Yeidy Rivero, "Erasing Blackness: Media Construction of 'Race' in *Mia Familia,* the First Puerto Rican Situation Comedy with a Black Family," *Media, Culture, and Society* 24:4 (July 2002): 481–91.

45. Purnima Mankekar, *Screening Culture, Viewing Politics: An Ethnography of Television, Womanhood, and Nation in Postcolonial India* (Durham: Duke University Press, 1999).

46. Szu-ping Lin, *On Prime Time Television Drama and Taiwanese Women: An Intervention of Identity and Representation* (Ph.D. diss., University of Wisconsin, Madison, 2000).

47. John Frow and Meaghan Morris, eds., *Australian Cultural Studies: A Reader* (St. Leonards, Aus.: Allen and Unwin, 1993), pp. xvi–xvii.

48. John Corner, "Media Studies and the 'Knowledge Problem,'" *Screen* 36.2 (summer 1995): 147–55; Richard Johnson, "What Is Cultural Studies Anyway?" *Social Text* 16 (winter 1986/87): 38–80.

William Boddy is a professor in the Department of Communication Arts at Baruch College and in the Certificate Program in Film Studies at the Graduate Center, both at the City University of New York. He is the author of *Fifties Television: The Industry and Its Critics* and numerous articles and book chapters on media history. He is currently completing a social history of twentieth-century electronic media.

Charlotte Brunsdon teaches in the Department of Film and Television Studies at the University of Warwick. She is the author of *Screen Tastes* and *The Feminist, the Housewife and the Soap Opera* and the coauthor of *The Nationwide Studies.*

John T. Caldwell is an author and filmmaker and teaches television and media studies at the University of California, Los Angeles. He is the author of *Televisuality: Style, Crisis, and Authority in American Television; Electronic Media and Technoculture;* and *Identity/Globalization/Convergence: Ethnic Notions and National Identities in the Age of Digital.* He is the producer and director of the award-winning documentary films *Freak Street to Goa: Immigrants on the Rajpathî* and *Rancho California (por favor).*

Michael Curtin is a professor of Communication Arts at the University of Wisconsin, Madison. He is the author of *Redeeming the Wasteland: Television Documentary and Cold War Politics,* and the coeditor of *Making and Selling Culture* and *The Revolution Wasn't Televised: Sixties Television and Social Conflict.* He is currently writing a book about the globalization of Chinese film and television and, with Paul McDonald, coediting a book series for the British Film Institute called International Screen Industries.

Julie D'Acci is a professor in the department of Communication Arts at the University of Wisconsin, Madison. She is author of *Defining Women: The Case of Cagney and Lacy* and is currently working on a book about cultural studies, media studies, and methodology.

Anna Everett is an associate professor of Film, TV, and New Media in the Film Studies Department at the University of California, Santa Barbara. She is the author of *Returning the Gaze* and *The Revolution Will be Digitized: Afrocentricity and the Digital Public Sphere.* She is active in SCMS's Black Caucus, Information Technology Committee, Program Committee, and she serves on the executive board of Console-ing Passions.

Jostein Gripsrud is a professor in the Department of Media Studies at the University of Bergen. He is the author of *The Dynasty Years* and editor of *Television and Common Knowledge.*

John Hartley is dean of the Creative Industries Faculty at Queensland University of Technology, Australia, and was previously head of the School of Journalism, Media and Cultural Studies at Cardiff University in Wales. He is the author of *Popular Reality, Uses of Television,* and *A Short History of Cultural Studies,* the coauthor of *The Indigenous Public Sphere,* and the coeditor of *American Cultural Studies: A Reader.*

Anna McCarthy is an associate professor of Cinema Studies at New York University. She is the author of *Ambient Television: Visual Culture and Public Space* (Duke University Press). Her current research investigates the commercial television activities of corporate activists, labor leaders, and cold war liberals in postwar America.

David Morley is a professor of Communication at Goldsmiths College, University of London. He is the author of *The Nationwide Audience; Family Television; Television, Audiences and Cultural Studies;* and the co-author of *Spaces of Identity* and *The Nationwide Television Studies,* and the coeditor of *Stuart Hall: Critical Dialogues in Cultural Studies* and *British Cultural Studies*. His most recent book is *Home Territories: Media, Mobility and Identity*.

Jan Olsson is a professor in the Department of Cinema Studies at Stockholm University. He is the author of several books and numerous essays, most of them on topics related to silent cinema. He is the founding editor of the film journal *Aura* and coeditor of the book series Stockholm Studies in Cinema published by John Libbey. He is currently involved in a project on film exhibition in Los Angeles.

Lisa Parks is an associate professor of Film, TV, and New Media in the Film Studies Department at the University of California, Santa Barbara. She is the coeditor of *Planet Television* and author of a book on global television and visual culture (forthcoming from Duke University Press).

Priscilla Peña Ovalle is currently pursuing a Ph.D. in Critical Studies at the University of Southern California. Her research focuses on the representation of the Latina body in American dance films. With a background in television and film production, she presently designs interactive digital media.

Jeffrey Sconce is an associate professor in the School of Communications at Northwestern University and the author of *Haunted Media: Electronic Presence from Telegraphy to Television* (Duke University Press). He is currently writing a book on television style.

Lynn Spigel is a professor in the School of Communications at Northwestern University. She is the author of *Make Room for TV* and *Welcome to the Dreamhouse* (Duke University Press). She has also edited several anthologies on media and culture and is currently writing *High and Low TV: Commercial Television and Modern Art*.

William Uricchio is a professor of media at the Massachusetts Institute of Technology. He is the coauthor of *Reframing Culture* and the coeditor of *The Many Lives of the Batman*.

Anthology format, of television narrative, 96
Anticommercials, 203–204
Appadurai, Arjun, 270, 305–306, 309, 406–408
Architecture, series, 38–39, 101
Archives: lack of, 395–396; as "legacy" holdings, 48
Arlen, Margaret, 366
Art: and color television, 367; and commercial television, 357, 375–376; as entertainment, 351; and everyday life, 356; and expression on television, 374–375; and network control, 368–373; pitching as, 57–59; public perception of, 354–356; television as, 93, 375
Art education, using television for, 373–376. *See also* Educational television
Articulation, theory of, 434–439
Artifacts, cultural: television programs as, 436–437
Audience: as consumer, 17; of global media flow, 309; of radio, 362–363; rights of, 397; in Sweden, 250, 267–268; and waiting area television, 189, 191
Audience, television: and community, 95; and conjectural mode, 109–110; as feminine, 359–360; focus on national, 280; and Internet, 13–14, 50–51; literacy of, 403; and museums, 351, 359, 362; as a public, 390; and Sandrew Television Week, 264–267; tastes of, 360–361
Audience interaction. *See* Interactivity; Quiz shows
Augé, Marc, 318
Ausländer, and *Heimat,* 318
Authorship, corporate, 401–402. *See also* Writing
Availability, program, 173–174, 220
Avant-garde, television as, 375
"Aztlan," 337

Baird, John Loggie, 258
Bakhtin, Mikhail, 330
Ballmer, Steve, 118
Barnouw, Eric, 19, 133
Barr, Alfred, 364, 370
Battcock, Gregory, 376
Batty, Phillip, 316
Bauman, Zygmunt, 304, 307
Baywatch, 280
Bazalgette, Peter, 86–87
BBC2, programming on, 86
Becker, Ron, 435
Becket, Samuel, 193
Begag, Azouz, 318
Behavior, viewing, 42–43, 218–219, 251
Benjamin, Walter, 198
Benn, Linda, 10–11
Benton, Thomas Hart, 366
Bergen, Candice, 143
Bernoff, Josh, 118
Bey, Hakim, 233, 238
"Big Three" networks, 66–69, 134, 167, 171. *See also specific networks*
Blacks: and computer literacy, 233–234; in prime-time, 68; programming for, 16; and television, 410–411; and *Who Wants to Be a Millionaire?,* 141
Black women: and political liberation, 228–229; uses of Internet by, 13, 160–161, 227–228, 238. *See also* Million Woman March
Bobo, Jacqueline, 436
Boddy, William, 4–5, 20, 39, 96, 136, 139
Bodroghkozy, Aniko, 316
Boredom, in waiting areas, 194. *See also* Waiting
Born in East L.A., 330
Boundaries, symbolic: of home, 304, 312–313; of space, 315–316
Bourdieu, Pierre, 18–19, 21, 362, 387
Branded content, 70, 121–122
Brand identity, decline of, 53
Branding, 5, 46–47; and network affilia-

Commercialism, and museums, 357–359, 368–373

Commercial sponsorship. *See* Advertising

Commercial television: and art, 357, 375–376; tradition of, 1

Communities: and audience, 95; and DEN, 142, 151; on the Internet, 315, 326–327, 335; and Oxygen Media, 142; and sense of home, 309–314; and television, 408

Commuter Channel, 202–205

Competition, between channels, 173–174, 220

Computer literacy, black, 233–234. *See also* Literacy; *Oprah Goes Online*

Computers: and television program forms, 114; watching television on, 217–218

Computer users, perception of, 137–138

Coney, Asia, 225–226, 235, 237

Conglomerating textuality, 46–47, 50–53, 66–71. *See also* Convergence

Conjectural narrative, in American television, 107–110. *See also* Narrative

Connoisseurs, versus housewives, 359–368. *See also* Tastes, of television audience

Consolidation, of corporate media, 14

Consumer resistance, to advertising, 125–126, 170. *See also* Personal video recorders; Remote control device

Consumers, women as, 146

Contempt, for television, 152–153

Content: branded, 70, 121–122; and convergence, 41–71; migrating, 46–47

Control: over advertising, 170; of copyright, 282–283; versus disruption, 169. *See also* Disruption; Remote control device

Convergence, 5, 41–71; aesthetics of, 43–45; and the "Big Three" networks, 134; and class, 137–138; consequences of, 179; culture of, 6; and digitalization,

213; failure of, 114; forms of, 47–66; and gender, 133–153; as historical phenomenon, 245–246; and identity, 247; as local culture, 45–47; and television Web sites, 53; texts, 46–47

Cooke, Alistair, 366

Copyright, control of, 282–283

Coren, Alan, 81

Corner, John, 165, 439–440

Corporate authorship, 401–402

Corporate media, consolidation of, 14

Corporate university, as crisis in humanities, 419

Couch potato, introduction of term, 171

Couric, Katie, 56

Coverage, media: of civil rights movement, 227; and the Million Woman March, 224–227, 232–233; of Sandrew Television Week, 265–266

Creative activity, during radio era, 275–276, 278

Crisis, in waiting area programming, 198–199

Cross-media/network stunt, 62–64

Cultural artifact, television as, 436–437

Cultural conditions, and media technologies, 210–211

Cultural form: broadcasting as, 211–213, 221; changes in, 159

Cultural icons, Pocho.com's use of, 325

Cultural identity: and Pocho.com, 334; and sense of home, 304. *See also* Identity

Cultural problem, television as, 94

Cultural space, and connections, 306

Cultural struggles, within television, 411

Cultural studies: in America, 420–422; and crisis in the humanities, 419–420; points of view of, 427; and television studies, 8–10, 346–347, 418–440, 423–424, 434

Culture: and changes in media, 1; and convergence, 137–138; demise of, 18–19; of production, 37–38; as rooted in

time and space, 304; television as
form of, 40
Culture model, circuit of, 425, 429–433
Cumulative narrative, 98–102
Curtin, Michael, 20, 165, 246

D'Acci, Julie, 22, 346–347
Dahlgren, Peter, 412
D'Amico, Victor, 363
Damon, Matt, 123
Daniels, David, 56–57
Danish television, Swedish access to,
251–252
Davi, Ajit, 173
Davies, Michael, 124
Davis, L. J., 114
Davis, Stuart, 364
Dawson, Andrew, 304
Dawsonscreek.com, 51–53
Daytime programs, in evening slots,
77
DeBord, Guy, 203
De Certeau, Michel, 230–231, 233
Democracy, television as part of, 408–
409
Democratic, print media as, 388
Demographic ghettos, 15–16
Demographics, 2, 39–40, 98–99
DEN (Digital Entertainment Network),
134, 148–153
Design by Five, 81
Development, show: and "shelf life," 47–
48. *See also* Writing, for television
D'Harnoncourt, Rene, 358, 370
Dickens, Peter, 307
Digital communications, social impact
of, 160
Digital divide, 13–14, 230
Digitalization, 213–218
Digital technology, 41–742, 120–127, 175,
210–211
Digital television, 65–66, 215–217
Dimmock, Charlie, 82
DIRECTV, 119–120

Dislocation, and electronic media, 245.
See also Space
Disruption: remote control as, 168–172,
179 (*see also* Remote control device);
television in public space as, 186
Distraction, television as, 194–195
Diversity: and conglomeration, 66–71;
and quiz shows, 140–141
Doane, Mary Anne, 189, 199
Doctor Who, 216
Documentaries, as education, 396
Docu-stunts, 62–63
Don, Monty, 82
Doordashan (Indian national television),
438
Dornan, Bob, 333
Double Agent, 176
Dumbing down debate, and British tele-
vision, 86–90
Dystopianism, technological, 12–13

Eco, Umberto, 397
Educational television: for art, 363, 373–
376; documentaries as, 396; and
MoMA, 358–359; potential of, 345; for
women, 361–362
8–9 slot, on British television, 75–90
Ellis, John, 8, 10, 85, 94, 165
Emerson, Faye, 370
"Emmy Ribbon Campaign"
(Pocho.com), 331, 333
"Encoding/decoding," as model, 425–426
Enforcement, of copyright control, 282–
283
Environment, television as object in,
186–188, 190. *See also* Television set
Enzensberger, Hans Magnus, 397
Episodic series, 96–97, 101
ER, 98, 105–107
Esping, Erik, 254–256, 266
Europe, television in, 214, 219–221
Evening broadcasts. *See* Prime-time
programming
Everett, Anna, 13, 160–161

Guild, Tricia, 81
Gurevitch, 421
Gwenellin-Jones, Sara, 110
Gyngell, Bruce, 316–317

Häger, Bengt, 264
Hall, Stuart, 9, 419, 421, 425–427
Hall, Tanya, 235
Hamer, Fannie Lou, 227–228
Hannerz, Ulf, 305, 307
Hartley, John, 10, 20, 165, 346, 421
Harvey, David, 17
Heath, Stephen, 165
Hebdige, Dick, 421
Heed, Börje, 265
Hegemony, theory of, 434–439
Heimat, and global media, 303–319
Hermes, Joke, 409
Herzog, Herta, 84
Highbrow, classification of, 360–361
Hill, Anita, 228
Hill, Logan, 13–14
Hilmes, Michael, 275
Hiltzik, Michael, 50
Hirsch, Eric, 310
Hispanic, as term, 325, 338
History, television: assumptions about,
    345–346; and broadcasting, 290–291;
    of interactive television, 39, 113–120;
    and nationalism, 20; object of, 246;
    Swedish, 256–257
A History of Reading in the West
    (Petrucci), 392
Hoggart, Richard, 9, 412
Hollywood: changes in, 280–283; and
    Hong Kong, 292; as media capital,
    275–279, 292; media from, 296; radio
    in, 275, 277
Holston, James, 406–408
Home: sense of, 246, 303–319; symbolic
    boundaries of, 304; television as object
    in, 186 (*see also* Television set). See
    also *Heimat*
Homemaking, and fine art, 366–367

Home video, and television literacy, 404
Hong Kong: broadcast television in, 286;
    and Chinese culture, 285, 293–294,
    296; and Hollywood, 292; identity of,
    287; as media capital, 272–274, 284;
    population growth in, 284; television
    in, 270–271, 283–288, 292–293; youth
    culture in, 285–286
Hotel television, 163–164
Households: and boundaries, 312–313;
    ownership of, and evening program-
    ming, 77; uses of information in, 310.
    See also Home
Housewives, versus connoisseurs, 359–
    368. *See also* MoMA
Hull, Gary, 236–237
Humanities, crisis in the, 418–440
Humor, stereotypes in, 335–336
Huntington, Samuel, 295

Icons, cultural: Pocho.com's use of, 325
Identity: and citizenship, 407–411; brand,
    53 (*see also* Branding); and conver-
    gence, 247; of digital technologies, 175;
    of Hong Kong, 287; and the Internet,
    327, 339–340; of Mexican Americans,
    324–326; and Pocho.com, 325–326,
    329, 330, 334; and self-imaging, 327;
    and sense of place, 317; and sense of
    home, 304; of television, 165–166
Indian national television (Doordashan),
    438
In Living Color, 330
Intellectuals, and television, 21–22, 364
Interactive television: and advertising
    form, 113–127; and cable networks, 3;
    failed attempts at, 20–21; history of,
    39, 113–120; and Microsoft, 114–120;
    and programming, 138–139
Interactivity: and digitalization, 213–214;
    and quiz shows, 139–140; and televi-
    sion audiences, 50–51; value of, 53
Interdisciplinary, television studies as,
    439–440

"Making-of" stunt, 62–63

Malcolm in the Middle, 106–107

Malmberg, Mark, 56

Malraux, Andre, 371

Mandela, Winnie, 232

Mander, Jerry, 387

Mankekar, Purnima, 438

Mann, Michael, 58

Mansfield, Nick, 419

Markle Foundation, 145

Marshall, T. H., 406

Marthastewart.com, 146

Martin-Barbero, Jesus, 273

Marvel Comics, 109

Marx, Karl, 425

"Masquerade" stunt, 62

Mass audiences, versus narrowcasting, 2–3

Massey, Doreen, 274, 305, 307, 317–318

Material geography, 315–319

McCaffrey, Barry, 125

McCarthy, Anna, 7, 160, 261

McChesney, Robert, 14

McDaniel, Hattie, 230

McLuhan, Marshall, 142

McMenamin, John, 191

"Meat locker" plot, 104–105

Medhurst, Andy, 76–77, 82, 88

Media capitals, 270–296; characteristics of, 273–274; Chicago as, 275–279, 291, 294–295; comparison of, 246; and globalization, 274; Hollywood as, 275–279, 292; Hong Kong as, 284; and radio, 275; studying, 272, 274, 290–296

Media citizenship, 406–408

Media coverage. *See* Coverage, media

Media delivery systems, changes in, 1

Media outlets, statistics on, 5

Media ownership, restrictions on, 14–15

Media republicanism, 388–390

Media study model, circuit of, 431–433. *See also* Television studies

Media violence, debates over, 151–152

Medical offices, waiting area television in, 195–197. *See also* Waiting

Medium: popularity of, 399; push and pull, 45–46; speed of, and trustworthiness, 390–391

Mellencamp, Patricia, 10, 190, 198, 232–233

Men, and television, 143

Mercer, Kobena, 316

Merchandizing, and future of television, 52–53, 70

Mexican Americans: identity of, 324–325; as subject of political discourse, 324; uses of the Internet by, 13, 247 (*see also* Pocho.com)

Microsoft, and interactive television, 114–120, 136

Middlebrow, classification of, 360–361

Midlands Television Research Group, 84

Miller, Jonathan, 76, 85, 87–88

Miller, Laura, 227

Million Man March, 225, 227

Million Woman March, 13, 224–238; after, 235–238; camcorder videotape of, 231–232; critiques of, 236–238; intentions of, 225; and media coverage, 224–227, 232–233; success of, 235; use of the Internet in planning, 226–227

Mills, C. Wright, 8

Mills, Kay, 228

Mills, Pam, 214

Minow, Newton, 279, 357, 375

Miss Television USA, 349–350

Mitra, Ananda, 326–327, 335

Mobile privatization, 137, 314

Mobility: decline of, 307–308; in modern world, 306–307; and new media technologies, 13; physical versus virtual, 308–309; and place-based programming, 191–192

Models, for television studies, 424–430

Modern art, 354–356, 374. *See also* MoMA

Modleski, Tania, 98, 193

Library of Congress Cataloging-in-Publication Data
Television after TV : essays on a medium in transition /
edited by Lynn Spigel and Jan Olsson.
p. cm. — (Console-ing passions)
Includes bibliographical references and index.
ISBN 0-8223-3383-x (cloth : alk. paper)
ISBN 0-8223-3393-7 (pbk. : alk. paper)
1. Television broadcasting. 2. Television. 3. Television—
Technological innovations. I. Spigel, Lynn.
II. Olsson, Jan. III. Series.
PN1992.5.T365 2004   302.23'45—dc22   2004006835